Traveling
Michigan's Sunset Coast

Exploring Michigan's West Coast Beach Towns
- From New Buffalo to Mackinaw City

Julie Albrecht Royce

Thunder Bay Press

Holt, Michigan

Traveling Michigan's Sunset Coast
Exploring Michigan's West Coast Beach Towns
-From New Buffalo to Mackinaw City

Published by
Thunder Bay Press
Holt, Michigan 48842

ISBN 10: 1933272090
ISBN 13: 9781933272092

First Thunder Bay Press printing, April 2007

Printed in the United States of America

*Dedicated to Bonnie Albrecht,
everyone needs a fan
- even if she is your mother.*

Thanks for your love and unfailing support.

Acknowledgements

I am deeply grateful to my husband, Bob, without whom this book would not have been possible. His willingness to sit in the car and read his *Financial Times* while I engaged in long conversations with shop owners is a testament to his endurance. He was a zealous guinea pig for every food establishment I wanted to try. He did the drudge work of verifying numbers, and his computer skills allowed the book to become a reality. The photos he took are peppered throughout. His encouragement never lagged. We would be driving along after a full day visiting some beautiful beach town and I would close my eyes and relax, ready to call it done. I would then hear him say, "Hey, there's a place I think you need to check," and he would pull over and I would start again.

I am indebted to Courtney Phillips (my nearly perfect daughter) for giving so generously of her time. She proofread several parts of the draft and offered many valuable editing suggestions that make the book more readable. Jes Phillips, my equally perfect son, also offered input.

I appreciate the assistance of everyone who took his or her time to read various sections of this guide in an attempt to catch my errors or point out places I had missed: Andrea Beach and Rick Albrecht, my sister-in-law and brother, offered immeasurable help with the Grand Haven section. They accompanied us to restaurants and without them I would never have found Fricano's or enjoyed a beautiful sunset on the deck of the Bil-Mar. They also let us stay at their lovely home while we traveled Lake Michigan's coast.

Dave Balas and Jim Sellman reviewed the Saugatuck/Douglas chapter and offered critical input. Dave was constantly confirming some additional piece of information that I was questioning. Gretchen Goehmann and Kinsey played tour guides extraordinaire when we visited their delightful Elk Rapids. Gretchen also reviewed the draft of Elk Rapids and suggested additional places she felt should be included. Marilyn Parr offered important assistance for the Ludington section and Linda Lewis provided helpful editing comments.

Rick Lahmann, President of the Leland Michigan Chamber of Commerce, generously shared his superior knowledge of his area and invited me to use his fantastic photos. His enthusiasm was catching and I found Leland a charming place to visit. Lloyd Petersen reviewed my piece on Bay Harbor and also offered a lovely photo. Steve Schneider provided a photo of the White River Light Station. All of the pictures in the book are there because of someone's generosity.

I received information from several chambers of commerce and visitors's centers and many of their staff members helped by reviewing specific sections of the guide: Jill Foreman reviewed Muskegon, Sally Laukitis reviewed Holland, Alice Fewins reviewed Frankfort, Sheryl Miller reviewed Pentwater, Jann Lindley reviewed the Leelanau Peninsula, and Diana Wall reviewed Manistee. To each of them my sincere thanks and to anyone I overlooked, my profound apologies. Other chambers of commerce and visitor's centers including White Lake, Petoskey, Charlevoix and Bay Harbor provided historical background and information regarding festivals. They also e-mailed photographs for inclusion in the guide.

Museum curators, Henry Roesler and the folks at the Arcadia History Museum were generous with their time as well. I thank each of them for their assistance and patience.

The Bower's Harbor Inn and the Lakeside Inn permitted me to use their ghost stories and Connie Williams at the Lakeside Inn sent a photo to go with the story.

The Department of Natural Resources provided great material for the chapter on "*Critters, Creatures and Other Living Things*."

My mother deserves special thanks for understanding I could not run off shopping every day if I entertained any hope of getting this project completed. It also meant that I gave her fewer opportunities to beat me at euchre.

Our dear friends, Susan and Joe Jurkiewicz, provided input on Saugatuck after they visited that lovely little town with a rough draft of my book in hand. More importantly they offered much needed encouragement and support, as well as many suggestions, along the way. Joe contributed several photographs to the project and they are sprinkled throughout the book.

Gary Martin, of Gary Martin Photography, kindly permitted me to use his beaufiul lighthouse photographs: the hauntingly beautiful winter shot of the lighthouse at St. Joseph (p. 359), the storm-battered South Haven lighthouse (p. 414), and the back cover photo of the Grand Haven lighthouses at sunset with sunbeams streaming through the clouds. Check Gary's website at www.coastalbeacons.com for more breathtaking photos.

Finally, I owe a debt of gratitude to the many people I met during my travels and who, in one way or another, helped me with this project. I simply cannot thank them all individually.

-Front Cover Photo Courtesy of Joe Jurkiewicz

TABLE OF CONTENTS

Overview

Welcome to Michigan's West Coast beach towns. Anywhere you travel you can expect to experience world class cuisine, sandy beaches, beautiful parks, unique museums, myriads of water activities, exciting shops, fascinating people – and those Million Dollar Sunsets. *Traveling Michigan's Sunset Coast,* will help you chart your course and provide reading material along the way.

This guide follows a continuous route north from New Buffalo, the sentry point as you enter Michigan, to Mackinaw City, at the tip of the mitten. The in-between towns can fill many summers with traveling pleasure. Savvy travelers are finding the fun does not stop Labor Day weekend. Wine festivals, the color tour and winter sports entice you to try Michigan's other exciting seasons.

Part One of Following Lake Michigan's Million Dollar Sunsets provides detailed information for each city or village in this guide. It will help you plan a day trip, weekend getaway or summer-long holiday. Prices for hotels, motels, B&B's, and restaurants are intentionally not included. They vary radically based on a myriad of factors: Are you staying at hotels and motels off-season, mid-week or high season? Are you thinking of a light lunch or filet mignon and lobster tails at an elegant restaurant? Most descriptions, however, will provide indications of whether the prices are on the high end, moderate, or a real bargain. Basic or standard generally means no-frills.

I have included hours for retail establishments and restaurants. Obviously these may change slightly from year to year and significantly from season to season. But, if you are visiting a place you need to know if it is going to be open the night you are dying to sample their whitefish. In a few situations an owner simply would not or could not provide a phone number or specific hours. One retailer told me, "We're open 'til we close." What more could I say?

Travelers come with varying budgets and different agendas and there is something for everyone included within these pages. No one has paid to be included in this guide. It is an independent attempt to identify information that would be useful for travelers. If you find an error or something else you wish to share, please bring it to my attention at: P.O. Box 127, Lexington, MI 48450, or *royce@msu.edu.* Your input is welcome.

I have done everything I can within my time constraints to ensure the information was correct when this book went to press, but stores go out of business and hours are modified. I recommend you call to confirm anything that is critical to your trip.

Part Two of this guide, *"A Bit of History, A Bit of Background, and A Bit of Fun,"* takes you beyond the typical guide book. It provides you with a background and history of Michigan's West Coast and a unique flavor of the area to savor on your journey. You have your travel guide and "beach read" in one volume. Learn about Lake Michigan and the people who originally inhabited her shores. Consider the natural wonder of the sand dunes. See if you can spot some of the rare plants and animals native to this area. Become familiar with the lighthouses you will see along your journey and learn of the ships they could not save. Shudder at a ghost story straight from the shoreline or make the acquaintance of some of the coastline's most interesting people.

I hope you enjoy your travels along Lake Michigan's shore and that you come back often.

PART ONE

Traveling Michigan's Sunset Coast

Mackinaw City
Cross Village

Harbor Springs
Petoskey/Bay Harbor
Charlevoix
Northport
Leland   Suttons Bay
Glen Arbor   Elk Rapids
Empire

Acme
Traverse City

Frankfort/Elberta

Manistee

Ludington

Pentwater

Silver Lake

Montague/Whitehall

Muskegon
Grand Haven/Spring Lake

Holland
Saugatuck/Douglas

South Haven

Saint Joseph/Benton Harbor
Stevensville
Bridgman/Sawyer
Harbert/Lakeside
Union Pier
New Buffalo

Southwest Michigan

Anchoring the southwest corner of Michigan are a handful of quaint little towns including: New Buffalo, Union Pier, Lakeside, Harbert, Sawyer, Bridgman, and Stevensville. Mostly resort towns with summer cottages flaunting gingerbread trim, they offer antiques, shopping, B&Bs and great restaurants all tucked away in the dunes and beachscape. If you start your journey at New Buffalo, the gateway to Southwest Michigan, and travel the Red Arrow highway north, you will drive through these small beach towns. Even if you do not plan to make any one of them a final destination, you are sure to find interesting junkets along the way. If you diverge from the larger, busier towns and stay a while, you may find yourself richly rewarded for choosing to spend a bit of your vacation time with them. The largest cities in Southwest Michigan are St. Joseph and Benton Harbor.

The next several pages include listings for the Southwest Michigan beach towns you travel through as you head north on Red Arrow Highway along the Lake Michigan coast. After the Benton Harbor section there is a collective listing of "Other Things to Do in Southwest Michigan" including contact numbers and suggestions for travel further inland during your trip. Several small beach towns have wine tasting, but if you want to actually visit a winery and see the process, you may wish to drive to St. Julian's in Paw Paw. Likewise, if you decide to follow the entire wine trail, you may pick it up on the coast, but find yourself wandering inland for many of the stops.

For the bicycling enthusiast it is hard to imagine more pleasant scenery to provide the backdrop as you roll along past streams, brooks, farms, beach and marshes. You will find several routes following secondary roads through picture worthy hills. The back-roads bikeway system offers possibilities from five to sixty miles of mapped scenic roads.

From your first glimpse of the sandy beaches, parks and fantastic dunes, the stage is set. Along the way you will find props: galleries, wine tours, museums, shopping, and produce stands. Dining opportunities abound and you will be pleasantly surprised at the variety of international flavors awaiting you. All eateries in the area thrive on the wealth of locally grown crops. Michigan's Southwest is famous for its fresh fruit and has the distinction of being the largest non-citrus fruit growing area in the country. It would be hard to avoid a farmer's market where you can get freshly picked, juicy apples, peaches, strawberries and an assortment of other summer treats.

There is truly something for everyone and every taste.

New Buffalo

Population: Approximately 2,000.

Directions: Take I-94 to New Buffalo exit (US-12) just inside the Michigan Border on Lake Michigan.

Background and History

Today New Buffalo serves as the cornerstone to Lake Michigan's Beach communities. It is a harbor town bustling with the activity of its public beach, lake and riverside parks, boat launch and marinas. Condos and yachts predominate the shoreline.

In earlier years, Native Americans prized the land and water around New Buffalo for its bountiful fishing and hunting. The lake and rivers provided a water highway for canoes. The Miami, Iroquois and Pottawatomie fought for control of this area with the latter victorious.

The riches of the land tempted French fur traders who were later followed by missionaries intent upon converting the Native Americans.

In 1834, Captain Wissell Whittaker, bound for Chicago, tangled with one of Michigan's notorious Storms of November and the gale afforded no mercy. The waves hurled his schooner, the *Post Boy*, ashore near current day Grand Beach. The ship was a total loss, but captain and crew miraculously made it to safety and struck camp before starting off for St. Joseph to report the wreck of their ship

On his way, the captain was awed by the beauty of the New Buffalo Harbor. Besides finding it physically stunning, he considered its utilitarian potential as a port so great that he argued it could rival Chicago.

In 1835 Whittaker returned with friends and family and began buying land and laying out plans for a city. He gained partners in his endeavor and the land quickly rose in value. Efforts were proceeding according to Whittaker's dream until the severe 1841winter brought an end to his speculative land development. After that, New Buffalo, which Whittaker had named for his prior home of Buffalo, New York, struggled for many years.

The Michigan Central Railroad was completed in 1849 and helped the economy rebound slightly. However, it was not until the turn of the century that the area gained recognition for its resort potential and began catering to tourists and summer residents.

Michigan recognized New Buffalo as the "Gateway" to the state and in 1934 built a tourist information center there. Its current location on I-94 remains the busiest tourist center in Michigan.

In the 1960s harbor dredging began and by 1975 New Buffalo's safe harbor was ready to offer sanctuary to boats seeking refuge from storms. The harbor never became serious competition to Chicago as

Whittaker had envisioned, but it is busy with marine activity and it is a prime travel destination.

The streets are lined with specialty stores and unique eateries. The lakefront park is a perfect place to watch the sailboats or a sunset, or perhaps feed the wild gulls, geese and ducks that flock to the shores to take advantage of tourists' generosity.

Food/Restaurants

The Beachwood, 19347 West US-12, (269) 469-5300. Casual dining offering seafood, steaks, chops, chicken and pasta. Open Wed to Sun from 5:00 pm.

Brewsters' Italian Café, 11 West Merchant Street, (269) 469-3005. In business for 15 years. Features an Italian inspired and ever-changing menu. Several locals claimed this as their favorite restaurant when asked about great places to eat. The parking lot is on Whittaker, the main drag in town. Open 7 days at 8:00 am for coffee and fresh baked goods. They serve lunch and dinner. They close Sun to Thurs at 10:00 pm and Fri and Sat at 11:00 pm.

Capozio's Pizza and Italian, 13982 Red Arrow Highway, (269) 469-4001. Pastas, sandwiches and Italian fare since 1945. Open 7 days 4:00 pm to closing.

Casey's Bar and Grill, 136 North Whittaker Street, (269) 469-5800, www.caseysbar-grill.com. Area landmark, casual atmosphere with worn wooden floors, pressed tin ceilings and a 42-foot art deco bar. Moderate prices. The Portabella Ravioli was superb as was the Lake Perch, although steaks are their specialty. Open 7 days, Mon to Thurs 11:30 am to 10:00 pm, Fri and Sat 11:30 am to 11:00 pm and Sun noon to 11:00 pm. In the winter they may close slightly earlier.

Chocolate Café, 126 Whittaker. Cheesecakes, coffee drinks, hot chocolates, candies, sandwiches and breakfast. Open 7 days, Mon to Thurs 7:00 am to 10:00 pm, Fri and Sat 7:00 am to 11:00 pm and Sun 7:00 am to 10:00 pm.

David's Deli, 30 North Whittaker. WIFI. Breakfast all day. Prepared picnics for the beach. Open 7 days, 7:00 am to 6:00 pm.

Dinner's Ready, 424 East Buffalo Street. (269) 469-1702. Elegant foods prepared by chef Diane Botica; ready to take with you.

El Rancho Grande, 310 East Buffalo Street, (269) 469-9600, www.elranchogrande.com. A family restaurant serving authentic Mexican food including: fajitas, burritos, tamales, tacos (try the Taco Duncan) and top-notch frozen margaritas. The key to their success is the fresh ingredients. This is another place recommended by locals. Open 7 days, Memorial Day to Labor Day. Open Mon to Fri 11:00 am,

Sat and Sun at 1:00 pm-but somewhat dependent on the crowd. Winter: closed Mon and Tues and open all other days at 5:00 pm.

Hannah's Restaurant, 115 South Whittaker Street, (269) 469-1440. Specialties include Roast Duck or Roast Pork served with sauerkraut and homemade dumplings. Open 7 days, 11:00 am to 11:00 pm during the summer. Closes an hour earlier during the winter. Also serves breakfast and brunch on Sat and Sun 8:00 am to 3:00 pm Memorial Day to Labor Day. Hannah's can accommodate large groups.

Michigan Thyme Café, 107 North Whittaker Street, (269) 469-6604. In July 1995, the current owner purchased an empty century-old building that was in desperate need of repair and turned it into a café that opened mere months later selling gourmet foods and men's and women's clothing. The Café and deli offer fantastic deserts as well as homemade soups, salads, sandwiches and quiche.

O'Brien's at Whittaker Woods Golf Community, 12578 Wilson Road, Exit one off I-94. Casually elegant décor. Pianist on Friday and Saturday evenings. Open for lunch, dinner and Sunday Brunch.

Oinks, 227 Buffalo Street. (269) 469-3535. This has been the place to get ice cream for two decades. They have a walk up window or you can go inside and take a look at the fudge, candy and gifts they carry along with their 55 flavors of ice-cream. Open 7 days, Mon to Thurs 11:00 am to 11:00 pm and Fri to Sun 11:00 am to 11:30 pm.

Pierre Anne Creperie, 9 South Barton Street (one block west of Red Arrow Highway and Whittaker), (269) 469-9542. Lunch/brunch establishment featuring sweet or savory (ham, cheese etc.) crepes. Other delicious options: quiche, salads and homemade soups. Open Wed to Sun 11:00 am to 4:00 pm April to November.

Redamak's Tavern, 616 East Buffalo Street, (269) 469-4522, www.redamaks.com. No credit cards accepted. According to residents of New Buffalo, this is the place to get hamburgers. The waitstaff invites you to "Bite into a legend." You decide if it deserves the hype. They have been in the hamburger business since 1946 and the current owners have been there since 1975. Open extended summer season; generally early March to late October. Hours vary slightly by the month, but generally open lunch and dinner.

Retro Café, 801 West Buffalo Street, (269) 469-1800. As expected from the name you get retro décor and retro music. You also get all food prepared from scratch and outdoor dining in the summer. The smell of cinnamon rolls will lure you inside in the morning. Breakfast served 7 days from 8:30 am to 3:00 pm and lunch from noon to 3:00 pm. Closed Tues in January and February.

Rios Mexican Food, 901 West Buffalo, (269) 469-8011. Many people recommended this place as their very favorite spot to eat in New

Buffalo. You may be surprised when you see it; it looks like a typical little fast food joint. You can use their drive through or walk up to the window to order, and then wait for some of the best Mexican food around. They have a couple of small, outside tables if you are inclined to eat on the premises. The food is several steps up from the chain they resemble. Open 7 days, 11:00 am to 10:00 pm during the season and in the winter from 11:00 am to 8:00 pm.

Rosie's, 128 North Whittaker Street, (269) 469-4382. No frills diner atmosphere that has no trouble packing 'em in for breakfast. For lunch try their sandwiches, burgers, salads, perch, dumplings and gravy or house special: "Grandma's Meatloaf." Open breakfast (served all day) and lunch 7:00 am to 2:00 pm. No credit cards.

The Stray Dog Bar and Grill, 245 North Whittaker, (269) 469-2727, www.eatatthedog.com. Waterfront dining and a rooftop patio make this a great place to catch lunch or dinner. Live entertainment on weekends. Menu features salads, sandwiches, platters, ribs, pizza, and burgers. Opens at noon 7 days.

Terrace Café and Lounge, (Located in the Harbor Grand Hotel), 111 West Water Street, (269) 469-7700 or toll-free (888) 605-6800. Stone fireplace, small café atmosphere, outdoor patio, waterfront dining and award winning tortes, pies and desserts. Open daily from 5:00 pm.

Lodging *(Also see Campgrounds below)*

Best Western Plaza Hotel, Exit 1 off I-94, (269) 469-4193, www.bestwestern.com. Extras: deluxe continental breakfast, indoor pool and spa, exercise room, laundry, close to lake.

Comfort Inn of New Buffalo, 11539 O'Brien Court, (269) 469-4440 or toll-free (800) 4CHOICE. Extras: indoor pool, continental breakfast, pets allowed, Jacuzzi suites, microwaves and refrigerators in deluxe suites and satellite television.

Grand Beach Inn, 19400 Ravine Drive, (269) 469-0097 or toll-free (800) 936-0034. A 1914 Inn located on 4 acres and able to accommodate up to 45 people in its 16 rooms and suites. Heated pool and large common area with fireplace. Activities for all ages.

Harbor Grand Hotel and Suites, 111 West Water Street, (269) 469-7700 or toll-free (888) 605-5900, www.harborgrand.com. Steps from the beach. Indoor pool and Jacuzzi, massage therapy center, some rooms with fireplace and whirlpool baths. Waterfront dining available at the Terrace Café (see above).

Holiday Inn Express Hotel & Suites, 11500 Holiday Road, hienewbuffalo@triton.net, www.lodgingmichigan.com, (269) 469-1400 or toll-free (800) HOLIDAY. Extras: indoor heated pool and whirlpool, game room, 24-hour free coffee and tea, free local calls, 2-line speaker phones, spa and suite-rooms available.

New Buffalo's Pink House, 205 West Mechanic Street, (219) 923-5997, www.harbourcountry.org/pinkhouse.htm. Restored Victorian with 4 bedrooms that can accommodate 11.

Pleasure Isle Penthouse, New Buffalo Harbor, (269) 469-3000. Two-bedroom units available by the week or month, year round.

Museums and Galleries

Block Fine Arts Gallery, 105 B North Whittaker Street, (269) 469-2039. The focus of this gallery is on the beginning and mid-market collector. You will find contemporary art and fine crafts by new and emerging artists working in a number of mediums, including sculpture, ceramics, textiles, porcelain, prints, photography and more. Open 7 days, 10:00 am to 6:00 pm. Fall hours reduced and winter open primarily weekends.

Clipper Ship Gallery, 116 North Whittaker Street, (269) 469-2590. Nautical themed paintings, gifts and accessories. Open 11:00 am to 6:00 pm, longer on weekends.

Courtyard Gallery, 813 East Buffalo Street, (269) 469-4110, info@courtyardgallery.com. Original upper end, high-quality fine art, including: paintings, bronze, blown glass, photography and more. Fantastic gourd vases and art by Whitney Jackson-Peckman. Open Mon to Sat 11:00 am to 6:00 pm, Sun 11:00 am to 5:00 pm and closed Tuesday. Also by appointment.

The Harbor Muse, 19135 West US 12, (269) 586-2212. A place to find gifts for infants, children and adults. Choose from handcrafted jewelry, one-of-a-kind scarves, handbags, travel hats, spa products and beautiful greeting cards. Open 10:00 am to 6:00 pm 7 days.

The New Buffalo Railroad Museum, 530 South Whittaker Street, (269) 469-5409. This museum is housed in a replica of the Pere Marquette Depot, which stood nearby. You will find furnishings and artifacts from the original depot, photographs and memorabilia of the New Buffalo area, model train layout with replicas of the Pere Marquette Roundhouse and other historic New Buffalo buildings, a World War II troop sleeper and a C&O box car restored to house additional displays. Open Mon to Fri 9:00 am to 5:00 pm and weekends 10:00 am to 3:00 pm.

Wow Art Gallery, 529 West Buffalo Street, (269) 469-1938. Primarily contemporary art. Gallery is operated by Rick Ott who displays his acrylic abstracts and Angela Reichert who does mixed media collages. The gallery also handles the work of about 30 other artists and displays their glass, ceramic, sculpture and jewelry pieces.

They do not post hours so you just have to check to see if they are open on any given day, although Rick says they are open most of the time.

Theatre

New Buffalo Performing Arts Center, at the high school, 1112 East Clay Street, (269) 469-6046. 450-seat capacity summer theatre and concerts. Call for further information.

Antiques

Da Barn, 510 East Buffalo Street, (269) 469-0333. Buys estates. Sells inexpensive to high end. Prices negotiable. You can find architectural artifacts, wrought iron pieces, rugs, upholstered furniture, lighting, picture frames, primitives, distressed painted furniture and lots of one-of-a-kind items. Open Sat and Sun noon to 6:00 pm or by appointment, call (312) 951-0001.

Other Shopping

C M Gift and Christmas Shop, 14 North Whittaker Street, (269) 469-2890. A small shop with a variety of Christmas items. Open Mon to Sat 10:00 am to 6:00 pm and Sun noon to 5:00 during the summer. Possibly longer hours during the holidays. Reduced winter hours.

The Cool Pepper, 100 C North Whittaker Street, (269) 586-2290. Specializes in gourmet fruit and tomato based salsa, hot sauces, dips and marinades. Also carries blown-art glass, original prints and more. Open 7 days at 11:00 am.

Global Arts Custom Imports, 430 Whittaker Street (warehouse), (269) 469-9180 and 17648 US Hwy 12 (showroom), (269) 469-1109. Indonesian, Chinese, Moroccan and Vietnamese imports including textiles, wall art, handicrafts, rugs, furniture, pottery, garden statues, lamps and more. Open Mon to Sat 10:00 am to 6:00 pm and Sun 11:00 am to 5:00 pm.

I Love Toy Trains/The Toy Store, 16 South Smith Street, toll-free (800) 892-2822. Features Lionel Trains, toys, books, videos, John Deere toys and more. Open May to Labor Day: Tues to Sun 11:00 am to 5:00 pm. September to December 31st: Thurs to Sun 11:00 am to 5:00 pm. January to April: Fri to Sun 11:00 am to 5:00 pm.

Indian Summer Imports, 126 South Whittaker Street, (269) 469-9994. Women's clothing and jewelry from around the world. Clothing made from organic cotton, gauze and hemp. Open 7 days.

Joe Jackson's Michigan Fruit Stand, features mainly Michigan grown produce and perennials. (Although I am reasonably sure we do not grow bananas in this lovely state.) Open daily 8:00 am to 8:00 pm in the summer. Funky stand and a fun place to stop. (Photo next page.)

Joe Jackson's Michigan Fruit Stand   *Photo by Bob Royce*

Lyssa, 28 North Barton, (269) 469-1162. A curiosity shop. Inventory includes Vera Bradley bags, Irish and Scottish sterling silver jewelry, Woodbury Pewter, linens, English bath products, men's neckties and golf hats, toys, accessories and handcrafted American gift items. Open daily except Tues.

The Purple Moon, 122 North Whittaker, (269) 469-4980. Embroidered and silk screened casual wear. Open Mon to Fri 11:00 am to 5:00 pm, Sat and Sun 10:00 am to 5:00 pm and closed Tues.

The Sailor's Wife, 110 North Whittaker Street, (269) 469-3440. Fashion and beauty collection. They claim to offer a "shopping adventure" with fashions from around the world. Open Mon to Fri 10:30 am to 6:00 pm and Sat and Sun 10:00 am to 6:00 pm.

Sweetwater Boating, 38 North Whittaker Street, (269) 469-6560. Boating supplies, beach needs, toy rafts, inflatables, life jackets, swim suits and cover-ups, gift items, and as incongruous as it seems in the middle of July, three fully decorated Christmas trees next to the swim suit rack. Open 9:00 am to 10:00 pm, reduced winter hours.

Third Coast Surf Shop, 22 South Smith Street, (block from Oink's Ice Cream), (269) 932-4575, www.thirdcoastsurfshop.com. Yes, you can surf on Lake Michigan and this shop will prepare you for the adventure. They sell surf wear, boards, beach accessories and gifts. They also rent beach cruiser bikes, surfboards, boogie boards, skim boards, sand boards and even wetsuits. Besides the encouragement and rentals, they provide lessons for surfing and skim boarding. Hours vary, but generally in the summer they are open 9:00 am to 8:00 pm, 7 days.

Whittaker House, 26 North Whittaker Street, (269) 469-0220. www.whittakerhouse.com. Upscale clothing store carrying men's and women's fashions, jewelry, purses, straw hats, cards, sandals, sunglasses and lotions. You will find both sportswear and evening wear. Open 7 days, Mon to Sat 10:00 am to 6:00 pm and Sun 11:00 am to 5:00 pm. In the summer they stay open until 7:00 pm on Sat and Sun.

You're Invited Cards and Gifts, 104 North Whittaker Street. Paper goods, cards, invitations and knickknacks. Open Mon to Thurs 10:00 am to 6:00 pm, Fri and Sat 10:00 am to 9:00 pm and Sun noon to 6:00 pm. Closed Tues.

Parks

New Buffalo Lakefront Park and Beach, at the end of Whittaker Street across the bridge, (269) 469-1522. Designated swimming areas with life guards Memorial Day to Labor Day from 10:00 am to 6:00 pm. Picnic tables, grills, playgrounds and a pavilion.

Marinas, Boat Launches and Charters

Harbor Country Charters, (269) 469-8422. Shoreline pleasure cruises for up to six people on a 42-foot Sea Ray. You can charter an hour, half day or full day trip and you can request port to port option. Call for details.

New Buffalo Municipal Marina, Located in the harbor at the end of Whittaker Street, (269) 469-1522. Offers transient docking, no reservations, first come, first served. There is a maximum of 55 feet. Amenities: showers, water and electric hookup, and pumpouts. Office open 7 days, 8:00 am to 6:00 pm during the season.

New Buffalo Public Boat Launch, Galien River across from the city beach, (269) 469-1522. 24-hour a day access to Lake Michigan from its eight ramps. Attendant on duty Mon to Fri 10:00 am to 6:00 pm. Sat and Sun 6:00 am to 8:00 pm.

Festivals

St Mary of the Lake Festival, May. 718 West Buffalo Street, (269) 469-1515. Carnival with rides, silent auction, prizes, food booths, book fair and live entertainment.

Golf

Whittaker Woods, 12578 Wilson Road, (269) 469-3400. www.golfwhittaker.com An 18-hole, par 72 golf course open to the public. Considered one of Michigan's ten most challenging courses and it may test your patience and temper.

Union Pier

Directions: Four miles north of New Buffalo on Red Arrow Highway.

Background and History

In 1861 John Gowdy moved from his home in New York to the site that would become Union Pier. He was immediately struck by the lush natural beauty of the forests surrounding him. Spectacular trees measuring up to five feet in diameter and sometimes 60 feet to the lowest branches represented a source of cheap lumber; Gowdy saw a fortune waiting to be harvested.

Capitalizing on the potential fortune required finding a way to cut the mighty giants and then transport them to market. Gowdy and his partners were able to resolve the first problem with no more than strong backs and a few simple tools.

Getting the felled trees to their logical destination, Chicago, presented a bit thornier dilemma. The savvy businessmen recognized the need for a ship to haul the cargo and a pier for docking. They set about constructing a 130-ton schooner on the beach and then built Union Pier at the foot of Berrien Street to provide their ship with docking facilities. The pier ultimately gave its name to the area.

Success seemed a foregone conclusion and the area prospered and with growth came a larger sawmill and a new industry: a brick factory.

The horrific Chicago fire of 1871 only increased the demand for cordwood, timber and bricks. Union Pier was financially secure until the depletion of the forests, coupled with the washing away of the pier, forced the little village to look for a new economic foundation. The fertile soil left in the wake of forest removal was perfect for fruit farms and agriculture.

The 1900s brought an even more lucrative business; one shared by all sister beach cities on Michigan's West Coast – exclusive resorts and tourism! Chicagoans needed to get away even more than they had needed bricks and lumber.

Today time is clarified by Southwest Michiganders as Michigan time to distinguish it from Chicago time out of respect for the resorters and tourists from the Windy City who arrive in droves. Times in this guide are Michigan time.

Food/Restaurants

Casual Chef Café, 16090 Red Arrow Highway, (269) 469-1200. It can get busy but some patrons swear by this place. One particular favorite is the clam chowder. Open Lunch every day except Wednesday, Dinner Thurs to Sun and breakfast Sat and Sun.

Millers Country House Restaurant, 16409 Red Arrow Highway, (269) 469-5950. Multi-ethnic influences enrich the menu of steaks, ribs, pastas and fresh seafood. Wonderful homemade desserts top off your dining experience. There is also a lighter bar menu with sandwiches, burgers, salads, fried chicken and fajitas. The dining rooms offer lovely views or you can choose to sit on the dining deck and enjoy a drink in the beautifully landscaped gardens. Open daily at 5:00 pm with lunch and brunch served on the weekend from noon.

Ramberg's Bakery, 9811 Union Pier Road, (269) 469-1010. Place to find donuts, breads, cookies, pies, muffins, strudel, coffee cakes and sugar free cookies and muffins. Open Mon to Sat 7:30 am to 2:00 pm. Weekends only in the winter.

Red Arrow Roadhouse, 15710 Red Arrow Highway, (269) 469-3939. Very casual, rustic, but comes with high recommendation from locals. Open Mon to Thurs 5:00 pm to 10:00 pm, Fri 5:00 pm to 11:00 pm, Sat noon to 11:00 pm and Sun noon to 10:00 pm.

Timothy's, 16220 Lakeshore Road, (269) 469-0900. Excellent seafood prepared in interesting and delicious ways. Consider the Miso Glazed Wild King Salmon. Open 7 days, July and August, 6:00 pm to 11:00 pm, June and September open Tues to Sun 6:00 pm to 11:00 pm Remainder of the year open Wed to Sun 6:00 pm to 11:00 pm.

Tuscany Ristorante, 16321 Red Arrow Highway, (269) 469-9094. Great Italian food moderately to expensively priced. Open Mon to Fri 6:00 pm to 10:00 pm, Sat and Sun 1:00 pm to 10 pm. Reduced off-season hours.

Whistle Stop, 15700 Red Arrow Highway, (269) 469-6700. An espresso bar and deli with outside seating. Box lunches available or consider beach delivery. Also sells wine and other goodies you might want to take on a picnic. Open 7 days, Sun to Thurs 8:00 am to 8:00 pm, Fri and Sat 8:00 am to 10:00 pm.

Lodging

Garden Grove B&B, 9549 Union Pier Road, (269) 469-6346 or toll-free (800) 613-2872, www.gardengrove.net. There are four rooms in the main house and three in the newly completed, detached carriage house where double Jacuzzis, wet bars, mini refrigerators and a microwave are standard. Also internet available. Nearly an acre of beautiful grounds provides tranquil setting for your special getaway. Enjoy the decks, hot tub and watching more than 30 species of birds that come to the many feeders.

The Inn at Union Pier, 9708 Berrien Street, (269) 469-4700, www.innatunionpier.com. 16 rooms, each with private bath, central air and ceiling fan, many with fireplaces, porches or balconies overlooking the landscaped grounds. Less than a block to Lake Michigan.

Pine Garth Inn, Villa and Guesthouses, 15790 Lakeshore Road, (269) 469-1642 or toll-free (888) 390-0909, www.pinegarth.com. A restored English Inn that was originally the summer estate of a Chicago industrialist. "Garth" is a middle-English term for enclosed garden, and the restoration created one for you to enjoy. The Inn offers seven guest rooms. The carriage house has one bedroom, full kitchen, deck, grill and hot tub-just steps from the lake.

River's Edge B&B and Cottages, 9902 Community Hall Road, (269) 469-6860 or toll-free (800) 742-0592, www.riversedgebandb.com Eight rooms and two cottages situated on 30 acres bordering the Galien River. You can canoe, hike, or in the winter, cross-country ski. Extras: Jacuzzis and stone fireplaces.

Sandpiper Inn, 16136 Lakeview Avenue, (269) 469-1146 or toll-free (800) 351-2080, www.sandpiperinn.net. Eight guest rooms. Lovely living room overlooking the lake. Walk down the terraced stairs to the private beach. Jacuzzi tubs, verandas and extraordinary views.

Warren Woods Inn, 15506 Red Arrow Highway, toll-free (800) 358-4754, www.warrenwoods.com. Country French Inn built in 1853 and situated on five acres, only a short walk to the beach. Heated pool with outdoor hot tub. Available by the week in the summer and can accommodate ten to thirty guests.

Galleries

Acorn Gallery, 16142 Red Arrow Highway, (269) 469-5278. Displays works of regional artists with exhibitions that change throughout the year. You will find jewelry, ceramics, baskets, hand printed silk, blown glass and fine crafts. They claim to have fine art with a sense of humor. Open Thurs to Mon 11:00 am to 6:00 pm.

Other Shopping

De Wolfe's Boutique, 15412 Red Arrow Highway, (269) 469-7727. Casual clothing, sunhats, sunglasses, handbags, linen separates, Eileen Fisher, Flax. Open 7 days, Mon to Sat 11:00 am to 5:00 pm and Sun 11:00 am to 4:00 pm. Closed October to April.

Patty's Picks, 16117 Red Arrow Highway (269) 469-1919, www.pattyspicks.com. Children's clothing, home accents, gift items and other good things for the home and the soul. Open 7 days, 10:00 am to 6:00 pm Memorial Day to Labor Day. Winter hours reduced.

Other Things to See and Do

St. Julian's Wine Tasting Room, 9145 Union Pier Road (I-94 Exit 6, north, turn right at St. Julian), (269) 469-3150. Free wine tasting.

Open 7 days, regular hours: Mon to Sat 10:00 am to 6:00 pm and Sun noon to 7:00 pm. Open until 7:00 pm daily from May through September. The St. Julian Winery offers tours in Paw Paw. (See Other Things to See and Do in Southwest Michigan, p. 40.)

Round Barn Winery Tasting Room, 9185 Union Pier Road (Next door to St. Julian's Wine Tasting Room), (269) 469-6885. www.RoundBarnWinery.com. Free wine tasting. Open 7 days, Mon to Sat 11:00 am to 6:00 pm and Sun noon to 6:00 pm. Consider the Wine Trail (See Other Things to See and Do in Southwest Michigan, p. 40.)

Photo Courtesy of Joe Jurkiewicz

Lakeside

Directions: Where Union Pier ends Lakeside begins! Five miles north of New Buffalo on Red Arrow Highway.

Background and History

It is believed the early Native Americans named the area north of New Buffalo, Chikaming. In the Algonquin language, the words Chigike-Chiamiu literally translate to "by the side of the great expanse" or more loosely to "on the shore of the sea." Translations may not be exact, but in this case, "on the shore of the sea" seems appropriate.

John Wesley Wilkinson arrived at Chikaming in the 1850s and established Wilkinson's Trading Post and Boarding House, both of which were lucrative local businesses for many years. The small community was named Lakeside in 1874.

The economic history of the small village was similar to that of so many others along the Michigan coast. Forests drew the attention of lumber barons seeking to make a fortune and some got rich. When timber was depleted farming took over. The sandy, somewhat acidic soil was perfect for growing fruit. Eventually, however, most coastal towns realized their fortunes lay in the establishment of resorts where the wealthy built second homes. Tourists, who flocked to the beautiful beaches to wade in the water, play in the sand and watch the sun set majestically in the west, brought a much needed infusion of money to the area.

Food/Restaurants

Blue Plate Café, 15288 Red Arrow Highway, (269) 469-2370. The brightly colored orange and green building will catch your eye as you are driving along Red Arrow Highway. Offers both inside and outside seating. They make their own pancake mix and this is a good place to have breakfast. Fresh foods are the secret to their great dishes. Open Mon and Thurs to Sat 8:00 am to 3:00 pm (2:00 pm in the winter) and Sun 9:00 am to 2:00 pm. Closed Tues and Wed.

Lodging

The Lakeside Inn, 15281 Lakeshore Road, (269) 469-0600, www.lakesideinns.com. Originally known as Ames Grove, this property was a picnic ground and recreation area beginning in 1889. John Aylesworth purchased the property in 1901 and opened the inn approximately 1915. Currently there are 31 guest rooms and a 100 foot front porch lined with rockers facing beautiful Lake Michigan. This inn is a state registered historic hotel sitting high on the bluffs. The Lake beckons you to cross the street, descend the steps, and enjoy the private beach. The Inn has a fascinating history (check its internet site) and its own resident but harmless ghost. (See Ghosts and Monsters, Part II, p. 411 of this guide).

The White Rabbit B&B, 14634 Red Arrow Highway, (269) 469-4620 or toll-free (800) 967-2224, www.whiterabbitinn.com. Previously a small hotel, each room has a private whirlpool bath. Owners have two dogs and two cats and welcome pets (dogs and cats) in their two cabins.

Museums and Galleries

Wilkinson Heritage Museum at Wilkinson Village, 15300 Red Arrow Highway (located in the former trading post built by city founding father John Wilkinson). This little museum houses artifacts from the Wilkinson family and a history of the Lakeside area. Period dolls, furniture, clothing and jewelry are on display and you can view early photos of the area. Open 10:00 am to 6:00 pm daily.

Antiques

Lakeside Antiques, 14866 and 14876 Red Arrow Highway, (269) 469-4467 and (269) 469-7717. Two buildings, one business. A place to find Oriental rugs, crystal chandeliers and French antiques scoured from Paris flea markets and others spots around the world. Several dealers display here and each one brings a new look. Consigned merchandise changes each week. Open every day in the summer (May to September) Fri to Mon year round.

Other Shopping

Abigail Heche, 14866 Red Arrow Highway, (269) 469-0447. Highly talented, like her big sister, Anne, Abigail creates beautiful, high-end jewelry for stars and common folks alike. She uses high quality gemstones and other materials to fashion her subtle but exquisite pieces. Open 11:00 am to 7:00 pm (approximate).

It's a Breeze, 15300 Red Arrow Highway, (269) 469-6671. Place mats, jewelry, hand bags, rugs, lotions, furniture, soaps, hemp runners, candles and washable silk scarves. Open Memorial Day to Labor Day 10:00 am to 6:00 pm. Weekends only in the winter. Hours may vary so call to confirm.

Harbert

Directions: Three miles north of Lakeside on Red Arrow Highway. Exit 6 off I-94 from Chicago.

Background and History

The tiny community of Harbert was founded in the 1850s by John Glavin. Glavin, a local farmer, was riding a train between Chicago and Detroit and noted the flat, barren land in the area. He thought it would be a good place to locate a train depot. Unfortunately for Glavin, it was a wealthy industrialist from Chicago who had the money to carry out the dream. Along with the village's gratitude, the industrialist was afforded the honor of naming the small town which became Harbert and not Glavin.

Orchards and vineyards were the economic mainstay of the region and the trains transported the fresh fruits to Chicago for consumption.

Carl Sandburg wrote much of his Pulitzer Prize winning Abraham Lincoln history while living at his Harbert home. (See *Famous, Infamous* in Part II, p. 440 of this guide).

It is believed that the judge who heard Al Capone's case hid his son in Harbert during the trial to keep him safe from Al's long reach.

Food/Restaurants

Café Gulistan, 13581 Red Arrow Highway, (269) 469-6779. Gulistan means roses in Kurdish and the restaurant beckons with beautiful flowers planted in front. Restauranteur, Ibriham Partak, a Turkish American immigrant, was besieged with hardship, imprisoned as part of the War on Terror and Café Gulistan closed. The restaurant's loyal customers were outraged at what they considered a miscarriage of justice and are happy he is back serving up Middle-eastern meals. Open Tues to Thurs 4:00 pm to 10:00 pm, Fri and Sat 4:00 pm to 11:00 pm and Sun 1:00 pm to 10:00 pm.

Chameleon, 13622 Red Arrow Highway (located in the Market Tower), (269) 469-0549. WIFI. Selection of sandwiches on your choice of bread. Coffee club for the cappuccino or latte crowd. The specialty drink, Chicaming Chococcino is a nice way to get your caffeine in a sweet way. Open Mon, Tues and Thurs 8:00 am to 5:00 pm, Sat and Sun 8:00 am to 6:00 pm.

Harbert Swedish Bakery and Luisa's Café, 13698 Red Arrow Highway, Café (269) 469-1777, Bakery (269) 469-1010. Nice selection of baked goods including kolachkis, coffee cakes, donuts, cookies and breads in the bakery. The café serves breakfast, lunch and brunch. Blueberry-Mascarpone Crepes with blueberry sauce and whipped cream can make a hard-core breakfast-skipper drool. The café is open

Mon and Thurs 7:00 am to 3:00 pm, Fri to Sun 7:00 am to 6:00 pm and closed Tues and Wed. Bakery open Thurs to Mon 7:30 am to 3:00 pm.

Galleries

Craig Smith The Gallery, 13648 Red Arrow Highway, (773) 750-7528. Craig Smith has opened his second gallery in the area and it is a beauty: 4000 square feet of art displayed in a museum like setting. Leisurely perusing the art is a pleasure. Opens between 10:00 am and 11:00 am and closes at 5:45 pm. Closed Wed. Hours reduced after Labor Day.

Jill Underhill Gallery, 13462 Red Arrow Highway, (269) 469-8000, www.jillunderhill.com. Outdoor sculptures, oil paintings, fine arts and crafts by many nationally recognized artists. Open weekends noon to 6:00 pm.

Judith Racht Gallery, 13707 Prairie Road (near Red Arrow Highway), (269) 469-1080, www.judithrachtgallery.net. Each summer month brings a new exhibit of contemporary art. Labor Day they have an event called Outsiders Outside where untrained artists who have an avocation or calling can exhibit their pieces. They draw artists from all over the country. The little shop across the street is part of the gallery and displays primarily textiles, rugs and quilts. It is believed that the building was once owned by Carl Sandberg's daughter.

Antiques

Harbert Antique Mall, 13887 Red Arrow Highway, (269) 469-0977. More than 50 dealers offering all periods of furniture from primitive to traditional to modern. You can also find pottery, silver, art glass, crystal, linens, lamps, lighting and art. Open 7 days, Mon to Sat 10:00 am to 6:00 pm and Sun 11:00 am to 6:00 pm, year round.

Marco Polo, 13630 Red Arrow Highway, (269) 469-6272. An assortment of interesting antiques and other intriguing objects spanning a time frame of the 18th century to current. Open weekends 11:00 am to 5:00 pm, year round.

Other Shopping

Dorajane, 13658 Red Arrow Highway (located in the Market Tower), (269) 612-1600. Ladies' boutique with nice selection of jewelry and accessories. Open Thurs to Tues 11:00 am to 6:00 pm. Hours may be reduced in the winter.

The Open Trunk, 13650 Red Arrow Highway (located in Market Tower), (269) 469-1950. Home furnishings including: hand crafted tables and lamps, jewelry, art, antiques and other funky stuff. Open 11:00 am to 6:00 pm, 7 days during the summer. Open weekends only in the winter.

Sawyer

Directions: Exit 12 off I-94. Two and a half miles north of Harbert on Red Arrow Highway.

Background and History

In the mid-1800s an Ohio Judge, Silas Sawyer, decided it was time to leave the bench and experience a more tranquil life style. Sawyer purchased 100 acres on which he intended to create an orchard. He cut the original timber and hauled it to the nearby pier for shipment to Chicago.

Sawyer has remained an agricultural center and lovely vineyards grace its rolling fields. Today Sawyer is known for the Warren Dunes. A few antique shops provide the traveler with a diversion from the lake, dunes and beach, although none can compete with the area's natural beauty as a tourist draw.

It is the northernmost village in the group of eight collectively known as Harbor Country.

Food/Restaurant

Horsefeathers, 12857 Three Oaks Road, (269) 426-3237. Contemporary American food. Try the Harbor Chicken Marsalis. Open Mon to Thurs 11:30 am to 10:00 pm, Fri 11:30 am to 11:00 pm, Sat noon to 11:00 pm and Sun 11:00 am to 10:00 pm.

Lodging

Super 8 Motel, 12850 Super Drive, (269) 426-3237. 61 rooms. heated indoor pool and some whirlpool rooms.

Antiques

Dunes Antique Center, 12825 Red Arrow Highway, (269) 426-4043, www.dunesantiques.com. 20,000 square feet of Americana to Modernism and 70 dealers. You can shop for furniture, art, pottery, crystal, primitives, linens, china, sterling silver, books, jewelry and more in this old building that was reputedly a speakeasy in an earlier life. In the early 1900s loggers rented rooms upstairs in the building. Open year round, 10:00 am to 6:00 pm, closed Tues.

Steward James Antiques and Galleria, 12619 Red Arrow Highway, (269) 426-3313. Antiques, art, primitives and generalized folk art, African art, backyard garden, furniture, lamps and other interesting objects. Open 7 days, Mon to Fri noon to 5:00 pm. Weekends 11:00 am to 6:00 pm. Reduced winter hours, call to confirm.

Tara Hill Antique Mall, 12816 Red Arrow Highway, (269) 469-8673. Open seasonally May through October, Mon to Sat 11:00 am to 6:00 pm, Sun 1:00 pm to 5:30 pm. Closed Fri.

Timeless Treasures Antiques, 12908 Red Arrow Highway, (269) 469-3636. Lots of Depression glass and a little of everything else. Open 7 days, 11:00 am to 6:00 pm (sometimes later in the summer). Weekends in the winter. (See Ghost stories, Part II, p. 409 for a related story.)

Other Shopping

Mums the Word Craft Store, 12388 Red Arrow Highway, (269) 426-8880. Offers hardy mums and other seasonal flowers when in bloom, but this is primarily a craft store displaying a variety of handmade items taken on consignment. You will find everything from furniture to doll clothes. Open 10:00 am to 5:00 pm 7 days. Closed January to March.

Joe Jackson's Fruit Stand, Next to the turnoff to the Dunes on Red Arrow Highway. (See listing under New Buffalo, p. 9 for details.)

Photo Courtesy of Joe Jurkiewicz

Parks and Campgrounds

Covert Park Beach and Campground, 80559 32nd Street (next to Warren Dunes between Sawyer and Bridgman), (269) 764-1421, www.covertpark.com. Township Park with ¼ mile of private sandy beach. The entrance to the campground takes you a short lovely drive down a tree canopied road. Amenities: water and electric, bathhouse, store, picnic tables, playgrounds, dump station, ice, firewood and new camping cabins. Day use welcome.

Bridgman

Population: Approximately 2,400.

Directions: Exit #16 off I-94 to Red Arrow Highway. Fifteen miles north of New Buffalo on Red Arrow Highway.

Background and History

In the late 1600s the French became the earliest European explorers to the area and they found sand dunes, marshes, and forests awaiting them on the shores of Lake Michigan. It took another century and a half before the first settler, John Harner, arrived in 1830. Known then as Laketon, a small village grew around the sawmill.

The village was renamed Charlotteville after prominent citizen, Charles Howe's wife. However, in 1870, George Bridgman plotted an area about a half mile east of Charlotteville and named it after himself. Bridgman had the good fortune or good sense to plot his land directly in the path of the Chicago and West Michigan Railroad, a fact that gave rise to growth in Bridgman and decline of Charlotteville, the latter eventually disappearing altogether.

At the end of the 19th century, Russian and German immigrants began populating the area and working on fruit farms and in other industries. In 1949 Bridgman became a city and today it covers three square miles. The lake attracts tourists by the hundreds in the hot summer months. Permanent residents are drawn to upscale living in beautiful homes built on the dunes. A sidewalk connects the city with Weko beach making the walk to the beach an easy one.

Food/Restaurants

D'Agostino's Italian Restaurant and Navajo Lounge, 8970 Red Arrow Highway, (269) 465-3434. Italian and American dishes. Fine dining or just pizza. They even have fried pickles. Open Mon to Thurs 5:00 pm to 11:00 pm, Fri and Sat 5:00 pm to midnight.

Getaway Bar and Grill, 9489 Red Arrow Highway, (269) 465-5932. Family atmosphere. Good hamburgers, good prices and Chicago Cub's paraphernalia as ambiance. Voted #1 Sports Bar by the local paper. A decent place to get a sandwich or burger and enjoy the live entertainment on the patio. Open 7 days, Mon to Sat 11:00 am to 2:00 am and Sun noon to 2:00 am.

Hyerdall's Café, 9673 Red Arrow Highway, (269) 465-5546. Opened in 1927 and drawing families looking for fresh food ever since. Open 7:00 am to 8:00 pm or 9:00 pm during the summer.

Parks, Beaches and Campgrounds

Warren Dunes State Park, south of Bridgman, exit 12 off I-94, (239) 426-4013. The rugged sand dunes rise majestically above Lake Michigan and are the focal center of the park. There are 197 camping sites and three mini-cabins available to campers. Hang gliding is a favorite activity in the park.

Weko Beach, exit 16 off I-94, then north on Red Arrow Highway and west on Lake Street, (269) 465-3406 or (269) 465-5144 for camping information. 900 feet of Lake Michigan beach. Amenities: concessions, beach house, changing areas, restrooms, boat launch, volleyball, lovely boardwalk and two magnificent sand dunes. There are 70 campsites available with electric, 48 have water. 25 rustic sites and four camping cabins are also available. *Taps* is played each night at dusk on summer evenings. Entrance fee to beach.

Other Things to See and Do

Captain Mike's Fun Park, Red Arrow Highway, 1½ miles north of Warren Dunes State Park, (269) 465-5747. Go-Karts, mini-golf, bumper boats, batting cages and game room. Open 7 days at 11:00 am.

Jones' Blueberries, 9245 Gast Road, Exit 16 off I-94, north on Red Arrow Highway to the stoplight, right 1.1 miles to Gast Road and left after a half mile. (269) 465-4745, www.jonesberryfarm.com, jones@jonesberryfarm.com. You can pick berries yourself or enjoy those already picked for you. Also sells, jellies, jams, and peaches.

Shafer Orchards, 207 Shafer Road, Exit 16 off I-94, north on Red Arrow Highway, right on Lake Street, five miles to Hills Road and then follow the signs.

Tabor Hill Champagne Cellar, 10243 Red Arrow Highway, (269) 465-6566, www.taborhill.com. Free wine tasting. You can also drive to Tabor Hill's winery and restaurant at 185 Mount Tabor Road, Buchanan, toll-free (800) 283-3363, or consider the wine tasting tour (See Other Things to See and Do in Southwest Michigan, p. 40.)

Festivals

Free Concerts at the Beach House, June through September.

Lake Michigan Shore Wine Festival, June, Weko Beach. Sponsored by the Southwest Michigan Wine Trail. Live music, food, and Michigan wines. Call toll-free (800) 716-WINE for more details.

Golf

Pebblewood Country Club, 9794 Jericho Road, (269) 465-5611. An 18-hole, par 68 golf club. Open to the public.

Stevensville

Population: 1,200.

Directions: 6½ miles north of Bridgman on US-12/Red Arrow Highway, or exit 22 of I-94. (21 miles north of New Buffalo.)

Background and History

The town of Stevensville was named for Thomas Stevens who purchased 160 acres of land there in 1869. Mr. Stevens struck a deal with the Chicago and West Michigan Lake Shore Railroad Company to have a railroad depot built on a portion of his property. The contract required the depot to be named after Stevens and noted he was to be paid $1.00 for the land.

By having a depot located at this spot, Mr. Stevens assured himself transportation to get his fruit crops to market.

Stevens had the land platted in 1870 but the plat was not recorded until 1872 and another decade passed before the Michigan Senate in 1893 formally acknowledged the Village of Stevensville as a chartered village.

Another early Stevensville pioneer was John Beers who came to the area from New Jersey in the same year as Stevens. After a failed peach crop, Beers decided to enter Medical School at Northwestern University and later returned to Stevensville to set up his practice.

In addition to farming and practicing medicine, Beers was an active politician, serving as state senator and in many lesser political offices.

Food/Restaurants

5 O'clock Sports Bar and Restaurant, 5000 Red Arrow Highway, (269) 429-3273. Serves sandwiches, hamburgers, wings and salads, or you can opt for a full dinner of pork chops, prime rib or Lake Perch among other selections. TVs are the primary ambiance. Open Mon to Sat 11:00 am to 2:00 am (kitchen closes at 10:00 pm during the week and 11:00 pm on weekends). Sun noon to 2:00 am.

Fireside Inn, 4296 Red Arrow Highway (adjacent to Park Inn Hotel), (269) 429-2420. House specialty is the slow roasted prime rib. Open Tues to Sat 10:30 am to 9:00 pm and Sun. 8:30 am to 9:00 pm. Closed Mon.

Grande Mere Inn, 5800 Red Arrow Highway, (269) 429-3591. Popular local spot with Lake Perch specialty. Views of Lake Michigan. Open Tues to Sat for dinner, 4:30 pm to closing.

Santaniello's Restaurant, 2262 West Glenlord Road, (269) 429-3966. Authentic Italian dinners including: rack of lamb, grilled rib eye, catfish, shrimp scampi, fettuccini, mostacciolo, Italian Venezia, rigatoni, lasagna or just pizza. With dinner you will get a free basket of foccacia bread. It is a challenge to resist eating so much foccacia that you are too full for the main course. Open Tues to Sun 4:00 pm to 10:00 pm. Closed Mon.

Lodging (Also see Campgrounds below)

Baymont Inn & Suites, 2601 West Marquette Woods, (269) 428-9111 or toll-free (800) 301-0200. About a mile from Lake Michigan. Extras: continental breakfast, pets welcome, vouchers to Southshore Health and Racquet Club.

Candlewood Suites, 2567 West Marquette Woods, (269) 428-4400. Extended stay hotel with spacious studio and one bedroom suites just minutes from Lake Michigan. Extras: full kitchen in suites, high speed internet, free use of washers and dryers, DVD player with free DVD library, a private patio with grills, hot tub and fitness center.

Chalet on the Lake, 5340 Notre Dame Avenue, (269) 465-6365, www.chaletonthelake.com. Located on the shores of Lake Michigan, these cottage chalets offer a private beach, swimming pool, volleyball, basketball, tennis courts, shuffleboard, playground and horseshoes.

Comfort Suites, 2633 West Marquette Woods, (269) 428-4888, www.stjoecomfortsuites.com. Extras: indoor pool, whirlpool, sauna, sun deck, rooms with heart-shaped Jacuzzi and fireplace, fitness center, business center, free high speed internet, laundry, coffee makers, loft suites, kids suites available.

Hampton Inn, 5050 Red Arrow Highway, Exit 23 off I-94, (269) 429-2700 or toll-free (800) 426-7866, www.hampton-inn.com. Extras: deluxe breakfast bar, indoor pool, high speed internet, whirlpool suites available and passes for off-site gym.

Park Inn, 4290 Red Arrow Highway, Exit 23 off I-94, (269) 429-3218 or toll-free (800) 670-7275, www.parkinn.com. Extras: free high speed internet, indoor/outdoor pools, hot tubs, complimentary full breakfast and pet-friendly.

Parks, Beaches and Campgrounds

Glenlord Beach, Exit 23 off I-94, north on Red Arrow highway and west on Glenlord Road. Situated on a high bluff overlooking Lake Michigan you can enjoy the most spectacular views in all of Southwest Michigan from the observation decks. Restrooms available. Swimming is not allowed at this site because of beach erosion.

Grand Mere State Park and Nature Area, exit 22 off I-94. The park is comprised of 1,000 acres; the nature center covers slightly over a third of that acreage. The nature area is a favorite place for bird-watchers. At the entrance there is parking and the beach is about ten minutes down the self-guided path. You will need a permit and it can be obtained at Warren Dunes State Park. Amenities: shelters, restrooms and paved trails.

Lincoln Township Park and Nature Center, Red Arrow Highway and Notre Dame Road just south of Stevensville. Amenities: boardwalk, access to the beach, picnic area and restrooms.

Stevensville: Early Days
Photo Courtesy of the Village of Stevensville

Festivals

Discover Stevensville Days, June. Four days of family fun with fireworks, street dances, arts and crafts, parade and all kinds of food.

St. Joseph

Population: 8800.

Directions: Exit 23 off I-94 and 5 miles on Business I-94. (28 miles north of New Buffalo on M-63).

Background and History

In 1679 French Explorer La Salle and fourteen fellow adventurers constructed a fort on a bluff overlooking the St. Joseph River. They did not stay long and the area remained unsettled except for a mission established in about 1700 at the mouth of the river. This mission was described in Catholic Church records as "The Mission of St. Joseph of Lake Michigan." St. Joseph was the Patron Saint of Canada which was called New France at that time. New France sent Jesuit priests to convert Native Americans living in the area. Pottawatomie migrated to the area in 1721.

William Burnett established a trading post in 1785 and became the first European settler to the area. In 1805 William Hull was made Governor of the newly formed Territory of Michigan. The largest Native American settlements of the time were in the northeast portion of St. Joseph County and the southeast part of Kalamazoo County.

Legends passed on by Native Americans to the European settlers, and by the settlers to their children, suggest fierce battles took place between various tribes for possession of the land in this area. The fertile soil produced abundant maize, the dense forests provided plentiful game and the lake was full of fish. These natural resources made the area extremely valuable.

The last battle is believed to have been fought in 1801, just after the turn of the century. The Pottawatomie had lived peacefully for a long time with their neighbors, the Ottawa of Kalamazoo Valley. The Shawnee broke the peace, motivated by their desire to possess the rich wilderness land. They made a sneak attack on the unsuspecting Pottawatomie, defeating them and attempting to drive them from the area. However, as the Pottawatomie fled they carried with them Princess Mishawaka, daughter of the fierce Shawnee leader, Chief Elkhart. Ultimately the princess found happiness with her scout captor. The Pottawatomie, eager to regain their land, struck an alliance with the Ottawa of Kalamazoo County and the Ottawa of the Grand River Valley area. The strength of the three tribes drove out the Shawnee and peace returned.

In the early 1800s an elderly, enterprising Native American Chief established a toll station on the old trail near Mottville and charged all travelers a fee to pass.

Apparently European settlers introduced the Native Americans to whisky and by 1821 Ottawa Chief Topinabee sold most of what is now St. Joseph County to the settlers. The terms of the deal provided the Ottawa with annual payments of $5,000 a year for 20 years, $1,500 a year for a blacksmith and a teacher and $1,000 a year forever.

There was a growth spurt after the Carey Mission Treaty of 1828. The developing village was named Newberryport in honor of a prominent businessman who lived there. The village incorporated in 1834 and was renamed St. Joseph.

The city became the permanent county seat in 1894, about the same time resorters and tourists began discovering St. Joseph. Hotels sprang up to accommodate visitors and the Silver Beach Amusement Park opened to provide entertainment.

The area's rivers and streams feed the St. Joseph River contributing to its grandness. Steamers, freighters and pleasure boats have long found St. Joseph an ideal Lake Michigan port.

Food/Restaurants

Barney's Boathouse, 600 Fisherman's Road, (269) 983-3456. A crazy kind of place with a Jimmy Buffet atmosphere. All you can eat fish after 5:00 pm each night. DJ and dance floor. Satellite TV so you can catch major sporting events. Not for everyone, but has its loyal following. Open 7 days, 5:00 pm to 2:00 am.

Bistro on the Boulevard, 521 Lake Boulevard, (at the Boulevard Inn) (269) 983-3882. Sophistication and excellent food are the trademarks of this French Bistro. You can dine al fresco on the deck or in the dining room; either way enjoying the spectacular views offered by the Bistro's prime location on a bluff overlooking Lake Michigan. Dishes are elegantly prepared and take advantage of local fresh ingredients. The dinners are a bit pricey, but you can choose "lighter fare" at more moderate prices. This is a great restaurant for a special evening not a quick bite on the run.

Broad Street Café, 614 Broad Street, (269) 983-7646. Good place to grab breakfast or lunch. Open 7 days, Mon to Fri 6:30 am to 3:00 pm, Sat 7:00 am to 4:00 pm and Sun 8:00 am to 3:00 pm.

Cabana's Ice Cream, 512 Broad Street, (269) 983-5669. Inside and outdoor tables, close to the beach. Sandwiches, cotton candy, pizza, yogurt and many flavors of ice cream. Seasonal: March to September. Open 11:00 am to 11:00 pm 7 days.

Cafe Tosi, 516 Pleasant Street, (269) 983-3354. The smell of rich, freshly brewed coffee and aromatic, warm bread lures you inside where you will find soups, sandwiches, grilled panini and desserts to make you happy you ate here. Open Mon 7:00 am to 7:00 pm, Tues to Fri 7:00 am to 8:00 pm, Sat 8:00 am to 8:00 pm, Sun 8:00 am to 4:00 pm.

Chan's Garden, 310 State Street, (269) 983-2609. Asian food. Open Mon to Thurs 11:00 am to 10:00 pm, Fri 11:00 am to 10:30 pm, Sat noon to 10:30 pm and Sun 11:30 am to 10:00 pm. In the winter they play it by ear, but generally close a bit earlier.

Chocolate Café and Museum, 300 State Street, (269) 983-9866. A place for all things chocolate. Open Mon to Wed 8:30 am to 10:00 pm, Thurs and Fri 8:30 am to 11:00 pm, Sat 8:30 am to midnight and Sun 9:00 am to 11:00 pm.

Clementine's Too, 1235 Broad Street, (269) 983-0990. Located on the St. Joseph River, decorated with nautical memorabilia and providing a patio from which you can watch the yachts and marine activity. Same menu as the original Clementine's located in South Haven, including everything from munchies to sandwiches to full entrees including steaks and seafood (try the Tin Pan Walleye or Lake Perch) all presented in a casual atmosphere. Open 7 days, Mon to Sat 11:00 am to 11:00 pm and Sun noon to 11:00 pm.

Dale's Donut Factory, 3687 South Lakeshore Drive, (269) 429-1033. Great bakery with the emphasis on donuts. If you go late in the day they will be sold out. Try the tiger tails or cherry rosebuds. Also offers homemade bread and has a lunch counter for soup and sandwiches. Open Mon to Fri 5:00 am to 5:00 pm and Sat 5:00 am to 2:00 pm. Closed Sun.

Golden Brown Bakery Café, 201 State Street, (269) 983-2002. Fresh bakery donuts, muffins, bread and cookies along with a good place to have a breakfast sandwich or a panini for lunch. Open 7 days, Mon to Thurs 6:30 am to 7:00 pm, Fri and Sat 6:30 am to 8:00 pm and Sun 8:00 am to 2:00 pm.

Kilwin's Chocolates, 316 State Street, (269) 982-1330. Hand-paddled Mackinac Island Fudge, 32 flavors of premium ice cream, old fashioned malts and shakes, smoothies, sundaes and ice cream pie. Handmade waffle cones, caramel apples, pecan, cashew and peanut brittle, caramel corn, chocolate dipped cherries and strawberries, turtle sticks, chocolate dipped Oreo cookies and pretzels and custom made gift baskets. Their motto, "Life is short, eat dessert first." Open 7 days, (summer hours): Mon to Sat 10:00 am to 10:00 pm and Sun noon to 10:00 pm. Reduced winter hours.

Mansion Grille by the Lake, 3029 Lake Shore Drive, (269) 982-1500. Fine dining, a lovely menu and a local favorite. Dinner entrees range from moderate to expensive. Open: Lunch Tues to Fri 11:00 am to 2:00 pm. Dinner: 7 nights 4:30 pm to 10:00 pm. (See related ghost story, p. 410, Part II of this guide.)

Pump House Grille, 214 State Street, (269) 983-0001. Specializing in steaks and ribs. House specialty is slow cooked prime rib from their custom smoker. You have to be intrigued by a deep fried pickle served with ranch dressing dip. Not bad actually. Eight beers on tap and a world class, top-shelf martini served in your own personal shaker. Open lunch and dinner, Sun to Thurs 11:00 am to 10:00 pm, Fri and Sat 11:00 am to 11:00 pm.

Schu's Grill & Bar, 501 Pleasant Street, (269) 983-7248. Contemporary, American dining where families are welcome and there is a children's menu. Casual atmosphere and views of Lake Michigan. Moderate prices. Open 7 days in the summer, Mon to Thurs 11:00 am to 10:00 pm, Fri 11:00 am to 11:00 pm, Sat noon to 11:00 pm and Sun noon to 8:00 pm. Winter: Mon to Thurs 11:00 am to 9:00 pm, Fri and Sat 11:00 am to 10:00 pm and Sun noon to 8:00 pm.

Silver Dollar Café, 412 State Street, (269) 983-4842. Great burgers and other home cooked menu items. Open Mon to Wed 10:00 am to midnight, Thurs 10:00 am to 1:00 am, Fri and Sat 10:00 am to 2:00 am and Sun noon to midnight.

Spinnakers, 105 Main Street, (269) 983-2000. This contemporary restaurant offers a large selection of menu items to appeal to every taste and degree of hunger: soups, salads, sandwiches, fresh seafood including: salmon, steaks and chicken, as well as a slice of homemade pie or cake to top it off. Moderate prices. If you have special dietary needs they will do their best to accommodate. Entertainment. Open 7 days, 11:00 am to 11:00 pm (Sun brunch until 3:00 pm).

Stooges Restaurant, 227 Main Street, (269) 983-6618. With pictures of Larry, Moe and Curly looking on, you can enjoy good food at inexpensive to moderate prices in a casual atmosphere. Serves breakfast, lunch and dinner 7 days. Open Sun to Thurs 6:00 am to 9:30 pm, Fri and Sat 6:00 am to 10:30 pm. Bar stays open later.

That's New Orleans Deli II, 4142 M-139, (269) 556-3354. A deli where you can find inexpensive Cajun style food. Open: Mon to Sat 11:00 am to 8:00 pm. Closed Sun.

Tootie and Dreamers, 304 State Street, (269) 983-5228. Café and retail store. Merchandise includes: aromatherapy and natural personal care products, unique gifts and incense. Open Mon to Fri 8:00 am to 6:00 pm, Sat 10:00 am to 5:00 pm. **Café** with salads, soups, vegan dishes and traditional vegetarian. Open Mon to Fri 8:00 am to 2:30 pm.

Vickie's Sandbar, 2701 Lakeshore Drive, (269) 983-9977. Billiards, burgers and beer. Home of the Scoop Burger (a scoop of soft cheese on the hamburger). Neighborhood bar feeling. Daily lunch specials, 25 cent wings on Wed, D.J. Tues and Thurs and Karaoke on

Wed, Fri and Sat from 10:00 pm to 1:30 am. Open Mon to Sat 10:00 am to 2:00 am and Sun noon to 2:00 am.

Lodging *(Also see Campgrounds below)*

The Boulevard Inn, 521 Lake Boulevard, (269) 983-6600 or toll-free (800) 875-6600, www.theboulevardinn.com. Extras: full breakfast, wireless internet access in public areas, refrigerators, wet bars, microwaves and full-size refrigerators in deluxe suites. The Boardroom Suite is 900 square feet with space for in-room meetings or entertaining. The Inn is situated on a bluff overlooking the sugar-sand beach of Silver Lake Park, the lighthouse and those spectacular Lake Michigan sunsets. Special packages available.

Econo Lodge, 2723 Niles Avenue, (269) 982-1310. 40 rooms and an outdoor pool.

Holiday Inn Express Hotel & Suites, 3019 Lakeshore Drive, (269) 982-0004 or toll-free (800) HOLIDAY, www.sjholidayinn.com. Overlooking Lake Michigan. Extras: indoor pool/spa, sun deck, fitness room, deluxe breakfast, 2-room suites for families with children, lake view rooms with spa, DSL wireless internet, in-room movies.

Quality Inn, 100 Main Street, (269) 983-7341. 49 rooms. Extras: some whirlpool rooms, heated indoor pool, whirlpool, sauna and exercise room.

Riverbend Retreat, 254 Jakway Avenue, (269) 926-2220, www.riverbendretreatbb.com. Perched on a bluff overlooking the St. Joseph River in a secluded area of woods and wetlands. It offers private decks and rooms overlooking the river. Lovely gardens. Each room has a private bath. Gourmet breakfast served.

South Cliff Inn B & B, 1900 Lakeshore Drive, (269) 983-4881, www.southcliffinn.com, inninfo@southcliffinn.com. An English style inn with colorful perennial gardens and large decks for relaxing and viewing the spectacular sunsets from a bluff overlooking Lake Michigan. Seven rooms each with a private bath and some with fireplaces and whirlpools. The breakfast is prepared by a retired chef who is the current owner. The B&B has received the "Readers Choice" award for Best B&B in Southwest Michigan for eight consecutive years. *Chicago Magazine* called it one of the 40 ways to pamper yourself.

Museums and Galleries

Box Factory for the Arts, 1101 Broad Street, (269) 983-3688, www.boxfactoryforthearts.org. Historic factory building originally constructed at the turn of the century and used for manufacturing boxes for various decorative and specialty purposes. It continued that function until 1989. Today it houses a mixed media facility for the arts where you are invited to watch artists work. Browse the studios and shop for one-of-a-kind items for yourself or to give as treasured gifts. The facility is owned by the Berrien Artist Guild and provides studios for 20 local artists. Saturday nights there are musical performances. Open Mon to Sat 10:00 am to 4:00 pm and Sun 1:00 pm to 4:00 pm.

Curious Kids' Museum, 415 Lake Boulevard, (across from Silver Beach), (269) 983-2543, www.curiouskidsmuseum.org. Voted Reader's Choice *Best Museum in Southwest Michigan* and *Best Place to Take Kids*. This hands-on museum encourages kids to touch, see, hear, smell, and even taste with over 100 exhibits and activities. Your children will love: Kids in Outer Space, the awesome Apple Orchard, the Great Lakes Ship and the Dinomania exhibits. Learning becomes fun as they experience science, culture, history and technology through their five senses. Open September to June, Wed to Sat 10:00 am to 5:00 pm, Sun noon to 5:00 pm. Expanded summer hours.

Fort Miami Heritage Center, Corner of Main and Market Streets, (269) 983-1191 or (269) 983-7227. Greek Revival Building on the site of the historic First Congregational Church, incorporates architectural elements salvaged from local houses scheduled for demolition. There is an exhibit hall and research library as well as a gift shop on premises. Open Tues to Fri 10:00 am to 5:00 pm or by appointment.

Gallery on the Alley, 611 Broad Street, (269) 983-6261. A place to check art and fine crafts from 175 American artists with a wide selection of jewelry and mediums from whimsical to fine art. They have Yardbird and Story People. Open 7 days, Mon to Sat 10:00 am to 5:30 pm and Sun noon to 4:00 pm.

Krasl Art Center, 707 Lake Boulevard, (269) 983-0271. Bringing people and art together for 25 years. Monthly exhibitions, trips, and a gallery shop. Open 7 days, Mon to Thurs 10:00 am to 4:00 pm, Fri 10:00 am to 1:00 pm, Sat 10:00 am to 4:00 pm and Sun 1:00 pm to 4:00 pm.

Priscilla U. Byrns Heritage Center, 601 Main Street, (269) 983-1191, www.fortmiami.org, www.michiganfruitbelt.org. A celebration of Michigan's fruit belt. Open May to September, Tues to Sat 10:00 am to 4:00 pm and Sun noon to 4:00 pm.

Theatre

Twin City Players Theatre, 600 West Glenlord Road, (269) 429-0400. Small theatre troupe that has performed for more than 70 years. Community theatre at its very best, this theatre tackles both comedy and drama. Call for details of current productions.

Antiques

Days of Yore Antiques, 215 State Street, (269) 983-4144. Collectibles (including Coke), memorabilia, and antiques including: jewelry, glassware, furniture, lamps, primitives, 45s and LPs. Summer open 7 days, Mon to Sat 10:00 am to 6:00 pm and Sun 11:00 am to 5:00 pm. January to March open Mon to Sat 10:00 am to 5:00 pm.

Elephant's Breath Antiques, 203 State Street, (269) 982-5210. Specializing in Mission and Vintage Oak. Collectibles, furniture, chairs, chests, desks, cabinets, fine china and porcelain. Open Mon to Fri 11:00 am to 5:00 pm (except closed Wed), Sat 10:00 am to 6:00 pm and Sun noon to 5:00 pm.

State Street Antiques, 410 State Street, (269) 983-7422. Antiques from the 40s predominate. Some Victorian jewelry and vintage purses. Open year round, Tues to Sat 11:00 am to 5:00 pm and Sun noon to 4:00 pm. Also by appointment.

Other Shopping

There are 75 shops in downtown St. Joseph. Check out those listed here and explore others you find along the way.

Bears greet you on the downtown corners.   *Photo by Bob Royce*

Bloomies Flower Studio, 400 State Street, (269) 983-000, www.bloomiesetc.com. You could walk past this shop several times before deciding to enter. Flower shops do not normally entice travelers, but there are so many interesting things beckoning. Besides flowers, plants and arrangements, you will find gourmet foods, gift items, limited but unusual wrought iron chairs, stools, Michigan Freshwater Foods, teas, metal tables, mirrors, Junkart, American Graffiti and much more. Open Mon to Fri 9:00 am to 5:00 pm, Sat 10:00 am to 5:00 pm and Sun noon to 5:00 pm. Closed Sun in winter.

Form, 210 State Street, (269) 982-7025. Unique collection of gifts and decorative accessories. Great collection of clocks and kitchenware. The pottery is beautiful and split between handmade and production made. Lovely art objects. Open 7 days, Mon to Sat 10:00 am to 6:00 pm and Sun noon to 5:00 pm.

Items, 318 State Street, (269) 983-3081. A woman's boutique with a limited but interesting inventory of jewelry, handbags, clothing, and shoes. Open Mon to Wed 10:00 am to 7:00 pm, Thurs to Sat 10:00 am to 8:00 pm and Sun 11:00 am to 5:00 pm. They close at 5:00 in the off-season and close completely during the "heart of the winter."

Moxie Boutique, 321 State Street (269) 325-4270. New boutique opened summer of 2006. Has a nice line of clothing and accessories. Open Mon to Sat 10:00 am to 6:00 pm and Sun noon to 4:00 pm.

My Sentiments, 312 State Street, Suite A, (269) 982-7366. Lawn and garden stakes, lotions and handmade one-of-a-kind jewelry. Open 7 days, Mon to Sat 10:00 am to 6:00 pm and Sun 11:00 am to 4:00 pm. Christmas to Easter hours are reduced or closed so call first.

Perennial Accents, 220 State Street, www.perennialaccents.com, (269) 983-5791. Home accents, garden items, bath and body, kitchen items and jewelry. Open Mon to Thurs 10:00 am to 8:00 pm, Fri and Sat 10:00 am to 9:00 pm and Sun 11:00 am to 5:00 pm.

The Toy Company, 208 State Street, (269) 983-0600. Specialty toys with a focus on things you would not find in a "white bread" kind of toy store. Toys from Japan, Germany and the United Kingdom. Lots of wooden toys and trains. Open Mon to Fri 10:00 am to 9:00 pm, Sat 10:00 am to 6:00 pm and Sun 11:00 am to 6:00 pm. Winter hours: Mon to Wed 10:00 am to 6:00 pm, Thurs to Sat, 10:00 am to 8:00 pm and Sun 11:00 am to 5:00 pm.

Urban Home, 212 State Street, (269) 983-0300. Innovative home accessories including furniture, lamps, prints and serving items. Open Mon to Sat 10:00 am to 6:00 pm (approximately) and Sun noon to 6:00 pm, sometimes later if customers are still shopping.

Your Favorite Things, 1320 State Street. Primarily gifts, Christmas items and teddy bears. Open 7 days, Mon to Sat 10:00 am to 6:00 pm and Sun 2:00 pm to 5:00 pm.

Parks, Beaches and Campgrounds

Knauf Nature Trail, access off Vineland Road at June Trace, ends at Niles Road. The trail takes you through a wide range of habitats in a minimal amount of acreage (34 acres). Many plants and creatures find a stream, forest, marsh or meadow to suit their tastes.

Kiwanis Park and the John and Dede Howard Skatepark, Pearl Street near Langley Avenue. Amenities: picnic tables and shelter, playground, basketball and tennis courts and a skatepark. Hours are seasonal.

Lake Bluff Park runs along Lake Boulevard downtown St. Joseph. Unparalleled views of Lake Michigan, Silver Beach, and the St. Joseph River. Amenities: walking trail, picnic tables, benches and historic monuments.

Lion's Park, below the bluff in downtown St. Joseph, south on Lions Park Drive. Amenities: parking and sidewalks, sheltered pavilions, playground and restrooms and a terrific view of the St. Joseph piers and lighthouse.

Lookout Park, Lakeshore Drive off Hilltop Road. Amenities: great views of Lake Michigan, picnic facilities and a viewing deck. (No swimming beach.)

Riverview Park, 2927 Niles Road (south of St. Joseph). 107 acres on the St. Joseph River. Amenities: baseball diamonds, playground, nature trails and boat access. Shelters can be reserved.

Silver Beach, below the bluff in downtown St. Joseph on Lake Street. Large parking lot off Broad Street. Amenities: men's and women's bathhouses, bike racks, playground, volleyball courts, visitors' center and a 1,600 foot beach for swimmers. Lifeguards are on duty during the summer. Fee at entrance.

Tiscornia Park, north of St. Joseph River Channel off Upton and Marina drives. Amenities: public beach and access to the North Pier and lighthouse, restrooms available and a place to fish. Fee charged.

Park in St Joseph   *Photo by Bob Royce*

Marinas, Water Sports, Boat and Jet Ski Rental

Brian's Marina, 285 Anchors Court, (269) 983-0760. Full service marina: 200 boat slips, 75 unit drydock stack storage, heated inside storage and service.

Outpost Sports, 800 Lions Park Drive, (269) 983-2010. Rent a kayak and get expert kayaking advice. Sat at 9:00 am get a free lesson.

St. Joseph/West Basin Marina, (269) 983-5432. 78 rental slips and 2 transient slips. Open year round, 7:00 am to 7:00 pm.

Cruises and Charter Fishing

Silverking Sportfishing Charters, Lake Michigan, (269) 983-7816, www.silverkingsportfishing.com, silverkingfish@aol.com. Ken Neidlinger has captained charter trips for 30 years. In the winter and spring he fishes in the St. Joseph River and in the summer and fall in Lake Michigan. His customers have included Bobbie Knight and Al Unser Jr. He will guide you to the best location to find salmon or trout (for which his charter holds the record at 40 pounds, 8 ounces).

Other Things to See and Do

Hug and Stuff and Gotta Go Pottery, 519 Broad Street, (269) 982-8010. A bit of fun for the younger set, as they make their very own stuffed animal, mug or other special gift. Open Mon to Fri 11:00 am to 5:00 pm, Sat 10:00 am to 5:00 pm and Sun noon to 4:00 pm.

Nye's Apple Barn, 3151 Niles Road, Exit 27 off I-94, (269) 429-5056. Sells fresh fruits and vegetables in season.

Festivals

Magical Ice Carving Festival of St. Joseph, February. The most serious ice carvers come to join the competition making this an amazing weekend full of fun.

Blossomtime Grand Floral Parade, May.

Memorial Day Parade, May.

Municipal Band Concerts, June. John E. N. Howard Band shell.

Krasl Art Fair on the Bluff, July.

Venetian Festival on the River, July.

Chalk on the Block Festival, August.

Harvest Festival, September.

Halloween Festival, October.

Luminary Festival, November.

Reindog Holiday Parade, December.

Golf

The Oaks, 3711 Niles Road, (269) 782-5827. An 18-hole, par 72 golf course with bar, snack bar, watered fairways, club rentals, driving range and pro shop.

Benton Harbor

Population: Slightly over 11,000.

Directions: North of St. Joseph. Exits 28 and 29 off I-94. (30 miles north of New Buffalo on M-63.)

Background and History

Often called the twin to its resort and tourist oriented sister, St. Joseph; Benton Harbor has strong ties to agriculture and industry. It is the site of Whirlpool Manufacturing.

Originally named Brunson Harbor, Benton Harbor was founded in 1860 by Sterne Brunson, Henry Morton and Charles Hull. In order to develop the site on the banks of the St. Joseph River and make it livable and productive, the men had to dig a canal to the harbor.

The home of the Henry Morton family is a registered Michigan Historic Site and the oldest home in the city. It provided shelter to four generations of this early founding family.

Benton Harbor began mainly as marshy swampland bordering the Paw Paw River. In 1863 the three original founders platted the village. The city was later renamed Benton Harbor in recognition of Thomas Hart Benton, a Missouri senator who is credited with supporting Michigan's 1835 bid to become a state.

Many famous people were born in Benton Harbor including: two actor/comedians, Arte Shaw and Sinbad; three professional basketball players, Anthony Miller, Quacy Barnes and Robert Whaley; a jazz pianist, Gene Harris (in whose honor there is a festival each summer); a rhythm and blues singer, Jerome Woods; and professional wrestler, Bobo Brazil among them.

Benton Harbor was home to the City of David, the third oldest Christian community in the United States. The City of David had a famous baseball team that is part of Benton Harbor's historic roots.

Food/Restaurants

Hacienda Mexican Restaurant, 1599 Mall Drive, (269) 927-4593. House specialties include the Fettuccini Fernando (a classic pasta dish with Mexican spices) and Adobo Enchiladas. There are appetizers, salads and great margaritas including the margarita meltdown. Open 7 days, Mon to Sat 11:00 am to 11:00 pm and Sun 11:00 am to 10:00 pm.

Sophia's House of Pancakes, 1647 Mall Drive, (269) 934-7688. Voted Reader's Choice best breakfast in Southwest Michigan three years in a row. Serves breakfast, lunch and dinner. Open 7 days, 6:00 am to 9:00 pm.

Texas Corral Steakhouse and Saloon, 1830 Pipestone Road, (269) 934-7445. Open 7 days, Mon to Thurs 3:00 pm to 10:00 pm and Fri to Sun noon to 11:00 pm.

Lodging (Also see Campgrounds below)

Best Western Inn and Suites, 1598 Mall Drive (Exit 29 off I-94), (269) 925-1880. 52-rooms. Extras: heated pool, sauna and whirlpool.

Comfort Suites, 1825 Meadow Brook Road (exit 29 off I-94), (269) 925-8800 or toll-free (800) 4-CHOICE, www.choicehotels.com. Extras: indoor pool and spa, free HBO, fitness room, free local calls, Jacuzzi suites available, continental breakfast buffet, data ports and voice messaging.

Courtyard Marriott, 1592 Mall Drive (Exit 29 off I-94), (269) 925-3000 or toll-free (800) 321-2211. Extras: fitness room, outdoor pool, indoor and outdoor spa. Courtyard Café offers breakfast at reasonable prices.

Holiday Inn Express Hotel & Suites, 2276 Pipestone Road, (269) 927-4599 or toll-free (800) HOLIDAY. Extras: heated pool, exercise room and whirlpool.

Motel 6, 2063 Pipestone Road, (269) 925-5100 or toll-free (800) 466-8356.

Red Roof Inn, 1630 Mall Drive, (269) 927-2484 or toll-free (800) 843-7663. Extras: video games (fee) and pets allowed.

Super 8 Motel, 1950 East Napier Avenue, (269) 926-1371 or toll-free (800) 800-8000.

Theatre

Gene Harris Coming Home-Coming Together Concert, Free open-air-concert in the City Center. Internationally renowned jazz pianist, Gene Harris was born and raised in Benton Harbor and each summer his exceptional life and music are celebrated.

Mendel Center Mainstage, campus of Lake Michigan College (Exit 30 off I-94), (269) 927-1221. Performances by well-known entertainers which in the past have included Smokey Robinson, Bill Cosby and B. B. King. The Mainstage offers Broadway Theatre. Also the Southwest Michigan Symphony Orchestra performs both classical and pop concerts. For Symphony information, call (269) 982-4030.

Parks, Beaches and Campgrounds

Jean Klock Park, Klock Road exit of M-63. Amenities: paved parking, boardwalk, volleyball courts, pavilion, shelter with picnic tables, concession area, playground, bathhouse, and observation tower.

Sarett Nature Center and Brown Sanctuary, 2300 Nature Center Road, (269) 927-4832. The sanctuary is a 300-acre wildlife preserve located on the floodplain of the Paw Paw River; it includes ponds, marshes and swamp forests in its large wetland area. It is home to much wildlife, including the great horned owl. The Brown Sanctuary is located about a mile downstream from the nature center's headquarters and is the place for bird-watchers. The rare black tern and the American bittern have nested here. In addition you will spot: ducks, geese, rails, coots, gallinules and green back herons. Sarett is open Tues to Sun and closed on Mon. **Mud Lake Bog**: a 550 foot boardwalk allows an interesting tour along the bog's mass of vegetation floating on the water, including carnivorous plants and other unique plants and wetland animals. Tours can be arranged through Sarett Nature Center.

Marina

Pier 1000 Marina, 1000 Riverview Drive, (269) 927-4471. Provides: rental docks, summer rack service, gas and diesel, pumpout, ship store, service, bathhouse, laundry, pool and clubhouse. Open year round.

Golf

Hidden Pointe Miniature Golf, 1062 Nickerson Avenue (Exit 28 off I-94), (269) 926-1358. 18-holes of miniature golf, batting cages (softball, baseball), go-carts and a small arcade.

Lake Michigan Hills Golf Course, 2520 Kerlikowski Road, www.lakemichiganhills.com, (269) 849-3266 or toll-free (800) 247-3437. An 18-hole, par 72 course with wonderful layout, mature trees, elevation changes and great greens. Also offers a pro shop, PGA lessons, driving range and restaurant.

Other Things to See or Do in Benton Harbor

Blue Creek Berries, 645 South Blue Creek Road (Exit 30 off I-94), east on Napier two miles to Blue Creek Road, north 1½ miles, (269) 782-8073 or (269) 424-3821. U-Pick or already picked and cleaned for you. You can also purchase blueberries by the pint or pound at their produce stand on the corner of Blue Creek and Napier.

Lake Michigan Shore Wine Trail. See below under "Other Things to See and Do in Southwest Michigan."

Festivals

Blossomtime Grand Floral Parade, May.

Gus Macker Tournament, June. Open to participants and observers.

Gene Harris Coming Home, Coming Together Concert, June.

Benton Harbor Children's Art Fair, July. Hands-on artists' experience for future Rembrandts and Monets.
Community Holiday Lighting Celebration, December.

Other Things to See and Do in Southwest Michigan

(including a few stops that veer away from the coast).

Backroads Bikeway, country roads for the cycling enthusiast. Most routes are mapped from Three Oaks, but several run through New Buffalo and Lakeside and you can pick them up or join them there as you travel the coast. The twelve different trails range from 5 to 60 miles, offering fun for the beginner and experienced rider as they cycle through picturesque hills beside streams, farms and meadows. The Three Oaks Bicycle Museum at 1 Oak Street in downtown Three Oaks has information regarding the trails, or you can send a SASE requesting a copy of their brochure with maps for all twelve trails. The address is: Backroads Bikeway, P.O. Box 366, Three Oaks, MI 49128.

Fort St. Joseph Museum, 508 East Main Street (behind City Hall), Niles, (269) 683-4702. Collections ranging from pictographs drawn by the famous Sioux Chief Sitting Bull to Fort St. Joseph excavation artifacts to Victorian decorative arts. The museum attempts to tell the story of early Niles and its contributions to the area and the world. The museum is housed in the Chapin Mansion. Open Wed to Sat 10:00 am to 4:00 pm. Closed major holidays.

Historic Courthouse Square, 313 North Cass Street, Berrien Springs, (269) 471-1202, www.berrienhistory.org. An 1839 log house, courthouse, sheriff's office, jail plaza and the Herb and Heritage Garden. Also a museum shop. Open seasonally from June 15th to September 15th, Tues to Fri 9:00 am to 6:00 pm, Sat and Sun 1:00 pm to 5:00 pm.

Southwest MI Wine Trail, www.miwinetrail.com. Much of Southwest Michigan is devoted to raising grapes and visitors are treated to a wonderful collection of wines and wineries. About 95% of the vineyards in Michigan are along the Lake Michigan coastal area from New Buffalo to Fennville. Covering the countryside from the state line north to Saugatuck, and from the lakeshore east to the vineyards beyond Paw Paw, there are nearly 12,000 acres of grapes. With the cool temperate climates and sandy clay soil of similar wineries in Germany and France, the Southwest Michigan area suits the vineyards perfectly.

Several times a year a dozen or so wineries, vineyards and tasting rooms allow participants to sample wines, taste local cuisine, and gain instruction on how to pair food with various wines. Special events include Cupid's Arrow (February), Spring into Summer (April) and Holiday Spice (November). Enjoy food, award-winning Michigan wine and the ambiance of a number of wineries along the trail. Step up to the wine bar to sample and learn about each winery's varieties before you purchase. To get you started, here are a dozen wineries to consider:

- *Black Star Farms Tasting Room*, Kalamazoo Street, Paw Paw, wine@blackstarfarms.com, www.blackstarfarms.com, (269) 655-8565.
- *Contessa Wine Cellars*, 3235 Friday Road, Coloma, (Exit 39 off I-94), (269) 468-5534. Open 7 days noon to 5:00 pm.
- *Domaine Berrien Cellars,* 398 East Lemon Creek Road, Berrien Springs, (269) 473-9463, www.domainberrien.com. Open May through December, Wed to Sun, noon to 5:00 pm. Call for winter hours.
- *Fenn Valley Vineyards and Wine Cellars*, 6130 122nd Ave, Fennville, www.fennvalley.com, winery@fennvalley.com, toll free (800) 432-6265. Award winning wines since 1973. Open Mon to Sat 11:00 am to 5:00 pm, Sun 1:00 pm to 5:00 pm. Sometimes open an hour later during July to October.
- *Karma Vista Vineyards and Tasting Room*, Ryno Road, Coloma, (Exit 39 off I-94), www.karmavista.com (269) GOT WINE. "The Zen and the art of Merlot maintenance."
- *Lemon Creek Winery and Fruit Farm*, (269) 471-1321, www.lemoncreekwinery.com. Open May to November, Mon to Sat 10:00 am to 6:00 pm and Sun noon to 6:00 pm. Open December to April, Fri to Sun noon to 5:00 pm.
- *Round Barn Winery and Distillery*, 10983 Hills Road, Baroda, www.roundbarndistillery.com, toll-free (800) 716-WINE. Open year round, Mon to Sat 11:00 am to 6:00 pm and Sun noon to 6:00 pm.
- *St. Julian Tasting Room at Union Pier*. (Exit 6 off I-94), (269) 469-3150. Free tasting and retail outlet. Open Mon to Sat 10:00 am to 6:00 pm and Sun noon to 6:00 pm.
- *St. Julian Winery*, 716 South Kalamazoo Street, Paw Paw, (Exit 60 off I-94), www.stjulian.com, toll-free (800) 732-6002. Free tasting. This is the largest, oldest and most award-winning winery in Southwestern Michigan. In a good year they process 6,000 tons of fruit and their press handles 33 tons of grapes in 2½ hours. Tours are offered Mon to Sat 10:00 am to 4:00 pm, but the bottling process can only be seen Mon to Thurs. You begin the tour with an eight minute film describing the process. Old wine making equipment is on display. Open Mon to Sat 9:00 am to 5:00 pm and Sun noon to 5:00 pm.
- *Tabor Hill Tasting Room* at Bridgman, toll-free (800) 283-363, www.taborhill.com.

- **Tabor Hill Winery and Restaurant**, Mt. Tabor Road, toll-free (800) 283-3363, www.taborhill.com.
- *Warner Vineyards*, 706 South Kalamazoo, Paw Paw (269) 657-3165. Open for tours and tasting: Mon to Sat 10:00 am to 5:00 pm and Sun noon to 5:00. Also has the Waterworks Station Café for casual gourmet dining and live music on Friday and Saturday (269) 657-5165 and the Vineyard Gallery open Thurs to Sat 10:00 am to 6:00 pm and Sun noon to 6:00 pm.

Van Buren County Historical Museum, 58471 Red Arrow Highway, Hartford, (269) 621-2188. The museum is located in the historic 1884 Van Buren County Poorhouse and contains three floors of historical memorabilia and a log cabin, blacksmith works and a gift shop. Open June through September, Wed and Sat 10:00 am to 4:00 pm and Sun 1:00 pm to 4:00 pm.

Additional Contacts in Southwest Michigan

Bridgman Area Chamber of Commerce, 4261 Lake Street, Bridgman, www.bridgmanarea.org, info@bridgmanarea.org, (269) 465-4413.

Lakeshore Chamber of Commerce, 4290 Red Arrow Highway, Stevensville, (269) 429-1170. www.LakeshoreChamber.org or e-mail them at info@lakeshorechamber.org. They provide information on Stevensville and surrounding communities.

State of Michigan Welcome Center, I-94 as you enter Michigan in New Buffalo, (269) 469-0011.

Southwest Michigan Tourist Council, 2300 Pipestone Road, Benton Harbor, www.swmichigan.org, info@swmichigan.org, (269) 925-6301.

St. Joseph Today, 120 State Street, St. Joseph, (269) 985-1111. Covers St. Joseph and Benton Harbor.

South Haven

Population: 5021 as of 2000 census.

Directions: US-31/I-196 North (Exit 38-B), M-43 west to South Haven. (54 miles north of New Buffalo and 65 miles south of Muskegon using US-31.)

Background and History

In 1787 Ottawa, Miami and Pottawattamie Native American tribes began using the area around South Haven as a place for trading. They called it "Ni-Ko-Nong," or "beautiful sunsets." They kept their birch bark canoes in the sands along the lake.

In 1833, the United States government granted J.R. Monroe a land patent for 65 acres along the shoreline of Lake Michigan. Monroe married Fanny Rawson and the newlyweds traveled by lumber wagon through the wilderness to the log cabin J.R. had built for his bride.

The Monroes were disappointed that the village they expected to help create around their home in South Haven never materialized. They abandoned their home and their dream and moved to Lawrence, Michigan. Their timing had been off by a couple of decades. In the 1850s the first permanent settlers arrived, and in 1869 South Haven was officially "founded."

The establishment of the city coincided with the building of a sawmill which in turn caused construction of a hotel, a school, additional homes, and stores to provide needed goods and services to the new settlers.

Lumbering was the impetus creating the city; it was also its economic sustenance for four decades. After the lumbering era ended the areas cleared of timber were used by fruit farmers to spark an industry that flourishes today. The first annual Peach Festival was held in 1930 and today's Blueberry Festival continues to draw eager visitors to South Haven to share the fun.

Both passenger and freight ships stopped at South Haven during its early days and the South Haven Pier and Lighthouse guided ships to the safety of the harbor during violent Lake Michigan storms. (See Part II, Lighthouses p. 359 and Ghost Stories p. 412.)

By the early 1900s South Haven became known as "The Catskills of the Midwest" and a swell of second homes grew into large resorts.

Today South Haven offers a visitor sugar-sand swimming beaches and unlimited boating and marine activity. It encompasses 120 square miles of beautiful countryside including: woodlands, ravines, fields and the famous dunes. It is the western stop on the Kal-Haven Trail, loved by both bicyclers and snowmobilers. A visitor can experience a wine tour and tasting, pick fruits and veggies for evening dinner or simply enjoy the fruits of someone else's labor by purchasing fresh produce at one of the many farm markets dotting the landscape.

South Haven is a dog friendly city and your best friend is welcome in all stores downtown except pharmacies and restaurants (or other food establishments because of health regulations).

South Haven Lighthouse and Pier   ***Photo by Bob Royce***

Food/Restaurants

Ambrosia to Go, 6291 111th Avenue, toll-free (866) 703-9904, ambrosiagourmetkitchen@netzero.net. Pleasing selection of imported cheeses. Picnic baskets and gift baskets put together for you. Open 7 days, 10:00 am to 6:00 pm.

Café Julia, 561 Huron Street, (269) 639-7988. Breads, pastries, specialty coffees, outdoor café and internet. Open 7 days, Sun to Thurs 7:00 am to 9:00 pm, Fri and Sat 7:00 am to 10:00 pm.

Captain Nemo's, 405 Phoenix Street, (269) 637-5372. Serves breakfast, lunch and dinner. Seafood, sandwiches or just an ice cream cone. Inexpensive. Open Mon to Fri 5:30 am to 11:00 pm. Open summer weekends until midnight.

The Chocolate Café, 406 Phoenix Street, (269) 637-1700. Katherine Hepburn reportedly once said, *"What you see before you, my friend, is the result of a lifetime of chocolate. A pound a day often."* What a woman and what a place: Turtle Sundaes, Turtle Cheesecakes, or something simple like Milk n' Fudge (a glass of cold milk and a big old slice of fudge). You can also get soups, salads and sandwiches (all non-chocolate). Open Sun to Thurs 8:30 am to 10:00 pm, Fri and Sat 8:30 am to 11:00 pm.

Clementine's, 500 Phoenix Street, (269) 637-4755. Family friendly restaurant. Gets great ratings from locals and visitors. Try to save room for their famous hot apple dumpling. Clementine's is located in the old Citizen's Bank building and surrounds you with antiques, tin ceilings and ornate wood trim. The bar looks like it came from an old-time saloon. Black and white photos line the walls, revealing the city's history and paying silent tribute to days gone by. Open Mon to Thurs 11:00 am to 10:00 pm, Fri and Sat 11:00 am to 11:00 pm and Sun noon to 11:00 pm.

Creole Tavern at the Idler Riverboat, 515 Williams Street (docked at Nichols Landing on the Black River), (269) 637-8435. Blackened Prime Rib is a favorite, but they also serve a wide range of other menu items including fish and pastas. Seasonal from May to September. Open Fri and Sat 11:00 am to 2:00 pm for lunch and 5:00 pm to 10:00 pm for dinner. Sun 11:00 am to 3:00 pm for lunch and 4:00 pm to 9:00 pm for dinner.

Fish Tale Pub and Grill, 38 North Shore Drive, (269) 637-5123. Nautical ambiance and a place boaters and sun bathers head after a day at the beach. Fish, beef and ribs. Hours and days vary with the season. Call for exact hours. On weekends reservations suggested.

Golden Brown Bakery and Cafeteria, 421 Phoenix Street, (269) 637-3418. The carrot (or any other) donut will leave you wanting a second. Variety of baked goods, fudge and a lunch menu. Open 7 days, Mon to Sat 6:00 am to 5:30 pm and Sun 8:00 am to 2:00 pm.

Harborside Bistro, 402 Phoenix Street, (269) 637-5400. World class brunch on Sunday according to loyal customers. Casual restaurant with moderate prices. Full dinners or just a sandwich. Try to save room for dessert: Blueberry Cobbler with Crème Auglaize. Open 7 days, Mon to Sat 11:30 am to closing and Sun 10:00 am to closing.

Hawkshead Restaurant, 523 HawksNest Drive, (269) 639-2121. Repeatedly voiced as a favorite by locals. This restaurant has a reputation as THE place to eat when you are looking for fine dining. It is named for the ghost town that bordered the north end of the property in earlier days. The dining room overlooks lush landscape and a forested ravine, the perfect backdrop for enjoying one of their martinis while you wait for dinner. Long time customers swear by the Crab Cakes with Curry Mayo, Basil Lobster or the Roasted Duck (crisp, candied-pecan glaze with a port cherry sauce). The Sweet Potato Mash with Brown Sugar Glaze is a delicious side dish. The best advice is: Go for the special of the day. Whatever it is, they worked on it all day and it will be superb. You can get lighter fare at the pub. Open 7 days, 11:00 am to 10:00 pm. Winter hours: Wed to Sat opening at 5:00 pm.

Sherman's Ice Cream, 1601 Phoenix Road, (269) 637-8251, www.shermanicecream.com. A single is as big as a triple anywhere else. The praline pecan is the best you will ever taste. Malts, shakes, sundaes, banana splits, dine-in or carry-out - just make sure you stop. This place has nearly a century long love affair with the city and it is easy to see why it is a favorite of locals and tourists alike. Open 7 days, Mon to Sat 11:00 am to 11:00 pm and Sun noon to 11:00 pm. Closed the last week of October through the first week in March.

Phoenix Street Café, 523 Phoenix Street, (269) 637-3600. Hamburgers, deli sandwiches, omelets, salads, vegetarian. Breakfast all day. Also has daily specials. Open 7 days, 7:00 am to 2:00 pm.

Tello's Trattoria, 7379 North Shore Drive, (269) 639-9898, www.tellostrattoria.com. Moderately priced eatery with entertainment (see Theatres below). This is another place recommended by locals. Pizza, Italian, sandwiches, hamburgers and salads. Opens Mon to Sat 11:30 am and opens at noon on Sun, year round.

The Thirsty Perch, 272 Broadway, (269) 639-8000. Consider starting with Mushroom Soup. Then, although they have excellent steaks, it just seems you should try the Endless Perch. Opens 11:30 am, 7 days a week, year round.

Tom's Buffet, 364 Broadway Street, (269) 639-1666. Chinese restaurant that is a favorite locally. Great Mandarin dishes. Open Mon to Fri 11:00 am to 10:00 pm, Sat noon to 10:00 pm and Sun noon to 9:00 pm. Closed on Tues.

Vineyard Italian Restaurant and Pizza, 259 Broadway Street, (269) 637-5732. Pasta, veal, steaks, chicken, fish and pizza. Open daily at 4:00 pm, year round.

Lodging (Also see Campgrounds below)

A&R's North Beach Vacation Cottages and Inn, 282 North Shore Drive, (269) 637-8972. Two and three bedroom cottages, five bedroom house and three bedroom coach house with new 10' x 30' deck. Fully furnished. Complete kitchen. Lake view from deck.

Carriage House at the Harbor B&B, 118 Woodman Street, (269) 639-2161. Eleven individually appointed guest rooms, each with a fireplace, private bath (many with whirlpool), TV/VCR. Hot breakfast and an hors d' oeuvre buffet served daily.

Comfort Suites, 1755 Phoenix Street, (269) 639-2014, www.choicehotels.com/hotel/mi242. 61 suites. Extras: free internet, separate work and sleep spaces, business center, heated indoor pool, fitness center, complimentary USA Today and continental breakfast.

Cottage Rentals of South Haven, 225 Broadway, Suite 7-107. (866) 455-7829. They will help you locate a cottage for your vacation.

Country Place B&B, 79 North Shore Drive, (269) 637-5523 or toll-free (877) 866-7801. Restored 1860s Greek Revival-style home located on two acres of woodland with beach access to Lake Michigan a half block away. Five guest rooms each with private bath. Also two cottages. Full breakfast with guest rooms.

Hampton Inn, 4299 Cecilia Drive, (269) 639-8550. 62 rooms, some with whirlpool, hot breakfast, coffee in lobby, indoor pool, spa, exercise facility, laundry, USA Today, free local calls and cable.

Holiday Inn Express, 1741 Phoenix Road, (269) 637-8800, www.holidayinn-express.com. 62 guest rooms. Located near Kal Haven Trail. Extras: continental breakfast, free wireless high speed internet, indoor heated pool and exercise room.

Inn at Hawks Island, 523 HawksNest Drive, (269) 639-2146, www.hawksheadlinks.com. Restored English Tudor mansion at the golf course. Oak banister leads to nine elegant rooms each with private bath. Extras: TV, air-conditioning, some fireplaces and continental breakfast served to the rooms.

Inn at the Park B&B, 233 Dyckman Avenue, (269) 639-1776 or toll-free (877) 739-1776, www.innpark.com. Nine rooms, each with fireplace and private bathroom (some with whirlpool baths). Lovely Victorian one block from beach, shops and restaurants. Full breakfast with one of many signature dishes awaiting you at the start of the day.

Jaqua Realtors and Vacation Places (rentals), 513 Broadway Street, www.jaquarealtors.com, (269) 637-6537 or toll-free (888) 764-2836. Offers wide range of rental options: homes, condominiums and cottages. Rental duration: weekly, monthly, weekend and off-season.

Jensen Motel, 7366 North Shore Drive, (269) 637-3544, www.jensenssh.addr.com. 14 clean, affordable, no-frills rooms and more than 100 campsites for RVs. (See campgrounds below.)

Lake Bluff Inn and Suites, 76648 11th Avenue, (269) 637-8531 or toll-free (800) 686-1305, www.lakebluffinnandsuites.com. Double, queen, king or luxury suites. Extras: recreation building, some kitchenettes and two-bedroom suites, free high-speed internet, hot tub and sauna and some lake view suites with fireplace.

Last Resort B&B Inn, 86 North Shore Drive, (269) 637-8943 or toll-free (866) 637-8943, www.lastresortinn.com. Constructed in 1883 by Civil War Captain Barney Dyckman as South Haven's first resort inn, it continued in that capacity until 1959 when it was closed and left vacant for two decades. In 1979 it was renovated, reopening in 1983 as South Haven's first bed and breakfast inn. The inn is situated between Lake Michigan and the City Marina, one half block from each. It is only a few minutes walk to downtown shops and restaurants. Offers 14 rooms. Closes from November through April.

Lighthouse Inn, 1555 Phoenix Street, (269) 639-9900. 90 rooms, some with whirlpools. Extras: heated indoor pool, whirlpool and exercise room.

Martha's Vineyard B&B, 473 Blue Star Highway, (269) 637-9373, www.marthasvy.com. Winner of 2005 Inn Traveler Award for Most Romantic Hideaway. Built in 1852 the Inn offers five guest rooms in the main house, each with private bath, fireplace, and veranda. Three whirlpool suites in the guest house. A four-course, gourmet breakfast is served each morning. Niceties such as Martha's Vineyard bathrobes, down comforters and pillows await you. You can request an in-room massage or order a gourmet picnic basket.

MichiMonaMac Lakeshore Cottages, 337 North Shore Drive, On Lake Michigan, (269) 637-3003, www.mmmlakeshorecottages.com. Six cottages. Cable TV, VCR, kitchens and lakefront units with fireplaces overlooking the lake.

Monroe Manor Inn Bed and Breakfast, 72861 8th Avenue, (269) 637-6547, www.monroemanorinn.com. Tranquil five acre historic mansion built in 1884. Completely modernized and restored, preserving the charm of a more relaxed era while providing all the modern conveniences you want. Five large rooms, luxury linens and a fireplace in each room. Take your breakfast on the wrap-around porch.

North Beach Inn, 51 North Shore Drive, (269) 637-6738. Lovely Victorian built as a private home in the 1890s for J. Basten Upham, a prominent Bostonian. It is one of South Haven's oldest homes. Open May through October.

Old Harbor Inn, 515 William Street (269) 637-8480 or toll-free (800) 433-9210, www.oldharborinn.com. Waterfront hotel with convenient location and individually appointed rooms with views of the harbor. Many rooms have private balconies and some have a whirlpool and fireplace. Small indoor pool and hot tub. Light continental breakfast served in the lobby.

Ramada Lighthouse Inn Banquet and Conference Center, 1555 Phoenix Street, www.lighthouseinnsouthhaven.com, (269) 639-9900. Extras: indoor heated pool, hot tub, deluxe breakfast bar, exercise room and high speed internet.

Sand Castle Inn B&B and condos, 233 Dyckman Avenue, (269) 639-1110. Ten guest rooms, each with private bath and fireplace. Steps from Lake Michigan. Guests have enjoyed this Inn since the late 1800s. Victorian front porch with swing, white wicker furniture and a ceiling fan. Most rooms have fireplaces and private decks. A full breakfast awaits you in the morning and hors d'oeuvres are served in the afternoon. Outdoor swimming pool. Rental condos available.

Sleepy Hollow Resort, 7400 North Shore Drive (269) 637-1127, www.sleepyhollowbeach.com. Offers a variety of units including cottages and condominiums from one to three bedrooms, many with views overlooking Lake Michigan. Plenty of activity to keep the entire family busy: heated, outdoor, Olympic size swimming pool, 1000 feet of private beach, tennis courts and daily programs for children.

Victoria Resort B&B, 247 Oak Street, (269) 637-6414, www.victoriaresort.com. Historic South Haven B&B only a block and a half from Lake Michigan. Originally a two-story home built on five acres owned by Albert and Anna Glassman who expanded it to include rental units. In 1966 the property was sold and remained empty for nearly two decades before becoming a B&B. Offers five rooms from super luxurious featuring fireplaces and whirlpool tubs to simpler amenities. All come with gourmet breakfast and all have private baths. You may also consider one of their eight cottages or their bungalow. The grounds include an in-ground pool and tennis courts.

Yelton Manor B&B, 140 North Shore Drive, (269) 637-5220, www.yeltonmanor.com. Actually two Victorian mansions with 17 guest rooms, each with private bath. Expansive and lovely gardens, beautiful parlors and porches and all of the antiques and art you would expect in a fine B&B that gets accolades from *Inn Traveler Magazine*. Honored in the Top Ten B&Bs in the USA by *Amoco Motor Club*. Elegant fireplace and whirlpool rooms, lake views, porches, lovely parlor, and antiques. You can curl up with a book from the thousands in the library, consider a current video or listen to music that suits your taste and mood.

Museums and Galleries

Blue Star Pottery, 337 Blue Star Highway, (269) 637-5787, www.bluecoastartists.com. Open Fri to Sun 11:00 am to 5:00 pm, May to November.

Brave Wolf Gallery, 417 Phoenix Street, (269) 639-0770. Native American art and art of the Southwest. Merchandise made in the USA and includes: crafts, artist signed pieces, hand-crafted jewelry and more. Open Mon to Fri 10:30 am to 6:00 pm, Sat 10:30 am to 7:00 pm and Sun 11:00 am to 4:00 pm. Hours may vary slightly with the season.

Crescent Moon Gallery & Gifts, 413 Phoenix Street, (269) 637-5119, crmoon@comcast.net. Carries some women's clothing, jewelry, and accessories. Also carries art, pottery and decorative faces. Open Sun to Thurs 10:00 am to 7:00 pm, Fri and Sat 10:00 am to 9:00 pm. Slight variation in hours seasonally.

Lattner Studio, 319 Blue Star Highway, (269) 637-1810, www.lattnerstudio.com. Vibrant paintings inspired by the natural surroundings of the Lake Michigan coastline. Open Tues to Thurs 10:00 am to 3:00 pm, most Sat 10:00 am to 3:00 pm. By appointment May to November.

Liberty Hyde Bailey Museum, 903 Bailey Avenue (Off Blue Star Highway and Aylworth Avenue), (269) 637-3251 or (269) 637-3141. The Bailey Museum is a National Historic Site marking the birthplace of world famous botanist and horticulturist Liberty Hyde Bailey. Bailey designed the nation's first horticultural laboratory at Michigan State University. The museum houses articles used by the Bailey family and other pioneer families of South Haven. It also displays spinning wheels, an operational cylinder phonograph, pianos, South Haven high school yearbooks and copies of Bailey's books. Open March through December, Thurs to Mon 1:00 pm to 5:00 pm. January and February open Sat and Sun 1:00 pm to 5:00 pm.

Michigan Maritime Museum, 260 Dyckman Avenue, (269) 637-8078. Exhibits featuring the people who sailed the Great Lakes. There are several buildings in the complex. One exhibit includes a gallery collection entitled, "Sailing through Time." Two U. S. Coast Guard buildings display period rescue equipment and three wooden rescue craft. The Boat Shed hosts workshops on ship building and sailing. Visitors are invited to ask questions, watch the work being conducted and even offer a hand if they like. You can climb aboard the historic replica sloop, the *Friends Good Will*. The original *Friends Good Will* was built in Detroit in 1810 as a merchant vessel. The sloop was chartered by the federal government to take military supplies to Fort Dearborn at what is now Chicago. She was returning with furs and skins when lured into the Harbor of Mackinaw Island by the British who confiscated the ship and cargo. She was renamed *Little Belt* and pressed into service fighting for the Royal Navy until 1813. For those interested a 90 minute sailing experience awaits. It is an adventure that will not soon be forgotten. Or consider the sunset sail. Museum open year round, Mon to Sat 10:00 am to 5:00 pm and Sun noon to 5:00 pm.

South Haven Center for the Arts, 600 Phoenix Street, (269) 637-1041, southhavenarts.org, Offers art exhibitions and special events. Open Tues to Thurs 10:00 am to 5:00 pm, Fri 10:00 am to 4:00 pm, Sat and Sun 1:00 pm to 4:00 pm.

Vesuvius, 1173 Blue Star Highway, (269) 227-3970, www.vesuviusgallery.com. Fine arts and crafts for your home and garden. Open May, June, September and October: Fri to Sun 11:00 am to 6:00 pm. July and August: Wed to Sun 11:00 am to 6:00 pm. Sometimes open longer on holiday weekends.

Theatre

The Legend Theater, 7579 North Shore Drive (at Tello's Trattoria), (269) 637-7829. Village theater productions starting in July and running for ten weeks with new shows every three days.

Our Town Players, 500 Erie Street, (269) 639-8228. Sponsors outside artists and stages its own productions at the Listiak Auditorium at Central School. Call for details.

Antiques

Ambrose & Manning Antiques, 520 Phoenix Street, (269) 639-1644. Antiques including: household items, glassware, chairs, tables, retro and some items that are not quite antiques. They also carry Irish themed merchandise including shamrock beaded purses.

Murphy's Antique Mall, 321 Center Street (Downtown), (269) 639-1662. Two floors with over 100 dealers. Open Wed to Sat 11:00 am to 6:00 pm and Sun 1:00 pm to 6:00 pm. Closed Tues.

Shooting Star Gifts and Antiques, 209 Center Street, (269) 639-0015. Mixture of unique and artsy pieces and general antiques. Open Mon to Sat 10:00 am to 9:00 pm and Sun 11:00 am to 9:00 pm. Open noon to 5:00 pm in the winter.

Sunset Junque, 856 Blue Star Highway, www.sunsetjunque.com, (269) 637-5777. Antiques and not-quite-antiques as well as some downright junk. Open 7 days, mid-May to Labor Day, 10:00 am to 6:00 pm. During the spring and fall open weekends or by chance.

Willow Bend Antiques, 1678 68th Street, (Blue Star Hwy), Glen, (616) 836-5084 (cell). Garden iron, antiques, cement statuary, estate pieces. Open April to November, Mon 11:00 am to 6:00 pm, Thurs to Sat 11:00 am to 6:00 pm and Sun 12:30 pm to 6:00 pm. Extended hours July and August, open 7 days at 10:00 am.

Other Shopping

Beach House Designs, 517 Phoenix Street, (269) 639-2191. Beach wear and accessories, umbrellas (in case the day does not turn out as nice as you hoped), winter shoes and coats for the off-season, home accessories, clothing for the entire family, books, chairs and lots of original merchandise. Open Mon to Sat 9:00 am to 9:00 pm and closed Sun. Winter Mon to Fri 10:00 am to 5:00 pm, weather permitting.

Bee You Tee Ful Fashions, 406 Phoenix Court #1, (269) 637-7700. Fashions for women (California Girls). Open 7 days, 10:00 am to 9:00 pm.

Biddy Murphy Celtic Gifts, 610 Phoenix Street, (269) 639-8585, www.biddymurphy.com. A wide assortment of Celtic gifts and all things Irish: jewelry, clothing, pottery, crystal, Guinness wear and unique gifts. Open 7 days, 10:00 am to 8:00 pm.

The Blueberry Store, 525 Phoenix Street, (269) 654-2400. Carries blueberry, blueberry-cherry and blueberry-raspberry preserves. Also dishes with a blueberry motif, sweatshirts and t-shirts with blueberries and even a blueberry wine - all a tribute to the importance of the blueberry crop to the region. Open Mon to Sat 10:00 am to 5:00 pm and Sun noon to 4:00 pm.

Blue Eyed Girl, 406 Phoenix Court. Fashions for women and children and household items. Open Mon and Wed to Sat 10:00 am. Sun open at noon. Closing time varies. Closed Tues.

Cotton Bay, 425 Phoenix Street, (269) 637-2223. Moderately-priced casual, resort wear for women. Also, jewelry, accessories and beachwear. Open daily 10:00 am, closes at 6:00 pm during the week and 9:00 pm on weekends.

Darcy's General Store, 515 Phoenix Street, (269) 637-3939. Started out selling Spiegel Catalog return items, but now looks like a carpet store run amok. This is a great store. It has rugs on all four floors and the higher you climb the less expensive they become. On the 4th floor there were some steals. Also carries toys and household goods, as well as bathing suits to bedroom suites. Check out the Demented Diva. I fell in love with a bright yellow and orange beach chair. Open 7 days, Mon to Sat 9:00 am to at least 5:00 pm and Sun 11:00 am to 4:00 pm.

Day Lily, 411 Phoenix Street, (269) 637-2088. Home decorating pieces and simple pleasures for the home and cottage. Special cat lovers section. Open 7 days, Mon to Thurs 10:00 am to 9:00 pm, Fri and Sat 10:00 am to 10:00 pm and Sun 10:00 am to 7:00 pm. Slightly reduced hours in the winter.

Decadent Dogs, 505 Phoenix Street, (269) 639-0716, or toll-free (866) 4K9-kids, wwwdecadentdogs.com. Everything to pamper your pooch. This is the ultimate pet boutique. The store opened to fill a niche for everything you could want for your four-legged friend: sweaters, boots, beds and toys. Open summer, 7 days, 10:00 am to 9:00 pm. Winter: Mon to Sat 10:00 am to 5:00 pm and Sun 11:00 am to 5:00 pm.

Harbor Toy Company, 409 Phoenix Street (269) 637-9300, www.harbortoyco.com. Educational toys, kites, travel games, board games, puzzles and a whole lot more to delight your children. Open 7 days, 9:00 am to 10:00 pm. Hours slightly reduced in the winter.

Hidden Room Book Store, 518 Phoenix Street, toll-free (877) 637-7222. All kinds of used books as well as some new. Open 7 days, May to August 10:00 am to 5:00 pm. Closed Tues and Wed September to December. Closed completely January and February Closed Tues to Thurs in March and April.

Marigolds, 406 Phoenix Court, (269) 639-2560. South Haven's only micro-nursery: plants and garden items. Open Mon, Wed, Thurs and Fri 10:00 am to 5:00 pm, Sat 9:00 am to 5:00 pm and Sun noon to 4:00 pm. Closed Tues.

Natures' Country Cupboard, 509 Phoenix Street, (269) 637-9277. Unique gifts, natural and gourmet foods, coffee, fudge, home accents and aromatherapy. Open 7 days, 9:00 am to 5:00 pm. Hours may vary slightly. Sometime closes in January and February.

Oh My Darlings, 508 Phoenix Street, (269) 637-7900. A kids' store with candy, great stuffed animals, baby layettes and children's clothing. Opens at 10:00 am daily and often stays open until Clementine's Restaurant (next door) closes for the day.

The Painted Turtle, 405 Phoenix Street, (269) 637-1598. Niceties, necessities and things to fill you with wonderment. Lots of gift items. They claim five out of four people shop here, so some customers must come more than once. Open 7 days, 10:00 am and closes when the customers are gone.

Props, 528 Phoenix Street, (269) 637-7337, props@i2k.com. Their philosophy is that your home is your stage and they will help you add some drama. Great home accents. Open 7 days, 10:00 am to 6:00 pm during the summer.

Rambling Rose, 411½ Phoenix Street, (269) 639-7216. Home accessories and treasures. Open 7 days, 10:00 am to 6:00 pm. Reduced winter hours.

Renaissance and Papyrus, 507 Phoenix Street, (269) 637-7033. Two shops in the same location. Renaissance carries clothes, linens, Basic Threads and Papillion. Papyrus has paper, jewelry, books and lotions and potions. Check out the upstairs. Open 7 days, Sun to Thurs 10:00 am to 9:00 pm and Fri and Sat 10:00 am to 10:00 pm.

Tucks of Saugatuck, Center Street a couple doors down from Phoenix Street. Christmas store, some Halloween, some general merchandise, great ceramic plaques and a few stuffed animals. Main store is in Saugatuck. Open 7 days, 11:00 am to 5:00 pm.

Whimsy, 415 Phoenix Street, www.whimsygiftshop.com, (269) 639-0379. Harden art, natural products and lots of gifts for the imagination. Open 7 days, Mon to Thurs 10:00 am to 6:00 pm, Fri and Sat 10:00 am to 7:00 pm and Sun 10:00 am to 5:00 pm (and sometimes later). Open year round, but may close earlier in the winter.

South Haven Beach   *Photo by Bob Royce*

Parks, Beaches and Campgrounds

Cousins' Campground, 7317 North Shore Drive, Corner of Blue Star Highway and North Shore Drive, (269) 637-1499. Amenities: play area, pavilion and flush toilets.

Dyckman Park, Packard Park North Beach and Oak Street Park. Surrounding the harbor (north and south sides) at South Haven. Swimming beaches and playground. Parking fee for non-residents.

Heritage Water Trail, www.vbco.org/watertrail.asp. The 20 mile Bangor to South Haven Heritage Water Trail is a navigable waterway including the Black River, other rivers, lakes and canals. It offers put-in points, take-out points, rest stops, maps and information on paddling conditions. It is intended to be an educational/interpretive program. To enrich your experience nearby museums are identified. The trail is still under development. The goal is to promote environmental awareness and help people enjoy nature and history while relaxing and having a good time. Currently about ¾ of the way completed, the trail will probably be finished in 2007. You can rent canoes along the way.

Jensen's Campground, North Shore Drive, (269) 637-3544. Located ¾ mile from Lake Michigan. Amenities: modern showers, electric and water hook-ups available to half the sites, full hook-ups, internet, picnic tables, fire ring, dump site, fish cleaning station and freezer for fish, laundry facilities, recreation hall and pets welcome.

Kal-Haven Trail State Park, accessed at Wells and Bailey Streets in South Haven, (269) 674-8011, www.kalhaventrail.org. The Kal-Haven Trail is a narrow strip that runs 34 miles from 10th Street near Kalamazoo to South Haven providing a route for the hardier cyclist to enjoy beautiful woods and farmland, a covered bridge, a camel back bridge, the Bloomingdale Depot, and a host of plants, flowers, birds and wildlife. The trail is a favorite spot for hikers and snowmobilers.

North Beach, North Shore Drive. Amenities: lifeguards, picnic tables, restrooms and volleyball.

Van Buren State Park, Exit 13 off I-196, north on Blue Star Highway, www.michigan.gov/dnr, (269) 637-2788 or toll-free (800) 44-PARKS. Located 3 miles south of South Haven on 400 acres of land along the Lake Michigan shoreline. The park has high dune formations and one mile of sandy beach. Amenities: picnic area, parking lot (550 cars), restrooms, changing areas, concession stand, hiking trail and an undeveloped 70-acre dune area. Entrance fee. Campground with 220 modern campsites. Sites have electricity, a picnic table and a fire ring.

Waterfront Skate Park, across from South Beach. Skateboarding and in-line skating.

Winding River Campground, Eighth Avenue, Exit 20 off I-196, then east to County Road 689 to Eighth Avenue and east one mile, (269) 637-8940.

Marinas, Water Sports, Bike, Boat and Jet Ski Rental

Rock-a-Road Cycle, 315 Broadway, (269) 639-0003. The place to rent a bicycle for your trail or backroads riding.

Public Boat Launch at Black River Park, Dunkley Avenue, (269) 637-3523. Boat launch facilities with automated gate entry. Picnic tables, fish cleaning station and public restrooms.

South Haven Marina, 345 Water Street #2, (269) 637-3171. 104 transient slips. Amenities: bathrooms, showers, water/electric and pump-out.

Tom's Jet Ski and Boat Rentals, 4891 68th Street, (269) 906-1754 or (269) 228-2628. Open June 1st to September 31st, Sat and Sun only. During the week they take reservations for weekend. Cash only. Waverunners, ski boat, fishing boat and dinghies.

Cruises, Charters, and Ferries

Captain Nichols Fishing Charters, 515 Williams Street, (269) 637-2507.

Finsation Charters, (269) 353-7171, boat (269) 207-1233. Captain Kevin Laaksonen gives you the opportunity to experience the thrill of salmon and trout fishing while enjoying yourself on his fully-equipped 31-foot Tiara.

Finn Fighter Sports Fishing, (269) 637-8282 or toll-free (800) 655-8585, or Captain Wally (269) 214-6934, www.finfighter.com Captain Wally docks at the Black River Yacht Club. Check the internet site for wonderful fish recipes. Open Mon to Fri 8:00 am to 5:00 pm to schedule reservations.

IT-IL-DO Charters, 1009 Hazel, Captain Jim Bard (269) 214-0051 and Captain Chad Bard (269) 214-6934, www.itildocharters.com.

The Bards have a long history of fishing in the area. Their grandfather was a commercial fisherman from the 1940s to the 1970s. They offer fishing charters and sunset cruises out of the ports of South Haven and Grand Haven. Sportfishing for Chinook, Salmon, Coho Salmon, Steelhead (Rainbow Trout), Lake Trout, Brown Trout and Lake Perch. Charters are generally for six hours.

Other Things to See and Do

Barden's Farm Market, 73398 County Road 388, Exit 20 off I-196, west 1/5 of a mile, (269) 637-2880. Strawberries, tomatoes, sweet corn and peaches. June to September, 7 days, 9:00 am to 7:00 pm.

Carriage Company, (269) 657-9000 or toll-free (800) 379-9100. Horse drawn carriage rides along Lake Michigan's shoreline and the river. Book early. Usually available on the corner by Clementine's.

DeGrandchamp's Blueberry Farm, 15575 77th Street, Exit 18 off I-196, three miles south of South Haven, (269) 637-3915, www.degrandchamps.com. Largest U-pick and farm market in the area. Also provides picnic tables, restrooms and bus/car/camper parking. Raspberries in July, cranberries in October and a lot in between. Open July through August, 7 days, 8:00 am to 6:00 pm. May reduce hours after August.

Dutch Farm Market, 6967 109th Avenue, Exit 26 off I-196. (269) 637-8334. Open mid-May through November 1st.

Fideland Fun Park, 68099 Phoenix Street, (269) 637-3123. Fastest high-bank Can Am Go-Kart track in the state, bumper boats, miniature golf, driving range, batting cages, off-road mini jeeps, kiddie cars, orbitron and arcade. Open summer 10:00 am to midnight.

Gingerman Raceway, 61414 Phoenix Road, (269) 253-4445. Simulated country road racetrack (nearly two-mile, eleven-turn motorsports complex). Open early April through mid-October, Mon to Thurs 8:00 am to 5:00 pm and Fri to Sun 7:00 am to 5:00 pm.

Hole in the Wall Paintball Field, 24262 66th Street, Bangor, (Between South Haven and Bangor), (269) 353-2978. Private games and rental equipment available. Appropriate for ages 12 and up. Walk on games every Saturday and Sunday, year round between 10:00 am and 5:00 pm. Open during the week by appointment.

Lakeside Entertainment Center, 09921 Blue Star Highway, (269) 637-4354. Restaurant, bowling center, mini-golf and arcade.

Festivals

Cottage Walk, June.
Harborfest, Father's Day Weekend.
Annual Fine Art Fair, July. Stanley Johnston Park.

South Haven Fourth of July Celebration, July.
Festival of Cars, July.
Garden Walk, July.
Van Buren County Youth Fair, mid-July.
National Blueberry Festival, 2nd full weekend in August. www.BlueberryFestival.com. This is their big one. There are events for the entire family including games for children, a sandcastle contest, pancake breakfast, fish boil dinner, parade, 5K run/walk, port activities, blueberry bake-off, hog roast dinner and big name entertainment.
Annual All Crafts Fair, Labor Day Weekend.
Antique Engine and Tractor Show, Weekend after Labor Day.

Golf

Fideland Fun Park Miniature Golf, CR-388, (269) 637-3123. (See above under Other Things to See or Do.)

Hawkshead, 523 Hawksnest Drive, www.hawksheadlinks.com, (269) 639-2121. An 18-hole par 72 course designed by Arthur Hill and open to the public. Reservations recommended.

Downtown South Haven   *Photo Courtesy of Joe Jurkiewicz*

Contacts

South Haven Visitor's Bureau, 546 Phoenix Street, (269) 637-5252 or toll-free (800) SOHAVEN, www.southhaven.org.

Southwest Michigan Tourist Council, 2300 Pipestone Road, www.swmichigan.org, info@swmichigan.org, (269) 925-6301.

Saugatuck/Douglas

-including a few stops in Fennville

Population: Saugatuck slightly over 1,000 as of 2000 U.S. Census. Douglas 1,200.

Directions: Exit 41 off I-196, between South Haven and Holland. From Chicago: I-94 toward Detroit to I-196 North (exit 21) to exit 36, continue on 68th Street/Blue Star Highway for 1.8 miles (Douglas) or 2.5 miles (Saugatuck). From Detroit: I-96 west 120 miles to Grand Rapids. Exit 46 onto I-196 west 24 miles to exit 41 toward Douglas/Saugatuck for ½ mile, turn right onto Blue Star Highway 1.8 miles (Douglas) or 2½ miles (Saugatuck).

Background and History

Although now considered the Art Coast of Michigan, the area around Saugatuck and Douglas (and ghost town Singapore) evolved from humble fur trading and lumbering origins. The area sprang to life in 1825 when a fur trading post was established there.

Singapore, founded in approximately 1830, was located on the river near the Lake Michigan Shore. Oshea Wilder, Singapore's city father, had dreams that his settlement would soon rival Chicago as a lake port and city. In 1846 two Great Lakes sailors purchased the heavily-wooded south bank of the Kalamazoo River near Douglas as a town site. They cleared the land and waited for settlers to come. They waited patiently, but not much happened until 1851 when the owner of a recently burned lumber mill in Singapore decided to move his operation to their location at what is now Douglas.

Life was not easy during the first 20 years for the small towns of Saugatuck, Douglas and Singapore. Residents spent their energy trying to merely survive. Prosperity was a ways off. By 1870, lumbering brought economic success to the area and the small town of Douglas was incorporated. That same year the Douglas Hotel was built.

The next year one of the most important events in early Michigan history occurred: the Chicago Fire. This unfortunate disaster created an almost inexhaustible need for lumber to aid in rebuilding. Every mill in Michigan, including those along the Kalamazoo River, responded to the strong market demand. The remaining mill in Singapore cut everything in sight, removing trees from the coastal dunes in the area. Ultimately that signaled the death knell for Singapore, the ghost town that during its life referred to Saugatuck as "the Flats."

Within four years the dunes, no longer grounded by the tree roots, buried the small village of Singapore. Up until the fire, the little town had boasted two hotels, several general stores and a renowned "wildcat" bank. After the fire many buildings moved to other locations when the sand started creeping in their doors, but the story persists that one resident refused to move, even as the sand enveloped his home. Eventually he had to enter and leave the dwelling by a second floor window; and still he refused to budge – until the sand reached his roof.

Two factors that greatly influenced other Lake Michigan coastal towns left Saugatuck and Douglas unaffected: both escaped the damage of the great fires of 1871 and 1881 that scorched so many of their sister cities; and, neither had a railway station.

In 1877 the last sawmill closed and the giant Douglas mill converted its production to baskets. This proved to be a stroke of genius, as the now cleared land was planted in fruit trees, and fruit growers needed baskets to hold and ship the picked fruit.

The new fruit business kept boat travel bustling along the Chicago route from Saugatuck and Douglas. When the fruit was unloaded in the Windy City, the boats returned with tourists anxious to escape the hot city and relax on the beautiful shores of Lake Michigan.

One local story reports that when an out-of-state party offered to buy land from area farmer, William McVea, McVea ran to his newly installed telephone and placed a call to a surveyor insisting that the surveyor come first thing in the morning: "These damn fools want to pay $500 for a pile of sand in my cow pasture." Many not-so-foolish investors wish they had that pile of sand today.

During the summer season, Illinois license plates are as prevalent as those from Michigan along elegant Lake Shore Drive. Early on, Saugatuck became a magnate for short-term visitors and many hotels and amusements were created for them. Douglas had relatively few day-trippers, but rather many conservative resort residents who stayed for the entire season. Even today Saugatuck is the more bustling, tourist-driven of the two; Douglas is a bit more relaxed and laid back with fewer tourists clamoring for entrance to each shop and restaurant.

An example of a luxury cruise ship is docked at Douglas and open for tours. If time permits, the Keewatin is an interesting stop.

The area is the B&B capital of Michigan. More Bed and Breakfasts are located in Saugatuck, Douglas and Fennville than in any other part of the state.

Brightly painted, quaint buildings extend a welcome to the wise travelers who include Saugatuck and Douglas in their travel plans. Shopping is fun, food is delicious and the beaches unparalleled.

Food/Restaurants

Arnie's Cottage Restaurant at Ravines Golf Club, 3520 Palmer Drive, Saugatuck, (269) 857-1616, www.ravinesgolfclub.com. Good basic food: sandwiches and full dinners in the evening. Open 11:00 am to 9:00 pm daily, April to October. Breakfast is served Sat and Sun from 7:00 am during the golf season. Hours may be reduced in winter.

Back Alley Pizza Joint, 22 Main Street, Douglas, (269) 857-7277. Open 7 days, Mon to Thurs 11:00 am to 10:00 pm, Fri and Sat 10:00 am to 11:00 pm and Sun noon to 10:00 pm. Closes an hour earlier in the off-season.

The Belvedere Inn and Restaurant, 3656 63rd Street, Saugatuck, (269) 857-5777. A fine dining establishment where you can bring your own wine. Great place for a special occasion. Only serves dinner and is open year round.

The Blue Moon Bar and Grille, 310 Blue Star Highway, Douglas, (269) 857-8686, www.BlueMoonBarandGrille.com. Moderately priced to expensive. Offers lunch, dinner, carry-out and on Sunday, breakfast. Contemporary American cuisine with international flair. Open 7 days, 11:00 am to 11:00 pm.

The Boathouse of Saugatuck, 449 Water Street, Saugatuck, (269) 857-2888. Moderate prices. BBQ, American, Mexican, steaks, sandwiches and seafood. Open 7 days, 11:30 am to 10:00 pm

Butler Restaurant, 40 Butler Street, Saugatuck, (269) 857-3501. Serves food and drinks year round. Open Mon to Sat 11:00 am to closing and Sun noon to closing (kitchen generally closes at 10:00 pm during the week and 10:30 pm on weekends).

Chequers of Saugatuck, 220 Culver Street, Saugatuck, (269) 857-1868, www.chequersofsaugatuck.com. British-style Pub and the place to get Fish & Chips. Lunch, dinner and carry-out. Open 7 days, Mon to Fri 11:30 am to 9:00 pm, Fri and Sat 11:30 am to 10:00 pm and Sun noon to 9:00 pm, year round. May stay open longer in summer.

Clearbrook Dining Room and Clearbrook Grill Room, 6494 Clearbrook Drive at 65th Street, Saugatuck, (269) 857-2000, www.clearbrookdining.com. The Dining Room at Clearbrook offers classic contemporary food in a fine dining setting and is fairly expensive. The Grill Room provides casual food and ambiance and is inexpensive to moderately priced. Dinner is served in the dining room 7 days, 5:30 pm to 9:30 pm. The Grill Room serves dinner 7 days, 4:00 pm to 9:30 pm. Hours reduced in the off-season. Call to confirm.

Charlie's Round the Corner Ice Cream Store, 134 Mason Street, Saugatuck, (269) 857-2100. Great place on a hot summer day.

Coral Gables, downtown Saugatuck overlooking harbor, (269) 857-2162. Moderately priced food. Outside seating during the summer. Dining, dancing, and entertainment. Open for lunch and dinner.

Crane's Pie Pantry and Restaurant, 6045 124th Avenue (SR-89 East of Saugatuck), Fennville, www.cranespiepantry.com, (269) 561-2297. Specializing in Michigan fruit pies. Open lunch and dinner with carry-out available. Mon to Fri 9:00 am to 8:00 pm, Sat 11:00 am to 6:00 pm. Reduced hours in the off-season.

Every Day People Café, 11 Center Street, Douglas, (269) 857-4240, www.everydaypeoplecafe.com. According to the *Chicago Tribune* in a piece they did on 7/19/05, this would be the place to eat if you had only one meal left. Many locals agree with that assessment; this is their favorite place to have a wonderful meal. Bar and a nice wine list. Moderate to expensive. Open Sun to Thurs 5:30 pm to 10:00 pm, Fri and Sat 5:30 pm to 11:00 pm. Brunch in the summer Thurs to Sun 8:00 am to 2:00 pm. Reduced winter hours. Closed Wed.

Ida Red's Cottage, 645 Water Street, Saugatuck. A good place for breakfast in a convenient downtown Saugatuck location. You can get breakfast until they close and lunch after 11:00 am. They make their own pancake batter using pure butter and buttermilk. No credit cards and a $3.00 per person minimum. Open 8:00 am to 2:00 pm daily.

Marro's Italian Restaurant, 147 Water Street, Saugatuck, (269) 857-4248, www.marrosrestaurant.com. Expensive but described by local patrons as unbelievable and amazing. Serving Italian favorites for 36 years. Open Tues to Sun 5:00 pm to 11:00 pm. Reduced off-season.

Mermaid Bar and Grill, 340 Water Street, Saugatuck, (269) 857-8208. Serving lunch and dinner. Waterfront views. The outdoor patio overlooking the Kalamazoo River is a popular place in the summer. Open 7 days, Sun to Thurs 11:30 am to 10:00 pm and Fri and Sat 11:30 am to 11:30 pm. Closed late October to late March or early April.

Monroe's Café and Grill, 302 Culver Street, Saugatuck, (269) 857-1242, monroescafe@verizon.net. The basil, sautéed onion and tomato omelet was excellent. If you are here later in the day you might want to try the baby back ribs with their special BBQ sauce. The café is decorated with Marilyn Monroe graphics. Breakfast, lunch and dinner.

Phil's Bar and Grille, 214 Butler Street, Saugatuck, (269) 857-1555. Serves broasted chicken, bistro-type appetizers, sandwiches and entrees as well as beer, wine and cocktails. Faithful customers swear Phil's has the best hamburger in town. Entrees are moderately priced and sandwiches inexpensive. A local hangout with a pleasant atmosphere. Open Mon to Thurs 10:30 am to 11:00 pm, Fri and Sat 11:30 am to 11:00 pm and Sun noon to 11:00 pm.

Pumpernickel's Eatery, 215 Butler Street, Saugatuck, (269) 857-1196. Relaxed atmosphere and you can dine on the patio and sun deck, weather permitting. Cocktails. Entertainment nightly in the summer. Moderate prices. Open 7 days for breakfast and lunch 8:00 am to 5:00 pm, and 7 days for dinner 5:30 pm to 10:00 pm, (summer only). Sunday Brunch buffet 9:00 am to 3:00 pm.

Restaurant Toulouse, 248 Culver Street, Saugatuck, (269) 857-1561, www.restauranttoulouse.com. French themed restaurant with continental food. You can enjoy lunch on the patio during the summer. Children's menu. Serving dinner only during the off-season.

Respite, 48 Center Street, Douglas, (269) 857-5411. Great place to get a cup of cappuccino or have breakfast or lunch. While you are there, check out the bathroom. Open 7 days, Mon to Thurs 7:30 am to 9:00 pm Fri and Sat 8:30 pm to 11:00 pm and Sun 8:30 am to 6:00 pm.

Sand Bar Saloon, 141 Butler Street, Saugatuck, (269) 857-2676. Serves Chicago style hotdogs, gyros, and sandwiches, including their special BBQ pork. Pool tables, jukebox and pinball. Live entertainment some Saturdays. Open lunch, dinner, and carry-out. Open 7 days, Mon to Sat 10:00 am to 2:00 am and Sun noon to 2:00 am, year round.

Saugatuck Brewing Company, 6785 Enterprise Drive, Unit 6, Douglas, (269) 857-7222, www.saugatuckbrewing.com. Micro-brewery with tasting bar and brewery tours.

Saugatuck Coffee Shop, located in historic Leland Alley behind the Butler's Pantry. (269) 857-COFE. Sandwiches and sweets. High speed internet available. Casually elegant.

Spectators Bar and Grill, 6432 Washington Street (Blue Star Highway), (269) 857-5001, www.spectatorsrestuarant.com. Sports Bar with TVs for you to catch your favorite sporting event. Serves lunch and dinner and provides carry-out.

SuCasa Super Mercado and Restaurant, 306 West Main Street (M-89) Fennville. Locals proclaim this the place for great Mexican food and worth the short side trip to Fennville. Not a trendy chain restaurant, but created to provide authentic Mexican food to seasonal labor population in the area. You walk through the grocery to get to the restaurant. Open 7 days, year round, 8:00 am to 9:30 pm.

Uncommon Grounds, 127 Hoffman Street, Saugatuck, (269) 857-3333, www.uncommongroundscafe.com. Indoor and outdoor seating and the coffee is strong. They claim they have fans as far away as Chicago. Also sells beans (or ground) by the pound. Nice selection of teas. Breakfast and luncheon menus. Sandwiches of the day and special plates like the hummus, pesto or curry chicken salad.

Wally's Bar and Grill, Hoffman Street, Saugatuck, (269) 857-5641. "Sandwiches and really good stuff." Open Mon to Sat 11:00 am to 2:00 am and Sun noon to 2:00 pm. Dinner served until 10:00 pm.

The White House Bistro and Winery, 149 Griffith Street, Saugatuck, (269) 857-3240, www.whitehousebistro.com. Has outdoor seating as well as indoor and on weekends provides entertainment. Serves lunch and dinner. Breakfast served on Saturday and Sunday.

Yum Yum Café, 98 Center Street, Lower Level, Douglas, (269) 857-4567. Coffee and gelatos. Try the banana caramel Praline gelato for a cool treat. You can also enjoy a lunch of paninis, wraps, soups or salads. Summer hours 7 days, Mon to Thurs 11:00 am to 7:00 pm, Sat 10:00 am to 10:00 pm and Sun 10:00 am to 7:00 pm.

Lodging (also see Campgrounds)

AmericInn Lodge & Suites, 2905 Blue Star Highway, Douglas, (269) 857-8581 or toll-free (800) 634-3444. Forty-six rooms, suites with whirlpool and fireplace available. Extras: extended continental breakfast, indoor pool recreation area with Jacuzzi and sauna and fireplace conversation area.

Bayside Inn, 618 Water Street, Saugatuck, (269) 857-4321. Casual elegance. Located on the water in downtown Saugatuck, the Bayside Inn is only a short walk to fine restaurants and shopping. Extras: all rooms have balconies; there is a common area with fireplace, luxury fireplace suites available and outdoor waterfront hot tub.

Beechwood Manor Inn, 736 Pleasant Street, Saugatuck, (269) 857-1587 or toll-free (877) 857-1587, stay@beechwoodmanorinn.com. Upscale accommodations just a few blocks from the heart of Saugatuck's busy downtown. The Inn was featured in Country Inns Magazine. Built for a diplomat in the 1870s it is on the National/State Historic Register. All rooms with private bath, cable TV, fine linens and full breakfast each morning. Open year round.

The Belvedere Inn & Restaurant, 3656 63rd Street, Saugatuck, info@thebelvedereinn.com, (269) 857-5777 or toll-free (877) 858-5777. A Saugatuck Award Winning Bed & Breakfast and Restaurant. European-Style Boutique Inn provides hospitality in casually elegant surroundings. The 1913 restored Inn sits on five acres of manicured gardens. Ten guest rooms with private baths and wonderful views.

Bentley Suites, 326 Water Street, Saugatuck, (269) 857-5416, bentleysuites@verizon.net. A luxury four-unit inn on the water in downtown Saugatuck. Extras: each spacious suite has a king-size bed, private patio and garden area or balcony overlooking the Kalamazoo River, wet bar, tiled bath with oversize whirlpool bathtub, fireplace, cable TV, telephone and elegant English furnishings.

Best Western Plaza Hotel, 3457 Blue Star Highway, Saugatuck, (269) 857-7178. Located 1½ miles from Saugatuck and surrounded by five acres of peaceful woods. 52 rooms. Extras: indoor swimming pool, whirlpool, exercise room, deluxe continental breakfast, free local calls, telephones with data ports, internet, satellite TV with HBO, king rooms with Jacuzzi/fireplace, laundry, and corporate, group or senior rates.

Birds of a Feather, 6068 Blue Star Highway, Saugatuck, toll-free (800) 852-1955, teresadingman@yahoo.com. Country estate with 11 suites. Extras: indoor pool, sauna, whirlpool, five acres by the woods, picnic area beside the pond, grills, and "all you can eat" breakfast.

Captains Quarters, 3242 Blue Star Highway, Saugatuck, (269) 857-2525 or toll-free (800) 499-2929. An on-location site in the filming of feature motion picture "*Singapore Harbor*," Captains Quarters offers clean, comfortable, air conditioned rooms. Extras: cable TV, quiet wooded setting.

The Cook & the Gardener, 6275 124th Avenue, Fennville, (269) 561-5451, thepats@acd.net. Five guest rooms each uniquely decorated with antiques. Five minutes from Saugatuck and ten minutes from South Haven. Ten acres of gardens on a country estate. Extras: fireplaces, barrier free first floor accommodations, a richly appointed balcony, Jacuzzi/fireplace suite available, full home-cooked breakfasts and special diets are accommodated.

Deer Creek Cottages, 300 Ferry Street, Douglas, (269) 857-5445, info@deercreekcottages.com. Bed and Breakfast style guest house with three stand-alone individual cottages. Cottages have pine flooring, private decks, full bath, and fully equipped kitchens and are nestled in the woods with an outdoor hot tub on the premises. Located between Douglas Beach, Oval Beach and the Saugatuck chain ferry.

Dunes Resort, 333 Blue Star Highway, Saugatuck, (269) 857-1401, mjones@dunesresort.com. The Midwest's largest Gay and Lesbian resort and entertainment complex. Situated on 20 acres with 80 hotel rooms, cottages, suites and a sprawling disco/bar complex. A nightclub, cabaret, outdoor patio bar and game room available. Large Pool/bar open daily in the summer. Open 7 days, year round.

The Glenn Country Inn & Country Suite, 1286 64th Street, Fennville, info@glenncountryinn.com. (269) 227-3045 or toll-free (888) 237-3009. Michigan's Premier pet friendly B&B. Five large guest rooms. Peaceful and serene in a rural setting. Extras: some rooms with fireplaces and whirlpools, the Country Suite offers a furnished 2+ bedroom apartment with fully contained kitchen, gourmet breakfasts, personalized picnic baskets and private fine dining.

Goshorn Lake Family Resort, 3581 65th Street, Saugatuck, (269) 857-4808 or toll-free (800) 541-4210, glccresort@verizon.net. 23 housekeeping cottages on Goshorn Lake, many with wood burning fireplaces. Fully equipped kitchens, picnic tables and BBQ grills, swimming pool, sandy private swimming beach, volleyball, fire pit, horseshoes, basketball and row boats. Close to downtown Saugatuck, Lake Michigan beaches and golf courses. No pets. Weekly rentals mid-June to late August. Nightly rentals early and late season.

Heritage Manor Inn, 2253 Blue Star Highway, Fennville, toll-free (888) 543-4384, rdhunter@heritagemanorinn.com. Decorated in country and Victorian. Extras: buffet fireside breakfast, Jacuzzi, fireplace rooms and suites available, spacious two-bedroom town houses available, heated indoor pool, children's area, sand volleyball court, basketball hoop and picnic areas.

Hidden Garden Cottages, 247 Butler Street, Saugatuck, (269) 857-8109 or toll-free (888) 857-8109. Secreted in the heart of downtown Saugatuck just steps from shopping and dining. These romantic cottages are designed for two and are luxuriously appointed with artwork, fireplaces, two-person whirlpools, robes, down comforters and exquisite linens. Extras: VCR, movies, CD player, mini-kitchen and continental breakfast. Hidden Garden Cottages were featured in Travel Holiday Magazine as a romantic place to stay in West Michigan.

Hidden Pond Bed & Breakfast, P.O. Box 461, Fennville, (269) 561-2491. Retreat like setting on 28 acres of woods, perfect for bird watching, hiking, cross-country skiing, or just relaxing in a rowboat on the pond. Two guest rooms with private baths. Extras: full hot breakfast served at your leisure, fireplace, library, deck, sun porch, turndown service, candies, soft drinks, tea and chocolates.

The Hunter's Lodge, 2790 Blue Star Highway, Saugatuck, (269) 857-5402, hospitality@thehunterslodge.com. The Hunter's Lodge is a "Cottage Living" magazine suggested place to stay (October 2005) and a 2006 Historic Preservation Award Winning Property. Two miles to downtown. The Arts-and-Crafts style log cabin provides rustic charm and modern conveniences. Extras: snacks, a private entrance, cable TV, microwave, refrigerator, coffee maker and hand-crafted quilts.

Ivy Inn, 421 Water Street, Saugatuck, (269) 857-4643. Located in the heart of Saugatuck, across from the Kalamazoo River. Extras: cable TV, common room with library and fireplace, screened-in porch, patio and deluxe continental breakfast.

J. Paules' Fenn Inn, 2254 South 58th Street, Fennville, (269) 561-2836 or toll-free (877) 561-2836. Just minutes from Saugatuck, Holland, and Lake Michigan. Extras: full gourmet breakfast and private evening dining, fireplaces and baths with robes and Jacuzzi.

Kingsley House, 626 West. Main, Fennville, (269) 561-6425 or toll-free (866) 561-6425, romanticgetaways@kingsleyhouse.com. Featured in *Time* magazine, *New York Times* and newspapers across Michigan. Eight guest rooms (four are Jacuzzi/fireplace suites). Extras: romance spa packages, in-house spa and concierge services, fireplaces, four-story turret, breakfast in bed and wireless internet access.

The Kirby House, 294 Center Street, Douglas, (269) 857-2904 or toll-free (800) 521-6473, info@kirbyhouse.com. An 1890 Queen Anne Victorian Manor and a Registered Historic Site, the home boasts quarter-sawn oak woodwork, prism windows, tall ceilings with gently curved moldings, six-sided turret, wrap-around porch and five fireplaces. Extras: full gourmet breakfasts prepared by award winning chef, seasonal heated in-ground pool, Jacuzzi, free bikes, and internet.

Lake Shore Resort, 2885 Lakeshore Drive, Saugatuck, (269) 857-7121. Overlooking Lake Michigan with private beach. Extras: decks, heated pool, bikes, lake kayaks, putting green, beach chaise chairs and umbrellas, two miles of wooded nature trails, continental breakfast and cable TV. Near restaurants, shops, galleries, boat cruises, theater and golf. Five minutes to town. Open May through October.

Landings of Saugatuck Inn & Marina, 726 Water Street Saugatuck, landingsinn@aol.com, (269) 857-4550 or toll-free (888) 857-4550. Located on the Kalamazoo River in downtown Saugatuck with a view to the waterfront activities from your deck. Walking distance to fine shops, galleries and restaurants.

The Maplewood Hotel, 428 Butler Street, Saugatuck, (269) 857-1771 or toll-free (800) 650-9790, info@maplewoodhotel.com. Next to the Village Green in downtown Saugatuck, short walk to shopping and restaurants. Extras: some rooms with fireplace and Jacuzzi tubs, breakfast included, deck with heated pool and common room with wood burning fireplace. Rated "Excellent" by the American Bed and Breakfast Association.

Maple Ridge Cottages, 719 Maple Street, Saugatuck, (269) 857-5211, info@thepinesmotorlodge.com. Housekeeping cottages, each with two bedrooms and linens, one bath and fully equipped kitchen with dining area. Extras: cable TV/VCR, fireplace, deck with private hot tub and grill. Private parking. Open all year.

Mason Street Suites & Cottages, 320 Mason Street, Saugatuck, masonstreetsuites@verizon.net, www.masonstreetsuites.com, (269) 857-5553 or toll-free (866) 857-5553. Located in downtown Saugatuck, one block from shops, restaurants, galleries and waterfront activities. Each suite is individually themed. Extras: fireplaces, TV-VCR, kitchen facilities, hot tubs and sauna, and Jacuzzis. Also a Lightkeeper's private one room cottage with fireplace, private deck and hot tub.

Marywood Manor Bed & Breakfast & Cottages, 236 Mary Street. Saugatuck, Info@marywoodmanor.com, (269) 857-4771 or (616) 836-4546. Located on a quiet side street just two houses from downtown shops and restaurants. All accommodations are two room suites. Extras: refrigerators, beautiful perennial garden, large screened porch and full breakfast.

Northern Lights, 320 Blue Star Highway, toll-free (888) 857-8890. One and two bedroom suites around landscaped gardens with a large pool, cabana, spa and fire pits. Other extras: kitchenettes, fireplaces, patio and deck.

The Park House B&B, 888 Holland Street, Saugatuck, (269) 857-4535 or toll free (866) 321-4535 info@parkhouseinn.com. Ten guest rooms, each with private bath in Saugatuck's oldest residence, the Park House which was built in 1857. Extras: full breakfast, personalized concierge services and an in-room massage therapist.

The Pines Motorlodge and Cottages, 56 Blue Star Highway, Douglas, (269) 857-5211, info@thepinesmotorlodge.com. Retro charm in a boutique-type lodging experience. Extras: renovated rooms, non-smoking, goose down comforters, TV\VCR, refrigerators, microwaves, private baths, knotty pine ceilings and continental breakfast.

The River Suites, 650 Water Street, Saugatuck, (269) 857-8899. The River Suites are two luxury suites for rent by the day or week. Each has a private balcony overlooking the Kalamazoo River. Extras: full kitchen, fireplace, Jacuzzi tub and parking. Located above the River Market & Deli, just a few blocks from the center of town.

Rosemont Inn Resort, 83 Lakeshore Drive, Saugatuck, (269) 857-2637 or toll-free (888) 767-3666, rosemontinnresort@comcast.net. Elegant inn on Lake Michigan, selected by the *Chicago Sun Times* as "One of the Midwest's Top 10 Romantic Retreats." It offers fourteen rooms with spectacular lake views, three with in-room whirlpools. Extras: fireplaces, cable, CD players, full breakfast buffet, seasonal pool, indoor whirlpool and sauna, direct access to the beach, broadband wireless and complimentary bicycles. Open year-round.

The Newnham Sun Catcher Inn, 131 Griffith Street, Saugatuck, (269) 857-4249 or toll-free (800) 587-4249. Four rooms and three suites with fireplaces. Built about the turn-of-the-century, this Country-Style Inn features a wrap around veranda and is furnished with family antiques. Located one block from business district. Extras: sun deck, hot tub, heated swimming pool, full breakfast and A/C.

Saugatuck's Victorian Inn, 447 Butler Street, Saugatuck, toll-free: (888) 240-7957, vicinn@comcast.net. Located in the heart of down-town Saugatuck, the Victorian Inn is one of Saugatuck's fine older homes. Built at the turn of the century, the original Victorian splendor has been meticulously restored. Each room has a private bath. Extras: wrap around porches.

Shady Shore Inn & Cottages, 787 Lake Street, Saugatuck, (269) 857-7600, rentals@michiganvacation.org. Waterfront Inn & Cottages nestled in Saugatuck's historic district on 120 feet of Saugatuck Harbor frontage, steps from shopping, restaurants and nightlife. Remodeled

1871 shipbuilder's home offers three guest rooms each with private bath, cable and TV/DVD player. Gorgeous views and grounds. Open year round.

Shangri-La Motel, 6190 Blue Star Highway, Saugatuck, (269) 857-1453 or toll-free (800) 877-1453. Located in a quiet, wooded setting only five minutes from downtown. Extras: satellite TV, VCR, direct-dial phones, heated pool, picnic area with grill, lawn games and continental breakfast. Minutes from shopping, restaurants, art galleries, golf and beaches. Affordable rates.

Sherwood Forest Bed & Breakfast, 938 Center Street, Douglas, sf@sherwoodforestbandb.com, (269) 857-1246 or toll-free (800) 838-1246. 2006 Voted Best In Personal Luxury in Michigan by *Lake Magazine* readers. Turn of the century home surrounded by woods. Guest rooms with antiques and private baths. Extras: fireplace/Jacuzzi suites, heated pool, ½ block to Lake Michigan. Cottage also available.

Ship 'n Shore Motel & Boatel, 528 Water Street, Saugatuck, (269) 857-2194. The only motel located in the heart of downtown Saugatuck on the water. Many rooms with decks. Extras: heated pool, Jacuzzi and large lanai with fireplace, in room refrigerators, free internet and continental breakfast.

Suites of Saugatuck Condominium Resort, 560 Campbell Road, Saugatuck. (269) 857-5000. rental@michiganvacation.org. Atop the bluff between Lake Michigan and downtown Saugatuck, this condominium resort is between Oval Beach and Douglas Beach. One and two-bedroom suites, spacious grounds, pool, cable, DVD players, fully equipped kitchens and complimentary coffee.

Twin Gables Inn & Cottages, 900 Lake Street, Saugatuck, (269) 857-4346 or toll-free (800) 231-2185, relaxing@twingablesinn.com. Harbor view inn with fifteen rooms set up to make your stay relaxing and luxurious. Extras: breakfast with a water view, pool and hot tub.

Twin Oaks Inn, 227 Griffith Street, Saugatuck, (269) 857-1600 or toll-free: (800) 788-6188, twinoaks@sirus.com. An 1860s English Inn that combines the graciousness and beauty of antiques with modern conveniences. All rooms have private baths. Extras: TV/VCR (library of 700 films), common room with fireplace, screened porch, outdoor hot tub, horseshoes, bicycles and full breakfasts. Located downtown.

Valentine Lodge, 653 Campbell Road, Douglas, (269) 857-4598. Three-story Victorian Inn located between downtown Saugatuck and the beaches. The area is quiet and lends itself to running, biking or leisurely walks. Extras: two acres of shade-garden, breakfast buffet served weekends on the second floor screened-in porch. Open May 1st to November 1st.

Wickwood Inn, 510 Butler Street, Saugatuck, (269) 857-1465 or toll-free (800) 385-1174, innkeeper@wickwoodinn.com. Co-author Julee Rosso (*Silver Palate Cookbook*), along with her husband, Bill Miller, are hosts at this Inn where the emphasis is on delicious food. Located in the village of Saugatuck. In 2003 and again in 2004, the Inn achieved an "extraordinary to perfection," ranking, making it one of the "Top Fifty Small Resorts, Inns and Spas in the U.S." *Zagat* reviewers described it as having "décor that is perfect!" "Around every corner is something more breathtaking than the last." Extras: great food, fine art, and creature comforts. Guest rooms carry such themes as *Summer in Santorini*, *A Vineyard in Bordeaux*, *Uptown* or *Province*.

Museums and Galleries

Amazwi Contemporary Art, 246 Culver Street, Saugatuck, (269) 857-5551, www.amazwi.com. Original contemporary paintings from Africa, as well as sculpture and unique crafts. You will find art on canvas, paper, cardboard and wood using acrylics, chalk, charcoal, pastels and watercolors. Open 7 days, Mon to Sat 10:00 am to 7:00 pm and Sun 11:00 am to 6:00 pm. Typically only open weekends in winter.

Bentley's Fine Art & Antiques, 50 Center Street, Douglas, (269) 857-3339. Antiques, original vintage posters, bronzes, paintings, furniture and accessories. Open summer 7 days, 11:00 am to 5:00 pm. Closed in the winter.

Bruce Baughman Studio & Gallery, 242 Butler Street, Saugatuck, brucebaughmangallery.com, (269) 857-1299. Reverse painting and contemporary fine art by resident artist Bruce Baughman. Open summer 7 days, Mon to Sat 11:00 am to 5:00 pm and Sun noon to 5:00 pm.

Button Art Gallery, 161 Blue Star Highway, Douglas, (269) 857-2175. Opened in 1966; offers original paintings, bronzes and garden sculpture from artists across the country. Summer hours 7 days, Mon to Sat 11:00 am to 5:00 pm and Sun noon to 5:00 pm.

Czarina's Treasure, 403 Water Street, Saugatuck, (269) 857-7216, www.czarinas.com. Specializing in Lotton Art Glass, crystal vases, icons, bronzes and jewelry. Open 7 days, 11:00 am to 7:00 pm (may vary somewhat). Reduced winter hours.

DeGraaf Forsythe Galleries, 403 Water Street, Saugatuck, (269) 857-1882, www.degraaffineart.com. Contemporary international fine art and sculpture from distinguished world-wide sources. Summer open 7 days, Mon to Sat 11:00 am to 6:00 pm and Sun 1:00 pm to 5:00 pm. Winter hours vary.

Discovery Art Center, 347 Water Street, Saugatuck, (269) 857-8225. A cooperative gallery featuring area artists.

Gebben Gray Gallery, 120 East Main Street (M-89) Fennville, (269) 561-2004, www.gebbengraygallery.com. Represents regionally and nationally known contemporary abstract and representational artists. Open year round. Wed to Fri 11:00 am to 6:00 pm, Sat and Sun 11:00 am to 4:00 pm.

Good Goods, 106 Mason Street, Saugatuck, (269) 857-1557, www.goodgoods.com. Fine art and American craft wearables, jewelry, furniture, paintings and sculpture. Open Memorial Day to Labor Day 7 days, 10:00 am to 10:00 pm. Open off-season 7 days; reduced hours.

James Brandess Studios & Gallery, 238 Butler Street, Saugatuck, (269) 236-1937. Artist's studio featuring Saugatuck area landscapes, still-lifes and portraits. Art for everyone. This is a one-man gallery aimed at being affordable and letting new collectors into collecting. Open 7 days, 10:00 am to 9:00 pm. Closes winter 5:00 pm.

Janice Miles Gallery, 421 Water Street, Saugatuck, (269) 857-5202. Six artists display porcelain, watercolors and jewelry. Open 7 days, Sun to Thurs 11:00 am to 5:00 pm, Fri and Sat 11:00 am to 7:00 pm.

Joyce Petter Gallery, 161 Blue Star Highway, Douglas, (269) 857-7861 or toll-free (888) 808-7920, www.joycepettergallery.com. Open 7 days, Mon to Sat 10:00 am to 5:30 pm and Sun noon to 5:30 pm. Winter: Sat and Mon 10:00 am to 5:00 pm, Sun noon to 5:00 pm.

Johnny Blue Gallery, 36 Center Street, (269) 857-8571, Douglas. Johnny Blue is a metal sculptor and this gallery exhibits his work and that of six other artists. Great pieces; and prices are amazingly reasonable. Open 7 days, 11:00 am to 5:00 pm (usually later weekends). Closed Tues and Wed in the winter. Also by appointment.

Khnemu Studio-Dawn Soltysiak, 6322 113th Avenue, Fennville, (269) 236-9260, www.khnemustudio.com. The unique working studio and gallery of pottery artist Dawn Soltysiak. Open April to November, Wed to Sun 10:00 am to 5:00 pm. Reduced off-season.

Koorey Creations, 104 Hoffman Street, Saugatuck, (269) 857-8050 www.Kooreycreations.com Gallery of fine handcrafted jewelry designs, unique gemstones and original art. Open summer 7 days, Mon to Thurs 10:30 am to 5:00 pm and Fri to Sun 10:30 am to 8:00 pm. Check website for off-season hours.

Marcia Perry's Gallery and Sculpture Studio, 6248 Blue Star Highway, Saugatuck, (269) 857-4210, www.marciaperry-art.com. The sculptor's workplace and showroom featuring soulful fine art. Open summer: Wed to Mon noon to 5:00 pm. Extended show hours. Closed Tues. Winter open week-ends and by appointment.

Saugatuck/Douglas Historical Museum, 735 Park Street (at the foot of Mount Baldhead in the old pumphouse on the west shore of the

Kalamazoo River). Take the Chain Ferry to the Douglas side from Saugatuck. This is an award winning museum with special exhibits and an outdoor garden with grand views of Saugatuck harbor. Free admission. Museum is open 7 days, noon to 4:00 pm, Memorial Day through Labor Day and on weekends in September and October.

Saugatuck Gallery, 317 Butler Street, Saugatuck, (269) 857-1189. One of the Midwest's largest selections of affordable art. Open 7 days, Mon to Sat 10:00 am to 9:00 pm and Sun 10:00 am to 6:00 pm.

The S. S. Keewatin Museum, docked just south of the Saugatuck-Douglas Bridge at Union Street and Blue Star Highway, (269) 857-2464. When active the Keewatin berthed as many as 288 passengers and today visitors to the museum can see her 105 first class staterooms and relive the by-gone era of elegant steamship travel. Check the details including hand etched skylight windows, 120-seat walnut lined dining room and forward ladies' drawing room. You can also see the Captain's quarters as they were left by the last master of the ship. Tours at 10:30 am and 4:30 pm daily from Memorial Day to Labor Day.

Stewartia Studio, 2525 Blue Star Highway, Fennville, (269) 543-4029, stewartiastudio.com. Studio of Mark A. Dyer who creates art to speak to your soul even if it does not match your sofa. Open year round, Thurs to Mon 10:00 am to 5:00 pm. Closed Tues and Wed.

The Thimgan Hayden Gallery, 36 Center Street, Douglas, (269) 857-8494, www.thimganhayden.com. Classical oil paintings by Ms. Hayden who studied in Florence, Italy. Open Mon to Thurs by appointment, Fri and Sat 11:00 am to 7:00 pm and Sun 11:00 am to 5:00 pm. Winter hours reduced, call to confirm or make appointment.

Thistle Gallery, 10 West Center Street, Douglas, (269) 857-7500, www.thistlegallery.biz. Fused glass, pottery, textiles and photography. Open 7 days, 10:30 am to 7:00 pm.

The Timmel Collection, 133 Main Street, Saugatuck, (269) 857-7274, www.thetimmelcollection.com. Gallery of fine art representing 120 artists, sculptors and photographers. Open summer 7 days, 10:00 am to 5:00 pm. Open Sat and Sun afternoons from Halloween to Easter.

Water Street Gallery, 546 Butler Street, Saugatuck, (269) 857-8485. The venue for contemporary sculpture, ceramics, painting and photography. Open Thurs to Mon 11:00 am to 5:00 pm.

You'nique International Art Gallery & Gifts, 95 Blue Star Highway, Douglas, (269) 857-8485 or toll-free (888) 670-7797. Original paintings, limited editions, prints, photographs, ceramic, pottery, art glass, wood carvings and sculpture. Open summer 7 days, 10:00 am to 6:00 pm. Off-season open weekends 10:00 am to 6:00 pm.

Theatre

Mason Street Warehouse, 400 Culver Street, Saugatuck, (269) 857-4898. Obtain current information by phone, e-mail or web; info@masonstreetwarehouse.org, www.masonstreetwarehouse.org.

Theatre at the Red Barn, 3657 63rd Street, (269) 857-7707. Call for information; the Red Barn offers mainly workshops and lectures.

One of Saugatuck's many shops   *Photo Courtesy of Joe Jurkiewicz*

Antiques

Amsterdam Art and Science, 3483 Blue Star Highway, Saugatuck, (269) 857-3044. Home and garden items as well as interesting antiques. Open 7 days, April 1st to October 1st 10:00 am to 6:00 pm, October to January Thurs to Mon 10:00 am to 6:00 pm and December to April check hours on their answering machine.

Anderson School House, 6270 124th Avenue (M-89), Fennville, (269) 561-6610. Open 7 days a week, year round.

Antique and Garden Gallery, 2918 Blue Star Highway, Douglas, Cell (616) 836-5084. All periods and types of antiques, ship wheels, glassware, furniture and garden iron. Located in an old farmhouse with each room filled with merchandise. Also has cement statuary. Open April thru June and September thru November Thurs to Mon 11:00 am to 6:00 pm. Open July and August 7 days 10:00 am to 6:00 pm.

Bentley's Fine Arts, Antiques and Gifts, 50 Center Street, Douglas, (269) 857-3339. (See above under galleries.)

Bird Cage Antiques, 2378 Blue Star Highway (Corner of Blue Star and M-89), (269) 543-4732. Primarily French and English wardrobes and dining room sets. Open May to September 7 days, noon to 6:00 pm. Winter: open weekends and some weekdays, call to confirm.

Blue Star Antique Pavilion, 2948 Blue Star Highway, Douglas, (269) 857-6041, www.bstarantique.com. 50,000 square feet of dealer booths, consignment room and auction house. Good place to stop if you are searching for a special antique. Open 7 days, 10:00 am to 6:00 pm.

Circa (c.), 98 Center Street, Douglas, www.circahousewares.com, (269) 857-7676. Antiques, art, accessories and the Glitter Garden with gifts, Halloween and Christmas items. Open summer Mon to Sat 10:00 am to 5:00 pm and Sun 11:00 am to 5:00 pm.

Country Store Antiques, 120 Butler Street, Saugatuck, (269) 857-8601. General merchandise, a little of everything. Open Mon to Sat 11:00 am to 5:00 pm. Closed in the winter.

Elephant Trunk, 20 East Center Street, Douglas, (269) 857-4755. British Colonial antique furniture and accessories from India, Africa and the Far East. Open year round Thurs to Mon 11:00 am to 5:00 pm. Additional days and hours in the summer.

Groovy! Groovy!, located at the Pines Motor Lodge, 56 Blue Star Highway, Douglas, (269) 857-2171. Cottage antiques, arts and seasonal décor ranging from architectural to funky for both the home and garden. Open 9:00 am to 8:00 pm.

Old House Antiques, 112 Center Street, Douglas, (269) 857-1623. Victorian, Havilland, cut glass, estate Waterford, silver and military. Hours vary.

Other Shopping

Alle Rue No. 133, 133 Butler Street, Saugatuck, (269) 857-5543. Parisian boutique with sophisticated personal home accessories, embellishments and apparel. Great chenille animals perfect for a toddler because they are not only cute and cuddly, but washable. Open 7 days, 10:00 am to 7:00 pm. Only open weekends in the winter.

Amantes, 110 Butler Street, Saugatuck, (269) 857-3813. Women's apparel and accessories including jewelry, shoes and purses. The merchandise they carry is primarily from California and you will not see it in every department store you enter. Open 7 days, 10:00 am to 6:00 pm (generally) and slightly reduced winter hours.

American Spoon Foods, 308 Butler Street, (269) 857-3084. All natural, made in Michigan preserves, jams, butters, salsas, dried fruits, gelato and sorbetto. Open 7days, Mon to Sat 10:00 am to 5:00 pm and Sun noon to 4:00 pm.

Art and Angels, 226 Butler Street, Saugatuck, (269) 857-1485. Designer children's clothing, some jewelry, figurines and books. Open 7 days, 10:00 am to 9:00 pm. Hours reduced to weekends in the winter.

Art Glass Alcove, 142 Butler Street, Saugatuck, (269) 857-3431. Handcrafted jewelry, hats, home accessories, gourmet food, bath products and more. Open summer 7 days, 10:00 am to 9:00 pm. Reduced hours in the winter.

Bauble Bath, 132 Butler Street, Saugatuck, (269) 857-1656. Natural bath and skin products. Artsy jewelry, gifts and home accessories. Open May to Labor Day 7 days, 10:00 am to 9:00 pm (sometimes later during weekend). After Labor day 10:00 am to 6:00 pm. November to January 1st Mon 11:00 am to 5:00 pm, closed Tues and Wed. January 1st to April 1st Sat and Sun 11:00 am to 5:00 pm, April open Thurs to Mon 10:00 am to 5:00 pm, closed Tues and Wed.

Bedfellows of Saugatuck, 247 Butler Street, Saugatuck, (269) 857-5505. Intimate apparel, sleepwear and street wear. Open year round.

The Boutique @ Little Bohemia, 140 Butler Street, Saugatuck, (269) 857-5959. Open daily from 11:00 am to 9:00 pm, (hours not set in stone). Closes for the season at the end of November and opens in April with reduced hours.

Bright World Candle Company, 233 Culver Street, Saugatuck, (269) 857-1184. Candles, gifts and decorative accessories.

The Butler Pantry, 119 Butler Street, Saugatuck, (269) 857-4875, www.thebutlerpantry.com. Kitchenware, gourmet foods and fine wines. Open 7 days, Sun to Thurs 10:00 am to 6::00 p m, Fri 10:00 am to 7:00 pm and Sat 10:00 am to 8:00 pm. Open 7 days in winter but reduced hours.

Caribbean Colors and Nostalgia, 326 Butler Street, Saugatuck, (269) 857-1116, www.caribbeancolorsnostalgia.com. Caribbean folk art and fashions. American memorabilia specializing in signs.

Cheryl's, 132 Mason Street, Saugatuck, (269) 857-5595, www.cherylsstore.com. Original art, home and garden pieces and fashion accessories. Lots of one-of-a-kind items with good prices. Open 7 days, 10:00 am to 9:00 pm. Reduced winter hours.

Chios, 201 Culver, Saugatuck, (269) 857-2462. Clothing, formal dresses, shoes and accessories. Open 7 days, 10:00 am to 9:00 pm.

Delphinia's, 133 Butler Street (will be moving to 247 Butler Street), (269) 857-1942, www.delphiniabath.com. Luxurious linens and elegant bath items made from flower and plant oils: imported perfumes, colognes, soaps, lotions, candles, air diffusers and potpourri. Also Steiff heirloom-quality teddy bears. Open summer 7 days, 10:30 am to 9:00 pm. Reduced off-season hours. May close after Christmas.

Devine's, 220 Culver Street, Saugatuck. Rings, jewelry, mirrors and accents. Open 7 days, 10:00 am to 10:00 pm. Reduced hours during the off-season.

Diggs, 269 Center Street, Douglas. Home décor and one-of-a-kind antiques. Open 7 days, Mon to Sat 10:00 am to 5:00 pm and Sun 11:00 am to 5:00 pm.

East of the Sun, 252 Butler Street, Saugatuck, (269) 857-2640. Home accessories, children's books and toys. Also Christmas items. Open 7 days, Mon and Tues 10:00 am to 5:30, Wed to Sat 10:00 am to 8:00 pm and Sun 11:00 am to 5:30 pm.

Elle's Design, 109 Butler Street, Saugatuck, cell phone (616) 886-8818. Women's apparel and accessories. Open 7 days, Mon to Thurs 10:00 am to 6:00 pm, Fri and Sat 10:00 am to 8:00 pm and Sun 11:00 am to 6:00 pm. Reduced hours in winter.

Flamingo Island T-Shirt, 421 Water Street, Saugatuck. Create and customize your t-shirt. Some additional apparel items. Open 7 days, 10:00 am to 10:00 pm. Closed winter.

Fatcats of Saugatuck, 246 Butler Street, Saugatuck, (269) 857-1055. Lots of children's casual clothing. Tie died T's and sundresses. Open 7 days, 10:00 am to 9:00 pm.

The French Cottage, 33 Center Street, Douglas, (269) 857-2705, www.douglasmichigan.com. Home furnishings and accents. Open 7 days, Mon to Thurs 10:00 am to 5:00 pm, Fri and Sat 10:00 am to 8:00 pm and Sun 11:00 am to 4:00 pm. Slightly shorter days fall to December. January to April open Fri to Sun only.

Gary Daniels Home and Garden, 360 Water Street, Saugatuck, (269) 857-3700. Home interior, garden and other unique pieces.

Grandpa's Circus, 134 Butler, Saugatuck (269) 857-1319. Several rooms of very unique merchandise. One entire room devoted to clowns. Also, metal art, ceramic, jewelry, glassware, charms, sculptures and a wall of fish, to mention just a few of the highlights. Open summer 7 days, 9:00 am to 9:00 pm. Reduced winter hours.

Hoopdee Scootee, 133 Mason Street, Saugatuck, (269) 857-4141, www.hoopdeescootee.com. Clothing, gifts, gag gifts, jewelry, Fossil watches and other fun stuff. Open 7 days, Mon to Sat 10:00 am to 9:00 pm and Sun 11:00 am to 9:00 pm.

Inca, 146 Butler Street, Saugatuck. Upscale, trendy men's and women's clothing and accessories. Open 7 days 10:00 am to 9:00 pm in the summer.

International Home, 360 Water Street (Dockside Market), Saugatuck, (269) 857-2805, www.internationalhomesaugatuck.com. You will have the feeling you stepped into a gallery by the pleasant displays of clocks, gifts, and art for the home from all over the world.

Great design and even some jewelry. Open 7 days, Mon to Sat 10:00 am to 8:00 pm and Sun 10:00 am to 6:00 pm. Reduced to five days during the winter and closed in January.

Monet-like art on restroom facilities
Photo Courtesy of Joe Jurkiewicz

Lakeside Outfitters, 105 Butler Street, Saugatuck, (269) 857-9991. Trendy men and women's clothing; modern with European influence. (Like a trendier, upscale Gap.) Open 7 days, 10:00 am to 9:30 pm (with slight variance possible).

Landshark and Landshark Shoe Store, 306 Butler Street, Saugatuck, (269) 857-8831. Men and women's casual clothing and beach apparel, sunglasses, hats and other paraphernalia. Open 7 days, Mon to Thurs 10:00 am to 10:00 pm, Fri to Sun 9:00 am to 10:00 pm.

Maurilios, 222 Butler Street, Saugatuck, (269) 857-1571. Men's and women's boutique. High fashion with a creative designer flair, accessories and fun things. Known for shoes and purses. Open Mon to Thurs 10:00 am to 8:00 pm and weekends 10:00 am to 9:00 pm.

Nostalgia, 326 Butler Street, Saugatuck. Caribbean and other clothing and memorabilia. Some toys. Open 7 days, 9:30 am to 10:00 pm. Open in the winter, but with reduced hours.

Possessions, 31 Center Street, Douglas, (269) 857-1925. A store for self, home and garden with items to delight the spirit. Open 7 days, Sun to Thurs 11:00 am to 5:00 pm, Fri and Sat 11:00 am to 9:00 pm.

Sand Castle Dockside, 360 Water Street, Saugatuck, (269) 857-2323. Gifts and unique toys to stir a child's imagination. Open 7 days, Mon to Thurs 11:00 am to 6:00 pm, Fri and Sat 11:00 am to 7:00 pm and Sun 11:00 am to 6:00 pm.

Santa Fe Trading Company, 325 Butler Street, Saugatuck, (269) 857-1359, www.santafetradingco.com. A store that tries to capture the spirit of Santa Fe with a unique blend of specialty items. Open 7 days, Mon to Sat 10:00 am to 9:00 pm and Sun 11:00 am to 9:00 pm. Open daily thru the end of the year. January and March only open Fri to Sun.

Saugatuck Spice Merchants, 115 Butler Street, Saugatuck, (269) 857-3031, www.spicemerchants.biz. Over 200 fresh spices, herbs and specialty blends. Also loose teas and accessories. Unique gifts and custom gift boxes. Open Memorial Day to Labor Day 7 days, 10:30 am to 6:00 pm. Labor Day to the holidays 7 days, 11:00 am to 5:00 pm. Only open weekends in later winter.

Saugatuck Traders, 214 Butler Street, Saugatuck, (269) 857-4005. High-end sportswear like Tommy Bahama and Lacoste. Open 7 days, Sun to Thurs 10:00 am to 9:00 pm and Fri and Sat 10:00 am to 10:00 pm. Open everyday until January then only long weekends.

Singapore Bank Bookstore, 317 Butler Street, Saugatuck, (269) 857-3785. New books and beach books for readers of all ages.

Tabor Hill Wine Port, 214 Butler Street, Saugatuck, (269) 857-4859, www.taborhill.com. Wine tasting and gift shop with discounts for case purchases. Open 7 days, Mon to Sat 10:00 am to 7:00 pm and Sun noon to 6:00 pm. Reduced winter hours.

Tiki Hut, 303 Butler Street, Saugatuck, (269) 857-8392. Beach store for entire family: cotton skirts, jewelry, belts, hand-made purses. Open 7 days, 10:00 am to 9:00 pm. Open weekends only in winter.

T-Shirt Shoppe, 107 Butler Street, Saugatuck, (269) 857-4254. Exactly what the name suggests.

Uncharted Courses, 314 Butler Street, Saugatuck, (269) 857-4330, www.unchartedcourses.com. Nautical art and merchandise for the sportsman, outdoorsman and the beach house. Open 7 days, 10:00 am to 6:00 pm with reduced winter hours (mainly weekends only).

Urban Cottage, 131 Mason Street, Saugatuck, (269) 857-4553. www.urbancottageofsaugatuck.com. Great accessories and gift items. Open summer 7 days, 10:00 am to 9:00 pm. Reduced off-season hours.

Ver Plank, 133 Butler Street, Saugatuck, (269) 857-1677. 40 years in business. Jewelry, picture frames, lotions and potions, candles, floral arrangements, Tile Styles tiles. Open 7 days, 10:00 am to 9:00 pm (or later). Reduced winter hours.

The Village Store, 201 Butler Street, Saugatuck, (269) 857-1874. Clothing, accessories, hammocks, jewelry, toys, chimes, shoes and more. Open 7 days, Mon to Sat 9:00 am to 10:00 pm and Sun 10:00 am to 8:00 pm. Closes evenings at 6:00 pm and all day Sun in the winter.

The Wild Dog, 241 Butler Street, (269) 857-5090. Cool ideas for pets and their people. There is a real "people" jewelry store in the back. Open 7 days, 10:00 am to 9:00 pm during the summer.

Wine Sellers of Saugatuck, 247 Butler Street, Saugatuck, (269) 857-7815. Wine, beer, gourmet food, cheese, gifts and cigars. Open 7 days, Mon to Sat 10:00 am to 9:00 pm and Sun 11:00 am to 8:00 pm.

Parks, Beaches, and Campgrounds

Douglas Beach Park. Take West Center and turn right on 70th Street, Douglas. Bath house and stairs to the beach.

Mount Baldhead. Take the hand-pulled, chain ferry across the Kalamazoo River (access downtown Saugatuck) and then ascend the 282 steps to the top of Mount Baldhead. The trek is guaranteed to leave all but the very fittest huffing and puffing at the top. Mercifully there are benches along the way and there are no rules against resting. The view from the top is nothing short of spectacular as you look down on the forested sand dune. Take plenty of sunscreen, it may take you a while and on a hot day the sun can be fierce.

Oval Beach Recreation Area, near Park Street, Saugatuck, (269) 857-1701. *Conde Nast Traveler* rated it one of the 15 best shorelines in the world. The beautiful beach has a great feeling of seclusion. Picnic tables, life guard, concession stand and a beach house are available

Saugatuck Dunes State Park, from Saugatuck, take BR-31 to 65th Street north to 138th Avenue, west to the park entrance. This area of rugged dunes on Lake Michigan was acquired in 1971 from the Augustinian Order that once used the buildings as a seminary. Today it is a day-use park (no camping permitted). The park's major draws are its beautiful swimming beach (2½ miles of shoreline) and 300-acre natural area which contains a coastal dune system with three endangered plant species, numerous bird species and 13 miles of sandy hiking trails. Pets are permitted on the trails. This is a relatively undeveloped park. It offers picnic tables, grills and a picnic shelter.

Shore Acres Township Park and Recreation Area, 64th Street to 138th Street, near Saugatuck State Park. Recreation area, jogging, walking and sports fields. The park is across from the Felt Mansion.

Marinas, Water Sports, Boat and Jet Ski Rentals

Best Chance Charters, Water Street, Saugatuck, (269) 857-4782, www.bestchancecharters.com. Whether you are a novice who needs special help or an old hand at fishing, the ten boats in the Best Chance fleet are waiting to serve you. They range from 27-feet to 36-feet and provide bunks and restrooms. They are captained by licensed and experienced Lake Michigan anglers. Fish for salmon, brown trout, lake trout, king salmon and some walleye.

Big Lake Outfitters, 640 Water Street, Saugatuck, (269) 857-4762, www.biglakeoutfitters.com. Rents kayaks, bikes, boats and carriers for all of your fishing equipment.

Running Rivers Kayak Rentals, Center Street, Wade's Bayou Memorial Park, Douglas, (269) 673-3698. Recreational kayaks with large cockpits, 9-foot to 14-foot tandem recreational kayaks that hold two adults and a child, and fast touring kayaks with spray skirts. Special packages and group deals. Open May to Labor Day, 9:00 am to 6:00 pm, evening hours and other times by appointment.

Saugatuck Harbor of Refuge, (269) 842-5510. Open 24 hours.

Sergeant Marina, 31 Butler Street, Saugatuck, (269) 857-2873. Seasonal and transient slips available. Gas and diesel available.

Tower Marina, Douglas, (269).857.2151. Full service marina with more than 500 deep water slips. Amenities: picnic areas, children's playground, showers, washrooms, heated outdoor pool and ship store.

Charters, Cruises, and Ferries

Harbor Duck Adventures Company, Coughlin Park at Culver and Griffith, (269) 857-DUCK, www.harborduck.com. You can board in either Saugatuck or Douglas. Learn about the history of these two towns while aboard a transformed WWII army amphibious vessel.

Hoppenero Charters, 405 Park Street, Slip No. 5, Saugatuck, (269) 806-0495, hoppenero@mindspring.com. Fishing and cruise charters on Lake Michigan.

Profishient Charters, 216 St. Peters Drive, Douglas, (616) 836-5736, www.profishientcharters.com. Sport fishing on Lake Michigan.

Star of Saugatuck Boat Cruises, 716 Water Street, Saugatuck, (269) 857-4261. One-an-a-half hour scenic, narrated cruise aboard an authentic sternwheeler paddleboat. Refreshments and restrooms aboard.

Yacht Charters, 360 Water Street, Saugatuck, (616) 399-8203, www.yachtboatcharters.com. 55-foot luxury yacht with room for 35 passengers for business, anniversary, birthday or other occasions.

Other Things to See and Do

Crane's Orchards, 6054 124th Avenue, Fennville, (269) 561-8651, www.cranesorchards.com. The history of Crane's orchards can be traced as far back as the late 1800s when H. H. Hutchins cleared and planted the property along a beautiful inland lake he named Hutchins Lake. Today the fruit orchards produce nearly all of the fruit that the Pie Pantry uses for their delicious and renowned pies. You can pick apples, peaches and sweet cherries while enjoying scenery that will stay in your memory forever. The farm has a corn maze (last year's featured the Wolverine and Spartan head), hayrides in the fall and other activities to add fun to your vacation. Hours for U-pick: 7 days, 10:00 am to 6:00 pm when fruit is ready. Hayrides: October weekends noon to 6:00 pm.

Fenn Valley Tasting Room, 310 Butler Street, Saugatuck, (269) 857-5470. Free wine tasting. Open 7 days, Mon 10:00 am to 6:00 pm, Tues to Thurs 11:00 am to 6:00 pm, Fri 10:00 am to 6:00 pm (sometimes 7:00 pm) and Sun noon to 6:00 pm. (See Other things to do in Southwest Michigan p. 40 of this guide.)

Harbor Duck Adventures Company, 400 Culver Street, Saugatuck, (269) 857-3825. (See above under cruises.)

Saugatuck Area Scenic Tour. A great way to savor the natural beauty of the area. Leave Saugatuck traveling east on Old Allegan Road. Take 57th Street south and the next street west to south on 58th Street. Travel over the one lane bridge at New Richmond. Continue traveling 58th Street to M-89 and turn left (east) through Fennville. At 56th Street, turn south to 118th Street, west (past the game reserve and Allegan Woods). Turn north on 67th Street (a good place to detour to Fenn Valley Winery if the urge strikes you) and take M-89 east to Crane's U-Pick Orchards and Restaurant. Return on M-89, west to the Blue Star Highway, north (past Douglas), back to Saugatuck. The tour covers a distance of 25 miles and will take you about an hour – longer if you make stops along the way.

Saugatuck Chain Ferry, Water Street downtown. Takes you across the Kalamazoo River. A pleasant way to reach the beaches.

Saugatuck Dune Rides, 6495 Washington Road, Saugatuck, (269) 857-2253, www.saugatuckdunerides.com. 35 minute scenic ride through the Saugatuck dunes. Open 7 days, May through September Mon to Sat 10:00 am and Sun at noon. Weekends only in October.

Saugatuck Guided Walking Tour, Tourist Center, Saugatuck. During the summer tours are Wed to Sun 2:00 pm to 5:00 and they last one hour. Or, you can pick up a map and take your own walking tour.

Festivals

Waterfront Film Festival, June. You will find filmgoers, actors, producers and directors as outstanding independent films from all over the United States are screened in casual, intimate settings.

Summer Recital Series, July and August. All Saints Episcopal Church.

Golf

Clearbrook Golf Club, 6494 Clearbrook Drive, (269) 857-2000. Started in 1926 this mature par-72 course plays to 6531 yards and a 131 slope. It features a variety of intriguing holes to test every club in your bag. You will drive down pine and hardwood lined fairways and encounter the meandering *clear brook* for which the course is named. The hilly slopes make this course a challenging one. Amenities include: a driving range, two putting greens, a chipping green, a practice bunker, two restaurants and expert instruction.

Laketown Golf and Conference Center, 6069 Blue Star Highway, Saugatuck, (269) 857-5730. This facility provides a site for practicing, learning and enjoying the game of golf regardless of season or weather. The practice range is all-weather and simulates an actual golf course with graduated target greens, laser-measured for accurate yardage. There are 24 heated and sheltered T-boxes to help you brave cold and damp weather. There is a 5,000 square foot green for chipping, putting and bunker play. Also an 18 hole mini golf course designed to entertain golfers of all ages and abilities. Children love it. Amenities: individual club fitting, instruction and rental clubs.

Ravines Golf Club, 3520 Palmer Drive, (269) 857-1616. A signature Arnold Palmer 18 hole golf course where the interplay between sport and beautiful natural surroundings make for a memorable day. You will experience six miles of cart path between the first tee and the 18th green. Amenities: state-of-the-art practice facility, golf pros to assist you in improving your game, clubhouse with full beverage service.

West Shore Golf Club, 14 Ferry Street, Douglas, (269) 857-2500. One of the ten oldest golf courses in the state, the course opened in 1916 and was expanded to 18 holes in 1932. The 5298 course plays to par 66. It features a winding creek, tree lined fairways and challenging elevations. Amenities: pro shop, rental clubs available, banquet facilities and a cocktail lounge.

Contacts

Saugatuck/Douglas Convention and Visitor's Bureau, 2902 Blue Star Highway, (269) 857-1701, www.saugatuck.com.

Holland

Population: 35,000.

Directions: **From Detroit and Lansing:** I-96 West to Holland/Zeeland Exit 55 (at Grand Rapids) west. Follow Chicago Drive west (44 miles) until it becomes 8th Street. **From Chicago:** I-94 east to I-196 (exit 34). Follow I-196 to US-31 north to Holland. Stay on US-31 (follow signs to Muskegon). Make a Michigan-turn at the stoplight at 8th Street and US-31 and continue to downtown.

Background and History

In September 1846, a group of sixty Dutch immigrants cast their fate to the steerage section of the sailing brig, *Southerner*, and headed for New York, their first port of call in America. Their leader, Reverend Albertus C. Van Raalte, who was bringing his wife and five children to a strange new place, prayed he was taking them to religious freedom and opportunity.

From New York the Van Raaltes made their way to Detroit. Albertus then went on alone to search for the perfect place to settle his family and start his Dutch Colony in the new world. He was convinced he had found it at the mouth of the Black River which flowed into Black Lake and on into the beautiful Lake Michigan.

Within six months the colony had grown to nearly 800, all of whom initially agreed with Van Raalte that he had found the perfect spot for their settlement. The first summer may have changed the minds of many of the immigrants when the undrained swamps of the area produced illness, death and despair. Housing and food was in woefully short supply. Many believed Van Raalte had brought them to this strange new country to die. Van Raalte ministered to his colony providing them with daily doses of quinine and other medicinal concoctions. Somehow most survived.

Changing the fortune of the little group and aiding in their survival was the beautiful, warm fall and mild winter of 1847. By spring they were able to begin building - and build they did. By 1852, in addition to their cabins, they had a tannery, a tailor, two hotels, seven stores, a blacksmith shop, machine shops and even a jewelry store.

The New Hollanders next turned their attention to two projects that demonstrate their foresightedness. They needed a channel to connect them to Lake Michigan so they could transport goods. They sought government assistance for the project, but when it was not forthcoming, they dug it by hand. The second project they tackled was manually constructing the River Avenue Bridge. Their strong Dutch work ethic and ingenuity became the cornerstone of the city's success.

The first Holland Harbor Lighthouse was built in 1872. It is nicknamed Big Red. (See Lighthouses, p. 360 in Part II of this guide.)

Today the greater Holland area is a thriving, award-winning community, home to hundreds of businesses, 1,500 acres of park, Lake Macatawa, and many local attractions and events to tempt travelers.

Holland's galleries offer something for every art lover and collector's taste. There are autumn and winter gallery walks. Holland has heated sidewalks to make winter shopping easier. Because of the deep religious influence in Holland, you will find more restaurants and businesses closed here on Sunday than in other coastal towns.

Repairing Holland's heated streets   *Photo by Bob Royce*

Food/Restaurants

Alpen Rose Restaurant and Café, 4 East 8th Street, (616) 393-2111. European-style restaurant featuring fine, casual and family dining. Also a Sunday Brunch. In addition to the soups, salads and sandwiches, the chef creates elegant dishes for dinner. Specialty pastries, cakes, and desserts. Open Mon to Sat 7:30 am to 9:00 pm, Sun brunch 10:00 am to 2:00 pm.

Beechwood Inn, 380 Douglas Avenue, (616) 396-2355. House specialties are Swiss Steak and Lake Perch, but also offers buffalo burgers and lighter fare. Sailing and beach décor. Open Mon to Thurs 11:00 am to 11:00 pm, Fri and Sat 11:00 am to midnight.

Ben and Jerry's, 62 East 8th Street. An ice cream place that needs no description. Open 7 days, Mon to Thurs 11:00 am to 10:00 pm, Fri and Sat 11:00 am to 11:00 pm and Sun noon to 9:00 pm.

Boatwerks Waterfront Restaurant, 216 Van Raalte Avenue, (616) 396-0600. Waterfront dining, casual, but upscale, with steaks, pastas, burgers, sandwiches, and seafood. They also have specials. Outside dining is available when weather permits. Open Mon to Thurs 11:00 am to 10:00 pm, Fri and Sat 11:00 am to 11:00 pm. Closed Sun.

Brann's Steakhouse, 12234 James Street, (616) 393-0028. Steaks, chicken, shrimp and salads. Décor includes mannequins dangling from the ceiling. Open 7 days, Mon to Thurs 11:00 am to 10:00 pm, Fri and Sat 11:00 am to 11:00 pm, Sun 11:00 am to 9:00 pm.

Butch's, 44 East 8th Street, (616) 396-8227. A favorite for deli selections during the day, Butch's transforms into fine dining for the evening. Extensive wine list and local beers. You can choose a casual dinner in the pub or reserve a table. Open lunch: Mon to Sat 11:00 am to 3:00 pm. Dinner: Mon to Thurs 5:00 pm to 9:00 pm, Fri and Sat 5:00 pm to 11:00 pm. Closed Sun.

Calypso's, 650 East 24th Street (In the Holiday Inn), (616) 396-0709. Pork, jerk chicken, full dinners or sandwiches, all with an Island flavor. Open year round, Mon to Fri 6:00 am to 2:00 pm and 5:00 pm to 10:00 pm. Sat and Sun 7:00 am to noon and 5:00 pm to 9:00 pm.

China Inn North, 2863 West Shore Drive, (616) 786-9230. Chinese Cuisine. Also a second location: **China Inn South**, 457 East 32nd Street, (616) 393-8383. Excellent Chinese food cooked to order rather than left to dry out and cool on a buffet table. Try the fried rice. Open 7 days a week for lunch and dinner.

China King Buffet, 1006 Washington Street, (616) 393-6868. If you are looking for lots of decent food at a reasonable price, this might be your place. Open 11:00 am to 10:00 pm (or later) 7 days.

Chinese Thai Cuisine, 301 North River Avenue, (616) 392-5990. As the name suggests offers both Chinese and Thai dishes. Fast food. Open Mon to Sat 11:30 am to 3:00 pm and 5:00 pm to 9:00 pm (closed Tuesday) and Sun noon to 8:00 pm.

Coldstone Creamery, 5 West 8th Street, (616) 396-5940. Rich, wonderful ice cream. Open 7 days, Sun to Thurs 11:00 am to 10:00 pm, Fri and Sat 11:00 am to 11:00 pm.

Crazy Horse Steakhouse, 2027 North Park Drive, (616) 395-8393. A local favorite for steak, chicken and salads. Open Mon to Thurs 11:00 am to 9:30 pm, Fri and Sat 11:00 am to 10:00 pm. Closed Sun. Hours may vary.

Curragh Irish Pub and Restaurant, 73 East 8th Street (616) 393-6340. Menu of Irish favorites and the beer to go with any choice. Open 7 days, Mon to Thurs 11:00 am to 1:30 am, Fri and Sat 11:00 am to 1:30 am and Sun 10:00 am to 2:00 pm.

deBoer Bakery and Café, 11539 East Lakewood Blvd. (616) 546-3000. Homemade Dutch pastries. Also sandwiches and deli items.

Don Miguel, 11975 East Lakewood Boulevard, (616) 392-2965. A local favorite for Mexican food that is better than the building would suggest. Excellent tacos. If you like your salsa hot, theirs will get happy tears flowing. Open 7 days, breakfast, lunch and dinner.

Duffy's Schooner, 393 Cleveland Avenue, (616) 394-1285. Family-style restaurant serving hearty dinners. Early bird specials from 3:30 pm to 5:00 pm. Open 7 days, Mon to Sat 6:00 am to 9:00 pm, Sun 8:00 am to 2:00 pm. Sat and Sun buffet 8:00 am to 2:00 pm.

8th Street Grille, 20 West 8th Street, (616) 392-5888. Decorated with local memorabilia. Serves burgers, sandwiches and hand-dipped shakes. All you can eat soup bar. Open 7 days, Mon to Thurs 11:00 am to 10:00 pm, Fri and Sat 11:00 am to 11:00 pm and Sun 11:00 am to 4:00 pm. Closes Sun in winter.

84 East Pasta Etc, 84 East 8th Street, (616) 396-8484. www.84eastpasta.com. Located in historic Brownstone Alley. House specialty is Spaghetti Pie, but they also serve other pasta dishes and pizza in a casual family atmosphere. Open Mon to Thurs 11:00 am to 10:00 pm and Fri and Sat 11:00 am to 11:00 pm.

Fricano's Too, 84 River Avenue (616) 392-6279. Specializes in thin-crust pizza. The original is in Grand Haven. The pizza is good, no frills and cheap. Service is not always the best, especially when they are busy and they make no apologies for it. Still, in spite of it, they have a huge loyal following. Open Mon to Sat 5:00 am to midnight.

Froggie's, 80 East 8th Street, (616) 546-3764. Frog-themed place to get a Chicago-style, all beef hot dog, fries or hamburger. Also dipped ice cream. Open 7 days, year round, 11:00 am to 9:00 pm.

The Good Earth, 14 East 7th Street, (616) 396-3061. Specialty coffees as well as bagels, sandwiches and soups. Open Mon to Fri 6:00 am to 7:00 pm, Sat 7:00 am to 4:30 pm and closed Sun.

Goog's Pub & Grub, 667 Hastings Avenue, (616) 546-3422. A place to grab a bite and watch the game. The broasted chicken, 23 different hamburgers and pizza all get good marks. Open lunch and dinner.

Gregordog, 210 College Avenue (616) 396-1900 and second location at 1817 Ottawa Beach Road. Only open seasonally and for take out at Ottawa Beach, but a good place to grab a lunch to take to the beach (picnics to go). Downtown open year round and you can eat-in or outside (in the summer). Open Mon to Thurs 11:00 am to 7:00 pm, Fri and Sat 11:00 am to 8:00 pm and closed Sun.

Huynh Vietnamese and Thai Restaurant, 143 Douglas Avenue, (616) 928-0297. Huynh escaped Vietnam in 1979, came to the U.S. got a college education, learned a new language and realized his dream of opening a restaurant. Dine on authentic Vietnamese and Thai cuisine or order carry out. Free delivery. Open 7 days, Mon to Sat 10:30 am to 9:00 pm and Sun 10:00 am to 7:00 pm. Closed Tues.

Jackie's Place, 541 17th Street, (616) 392-6775. Family dining. Open Mon to Fri 5:45 am to 8:00 pm, Sat 5:45 am to 11:00 pm and closed Sun.

James Street Inn, 255 James Street, (616) 399-0101. Specializes in American favorites with a varied menu that includes: appetizers, soups, salads, sandwiches, burgers, BBQ, Mexican, wraps and breakfast. Open Mon to Sat 6:00 am to 10:00 pm. Closed Sun.

JJ Finnegan's, in the Westshore Mall, (616) 392-9800. Large menu of Irish dishes. Open 7 days at 11:00 am. Closes: Mon 9:00 pm, Tues and Thurs to Sun 1:00 am and Wed 10:00 pm.

JP's Coffee and Espresso Bar, 57 East 8th Street, (616) 546-9412, www.jpscoffee.com. Great coffee and baked goods as well as lunch. Open 7 days, Mon to Fri 6:00 am to 11:00 pm, Sat 7:00 am to 11:00 pm and Sun 11:00 am to 4:00 pm.

Kilwin's, 24 East 8th Street, (616) 393-8961. Chocolates, fudge and ice cream. Open Mon to Sat 10:00 am to 10:00 pm and closed Sun.

The Legends Grille, 4600 Macatawa Legends Boulevard, (616) 212-2640. Located at the Macatawa Legends Golf Course. Specializes in American favorites. Open 7 days, Mon to Thurs 11:00 am to 7:00 pm, Fri and Sat 10:00 am to 9:00 pm and Sun 9:00 am to 4:00 pm.

Margarita's, 495 West 17th Street, (616) 394-3069. Great place for Mexican food. Open 7 days, Mon to Thurs 10:00 am to 9:00 pm, Sat 7:00 am to 10:00 pm and Sun 7:00 am to 9:00 pm.

New Holland Brewing Company, 66 East 8th Street, (616) 355-6422. Offers a full menu and award-winning micro-beers. Open Mon to Thurs 11:00 am to midnight, Fri and Sat 11:00 am to 1:00 am. Closed Sun.

Ottawa Beach Inn, 2155 Ottawa Beach Road, (616) 399-9220. The crowd enjoys the sizzler steaks and the Lake Perch dinners. During the summer, visitors come for the outdoor chicken BBQ. Open Mon to Thurs 11:00 am to 10:00 pm, Fri and Sat 11:00 am to 11:00 pm. Closed most Sundays.

Parkway Inn, 1642 South Shore Drive, (616) 335-9319. A favorite spot to grab a great burger, wrap, or salad. Also have full dinners. Open Mon to Sat 7:00 am to 10:00 pm. Closed Sun.

Pereddies, 447 Washington Square (616) 394-3061. Quaint neighborhood restaurant with Italian specialties. Old world recipes and fresh baked bread make you forget dieting for another day. Their deli displays proscuitto, capocollo, martadella, fresh mozzarella and a huge selection of other cheeses. They stuff their own feta, gorgonzola and garlic olives and make their own pasta salads daily. Open for lunch and dinner. Take out available.

Pietro's, 175 East 8th Street, (616) 396-1000. In 1906 Pietro brought his wife Regina to America where she baked bread and pasta and he made wine. From those humble beginnings the tradition began. The place for Italian food in the city. The wood fired pizza is excellent if you are not in the mood for a full dinner. Portions are large and it is unlikely you can save room to indulge in the Chocolate Volcano–at least not without help from everyone else at your table. Everyone oohs and aahs over the food. Open 7 days, Mon to Thurs 11:30 am to 10:00 pm, Fri and Sat 11:30 am to 11:00 pm and Sun 11:30 am to 9:00 pm.

Piper, 2225 South Shore Drive, www.PiperRestaurant.com, (616) 335-5866. All diners have a view of Lake Macatawa. Casual dining with a variety of menu items including prime rib, calamari or just a pizza. On the expensive side, but moderately priced items also available. They have a tapa time. Open 7 days for dinner at 5:00 pm.

Remember When Cafe, 1146 South Shore Drive, (616) 355-8422. A hometown restaurant that is perfect for grabbing a hearty breakfast. They also serve lunch. Inexpensive food in a diner atmosphere. Summer hours 7 days, Mon to Sat 6:00 am to 3:00 pm and Sun 8:00 am to 1:00 pm.

Russ' East, 361 East 8th Street, (616) 396-2348. (Also has locations at 210 North River Avenue and 1060 South Lincoln.) A place to consider when you just want a burger or a sandwich. They also offer dinners. This is a chain of restaurants on the west side of Michigan. Breakfast, lunch and dinner. Closed Sun.

Thai Palace, 977 Butternut Drive, (616) 994-9624. Freshly prepared, authentic Thai food. Try the Pad Po-Tak or if you want to experience several specialties get the Thai Palace Combination with chicken sa-tay, two fish cakes and three shrimp rolls. Open Tues to Sat 11:00 am to 10:00 pm and Sun 11:00 am to 9:00 pm. Closed Mon.

Till Midnight Restaurant and Bakery, 171 East 24th Street, (616) 392-6883. This bistro has an impressive wine list to accompany its unique dinners and made-from-scratch entrees. Open lunch Mon to Fri 11:30 am to 2:00 pm and dinner Mon to Sat 5:00 pm to 10:00 pm with an all-day menu served until midnight. Bakery open 7:00 am to 7:00 pm.

Tres Lobos, 381 Douglas Avenue, (616) 355-7424. Award-winning Mexican restaurant offering sizzling fajitas, great wet burritos, quesadillas and their special parrilladas. Open Sun to Thurs 11:00 am to 9:00 pm, Fri and Sat 11:00 am to 10:30 pm and closed Mon.

Unkh's, 332 East Lakewood Boulevard, (616) 394-0020. Sushi, Udon, seafood and daily chef inspired specials make this a delightful place to experience Japanese cuisine. Open lunch Mon to Fri 11:00 am to 2:00 pm, dinner Mon to Sat 5:30 pm to 9:00 pm. Closed Sun.

Via Maria, 13 West 7th Street, (616) 494-0016. Homemade Italian-inspired dishes including wood-fired pizzas, steaks, seafood, sandwiches, salads, baked goods and desserts. Open Mon to Thurs 11:30 am to 9:00 pm, Fri and Sat 11:30 am to 10:00 pm. Closed Sun. Bakery opens at 7:00 am and remains open until the restaurant closes.

Village Inn, 934 South Washington Avenue, (616) 392-1818. Choose your pizza with one of four crust options or enjoy an oven baked sub. Also offers pasta and Mexican specialties. Several large screen TVs. Open 7 days, Mon to Fri 11:00 am to 1:30 am, Sat noon to 1:30 am and Sun 3:30 pm to 10:00 pm.

Wild Chef Japanese Steak House, 2863 West Shore Drive, Suite 112, (616) 399-8398. Features sushi and hibachi steaks. Tempura Salmon is a good choice and if you bring children there is a menu just for them. Open 7 days, Mon to Thurs 11:00 am to 10:00 pm, Fri and Sat 11:00 am to 10:30 pm and Sun 11:00 am to 9:30 pm.

Windmill Restaurant, 28th West 8th Street, (616) 392-2726. Serves breakfast all day. Also has burgers and sandwiches for lunch. Even during the week, the place is packed for breakfast and the full meal is under $3.00. This is definitely a no-frills, hearty-food kind of place. They have a hash brown omelet that locals say is terrific and a bacon, lettuce, tomatoes and egg salad on toasted homemade whole wheat bread. It is not the usual combination, but the delight in the eyes of the woman describing it make it worth a try. Open 7 days, Mon to Sat 5:00 am to 4:00 pm and Sun 7:00 am to 2:00 pm.

The Wooden Shoe, 441 US-31, (616) 396-4744. A place for breakfast, featuring American dishes. Also serving lunch and dinner. Gets mixed reviews, but they have been in business for 38 years and many local patrons swear by the breakfast. Open 7 days, Mon 5:30 am to 2:00 pm, Tues to Sat 5:30 am to 9:00 pm, Sun 7:00 am to 2:00 pm.

Lodging (Also see Campgrounds below)

Best Western Inn, 2888 West Shore Drive, (616) 994-0400, toll-free (800) 937-8376, www.bestwesternholland.com. 80 rooms, walking distance to Westshore Mall and restaurants. Allows pets. Extras: indoor pool and exercise room, meeting room, internet and deluxe continental breakfast.

Bonnie's Parsonage 1908, 6 East 24th Street, (616) 396-1316, www.bbonline.com/mi/parsonage. Opened in 1984. Was originally built as a parsonage to one of Holland's Dutch churches. The dark woodwork, pocket doors, and leaded glass all enhance the interior beauty. Two guest rooms with private baths and possible third room with shared bath. Full breakfast. No pets and no smoking.

Comfort Inn, 422 East 32nd Street, (616) 392-1000, toll-free (800) 228-5150, www.comfortinn.com. 71 rooms. Extras: outdoor pool, continental breakfast and wireless internet.

Country Inn by Carlson, 12260 James Street, (616) 396-6677 or toll-free (800) 456-4000, www.countryinns.com/hollandmi. 116 rooms. Extras: indoor pool, deluxe continental breakfast and wireless internet.

Days Inn, 717 Hastings Avenue, (616) 392-7001, toll-free (877) 251-8097, www.daysinn.com. 60 guest rooms. Easy access to downtown Holland and the lake, outdoor pool and internet access.

Dutch Colonial Inn B&B, 560 Central Avenue, (616) 396-3664, www.dutchcolonialinn.com. The Inn received the Holland Area Beautiful Award and was voted #1 B&B in Holland. Built in 1928, it is a Dutch Colonial home, originally a gift to a lucky bride and groom from their parents. Check out the suites on the internet. The Tulip Suite is two levels with an entertainment center, gas fireplace, whirlpool tub and other special touches to enhance any romantic occasion.

Econo Lodge, 409 US-31, (616) 392-7073, toll-free (888) 258-3140. 81 guest rooms with restaurants nearby. Allows pets. Extras: continental breakfast.

Fairfield Inn, 2854 West Shore Drive, (616) 786-9700, toll-free (800) 228-2800, www.fairfieldinn.com. 64 guest rooms. Near Westshore Mall, Holland Town Center, attractions and restaurants. Extras: deluxe continental breakfast, indoor pool and internet.

Hampton Inn, 12427 Felch Street, (616) 399-8500, toll-free (888) 933-8500, www.suburbaninns.com. 178 guest rooms. Bar and grill on premises. Extras: indoor pool, indoor and outdoor hot tubs, exercise room, video arcade, continental breakfast, extended stay suites, internet, 2-line phones, data ports and Sharkee's Bar and Grill open at poolside.

Haworth Inn, 225 College Avenue, (616) 395-7200, toll-free (800) 903-9142, www.haworthinn.com. 50 guest rooms with indoor entrances. Located downtown in the city of Holland. Extras: deluxe continental breakfast, banquet and meeting rooms and exercise room.

Holiday Inn and Conference Center, 650 East 24th Street, (616) 394-0111, toll-free (800) 279-5286, www.holiday-inn.com. 168 guest rooms with island theme. Restaurant on premises. Extras: indoor pool, sauna, exercise room, games, banquet and meeting rooms, and internet.

Holiday Inn Express, 12381 Felch Street, (616) 738-2800, toll-free (866) 315-6182, www.suburbaninns.com. 118 guest rooms. Quality Excellence Award Winner in 2004-2005. Extras: refrigerator and microwave in each room, Michigan-shaped indoor pool, sauna, exercise room, game room, deluxe continental breakfast, meeting room, 2-line phones, cordless data ports and internet.

The Inn at Old Orchard Road, 1422 South Shore Drive, www.theinnatoldorchardroad.com, orchardroad@chartermi.net. (616) 335-2525. 1906 Dutch farmhouse. Modestly priced rooms as B&Bs go. The Pecan French Toast sounds wonderful.

Lake Ranch Resort, 2226 Ottawa Beach Road, (616) 399-9380, www.lakeranchresort.com. 19 rooms within a mile of Holland State Park, accessible by bike path. Extras: waterfront location, outdoor pool, volley ball courts, grills, fish cleaning station. Seasonal.

Microtel Inn and Suites, 643 Hastings Avenue, (616) 392-3235 or toll-free for reservations (800) 771-7171, www.microtelinn.com. 83 guest rooms. Built in 2005. Located near US-31 with easy access to downtown Holland and the lakeshore. Extras: continental breakfast, free high-speed internet, long distance and local phone calls.

Residence Inn by Marriott, 631 Southpoint Ridge, (616) 393-6900, toll-free (800) 331-3131, www.residenceinn.com. 78 suites with indoor entrances. North of I-196 off M-40, and close to Holland attractions. Allows pets. Extras: breakfast and evening socials, meeting room, indoor pool and internet.

Rosewood Pointe Retreat and Cottages, 806 North Shore Drive, www.rosewoodpointe.com. (612) 501-2548. Rosewood Pointe is located on the north side of beautiful Lake Macatawa, five miles from Holland. Minutes from Lake Michigan, the resort is nestled among stately oaks and fragrant pines. The resort consists of four large cottages (sleeps 4-7), the Retreat House (sleeps 25-30), the Waikato House (sleeps 6-10) and the two story, lakefront, Kiwi House (sleeps 9-11), which all sit on a gentle rise overlooking a private, sandy beach. The area is secluded, providing a great opportunity to get away and relax. Extras: boating, fishing, swimming, volleyball, horseshoes, biking and several fire pits for evening campfires.

Shaded Oaks B&B & Cottages, 444 Oak Street, (616) 399-4194, shadedoaks@chartermi.net, www.shadedoaks.com. Two luxury (but pricey) suites and a cottage. All the bells and whistles including: double soaking tub in front of fireplace, flat screen TV, double shower, cable, DVD, VCR. Cottage has grill and washer/dryer. Close to Lake Macatawa. Walking distance to state park, lighthouse and bike paths.

Summer Place Resort Properties, 2029 Lake Street, (616) 399-3577, www.summerplaceresort.com. Summer Place Resort Properties rents furnished resort homes and cottages for your vacation. Currently they have eight properties available. Most are either located along Lake Macatawa or have views of the water. Homes have all the conveniences you expect. Summer season runs June through August.

Museums and Galleries

Cappon House and Settler's House, 9th Street at Washington Avenue toll-free (888) 200-9123. Victorian home of Holland's first mayor and the one room dwelling of a working class family. You will feel what it was like to live in another era. Open November through May, Fri and Sat 1:00 pm to 5:00 pm. Open June to October, Wed to Sat 1:00 pm to 5:00 pm. Extended hours during the Tulip Festival.

Castle Park Gallery, 8 East 8th Street, (616) 395-0077. More than 150 national artists and craftspeople display their jewelry, pottery, watercolors, glass and metal here. The kaleidoscopes were lots of fun. Open 7 days, Mon to Wed 10:00 am to 6:00 pm, Thurs to Sat 10:00 am to 9:00 pm and Sun noon to 4:00 pm with slight seasonal variation.

DePree Gallery, 160 East 12th Street (at Columbia Avenue), (616) 395-7500, www.hope.edu/arts. Houses the Hope College Arts Department and holds special exhibits. Call for information. Open summer Mon to Fri 10:00 am to 5:00 pm, school year Mon to Sat 10:00 am to 5:00 pm and Sun 1:00 pm to 5:00 pm.

The Drouillard Thomas Galleries, 420 West 17th Street, (616) 399-8184 or toll-free (800) 809-8501. Contemporary and eclectic art at reasonable prices. Open Wed to Sat noon to 7:30 pm or other times by appointment.

Holland Museum, 31 West 10th Street at River Avenue, (888) 200-9123, www.hollandmuseum.org. Holland history and heritage, children's room and special exhibits. Open Mon, Wed, Fri and Sat 10:00 am to 5:00 pm, Thurs 10:00 am to 8:00 pm and Sun 2:00 pm to 5:00 pm. Closed Tues.

Lake Effect Gallery, 29 West 8th Street, (616) 393-3025. Gallery, studio and framing. Art of about 20 local artists with lots of local scenes. Also rugs and jewelry. Open Mon to Thurs 10:00 am to 5:30 pm, Fri 10:00 am to 8:00 pm, Sat 10:00 am to 5:00 pm. Closed Sun.

Moynihan Gallery and Framing, 28 East 8th Street, (616) 394-0093. More than 3,500 square feet for displaying a variety of artists' works and art forms. Open 7 days, Mon to Fri 10:00 am to 9:00 pm, Sat 10:00 am to 6:00 pm and Sun 11:00 am to 4:00 pm.

Reflections Fine Art Gallery, 172 South River Avenue, (616) 396-6416. No original art, but exclusive handling of major publishers including Millpond Press. Open Mon to Sat 10:00 am to 9:00 pm (Sat closes at 6:00 pm), and Sun 11:00 am to 4:00 pm.

Uptown Gallery and Frame Shop, 205 Columbia Avenue, (616) 392-4756. Contemporary and whimsical art. Original paintings and art objects by well-known local artists, limited edition prints and fine art posters. Open Mon to Thurs 10:00 am to 5:30 pm, Fri 10:00 am to 8:00 pm and Sat 10:00 am to 5:00 pm.

Theatre

Holland Civic Theatre, 50 West 9th Street, (616) 396-2021, www.hollandcivictheatre.org. Call for current information.

Holland Symphony Orchestra, (616) 494-0256, 150 East 8th Street, www.hollandsymphony.org. Call or go online for current info.

Antiques

Great Lakes Antique Mall, 2975 West Shore Drive, (616) 994-9545. Offering coins, furniture, glassware, jewelry, books, and much more. 18,000 square foot showroom. More than 100 dealers. Open 7 days, Mon to Sat 10:00 am to 6:00 pm and Sun noon to 5:00 pm.

Harvest Antiques and Collectibles, 12330 James Street (Holland Town Center), (616) 395-0823. (This used to be called Harvest Antiques in the Holland Outlet Center, but the Outlet Center has been renamed the Town Center–same place, just a different name.) 60 dealers, 85 booths, a bit of everything antique or almost antique. Open 7 days, Mon to Sat 10:00 am to 8:00 pm and Sun 11:00 am to 6:00 pm.

Nob Hill Antiques, 4585 60th Street, (616) 392-1424. Describes its merchandise as antiques and fine goods. Also serves coffee, tea and pastries. Open Wed to Sat 11:00 am to 5:00 pm, Sun noon to 5:00 pm.

Wooden Shoe Antique Mall, US-31 at 16th Street, (616) 494-SHOE. Carries primitives, glassware, collectables, folk art, post cards, books and more. Open 7 days, Mon to Sat 10:00 am to 6:00 pm and Sun 10:00 am to 3:00 pm.

Other Shopping

The Bridge, 18 West 8th Street, (616) 392-3977. Gifts that give twice: Hope for third world artisans and a unique gift for your special person. This is a mission project working to help the world's poor and hungry. They carry great gift bags, wall-hangings, jewelry, and home accents from around the world. Open Mon to Fri 10:00 am to 8:00 pm, Sat 10:00 am to 6:00 pm and closed Sun.

Cottage Corner, 170 South River Avenue, (616) 494-9880. Cottage-style furnishings and accessories and shabby-chic - all hand painted. Open Tues to Sat 10:00 am to 5:00 pm.

Crow's Cottage and Eclectic, 1504 South Lakeshore, (616) 335-4751. Local art and artifacts. Open Tues to Sat 10:00 am to 5:30 pm.

Debbie and Company, 12330 James Street. Educational toys, games, teaching materials, children's books and teaching tools for parents. Open 7 days a week.

Fayes at Mira, 21 8th Street, (616) 396-8333. Classic clothing with a flair, a little on the edge. The owner carries clothes to help you express your own personal style, casual to evening wear and a nice selection of jewelry. Open Mon to Wed 10:00 am to 6:00 pm, Thurs and Fri 10:00 am to 8:00 pm, Sat 10:00 am to 5:00 pm and closed Sun.

Harbor Wear, 13 East 8th Street, (616) 335-7937. Holland logo sportswear, Life is Good and Fresh Produce. Open 7 days, Mon to Sat 10:00 am to 9:00 pm and Sun 11:00 am to 4:00 pm. Winter hours Mon to Sat 10:00 am to 6:00 pm (Fri until 9:00 pm). Closed Sun.

Holland Peanut Store, 46 East 8th Street, (616) 392- 4522. Carries Fabiano's famous nutty paddle pots and other imported candies and sweet treats. Open Mon, Thurs and Fri 9:30 am to 9:00 pm, Tues, Wed and Sat 8:30 am to 5:30 pm. Closed Sun.

Home and Company, 190 South River Avenue, (616) 393-0305. Glassware, rugs, household accents, infants and children items, rocking chairs, robes and even a Christmas vault. Open Mon to Fri 10:00 am to 9:00 pm, Sat 10:00 am to 6:00 pm and Sun noon to 4:00.pm.

JB and Me, 36 West 8th Street, www.jbandme.com, (616) 392-8902. Large store with clothes, accessories, gourmet items, beach wear, bags, shoes, sweaters, accessories and a second store: JB Sole Mates at 48th East 8th. Feels like a cross between a small boutique and a large department store. Open Mon to Sat 10:00 am to 9:00 pm. Closed Sun.

Jos A. Bank, 12 West 8th Street, (616) 393-6287. High-end men's casual and dress clothing. Open 7 days, Mon to Fri 10:00 am to 9:00 pm, Sat 10:00 am to 9:00 pm and Sun noon to 6:00 pm.

Karla's Place, 450 Washington Square, Unique neighborhood boutique with vintage clothing, jewelry and home accents. Open Tues, Wed and Fri 10:00 am to 6:00 pm, Thurs 10:00 am to 8:00 pm, Sat 10:00 am to 3:00 pm and closed Sun and Mon.

Lokker Rutgers, 39 East 8th Street, (616) 392-3237. This *Centennial Retailer* carries men and women's clothing, moderate in both style and price. Men's classics, women's updated. Also carries men's tall. Open Mon to Wed 10:00 am to 6:00 pm, Thurs and Fri 10:00 am to 8:00 pm and Sat 10:00 am to 5:00 pm. Closed Sun.

Main Sport, 60 East 8th Street. Men and women's sportswear, including casual sportswear and Winter Ski Shop. Open Mon, Tues and Thurs 10:00 am to 5:30 pm, Wed 10:00 am to 4:00 pm, Fri 10:00 am to 8:00 pm, Sat 10:00 am to 5:00 pm. Closed Sun.

Model Drug and Apothecary Gift Shop, 35 West 8th Street, (616) 392-4707. This drug store really does have a gift shop – not just a counter of souvenirs in a pharmacy. You will find an interesting selection of home accents, toys, jewelry and candles. Open Mon, Tues and Wed 9:30 am to 8:00 pm, Thurs and Fri 9:30 am to 9:00 pm and Sat 9:30 am to 6:00 pm. Closed Sun.

Northern Rustics, 15 West 8th Street, (616) 928-0234. Rustic, lodge-style furnishings for the home and cabin, as well as gifts and accessories. Open Mon, Thurs and Fri 10:00 am to 8:00 pm, Tues, Wed and Sat 10:00 am to 5:00 pm and closed Sunday.

The Outpost, 25 East 8th Street, (616) 396-5556. Every conceivable piece of camping gear, sporting equipment and sportswear. Open Mon and Thurs 10:00 am to 8:00 pm, Tues and Wed 10:00 am to 5:30 pm, Fri 10:00 am to 9:00 pm, Sat 9:30 am to 5:30 pm. Closed Sun.

The Picket Fence, 17 East 8th Street, (616) 395-4120. A variety of home décor, gifts and jewelry. Open Mon to Wed and Sat 10:00 am to 5:30 pm, Thurs and Fri 10:00 am to 8:00 pm. Closed Sun.

Reader's World, 194 South River Avenue, (616) 396-8548. Newspapers (including the *New York Times*), comics, paperbacks and hardbacks and a huge selection of magazines. Open Mon to Fri 9:00 am to 9:00 pm, Sat 9:00 am to 6:00 pm and Sun 8:00 am to 5:00 pm.

Sandcastle for Kids, 2 East 8th Street, (616) 396-5955 or toll-free (800) 446-0790. Toys and gifts for the younger set: dolls, puzzles, games and books. Open Mon to Fri 10:00 am to 9:00 pm and Sat 10:00 am to 7:00 pm. Closed Sun.

The Seasoned Home, 208 College Street (616) 392-8250. A unique specialty shop featuring over 200 premium blends of spices and seasonings. Also carries kitchen accessories, cookware, bake ware, cookbooks, home décor items, gourmet foods and imported teas. Open Mon to Wed 10:00 am to 5:30 pm, Thurs and Fri 10:00 am to 8:00 pm, and Sat 10:00 am to 5:00 pm. Closed Sun.

Shaker Messenger Folk Art, 210 South River Avenue, (616) 396-4588. An eclectic collection including: Shaker folk art, food pantry, souvenirs, Bauer Pottery and guest artists visiting several times a year. They only carry American made goods. The pantry has jams, jellies, ice cream toppings, gourmet coffee, vinegars, salad dressings, dips and other interesting foods. Open Mon, Thurs and Fri 10:00 am to 8:00 pm, Tues, Wed and Sat 10:00 am to 6:00 pm and Sun noon to 5:00 pm.

Talbot's, 23 West 8th Street (616) 494-0217. Upscale chain of fashionable women's clothing and shoes. Open Mon to Fri 10:00 am to 9:00 pm, Sat 10:00 am to 6:00 pm and Sun 10:00 am to 6:00 pm.

Tikal, 6 East 8th Street, (616) 396-6828. Unique imported women's clothing. Open Mon, Thurs and Fri 10:00 am to 9:00 pm, Tues and Wed 10:00 am to 8:00 pm, Sat 10:00 am to 5:30 pm and closed Sun.

The Tin Ceiling, 10 East 8th Street, (616) 395-2623. Unique specialty gifts featuring Scandinavian, April Cornell, McCall's Country Canning, Mary Engelbreit, Woof and Poof, and Heatwood Creek. Open Mon to Wed 10:00 am to 6:00 pm, Thurs and Fri 10:00 am to 8:00 pm and Sat. 10:00 am to 6:00 pm. Closed Sun.

Ottawa Beach General Store, 2256 Ottawa Beach Drive, Cold beer, ice cream, candy, sub shop, deli, gifts, collectibles and antiques. Open 7 days, 8:00 am to 10:30 pm in the summer.

Studio K Clothing Company, 47 East 8th Street, (616) 393-7900. Very contemporary women's apparel. Open Mon 10:00 am to 8:00 pm, Tues and Wed 10:00 am to 5:30 pm, Thurs and Fri 10:00 am to 8:00 pm and Sat 10:00 am to 5:00 pm. Closed Sun.

Teerman's, 20 East 8th Street, www.teermans.com, (616) 392-1831. A wide selection of crystal, dinnerware, casual furnishings, patio furniture, wicker, rattan, housewares and everything imaginable for the kitchen, gift items, clocks and electronics. This is a department store with resort overtones. Open Mon and Thurs 9:30 am to 9:00 pm, Tues, Wed, and Sat 9:30 am to 5:30 pm, Fri 9:30 am to 9:00 pm. Closed Sun.

Tree House Books, 37 East 8th Street, (616) 494-5085. Open: Mon to Wed 9:30 am to 8:00 pm, Thurs to Sat 9:30 am to 9:00 pm and Sun noon to 5:00 pm. Reduced hours in the winter.

The Wee Dollhouse, 128 South River Avenue, (616) 392-4321. Dollhouses and all of the miniature furniture and accessories to go with them. Open Mon to Fri 11:00 am to 5:00 pm and Sat 11:00 am to 3:00 pm. Closed Sun.

Yeta's, 29 West 8th Street, (616) 393-5950. Women's fine fashion in sizes 14 to 24. Open Mon to Wed 10:00 am to 5:30 pm, Thurs and Fri 10:00 am to 8:00 pm and Sat 10:00 am to 5:30 pm. Closed Sun.

Parks, Beaches, and Campgrounds

Centennial Park, River Avenue between 10th and 12th Streets. Lovely Victorian City Park with fountains, flowers, mature trees, benches and a gazebo. Historical markers; one recounts the founding of Holland. Summer concerts are held in this park.

Columbia Park, 9th Street and Columbia Avenue. Locally designed and a skateboarder's paradise.

Dog Park, 1286 Ottawa Beach Road. A place to indulge your pet with separate fenced areas for large and small dogs. Rover will also enjoy the toys and water.

Drew's Country Camping, 12850 Ransom Road, (616) 399-1886, www.drewscountrycamping.com. Located 4½ miles north of Holland. All sites have water, electric and picnic table. Grounds have a pool, playground and ball field. For a nominal fee: ice, laundry facilities and firewood. Camp store for other supplies.

Dunton Park, 270 Howard Avenue west of North River Avenue. Access to Lake Macatawa and a popular place to picnic or fish. Also has boat launch.

Dutch Treat Camp and Recreation, 10300 Garden Street, (2¼ miles East of Hwy 31 on East/West Business I-196, exit 55 off I-196), Zeeland, (616) 772-4304, www.dutchtreatcamping.com. Minutes from Holland attractions and 8 miles to Lake Michigan beaches. 3-night minimum stay during 2nd weekend of Tulip Time and holiday weekends. Amenities: paved roads, bathrooms, showers, laundry, fire rings, picnic tables, ice, firewood, telephone on some lots, pay phones, vending machines, playground, swimming pool, volley ball, paddle boats, recreation room, hayrides on Saturday night and a small store.

Holland State Park, 2215 Ottawa Beach Road, (616) 399-9390, Reservations at: (800) 44.PARKS. Beautiful sandy beach and a great place to view the local lighthouse, Big Red. (See p. 360 in Part II for related story.) Two large campgrounds, picnic areas, a playground, beach house, boat launch and concession stands. One of Lake Michigan's most popular parks.

Kirk Park, 9815 North Lakeshore Drive (15 miles north of Holland State Park in West Olive), (616) 738-4810. 2,000 feet of sandy beach and scenic dune overlooks. A perfect place for a summer swim. You can also hike the wooded trails. Pets allowed on the trails and the beach. Covered pavilion, playground and day permits available.

Kollen Park, West end of 10th Street at Van Raalte Avenue. Close to downtown on the shores of Lake Macatawa. Beautiful shade trees and benches along lake walkway create a pleasant place to watch the summer activity. Playground, restrooms, grills and picnic tables.

Lake Macatawa Beach and Park, East of Holland State Park on Lake Macatawa, (800) 447-2757. Swimming and hiking, 211 camping sites and a boat launch available to campers.

Matt Urban Park, 270 East 32nd Street. Neighborhood sports complex where soccer and baseball are played.

Moran Park, 22nd Street and Pine Avenue. Playground, tennis courts, shuffleboard and baseball.

Oak Grove Campground and Resort, 2011 Ottawa Beach Road, www.michcampgrounds.com/oakgrove. (616) 399-9230. Family resort located within walking distance of Lake Macatawa and Lake Michigan beaches. Close to fishing, boating, golfing and miles of paved bike trails. Beachside bike rentals where you can rent tandems, 21-speeds, single-speeds, kid's bikes, baby seats and burley carts. Extras: heated swimming pool, whirlpool, game room, basketball, playground and high speed internet. Open May through October.

Sanctuary Woods Preserve, west end of 32nd Street. Hiking through wooded dunes and trails. You can take your dog. Has dune stairs and lovely views of both Lake Michigan and Lake Macatawa.

Smallenburg Park, Fairbanks Avenue at 14th Street. Playground, picnic facilities. Offers ice-skating in the winter.

Tunnel Park, North Lakeshore Drive, 2 miles north of Holland State Park, (616) 738-4810. Got its name because it creates a tunnel through the dunes. There is a dune stairway to Lake Michigan. Pets are only allowed in the park after the summer season. (They are permitted from October through April.)

Van Raalte Farm Park, 24th Street, 1 mile east of US-31 (16th street). City park with picnicking and hiking during the warm months and cross-country skiing and sledding during the winter.

Window on the Waterfront, 50 Columbia Avenue (at 6th Street). Charming downtown Holland Park. Enjoy the walkway overlooking the Black River and Windmill Island. Paved trail winds along the Macatawa River, perfect for walking or biking. Wildlife can be spotted from several observation points. A favorite place to bird-watch.

Winstrom Park, Perry Street at 160th Avenue, (616) 738-4233. Frisbee golf.

Marinas, Water Sports, Cruises, Boat and Jet Ski Rentals

Cresent Shores Marina, 545 Cresent Drive, (616) 392-9951. Boat launch can accommodate larger boats. Transient slips. Pool, hot tub, deck and picnic area.

Holland Harbor of Refuge, (616) 842-5510. Open 24 hours.

Holland Princess, Howard Avenue west of River Avenue, (616) 393-7799, www.hollandprincess.com. Paddleboat rides on Lake Macatawa from Dunton Park. Popular two-hour dinner cruises with cash bar.

Holland Water Sports, 1810 Ottawa Beach Road, www.hollandwatersports.com, (616) 399-6672 (reservations) or (616) 786-2628 (information). Rent a SeaDoo, boat, water skis or go tubing on Lake Michigan.

Macatawa Boat House Kayak and Canoe Rental, Ottawa Beach Road (across from Holland State Park), (616) 834-3033.

Other Things to See and Do

Beachside Bike Rentals, 2011 Ottawa Beach Road, (616) 399-9230. Place to get a bike if you did not bring one.

Craig's Cruisers, Chicago Drive at US-31, (616) 392-7300, www.craigscruisers.com. Go-Karts, kiddie rides, batting cages, bumper boats, miniature golf, game room. Open summer 7 days, 10:00 am to 11:00 pm.

Crazy Bounce, 12255 Felch Street, www.crazybounce.com, (877) 399-8150. Air-filled canvas slides, velcro wall, slides, dodge ball, crazy inflatable structure and boxing rings. Supervised. Open Mon and Wed

9:00 am to 11:00 am toddler time, 11:00 am to 9:00 pm open-bounce, Tues and Fri open-bounce 9:00 am to 9:00 pm, Thurs and Sat 9:00 am to 3:00 pm open-bounce, 3:00 pm to 9:00 pm reserved for private parties (if no parties, open-bounce) and Sun open-bounce noon to 8:00 pm. Open year round.

The DeGraaf Nature Center, 600 Graffschap Road, (616) 335-1057. Open year round. Has weekly events and provides you with an opportunity to enjoy woodlands, shrubs, marshes and trails. There is an interpretive center. Nice place for hiking and cross-country skiing.

DeKlomp Wooden Shoe & Delft Factory, 12755 Quincy Street (US-31 at Quincy Street), (616) 399-1900, www.veldheertulip.com. The only Delftware Factory in the United States. Free factory tours. Wooden shoe carving and an American buffalo herd. Hand-painted Delftware and gift shop. Beautiful gardens. Open April through December Mon to Fri 8:00 am to 6:00 pm, Sat and Sun 9:00 am to 5:00 pm, January through March, Mon to Sat 9:00 am to 5:00 pm. Extended hours during Tulip Time.

Dutch Village, US-31 at James Street, (616) 396-1475 or toll-free (800) 285-7177, www.dutchvillage.com. Family theme park and a recreated 1800s Netherlands town with Dutch architecture, canals, and farm animals. Activities include: Dutch folk dancing, walking through spectacular gardens, educational movies, petting zoo, rides for children and museums. Also has a gift shop with imports from around the world. Open end of April through mid-October, 7 days, 10:00 am to 5:00 pm.

The Edge Ice Arena, Holland Avenue east of US-31, (616) 738-0733. Indoor ice skating.

Farmer's Market, 8th Street Market, (616) 355-1130. More than 50 booths offering locally grown produce. Open Wednesday and Saturday, May to December, 8:00 am to 5:00 pm.

Holland Community Aquatic Center, Maple Avenue at 22nd Street, (616) 393-7595, www.hollandaquaticcenter.org. Michigan's largest aquatic center and water park with a 50 meter pool, fitness room and lap-swimming. Open year round.

Lost City Laser Tag Arena, Holland Town Center at US-31 and James Street, (616) 396-6746. 5,000-square-foot arena, video games, virtual reality, networked PC games and snack bar.

Veldheer Tulip Gardens, US-31 at Quincy Street, (616) 399-1900. Holland's only Tulip Farm, boasting 30 acres of tulips.

Walking Tour of Holland's Statues, varied locations throughout the city including:

Ben Franklin, A wise-looking Ben sits on a park bench on River Street reading the Declaration of Independence. Mark Lundeen created the work.

Ben Franklin Statue   *Picture by Bob Royce*

Contemplation, life-size bronze sculpture of the artist's sister sitting on a bench with a book. Artist: Billie Houtman Clark. 10th and College.

Grandpa's Workbench, in the courtyard of Evergreen Commons, portrays a Grandfather building stilts with his grandchildren. Sculptor: Gary Alsum. Located at the foot of River Avenue.

Immigrant's Statue, at Lake Macatawa, captures immigrants arriving on the shores of Lake Macatawa. The statue was a gift of the Dutch Province of Drenthe, presented to Holland in 1997 to commemorate Holland's Sesquicentennial. The artist was Bert Kievit.

Joy of Music is a group of five, including three musicians and two singing children. It is located in Alpenrose Park. The sculptor was George Lundeen.

Padnos Sculptures, created from scrap metal with assistance from Stuart Padnos at Louis Padnos Iron and Metal Company. Padnos' sculpture of a Dutchman wearing wooden shoes and holding tulips is located at 7th and Lincoln. His other sculptures are located on Pine Avenue between 3rd Street and 7th Street.

Perro Del Sol, colorful steel work created by Hope College professor, Billy Mayer. River Avenue at 12th.

The Pledge of Allegiance, a group of children honoring the flag. Artist: Glenda Goodacre. 8th and College.

The Protector depicts a police officer dressed in a Holland Police Department uniform. He is holding the hand of a small girl. The statue was donated to the city and paid for through personal and corporate donations. Artist: Neil Brodin. Location: 8th and Pine.

Queretaro Fountain. Donated by Holland's sister city Queretaro, Mexico in 1999 as a symbol of the friendship between the two cities. 11th street near Kollen Park.

Secret Garden, life-size sculpture of two young girls sitting on a bench reading a book. Artist: Mark Lundeen. Located: 10th and Central.

Statues of Hope College, several statues on Hope Campus between College and Columbia from 9th to 13th Streets.

The Valentine, located on the grounds of Freedom Village. Romantic statue portraying an older couple sharing a valentine. George Lundeen created the statue.

Water Lily, a young girl sits on a stump holding a water lily from which water flows into the pool below. Artist: Rosalind Cook. Located at 6th and Central.

Van Raalte Statue was created for the city's sesquicentennial in 1997. The statue of Reverend Albertus C. Van Raalte faces Hope College and Pillar Church, both founded by Van Raalte. 10th Street at Centennial Park.

Windmill Island, Lincoln Avenue at 7th Street, (616) 355-1030. 240-year-old authentic windmill. Guided tours, 1929 antique carousel, candle carvers at work, historical multi-media presentations, Frisian horses and cows, greenhouses, Little Netherlands Museum, Klompen dancing, Dutch games and other special events. Open daily from mid-April through mid-October. Haunted windmill last two weeks in Oct.

Golf

The Links at Rolling Meadows, 1259 Saint Andrews, (616) 395-5926. 9-hole course. Open to Public. Pro shop, no restaurant.

Sundae Sundae Golf Course, 631 East Lakewood Boulevard, (616) 396-8085. Miniature golf. Open Sun to Thurs 10:00 am to 10:00 pm, Fri and Sat 10:00 am to 11:00 pm.

West Ottawa Golf Club, 6045 136th Street, (616) 399-1678. 27-hole golf course, open to public. Snack bar, small pro shop and lessons.

Winding Creek Golf Club, 4514 East Ottogan Street, (616) 396-4516. 27-hole golf course, open to public. Pro shop and lessons.

Contacts

Holland Area Convention and Visitors Bureau, 76 East 8th Street between Columbia and College Avenues, toll-free (800) 506-1299, www.holland.org, info@holland.org. Information regarding accommodations attractions and current dates for festivals and events. Open year round, Mon to Fri 8:00 am to 5:00 pm. Open Sat 10:00 am to 4:00 pm mid-April through October.

Holland Chamber of Commerce, 272 East 8th Street, (616) 392-7379, www.hollandchamber.org, info@hollandchamber.org.

Grand Haven
-Including Spring Lake and Ferrysburg.
Population: Slightly over 11,000 in 2000.
Directions: Twenty-two miles north of Holland on US-31. From Grand Rapids, Lansing or Detroit take I-96 West to US-31 South 10 miles.

Background and History
Fur trading gave birth to Grand Haven or "Gabagouache" as it was then known. In the language of the Ottawa, the word Gabagouache described the widening of the river and the slowing of the current as the flow reached Lake Michigan. In the early 1600s the area was a major trade route for the Ottawa as they took advantage of Michigan's largest river (the Grand) snaking its way into the interior of the state. For nearly two centuries Gabagouache was economically dependent on pelts.

By the late 1700s John Jacob Astor's American Fur Company was operating twenty trading posts in Western Michigan and Gabagouache was Astor's principal post with a dated existence back to at least 1809.

From 1809 to 1821, Astor's posts were managed by Madame Madeline La Framboise who was half-French and half-Ottawa. When she retired to Mackinac Island her job was turned over to Rix Robinson who is often credited with laying the foundation for settling Western Michigan. In later years Robinson served as a Michigan State Senator.

In 1822 William Ferry, a Presbyterian minister, became the first permanent resident of the area and appropriate to his profession he built the first area church. Neighboring Ferrysburg is named in his honor.

In the early 1800s white pine was crowned king, replacing the fur industry. Sawmills required a transportation system to get lumber to markets and Grand Haven's strategic water vantage point met the need.

By 1834, Ferry and Robinson began developing the town. They formed the Grand Haven Company and platted and sold lots. Gabagouache became Grand Haven in 1835, taking its name from the fact that it provided a large, safe haven for ships at the mouth of the Grand River. By 1837 the town had more than two-hundred residents.

By 1870 the population burgeoned to six-thousand and lumbering still supported the economy. Several sawmills, a shingle mill and a sash and door factory were located in Grand Haven; in that year the Grand Trunk Western Railroad constructed a depot along the waterfront. Today the depot is a fascinating museum.

The late 1800s gave a clue of what was to come. Grand Haven became a popular health resort, famous for its Magnetic Mineral Spring. Grand Haven did not suffer as much with the demise of the lumber industry as did her sister cities. She had been transforming into an active port renowned for sport fishing as well as a tourist hotspot. The Grand Haven Lighthouses were first built in 1839 on the south pier marking the channel into the river. There are currently two lighthouses, each painted red. The outer light was built in 1875 and the inner light was built in 1905. They are connected by a lighted catwalk which runs along the pier to the shore. (See p. 360, Part II for additional detail.)

Grand Haven is home to the U. S. Coast Guard Station which coordinates all Lake Michigan Coast Guard activity. The Coast Guard came to Grand Haven in 1932 and its presence has been significant ever since.

It is an easy task for travelers to plan a busy itinerary taking in local sites and activities. The problem will be budgeting available time to allow everything they want to see or do. The choices are varied. They can explore the river bayous by canoe or kayak. They can walk Grand Haven's scenic two-and-a-half mile boardwalk, or they can rent a bicycle and peddle their way around miles of beautiful countryside.

Expect to fall in love with Grand Haven and the smaller Ferrysburg and Spring Lake. When they lay claim to your heart, you will find yourself filled with the desire to make repeat visits.

Food/Restaurants

Arboreal Inn, 18191 174th Avenue, Spring Lake (616) 842-3800, A cozy Cape Cod is the setting for excellent continental food. Moderate to pricey, but worth it. Extensive wine list. Open dinner only, Mon to Thurs 5:00 pm to 9:00 pm, Fri and Sat 5:00 pm to 10:00 pm.

Bil-Mar Restaurant, 1223 Harbor Drive, (616) 842-5920. Perch and Prime Rib are the house specialties. The outdoor deck has a different menu (burgers, nachos and more casual fare) and it is the place to be on a hot summer day. You can walk from the beach to the deck in your swimming suit and flip-flops or even barefoot, and watch the sunset while enjoying a refreshing drink. Open for lunch Mon to Sat 11:00 am to 2:30 pm, dinner Mon to Thurs 5:00 pm to 10:00 pm, Fri and Sat 5:00 pm to 10:30 pm. Closed Sun (except Mother's Day and Easter). Slightly reduced hours in the off-season.

Butch's Beach Burritos, 726 Harbor Drive, (616) 842-3690. Inexpensive Mexican food. Lunch, dinner and take-out.

Clover Bar, 601 South Beechtree Street, (616) 846-3580. Dinner and take-out: subs, salads, Italian night (Thurs) and pizza. Open Mon to Wed 4:30 pm to 11:00 pm, Thurs to Sat 4:30 pm to midnight.

Cobb's Chicken and Seafood, 305 North Beacon Boulevard, (616) 842-8421. Chicken and seafood; lunch, dinner and fast food. Take-out only. Open Mon to Sat 11:00 am to 9:00 pm and closed Sun.

Coffee Gallery, (See below under galleries.)

The Coffee Grounds, 41 Washington Avenue, (616) 844-3078. Gourmet coffee, tea, cold drinks and dessert. Free WIFI. Open 7 days.

Dee-Lite Theater Bar and Grill, 24 Washington Avenue, (616) 844-5055. Fantastic breakfasts, Tex-Mex and fresh seafood. Most items are inexpensive to moderately priced. The Original Farmer's Breakfast will leave you stuffed long into the day. Wide range of foods: American, Asian, Japanese, Thai, Californian, Italian, Mediterranean, Tex-Mex, vegetarian or a plain old hamburger. This is a great place to grab a bite for any meal, but the lines often start early, especially Sunday morning. In the summer there is outside sidewalk seating where you can watch the world go by. Open summer 7 days, 6:00 am to 11:00 pm. Open year round, hours slightly reduced in off-season.

Elegance of the Season, 216 Washington Avenue, (616) 296-1059, www.eleganceoftheseason.com. Bakery, coffee, lunch, brownies, cheesecake and other wonderful desserts, Michigan syrups, honeys and jams. Also a catering service. Open Mon 8:30 am to 2:00 pm, Tues to Sat 8:30 am to 6:00 pm. Closed Sun.

Fortino's, 114 Washington Avenue. Old world shopping since 1907. Kids love the selection of candies. Gourmet and food items. Open Mon to Thurs 10:00 am to 8:00 pm, Fri and Sat 10:00 am to 9:00 pm. Closed Sun.

Front Porch Ice Cream, 618 Savidge Street, Spring Lake (616) 846-2460. 42 kinds of ice cream. Open 7 days, 11:00 am to 10:00 pm, summer only (closes in October).

Fricanos Pizza Tavern, 1400 Fulton Avenue, (616) 842-8640. Interesting pizza joint that you would probably never stumble on without some help. This former boarding house does not exactly reach out and welcome you as you stand wondering what you are doing there. The menu is the paper placemat. Fricanos has one menu item: pizza. There is one size and one crust (very thin - so thin in fact, that they cut the pieces with scissors rather than a pizza cutter). You can not order a salad with your pizza (or anything else to eat for that matter). You can get beer, wine and cocktails. The service can be rather brusque during busy periods and they make no apologies. Still, you may have to wait an hour to get in and the crowds keep coming back. No credit cards. Open Mon to Sat 5:00 pm to midnight. Closed Sun.

Great Harvest Bread Company, 120 Washington Avenue, (616) 847-6700. Great box lunches with gourmet sandwiches to take to the beach, and you can always get a free slice of bread. Open 7 days in the summer and Tues to Sat noon to 6:00 pm during the off-season.

Jack's Restaurant and Lounge, 940 West Savidge Street, (In the Holiday Inn) Spring Lake, (810) 846-1370 or (616) 846-1000, www.higrandhaven.com. Waterfront dining with lovely views and a wide variety of entrees. Entertainment most nights in the Tiki Bar and Night Club. Open 7 days, Mon to Thurs for breakfast 8:30 am to 11:00 am, lunch 11:00 am to 4:00 pm and dinner 4:00 pm to 10:00 pm. Fri opens at 6:30 am for breakfast, Sat at 8:00 am. Fri and Sat lunch and dinner hours the same as Mon to Thurs. Sun breakfast 8:00 am to 2:00 pm, lunch 2:00 pm to 5:00 pm and dinner 5:00 pm to 9:00 pm.

Jumpin' Java, 215 Washington Avenue, (616) 842-9534. Lunch and gourmet coffee, smoothies, and snacks. Some entertainment. Free WIFI. Open 7 days, Mon to Thurs 6:30 am to 11:00 pm, Fri and Sat 6:30 am to midnight and Sun 8:00 am to 11:00 pm.

The Kirby House, 2 Washington Avenue, (616) 846-3299. Three different dining experiences: The Kirby Grill offers casual family dining and an eclectic menu. Live music Friday and Saturday. Lunch, dinner and take-out. The Grill Room features fine dining, steaks, chops, and fresh seafood and is a more expensive dining experience. Open for dinner only. Reservations recommended during peak times and high season. The Pizzeria is upstairs from the restaurant, on the roof with both inside and outside seating, and offers casual family dining with the emphasis on authentic wood-fired pizza and salads. The Kirby Grill is open Mon to Sat 11:30 am to 11:00 pm and Sun 11:30 am to 10:00 pm. The Grill Room opens at 5:00 pm.

Mojo Java Lounge, 510 West Savidge Street, Spring Lake, (616) 842-MOJO. They claim to provide you with a shot of Karma for life's journey. Intimate ambiance. Breakfast all day, pastries, salads and decadent desserts. Live entertainment on Friday and Saturday nights. Open 7 days, Mon to Thurs 6:00 am to 10:00 pm, Fri 6:00 am to 11:00 pm, Sat 7:00 am to 11:00 pm and Sun 8:00 am to 10:00 pm.

Old Boy's Brewhouse, 961 West Savidge Road, Spring Lake, (616) 850-9950. Pub with karaoke Thursday and live music Friday and Saturday. A fun place to bring the entire family for good, old American food. Microbeers around their crackling fire in the late autumn may be your perfect way to unwind. Outdoor deck overlooks Spring Lake Channel. You can also take a more active approach to letting off steam and shoot a game of pool or try the dance floor. Moderate prices. Open 7 days, Mon to Thurs 11:00 am to 11:00 pm, Fri and Sat 11:00 am to midnight and Sun noon to 8:00 pm.

Pavilion's Wharf Deli, 16 Washington Avenue, (616) 842-9500. Sandwiches on fresh baked bread. The deli offers a good selection of meats and cheeses, vegetarian sandwiches and soups for a tasty and inexpensive lunch. Open 7 days for lunch and Sun breakfast and lunch.

Pier Peddler, 709 South Harbor Drive, (616) 897-3022. Grab an ice cream cone or yogurt as you walk the beach. Located on the Boardwalk in Grand Haven.

Pine Street Café and Boiler Room Bistro, 401 Pine Street, Ferrysburg, (616) 847-6080. Family-style restaurant serving steaks, seafood and pasta. Breakfast, lunch, dinner and take-out. No frills kind of place where you can get inexpensive, hearty food. Open for breakfast and lunch Mon to Sat 6:00 am to 2:00 pm and Sun 8:00 am to 2:00 pm. Dinner Thurs and Fri 4:00 pm to 8:00 pm.

Porto Bello, 41 Washington Avenue. (616) 846-1221. Italian eatery with tasty pastas, pizza and beef and veal dishes. Entertainment Thursday to Saturday. Outside seating when weather permits. Open 7 days, Mon, Tues, Wed and Thurs 11:00 am to 10:00 pm, Fri and Sat 11:00 am to 11:00 pm and Sun noon to 10:00 pm. Slightly reduced hours in the winter. Closes in the dead of winter.

Ray's Beef Burgers, 20 North Beacon, (616) 842-3400. Fast food joint and a place to get inexpensive, tasty burgers.

The Rosebud of Grand Haven, 100 Washington Avenue, (616) 846-7788. Located in the old post office. Fresh seafood, steaks, pasta, pizza and prime-rib. Live entertainment Thursday to Saturday. Outside sidewalk seating in summer; good food and moderate prices keep 'em coming back. Open Mon to Sat 11:30 am to 2:00 am and Sun 11:00 am to 2:00 am. Kitchen closes at 10:00 pm in the summer.

Russ' Restaurant, 1313 South Beacon Boulevard, (616) 846-3330. Family dining. Western Michigan chain restaurant with good burgers and inexpensive food. Breakfast, lunch, dinner and take-out.

Santo Stephano Sweets, 210 Washington Avenue (entrance in back), (616) 844-9060. Italian desserts, gelato, sorbetto and other confections. Open Mon to Thurs 9:00 am to 10:00 pm, Fri and Sat 9:00 am to 11:00 pm. Reduced winter hours.

Snug Harbor, 311 South Harbor Drive, (616) 846-8400. Steaks done to taste perfection, seafood and Mexican entrees - all in a lively atmosphere. Popular with locals (many swear it is the best restaurant in town) and tourists. Some entertainment. Outside deck overlooking the channel. Open 7 days, Mon to Thurs 11:00 am to 10:00 pm, Fri to Sun 11:00 am to 11:00 pm.

Sweet Temptations, 1003 South Beacon, (616) 842-8108. Ice cream store (great ice cream in lots of mouth-watering flavors) but much more. Caramel corn drizzled in chocolate, super cakes, caramel and fudge covered apples and Monster Munch. What is not to like? Open 7 days, 11:00 am to 10:00 pm (may close early if it is raining).

Thali Bistro, 211 North 7th Street, (616) 844-3040. Colonial influenced, authentic Sri Lankan and Indian flavored French Cuisine. International beer and wine. Their dishes use organic fresh vegetables. Pavilion outdoor patio. Open Tues to Sat, noon to 3:00 pm for lunch and 5:00 pm to 9:00 pm for dinner.

Tip-a-Few Tavern, 10 Franklin Avenue, (616) 846-2670. Inexpensive food and full bar. You will see Harleys and Buicks parked in front and the joint is definitely not upscale; in fact, it is a bit of a dive, but some would still say they have the best wet burrito in Grand Haven. Give it a try - at least once, then you will have a new experience to talk about or you will be hooked. Serves lunch, dinner and take-out.

Two Tonys Taverna Grille, 723 East Savidge Street, Spring Lake, (616) 844-0888, or (616) 844-1888. This is a newcomer to the restaurant scene in the tri-cities and it is getting some rave reviews and a few comments suggesting there may be a couple of kinks to get worked out. One Tony is Italian and one Tony is Greek, hence the name and the cuisine. You might consider the Tortellini Con Pollo. Open Mon to Sat at 11:00 am. Closing time may vary. Closed Sun.

Vic's, 14975 Cleveland, Spring Lake, (616) 846-0338. Mexican and American entrees. Open for breakfast Mon to Fri 6:00 am to 11:00 am, Sat 6:00 am to noon and Sun 7:30 am to 1:00 pm (great skillet breakfasts). Lunch served everyday and dinner served Sun to Thurs to 10:00 pm and Fri and Sat to 11:00 pm.

Lodging *(Also see Campgrounds below)*

Best Western Beacon Inn, 1525 South Beacon Boulevard, www.bestwestern.com/beaconinn, (616) 842-4720 or toll-free (800) 528-1234. 107 rooms offering choice of king whirlpool suites, king business suites and standard guest rooms. All rooms have two queen or one king bed. Extras: indoor heated pool, hot tub, sundeck and continental breakfast.

Blue Water Inn and Suites, 1030 Harbor Drive, (616) 846-7431. Located directly across from the beautiful beach of Grand Haven State Park. Extras: many rooms have kitchenettes, weekly rates available.

The Boyden House Inn, 301 South Fifth Street, (616) 846-3538, www.bbonline.com/boyden. Queen Anne Style Victorian, circa 1874. Step inside to find yourself transported back in time to the gracious and beautiful architectural design and rich construction of a bygone era. Each room is uniquely decorated, exuding its own special charm. Extras: VCR or DVD in each room, internet service available (if you absolutely can not leave quite everything behind), massage therapist, private dinners on request, concierge service for restaurant, theatre, and special events, guest kitchen available, candlelight gourmet breakfast can be requested and they honor special dietary needs.

Castle B&B, 200 Prospect, (616) 296-1161 or toll-free (877) 696-1161. www.thecastle.com. Perched on Five Mile Hill, the Castle was constructed in 1928. From its decks and porches you get a panoramic view of Lake Michigan and Grand Haven's beautiful sand beach. Full breakfast included.

Days Inn, 1500 South Beacon Boulevard, (616) 842-1999. Guestroom amenities include a microwave, refrigerator and high speed internet access. Extras: indoor swimming pool, spa tub and room service from Damon's grill during certain hours.

Fountain Inn, 1010 South Beacon Boulevard, (616) 846-1800 or toll-free (800) 745-8660. 47 guestrooms. Extra: continental breakfast. A place to consider if you are looking for less expensive lodging.

Harbor House Inn, 114 South Harbor Drive, (616) 846-0610 or toll-free (800) 841-0610, www.harborhousegh.com. Victorian charm on the Waterfront. Warm, inviting rooms that will make your stay special. All rooms with private bathrooms, telephones with modem outlets, internet access, TV and VCR. 11 of the 17 rooms offer whirlpool tubs and fireplaces. Each room has one king or queen bed.

Holiday Inn, 940 Savidge Street, Spring Lake, (616) 846-1000, www.higrandhaven.com. Close to Lake Michigan. Extras: some waterfront views, heated indoor pool, hot tub and fitness center.

Khardomah Lodge, 1365 Lake Avenue, (616) 842-2990, www.khardomahlodge.com. Just a few steps from Lake Michigan and tucked into a wooded dune. The lodge became a Historic Site in 2000. It has been welcoming guests for almost a century. The Inn was named for a Native American chief who was friends with the original owners. Offers 15 rooms, suites, and a cottage, each uniquely decorated with vintage items, quilts and hooked rugs.

Lakeshore B&B, 11001 Lakeshore Drive, (616) 844-2697. www.bbonline.com/mi/lakeshore. This fully restored 6,500 square foot mansion was built in 1941 on 200 feet of private Lake Michigan beach frontage. You will be mesmerized by the gorgeous lake views from every room. Three guestrooms.

Looking Glass Inn, 1100 Harbor Drive, (616) 842-7150 or toll-free (800) 951-6427, www.bbonline.com/mi/lookinglass. High on a dune overlooking Grand Haven State Park, Lake Michigan and the lighthouse, this three-story home affords spectacular views. You can hop aboard their electric, six-person trolley that drops you at the front door while affording you a breathtaking spectacle along the way. Four rooms and a cottage are available.

Washington Street Inn, 608 Washington Avenue, (616) 842-1075, www.bbonline.com/mi/washinn. Built in 1902, the Inn is an example of the American-Four-Squares-Style. Its leaded-glass windows, spacious archways, original oak woodwork and hardwood floors typify a quality home from the turn-of-the-century. Five rooms, three with separate baths, two that share a bath.

Museums and Galleries

41 Gallery North, 110 Washington Avenue, (616) 842-5759. Limited edition works by local artists. Lighthouses. Open summer 7 days, 10:00 am to 9:00 pm. Winter 10:00 am to 6:00 pm (Fri 9:00 pm).

The Bicycle Museum, 119 Washington Avenue, (616) 842-1418, www.thebicyclemuseum.com. A new museum displaying 75 bicycles including the 1939 World Fair Elgin. Open Mon to Sat 1:00 pm to 6:00 pm. Closed in the winter.

Carlyn Gallery, 207 Washington Avenue, (616) 842-7744. Fine art and antiques. Handcrafted work from many media. Open 7 days, Mon to Sat 10:00 am to 5:30 pm and Sun 1:00 pm to 4:00 pm.

The Coffee Gallery, 17750 Fruitport Road, Spring Lake, (616) 850-9500. This place may be one of the "sleepers" of your trip. The coffee shop you expect. But what is really amazing is the art. This is a real gallery. They display exquisite glass pieces by Rollin Karg, Louie Via, Wes Hunting and Tom Philabaumm. In fact, you will see work by 60 artists from all over the U.S. The upstairs galleries have the feel of a small museum. Of course you can also enjoy premium coffees, specialty drinks, deli sandwiches, soups and salads. Entertainment on Saturday from 6:00 pm to closing. Open Tues to Fri 7:00 am to 5:00 pm, Sat 7:00 am to 5:00 pm and Sun 8:00 am to 4:00 pm.

The Gallery Upstairs, 715½ Washington Avenue, (616) 846-5460. Original local art in all price ranges. You will find paintings, glass, pottery, photography and jewelry. Open Mon to Fri 10:30 am to 5:30 pm and Sat 9:00 am to 3:00 pm.

The Gallery Uptown, 201 Washington Avenue, (616) 846-5460, www.galleryuptown.net. Works of 24 artists. Open 7 days, Mon to Fri 10:00 am to 8:00 pm, Sat 10:00 am to 6:00 pm and Sun noon to 4:00 pm. Reduced winter hours.

Tri-Cities Historical Museum, 1 North Harbor Drive, downtown Grand Haven on the lakeshore, www.tri-citiesmuseum.org, (616) 842-0700. Follow the history of Grand Haven from the Native Americans to the pioneers; including the lumberjacks and the French voyageurs. The lifestyle of each era is revealed through exhibits showcasing period rooms, medicine, agriculture, lumbering methods, maritime history and tourism. The museum is a view to the history of Northwest Ottawa County. Located in two separate buildings, each with historic ties to the area, the museum has continued growing since it was started back in 1959. In 1972 it occupied the former Grand Trunk Railroad Depot which was built in 1870. This remains the lakeside location and it has a new Maritime Gallery with wonderful ship models. The Depot/Lake location simply outgrew its space and in July, 2004, the doors to a second site opened: **The Akeley Building, constructed in 1871, located at 200 Washington**. Both locations display artifacts from the life and times of the people, places and events that shaped this area's history. If you want to expand on the short history included at the beginning of this Grand Haven section, you only have to stop at this museum's locations. There are also temporary exhibits which change from time to time. No admission charge. Do not forget to check the museum gift shop. It has great collectibles, toys, books and gifts. Open year round, Tues to Fri 9:30 am to 7:30 pm, Sat and Sun 12:30 pm to 7:30 pm, closed Monday. In the winter the museum closes at 5:00 pm.

Antiques

Depot Antiques, 14599 M-104, Spring Lake, (616) 847-7100, www.depotantiques.net. A little of everything: primitives, country furniture, formal furniture, rustic, architectural pieces, garden treasures, nautical, military, pottery, canoes, airplane propellers, mantels and signs. Open 7 days, Mon to Sat 10:00 am to 5:00 pm and Sun noon to 5:00 pm.

Harbor Antiques, 41 Washington Street, (in the Harbourfront Building), (616) 846-4404. Vintage clothes, stained glass, quilts, jewelry, cut crystal, glassware and furniture. Lovely shop with nicely arranged displays. Open Mon to Sat 10:00 am to 6:00 pm and Sun noon to 5:00 pm. Closes half hour earlier in the winter and is closed Sun.

Spring Lake Antique Mall, 801 West Savidge (M-104) Spring Lake, (616) 846-1774. Looks like an old metal trailer from the outside, but inside it is well-organized with a wide range of quality antiques and collectibles from about 80 dealers. Furniture, china, coins, vintage and period items, primitives, and home decorations. Open 7 days, Mon to Sat 10:00 am to 5:00 pm and Sun noon to 5:00 pm.

Other Shopping

Aberdeens, 133 Washington Avenue, (616) 850-8820, www.aberdeenschildren.com Clothing for children. Open Mon to Fri 10:00 am to 8:00 pm, Sat 10:00 am to 5:30 pm and Sun noon to 5:00 pm. Closed Sun in the winter.

Abigail Evans, 134 Washington Avenue, (616) 846-6550. Bath accessories, home décor, gourmet gifts, baby gifts and kitchenware. They self-describe as "Elegant home décor for your casual lifestyle." Open Mon to Thurs 10:00 am to 8:00 pm, Fri 10:00 am to 9:00 pm, Sat 10:00 am to 8:00 pm, Sun noon to 5:00. Winter hours slightly reduced.

Bayberrie Tree, 111 Washington Avenue, (616) 847-8605. Gift items, jewelry, handcrafted furniture and home accessories. Open 7 days, Mon to Fri 10:00 am to 9:00 pm, Thurs 10:00 am to 8:00 pm, Sat

10:00 am to 5:30 pm and Sun noon to 5:00 pm. Winter Mon to Fri 10:00 am to 5:30 pm.

Bodacious Babes Emporium and Tea Room, 107 Washington Avenue, (616) 935-1144, www.bodaciousbabesemporium.com. Lovely place to have a cup of freshly brewed afternoon tea and a delectable dessert. You can also browse their collection of Polish pottery, Persian rugs and antiques. Open 7 days, Mon to Wed 10:00 am to 7:00 pm, Thurs and Fri 10:00 am to 9:00 pm. Sat and Sun 10:00 am to 6:00 pm.

Buffalo Bob's General Store, 136 Washington Avenue, (616) 847-0019. Unique gifts, housewares, apparel, shoes, sunglasses, beach bags, belts, blue jeans and sandals. Open Mon to Fri 10:00 am to 7:00 pm and Sat 10:00 am to 6:00 pm. Closed Sun.

The Calico Cat, 10 Washington Avenue, (616) 846-5830. Collectibles, gifts, soaps, purses, and traditional home furnishings, as well as lots of linens (hot pads, tablecloths, drapes, dish towels, pillows, quilts and shower curtains). Open Mon to Wed and Sat 10:00 am to 5:30 pm, Thurs and Fri 10:00 am to 9:00 pm.

The Ceramic Café, 202 Washington Avenue, (616) 846-4484. If your kids need a change of pace you might bring them here to design their own plates, jewelry boxes, piggy banks, statues or mugs. Age six to adult, but this not alternate babysitting. They will ship your items to your home after the firing.

The Creative Fringe, 210 Washington Avenue, (616) 296-0020, www.thecreativefringe.com. Beads, stringing, jewelry, metal clay and lampworking, craft and party supplies.

Dockside Clothing, 1 Washington Place. Fashions for men and women, sportswear and casuals and accessories. There are two separate shops as part of this business, but they are located close to each other in Harbourfront Place. Open 7 days, Mon to Sat 10:00 am to 9:00 pm and Sun noon to 4:00 pm. Reduced winter hours: noon to 5:00 pm.

Down to Earth, 105 Washington Avenue, (616) 846-7781. Really cute clothes as well as candles, home accents and unique merchandise you will not see in every other shop. Open 7 days, Mon to Sat 10:00 am to 8:00 pm and Sun 11:00 am to 6:00 pm. Reduced winter hours.

East Village Wine Shoppe, 723B Savidge, Spring Lake. Open Mon to Thurs 11:00 am to 8:00 pm, Fri and Sat 10:00 am to 9:00 pm. Closed Sun.

Flotos Gifts, 123 Washington Avenue, (616) 842-7580. Wickerware, Christmas items, gift items, clothes, nautical souvenirs, and items by local artists. Open Mon to Sat 10:00 am to 7:00 pm (or later), and Sun noon to 5:00 pm. Not open evenings off-season.

Jax Threads, 116 Washington Avenue, (616) 842-2218, www.jaxthreads.com. Progressive, sassy, contemporary clothing. Open

7 days, Mon to Wed 10:00 am to 6:00 pm, Thurs to Sat 10:00 am to 7:00 pm and Sun noon to 5:00 pm.

Harbourfront Place, corner of Harbor and Washington. A marketplace in an award-winning renovation of the century-old piano factory. Both shopping and dining. Individual establishments listed separately.

Harborwear, 210 Washington Avenue, (616) 842-0030. Resort and casual wear. Beach clothing, T's and sweatshirts with Grand Haven logo. Also, Life is Good label. Open 7 days, Mon to Sat 10:00 am to 9:00 pm and Sun 10:00 am to 4:00 pm.

Mackinaw Kites and Toys, 106 Washington Avenue, (616) 846-7501, www.mackite.com. Casual clothing and surf shop as well as kiteboards and lots of non-battery, unique toys. Open 7 days, Mon to Sat 9:00 am to 9:00 pm and Sun 11:00 am to 7:00 pm. Reduced winter hours, but open year round.

The Michigan Rag Company, 121 Washington, (616) 846-3510 or toll-free (800) 373-1451, www.michiganrag.com. Silk screened clothing. Open 7 days, Mon to Sat 10:00 am to 9:00 pm and Sun 11:00 am to 5:00 pm. Not open evenings or Sun in the winter.

Ooh La La, 128 Washington Avenue, (616) 847-4401. Swimwear and lingerie. Open 7 days, Mon to Sat 10:00 am to 9:00 pm and Sun noon to 5:00 pm. Closes at 7:00 pm in the winter and closed Sun.

R House Country Gift Shop, 704 East Savidge, Spring Lake, (616) 847-3530. One of West Michigan's largest country shops carrying handcrafted furniture, framed prints, afghans, candles, crafts, and floral arrangements. Open Mon to Fri 10:00 am to 6:00 pm (Tues to 8:00 pm), and Sat 10:00 am to 5:00 pm. Closed Sun.

The Saltbox, 109 Washington Avenue, (616) 842-9060. Miscellaneous inventory but, for example, the light switch plates are cooler than any you will see elsewhere. Open 7 days, Mon to Fri 10:00 am to 9:00 pm, Sat 10:00 am to 8:00 pm and Sun 11:00 am to 5:00 pm. Hours reduced after Labor Day.

The Schooner, 211 Washington Avenue, (616) 842-3530. This is the place for the maritime enthusiast to find nautical artifacts, decorated furniture and accessories. Open Tues to Fri 10:00 am to 5:00 pm, Sat and Sun noon to 4:00 pm. Open in the summer until 9:30 pm.

Ship Store, 110 Washington Avenue. Primarily boat supplies, but also nautical gifts and consignment photographs. Open 7 days, Mon to Fri 10:00 am to 7:00 pm, Sat 10:00 am to 5:00 pm and Sun noon to 4:00 pm. Reduced winter hours.

The Store of Grand Haven, 16 Washington Avenue, (616) 846-9959. Contemporary clothing for today's woman. Upscale. Dresses, jewelry, accessories. Open Mon to Fri 10:00 am to 8:00 pm, Sat 10:00 am to 6:00 pm and Sun 10:00 am to 5:00 pm. Reduced winter hours.

That Hat, 1 Washington Avenue (Harbourfront Place), (616) 846-HATS. The place to find hats for everyone in the family. Also some pottery, jewelry and sculptures. Open Mon to Thurs 10:00 am to 7:00 pm, Fri and Sat 10:00 am to 8:00 pm and Sun noon to 4:00 pm.

Parks, Beaches and Campgrounds

Grand Haven Skate Park, located in Mulligan's Hollow next to Imagination Station off Harbor Drive, (616) 850-6800. Ramps include both a large and small half pipe, 16-foot by 16-foot flat-top pyramid, grind-rails and G-ramps. Helmets and signed waiver mandatory. Park is supervised 7 days from 2:00 pm to 10:00 pm, Memorial Day weekend to Labor Day weekend.

Grand Haven State Park, 1001 South Harbor Drive, (616) 847-1309. Located one-half mile from downtown, this beautiful 48 acre park features the shore of Lake Michigan along the west side of the park and the Grand River along the north side. The park consists entirely of beach sand and paved seasonal camping sites with unparalleled views of Lake Michigan and the Grand Haven pier.

Grand Trunk Station of Lakeside Trail, Off Fruitport Road. In-line skate, skateboard, bicycle or walk. Benches along the way.

Hemlock Crossing/Pine Bend Park, 239 acres of woods and wetlands along the Pigeon River. More than six miles of trails for hiking and cross-country skiing. Enjoy the scenic overlooks or rent a kayak or canoe and explore the river. There is no entry fee and both parks are open year round. (Pine Bend is a secondary access on the west end of the property.) Located on 156th street, south of Croswell.

Imagination Station, Mulligan's Hollow (Mulligan Drive off Sherman). A 10,000 square foot playground of fun. It was designed by children and constructed by the community.

Kirk County Park, Two miles south of Grand Haven, Kirk Park is known for its forested beauty, sandy beaches and walking trails through the dunes. Bath house, big picnic area and in the winter cross-country skiing and snow shoeing.

Linear Park, Jackson to 3rd Street (left on Harbor Island). Great walking, jogging park with views of the channel and boat activity.

Pigeon Creek Park, between 128th and 120th Avenues. From US-31, take Stanton Road 3 miles east to the park entrance, (Grand Haven State Park). The trails wind through more than 400 acres of rolling, forested, land surrounding the Pigeon Creek. It is a great place for cross-country skiing with a warming lodge and ski rentals. For joggers there is a 4K lighted trail.

Rosy Mound County Park, On the Lake Michigan shoreline just south of Grand Haven. This is a natural area that encompasses an example of the Great Lakes dune system with its beach, foredunes, and dunes. Boardwalk and trail. Short walk through the dunes to the beach.

Grand Haven Beach   *Photo by Bob Royce*

Marinas, Water Sports, Boat and Jet Ski Rental
Grand Haven Municipal Marina, (616) 842-2550. 51 transient slips. Open 8:00 am to 4:00 pm.

Grand Isle Marina, One Grand Isle Drive, (616) 842-9330. Full service marina offering boat launching areas, store, fuel and maintenance.

Cruises and Charter Fishing
Book 'Em Dan-O Charters, 301 North Harbor Drive (at Chinook Pier on the Grand Haven Boardwalk), (616) 293-4064. Great Lakes charter fishing out of Grand Haven.

Fish 'N Fun Charters, Chinook Pier, Slip 9, (616) 850-0454. This charter will take you sport fishing for salmon, trout, or perch aboard the 33-foot Trojan Express with the latest in navigation and fishing technology. You can also charter scenic cruises of Spring Lake, the Grand River and the eastern shore of Lake Michigan.

IT-IL-DO Charters, 1009 Hazel Street, South Haven, offers charters out of Grand Haven too. See listing under South Haven/Charters p. 56.)

Harbor Steamer, downtown Grand Haven at the Chinook Pier Landing, (616) 842-8950, www.harborsteamer.com. Explore the Grand River and Spring Lake while relaxing aboard a replica of the stern wheel and paddle wheel river boats of America's past. You will also be provided with a historic narrative and music while on board. The boats have a full service bar and dining cruises are scheduled throughout the season. You can reserve an exclusive charter for a large group.

Other Things to See and Do

A& L Farms, 11901 144th Avenue (616) 842-1987. If you want to get fresh blueberries (July and August).

Bicycle Rides, There are over 100 miles of bike paths throughout Northwest Ottawa County. Popular paths and trails run along Lake Michigan's shoreline on Lakeshore Drive between Grand Haven and Holland, circling Spring Lake, and along the Grand River to Eastmanville. Maps are available at the Chamber of Commerce.

Craig's Cruisers, Pontaluna and US-31, five miles north of Grand Haven (231) 798-4936. Go-Karts, batting cages, mini-golf, bumper boats, Laser Storm, Kiddie-Karts and more. Open year round.

Farmers Market, (616) 842-4910. Downtown on Harbor Drive. Mon 11:00 am to 6:00 pm or the Wed and Sat Market under the bright blue canopy near Chinook Pier at 8:00 am. Garden fresh produce, flowers and more. The market is open from June through October.

Grand Haven Waterfront Stadium, on the Waterfront Boardwalk, (616) 842-2550. Host to many summer activities including the Musical Fountain, big band dances, worship services, Anchorage Cup Sail Races, Powerboat Runs, Trawlerfest and Coast Guard Festival activities.

World's Largest Musical Fountain, at Washington and Harbor, (616) 842-4910. A synchronized display of water and lights on the harbor. Every summer evening at dusk. Special performances on Fridays and Saturdays during Tulip Time and in September. It is one of the "musts" when visiting Grand Haven.

Ride the Harbor Trolley and Transit, catch it at the Chinook Pier, (616) 842-3200. Offers transportation services between the Tri-Cities of Spring Lake, Grand Haven and Ferrysburg. You will get a narrated tour of the area. Operates 7 days from Memorial Day weekend to Labor Day.

Stroll the Waterfront Boardwalk, 2½ miles of the Grand Haven harbor starting with the shops at Chinook Pier. You pass restaurants, marinas, charter fishing boats and parks and end at the lighthouses on the pier. The Boardwalk intersects with downtown shops and restaurants. Great place to jog or maybe meander along, holding hands with someone special. No matter how you do it, the views will be worth every minute you spend.

Festivals

The Coast Guard Festival, August. Honors the U.S. Coast Guard with parades, a midway, entertainment and street dancing, plus a whole lot more. Major fireworks on the final Saturday. This is Grand Haven's really big festival.

Coast Guard Memorial with Coast Guard Building in Background
Photo by Bob Royce

Golf

Fore Seasons Indoor Golf, 1097 Jackson Street, (616) 850-9000. Call for tee times.

Grand Haven Golf Club, 17000 Lincoln Street, (616) 842-4040, www.grandhavengolfclub.com. Golfers consider this a must play course. It has been written up in nearly all golf magazines. Rated among the top 50 public golf courses by *Golf Digest* for ten years. It was designed in 1965 by Bruce Matthews Sr. After a round of golf, stay for a cold beer and great food at the Falcon's Nest restaurant.

Contacts

Grand Haven Chamber of Commerce, 1 South Harbor Drive, (616) 842-4910.

Muskegon

Population: Approximately 42,000.

Directions: Three hours from either Detroit or Chicago. **From Detroit, Lansing and Grand Rapids**: Follow I-96 West to US-31. From Chicago: Follow I-94 towards Detroit; merge into I-196/US-31 North.

Background and History

In spite of its miles of sugar-sand beaches along Lake Michigan, Muskegon does not enjoy the resort or tourist glory of other lake communities like Traverse, Holland, Petoskey or Mackinaw. The reason is at least partially due to its industrial persona which in the mid-1900s was associated with foundries. Its history has been summed up as pelts, pines and piston rings. Such a glib characterization shortchanges Muskegon and travelers to this area as well.

It would be a shame to ignore Muskegon's rich history, wonderful parks (the beach at Pere Marquette Park has been on *USA Today*'s list of cleanest beaches in the U.S.), museums and cultural events.

It is believed that the first people to the Muskegon area were nomadic hunters who came seven to eight thousand years ago following the retreat of the glaciers. Woodland cultures, such as the Hopewellian, came after the hunters and they dominated the area about two-thousand years ago.

Europeans began recording the history of the area when it was still primarily occupied by Ottawa and Pottawatomie tribes. Ottawa Chief, Pendalouan was a leading participant in the French inspired campaign against the Fox Indians of Illinois in the 1730s. The Chief and his people lived in the vicinity of Muskegon in the 1730s and 1740s.

The name Muskegon is derived from the Ottawa term "Masquigon" meaning "marshy river or swamp." The Masquigon (or Muskegon) River is identified on early French maps of the late 17th century confirming that by then the French had reached the west coast of Michigan.

While it is uncertain exactly when the first Frenchman visited the Muskegon area, we do know that Father Jacques Marquette traveled northward through this area on his last trip to St. Ignace in March 1675. A party of French soldiers under the command of La Salle's lieutenant, Henry de Tonty, passed through in 1679.

History documents French fur-trading activity during the next century, but the exact locations of the forts cannot be pinpointed. By the early 1800s we know there were posts created around Muskegon Lake where traders were drawn by the large number of beaver in the river networks. Credit for the first trading post goes to Madeline LaFramboise in 1810. Her husband, Joseph, had been making trips to the area since 1783. In 1812 Jean Baptiste Recollet established a post near what is now North Muskegon.

It was not until the mid-1800s that Muskegon seemed to catch on; and, then it was directly linked to the realization that the timber in the area meant great riches for anyone coming from the East with enough of a stake to erect a lumber mill. The typical lumberman was in good health and young. Generally he was between twenty and thirty-years-old and came from New England, New York, or Pennsylvania and had done well enough in his prior endeavors to finance his lumber venture.

The lumber boom actually blossomed ahead of its time because there was no adequate means of transportation to the area. Stagecoach was slow and the railroad was not yet a transportation presence. However, by the mid-1800s Muskegon's port rivaled that of Chicago.

By 1869 railroad fever hit and various lines made Muskegon a stop on their route. Inside the city, however, even fifteen years after the railroad, horses and mules pulled streetcars along three and a half miles of track. It was 1890 before they were replaced by electric cars.

Muskegon became known as the "*Lumber Queen of the World.*" After the fire of 1871, the city of Chicago rebuilt with local timber. During the lumbering era, Muskegon boasted more millionaires than any other town in America.

Around the turn of the 20th century as the lumber industry died, a community catering to entertainers sprang up along the massive sand dune known as Pigeon Hill in a section of the city known as Bluffton. (See Sand Dunes p. 350 and Famous People, p. 434 Part II of this guide.) In 1903 the Keatons (Buster and his parents) and other vaudevillians began to summer in the area.

Today, you can follow the history of Muskegon through a guided walking tour, or by visiting its fascinating museums including: The Muskegon County Museum, the Hackley House and the Hume House. These homes were built by lumbar barons of the era. Charles Hackley's name is virtually synonymous with Muskegon; his legacy lives on through family donations and gifts to the city. You can take a self-guided walk and explore the best and most interesting sites of Muskegon's past.

But, whatever else you do, you will want to visit Muskegon's beaches and parks. They are some of the greatest along the west coast.

Food/Restaurants

Bayside Beanery Coffeehouse, 2009 Lakeshore Drive, (231) 755-0506. Indonesian and Costa Rican coffees along with Lattes and other hot and cold drinks and a selection of pastries. Across from Great

Lakes Marina. Open 7 days, Mon to Fri 7:00 am to 5:00 pm, Sat 8:00 am to 10:00 pm, Sun 8:00 am to 5:00 pm. Hours change in off-season.

Brann's Steakhouse and Grille, 5510 Harvey, (231) 798-1399, www.branns.com. Located at the entrance to Lakes Mall. Wide variety of traditional, casual food entrees plus a few unusual dishes. If you do not want to dine in, they will box it to go. Munchies, soups, salads, wraps, ribs, burgers, sandwiches, choice steaks, chicken, pasta, seafood, full bar, milkshakes and kids' menu. Lunch served daily, 11:00 am to 3:00 pm, dinner 4:00 pm to closing.

City Café, 411 West Western Avenue (231) 725-7769. European influenced American-style bistro. Located in the historic Frauenthal Performing Arts Center. Soups, gourmet salads, panini sandwiches, prime rib, pastas and desserts. Open Mon to Thurs 11:00 am to 8:00 pm, Fri 11:00 am to 10:00 pm, Sat 5:00 pm to 10:00 pm. Closed Sun.

Finley's American Grill, 3065 Henry Street, (231) 733-9928. House special: Baby Back Ribs. Also steaks, chicken and seafood dishes available. Open Mon to Thurs 11:00 am to 10:00 pm and Fri and Sat 11:00 am to 11:00 pm.

Harbor Steakhouse, 939 3rd Street, inside the Holiday Inn, Muskegon Harbor. (231) 720-7123. Casual atmosphere offering American cuisine. Open 7 days for breakfast, lunch and dinner. Sunday breakfast buffet with made to order omelets and fajitas.

The Hearthstone Bistro and Bar, 3350 Glade Street, (231) 733-1056, www.hearthstonerestaurant.com. A favorite area haunt since 1975. Soups, sandwiches, char-grilled steaks, homemade matchstick fries, grilled fish, pastas, salads, children's menu and a full bar. Open 7 days, Mon to Thurs 11:00 am to 10:00 pm, Fri and Sat noon to midnight and Sun 5:00 pm to 10:00 pm.

House of Chan/Joe's Steakhouse, 375 Gin Chan Avenue (Norton Shores), (231) 733-4346. Full service menu including: steak, lobster, sandwiches and excellent Chinese dishes. Buffet if you prefer not to be limited. Lunch Tues to Fri. Dinner Tues to Sun and a Sunday Brunch.

Pints and Quarts Pub and Grill, 950 West Norton Avenue, (231) 830-9889, www.pintsandquarts.com. Starters, homemade soups, salads, burger baskets, sandwiches, Mexican, perch, specialty drinks and a wide assortment of beers and ale by the pint or quart. Open Mon to Wed 11:00 am to 11:00 pm, Thurs and Fri 11:00 am to 2:00 pm and Sat noon to 2:00 am. Closed Sun.

Rafferty's Restaurant, 730 Terrace Point Boulevard, (231) 722-4461, www.shorelineinn.com. Casual fine dining. Start with one of their homemade soups, followed by Tuscan salad and then the Pretzel Crumb Walleye. Music on the dock Saturdays in the summer and free docking for dinner guests. Open 7 days, Mon to Thurs 11:30 am to

10:00 pm, Fri and Sat 11:30 am to 11:00 pm and Sun 10:30 am to 8:00 pm. Extended summer hours. Closes an hour earlier in the winter.

Russ's Restaurant, North, 1499 East River Road, (231) 744-4856, www.RussRestaurants.com. The first of this West Michigan family chain was founded in 1934. Munchies, soups, salads, sandwiches, burgers, omelets, dinners, kids menu and specials. Inexpensive. Open Mon to Thurs 6:00 am to 10:00 pm, Fri and Sat 6:00 am to 11:00 pm. Closed Sun. (Second location at 3225 Henry Street, (231) 739-2214).

The Sardine Room, 2536 Henry Street, (231) 755-5008, www.sardineroom.com. Homemade soup and sandwiches, fresh seafood, steaks, chops and baby back ribs. The owners describe it as a "little bit Chicago and a little bit New Orleans." Many regulars drive from Grand Rapids, Ludington, Pentwater and Holland to dine here. Open 7 days, Mon to Thurs 11:00 am to 11:00 pm, Fri and Sat 11:00 am to midnight and Sun 4:00 pm to 9:00 pm.

Toast 'N' Jams, 3462 Henry Street, (231) 737-5267. Clean, bright, modern, open, airy and full of locals. At first it was difficult to figure out why this place was called Toast 'n Jams since the jam on the table was Smuckers, but they do have their own label of preserves or jams called "Toast and Jams" for sale. The omelets are excellent and the Cinnamon Raisin French Toast is a good choice. The retro-looking interior is not overdone and this is a fine place to get breakfast or lunch. Open Mon to Fri 6:00 am to 3:00 pm and Sat 7:00 am to 2:00 pm.

Topo's, 2675 Henry Street, (231) 759-8676, www.topospizza.com. Northern Italian cuisine in a casual setting. New York and Chicago style pizza made with fresh ingredients. Italian lunch buffet Mon to Sat. Open Mon and Tues 11:00 am to 10:00 pm, Wed and Thurs 11:00 am to 11:00 pm, Fri 11:00 am to midnight, Sat noon to midnight and Sun 4:00 pm to 9:00 pm.

Lodging (Also see Campgrounds below)

Amerihost Inn, 4677 Harvey Road, (231) 798-0220 or toll-free (800) 434-5800, www.amerihostinnmuskegon.com. Extras: indoor pool, deluxe continental breakfast, hot tub, sauna and exercise room.

Comfort Inn, 1675 East Sherman Boulevard, (231) 739-9092, www.comfortinn.com. Extras: indoor/outdoor pools, whirlpool, sauna, exercise facility, game room, deluxe continental breakfast and internet.

The Cornerhouse Inn, 3350 Glade Street, (231) 733-1056, www.hearthstonerestaurant.com. Competitive rates. Extras: close to beaches, most rooms have microwaves and refrigerators available.

Fairfield Inn and Suites by Marriott, 1520 Mount Garfield Road, (231) 799-0100, www.marriott.com/MKGNS. 83 room hotel adjacent to Lakeshore Marketplace Mall. Extras: whirlpool suites, exercise facility, free high-speed internet, indoor pool and hot tub.

Hackley-Holt House B&B, 523 West Clay Avenue, (231) 722-0278 www.bbonline.com/mi/hhhbb. Four guestrooms, each with private bath. Full breakfast. Treats always available. The house was built in 1857 for Joseph Hackley and was considered one of the finest residences of the time. It is an Italianate-style home on the National and State Register of Historical Places. It is located in historic Heritage Village set amidst beautiful perennial gardens. It boasts a large wrap-around porch. The parlor features the original stained glass windows.

Hampton Inn, 1401 East Ellis Road, (231) 799-8333 or toll-free (800) HAMPTON, www.hampton-inn.com/hi/Muskegon. 81 room hotel adjacent to Lakeshore Marketplace Mall. Extras: spacious whirlpool suites, indoor pool and hot tub.

Holiday Inn Muskegon Harbor, 939 Third Street, (231) 722-0100. Full service hotel with 201 luxury rooms. Extras: remodeled pool area, fitness center, high speed internet and lake views.

Langeland House, 1337 Peck Street, www.langelandhouse.com, (231) 728-9404. Historic Victorian home furnished with maritime art and artifacts. Three rooms on second floor share a bath, although you can also use the downstairs bath. Breakfast, robes and cookie snack.

Port City Victorian Inn B&B, 1259 Lakeshore Drive, (231) 759-0205 or toll-free (800) 274-3574, www.portcityinn.com. Elegant historic 1877 Queen Anne-style home overlooking Muskegon Lake and yacht harbor. Full breakfast, vintage antiques, luxury suites with two person whirlpool and many other amenities. Rated one of the *"Best in the Midwest"* by Arrington's B&B Journal. Step back more than a century when you step through the front door into the grand foyer of this Victorian mansion built for Alexander Rodgers Senior. Five bedrooms, each with private bath, welcome guests to enjoy the old world elegance, grace and charm that define this vintage mansion.

Quality Inn, 150 Seaway Drive, (231) 739-9429. Affordable rooms, continental breakfast, *USA Today*, local calls and indoor pool.

Shoreline Inn and Suites, 750 Terrace Point, toll-free (866) 727-8483, www.shorelineinn.com. European flavor to this Victorian hotel with modern conveniences. Extras: pools, fireplaces, hot tubs, exercise room and continental breakfast.

Museums and Galleries

Art Cats Gallery, 1845 Lakeshore Drive, (231) 755-7606. The owner of this gallery creates whimsical pieces and 30 other artists present their works of jewelry, pottery, mosaics, glass and sculpture here. Open Mon to Fri 11:00 am to 5:00 pm, Sat 10:00 am to 5:00 pm, second Sunday noon to 5:00 pm, or by appointment.

The Fire Barn Museum, Clay Avenue between Fifth and Sixth Streets, (231) 722-0278. The C.H. Hackley Hose Company No 2 was formed in December 1875. Twelve volunteer firemen were sponsored by Charles Hackley in the first of what would be many gifts he made to the city. Initially the firefighters used hand drawn carts which they later traded for horse drawn carts as they rushed to respond to neighborhood fires. The museum is a living memorial to the brave men and women who have served as Muskegon firefighters over the years. Open May through October, Wed to Sun noon to 4:00 pm.

The Great Lakes Naval Memorial and Museum, 1346 Bluff, (231) 755-1230, www.glnmm.org. Tour the *U.S.S. Silversides* and the USCGC *McLane*, two World War II Ships. The *U.S.S. Silversides* served with the Pacific Fleet along Japan's coast, the East China Sea, and through key enemy shipping routes. Her mission was to stop raw materials and supplies going to Japan. The USCGC *McLane* was authorized by President Calvin Coolidge's administration to enforce prohibition. This museum has an overnight encampment program that is a great way for a scout or other group to enjoy an unusual learning experience. June to August open 7 days, 10:00 am to 5:30 pm. April and October Sat and Sun 10:00 am to 5:30 pm. May and September Mon to Fri 1:00 pm to 5:30 pm and Sat and Sun 10:00 am to 5:30 pm.

Historic Hackley Home
Photo Courtesy of Muskegon County Convention and Visitors Bureau

Hackley & Hume Historic Site, Northeast corner of Sixth Street and Webster Avenue, (231) 722-7578. These are the two homes of Muskegon's most famous lumber barons: Partners Charles H. Hackley and Thomas Hume. In 1887 Hackley purchased the lots on which these homes stand and construction took place over the next two years. You will experience the history of the lumbering era, these two families, and the beauty and charm of these Queen Anne Victorian homes with their exquisite late 19th century craftsmanship. Open May through October, Wed to Sun noon to 4:00 pm.

Jilly's, 1812 Lakeshore Drive, (231) 755-1515. Whimsical figurines and porcelain clay ornaments. Lovely fused glass jewelry, driftwood art and wall pieces by local illustrator Jill Barnes who does custom pieces. (Same location as Through the Looking Glass below.)

Muskegon County Museum, Southwest corner of Clay Avenue and Fourth Street, (231) 722-0278. This is the main museum building (Hackley & Hume Historic Site and the Firehouse Museum are also part of the Museum complex) and it is a treasure trove of Muskegon history including: nine dioramas from 1937 tracing the early history of the area, the Coming to the Lakes exhibit which displays 10,000 years of history including a 21 foot mastodon, a gallery for examining a dune, grassland, wetland, forest and urban habitat and a hands on science center where you can create a tornado. Free admission. Open Mon to Fri, 9:30 am to 4:30 pm, Sat and Sun 12:30 pm to 4:30 pm.

Muskegon Museum of Art, 296 West Webster Avenue, (231) 720-2570, www.muskegonartmuseum.org. Permanent collection of fine American and European paintings, sculpture, prints, and drawings. Also changing exhibits and special programs to entice the museum-goer. Guided tours available by appointment. Open Tues to Sat 10:00 am to 4:30 pm (later on Thurs) and Sun noon to 4:30 pm. Closed Mon.

S.S. Milwaukee Clipper, 2098 Lakeshore Drive, (231) 755-0990. She was called the Queen of the Great Lakes and you can take a guided tour through four of her six decks. Open Memorial Day weekend through Labor Day, Fri to Sun 2:00 pm to 7:00 pm.

Through the Looking Glass, 1812 Lakeshore Drive, (231) 755-0735. Functional pottery and life size metal garden sculptures. Open Mon to Thurs noon to 5:30 pm, Fri and Sat noon to 4:00 pm. Closed Sun.

USS LST 393, Mart Dock on the waterfront, just off Shoreline Drive, (231) 730-1477. The tour will take from 30 to 45 minutes and you can explore the technology and living conditions of WWII sailors. She is one of only two remaining LST's from WWII. Open for tours May through September 7 days, 10:00 am to 4:00 pm.

Theatre

West Shore Symphony Orchestra Concert Series, Tickets available at Frauenthal Box Office or Star Tickets Plus at toll-free (800) 585-3737, www.wsso.org.

Antiques

Airport Antique Mall, 4206 Grand Haven Road, (231) 798-3318. More than twenty dealers. Open 7 days, Mon to Sat 11:00 am to 5:30 pm and Sun noon to 5:30 pm.

Muskegon Antique Mall, 5905 Grand Haven Road, (231) 798-6441. Located in a new building, this mall houses 50 dealers and a wide variety of merchandise. Open 7 days, Mon to Sat 11:00 am to 6:00 pm and Sun 1:00 pm to 6:00 pm.

Other Shopping

Heart and Hand/The Creamery, 1437 Holton Road, (231) 744-0052. Largest country shop (with 7,000 square feet) on the west side of the state. Gifts, collectibles, floral, candles - and even an ice cream parlor next door (the Creamery). Store open 7 days, Mon to Fri 10:00 am to 6:00 pm, Sat 10:00 am to 5:00 pm and Sun noon to 5:00 pm. The Creamery is open 7 days, Mon to Sun 1:00 pm to 10:00 pm.

Lakes Mall, US-31 at the Sternberg Road Exit, (231) 798-7154, www.thelakesmall.com. 70 stores if you need a mall experience.

Note: *Much of downtown Muskegon is under reconstruction so there is not a downtown area with cute little shops like there are in several other lake towns. Hopefully that will change in the future.*

Parks, Beaches and Campgrounds

Kruse City Park, Sherman at Beach Street. Enjoy the dunes on the walkways or overlooks in this great park. Also provides restrooms, playground, picnic tables and shelter, nature trails, basketball courts and about a mile of beach with a designated dog beach.

Margaret Drake Elliot City Park, Beach Street just north of Pere Marquette Park. Amenities include: playground, bathrooms and a shelter/picnic area that can seat eighty people and can be reserved.

The Monet Garden of Muskegon, Corner of Clay Avenue and Fifth Street, (231) 724-6361, www.muskegonmastergardeners.org. Called a "Pocket Park," these gardens are a tiny replica of the famous Monet Garden of France. When you are downtown visiting museums, take a minute to peek at these beautiful miniature gardens.

Muskegon State Park, 3560 Memorial Drive, US-31 to the M-120 Exit in North Muskegon and follow signs to the park, toll-free (800) 44PARKS. Provides a great expanse of beautiful Lake Michigan sandy beach that is as gorgeous as any in the state. Forested dunes stretch to meet the shoreline. The park contains three campgrounds. Amenities: electricity, shower/toilet and picnic tables. There are also two mini-cabins. Day visitors love the beach for swimming or just soaking up the rays. Enjoy hiking the twelve miles of marked trails. There is a lighted boat launch at Snug Harbor where trailered boats of all sizes can be launched. In the winter, visitors enjoy cross-country skiing, ice fishing and ice skating.

Musketawa Trail, (231) 821-0553, www.musketawatrail.org for additional information. The Rails to Trails Conservancy has led the way in converting the state's abandoned railroad corridors to trails. The Musketawa trail is a 26 mile paved recreational trail that runs from Muskegon to Marne, past farmlands and wetlands, over creeks and through villages. It is perfect for bikers, snowmobilers, horseback riders, inline skaters, cross-country skiers, hikers, wheelchair travelers, and nature lovers who want to enjoy meandering any part of the trail.

Pere Marquette Park, Beach Street and Lakeshore Drive. Facilities include: playground, life guard, restrooms, picnic tables, bath house, volleyball courts, handicap accessible walkway, snack bar and restaurant. The real draw of this beach is its amazing two and a half miles of beautiful sandy Lake Michigan frontage.

Pioneer Park, Entrance is on Orshal Road close to Scenic Drive. 213 modern campsites with water and electric hook-ups at every site. The campground can accommodate tents and RVs. No reservations are taken so first come, first served. Modern toilets and showers. Access to Lake Michigan. For the "day use" visitor the beach is ideal for any of your water activities and there are softball diamonds, volleyball area, and tennis and basketball courts. Hours: 7 days, 8:00 am to 10:00 pm from May 1st to September 30th. Day-use visitors must leave by 10:00 pm), 8:00 am to dark daily from October 1st to April 30th.

P. J. Hoffmaster State Park, 6585 Lake Harbor Road, (231) 798-3711. This 1,130 acre park offers forested dunes along three miles of Lake Michigan Shore. The sandy beach is spectacular. The campground is located in a wooded valley and has 293 sites with electric and modern shower/toilet buildings available. The day use area has picnic sites, a picnic shelter and, of course, the swimming beach. 10 miles of trails beckon the hiker or birdwatcher. Winter finds the cross-country skiers enjoying the marked three mile trail for intermediate skiers. Pets must be on a leash and are not allowed on the beach. The park also features the Gillette Sand Dune Visitor Center, a beautiful building that houses an exhibit hall depicting the ecological zones of the unique dune environment. There are nine multimedia presentations on the dunes and seasonal nature subjects in the 77-seat auditorium.

Marinas, Water Sports, Boat and Jet Ski Rental

Great Lakes Marina and Storage, 1920 Lakeshore Drive, (231) 759-8230, www.greatlakesmarina.com. 30 transient slips. Gas, diesel, pump-out, pool, laundry, grills, picnic area, restrooms and boat rentals.

Hartshorn Marina, 920 West Western Avenue, (231) 724-6785. Public marina, 54 transient slips, shore power, but no pump-out or gas.

Torresen Marina, 3003 Lakeshore Drive, (231) 759-8596. Sells seasonal slips but may have five to twenty transient slips. Primarily sailboats. Amenities: pump-out, travel lift, sailing lessons. No gas.

Cruises and Ferries

Day Trip (or longer) to Milwaukee. Taking the Lake Express (below) opens the possibility of a wonderful side trip. To whet your appetite, here are a few things to check out in Milwaukee:

- America's Black Holocaust Museum
- A. Mitchell Leather Manufacturing and Outlet
- Betty Brinn Children's Museum
- Cedar Creek Winery
- Historic Third Ward (shops, galleries, restaurants)
- Miller Brewing Company Visitor Center and Shop
- Milwaukee Art Museum (20,000 permanent holdings)
- Milwaukee Public Museum
- Mitchell Park or Whitnall Park
- Narrated Tour of Historic Milwaukee
- For further information, contact the Tourist Information Center, 8832 North Port Washington Road, #150, Milwaukee, WI 53217, (800) 575-9781, www.wisonline.com.

Lake Express, Muskegon Terminal, 1918 Lakeshore Drive, toll-free (866) 914-1010, www.lake-express.com. It takes 2½ hours to cross the lake by this high-speed ferry. Instead of fighting traffic you will have the opportunity to relax, sip a glass of wine, enjoy the lake or even catch a movie. The ferry connects Muskegon with Milwaukee.

Port City Princess, 560 Mart Street, (231) 728-8387 or toll-free (800) 853-6311. You choose the cruise experience you want: sunset, dining and dancing, luncheon, scenic tours or Sunday Brunch cruises. Also specialty cruises: Hawaiian Luau, Jammin' Jamaican, Pirates, Fireworks, Blues/Jazz, Big Band, Native American Cultural Show, Rock and Roll, Mexican Fiesta or Margaritaville.

Other Things to See and Do

The Farmer's Market, Seaway Drive (Business 31) at Eastern. The place to buy fresh Michigan produce, flowers, pastries and more. Open Tues, Thurs and Sat 7:00 am to 3:00 pm through December.

Great Lakes Downs, 4800 Harvey Street (intersection of I-96 and US-31), (231) 799-2400, www.greatlakesdowns.com. Michigan's only live thoroughbred race track.

The Hart-Montague Trail. 25.5 mile trail offering scenic overlooks, picnicking, and rest rooms. Mile markers help you chart your progress. (See listing under Montague p. 139.)

Ice Fishing. When Michigan's 11,000 inland lakes freeze over (usually by late December), you can try your luck ice-fishing for perch, walleye, pike, bluegill and other delicious fresh-water fish. You will need an ice auger to drill a hole, a seat of some sort (sitting on the ice is neither practical nor comfortable), a pole, a bit of luck and a fishing license (available at most sporting goods stores).

Michigan Adventure, eight miles north of Muskegon, take Russell Road exit off US-31, (231) 766-3377. It is Michigan's largest water park and you can fly, whirl, propel, cruise, topple, tumble, turn and slide through sixty water adventures. From tame to tumultuous and everything in between. One thing is certain: You will get wet. And, on a hot Michigan summer's day, that is just perfect. Open late-May until early-September, hours vary by date.

Muskegon Trolley Company, (231) 724-6430 for additional information. The Trolley only costs a quarter and getting to your destination is half the fun.

Muskegon Winter Sports Complex, 462 Scenic Drive, located at Muskegon State Park, toll-free (877) TRYLUGE, www.msports.org. One of only four Olympic luge training tracks in the U.S. The complex has 15 kilometers of cross-country ski trails; half of them are lighted for evening skiing. Trails wind through dense forests and the area's wind-blown dunes where skiers often encounter white-tailed deer and other critters watching them with rapt attention. Visitors can snowshoe trails, practice spins at the outdoor ice rink, and then warm up at the heated Sports Lodge. Equipment rentals, food service and a warming area with a fireplace await inside the lodge. The luge run is a must for any dare-devil or skier with an adventurous spirit. For first-timers, a 2½ hour training clinic is required: 15 minutes of instruction on proper form, steering and stopping techniques, and the remaining time devoted to taking runs down the lower half of the track where speeds reach a deceptive 15 miles per hour. Advance registration is required.

Walking Tours:

Muskegon provides the opportunity for lovely, historical, walking tours. Learn a bit, exercise a bit and relax a bit. Life is good when you are taking a leisurely stroll among Muskegon's historic sites.

Muskegon's Heritage Village Walking Tour. The tour area is bordered by First Street on the East, Sixth Street on the West,

Muskegon Avenue on the South and Western Avenue on the North. It features 23 sites including: Hume House, Hackley House, Hackly Hose Company, St. Paul's Church, Hackley Park, Muskegon Union Depot, Torrent House, Muskegon Board of Education Building, Frauenthal Center, St. Mary's Church and the Amazon Building, among others. (The Muskegon Heritage Association (231) 722-1363.)

Wagging the Tale, meet at Union Depot, 610 West Western Avenue, (231) 865-6319. Walking guided-tour of Muskegon's original upper-class neighborhood covers many of the same sites as the above Heritage Village Walking Tour. The tour takes approximately 1½ hours and includes refreshments. Tours offered July through August, Wednesdays and Saturdays, 11:30 am and 2:00 pm.

Festivals

Muskegon Summer Celebration, June. Music, midway, parade, arts and crafts, and national headliners.

Unity Christian Music Festival, August. Three days of the best in Christian Music.

Michigan Irish Music Festival, September. Where everyone can be Irish for a weekend.

Golf

Chase Hammond Golf Club, 2454 Putnam Road, (231) 766-3035, www.chasehammondgolfclub.com. 18 holes through a dense forest make for a challenging round.

Fruitport Golf Club, 6334 South Harvey, (231) 798-3355, www.fruitportgolfclub.com. 18 holes, 5,725 yards. Banquet facilities.

Putters Creek Mini-Golf, 40 North Causeway, North Muskegon (231) 744-1418. Mini-golf, arcade and go-karts on the beautiful Muskegon River.

Contacts

Muskegon Area Chamber of Commerce, 900 Third Street, Suite 200, (231) 722-3751, www.muskegon.org, macc@muskegon.org.

Muskegon County Convention and Visitors Bureau, 610 West Western Avenue, (800) 250-9283 www.visitmuskegon.org. Great people willing to help you in any way they can. The building is the Union Depot which opened in 1895 and served as a whistle stop during political campaigns. Check out the architecture while there.

Muskegon Summer Celebration, www.summercelebration.com, 231-722-6520.

Whitehall/Montague

Population: Whitehall: 2884.   Montague: 2407.

Directions: Approximately 15 minutes north of Muskegon on US-31, midway between Holland and Ludington and about an hour drive from each. **From Detroit**: (200 miles) I-96 West to US-31 North, take the Whitehall/Montague exit. **From Chicago**: (200 miles) I-94 towards Detroit, exit 34 onto I-196, 45 miles to exit 44 and north on US-31 for 52 miles.

Background and History

The residents of Whitehall and Montague received a special bonus from the giant glaciers that carved this area nearly 20,000 years ago. They were left with a special Sixth Great Lake: Their White Lake is a deep channel lake, approximately seven miles long and one mile wide. It provides a water connection from White River to Lake Michigan.

Early Native Americans chose to live in this area because the water routes enhanced their ability to travel. Later the connecting waters provided the same advantage to fur traders, lumbermen, settlers and, eventually, the tourists.

Montague got its first permanent settler in 1855 when Nathanial Sargent built his home there. In 1883 the little village was officially incorporated. Noah Ferry, one of the town founders, named it in honor of his father, William Montague Ferry, who had founded the cities of Grand Haven and Ferrysburg in neighboring Ottawa County.

Noah Ferry brought a post office to Montague and the street where it stands is named in his honor. The Ferry Reformed Church on Old Channel Trail is also named for Noah Ferry. Ferry joined the Union forces when the Civil War broke out and became captain of a company of 102 men known as the "White River Guard." In early 1863, he was promoted to Major, but that same year he was killed in battle against Robert E. Lee's forces at Gettysburg.

The same year Sargent built his home in Montague, William Barnhard bought property in Whitehall from the United States government in a land grant signed by President James Buchanan. Barnhart had been lumbering since 1844 and decided to set up business in the area. Around 1859 Charles Mears, another noted lumber baron of the area platted the village and named it Mears after himself. In 1862, the village was renamed Whitehall and five years later it was incorporated. There remains a Mears a few miles north near Silver Lake.

The lumber era of the 1800s brought a boom to the cities of Whitehall and Montague, standing on their opposite sides of the White River. In 1857 George Rogers built the first steam powered lumber mill in Montague. Rogers' life ended tragically a short time later when he fell overboard and drowned while crossing White Lake in the steamer *Oceana*.

During the heyday of lumber, the two cities were nearly as large as they are today. Their growth was advanced because great steamships could dock and pick up lumber for Chicago. It has been estimated that 85% of the timber used to rebuild Chicago after the horrific fire of 1871 came from the surrounding area and started its journey in White Lake. In the late-1800s there were 19 steam powered lumber mills around White Lake.

A gruesome train derailment on April 9, 1894 was one of the worst tragedies of the logging era. Seven men died of fatal burns when a locomotive rounded a curve and plowed directly into a tree that had fallen across the track.

By the close of the century the forests had been decimated and 1903 marked the last log drive of any consequence. With the close of the lumber era, the residents needed another source of support for their struggling economy and turned their attention to resorts and tourism. City folks from Chicago as well as many spots in Michigan longed to escape the hot, gritty summer of the big cities and refresh their bodies and spirits in the cooling waters and relaxed atmosphere of these quaint little towns near Lake Michigan. By 1890 the White Lake area was recognized as a premier tourist destination.

Train transportation helped tourism flourish; a ticket from Chicago to White Lake in the summer of 1917 cost $4.00 for a round trip. During the roaring 20s automobiles became the preferred means of transportation replacing steamers and trains for the journey. In a single day the entire family, along with as much luggage as they cared to pack, could arrive in White Lake from destinations as far away as Indiana and Illinois. Spending the summer, or at least a portion of it, in a fashionable resort on White Lake or nearby Lake Michigan was a testament to the new-found wealth of many Chicagoans.

Today tourists are captivated by the magnificence of the forests, dunes and beaches. Picturesque White Lake is admired for its esthetics and recreational opportunities more than its practical use in shipping. The white pine is valued for its natural beauty not its commercial value.

Whether your sport is kayaking, tubing, rafting, canoeing, fishing or waterskiing, this major hub of water activity is a perfect place to play.

The "World's Largest Weathervane" rises a majestic height of 48 feet on the north shore of White Lake. It weighs 4,300 pounds. Perched atop the weathervane is a replica of the *Ellenwood*, a lumbering schooner whose home port was White Lake. On October 1, 1901 the *Ellenwood* ran aground during a nasty, northerly storm. She was about eight miles north of Milwaukee and far from her home port. The crew abandoned her and headed for safety in the ship's yawl. The beleaguered ship was bashed and battered by the mighty waves, until she tore apart and sank. The next spring a portion of her wooden nameplate washed ashore at White Lake. The *Ellenwood* was determined it would rest in the watery grave of her home port.

A 22.5 mile rail trail opened in 1988 and beckons bicyclers, inline skaters and hikers alike. It is a paved recreation trail built on the former C & O Railroad right of way. The trail is handicap accessible. (See Other Things to See or Do, below.)

Townspeople welcome visitors to their many annual festivals including: music festivals, fishing contests and arts and crafts fairs.

Make time in your busy schedule to visit the historic White River Light Station, currently a museum open to the public. (See below for additional information.)

Food/Restaurants

Beth I's Pies, 8851 Water Street, Montague, (231) 893-2132. A place where the motto is "*Life is uncertain, eat dessert first.*" This establishment serves just desserts and the selection is delicious: cakes, cookies, cheesecakes, scones, biscotti, muffins, candy and pies. You gotta love a place like this. Open Tues to Sat 9:00 am to 2:00 pm.

The Book Nook and Java Shop, 8726 Ferry Street, Montague, (231) 894-5333. Coffee drinks, smoothies, soups, bagels, biscotti and fresh fruit. Also a wireless café and full service bookstore. Live music Friday and Saturday. Open 7 days, Mon to Thurs 9:00 am to 6:00 pm, Fri and Sat 9:00 am to 8:00 pm and Sun 9:00 am to 3:00 pm.

Chen's Chinese and Thai, 212 East Colby, Montague, (231) 893-6138. In addition to the Chinese and Thai dishes, there are a wide variety of desserts. Open for lunch and dinner buffets 7 days.

C.S. Extreme Ice Cream and Mini Golf, 8990 Water Street, Montague, Hudsonville Ice Cream, hot dogs, nachos and chili dogs. Summer: Mon to Sat 11:00 am to 10:00 pm and Sun noon to 10:00 pm.

The Dockside Grill at South Shore Marina, 6806 South Shore Drive, Whitehall, (231) 893-3935. Very casual atmosphere. Menu includes Brew City Fries, salads, sandwich baskets and daily specials to enjoy while overlooking White Lake. Live music on weekends. Seasonal Outside Restaurant. Open 7 days, Mon to Sat 11:00 am to 9:00 pm and Sun 11:00 am to 7:00 pm.

Dog n Suds Drive In, 4454 Dowling, Montague, (231) 894-4991, www.dog-n-suds.com. Views of White Lake. Eat in your car or at one of the umbrella-covered tables. Known for their creamy root beer, this authentic 50s Drive In is the last remaining Dog and Suds in Michigan, and still provides curb service. Thursday night is Cruise Night and customers turn out in classic cars.

Doug Born's Smokehouse and Sausage Kitchen, 10150 US Bus. 31 (Corner of Fruitvale Road, 300 feet west of the Bike Trail), Montague, (231) 894-2753. Home cured and smoked hams, bacon, Canadian bacon, beef bacon, chicken, turkey, dried beef jerky and fish. Offers deli sandwiches, fresh salad and other menu items. They also have a large stock of micro brew and imported beer, as well as a variety of Italian, German, Californian and Michigan wines. For the taste adventurous, they carry bison: ground, steaks and roasts. Open 7 days.

Gary's Restaurant, 8844 Water Street, Montague, (231) 894-6720. Local favorite for breakfast and lunch. Family atmosphere. Open 7 days, Mon to Fri 6:00 am to 3:00 pm, Sat 6:00 am to 11:30 am and Sun 7:00 am to 11:30 am.

JoAnne's Lumberjack Café, 8775 Water Street, Montague, (231) 894-5943. Homemade soups, breads and cinnamon rolls. Daily specials. Serving breakfast and lunch all day, 7 days a week. Open 5:30 am to 2:00 pm.

Lakeside Inn, 5700 North Scenic Drive, Whitehall, (231) 893-8315 or toll-free (888) 442-3304, www.lakesideinn.net. On the shores of White Lake featuring a full menu and daily specials. Enjoy a romantic sunset and a great meal starting with Scallop and Smoked Salmon Cakes with Remoulade Sauce. Then give in to the temptation of their house specialty: Slow Roasted Prime Rib. Save room for the Ice Cream Sundae Pie. They serve breakfast, lunch and dinner. Seasonal. Open from the end of June to Labor Day, Tues to Sat 6:00 am to 9:00 pm.

Lipka's Old Fashioned Soda Fountain, 8718 Ferry Street, Montague. Malts, shakes, sodas. Often the busiest place in town. Open Mon to Sat 9:00 am to 7:00 pm. Closed Sun.

The Local Pub, 111 West Colby, Whitehall, (231) 894-8269. Serving food and drinks for more than half a century. This is a favorite of locals who often enjoy the Lake Perch Dinner. Live bands and dancing on Friday and Saturday nights. Open year round, 7 days, Mon to Thurs 11:00 am to 2:00 am, Fri 7:00 am to 2:00 am, Sat 11:00 am to 2:00 am and Sun noon to 8:00 pm.

Old Channel Inn, 6905 Old Channel Trail, Montague, (231) 893-3805. A country inn that features good food at moderate prices. Menu includes steaks, seafood, soups and sandwiches. Another local favorite. Open year round, Memorial Day to Labor Day, Tues to Thurs noon to 10:00 pm, Fri and Sat noon to 11:00 pm and Sun noon to 10:00 pm. Labor Day to Memorial Day closed Mon and Tues, open Wed, Thurs and Sun noon to 9:00 pm and Fri and Sat noon to 10:00 pm.

Pekadill's, 503 South Mears, Whitehall, (231) 894-9551. 32 flavors of ice cream. Or, if you need something a bit heartier, you can enjoy soup and sandwiches in the outdoor garden. Seasonal. Open 7 days, Mon to Sat 11:30 am to 10:00 pm and Sun noon to 10:00 pm.

Pinhead's Great Food and Fun, 115 South Lake Street, Whitehall, (231) 894-4103. The name comes from the 12 bowling lanes. Has an arcade and billiards room. Wood-fired oven pizza, pastas, sandwiches, salads, Mexican and daily specials. Indoor or outdoor dining with views of White Lake. Open 7 days, Sun to Thurs 11:00 am to 10:00 pm, Fri 11:00 am to midnight and Sat 11:00 am to 2:00 am. Winter: Mon to Thurs 4:00 pm to 10:00 pm and the weekends remain the same.

Sam's Bistro, 306 East Colby, Whitehall (231) 893-3000. Enjoy the taste of the Mediterranean in the appetizers (hummus, feta hortariko), pizzas, pitas (shawarma), subs, kafta burger, salads (fattoush), and dinners (shish tawook, magmour). Open 7 days, Mon to Thurs 11:00 am to 10:00 pm, Fri and Sat 11:00 am to 11:00 pm and Sun 1:00 pm to 10:00 pm.

Scales Fish House and Steaks, 302 South Lake Street, Whitehall, (231) 893-4655, www.scalesfishhouse.net. The Sesame Fried Scallop Appetizer is the perfect way to start your dinner at this casual fine-dining restaurant. The Eggplant Parmesan offers an entrée that is a bit out of the ordinary. The fresh seafood entrees also deserve consideration. Open Lunch: Mon to Fri 11:30 am to 4:00 pm, Sat noon to 4:00 pm. Dinner: Mon to Thurs 4:00 pm to 9:00 pm, Fri and Sat 4:00 pm to 10:00 pm.

Sundance Saloon and Steakhouse, Double JJ Resort, 5900 Water Road, Rothbury, (231) 894-3900 or toll-free (800) DOUBLE JJ. Casual fine dining overlooking Carpenter Lake and the Thoroughbred Golf Course at the Double JJ resort. In addition to steaks there are chicken and seafood dishes. Open 7 days, Sun to Wed 8:00 am to 9:00 pm, Thurs to Sat 8:00 am to 10:00 pm. Reduced hours off-season.

Villa Venafro, 9521 Business US-31 North, Montague. (231) 894-9830. Italian and American dishes in a casual no-frills kind of atmosphere. Open 7 days, Mon to Sat 8:00 am to 10:00 pm and Sun 8:00 am to 1:00 pm.

Lodging (Also see Campgrounds below)

Best Western Inn and Suites of Whitehall, 2822 North Durham Road, (231) 893-4833 or toll-free (866) 737-8237. 74 guestrooms. Extras: internet, Jacuzzi suites, indoor pool, whirlpool and continental breakfast.

Cocoa Cottage B&B, 223 South Mears Avenue, Whitehall, (231) 893-0674 or toll-free (800) 204-7596, www.cocoacottage.com, innkeeper@cocoacottage.com. Restored Arts and Crafts bungalow with a chocolate theme: chocolate dishes, chocolate candy and rooms with such names as "The Hershey Room", the "Ghirardelli Room" and the "Godiva Room." Prides itself on attention to detail. Each room has a private bath; there is a whirlpool suite, wireless internet, fireplace, relaxing gardens and special seasonal packages. Guests rave about their breakfast and you can check out some of their recipes on their website.

Double JJ Ranch and Golf Resort, 5900 Water Road, Rothbury, (800) DOUBLEJJ. Full service resort-hotel, condominium, log homes and bunkhouse accommodations. Horseback riding, swimming pool, waterslide, golf, rodeo, snow tubing and sleigh rides (depending upon season). All inclusive packages available.

A Finch Nest, 415 Division Street, Whitehall, (231) 893-5323 or toll-free (866) 514-9355, afinchnest@chatermi.net, www.afinchnest.com. High ceilings and Victorian décor set the tone for this 1860s-Victorian cottage-turned-B&B. Three comfortable rooms with especially nice bathrooms, each with a whirlpool tub and modern shower. Extras: TV/VCR/DVD in each room, internet access, video library. Fresh coffee and tea available 24 hours. Bread baked fresh on premises.

Glaser's Glenn Log Cabin Resort, 6900 Hill Street, Whitehall, (231) 894-2491 or toll-free (866) 784-7829, www.glasersglenn.com, lynpyn@msn.com. Five rustic housekeeping log cabins overlooking White Lake. Extras: fireplaces, private beach. Rowboats available. Weekly rentals. Check the internet pictures to decide if these cottages are too rustic to suit your taste or maybe they are just what you are looking for. Open May to October.

Lakeside Inn Resort, 5700 North Scenic Drive, Whitehall, (231) 893-8315 or toll-free (888) 442-3304, www.lakesideinn.net. The Inn opened in 1913. Single rooms and some housekeeping units. Seasonal and on White Lake. Extras: heated pool, free docking and tennis courts. The Inn is steeped in history and located at the site of a former lumber mill known as Sprigg's Landing and then Green's Landing.

Maple Tree Inn, 323 South Mears Avenue, Whitehall, (231) 894-4091, Extras: Jacuzzi suites, internet access, cable TV, refrigerators, microwaves. Walking distance to shops. Single story, basic motel.

Michillinda Lodge, 5207 Scenic Drive, Whitehall, (231) 893-1895. www.michillindalodge.com. Located on a bluff overlooking Lake Michigan. Originally a turn-of-the-century estate, the Inn has 52 guest rooms. Extras: dining facilities, heated pool, tennis courts, miniature golf and shuffleboard.

Ramada Inn of Whitehall, US-31 at the Colby Road exit, (231) 893-3030 or toll-free (800) 893-3030, www.ramadawhitehall.com. 66

rooms. Extras: free hot breakfast, internet, remodeled in 2005, heated pool, exercise room and sauna, cable, whirlpool and efficiency suites.

Super 8 Motel of Whitehall, 3080 Colby, (231) 894-4848 or toll-free (800) 800-8000 or (877) 894-4848. 54 rooms. Extras: whirlpool suites available, cable TV, microwaves and refrigerators in some rooms, superstart breakfast and high speed internet in the lobby.

Weathervane Inn, 4225 Dowling Street, Montague, (231) 893-8931 or toll-free (877) 893-8931, www.theweathervaneinn.net. Waterfront hotel located on White Lake causeway between Montague and Whitehall. Adjacent to the bicycle/snowmobile path and the World's Largest Weathervane. 24-suites, most with Jacuzzi, fireplace, refrigerator, microwave. Also: breakfast, movies and free local calls. One extended stay suite.

White Sands Resort, 6235 Old Channel Trail, Montague, (231) 740-5071, whitesands@developmentrealty.com. Waterfront rentals on White Lake. Two and three-bedroom units available, linens provided, fully-equipped kitchens. Boat lifts available. One week minimum stay.

White Swan Inn B&B, 303 Mears Avenue, Whitehall, (231) 894-7926 or toll-free (888) 948-7926, www.whiteswaninn.com. Each room has a private bath and there is a whirlpool suite. Extras: cable TV/DVD, wireless internet, screened porch and full breakfast.

Museums and Galleries

Claybanks Pottery Studio, 7060 South Scenic Drive (six miles west of US-31 at New Era Road Exit, then three miles south on Scenic Drive, Highway B-15), (231) 894-4177. It's a bit of a ride, but the countryside is pleasant and you can watch as artisans make their functional and rakku pottery in a wooded setting near Lake Michigan. Open 7 days, May to November, 10:00 am to 5:00 pm.

Montague City Museum, Church and Meade Streets, Montague, (231) 893-3055. Experience the feel of the lumbering era through the artifacts displayed at this museum. Also displays the dress worn by Montague's Miss America, Nancy Ann Fleming. Open June to August, Sat and Sun 1:00 pm to 5:00 pm.

Terrestrial Forming Pottery Studio, 5385 Lamos at Michillinda Road, (231) 894-2341. Pottery for both function and art. Watch owner and resident potter, Peter Johnson, create his beautiful sculptural pottery. For 30 years he has been working on his old-English designed treadle-kick wheel. Peter mixes his own clay and glazes and fires his self-built kilns about every two months. He will be happy to give you a tour of his studio. He favors earth tone glazes reminiscent of the woodland Native Americans whom he studies. The barn-like studio is tucked into the woods near Lake Michigan. Open 7 days, Mon to Sat 10:00 am to 5:00 pm and Sun 1:00 pm to 5:00 pm.

Tiller's Art and Gifts, 108 West Colby, Whitehall, (231) 894-9484. A number of artists creating in various mediums display and sell their pieces at this studio and you may catch them with their work in progress. Focus is on local artists and the studio "fills in" with unusual gift items they purchase. There is a lovely garden behind the shop. Open Tues to Sat 10:00 am to 5:00 pm.

White River Gallery, 8701 Ferry Street, Montague, (231) 894-8659. Original works of over 20 West Michigan artists. You will view the art and fine crafts of an eclectic array of media. An opportunity to buy distinctive, unusual and beautiful gifts, for yourself or someone special. Summer hours begin June 1st: Tues to Fri 11:30 am to 5:30 pm, Sat 10:00 am to 4:00 pm and Sun noon to 4:00 pm.

White River Light Station Museum, 6199 Murray Road, Whitehall (231) 894-8265. The historic lighthouse was built in 1875 and currently houses a maritime museum. You can climb the old spiral stairs for a spectacular view of Lake Michigan and White Lake. Open Memorial Day to Labor Day, Tues to Fri 11:00 am to 5:00 pm, Sat and Sun noon to 6:00 pm. Open September on weekends only. (See p. 362, Part II for additional detail regarding lighthouse.)

White River Light Station   *Photo Courtesy of Steve Schneider*

Theatre

Howmet Playhouse, 304 South Mears, Whitehall, (231) 894-1966. Operated by the Blue Lake Fine Arts Camp, this theatre has 400 seats and offers summer productions (musicals, opera, ballet and Shakespeare) from June through August. Call for information.

Antiques

Colby Street Shops, 106 East Colby Street, Whitehall, (231) 750-2545. Art, antiques, collectibles, stained glass, pictures, wall art and tiffany lamps. Open Thurs to Mon 11:00 am to 6:00 pm.

Gloria's Antiques, 212 South Mears Avenue, Whitehall, (231) 670-5631. Vintage clothing and more. Open Tues to Sat 10:30 am to 5:30 pm. Open summer season through September.

Montague Antique Mall, 4586 Dowling Street, Montague, (231) 893-1260. Dealers with a variety of specialties including shabby chic, collectibles, vintage jewelry and clothes. Flea market every Friday from May to October, 7:00 am to 1:00 pm. Open June to September, 7 days, noon to 5:00 pm. October to January Wed to Sun noon to 5:00 pm.

Wild Flower Antiques II, 4575 Dowling Street, Montague, (231) 903-8705 Carries many interesting antiques. Summer open 7 days, Mon to Fri 10:00 am to 5:00 pm, Sat and Sun noon to 4:00. The owners also have **Wild Flower Refinishers and Antique Shop**, 875 Industrial Park Drive, Whitehall, and (231) 894-9016. They may refer you there to see additional antiques at their original showroom.

Other Shopping

102 West, 102 West Colby, Whitehall, (231) 894-1025. The building housing this store is beautifully restored to retain its historic flavor. Home décor items, framed prints, baskets, pottery, bath and body treats and a selection of gift items. It is a store to buy something you like and worry about where it will go or what you will do with it later. Open Tues to Sat 10:00 am to 5:00 pm. Closed Sun and Mon.

The Book Nook (See above under Food/Restaurants).

Colby's Designer Outlet, 107 East Colby, Whitehall, (231) 894-6677. Women's fashions (clothes, accessories and jewelry) at discounted prices. Carries Tommy Hilfiger, Jones of New York, Liz Claiborne, Guess, XOXO and other fashion names. Most items are $16.99 or less and come from Macy's and the Gap. (The outlet also has a summer location in Silver Lake and a store in Pentwater.) Open 7 days, Mon to Sat 10:00 am to 7:00 pm and Sun noon to 5:00 pm.

The Corner House of Gifts, 223 East Colby, Whitehall, (231) 893-5235, www.cornerhouseofgifts.com. Carries women's fashions, jewelry, cookware, and items for the home and garden. Also has collectibles: Cat's Meow Village, G. Debrekht, Pipka Santas, Shiela's Collectibles, Spencer Collin Lighthouses and Harmony Kingdom, David Winter Cottages, Nancy DeYoung Tiles (my favorite), Emile Henry, April Cornell, Tracy Potter and more. Also has cards, souvenirs, CDs, Vera Bradley bags and a seasonal Christmas room. So many rooms of merchandise that it would be impossible to give a complete overview. Open year round, Mon to Sat 10:00 am to 5:30 pm, Sun in July, August, and December noon to 4:00 pm. January, February and March only open Fri and Sat 10:00 am to 5:30 pm.

Factory Surplus Sales, 10112 US-31 Montague, (231) 894-6633. They advertise clothes for the entire family, including some hard to find sizes (Big & Tall and Petite). Name labels at discounted prices. If you need blue jeans, Carhart, hunting or work clothes this place has them. Not a great selection in women's fashion. Cannot compete with boutiques or department stores for stylish clothing. Open Mon to Sat 9:00 am to 5:30 pm, (Fri open to 8:00 pm) and closed Sun.

The General Store, 103 East Colby, Whitehall, (231) 894-2164. You will feel like you have stepped back a century when you shop the interesting merchandise of this unique store. Two floors of collectible dolls and bears, baskets, Robinson's Pottery, Seed Sack fashions, quilts, candles, purses, art, wood carvings, bird houses, dips, bread mixes and weather vanes. Open Mon to Sat 10:00 am to 5:00 pm.

The Mud Puddle, 819 East Colby, Whitehall, (231) 894-5817. Ceramics, gifts and garden. Open Tues and Wed 6:30 pm to 9:00 pm, Thurs and Fri 10:00 am to 4:00 pm and 6:30 pm to 9:00 pm and Sat 10:00 am to noon.

Outdoor Living Center, 124 East Colby, Montague. Beach and other toys, picnic baskets, garden accessories, outdoor cooking supplies and gift ideas. Open Mon to Fri 7:30 am to 5:30 pm and Sat 7:30 am to 3:00 pm. Closed Sun.

Payne's Emporium, 108 South Mears, Whitehall, (213) 894-1804. Friendly little shop with original artwork, collectibles, and unique home décor accessories including lamps and pillows, gift items and kitchenware. Large collection of cute and cuddly stuffed animals. Open Mon, Tue, Thurs, and Fri 10:30 am to 5:00 pm, Sat 10:00 am to 5:00 pm. Closed Sun and Wed.

Pitkin Drug and Gift Shoppe, 101 West Colby, Whitehall. Wide selection of home décor items, gourmet foods, clothing boutique, sweatshirts, afghans and lighthouses. They say they offer gifts with city flair. Open 7 days, Mon to Fri 9:00 am to 7:00 pm, Sat 9:00 am to 5:00 pm and Sun 9:00 am to 2:00 pm.

Power's Outdoors, 4523 Dowling Street, Montague, (231) 893-0687. www.powersoutdoors.com. Rugged gear for all seasons. Name brand clothing, footwear and accessories for everyone in the family. Also rents kayaks, bikes, skim boards, ice skates and snowshoes.

Todd's Pharmacy, 8744 Ferry Street, Montague, (231) 894-4573. Selection of gift items, sweatshirts and t-shirts. Open Mon to Fri 9:00 am to 7:00 pm and Sat 9:00 am to 5:00 pm.

Parks, Trails, Beaches, and Campgrounds

Trailway Campground, 4540 Dowling Street, Montague (between Montague and Whitehall, next to the World's Largest Weathervane), (231) 894-4903. 55 sites within walking distance of shopping and restaurants. Near boat launch and the Hart-Montague Bike Trail.

Manistee National Forest and White Lake's natural marshland provide habitats and homes to more than 100 Mute and Tundra swans. Outdoor enthusiasts can hike the area and enjoy the natural beauty. (See p. 180 for additional information on Manistee National Forest.).

White River RV Park and Campground, 735 Fruitvale Road, Montague (Located in Manistee National Forest next to the White River), (231) 894-4708, www.whiterivercampground.com. Camping cabins, RV (including many large full-service, pull-through) sites, and tent sites. Extras: swimming pool, camp store, recreation building, playgrounds, hiking trails.

Marinas, Water Sports, Boat and Jet Ski Rental

Crosswinds Marine Service, 302 South Lake Street, Whitehall (231) 894-4549. Offers charters, docking, diesel fuel, gas, parking, pump out, storage and repair. 96 seasonal and transient slips accommodating ships up to 100 feet. Also has a fish cleaning station, restaurant, picnic area with grills and cable TV.

Happy Mohawk Canoe Livery, 735 Fruitvale Road, Montague, (231) 894-4209. Scenic White River provides fun by canoe, raft, tube or kayak. Your adventure can last for an hour or two days and can be geared to any level of experience. Call for reservations.

Montague Marina, 4770 Goodrich Street, Montague, (231) 893-4737. Docking, 66 seasonal and transient slips. Clubhouse with galley, ice, showers, washrooms, picnic area, parking and charters. Seasonal.

Moxie Marine, 2 locations: 4464 Dowling, Montague, and 220 Lake Street, Whitehall (231) 894-2628, www.moxiemarine.com. 90 fixed and floating slips. Boat repair, ship store, sales, storage, seasonal cottages, bath house, fire pit, fish cleaning station, ice, picnic area with grills, wireless internet and walking distance to downtown.

Municipal Boat Launch, Launch Ramp Road, Montague, (231) 893-1155. Fish cleaning station and rest rooms available. Montague City Hall sells day-use passes.

Powers Outdoors (Rents kayaks, see above Other Shopping).

South Shore Marina Boat Rentals, 6806 South Shore, Whitehall, (231) 893-3935. Rent a 21 foot pontoon boat or 24 foot deck boat by the hour or day. Reservations recommended. Open 7 days, 11:00 am to 7:00 pm during the season.

White Lake Municipal Marina, 100 North Lake Street, Whitehall, (231) 894-9689 or (231) 894-4048. 50 slips. Docking, diesel fuel, gas, parking, pump out, ice, bath house with showers and large playground. Located at Goodrich Park. Seasonal.

Cruises, Charters, and Ferries

Fishmas Charters, 4628 Sandy Lane, Whitehall, (231) 894-8718, e-mail KenClarke@FishmasCharters.com, www.FishmasCharters.com. Captain Clark takes you sport-fishing year round. Specializes in walleye. Also runs charters for bass, northerns and panfish. Families welcome.

Lady Lou Charters, Montague, (231) 894-6928, e-mail: bobgbel@aol.com. Captain Bob Belinger takes charters on Lake Michigan for salmon and trout. Fully-equipped 26-foot Bertram Sportfish. 30 years experience.

Shelly-Lee Charters, 8934 Burrows, (231) 894-2101, cell: (231) 730-1004, www.bluewatermarinesvc.com, e-mail Schillerpp@aol.com. Captain Pat Schiller runs two boats and charters trips on White Lake, Lake Michigan and surrounding lakes. His quest is salmon, trout, steelhead, northerns, bass, perch, walleye and panfish. Family rates available and Captain Schiller has more than 20 years of experience. *(There is a charter boat association with 10 members (231) 343-9875 for more information.)*

Other Things to See and Do

Farmer's Market, Water and Church Street, Montague, (231) 893-1155. Seasonal local produce. Open Wed and Sat 8:00 am to noon.

Country Dairy, between New Era and Shelby, adjacent to the Hart-Montague Bike Path, (231) 861-4636, ex. 234 or toll-free (800) 243-7280, www.countrydairy.com. Tours (fee charged) of milk-bottling process. You can watch not only white and chocolate milk being processed, but vanilla and strawberry as well. The tour of this working dairy farm and milk processing facility includes the cheese making process and the Show Barn where the cows are fed and milked. You may even spot a new calf or two. The Country Dairy also serves three meals a day and invites the traveler to browse their selection of gifts. Open Mon, Tues, Thurs, Fri and Sat 9:00 am.11:00 am and 1:00 pm for tours. Also gives a wagon tour by appointment. Store open Mon to Sat 7:00 am to 8:00 pm and closed Sun.

Hart-Montague Bicycle Trail State Park, Business 31/Water Street, Montague, or John Gurney Park in Hart, (231) 893-4585. Michigan's first linear state park, this 22.5-mile paved recreation trail is used by bicyclists (bikes can be rented at many hotels and other businesses in the area), rollerbladers, skate-boarders, hikers, runners, walkers, and in the winter: snowmobilers and cross-country skiers. You can ride horses beside the trail, but not on the asphalt. You can do the entire trail or a piece of it, non-stop, or meander along pausing at shops or grabbing a snack at any one of many restaurants close-by. The trail is handicap accessible and weaves through White Hall, Montague and nearby communities.

The trail was originally a railroad track established in the late 1800s. In order to entice the railroad to the area, local residents raised $30,000 and provided the land for the right of way. They also provided the labor to grade the rail bed; a task that required picks, shovels and teams of horses. Ownership of the railroad changed several times over the years, but it was part of the C & O line in 1982 when it was abandoned. The railroad donated the land to create this trail.

Historic Walking Tour, Maps at the Welcome Center (C&O Railroad Depot), 124 West Hanson Street, Whitehall, (231) 893-4585. The tour will take you past 16 historic homes of founders of the communities. The yards and homes are privately owned and not open to the public, but a leisurely walk past them is the perfect way to experience the feel of these two little cities. You will also pass lovely churches with inspiring architecture.

Rainbow Ranch, 4345 South 44th Avenue, New Era, (231) 861-4445, www.rainbowranch-inc.com, info@rainbowranch-inc.com. Horseback riding and wagon rides. Riding lessons, sleigh rides in season and hot dog roasts. If horses are on your agenda, this is a place to check. Hours vary by season, call for details.

White Lake Music Shell, Launch Ramp Road, Montague, (231) 893-4585. Free concerts every Tuesday from June to August. 7:30 pm. Located on the shores of White Lake, the concerts vary to include: jazz, folk, country, swing and international groups.

Festivals

Arts and Crafts Festival, June. Arts and crafts as well as entertainment and a food court.

Nautical Flea Market, June.

Spencer Weersing Memorial Regatta, June. Sailors from across the state join in four races on Saturday and two on Sunday. Annual event.

Fourth of July Parade and Fireworks, July. Parade begins at Whitehall City hall and travels to downtown Montague. Fireworks begin at dusk over the northeast end of White Lake.

Celebrate the Arts Home and Garden Tour, July. An opportunity to tour White Lake gardens. Music, dance, artwork, food, and garden experts to answer questions. Held every other year.

Celebrate White Lake, July. A family oriented festival with antique boat show and historical displays. Held at Goodrich Park.

Cruz-'in', July. Classic and vintage cars cruise from downtown Whitehall to Montague. Food, dancing, and general fun.

Blueberry Festival, July. Pancake breakfast, arts and crafts shows, activities for children and trolley rides. Fruitland Township Park.

Arts in the Barn, August. Art auction, live demonstrations, music, food and wine. Held at Schiller/Lindrup Barn.

Maritime Festival, August. Children's activities, trout pond, shuffleboard tournaments, sailing regatta, shrimp boil, food tent and a variety of entertainment.

Labor Day Community Walk, Labor Day/September. The walk takes place on the Montague/Whitehall Bike Trail.

Montague Street Dance, September.

Fall Fest, September. Continuous entertainment to spice up this Farmer's market. Hayrides, bobbing for apples, food, arts and crafts.

Golf

Hickory Knoll Golf Course, 3065 West Alice Street, Whitehall, (231) 894-5535). 36-holes and the public welcome. No tee time necessary and they offer senior rates. Golf carts and equipment are available. Snack bar. Open 7 days dawn to dusk.

Old Channel Trail Golf Course, 8325 North Old Channel Trail, (6 miles west of US-31 at Fruitvale exit), Montague, (231) 894-5076, www.ForeOnTheShore.com. A 27-hole public golf course on Lake Michigan. Driving range, lakeside picnic area, 3-hole practice course, pro-shop, professional instruction and special events. Offers 3 and 7-day vacation memberships.

Thoroughbred Golf Club, Double JJ Resort, 5900 Water Road Rothbury (231) 894-3939 or toll-free (800) DOUBLEJJ. 18-hole championship golf course designed by Arthur Hill. Voted best "New Course" in Michigan and #3 in America by *Golf Digest*. *Golf Week* labels it one of American's Best. Full service pro-shop, PGA professional, diving range and practice greens. See Lodging and restaurants above for other amenities of Double JJ.

Contacts

White Lake Area Chamber of Commerce, 124 West Hanson Street, Whitehall, (800) 678-9702, www.whitelake.org.

Silver Lake

Directions: Highway B-15 (coastal highway) from Montague or US-31 to Mears (Monroe Road) exit. **From Detroit, Grand Rapids and Lansing**: take I-96 to US-31 North (on the outskirts of Muskegon), take the Hart/Mears exit (148) from US-31, turn west and follow the signs to Silver Lake Sand Dunes.

Background and History

The Silver Lake area is Michigan's Sand Playground: the recreational destination geared for fun. It offers so much action it deserves its own section in this guide. It is not, however, a separate city and the addresses of its restaurants and shops will be Mears, Shelby or Hart. Silver Lake has no post office and is not incorporated as a separate entity. Still, this little non-city is a perfect vacation spot.

The famous dunes of the area perch between the shores of Lake Michigan and Silver Lake. Silver Lake Park has 500 acres of drivable dunes. You can test your skill with your own 4-wheel drive vehicle or rent a jeep, dune buggy or quad from one of the many rental places in the area. If you prefer you can take a dune tour and leave the driving to someone else. Sand-surfing is yet another option.

The Silver Lake Dunes are a beautiful and interesting backdrop for a perfect hike. The Hart-Montague Trail lets you go a distance of twenty-two miles hiking, biking, or cross country skiing in season. A refreshing swim and a picnic are the perfect conclusion to an invigorating hike or ride.

Golfing enthusiasts will find courses to challenge any skill level. Miniature golf entertains the entire family. There are also go-karts, paddle boats and bumper boats waiting with your name on them.

The Little Point Sable historic lighthouse is open weekends and lets you climb the tower for an amazing view of this spectacular area.

Food/Restaurants

Golden Bakery and Video Arcade, North Shore Road, Mears, (231) 873-0276. Pizza, subs, strudel, cinnamon rolls and donuts. Also a few games and a pool table. Open summer 7 days, Mon to Thurs 8:00 am to 10:00 pm, Fri and Sat 7:00 am to 11:00 pm and Sun 7:00 am to 10:00 pm. Winter hours: Fri 4:00 pm to 10:00 pm, Sat 8:00 am to 11:00 pm and Sun 8:00 am to 4:00 pm.

Lakewinds Restaurant, 8407 West Silver Lake Road, Mears, (231) 873-0927. Casual dining: burgers, huge subs, soups, salads, appetizers, or dinner specials that include steak, perch or prime rib. Open summer 7 days, 8:00 am to 9:00 pm or longer if busy.

Par 5 Grill, 3666 Scenic Drive, Shelby, (231) 851-6555. Overlooks the 17th hole at Benona Shores Golf Course. Deck or inside dining. Homemade soups and fresh salad bar. (See golf courses below.)

Sands Restaurant, 8448 West Hazel Road, Mears (231) 873-5257, www.sands-restaurant.com, sandsrestaurant@verizon.net. Full menu and take-out window for pizza, chicken, breakfast and coffee. Weekend breakfast bar during the summer. Homemade jumbo cinnamon rolls for breakfast, half pound dune burger for lunch or a casual meal. Walleye or whitefish would be a good choice for dinner. Open 7 days, Sun to Thurs 7:00 am to 9:00 pm, Fri and Sat 7:00 am to 10:00 pm. Seasonal restaurant (closes after Halloween).

The Station, 8427 North Shore Road, Mears. Go-carts, ice cream, hamburgers, shakes and fries.

Whippy Dip, 591 North 18th Avenue, Mears, (231) 873-4715. Ice cream and sandwiches and open for your late night snacks. Open 7 days, 11:00 am to 11:00 pm, slightly reduced hours when slow and closed after the summer season.

Lodging

Dunes Resort, 1180 North Shore Road, Mears, (231) 873-5500, www.duneswaterfrontresort.com. On the beach. Amenities: enclosed heated-pool, hot tub, sun deck, recreation area, in-room whirlpools, refrigerators, private balconies, 100 foot dock, WIFI and guest laundry.

Sierra Sands Dunes Resort, 7990 West Hazel, Mears, (231) 871-1008 or toll-free (866) 873-1008. All rooms have microwave, refrigerator and data port access.

Silver Sands Resort, 8446 West Hazel Road, Mears (231) 873-3769, www.silversandsresort.net. Rooms, efficiency apartments and cottages. Daily or weekly rates, heated pool, playground, private beach.

Summer Wind Resort, 8484 North Shore Road, Mears (231) 873-3069, www.summerwindcondoresort.com. Cottages and condos on Silver Lake, overlooking the dunes.

Galleries

Dune Scapes, 527 North 18th Avenue, Mears, (231) 873-5171, www.dunescapephotography.com. Dune photography, purses, t-shirts, gourd art, baskets, photo frames and jewelry. Many gift items and some consignment art. Open summer 7 days, 10:00 am to 7:00 pm. Off-season, weekends from 10:00 am to 4:00 pm when business gets slower. By appointment in the winter.

Antiques

Silver Hills Antique Mall, 6780 West Fox Road, Mears (231) 873-3905. More than twenty dealers specializing in furniture, kitchenware, glassware, 50s items, china, books, linen and lace, primitives and antique farm and dairy displays. Located in a restored, century-old barn. Open Wed to Mon (closed Tues) Memorial Day through Labor Day 11:00 am to 5:00 pm, and open until 9:00 pm in July and August.

Other Shopping

Shelby Gem Factory, Industrial drive, (231) 861-2165, Shelby. Fifteen minute drive from the dunes to this factory where man-made rubies, sapphires, emeralds and diamonds sparkle like the real thing. Take a bit of bling home from your summer vacation. Open Mon to Fri 9:00 am to 5:30 pm and Sat noon to 4:00 pm.

Lewis Farm Market, New Era Exit ¼ mile east of US-31. (231) 861-5730. Fresh baked pastries, jams, syrup, honey, locally grown vegetables, fruit and other food items. Has a free petting farm. Open summer 7 days, Mon to Sat 9:00 am to 6:00 pm and Sun 11:00 am to 5:00 pm. Closes after October.

Sandbox, 8437 West Silver Lake Road, Mears, (231) 873-4828. Recreational toys, camping equipment, sporting goods and gifts. They describe themselves as a "fun store for fun people." Open 7 days, Sun to Thurs 10:00 am to 7:00 pm, Fri and Sat 10:00 am to 10:00 pm. Weekends only in September and closed in the winter.

Scooterville USA, Souvenir shop at Mac Dunes. (See listing under Dune Rides below).

Silver Lake Dune Town Specialty Shops, Between Craig's Cruisers and Jellystone Park. Several little shops, including: fudge shop, ice cream, bakery, clothing, and jewelry stores. The Colby Designer Outlet is open 7 days 10:00 am to 10:00 pm during the tourist season but closes after Labor Day.

Silver Lake T's, 8430 Silver Lake Road. Beachwear, resort apparel and gifts. Open 7 days 10:00 am to 10:00 pm. Closed winter.

Parks, Beaches and Campgrounds

HideAway Campground, 9671 West Silver Lake Road, Mears www.hideawaycampground.com, info@hideawaycampground.com. (231) 873-4428. Large seasonal, primitive campsites with electric and water. Pull-through sites available. Amenities: restrooms, showers, sanitation station, playground, swimming pool, game room, hiking trails, convenience store and security guard.

Sandy Shores Campground, 8595 West Silver Lake Road, Mears, (231) 873-3303, www.sandyshorescampground.com. 212 sites with private beach on Silver Lake. Amenities: heated outdoor pool, playground equipment, bathrooms, laundry and camp store.

Silver Creek RV Resort, 1441 North 34th Street, Mears, (231) 873-9200, www.silverlakesanddunes.net. New campground with 181 landscaped sites with full hook-up. Amenities: cable, telephone, pool, hot tub, kids' pool and gift shop. Closes October 31st for the season.

Silver Hills Campground Resort, 7594 West Hazel Road, Mears, (231) 873-3976 or toll-free (800) 637-3976. Families welcome in this quiet campground with heated pool. No music and no alcohol allowed.

Silver Lake State Park, 9679 West State Park Road, Mears, (231) 873-3083. A 3,000 acre park with 500 acres of driving dunes and staging area, and 25 acres of camping with more than 200 camp sites. Boat launch and swimming beach. Bathhouse, picnic tables, shelters, grills and firepits. Great place to explore, hike and fish. Vehicle permit required. Hunting (grouse, white-tailed deer, rabbit, and squirrels) allowed in designated areas in season. The park has four miles of Lake Michigan shoreline, mature forests and is the only park in Michigan that allows off-road and all terrain vehicles on designated routes.

Silver Lake Resort and Campground, 1786 North 34th Street, Mears, (231) 873-7199, www.silverlakeresortandcampground.com, camping@silvercreekrv.com. Nearly 200 campsites and 14 rustic camping cabins, bathhouse, playground, swimming pool, full hook-up sites include water, electric and sewer. Convenience store.

Timberlake Resort and RV Club, 4370 Ridge Road, Mears, (231) 873-3285, www.timberlake-resort.com. Overnight and membership camping. Amenities: pontoon boats and Lake Michigan access.

Yogi Bear's Jellystone Park, 8239 West Hazel Road, Mears, (231) 8873-4502. 200 campsites with electric, water and sewer hookups. Amenities: heated pool, pavilion, laundry facilities, movies, recreation room, playground, camp store, bath facilities, organized games, arts, crafts and activities, hayrides, horseshoes, basketball, shuffleboard and billiards. Also cabins for rent. Security patrolled.

Dune Rides and Rentals, Boat Rental and Jet Ski Rentals

Craig's Cruisers (See below, Other Things to See or Do.)

MacWoods Scenic Dune Tours, 629 North 18th Street, Mears, (231) 873-2817. Forty minute rides of the scenic dunes. Gift shop. No reservations required.

Parrot's Landing Jeep Rentals and Wild Bill's Quad Rentals, 8110 West Hazel, Mears (231) 873-8400, www.parrotslanding.com. Rent jet skis, ski boats, mopeds, quads and jeeps. Rentals by the hour, half-day or day. You drive, no guides provided.

Silver Lake Buggy Rentals, 8288 West Hazel Road, Mears, (231) 873-8833, www.silverlakebuggys.com. Explore the sand dunes in a two-seat dune buggy. Open 7 days, Memorial Day through Labor Day.

Wave Club Watersport Rentals, 1560 N. Shore Drive, Mears, www.silverlakesanddunes.net, (231) 873-3700. Rent all types of water equipment including: ski boats, wave runners, kayaks (both single and double), canoes, rowboats, motor boats, sandboards, pontoon boats and paddle boats. Open 7 days, 7:00 am to 8:00 pm.

Ready for a dune ride   ***Photo Courtesy of Jon Royce***

Other Things to See or Do

Craig's Cruisers, 8239 West Hazel Street, Mears, (231) 873-2511, www.craigscruisers.com. Go-Karts, miniature golf, bumper boats, paddle boats, game room, snack bar and gift shop. Open Memorial Day through Labor Day, 7 days, 10:00 am to 11:00 pm.

Hart-Montague Bike Trail. 22½ miles of walking, skating, biking, snowmobiling or cross country skiing depending upon the season. (See Montague, p. 139 for additional information.)

Oceana County Historical Park and Museum, two blocks west of downtown Mears, (231) 873-2600, www.oceanahistory.org, info@oceanahistory.org. Open Memorial Day to Labor Day, Sat and Sun 1:00 pm to 4:00 pm and Wed 1:00 pm to 4:00 pm July and August.

Rainbow Ranch, 4345 South 44th Avenue, located in New Era (take Stony Lake Road Exit off US-31 North, west three miles to 44th street and then ½ mile north), (231) 861-4445, www.rainbowranch-inc.com. Stable open to the public for horseback riding. The ranch has been operating since 1949; in addition to riding you can take lessons, enjoy a hay ride or sleigh ride (depending on season) and revel in the

146

fresh clean air. You will spot wildlife and enjoy the sounds and sights of nature. 70 horses at the stables.

Sandy Korners Adventures, 1762 North 24th Avenue, Mears, www/sandykorners.com, adventuretours@sandykorners.com, (231) 873-5048. Numerous adventures available: Dune Adventure and Beach Adventure (July and August), Fall Color Adventure, Manistee Adventure, Croton Dam Adventure, Drummond Island Challenge and Lake Superior Color Adventure. Take the wheel of a Jeep Wrangler for the thrill of driving up and over the spectacular Silver Lake Sand Dune Mountains for an unforgettable roller-coaster like ride. Reservations recommended. Open 7 days, May 14th through October 31st.

Golf

Benona Shores Golf Course, 3410 Scenic Drive, Shelby, (231) 861-2098. Two miles from the Silver Lake Sand Dunes this is a place for the entire family to enjoy golfing.

Colonial Golf Course, 2763 North 72nd Avenue, Hart, (231) 873-8333. 18 hole, par 72 course, full service bar and restaurant, groups welcome, driving range, senior discounts.

Golden Sands Golf Course, 2501 North Wilson, Mears, (231) 873-4909, www.goldensandsgolfcourse.com. 9-hole, par 33 course with a full driving range and a putting green. Two miles from Silver Lake Sand Dunes.

Oceana Golf Course, 3333 West Weaver Road, Shelby, (231) 861-4211. 18-hole course with small, quick, smooth-rolling greens.

Contacts

Silver Lake Sand Dunes Area Chamber of Commerce, 2388 North Comfort Dr., Hart, (231) 873-2247 or toll-free (800) 870-9786.

Lake Michigan Sand Dunes   *Photo by Jon Royce*

Pentwater

Population: Approximately 1,000.

Directions: **From Detroit, Lansing or Grand Rapids**: take I-96 West to US-31 North. Take Pentwater (Monroe Road) exit and drive 3 miles west. Pentwater is about 50 miles north of Muskegon.

Background and History

A quaint turn of the century town nestled on the shores of Lake Michigan, Pentwater has been nicknamed *"The Nantucket of the Mid-West."* Residents refer to it as "a little piece of heaven," and cherish its slower pace of life. Traffic comes to a halt to let ducks pass. The village has no stop lights and, as of yet, no fast food chains. Life is near-perfect along the sandy stretch of white-sand beach that entices travelers to Pentwater. Quaint shops, B&Bs, restaurants, antiquaries and a full plate of summer activities keep them busy once they arrive.

Pentwater Lake is two miles long and its width varies between ½ and ¾ of a mile. The lake's annual ice harvest cooled local ice chests during hot, steamy summers before modern refrigeration was available.

There are three explanations offered for how Pentwater was named. The first: Native Americans gave it a name meaning "penned-up" waters. The second: it is a variation of "paintwater" from the dark color of Pentwater Lake. And, the third: it comes from the word pentagram meaning five points and refers to Pentwater's five bodies of water: Lake Michigan, the Channel, Pentwater Lake, the flats and the Pentwater River. In the 1800s land in the area was home to about 800 Native Americans, predominantly Pottawatomie, Chippewa and Ottawa.

The town was originally named Middlesex by Charles Mears who built a sawmill there in 1856. Mears' accomplishments earned him the city's respect; often he is referred to as its founder. He was only twenty-three-years-old when he arrived in the White Lake Area in 1837. He made his fortune in virgin timber.

Mears first mill was located on Silver Creek and it quickly became a full-fledged lumber community. Mears built many lumber settlements before branching out into other businesses. He owned thousands of acres stretching from White Lake to Big Point Sable. Before ending his illustrious career he built fifteen mills and five harbors. He was a lumber baron with one of the largest operations in Western Michigan. It is not surprising that he is honored as the founding father of Pentwater. The first land in the Pentwater area sold for $1. to $1.25 per acre.

In truth, however, E.R. Cobb and Andrew Rector had already built a lumber mill and a boarding house on the south end of Hancock Street by 1853, three years before Mears happened on the scene. Their mill and boarding house were separate from Mears' settlement of Middlesex. On March 16, 1867 Cobb's village was incorporated and officially named Pent Water and Middlesex was eventually absorbed into Pent Water. But for many years the area west of Hancock continued to be called Middlesex. It may be more correct to say that Rector and Cobb first founded Pentwater and Mears was one of the area's most important and illustrious early citizens.

Mears established a ferry service across the channel in 1858. He also built a 660 foot long pier into Lake Michigan from the north bank of the channel, so even the largest boats could haul lumber to yards in Chicago and drop cargo in the village of Pentwater on their return trips. Mears' efforts to provide a deeper and wider channel were assisted by the federal government, when it 1868 it began a 20-year project to enhance the size of the channel.

In 1861 the first newspaper was printed in Pentwater. At the time the village boasted three stores, two steam sawmills, one printing press, several fisheries, two lawyers, one minister, and 300 village residents. It was, in fact, the only village in all of Oceana County.

Smoke from the Chicago fire of 1871 could be seen all the way to Pentwater and in 1889 Pentwater blazed with its own devastating fire. The conflagration started in a cigar store on the west side of Hancock Street. The surrounding stores, built of wood and only one story high, quickly went up in flames.

A lighthouse and a life-saving station were established in Pentwater to increase shipping safety. The Pentwater lights stand at the mouth of the Pentwater River, the southern boundary of Charles Mears State Park. (See p. 362, Part II for lighthouse information.)

The waters around Pentwater are believed to hold the skeletons of at least 40 ships. The 1940 Armistice Day storm is the most notorious to hit the area. It claimed 59 sailors that fateful, black, moonless night in November; winds of 80 miles an hour (with gusts reaching 110 miles), and 30 foot waves battered everything within reach. (See p. 387, Part II for shipwreck stories.)

The State Park located on the north side of the village bears Mears' name. His daughter, Carrie, deeded 600 feet of beach north of the channel to the state in 1920. That property marks the beginning of the Mears Park.

Food/Restaurants

The Antler Bar, 283 South Hancock, (231) 869-2911. Family-friendly tavern "where generations have met to eat good food, drink, and tell lies." Mexican dishes and bar food including hamburgers. Open 7 days, Mon to Sat 11:30 am to 2:30 am and Sun noon to 2:30 am.

Boat House Bar and Grille, 5164 West Monroe, (231) 869-4588. Daily lunch specials and a full bar. Appetizers, salads, home-made soups, hamburgers, sandwiches, and pizza. Carry-out available. Open 7 days, 11:00 am. Grill closes 11:00 pm. Karaoke Fri and Sat at 9:30 pm.

The Brown Bear, 278 South Hancock, (231) 869-5444. Known for its Bear Burger, a huge, two-handed monster, full of flavor. Family atmosphere. Serves alcohol: beer, wine, or mixed drinks. Open year round, Mon to Sat 11:00 am to 11:00 pm (grill closes at that time) and Sun noon to 11:00 pm.

The Cottage Garden Café, 40 Third Street, (231) 869-8188. Freshly prepared meat or vegetarian dishes that can be enjoyed on the screened porch with a view of Pentwater Lake. Also serves breakfast with popular Belgian waffles and other morning dishes. The desserts are a worthy finale to lunch. Open 7 days, from 7:30 am to 3:00 pm.

Goodstuffs, 111 South Hancock, (231) 869-5535. Fresh coffee and baked goods along with soups, sandwiches and their own Pentwater preserves. Consider the Pentwater Po' Boy or the George W (regardless of your political affiliation). Hours are not set in stone, but Mon to Sat generally about 9:00 am to 5:00 pm. Open later on Sun.

Gull Landing, 438 South Hancock Street, (231) 869-4215, www.pentwatermichigan.com/gulllanding. Casual dining with a view of Pentwater Lake. Outside seating available in the summer. Dinners and sandwiches (both the Reuben and the Grouper Rachel were excellent), and a soup and salad bar. Jazz Night on the Deck Wed and Sun in the summer. Open mid-June to mid-August Mon to Thurs 7:00 am to 10:00 pm, Fri to Sun 7:00 am to 11:00 pm. Off-season hours Mon to Thurs 7:00 am to 9:00 pm, Fri to Sun 7:00 am to 10:00 pm.

The House of Flavors, 210 South Hancock Street, (231) 869-4009, www.pentwaterflavors.com. More than just an ice-cream place, this establishment offers lunches and dinners. Still, they are best known as the place to get an old-fashioned ice cream sundae or other ice cream treat. Open 7 days, 11:00 am to 10:00 pm.

Lakeside Deli, 401 South Hancock, (231) 869-4728. Deli and party store next to the marina. Breakfast Pizza as well as other early morning options. Also daily lunch and dinner specials. Thursday BBQ ribs and Friday is seafood night. Outdoor seating available. Open 7 days, Sun to Thurs between 5:00 am and 6:00 am, closes at Midnight. Fri and Sat stays open until 2:00 am.

The Main Event, 9587 North Business US-31, (231) 869-5975. Serving three meals each day in a family atmosphere. House specialties are the Swedish pancakes and Camper's Breakfast. Open 7 days, Mon to Sat 8:00 am to 8:00 pm and Sun 8:00 am to 4:00 pm.

Nickerson Inn, 262 West Lowell Street, (231) 869-6731, www.nickersoninn.com. A romantic place to enjoy spectacular views of Lake Michigan sunsets from the all-season dining porch. You can also choose to enjoy your dinner by candlelight in the indoor dining room. The New Zealand Rack of Lamb is superb, the Beef Wellington is awesome and the Fennel Seared Scallops are scrumptious. You will likely need reservations. Open for dinner 7 days, 5:30 pm to 8:30 pm (last reservation accepted). Winter hours may be slightly reduced.

Photo Courtesy of the Nickerson Inn

Pentwater Dari Cream, 11 South Hancock Street, (231) 869-8121. This is more than just ice cream delights like Snickerdoodle Flurry or Bill's Shady Past. You can also order pizza, foot-long subs and wraps.

Rinaldi's Soft Serve and Beach Street Deli, 31 West Lowell Street, (231) 869-5130. Open for over 30 years. Soft serve and deli sandwiches. Also an arcade and 18-hole miniature golf course. An easy stop on your way back from the beach. Open 7 days during the summer, generally 10:00 am to 11:00 pm.

The Village Café and Pub, 347 South Hancock, (231) 869-4626. Enjoy a cocktail and casual dining on the oversized deck with a view of Pentwater Lake. Serves full dinners: steak, chicken or fish, including their Whitefish house specialty. Open mid-May to November 1st. Located downtown, it is a good place to hang out and have fun. Comedy Tues night and live rock bands on weekends. Hours: generally 7 days, 11:30 am to 9:30 pm (earlier or later depending on the crowd).

The Village Grounds, 240 South Hancock, (231) 869-5994, www.thevillagegrounds.com. They claim, "friends don't let friends drink bad coffee" so you should get yours from the Village Grounds. In addition to coffee, they serve specialty drinks including: tea, cocoa, frappes, and smoothies. Also sandwiches (panini, club, fajita, and a build your own option), along with a homemade soup and baked goods offered daily. Breakfast options such as the Breakfast Burrito and Breakfast Panini. Open 7 days, 7:30 am to 9:00 pm. Reduced off-season, Mon to Sat 8:00 am to 5:00 pm and Sun 8:00 am to 4:00 pm.

Lodging (Also see Campgrounds below)

Best Western/Pentwater Trace Inn and Suites, 7576 South Pere Marquette Hwy. (231) 869-8000 or toll-free (800) 780-7234, www.bestwestern.com. Courtyard graced by beautiful landscaping and fountains. Extras: heated indoor pool, whirlpool, 27-inch TV with expanded cable, free high-speed internet and exercise room.

Channel Lane Inn, 10 Channel Lane, (231) 869-5766, www.channellaneinn.com. Located in the village of Pentwater. All rooms have equipped kitchenette and a view of either the channel leading to Lake Michigan or Pentwater Lake. Some rooms are traditional motel style with two double beds and they also have larger rooms, master suites and a two bedroom house by Mears State Park. The Channel Lane Inn may change ownership within the next couple of years, but will most likely remain an inn.

Empty Nest Guest House B&B, 85 Ellery Street, (231) 869-4778, www.pentwatermichigan.com/emptynest. A short walk to Lake Michigan and downtown Pentwater. The guest suite has its own bathroom and separate outdoor entrance, microwave and refrigerator. This is not a traditional B&B with several rooms and a full breakfast, but more like a guesthouse with a continental breakfast.

Fernwood Inn B&B, 6131 Longbridge Road, (231) 869-4765, www.pentwatermichigan.com/fernwood. A quarter of a mile from boat launch. Two suites: one with a queen bed and private sitting area, the second with a queen bed and pull-out queen sofa as well as a private sitting area. Each with a private bath. Pet friendly. Located between Silver Lake and Pentwater.

Ferwerda's Resort, 7100 South Lakeshore Drive, (231) 869-5094, www.basslakeresortmi.com. Popular resort located on the west side of Bass Lake within walking distance of Lake Michigan. The same visitors come year after year.

Hexagon House B&B, 760 Sixth Street, (231) 869-4102, www.hexagonhouse.com. Situated on three beautifully manicured acres, the Inn offers five guest rooms each with private bath. Full breakfast. The owners refer to their uniquely shaped B&B as the "shape of serenity." They have bicycles, croquet, DVD players in each room and a DVD library, wrap-around-porch access from each room. Special romantic weekend packages, spa packages, retreat packages, murder-mystery dinner party, senior citizen discounts, whole house rental for reunion parties and dinner parties with the chef. Enjoy a warming glass˙ of wine in front of the fireplace in the Victorian parlor. Gift certificates and last minute specials. Lovely place to vacation. Open all year.

Photo Courtesy of the Hexagon House B&B

The Historic Nickerson Inn, 262 W. Lowell Street, (231) 869-6731, www.nickersoninn.com. Built in 1913 this near century-old home sits on a bluff overlooking Lake Michigan. It is built of hand-crafted blocks made of Lake Michigan sand. Each of the 10 period-decorated rooms has a private bath and individual temperature control. Lovely place to sit on the porch and absorb the view. Two blocks from Mears Park. A great place to stay in Pentwater. (See picture p. 151.)

Lake Shore Rental Management, 556 South Carroll Street, (231) 869-4256, www.lakeshoreweeklyrentals.com. Helps you find cottages available in the Pentwater area. From small, rustic lakeshore cottages to large, beautiful beachfront homes, this company handles rentals for individual owners. Rates are generally on a weekly basis.

The Pentwater Abbey B&B, 85 West 1ˢᵗ Street, (231) 869-4094, www.pentwaterabbeybb.com. The Abbey was built in 1868 and features country Victorian décor. Three rooms, each with a private bath. It is located two blocks from Lake Michigan. The owners say their guests liken it to a stay at Grandma's house.

The Pineric B&B, 279 East Sands, (231) 869-5471. Located in a pine forest a short walk to downtown Pentwater and Lake Michigan. Associated with "More to Life Christian Ministries." Open seasonally.

Smerts Resort, 6567 South Schlick Road, (231) 869-6972 or toll-free (800) 273-3979, www.3lakesrealty.com/smerts. Seven log cabins on 450 feet of Bass Lake frontage. Each cabin has a fieldstone fireplace and kitchenette. A number of repeat visitors year after year.

Museums and Galleries

Art on the Town features the art of eighteen local artists in such media as paintings, sculptures, jewelry, blown glass and ceramics. (See other shopping below.)

Caesar's Palette, 57 First Street, (231) 869-8880. Displays the works of sixteen local artists. Open 7 days, 10:00 am to 6:00 pm during the season and Thurs to Sat and by appointment in the off-season.

Gatherings, 110 South Hancock Street, (231) 869-5422. This gallery gets its name because it is a "Gathering of Friends" (artists, of course). It selects beautiful designs for inspired living. Open 7 days, 10:00 am to 7:00 pm, reduced to weekends fall through Christmas and Closed January to March.

House of the Setting Sun, South Main Street at Hancock and Fifth, and **Studio RBC**, 119 North Hancock Street, (231) 869-9916. Renee Connoy is associated with both galleries. Studio RBC was her original small gallery tucked away in an alley along the shopping district on Hancock. That location still functions as her studio, but she has moved into the larger and easier to find House of the Setting Sun, a spacious new location displaying artwork that is universal in nature and includes contemporary paintings, drawings, watercolors and sculpture. Open July to August 7 days 10:30 am to 4:00 pm or later. September through June Fri to Sun 10:30 am to 4:00 pm and weekdays by chance or appointment.

Our Gallery, 226 South Hancock Street, (231) 869-8211, www.ourgallery-petri.com. This lovely, bright gallery displays the art of Bert and Cheri Petri and other local and national artists. They also feature an '*Artist of the Month.*' Open through Christmas Mon to Sat 10:00 am to 8:00 pm, Sun noon to 5:00 pm. Reduced hours or by appointment from Christmas to April.

Pentwater Historical Society Museum, 327 Hancock Street (behind the building and in the lower level). This small museum contains interesting local history about the Armistice Day Storm, local buildings, shipping, Charles Mears and more. Open Mon thru Sat, mid-June to mid-September from 2:00 pm to 5:00 pm.

Antiques

Bearied Treasure Curiously Shop, 59 First Street, (231) 869-2327. Antiques and other interesting merchandise. Open 7 days, Memorial Day to Labor Day, 11:00 am to 7:00 pm (generally). Closed October 15th through May 15, unless by appointment.

154

Gifts of the Times (GOTT), 168 South Hancock, (231) 869-5162. Antiques, nostalgia, interior home accessories and lawn and garden items. Also scooters for rent. Open 7 days, Mon to Sat 11:00 am to 7:00 pm and Sun noon to 5:00 pm. Reduced winter hours.

Pelican Zim, 119 South Hancock Street, (231) 869-6006. Some antiques, but also shabby chic and a few unusual items. Open Mon to Sat 10:00 am to 6:00 pm, Sun 10:00 am to 4:00 pm, hours reduced slightly after Labor Day and closed after Christmas for a "few months."

The Secret Garden, 168 South Hancock Street, (231) 869-7300, www.thesecretgarden.pentwater.com. Antiques and collectibles for the home and garden. It is a place where the staff tries to assist you in making your own home and back yard a place to find happiness and tranquility. In addition to antique furniture, linens and glassware, the merchandise includes handcrafted floral arrangements, watercolors, twig furniture and a selection of books. Open 7 days, 11:00 am to 5:00 pm, closed after Christmas until Memorial Day.

Timberdoodle Antiques, 22 South Hancock Street. Unique gifts, vintage clothing, glassware and antiques. Open Mon to Sat 11:00 am to 5:00 pm. Closed Sun.

Other Shopping

Air Fun Kites, 167 Hancock Street, (231) 869-7004, www.air-fun.com. The beautiful dunes of Lake Michigan are the perfect place to fly a kite. Air Fun Kites is the perfect place to buy a kite for your kite-flying experience. Open Sun to Wed 10:00 am to 5:00 pm, Thurs to Sat 10:00 am to 8:00 pm during the season. Reduced hours off-season and January to March by appointment.

Art on the Town, 165 Hancock Street, (231) 869-8107. Art, handmade cards, jewelry and other original gifts. Open summer 7 days, Mon to Sat 10:00 am to 9:00 pm and Sun 11:00 am to 9:00 pm. Hours reduced in the fall and closed January to May.

Avenue on the Green, 240 South Hancock Street, (231) 869-2299, www.aveneueonthegreen.com. This mini-mall houses the Village Green Coffee Shop plus a spa and salon, unique jewelry accessories, Beachbulbs (a tanning salon) and the Happy Woman store.

Bone'z Beach Survival Gear, 2925 South Hancock Street, (231) 869-5383. All kinds of boards: skate boards, skim boards, body boards. Open 7 days, 10:00 am to 9:00 pm in the summer. Reduced hours in the fall and closed November through May.

Chez Moi/Bitchen Kitchen, 320 South Hancock Street, (231) 869-4522, www.chezmoipentwater.com. Anything you can imagine for you kitchen and many things that will leave you wondering. A great store in Pentwater! Located in a former house with the many rooms packed with interesting merchandise including: Crème Brule sets, tea pots, scales, tiffany lamps, mugs, salt and pepper shakers and mills, cloth bags, wallets, duffel bags, cutting boards and more. Open Mon to Sat 9:00 am to 9:00 pm in the summer and the remainder of the year Mon to Sat 10:00 am to 5:00 pm and Sun 11:00 am to 4:00 pm.

Colby's Designer Outlet, 438 South Hancock Street, (231) 869-5868. Some interesting fashion items, most under $16.98. (See listing under Whitehall p. 136 for additional information.)

Craze, 482 Hancock, (231) 869 2200. Junior and Missy size boutique. Open Sun to Thurs 10:00 am to 5:00 pm, Fri and Sat 10:00 am to 9:00 pm.

Decors by Sandra, 240 South Hancock Street, (231) 869-7961. Vintage jewelry, great and varied selection of greeting cards and much in between. Open Year round.

Durand Wine Company, 161 South Hancock Street, (231) 869-5520, www.durandwinecompany.com. Large selection of domestic and imported wines (over 1200 varieties). Also carries a nice selection of cheese and imported beers. They boast the ability to offer quality products at chain store prices. Discounts on purchases of six or more bottles of wine. Summer hours: Mon to Sat 10:00 am to 6:30 pm and Sun 10:00 am to 5:00 pm. Fall hours: Mon to Sat 10:00 am to 6:30 pm, Sun noon to 5:00 pm. Winter hours reduced slightly more.

Elise, 252 South Hancock Street, (231) 869-0252. Upscale boutique Open May to October, 7 days, Mon to Sat 10:00 am to 6:00 pm and Sun noon to 4:00 pm.

Gardener's Folly, 119 Hancock Street, (231) 869-7773, www.gardenersfolly.com. 2005 Retail Excellence Award Winner. Selection of garden, cottage, household, games, dishes, picnic baskets, wall art, jewelry, home accessories and more. Another wonderful store in Pentwater! Open 7 days, Mon to Sat 10:30 am to 5:00 pm and Sun 10:30 am to 4:00 pm.

Max and Chloe's, 119 South Hancock Street, (231) 869-8328. Clothing, jewelry and art. Hours change seasonally, but open all year. Summer generally open 7 days, 10:00 am to 7:00 or 8:00 pm. Closes at 4:00 pm on Sun unless there is a crowd.

Oldewick Post, 134 South Hancock Street, (231) 869-4322. Homemade fudge, espresso bar and a wide selection of gift items. Open 7 days, 9:00 am to 8:00 pm (or about those times). Reduced in the fall to 10:00 am to 6:00 pm and closed January through March.

Pentwater Toy Box, South Hancock Street, (231) 869-8697. The owners claim they "sell fun, right out of the box." A selection to please all ages. Open Mon to Wed 10:00 am to 5:00 pm, Thurs to Sat 10:00 am to 8:00 pm and Sun noon to 5:00 pm.

156

Pentwater Gourmet Popcorn and Cosmic Candy Company, 168 Hancock, (231) 869-4852, www.pentwaterpopcorn.com. A newcomer in town. If popcorn is your weakness you need to stop here. Kids will love the candy treats.

Pentwater River Outfitters, 42 West Second Street, (231) 869-2999, www.pentwaterriveroutfitters.com. The place to buy or just rent a bike (including tandems). Also rents one or two-person-kayaks. Sells beach and camping gear. Open 7 days, Memorial Day to Labor Day 10:00 am to 5:00 pm.

Provisions Sport Shop, 347 South Hancock Street, (231) 869-4626. Sporting goods, sportswear with such labels as Brandsilk and Woolrich. Hours generally 7 days, 10:00 am to 9:00 pm, reduced in the fall and closed November to April.

Rip Girl, 292 South Hancock Street, (231) 869-4863. Junior surfwear. Open 7 days, 10:00 am to 9:00 pm in the summer. Reduced hours in the fall and closed November through May.

Sassafras Tees, 298 South Hancock Street, (231) 869-4320. Resort wear for entire family. Open 7 days, 10:00 am to 9:00 pm in the summer. Reduced hours in the fall and closed November through May.

Parks, Beaches and Campgrounds

Charles Mears State Park, 400 West Lowell Street, (231) 869-2051, www.michigan.gov/dnr. Sandy swimming beach and campgrounds located on Lake Michigan. Beach has swings and bathhouse.

Hill and Hollow Campground, 8915 North Business US-31, (231) 869-5851, www.hillandhollowcamp.com. Large, wooded sites located 1½ miles north of Pentwater and a ten minute bike ride to Lake Michigan. Access to AJ's Family Fun Center (go-carts, arcade and miniature golf). Extras: two heated pools with sun decks, Galley Café, camp store stocked with ice, firewood, and other camping necessities, playgrounds with basketball and volleyball courts, softball field, horseshoe pits and a fish cleaning station.

Riverfarm Campground, 5480 West Wayne Road, (231) 869-8127, www.riverfarmcampground.com. Located on thirty wooded acres in Oceana County with large wooded sites, picnic tables, firepits, electric, tent campsites without electricity, hot showers, playground, ice, firewood, horseshoe pits and a volley ball court.

Whispering Surf Camping Resort, 7090 South Lakeshore Drive (231) 869-5050. Campsites since 1913 with a beach on Bass Lake and only a short walk to Lake Michigan.

Marinas, Water Sports, Boat and Jet Ski Rental

Charlie's Marina, 240 West 6th Street, (231) 869-5000, www.charliesmarina.com. Charlie's purchased Pentwater Point last year and has transient slips for your boat or yacht close to downtown shops and restaurants.

Pentwater Municipal Marina, Hancock Street, (231) 869-7028. Harbor Master on duty May 1st to October 31st, 7:00 am to 7:00 pm.

Pentwater River Rentals, 145 South Hancock, (231) 869-2999. The place to rent kayaks and bicycles.

Cruises, Ferries and Sportfishing

Sportsmen Sportfishing Charters, Municipal Marina, (231) 845-1722 or (231) 206-2820, www.sportsfishingcharters.com. Fish with Captain Brent Daggett aboard a 31-foot Chris Craft, fully-equipped to ensure the best opportunity to catch that trophy fish. You need a fishing license with trout and salmon stamp, or a daily license, your lunch and drinks, soft-soled shoes, sunglasses, sun block, camera, cooler (for your catch), warm jacket, and rain gear (if weather is at all "iffy"). All fishing equipment is provided.

Wizard Sportfishing Charter, Municipal Marina, (231) 638-7125. Wizard has been offering sportfishing charters for more than 20 years. They currently use a 34-foot, fully-loaded, Luhrs Sportfisherman.

Sailing aboard the Irish Wake, Snug Harbor Marina, (231) 629-0739, www.irishwakeenterprises.com. Sail Lake Michigan on this 30-foot Pearson Sailboat. USCG inspected. 90 minute sailing excursions open to the public from mid-May through mid-October. Private charters are also available.

Other Things to See and Do

AJ's Family Fun Center, 8942 North Business 31, (231) 869-5451. Go-Karts, Video Arcade, mini-golf, pavilion and playscape. Open Memorial Day to Labor Day, 7 days, 11:00 am to 11:00 pm.

Halcyon Nature Center, 780 Sixth Street, (231) 869-8221. Offers 2½ acres of native trees, pond (with two small islands), and nature trails with labeled flowers, rocks and trees. No charge, but stop at the entry house before entering the nature center. Group guided tours available.

Jomagrha Winery, 7365 South Pere Marquette Highway, (231) 869-4236, www.jomagrha.com, info@jomagrha.com. Located one mile from Lake Michigan and four miles north of Pentwater, this winery has a limited production of its French-hybrid plantings and other wines from the harvests of local vineyards. Tasting after April, Thurs to Mon 1:00 pm to 6:00 pm.

Rinaldi's Mini Golf (see listing under Food above).

Festivals

Annual Community Wide Garage Sale, Saturday of Father's Day Weekend.

Annual Pentwater Civic Band Concerts, Thursdays from June through Labor Day, 8:00 pm on the Village Green.

Annual Spring Fest Arts and Craft Fair, Second Saturday and Sunday in June on the Village Green.

Annual Strawberry Shortcake Festival, Saturday of Father's Day weekend, Village Square, 10:00 am to 4:00 pm.

National Asparagus Festival and Parade, Second full weekend in June beginning on Friday.

Pickin' in Pentwater, June through August, 7:00 pm on Village Green.

Annual Fireworks Show, July 3rd. Begins at dusk in Charles Mears State Park.

Annual Pie Contest and Auction, July 4th weekend. Everyone welcome to enter. Held on the Village Green.

Annual "one day" Fine Arts Fair, second Saturday in July, 9:00 am to 5:00 pm.

St. Vincent's Arts and Crafts Fair, fourth Saturday in July, 9:00 am to 4:00 pm.

Annual Pentwater Homecoming Celebration, second full weekend in August beginning on a Thursday, many events on the Village Green. A parade and fireworks on Saturday in Charles Mears State Park beginning at dusk.

Annual Merchants' Sidewalk Sale, last weekend in August beginning on a Friday.

Wine at the Harbor, second Saturday in September from 2:00 pm to 6:00 pm in Snug Harbor Marina.

Annual Fall Festival, last full weekend in September. Features an "Open Air" Arts and Crafts Fair, Saturday and Sunday. Beach Run 5K and 10K races on Saturday.

Golf

Driftwood Golf Course, Washington and Brye, (231) 869-5012. Open to the public. 9 holes, par 36, power carts, driving range and rental equipment.

Contacts

Pentwater Chamber of Commerce, 324 South Hancock, (231) 869-4150 or toll-free (866) 869-4150, www.pentwater.org, travelinfo@pentwater.org.

Oceana County Visitors Bureau, toll-free (800) 874-3982, www.oceana.net.

Ludington

Population: 8,357 as of 2000.

Directions: **From Lansing or Detroit**: I-96 West to Grand Rapids, US-31 North to US-10/East Ludington Avenue. **From Chicago**: I-94 East towards Detroit to I-196/US-31 North towards Holland, merge into US-31 North, to US-10/East Ludington Avenue.

Background and History

Ever since French Jesuit missionary and explorer Father Jacques Marquette first landed on the narrow peninsula dividing Lake Pere Marquette and Lake Michigan, Ludington's destiny has been tied to her water.

Father Marquette preached Easter Sunday, 1675, at a Native American village on the shore of the Illinois River. His health had deteriorated and death was imminent. His last earthly wish was to return to his beloved mission at St. Ignace, but on May 18, he collapsed and died in route. His remains were laid to rest in Ludington, or at least that is the story told here. A memorial and large iron cross mark the approximate location of his supposed grave. Historians are not so sure.

Frankfort claims Father Marquette died in their small village and, like Ludington, has erected monuments at the death site. A third story recounts that immediately preceding his death, Father Marquette planted a cross on a bluff overlooking Lake Michigan at the site that eventually became Cross Village. Regardless of where his remains were initially interred, there is agreement that his bones were later dug up and carried to St. Ignace where he wished them buried.

The area around Ludington was a wilderness in 1845 when Burr Casswell began setting traps and fishing the mouth of the Pere Marquette River. Captivated by the beauty that surrounded him, Casswell moved his family to the area two years later and began a small community known as Pere Marquette Village.

In 1849 the Casswells built a two story wood-frame house on their farm. In 1855 the first floor of their home was converted into the county's first courthouse. In 1976 the Mason County Historical Society restored the building which now stands as part of White Pine Village (see below under museums).

The town was later renamed for industrialist James Ludington who lived in the area and owned several logging operations in the late 19th and early 20th centuries. The city enjoyed an era of prosperity in the late 1800s due to both lumbering and the discovery of salt deposits nearby. By 1892, 162 million board feet of lumber and 52 million wood shingles had been produced by the Ludington sawmills. Logging was instrumental in turning Ludington into a major port for transportation of "green gold."

In 1897, the Pere Marquette Railroad constructed a fleet of ferries to transport rail cargo across Lake Michigan to Manitowoc, Wisconsin where the cargo cars resumed their rail journey. The fleet later expanded to carry automobiles and passengers across the Lake. In the mid-1950s, Ludington became the largest car ferry port in the world.

Today only one car ferry, the SS Badger, makes regular trips across the Lake from Ludington to Manitowoc. It is one of only two lake-crossing car ferries on Lake Michigan; Muskegon has the other.

As a visitor to this area, you may want to take the ferry to Manitowoc and spend the afternoon. (See Other Things to See or Do below.) Or, you may enjoy eighteen miles of hiking and biking trails through forests of hardwoods along Ludington State Park's seemingly endless stretch of Lake Michigan Beach. Big Sable Point Lighthouse, one of the tallest lighthouses on the Great Lakes, maintains its vigil along that sandy shore. (See p. 362, Part II for further information about the lighthouse.) You should also check out the Pumped Storage Project (See Other Things to See and Do below). It is a one-of-a-kind educational experience for the entire family.

Food/Restaurants

Anna Bach Chocolates and Danish Pastries, 102 West Ludington Avenue, (231) 843-9288 or toll-free (877) 363-6917. Authentic Danish coffee cakes and kringles. Delicious chocolates. Open summer: Mon to Sat 9:00 am to 8:00 pm and closed Sun. Winter hours reduced: Mon to Fri 10:00 am to 6:00 pm and Saturday 10:00 am to 6:00 pm.

Bortell's Fisheries, 5528 South Lakeshore Drive, (231) 843-3337. Named One of the Ten Best "Seafood Shacks" in America, this fish market allows you to purchase fresh or smoked fish to take home or have cooked on the premises. You can buy just fish (by the piece or by the pound) or a complete dinner. The menu includes walleye, catfish, trout, smelt, perch and whitefish from nearby waters. Strictly take-out, there is no dining room. Once you get your fish, find a picnic table, grab a bit of beach or sit under an ancient beech tree. Whatever your choice, Lake Michigan provides the best ambiance to be found anywhere. The fishery has been in business for over 100 years and is currently operated by the 5th generation of a local fishing family. Open 7 days, 11:00 am to 8:00 pm, Memorial Day to Labor Day.

Chef John's European Bakery and Café, 110 West Filer Street, (231) 843-3327. A unique restaurant and bakery offering tempting pastries and freshly prepared homemade soups, hearty deli sandwiches and specialty breakfasts served in a relaxed European café atmosphere with artistic surroundings. Open Mon to Sat 8:00 am to 4:00 pm.

House of Flavors, 402 West Ludington Avenue (231) 845-5785, www.houseofflavors.com. Serving wonderful homemade ice-cream is the mainstay of this chain. But, the House of Flavors also offers breakfast (served all day) and lunch and dinner with homemade soups and other freshly prepared items. In the 1960s, when it was the Park Dairy, local kids blew their straw papers at the ceiling where they stuck; a phenomenon that actually earned a story in Life Magazine. Open 7 days, 7:00 am to 10:00 pm.

James Street Station, 320 South James Street, (231) 845-7575. American and Mexican appetizers and entrees (including nachos), and standard bar food. Try the Philly Sandwich. The Station is a favorite with locals. Open Mon to Wed 4:00 pm to at least 11:30 pm, Thurs 4:00 pm to 2:00 am, Fri and Sat 11:30 am to 2:00 am. Closed Sun.

Jamesport Brewing Company, 410 South James Street, (231) 845-2522, www.jamesportbrewingco.com. A brew pub with many beers to consider. For dinner, try the Grilled Chicken Triple Sec, Cajun Chicken Pasta or one of the seafood features such as the Blackened Walleye. Save room for the Bananas Foster. Nightly specials. Open daily at 11:30 am and serves lunch and dinner.

Kuntry Kubbard, 5474 US-10 at old US-31, (231) 845-5217. Home-cooking with a wide range of options including: sandwiches, dinners (fish, meatloaf. chicken, steaks, veal, baskets, lasagna), baskets, children's menu, senior menu and a large selection of breakfast items. Open 7 days, 7:00 am to 9:00 pm.

The Landing Restaurant, 4079 West US-10 (Located in the Ramada Convention Center), (231) 845-7311. Whether you order a porterhouse steak with steamed shrimp or a veggie wrap with fries, the menu items are diverse enough to please every appetite. Open 7 days, 7:00 am to 2:00 am. Closed major holidays.

Lannigan's Café, 110 North James Street, (231) 845-7041. Serves sandwiches, soups and sweets. Open Mon to Sat 8:00 am to 3:00 pm. Closed Sun.

Le Serving Spoon, 130 West Ludington Avenue, (231) 843-6555. Serves breakfast specials, lunch crepes, and also offers bakery items. Open 7 days, Mon to Sat 8:00 am to 6:00 pm, Sun 8:00 am to 4:00 pm.

Luciano's Restaurant, 103 West Ludington Avenue, (231) 845-2244. Recommended by several local residents. Serves homemade Italian food such as Three Cheese Angel Hair Pasta with Scallops and Shrimp. You can get pizza by the slice. Open 7 days, Mon to Sat 11:00 am to 9:00 pm and Sun 11:00 am to 9:00 pm.

Michael's On the Avenue, 129 West Ludington Avenue, (231) 845-7411. Their motto is: Good Food, Good Times and Good Friends. Full service bar. Open Mon to Thurs 11:00 am to midnight, Fri and Sat 11:00 am to 2:30 am.

Old Hamlin Restaurant, 122 West Ludington Avenue, (231) 843-4251. Owned and operated by the same family since the early 1940s and a favorite among both locals and tourists. The name Old Hamlin, comes from the original restaurant which was located on Hamlin Lake just north of Ludington. They serve breakfast, lunch, and dinner buffets with American, Greek and Mexican specialties, and fresh homemade breads and pies. Carry-out available and full bar service. Open 7 days, 5:30 am to 9:00 pm.

PM Steamers, 502 West Loomis Street, (231) 843-9555, www.pmsteamers.com. Voted one of the top waterfront restaurants by *USA Today*. The signature Pepper Krab Bisque is the perfect way to start your meal. Even with all of the fancy food, the Wild Mushroom Meatloaf might catch your attention. The Vegetable Stir Fry suits the health conscious. Gracious staff and glorious sunset views. Open 7 days for lunch and dinner, 11:00 am to 10:00 pm. Closes two days a week beginning in October and is only open for dinner.

Scotty's Restaurant, 5910 East Ludington Avenue, (231) 843-4033. Scotty's casual, relaxed dining has a devoted following in Mason County. Homemade soups and entrees from Lake Perch to Prime Rib. Open lunch Mon to Fri 11:30 am to 2:00 pm, dinner Sun to Thurs 5:00 pm to 9:00 pm and Fri and Sat 5:00 pm to 10:00 pm. Closed Sun.

Sportsman's Restaurant and Irish Pub, 111 West Ludington Avenue, (231) 843-2138, www.sportsmansirishpub.com. Modestly priced but good bar food. Open year round Mon to Thurs 11:00 am to 11:00 pm, Fri and Sat 11:00 am to midnight and Sun noon to 10:00 pm.

Lodging (Also see Campgrounds below)

Abbey Lynn Inn B&B, 603 East Ludington Avenue, (231) 845-7127 or toll-free (800) 796-5421, www.abbeylynninn.com. 1890s Colonial Inn located near the beaches. Five rooms, each with private bath. Enjoy a special murder mystery weekend. Fresh cookies when you arrive. Elegant breakfast.

Cartier Mansion, 409 East Ludington Avenue (231) 843-0101 or toll-free (877) 843-0101, www.cartiermansion.com. A neo-classical mansion built in 1903 by Mr. Warren Cartier, a Ludington lumber baron. The mansion has been featured in *Historic Homes of America* and *Grand Homes of the Midwest* and is a premier place to stay in the city. The woodwork is beautiful and the home is furnished with lovely antiques and original chandeliers. Breakfast included. Seven guest rooms with a range of sizes (from large and spacious to small, former maid's quarters). Amenities vary by room.

Days Inn of Ludington, 5095 West US-10, (231) 843-2233 or toll-free (800) 329-7466, 62 rooms. Extras: kitchenettes available, suites with whirlpools, pets allowed, HBO, continental breakfast, internet and parking available for boats/trailers.

Four Seasons Lodging, 717 East Ludington Avenue, (231) 843-3448 or toll-free (800) 968-0180, www.lodgingandbreakfast.com. 28 rooms. Extras: kitchenettes, full gourmet breakfast, and special vacation packages available.

Greiner Motel, 4616 West US-10, (231) 843-3927 or toll-free (800) 968-1848, www.greinermotel.com. Basic, family owned motel with 22 rooms. Extras: car ferry shuttle and internet access.

Holiday Inn Express, 5323 West US-10, (231) 845-7004, or toll-free (866) 432-0209, www.stayludington.com. 102 rooms. Extras: indoor pool, car ferry shuttle, kitchenettes, special packages, whirlpool suites, pets allowed, continental breakfast, fitness and game rooms.

The Inn at Ludington, 701 East Ludington Avenue, (231) 845-7055 or toll-free (800) 845-9170, www.inn-ludington.com. Victorian home built in 1890 and currently standing at the edge of the historic "*Old Town*" area. Six rooms, each with private bath and lovely furnishings. The Great Lakes Victorian Suite has a warm fireplace. Special murder mystery weekends. Breakfast included.

Lakeside Inn of Ludington, 808 West Ludington Avenue, (231) 843-3458 or toll-free (800) 843-2177, www.lakesideinnludington.com. 52 rooms. Extras: special packages, heated outdoor pool, across from public beach and ferry shuttle.

Lakeview Cottages, 420 North Ferry Street, (231) 843-3578, www.lakeviewcot.com. Fully furnished cottages, from efficiency to two bedrooms, within walking distance of downtown Ludington, Stearns Park, and Lake Michigan. Seven units that can be rented by the day or by the week.

The Lamplighter B&B, 602 East Ludington Avenue, (231) 843-9792 or toll-free (800) 301-9792, www.ludington-michigan.com. This house was built around 1894 to serve as both home and office to Dr. Crosby, a local surgeon. Over the years it has taken on many uses, but is now restored to its former Victorian elegance. Five guest rooms each with private bath. Romance, murder mystery and other special packages. Full breakfast included.

Ludington House Victorian B&B, 501 East Ludington Avenue, (231) 845-7769 or toll-free (800) 827-7869, www.ludingtonhouse.com. Built in 1878, this Victorian offers eight guest rooms each with private bath. Full Breakfast included.

Ludington Pier House, 805 West Ludington Avenue, (231) 845-7348 or toll-free (800) 968-3677, www.ludingtonpierhouse.com. 28 rooms. Extras: indoor pool, vacation packages and across from Lake Michigan.

Nader's Lakeshore Motor Lodge, 612 North Lakeshore Drive, (231) 843-8757 or toll-free (800) 968-0109, www.nadersmotel.com. 39 rooms. Extras: car ferry shuttle, vacation packages, outdoor pool, whirlpool suites, kitchenettes, pets allowed and cable.

Nova Motel, 472 Pere Marquette Highway, (231) 843-3454 or toll-free (800) 828-3162, www.novamotel.com. Basic rooms. Whirlpool suites available, pets allowed, heated pool, whirlpool spa and HBO.

Ramada Inn & Convention Center, 4079 West US-10, (231) 845-7311 or toll-free (800) 272-6232, www.ramadaludington.com. 107 rooms. Extras: indoor pool, vacation packages, rock climbing wall, whirlpool suites available, pets, fitness room, internet and game room.

Snyder's Shoreline, 903 West Ludington Avenue, (231) 845-1261, www.snydersshoreinn.com. 44 rooms. Extras: outdoor pool, vacation packages, whirlpool suites available, breakfast, internet access and private balconies.

Stearns Motor Inn, 212 East Ludington Avenue (231) 843-3407 or toll-free (800) 365-1904, www.stearnsmotorinn.com. 50 rooms in downtown historic hotel. Extras: kitchenettes and efficiencies, whirlpool rooms available, fireplace suites, internet and fitness room.

Super 8 Motel, 5005 West US-10, (231) 843-2140 or toll-free (800) 800-8000, www.ludingtonsuper8.com. 85 rooms. Extras: indoor pool, car ferry shuttle, vacation packages, kitchenettes available, whirlpool and fireplace suites, pets allowed, breakfast, playground and picnic area, grills, waterslide, fitness room, game room and internet.

Ventura Motel, 604 Ludington Avenue, (231) 845-5124 or toll-free (800) 968-1440, www.ventura-motel.com. 25 rooms. Extras: car ferry shuttle, free early morning coffee, and freezer space for fish.

Viking Arms Inn, 930 East Ludington Avenue, (231) 843-3441 or toll-free (800) 748-0173, www.vikingarmsinn.com. Basic motel with 45 rooms. Extras: outdoor pool, vacation packages, whirlpool and fireplace suites available, breakfast, internet access and in-room coffee.

Vista Villa Motel, 916 East Ludington Avenue, (231) 843-9320 or toll-free (800) 358-2402, www.visitludington.com/vistavilla. Standard motel with 40 rooms. Extras: whirlpool suites available.

Museums and Galleries

Art Center, 127 West Ludington Avenue, (231) 845-0501. Open Mon to Sat 10:00 am to 5:00 pm. Closed Sunday.

Artist's Market, 925 South Washington Avenue, (231) 845-6648, www.artistsmarketonline.com. Original paintings, prints, pottery, photography and more. Complete line of artist supplies. Open all year, call for hours.

Hen House Studios @ the Mermaids Perch, 416 South James Street, (231) 690-6058. (See Mermaid's Perch, Other Shopping below.)

Majestic Art Gallery, 115 South James Street, (231) 843-2585. Open Wed to Sat 6:00 pm to closing.

Melting Sands Glass Studio, 5910 East Ludington Avenue, (Behind Scotty's Restaurant), (231) 794-9101, www.judscott.com. You are invited inside Jud Scott's working studio to watch the transformation of molten glass into beautiful artwork. Summer open Tues to Sat 10:00 am to 6:00 pm, or by appointment.

The Red Door Gallery, 310 West Ludington Avenue, (231) 843-4529 or (231) 392-4709. Contemporary fine art and crafts from Michigan. Open Mon to Sat 10:00 am to 5:00 pm, Sun noon to 4:00 pm. Closed Tuesdays.

White Pine Village, 1687 South Lakeshore Drive, (231) 843-4808, www.historicwhitepinvillage.org, info@historicwhitepinevillage.org. This historic village allows you to rediscover life in small-town Michigan as it was in the late 1800s. The entire family will enjoy this interesting and educational experience. The village features more than 25 buildings/sites of history on 23 acres. Artifacts of lumbering, music, farming, small rural villages, maritime, sports and the development of business and industry. Buildings include a sawmill, one room school, and a courthouse among many others. The village has numerous special events. Call the above number for details. Open Tues to Sun, 10:00 am to 5:00 pm. Closed Mon except for Memorial Day and Labor Day.

Theatre

West Shore Community College Cultural Arts Series, Center Stage Theatre, (231) 845-6211, ext 3344, www.westshore.edu. Dinner theatre, concerts and cultural presentations. Call for information.

Antiques

Cole's Antiques Villa, 322 West Ludington Avenue, (231) 845-7414, www.colesantiquesvilla.com. Approximately 5,000 square feet of space and nearly 30 dealers. Variety of quality antiques in pleasant displays. Summer open Mon to Sat 10:00 am to 5:00 pm, Sun noon to 5:00 pm. Closed Mon in September, Mon and Tues in October. Further reductions until closes completely January to beginning of summer.

Sunset Bay Antiques, 404 South James Street, (231) 843-1559. Vintage jewelry, clothing, stained glass, furniture, books and toys. Open Mon to Fri noon to 5:00 pm, Sat and Sun 11:00 am to 5:00 pm.

Other Shopping

ABC Kidz, 5905 West US-10 and 123 East Ludington Avenue (231) 843-3734. Clothing, furniture and toys for children. Oshkosh, Biti Kids and Hartstrings. Open 7 days, Mon to Fri 10:00 am to 5:30 pm, Sat 10:00 am to 5:00 pm and Sun noon to 4:00 pm.

Bella Casa, 103 East Ludington Avenue (231) 843-1011. Treasures for your home, kitchenware, gadgets, candles, gourmet foods, table linens, cookware, household furnishings and items for pampering yourself. Open 7 days, 10:00 am to 6:00 pm.

The Book Mark, 201 South Rath Avenue, (231) 843-2537. Largest selection of books, magazines and newspapers in the area. Has a special section featuring Michigan authors. You can also enjoy a cup of your favorite latte, cappuccino, mocha, frappe or smoothie with their fresh baked goods. Open 7 days, 8:00 am to 9:00 pm.

The Christmas Shop, 123 West Ludington Avenue, (231) 843-0968. If summer vacation makes you long for Christmas, this place has ornaments for every interest, hobby and sport. Open year round.

Evergreen Natural Foods Market, 106 West Ludington Avenue, (231) 843-1000. Besides natural foods they carry interesting gifts, jewelry and accessories. Open 7 days, Mon to Sat 10:00 am to 6:00 pm and Sun noon to 4:00 pm. (May be open longer in the summer.)

Fort Daul, 101 West Ludington, (231) 843-2890. Moccasins, souvenirs, gifts, jewelry and interesting merchandise for the entire family. Great murals on the outside of the building. Open 7 days, 11:00 am to 8:00 pm.

Gordy's, 109 West Ludington Avenue, (231) 845-9100, www.gordysskateco.com. Skateboards, skimboards, snowboards, rollerblades, sport shoes and sports clothing. Open 7 days, Mon to Sat 10:00 am to 8:00 pm and Sun 11:00 am to 6:00 pm.

Mariellen's Hallmark Store, 116 East Ludington Avenue, (231) 843-9460. Vera Bradley bags, music boxes, stuffed animals and, of course, cards and paper products. Open Mon to Sat 9:30 am to 9:00 pm.

Mermaid's Perch, 416 South James Street, (231) 843-6893. Toys, gifts and accents. Open Mon to Thurs 11:00 am to 6:00 pm (approximately) and Sun 1:00 pm to 5:00 pm.

Newberry Cottage, 104 West Ludington Avenue, (231) 843-6830, www.newberrycottage.com. Home and garden décor, pillows, antiques, painted furniture and floral designs. Open Mon to Sat 10:00 am to 8:00 pm, Sun 10:00 am to 6:00 pm. Closed Sun and Mon after Labor Day.

Sandcastles at the Beach, Ludington Avenue at the lake, (231) 843-3008. Garden items, t-shirts, gifts, accents, Swan Creek Candles. Open 7 days 10:00 am to 9:00 pm during the summer. Also a place to rent vacation cottages, condos and homes.

Seasons on the Shore, 110 West Ludington Avenue, (231) 843-8200. Home accents and gifts including: Mikasa Crystal, Polish Pottery, Wilton Armetal, Arthur Court and Coaster Stone. Also carries a large assortment of Ludington sweatshirts, t-shirts and souvenirs. Open 7 days, 10:00 am to 6:00 pm.

Ships Locker, 116 West Ludington Avenue, (231) 843-4514. Nautical gifts and accents. Varied hours, Memorial Day to Labor Day.

Wolf's Den, 880 West US-10, six miles east of Ludington, (231) 757-7000, www.wolf-log-homes.com. Primarily log homes, but also a selection of unique gift items by 14 talented artists. You will find: unique mirrors, chainsaw carvings, one-of-a-kind furniture, candles and more. Open 7 days, Mon to Fri 8:00 am to 5:00 pm, Sat 10:00 am to 4:00 pm and Sun noon to 4:00 pm.

Parks, Beaches and Campgrounds

Buttersville Park and Camping, 991 South Lakeshore Drive, (231) 843-3943. Park Amenities: camping, picnic area, grills, restrooms, playground, beach. Shelter can be reserved. 44 campsites with: electric hook-up, showers, boating access, fishing on site, swimming, playground, pets allowed and a sanitation station.

Cartier Campground, 1254 North Lakeshore Drive, (231) 845-1522, www.cpcampground.com. 164 sites, reservations accepted. Amenities: electric, water and sewer hook-up, modern restrooms, showers, boating access, store, fishing on site, playground, pets allowed and sanitation station.

Copeyon Park, South Washington Avenue, (231) 845-6237. Open year round. Amenities: picnic area, playground and fishing.

Kibby Creek Park, Pere Marquette Highway, (231) 843-6304. Open 24 hours. Amenities: picnic area, rustic restrooms, artesian well.

Ludington City Park, West Ludington Avenue, (231) 845-6237. Open 24 hours. Amenities: picnic area, tables and grills, restrooms, swings, play area and band shell by reservation.

Ludington State Park, End of Highway M-116 at Lake Michigan, www.midnrreservations.com, (231) 843-8671 or toll-free (800) 44-PARKS. Park closes to visitors at 11:00 pm. Park is 5,300 acres and a pass is needed to enter. 347 camp sites (reservations accepted), electric hook-up, modern toilets and showers, cabins available, boating access, fishing, and concessions. Other amenities: picnic areas, grills, fishing, beaches, bath houses, playground, canoe and boat rentals, swimming, hiking and biking trails, restaurant, internet access and general store. Pets allowed.

Mason County Campground, 5906 West Chauvez Road, (231) 845-7609. 279 acres with 54 campsites and reservations accepted.

Amenities: water and electric hook-ups, modern restrooms and showers, playground, sanitation station and pets allowed.

Mason County Picnic Area, West Chauvez off Pere Marquette Highway, (231) 843-9361. Open 9:00 am to 9:00 pm. Amenities: shelter, picnic area, playground, disc golf course and restrooms.

Memorial Tree Park, North Washington Avenue at Ivanhoe, (231) 843-9361. Open 9:00 am to 9:00 pm. Amenities: shelter (reservations needed), picnic area, grills, playground and ball field.

Nordhouse Dunes, a National Wilderness Area within the Manistee National Forest offering 3,450 acres of unique ecosystem that is the only designated wilderness in the Lower Peninsula. From Ludington take US-10 East to Stiles Road, turn north (left). At Townline Road turn right, then left on Quarterline Road. Turn west (left) on Nurnberg Road and follow it to the end.

Poncho's Pond, 5335 West Wallace Lane, (231) 845-7711. RV campground, Amenities: full hook-up, three pools (one adult-only outdoor pool, one indoor pool with spa and one outdoor family pool), a fishing pond, cable TV and family activities on the weekend.

Stearns Park Beach, North Lakeshore Drive, (231) 845-6237. Open all the time. Amenities: picnic area, grills, playground, beach and summer concessions.

Summit Park, South Lakeshore Drive, (231) 845-6304. Open 8:00 am to 10:00 pm. Amenities: shelter (reservation only), picnic area, grills, playground, restrooms, ball field, tennis court and beach.

Suttons Landing, Iris Road off Pere Marquette Highway, (231) 843-9361. Open 24 hours. Amenities: shelter, picnic area, restrooms, boat launch and boardwalk along the river.

Victory Township, Upper Hamlin Lake Victory Park Road. Open all the time. Amenities: picnic area, grills and boat launch.

Waterfront Park, South William Street between the City Municipal and Harbor View Marinas, (231) 845-6237. Newly developed City Park with an amphitheater. Bronze sculptures take the visitor on an interesting trip through local history. Other amenities: playground and picnic shelter. The Waterfront Walkway extends from downtown Ludington to the south end of William Street, north to Stearns Park.

Wilson Hill Park, Upper Hamlin Lake-Barnhart Road. Open dawn to dusk. Amenities: picnic area, grills, boat launch and ball field.

Marinas, Water Sports, Boat and Jet Ski Rental

Harbor View Marina, 400 South Rath Avenue, (231) 843-6032, www.harborviewmarina.com. Full service marina with seasonal and transient dockage available.

Ludington Municipal Marina, 400 West Filer Street, (231) 843-9611, www.ci.ludington.mi.us/departments/marina. 150 slip marina. 62 transient slips. Amenities: fish cleaning station, laundry, restrooms, showers, fuel, ice and internet access. Reservations accepted.

Ludington State Park Rentals, M-116, north of Ludington, (231) 845-8582. Rents boats at Cricket's Concessions during the season.

Trailhead Bike and Kayak, 216 West Ludington Avenue, (231) 845-0545, www.trailheadbikeshop.com. Rents kayaks and bicycles. Open 7 days, Mon to Fri 10:00 am to 6:00 pm, Sat 10:00 am to 4:00 pm and Sun noon to 4:00 pm. (Hours may vary slightly.)

Cruises, Charters, and Ferries

Camel Charters, (231) 843-1160, www.camelcharters.com. Sport fishing on Lake Michigan in 33-foot Chris Craft. All equipment furnished. Docked at Ludington Municipal Marina.

Lie-A-Lot Charters, (231) 845-1978 or toll-free (800) 850-1978, www.liealot.com. 33-foot Chris Craft. Full-service charter operation.

Ludington Area Charterboat Association, (231) 843-3474, www.ludingtoncharterboats.org. More than 60 licensed charter boats to introduce you to the thrill of big lake sport fishing.

Ludington Charter Service, (231) 690-1795 or toll-free (800) 845-6095, www.fishludington.com. Fishing charters and sunset cruises aboard a 38-foot Tiara yacht.

Slapshot Charters, (231) 425-6146. Captain Dave takes you fishing for King and Coho salmon, steelhead, brown trout and lake trout from a 30-foot Baha Sport Fisherman. Half day, full day or evening trips available.

S.S. Badger Car Ferry   *Photo Courtesy of S.S. Badger*

S.S. Badger, toll-free (800) 841-4243, www.ssbadger.com. A 410-foot car ferry (cars, motorcycles, and RVs) operating between Ludington and Manitowoc. (See picture on preceding page.) Spacious outside decks for walking or lounging. Restaurant and deli snack bar, children's play room, video arcade, free movies, entertainment and gift shop. (See below for things to do in Manitowoc.)

Other Things to See and Do

Amber Elk Ranch, 2688 West Conrad Road, (231) 843-5355, www.amberelkranch.com. A fascinating 130 acre elk ranch where the kids can enjoy watching the herd. The ranch started as the hobby of its owners and has grown into a successful business. Group tours available. Open Memorial Day to Labor Day, Sun to Fri 9:00 am to 6:00 pm, Sat 9:00 am to 8:00 pm. Reduced hours in the spring and fall.

Big Sable Lighthouse, Ludington State Park, (231) 845-7343, www.bigsablelighthouse.org. (See p. 362, Part II of this guide.)

Father Marquette Shrine, South Lakeshore Drive. This monument honors the Jesuit priest who was a big part of Michigan's history and one of the area's earliest founders. (See Background/History above.)

Historic Murals, www.ludingtonmurals.org. Located on downtown buildings. The murals offer an interesting way to become familiar with Ludington history. They depict locally famous people and places as well as wildlife scenes.

Llamas ETC, 5344 North Beaune Road, (231) 845-1487, www.llamasetc.com. A llama adventure offers a different kind of vacation experience.

Ludington Pumped Storage Project, 3525 South Lakeshore Drive, (231) 727-6381. It may look like a crystal clear lake at the top of a large grassy hill, but if you check out the base you will discover huge turbines that generate reliable, safe and economical electrical power for thousands of consumers. The pumped storage hydroelectric generating plant can produce power sufficient to service a city of 1.4 million people. It is an educational experience that will fascinate your whole family. You can view the plant's 824 acre reservoir from special observation decks. Open daily from dawn to dark from Memorial Day weekend through October.

Manitowoc Day or Weekend Trip. Manitowoc has a population of approximately 35,000 and is a nice-sized city for an afternoon or weekend visit. You can reach it by the S.S. Badger Car Ferry (See Above). In Manitowoc you can eat at *The Boatyard Café*, 101 Maritime Drive, (920) 682-7000 or toll-free (800) 654-5353, the *Courthouse Pub*, 1001 South 8th Street, (920) 686-1166, *Garnishes*

Restaurant, 1306 Washington Street, (920) 652-9109 or strike out on your own and investigate the varied dining opportunities.

If you plan to spend the night you might wish to make reservations before you leave and you can consider: *Holiday Inn Manitowoc*, 4601 Calumet Avenue, (920) 682-6000 or toll-free (800) HOLIDAY, the *Inn on Maritime Bay*, 101 Maritime Drive, (920) 682-7000 or toll-free (800) 654-5353 or *Westport B&B*, 635 North Eighth Street, (920) 686-0465 or toll-free (888) 686-0465, www.thewestport.com.

Among other attractions you may discover during your visit, you might want to stop at the *Rahr-West Art Museum*, 610 North 8th Street, www.rahrwestartmuseum.org (920) 683-4501, the *Rogers Street Fishing Village and Museum and Great Lakes Coast Guard Museum*, 2102 Jackson Street, Two Rivers, (920) 793-5905 and/or the *Wisconsin Maritime Museum*, 75 Maritime Drive, (920) 684-0218 or toll-free (866) 724-2356.

You will find antiques and other shopping at *Pine River Art, Antiques and Gifts*, 7430 City Highway CR-I-43 (Exit 144), (920) 726-4440, *Cook's Corner*, 836 South 8th Street, (920) 684-5521 or toll-free (900) 236-CHEF, and other shops in the area.

You might want to take the family to the *Lincoln Park Zoo*, 1215 Block of North 8th Street, (920) 683-4685 or the *West of the Lake Gardens*, 915 Memorial Drive, (920) 684-6110.

For additional information contact the *Manitowoc Area Visitor and Convention Bureau,* 4221 Calumet Avenue (920) 683-4388 or toll-free (800) 627-4896, www.manitowoc.info.

Ludington Festivals

Craft Show, June at Western Michigan Fairgrounds.

Ludington Gus Macker, June.

White Pine Village Pancake Supper/Maple Syrup Days, June.

AAUW Antiques & Craft Show July, at the Fairgrounds.

Freedom Festival Parade and Fireworks, July 4th.

Gander Mountain Offshore Classic Fishing Tournament, July.

Ludington's Music Festival, July.

Village Fish-Fry at Historic White Pine Village, July.

West Shore Art League's Fine Arts & Crafts Fair, July.

Western Michigan Fair, July.

Bike Night in Downtown Ludington, August.

Clown Band/Corn Roast, August, White Pine Village.

Craft Show at Western Michigan Fairgrounds, August.

Gold Coast Arts & Crafts Fair and *Carferry Festival*, likely to be held in August.

Ludington Lighthouse Triathlon-Duathlon, August.

Mason County Garden Club's Annual Garden Walk, August.
Outdoor Movie at Ludington City Park, July, every Thursday evening at dusk.
Lumbering Days, September, Whitepine Village.
Scotville Harvest Festival, September.
Autumn Days, October, Whitepine Village.

Golf

Hemlock Golf Club, 5105 West Decker Road, (231) 845-1300 or toll-free (888) 490-3673, www.hemlockgolfclub.com. Formidable 18-hole, 7,030 yard course sculpted from natural landscape. Rated among the Top Ten Best New Affordable Courses in America by *Golf Digest* in 2003.

Lakeside Links, 5369 West Chauvez Road, (231) 843-3660, www.lakesidelinks.com. 27-hole public course with bar and snack shop. Amenities: club and cart rentals, golf pro shop, lessons, senior and twilight specials.

Ludington Area Jaycees Mini-Golf Course, West end of Ludington Avenue, (231) 843-4663. 18-holes of mini golf located at Stearns Park along the Lake Michigan shoreline. Features "Landmarks of Ludington."

Contacts

Ludington Area Convention and Visitor's Bureau, 5300 West US-10 (231) 845-5430 or toll-free (877) 420-6618, www.ludington.org.

Manistee

Population: Approximately 6,500.

Directions: **From Chicago**: I-94 East to I-196 North to US-31 North to US-10 East then take US-31 North to Manistee. **From Detroit and Lansing**: I-96 West to US-131 North to Ludington/Clare to US-10 to US-31 North.

Background and History

Manistee is a Native American word but while its origin is clear, its meaning is not. It may mean "river at whose mouth there are islands." It may refer to the reddish/brown ochre used for ceremonial decoration of the face and body. Or, it may have a more symbolical meaning, and refer to the spirit of the wind blowing through the trees. The Historical Society of Manistee supports the last and more poetic interpretation.

Native Americans placed a high value on the Manistee River, and attempted to keep European settlers away from the river's mouth at Lake Michigan. However, by the Treaty of Washington in 1836 the land was ceded to the United States and settlers began arriving.

In 1840 John, Joseph and Adam Stronach chose the site of what is now Manistee and built the first permanent sawmill there one year later. The sawmill was the first foundational building block of the village that would soon thrive on the shores of Lake Michigan. Manistee was incorporated as a city in 1869.

On October 8, 1871, the same day as the infamous Chicago fire, flames of biblical fire-and-brimstone proportions also rained down on the small town of Manistee. The loss of property was estimated at $1,000,000.

The *Grand Rapids Eagle* carried stories of how the inferno started and the path the rampaging disaster took. Within the city limits lay a twenty-acre Hemlock forest; many of its trees were only partially standing and some were toppling in various stages of decay. Still more were already dead and littering the ground. This timber was "combustible as gun powder," the perfect tinder to start a major conflagration.

At 9:00 am the fire department was called to a dangerous fire burning at an old chopping area. The hardworking firefighters spent much of the day battling the flames and by evening they were exhausted, but able to congratulate themselves for containing and subduing the menace.

At 9:30 pm, devout congregants returned to their homes from an evening worship. They had offered prayers of thanks that their city had been spared. And then the fire alarm rang again. Monstrous gale-winds raged and the fire department rushed to the scene and tried a second time to contain the blaze. The fire threatened the mill of John Canfield, along with his boarding house and about thirty other buildings. The surrounding area, as part of the Canfield's milling operation, was covered with pine dust and cords of dry pine slabs – all of which became additional fuel for the raging inferno.

An unidentified reporter described it: "*Down from the circling hills on the lake shore pounced the devouring monster. The burning sawdust, whirled by the gale in fiery clouds, filled the air. Hundreds of dry, pitchy slabs sent up great columns of red flame, that swayed in the air like mighty banners of fire, swept across Manistee, two hundred feet wide, and almost instantly, like great fiery tongues, licked up the government lighthouse, built at a cost of nearly $10,000, and situated a hundred and fifty feet from the north bank of the river.*"

Soon the winds carried the fire to other sites and the blaze turned on the city from all directions. Pandemonium broke out. With Herculean but futile efforts, families tried to stave off the spread.

When the sun rose on Monday morning the city was in ruins: 1,000 people were homeless and many of them penniless as well. In spite of the damage, the city had reason to be grateful; there was no loss of life and very little serious injury. Cities along the west side of the state pitched in to help Manistee rebuild; they provided aid and supplies to help victims survive the next year.

Less than two years later, in 1873, the city had 5,000 residents, 20 sawmills, a daily line of steamers connecting to Milwaukee and Chicago, three telegraph lines, three schools, five churches, hotels, railroads in the planning stages, and nearly every type of merchandising establishment imaginable - including a candy store. The drive to rebuild Manistee seemed more intense than that for her initial growth before the fire. In 1880, lumberman, Charles Rietz helped rejuvenate the local economy when he successfully drilled for salt. Freighters soon hauled salt brine out of the port.

Victorian buildings, many that remain today, began gracing the downtown. Like a Phoenix rising from the ashes, Manistee again became a great place to live. Current residents would tell you it still is.

It is also a great place for a tourist to visit. Wander back in time; take a stroll down River Street. Manistee's central business district shows off lovingly restored Victorians - alive with activity from boutiques, restaurants, cafes and an eclectic mix of other shops.

Food/Restaurants

Four-Forty-West Restaurant, 440 West River Street, (231) 723-7902. Overlooks the lovely Manistee River. Enjoy a lunch or dinner of fresh seafood, steak or pasta. You might also wish to try the Sunday Brunch Buffet which features an omelet station and flaming desserts.

Extensive wine list. Open 7 days, lunch Mon to Sat 11:00 am to 4:00 pm, dinner 4:00 pm to closing (generally 10:00 pm), Sun brunch 10:00 am to 2:00 pm, and Sun dinner until 10:00 pm.

Goody's, 343 River Street, www.goodysjuiceandjava.com, (231) 398-9580. Smoothies, cappuccinos, lattes, baked goods, sandwiches and soup, with take-out available. This is the local internet café. Open 7 days, Mon to Sat 7:00 am to 6:00 pm and Sun 8:00 am to 5:00 pm.

Osprey Grill, 4797 US-31, toll-free (800) 867-2604. (See Manistee National Golf Resort below)

River Street Station, 358 River Street, (231) 723-8411. Friendly bar with a deck. Burgers, burritos, sandwiches, steaks and seafood with full bar service. Kitchen open Sun to Thurs to 10:00 pm, Fri and Sat to midnight (sometimes later) and bar open until 2:00 am.

Stafono's Restaurant, 50 Arthur Street, (231) 723-4400. Daily specials. Breakfast, lunch, dinner. Open 7 days, 6:00 am to 9:00 pm.

Tuscan Grille, 312 River Street, (231) 723-4200. Casual riverside dining with a deck and an emphasis on Northern Italian Cuisine. Nice wine list. Second story bar has live entertainment. Open 7 days, Mon to Thurs 11:00 am to 10:00 pm, Fri and Sat 11:00 am to midnight and Sun noon to 10:00 pm. Slightly reduced hours in the off-season.

The Willows, 2700 Orchard (Little River Casino), (231) 723-1536. Seats 221. Daily Little River Blue Plate Specials, all-you-can-eat specials, Sun to Thurs steak and shrimp special. Sun to Thurs prime rib and seafood buffet, and Fri and Sat kids' special with drink, choice of kid's meal and ice cream. Open 7 days, 7:00 am to 11:00 pm.

Lodging (Also see Campgrounds below)

Carriage Inn/Rodeway Inn, 200 US-31 North, (231) 723-9949. 69 rooms from standard singles to deluxe with hot tubs, overlooking Manistee Lake. Extras: cable, pool, continental breakfast, casino packages, shuttle and game room.

Days Inn, 1462 US-31 South, www.daysinnofmanistee.com, (231) 723-8385. 94 guest rooms. Extras: indoor pool, hot tub, deluxe continental breakfast, internet, free local and long distance (within 48 states), HBO, HBO2, game room, laundry and casino shuttle.

Little River Casino Resort, 2700 Orchard Highway, (231) 723-1536. 100 rooms in a small scale hotel away from it all. Extras: internet, heated indoor pool, sauna, playground and exercise room.

Little Riverside Motel and Marina, 225 North US-31 (231) 398-3420. Marina available for daily and seasonal dock rental. Extras: casino package, free shuttle, HBO/ESPN, refrigerator and microwave.

Manistee Inn and Marina, 378 River Street, (231) 723-4000 or toll-free (800) 968-6277, www.manisteeinn.com. Extras: fifteen guest slips for boats, riverside rooms, deluxe hot tub rooms, king or two double beds, VCR and continental breakfast.

Manistee National Golf and Resort, 4797 US-31 South in Manistee National Forest, (231) 398-0123 or toll-free (800) 867-2604. 42 room inn with 12 suites. Extras: hot tub rooms, indoor and outdoor pools, whirlpools, golf, ski and casino packages and deluxe continental breakfast. Osprey Grille is the on-premises restaurant..

Microtel Inn and Suites, 26 East Parkdale Avenue, (231) 398-0008 or toll-free (800) 260-2515. Extras: free long distance calls in continental U.S. and free high-speed wireless internet.

Super 8 Motel, 220 US-31 North, (231) 398-8888 or toll-free (800) 800-8000, www.super8.com. Extras: high-speed wireless internet access, 24-hour coffee, continental breakfast and free casino shuttle.

The Ramsdell Inn, River Street at Maple, (231) 398-7901, www.ramsdellinn.net. Ten rooms in a European, boutique-style hotel. Rooms are located on the upper three floors of Manistee's historic Ramsdell Building. Self-describes as an intimate Victorian hotel with attitude. Enjoy the 1891 Victorian architecture, stained glass windows, and elaborately carved woodwork. Simply a lovely place to stay. The Inn received the National Award for Renovations. Extras: robes, rooms with fireplaces, cable and data ports, but no pets and smoke-free.

Museums and Galleries

Manistee Art Institute, Exhibits at the Ramsdell Theatre, (231) 723-2682. Permanent home for Manistee's artistic legacy. Displays non-commercial exhibits from museums and private and corporate collections.

The Manistee County Historical Museum, A.H. Lyman Building, 425 River Street, (231) 723-5531. Collection of vintage artifacts, newspaper articles and photographs depicting the early days of Manistee County. Open summer Mon to Sat 10:00 am to 5:00 pm. Off-season Tues to Sat 10:00 am to 5:00 pm.

Our Savior's Historical Museum, 304 Walnut Street, (231) 723-9486. A Michigan Historical Site listed on the National Register of Historical Places, this church is the oldest Danish American Evangelical Lutheran Church in America. Call for tour schedules.

River Street Gallery, 384 River Street, (231) 398-4001. Original art from local, national, and more than 100 internationally acclaimed artists offering affordable art. Diverse selection of gifts, sculpture, jewelry, paintings, and accessories for the home. Open year round, Mon to Sat 10:00 am to 5:00 pm and Sun 11:00 am to 4:00 pm. Closed Sun and Mon from January through March.

SS City of Milwaukee, Moored in Manistee, (231) 723-3587, www.carferry.com. This railroad car ferry is a National Historic Landmark and open for tours that provide a glimpse of the "rails across the water" legacy. In its day it carried an entire freight train and 300 passengers across Lake Michigan, year round, through ice and storms. Call for tour schedules.

Theatre

Historic Vogue Theater, 383 River Street, www.aacinema.com, 231-398-3006.

Ramsdell Theatre, 101 Maple Street, (231) 723-7188. The place where James Earl Jones began his career. The architecture is beautiful, and this century old ornate building houses theatrical and symphony productions as well as exhibits from the Manistee Art Institute. Home of the Manistee Civic Players. Call for schedule of events.

Antiques

River Street Antiques, 382 River Street, (231) 723-9133. Several dealers carrying primitives, garden antiques and collectibles, Victorian, and country. Open year round, Mon to Sat 10:00 am to 6:00 pm. Closed Sun.

Port City Antique Mall, 351 River Street, (231) 723-4150. Primitives, collectibles, toys, post cards, jewelry, linens, pottery, books, glassware, clocks, quilts, stoneware and Victorian treasures. Open 7 days, Mon to Sat 11:00 am to 6:00 pm and Sun noon to 5:00 pm.

Cruise Ship Niagara Prince docked on the Manistee River at the Riverwalk.
Photo Courtesy of the Manistee Area Chamber of Commerce

Other Shopping

Alex Doucett's, 385 River Street, (231) 398-9552. Clocks, wine racks, hooks, wicker, rugs, iron beds and accessories. Open Mon to Sat 10:30 am to 5:30 pm.

Glik's, 400 River Street, (231) 723-1105. Department store with the emphasis on children and adolescents, not "grown-ups." Open 7 days, Mon to Sat 9:00 am to 9:00 pm and Sun noon to 6:00 pm.

Golden Apple, 336 River Street, (231) 398-0871. Educational merchandise and toys. A way to make learning fun if your children want something a bit mentally challenging while on vacation. Also has a teachers' room and t-shirts. Open 7 days, Mon to Sat 10:00 am to 7:00 pm. Closes Sun at 5:00 pm and slightly earlier in the winter.

Happy Chappy's, 450 Gloria Lane, (231) 398-4000. Northern Michigan wines and large import beer selection as well as imported English chocolates, Stone House Bakery Goods and imported English meat pies. Close to Manistee State Park. Summer hours 7 days, Tues to Fri 7:00 am to 10:00 pm and Sat to Mon 8:00 am to 10:00 pm.

The Hitching Post, 84 Cypress Street (US-31, (231) 723-8335 or toll-free (800) 851-5919, www.hitchingpost.com. Gift and garden shop, and year round Christmas store.

Hollyhock, 431 River Street, (231) 723-2051. Crystal, lamps, gifts, mirrors, framed prints and other home and kitchen accents. Open 7 days, Mon to Sat 10:00 am to 6:00 pm and Sun noon to 4:00 pm.

Hull's, 358 River Street, (231) 723-7333. Women's clothing and accessories. Open 7 days, Mon to Sat 10:00 am to 6:00 pm and Sun 11:00 am to 4:00 pm.

The Ideal Kitchen, 421 River Street, (231) 398-9895. The perfect place to shop for any kitchen accessory. Carries All-Clad, Wusthof, KitchenAid, Emile Henry and Rosle. Open Mon to Thurs 10:00 am to 6:00 pm, Fri and Sat 10:00 am to 8:00 pm and Sun noon to 4:00 pm.

Northern Spirits Gift Shop, 387 River Street, (231) 398-0131. Jewelry, beads, garden accessories, sweaters, yarns, and Native American items. Open 7 days, Mon to Thurs 10:00 am to 6:00 pm, Fri and Sat 10:00 am to 8:00 pm and Sun 11:00 am to 5:00 pm.

The Outpost, 359 River Street, (231) 398-5556. Sportswear and outerwear for men, women and children. Brands include: Columbia, Eddyline, Necky, Patagonia, Thule, Yakima, Wilderness Systems and North Face. Open Mon to Thurs 10:00 am to 6:00 pm, Fri 10:00 am to 8:00 pm and Sat 9:00 am to 8:00 pm. Closed Sun.

Ruth's Hole in the Wall Candy Shop, 351 River Street, (231) 723-7238. Candies, confections and canine cookies. Special orders for gift bags. Open Mon to Sat 11:00 am to 6:00 pm, Sun noon to 5:00 pm.

Surroundings, 423 River Street, (231) 723-0637. Smoke room with walk-in humidor, cigars, candles and gifts. Internet available. Open 7 days, Mon to Thurs 10:00 am to 6:00 pm, Fri and Sat 10:00 am to 8:00 pm and Sun noon to 4:00 pm.

Parks, Beaches and Campgrounds

Douglas Park and First Street Beach. Amenities: municipal boat launch, fish cleaning station, tennis, volleyball, basketball courts, baseball field, beach house, picnic area, three playground areas and the Lighthouse Park.

Fifth Avenue Beach. A place to begin a walk to the lighthouse and catwalk. Amenities: playground, beach house, volleyball and tennis courts, fishing from the pier and a picnic area.

Insta Launch Campground and Marina, 20 Park Avenue, (231) 723-3901 or toll-free (866) 452-8642, www.instalaunch.com. 181 campsites (rustic through full hook-up). Trailer/cabin rentals, fishing boat, kayak, canoe, paddleboat and pontoon rentals. Amenities: store, laundry, bathroom/shower facilities and playground.

Manistee National Forest, (800) 821-6263. The Manistee National Forest is located in the west-central part of Michigan and a small part of it borders the eastern shore of Lake Michigan. The 533,901 acres contain trees; rivers, miles of trails, a placid lake and eighteen developed campgrounds - one located on Lake Michigan's shores. Activities include: fishing, boating, biking, canoeing, hiking, tubing, swimming and bird watching.

There is a semi-primitive motorized area, featuring sites for car, tent, RV and motor home camping. (See also Nordhouse Dunes Wilderness Area under Ludington p. 169.) Three rivers wind through the Manistee National Forest to Lake Michigan: the Pine, Manistee, and Pere Marquette. The smallest is the Pine River, a fast flowing waterway to the Manistee River. The Pine is recommended only for experienced canoeists who do not mind taking an unplanned dip. The Manistee River is a wider, slower moving river. Fisherman claim the Pere Marquette River is the best fishing river in the Forest.

There are several hundred miles of trails winding through the Manistee National Forest. Some trails are designated for mountain bikes while others are specifically designed for off-road-vehicles. Many are reserved for foot traffic only.

Orchard Beach State Park, 2064 Lakeshore Road, (231) 723-7422. Situated on a bluff overlooking miles of sandy Lake Michigan shoreline and sparkling water, this 201 acre park has 176 campsites. Amenities: picnic table at each site, fire rings, electrical hook-up, sanitation station, two bathhouses, playground, fish cleaning facility, mini-cabin and self-guided nature trail. Camping facilities available from April 15th to December 1st.

Marinas, Water Sports, Boat and Jet Ski Rental

(See also **Insta Launch Campground** and **Manistee Marina Inn** listed above.)

Manistee Municipal Marina, (231) 723-1552. Marina borders the Riverwalk connecting the historic downtown district to Lake Michigan. 24 transient slips. Services: gas and diesel, pump-out, dock attendants, electricity, water, 50 AMP service, monitor Channel 9, snacks, restrooms, showers and laundry.

Solberg Marina, 267 Arthur Street, solberg@chartermi.net, (231) 723-2611. Full service marina: seasonal or transient slips and campsites.

Charters, Cruises and Ferries

Fire Plug Charters, (231) 398-9073 or (517) 260-5297, www.fireplugcharters.com. Captain Dan Golden will take you for half or full day charters for one to six people.

Manistee Area Charterboats, Corner of US-31 and 1st Street, (231) 398-9355, www.fishmanistee.com. Call or check their website for further information on how to charter a fishing trip.

Tilmann Outfitters and Charter Service, 2626 Bialik Road, (231) 723-6166 (home) or (231) 510-9345 (cell) www.tilmannoutfitters.com, captmichael@tilmannoutfitters.com. Big Manistee River guided fishing trips and sportfishing for salmon, steelhead and brown trout. Lake Michigan sport fishing for salmon, steelhead, lake trout and brown trout. All fishing equipment provided.

Other Things to See and Do

Biking Tours, Udell Hills Road in Wellston has 30 kilometers of cross country skiing, biking or hiking trails for all level of sports enthusiasts. Bicycles can be rented at the **Bent Crank Bike Shop**, 142 Washington Street, (231) 723-4155.

Historic Buildings Tours. Manistee has many interesting old buildings that have been maintained or returned to their original splendor: the Ramsdell Theatre, the Manistee Fire Hall and the Waterworks building are among them. You can pick up information and a walking tour guide at the Visitors' Center and Manistee Chamber of Commerce. (See Contacts below).

Little River Casino, intersection of US-31 and M-22, (231) 723-1535 or toll-free (888) 568-2244. More than 800 slot machines and 20 game tables, including: blackjack, craps, roulette, Caribbean Stud Poker and Let it Ride. Open 24 hours a day, 7 days.

Paintball Extreme Arena and Arcade, 77 Hancock Street, (231) 723-2811, www.paintballextreme.biz. 20,000 square feet devoted to your good time. Call for hours. Some times are open to the public and other times require reservations.

Trolley Ride Tours of Historic Manistee, 11 Cypress Street (231) 723-2575 or toll-free (800) 288-2286. Take a narrated trolley ride through the historical district.

Festivals

Spirit of the Woods Folk Festival, June.
Manistee National Forest Festival, June/July.
Bear Lake Days, July.
Manistee Lakeside Club Tour of Homes, July.
Arcadia Days, July.
Onekama Days, August.
Manistee County Fair, August.
Port City Festival, September.
Victorian Sleigh Bell Parade and Christmas Weekend, December. Horse drawn sleighs, cider at local merchants and everyone dressed in Victorian period style. This is a wonderful event in Manistee.

Golf

Manistee Golf and Country Club, 500 Cherry Road, (231) 723-2509, www.manisteegolfandcc.com. Open to the public. Established in 1901 and one of the oldest continually operating golf courses in Michigan. Three quarters of a mile of Lake Michigan Shoreline.

Manistee National Golf and Resort, 4797 US-31 South, toll-free (877) 271-4780, www.manisteenational.com. Two 18-hole courses to challenge every skill level. Pro shop with PGA professionals on staff.

Contacts

Manistee Area Chamber of Commerce, 11 Cypress Street, Manistee, MI 49660, (231) 723-2575 or toll-free (800) 288-2286, www.manisteecountychamber.com; chamber@manistee.com.

Manistee County Convention and Visitors Bureau, US-31 at First Street, (231) 398-9355 or toll-free (877) 626-4783, www.visitmanistee.com, chamber@manistee.com.

Frankfort
-and Elberta, Arcadia and Onekama
Population: Frankfort approximately 1500.
Directions: **From Lansing**: US-27 North to 115 West to Frankfort. **From Detroit**: I-75 North to Clare to M-115 West. **From Ludington**: M-22 North along the coast. Elberta, Arcadia and Onekama are south of Frankfort on scenic M-22.

Background and History
Frankfort extends its small town charm and friendliness and invites you to visit Benzie County - Michigan's smallest county. Gently rolling hills provide a scenic backdrop to the area's maritime beauty.

Frankfort has an ongoing dispute with Ludington over which is the site of the death and original grave of Father Jacques Marquette. A plaque in his honor stands in each city.

The first European settler to the area was Joseph Oliver who arrived in 1850. Early residents named the settlement Frankfort because it reminded them of Frankfort, Germany. The small city was originally part of Leelanau County.

1864 saw an influx of Norwegian immigrants to the area, beginning with Isak Peterson who was drawn by the excellent fishing opportunities. Initially the fishery provided the most important economic support for residents; they later turned to agriculture. Frankfort was incorporated as a village in 1874.

Pastor Rasmus Bull established the first Norwegian congregation of the Evangelical Lutheran Church in the country in Frankfort in 1873. The actual structure to accommodate his flock was built in 1884.

Elberta, was first settled in 1855 just south of Frankfort and was originally incorporated as South Frankfort in 1894. The village was renamed Elberta because Elberta peaches were grown there.

The Frankfort-Elberta port was opened in 1867 and by 1870 the channel was 200 feet wide and had both a south and north pier. In 1873 the United States Lighthouse Service established the first pier head light to mark the entrance to the harbor. Today you can visit Point Betsie Light by taking M-22 to Point Betsie Road. (See p. 363 Part II for information about the lighthouse.)

While the Great Lakes have long been considered a huge natural asset for shipping and transportation, they were also a detriment and barrier to overland transportation. A train sitting in a station in Manistee or Frankfort had to go all the way south to Chicago, round the Lake's southern end, and head north again. A distance of less than 100 miles as the crow flies became a land distance of four times that. The railroads considered that unacceptable and enterprising minds considered the alternatives. On November 24, 1892, a bold experiment began at South Frankfort. Loaded freight cars were carried across the open waters of Lake Michigan on a train car ferry. After that initial experiment, a car ferry fleet was built for this service and operated for a century out of the Frankfort-Elberta port.

Historian author Bruce Catton, who won a Pulitzer Prize for "*A Stillness at Appomattox*," died at his summer home in Frankfort in 1978.

Any history of Frankfort, no matter how abbreviated, must mention gliding. In the 1930s Frankfort was the site of the sailplane company selected to manufacture the first designated military training glider. The area has remained a soaring site ever since. It has hosted two national soaring meets and many Midwest gliding contests. A National Soaring Landmark stands in Frankfort reminding everyone of the popularity of soaring and gliding on the Sleeping Bear Dunes and Frankfort Beach.

A few miles south of Frankfort is the small village of Arcadia. Henry Starke, a German immigrant living in Milwaukee, became attracted to the Arcadia area while he was overseeing the Manistee Pier construction. He was drawn to the lush hardwood forests and by 1883 he had purchased about 2,000 acres of land and established the Starke Land and Lumber Company. Starke built a sawmill and a 1,000 foot pier into Lake Michigan. A jack-of-all-trades, he also built a railroad into the timberlands and operated a general store and ran his own ship, the *Arcadia*. In 1906 his sawmill burned and Starke made a decision to use the remaining local hardwoods to build furniture, and he opened the Arcadia Furniture Company which made bedroom furniture and remained in business until 1952.

Harriet Quimby, the first female aviatrix to cross the Atlantic lived part of her childhood in Arcadia. Today tourists enjoy the relaxed pace of this small village with its beautiful sunsets and peaceful way of life.

Food/Restaurants
The Betsie Bay Inn, 231 Main Street, www.betsiebayinn.com, (231) 352-8090. All-around-good-food in pleasant surroundings. Breakfast 7:30 am to 11:00 am, lunch 11:00 am to 4:00 pm, dinner 4:00 pm to 10:00 pm. Sunday breakfast buffet 8:00 am to 1:00 pm.

Blue Door Gourmet and Wine Shop, 323 Main Street, (231) 352-8050. Cheese, beer, lunches to go and other gourmet food. Open 7 days, Mon to Thurs 11:00 am to 6:00 pm, Fri and Sat 11:00 am to 9:00 pm and Sun noon to 3:00 pm.

Blue Slipper Bistro and Blue Slipper Pizzeria, 8058 Scenic M-22, Onekama, (231) 889-4045. Casual atmosphere with upscale lunch and dinner menus. Homemade pasta sauces, great appetizers, pizza and sandwiches as well as full dinners. Locals recommend this as their favorite restaurant in the area. Open year round, 7 days a week.

CoHo Café, 320 Main Street (231) 352-6053. Among the entrees: Almond Crusted Salmon and Fish Tacos. Open Mon to Sat 11:00 am to 2:00 pm for lunch and 5:00 pm to 9:00 pm for dinner. Closed Sun. Open seasonally April to November.

The Cool Spot, 310 Main Street, (231) 352-7312. Yogurt, ice-cream, fudge, caramel corn and candy. Open noon to 10:30 pm but hours may vary.

Crescent Bakery, 404 Main Street, www.crescent-bakery.com, (231) 352-4611. Breakfast served all day and great panini sandwiches for lunch. Also: doughnuts, pastries, espresso, cakes, desserts, Artisan bread and soups. Open 7 days, 7:00 am to 2:00 pm.

Dinghy's, 415 Main Street, (231) 352-4702. Appetizers, salads, burgers, sandwiches (excellent pulled pork), Mexican, ribs (another specialty), and Friday fish fry (walleye). Open Mon to Thurs 11:00 am to 10:00 pm, Fri and Sat 11:00 am to 11:00 pm, Sun noon to 9:00 pm.

Frankfort Deli, 327 Main Street, (231) 352-3354. Soups, subs, salads and desserts. Open May to October 7 days, 11:00 am to 5:00 pm.

The Fusion, 411 Main Street, (231) 352-4114. Try the Tour of Asia which gives you a sampling of Thailand, China, Vietnam, Japan and Korea on one plate. Great Sushi. This is the place all of the locals rave about. Open Summer 7 days, Sun to Thurs 11:00 am to 8:00 pm (or later), Fri and Sat 11:00 am to 9:00 pm (or later). Winter closed Mon.

Kilwin's, 413 Main Street, (231) 352-4750. Fudge and other confections. Open 7 days in summer.

Rhonda's Wharfside, 300 Main Street, (231) 352-5300. Enjoy a wonderful dinner while delighting in the view of Betsie Bay. Great choice: Shitake Dusted Sea Scallops (baked in mango chutney butter, served with sweet potato polenta). Open Wed to Mon 11:30 am for lunch 5:00 pm for dinner. Closed Tues.

Villa Marine Bar, 228 Main Street, (231) 352-5450. Homemade soups, appetizers, salads, sandwiches, platters, steaks, chops, seafood, breakfast and Mexican. Kitchen open 7 days, 11:00 am to 10:00 pm, 7 days. Closes an hour earlier in the winter.

Lodging

Arcadia House B&B, 17304 Northwood Highway (Scenic M-22), Arcadia, (231) 889-4394. Amenities: on-site masseuse, outdoor spa, wireless internet, private baths, parlor with fireplace and breakfast. Open year round. Four rooms plus 1000 square foot carriage house with cooking facilities. Just five blocks to Arcadia Beach.

Betsie Bay Inn, 231 Main Street, (231) 352-8090. A boutique inn. All rooms have private bath, cable TV, wireless internet and are non-smoking. Varied room sizes and amenities, from two-room, luxury-king suite with oversize hot tub and Swedish sauna, to simple queen room.

Harbor Lights Resort, 15 Second Street, (231) 352-9614 or toll-free (800) 346-9614, www.harborlightsresort.net. Condo rentals and motel rooms with Lake Michigan beach. Extras: indoor pool and spa, free wireless internet, HBO, daily and weekly rentals.

Museums and Galleries

Arcadia History Museum, 3340 Lake Street, (231) 889-4360 or (231) 889-4754 (cell). Located in a restored Victorian-style home built in 1884 by H. E. Gilbert and originally located on Norman Road.

Harriet Quimby State Historical Site, M-22 south of Arcadia to right on Erdman Road, Arcadia Township. Historical marker and the remains of the Quimby home stand at this location.

Joan Miller Impressionist Oil Paintings, 598 Michigan Avenue (entrance on Beech Street one block south of Lake Michigan), (231) 352-9955. Miller's studio is in the back of her home, nestled in the woods. Original oil paintings and note cards and matted prints from her paintings. Open year round, Mon to Sat 1:00 pm to 5:00 pm or by appointment.

Les Sirenes Galerie D'Art, 338 Main Street (231) 352-7640, www.lessirenes.com. Works of art from around the world including the batiks of Terri Haugen. Summer open 7 days, Mon to Wed 10:00 am to 6:00 pm (sometimes later), Thurs to Sat 10:00 am to 9:00 pm and Sun 11:00 am to 5:00 pm. Call for winter hours.

The Trick Dog Gallery, 1121 Furnace Street, Elberta, (231) 352-8364. Regionally influenced paintings, sculpture, block prints, mosaics and furniture of Greg Jaris. You can also get a cup of coffee and a sandwich. Open 7 days from May to Labor Day, 9:00 am to 5:00 pm. Thurs to Sun until Christmas.

Shopping

The Arcadia Ice House, Scenic M-22 at Arcadia Marine, (231) 889-4555. A building equivalent to the human jack-of-all-trades. This is an old-fashioned ice-cream parlor (sundaes, malts, shakes, sodas, banana splits, flurries and cones), a gas station and a gift store (Lily Pad) with Arcadia shirts and jackets, jewelry, candles, lamps, frogs, bears, moose, cards, and more. It is also a hardware. Small-town, one-stop shopping. Open 7 days, Mon to Sat 9:00 am to 6:00 pm and Sun noon to 6:00 pm.

Bay Wear, 332 Main Street, (231) 352-4489. Sports clothing. Open 7 days, Mon to Thurs 10:00 am to 8:00 pm, Fri and Sat 10:00 am to 9:00 pm and Sun 10:00 am to 8:00 pm. Open seasonally, April to November.

Betsie Bay Furniture, 311 Main Street, (231) 352-4202. This furniture store has a nice selection of custom linens, art, and unique accessories in addition to their cottage rustic and fine furniture. Open 7 days, Mon to Sat 10:00 am to 5:00 pm and Sun 11:00 am to 4:00 pm.

The Bookstore, 330 Main Street, (231) 352-9720. Largest bookstore in town and it offers a good selection by local authors. Open 7 days, Mon to Sat 9:00 am to 10:00 pm and Sun 10:00 am to 10:00 pm.

David's Harborside, 421 Main Street, (231) 352-4031. Clothing and gifts with an "up North" flavor. Open summer, 7 days, 10:00 am to 5:00 pm. Sometimes closes at 4:00 pm during the winter.

Hull's of Frankfort, 419 Main Street, www.hullsoffrankfort.com, (231) 352-4642. Name brand women's clothing from classic to casual. Distinctive accessories. They carry merchandise that allows them to dress any woman from nineteen to ninety in style. Open 7 days, Mon to Sat 10:00 am to 6:00 pm (often 'til 9:00 pm in the summer) and 10:00 am to 5:00 pm Sun. (Closes at 4:00 pm on Sun in the winter.)

It's the Berries, 336 Main Street, (231) 352-6120. Fashion, style and a bit of whimsy at this boutique. Open 7 days, Mon to Sat 10:00 am to 8:00 pm and Sun 11:00 am to 5:00 pm. Seasonal: April to October.

The Little Garden Shop, Scenic M-22 and 8 Mile in Onekama, (231) 889-4172. Gifts, garden supplies, antiques, fresh and silk flowers. Open 7 days, Mon to Sat 10:00 am to 5:00 pm and Sun noon to 4:00 pm in the summer.

MacBeth and Company, 8011 First Street, Onekama, (231) 889-0352. Great, unusual, upscale, creative merchandise including: clothing, dishes, kitchenware, cards, candy and much more. Definitely a fun little shop. Open 7 days, summer Mon to Sat 10:00 am to 6:00 pm and Sun noon to 4:00 pm, then weekends through Christmas.

Michigan Rag Company, 433 Main Street, (231) 352-7028. T-shirts, sweatshirts, pillows, fabric art. They do their own designing. Open Mon to Sat 10:00 am to 5:00 pm and Sun 11:00 am to 4:00 pm.

Momentum, 321 Main Street, (231) 352-8191. Casual clothing: shirts, jackets, slickers, shorts, T's, slacks, fleece at great prices. Open summer 7 days, 9:00 am to 10:00 pm. After Christmas open weekends. (See store description under Traverse City p. 247.)

Northern Lights, 312 Main Street, (231) 352-6443. Fascinating selection of merchandise including Victorian chandeliers, handcrafted benches, and authentic replicas of famous period items rooted in America's past. Carries works by Michigan artists including handcrafted gift tiles and framed prints. Large selection of handcrafted (in the best sense of that word), well-made items. Open Mon to Fri 10:00 am to 5:00 pm, Sat 10:00 am to 4:30 pm and closed Sun.

Olsen-Sayles Gift Shop, 331 Main Street, (231) 352-9915. Little of everything: glassware, food products such as Robert Rothschild and Red Barn (cheesecake mixes and scones), wild huckleberry jam, cookbooks, Yankee candles, miniatures, party needs, linens, toys, greeting cards and kitchen accessories. Open July to mid-August Mon to Sat 10:00 am to 8:00 pm and Sun 10:00 am to 5:00 pm. June closes during the week at 5:30 pm. Reduced off-season hours and closed January to March.

Wear It Out, 325 Main Street, (231) 352-8070. T-shirts, novelties, custom apparel. Also rents bicycles from this location. Open Mon to Sat 10:00 am to 6:00 pm. Closed Sun.

Yankee Clipper Trading Company, 318 Main Street, (231) 352-7321. Pottery, gifts, kitchen accents and art from Ireland. Open Mon to Sat 10:00 am to 4:00 pm. Seasonal April to September.

Parks, Beaches and Campgrounds

Bellows Park, across the street from Crystal Lake. Covered pavilion, BBQ grills and public beach.

Betsie Valley Trail. The bed of the former Ann Arbor Railroad winds through the countryside from Elberta on Lake Michigan into Thompsonville 27 miles to the southeast. Hikers, bikers and leisure walkers all experience the panoply of visually stimulating scenes. (See Wear It Out under shopping above for bike rentals).

Father Charlevoix (Cannon) Park, west end of Main Street across from Lake Michigan, Frankfort. Civil War cannon located on the edge of the park. Picnic tables and benches available. Close to beach.

Historic Waterfront Park, Shores of Betsie Bay, Elberta. Amenities include: performance pavilion, picnic pavilion, restored Life Saving Station, large BBQ grill and huge playscape for children.

Market Square Park, M-22, three blocks from downtown, Frankfort. Playground equipment, tennis and basketball courts.

Mineral Springs Park, between Main Street and Betsie Bay. Flowing well of mineral water, supposedly healthy but expect a strong taste. Covered pavilion.

Marinas

East Shore Marina, 324 Lake Street, (231) 352-7511. 70 lighted boat slips, fish cleaning pavilion, picnic area. Slips are rented on annual basis and only those not rented are available as transient slips.

188

Frankfort Municipal Marina, 412 Main Street, (231) 352-9051. 35 transient slips. Open May, June, September and October 8:00 am to 5:00 pm, July and August 8:00 am to 9:00 pm.

Charters

Let's go Fishin', 2365 South Shore East, www.slomosean.com, thecaptain@slomosean.com. (231) 352-5019 (boat) or (989) 274-6689 (cell), Captain Dick Murphy will take you fishing for chinook, rainbow, coho and brown trout. Fulltime fishing May to October.

Murphy's Law Charter Service, www.frankforttacklebox.com, (231) 352-7673. Murphy's Law is a 31-foot Tiara that you can charter for half or full-days or twilight. All fish cleaned and packaged.

Other Things to See and Do

Bird Watching, for more information contact the Audubon Club, P.O. Box 804, Frankfort, MI 49635, www.carlfreeman.com westphal@benzie.com. Individual birders have recorded up to 132 species in one day and 270 species have been recorded in the county.

Post Office, 615 Main Street. If you need to mail a postcard, take the extra steps to do it at the post office and check out the murals.

Golf

Arcadia Bluff Golf Club, 14710 Northwood Highway, Arcadia, toll-free (800) 494-8666, www.arcadiabluffs.com. Three-thousand-feet of Lake Michigan frontage provides the backdrop to this exceptional course. Clubhouse and dining room with lovely menu. Feels like a private course, but is open to the public.

Contacts

Benzie Convention and Visitors Bureau, (800) 882-5801, www.visitbenzie.com.

Frankfort-Elberta Area Chamber of Commerce, 400 Main Street, (231) 352-7251, www.frankfort-elberta.com, fcofc@frankfort-elberta.com.

Empire

Population: 378.

Directions: 22 miles north of Frankfort on M-22. **From Traverse City**: Take M-72 East for 23 miles.

Background and History

The little village of Empire was named for the steamboat, *Empire State*, which ran ashore on its sandy beaches more than a century ago. The *Empire State* was one of the largest ships on the Great Lakes and provided its passengers with luxurious accommodations. Its route was Buffalo to Chicago, carrying loads of immigrants bound for the western farmlands. On August 9, 1849, on a return trip from the Windy City, the *Empire State* was caught in a sudden, violent gale on Lake Michigan. She sprang a leak and was deliberately beached three miles south of Sleeping Bear. While out of service it is believed she served as the area's first school. After repairs, the *Empire State* sailed until 1857.

Like many other cities along the Manitou Passage and the northern part of Lower Michigan, the village of Empire was founded by lumber entrepreneurs. From 1870 to 1910 small villages and towns grew up around local sawmills.

In 1885, a small steam-powered sawmill was built on Empire's shore. Twelve miles south of the village, two docks stretched into Platte Bay. Railway cars from inland brought hemlock bark, white pine and the other lumber products to be loaded onto ships at these docks.

In 1887 the T. Wilce Company established the Empire Lumber Company. With one of the largest mills in the state it supported the Empire economy. Many Norwegian mill workers settled in the area near the Wilce Company and it became known as Norway Town.

The Empire Lumber Company's sawmill burned twice and the second time, in 1916, there was no need to rebuild it. The forests were depleted and the lumbering era had come to an end. A historic monument marks the remains (a bit of the foundation) of the mill in Empire Village Park.

Empire, once a bustling little town with hotels, a newspaper, seven stores and a bank, shrank into near obscurity. After the lumber boom fizzled, small dots-on-a-map villages like Empire turned to agriculture. Farmers finished clearing the land that had already been stripped of trees and started growing potatoes and grain crops. These early forays into farming were supplemented, and eventually overtaken, by fruit orchards.

On a hill above the village sits a white ball to remind Empire of the United States Air Force surveillance radar system that operated there for 30 years beginning in the 1950s. The Federal Aviation Authority

(FAA) maintains it today for air traffic control at the Cherry Capital Airport servicing Traverse City twenty miles away.

Tiny Empire's main claim to fame today is its Visitor Center to the Sleeping Bear Dunes National Lakeshore. Thousands of visitors pass through the center annually. From this origination point they travel north soaking up the beautiful parklands which occupy much of the shoreline of the Manitou Passage.

Food/Restaurants

Tiffany's Ice Cream, 10213 West Front Street (231) 326-5679. *Sandy Toes Welcome* at this small café where you can order "Breakfast at Tiffany's" from choices including: Strata of the Day, bagels, breakfast sandwich or house-made Granola. The remainder of the day you can get sandwiches and ice cream. Open 7 days at 7:30 am.

Joe's Friendly Tavern, 11015 West Front Street. Breakfast (full menu), lunch (Joe's Friendly Burgers, salads, sandwiches), dinner (fish, rib eye, vegetarian plate, Mexican) and children's menu. Open 7 days, Mon to Thurs 7:30 am to 2:00 pm, Fri and Sat 7:30 am to 11:00 pm and Sun 7:30 am to noon.

The Village Inn, 11601 South Lacore Road, (231) 326-5101. Local pub that offers pizza, complete dinners, grinders, sandwiches, burgers and salads. The "Sandpiper" is a house specialty sandwich (hot turkey, onion slaw and Swiss cheese on a sourdough bun with French fries or onion rings on the side). Open 7 days, year round, 11:00 am to 2:00 am.

Lodging (Also see Campgrounds below)

Lakeshore Inn Motel, 11730 South Lacore Road, (231) 326-5145. A nice, basic two-story motel within walking distance of the village.

Empire House B&B, 11015 Lacore Road, (231) 326-5524. 19th century farm house. Four rooms and a two-bedroom guesthouse. Screened porch and hearty continental breakfast.

Sleeping Bear B&B, 11977 South Gilbert, (231) 326-5375, www.sleepingbearbb.com, info@sleepingbearbb.com. A Country Inn located on four acres of gently rolling hills in Leelanau. The home was built in 1889 and restored to a B&B in 1990. It features five bedrooms, three with private baths (one with jetted tub and one with soaking tub) and two that share a bath. Covered front porch and full breakfast.

Museums and Galleries

The Blue Heron Gallery of Empire, West Front Street, www.jenniferflynngallery.com, jflynnart@bignetnorth.com (231) 882-4675 or (231) 326-2083. Jennifer Flynn works with various art media. Since 1987, her primary medium has been batik, prior to that she worked in watercolors. Her regular studio sits on Warren Hill in Benzie

County near Sleeping Bear Dunes National Lakeshore but her small gallery in Empire features works of Michigan artists. Open Tues to Sat 11:00 am to 5:00 pm.

Empire Area Museum, 11544 Lacore (M-22), (231) 326-5568, www.leelanau.co/Empirevillage.ASP. Four buildings reveal area history: turn of the century living is displayed in the main building, but there is also a one-room schoolhouse, a 1911 Fire House, and a barn housing horse-drawn farm equipment. Open July 1st to Labor Day 6 days, 1:00 pm to 4:00 pm (closed Wed). During the off-season only open Sat and Sun 1:00 pm to 4:00 pm.

Secret Garden, 10206 West Front Street, (231) 326-5428, www.secretgardenempire.com. A gallery with varied merchandise including: pottery, watercolors, oils, vases, chimes, accents, lamps and coasters. Work of more than 200 artists. Open 7 days, 10:00 am to 8:00 pm in the summer. Reduced winter hours. Closed March and April.

Antiques

Miser's Hoard Antiques, 10126 West Front Street, (231) 326-6081, skinner@coslink.net. Antiques, collectibles and estates. Lots of interesting and funky stuff. Open May to January 7 days, 10:00 am to 7:00 pm.

Other Shopping

The Sleeping Bear Store, M-22 Empire, (231) 326-5433, sleepingbearstore@earthlink.net. The place to get local souvenirs, surf supplies, film and fudge. Open late May through the color season.

Parks, Beaches and Campgrounds

Empire Township Campground, 7264 West Osborn Road, (231) 326-5285. 60 campsites, some electric, showers, dump station. Open May to September 15.

Empire Village Park, tucked behind the village at the intersection of M-72 and M-22. Crashing surf and sugar-sand beaches lure tourists to this marvelous little park. Amenities: playground, restrooms, picnic tables, free boat ramp, benches, basketball. Historic marker of the Empire Lumber Company which operated from 1887-1916.

Sleeping Bear Dunes National Lakeshore was created by an Act of Congress in 1970 and stretches 35 miles along Lake Michigan and covers 70,000 acres. Dunes, created by ancient glaciers, rise a towering 460 feet. The Sleeping Bear Dunes National Lakeshore provides more than a million travelers a year with a cacophony of sights, sounds, and experiences. You can climb the well-publicized trails and dune paths or venture out on your own in a secluded wonderland that is sparsely trafficked, rich with unexpected overlooks, quiet lakes, uncrowded beaches and you may even catch a glimpse a doe with her fawn.

Wildlife is abundant; you may stumble upon a species or two that you have never seen before. The rare Piping Plover, an endangered bird, nests on these beaches. (See p. 399 Part II for story of Piping Plover.)

Within the park are 20 inland lakes, beech and maple forests, two islands and the remains of more than 50 shipwrecks.

The Phillips A. Hart Visitor Center in Empire, 9922 Front Street, Empire, (231) 326-5134. The place to start your Dune Adventure. Take a minute to talk to the group of knowledgeable rangers who willingly share their expertise. The Center has models of the park to help you get your bearings. You can watch a short orientation film to get a better perspective of the area: its history and what you are likely to discover. The rangers will help you decide where to begin your exploration based upon your interests and their experience.

You can walk trails that were first walked by the early Native Americans who enjoyed the tranquility and beauty of the area thousands of years before you. The Dunes are a living museum and tribute to the factors that shaped this area of Northern Michigan. You will find the remains of sawmills, fueling docks, and old barns; each symbolic of the economy of its era. You are likely to encounter a scattering of fruit trees, early orchards planted in another time; representative of an industry that is still very much alive and vibrant in the newer orchards throughout Michigan's northwest.

In addition to walking the area you will find the following activities: camping, boating, cross-country skiing, swimming, fishing, picnicking, horseback riding, scenic drives, nature studies, bird-watching and canoeing. Restrooms and picnic tables are available throughout the park. No mountain bikes allowed. The Center is open year round except major holidays: Memorial Day to Labor Day 8:00 am to 6:00 pm and Labor Day to Memorial Day 9:00 am to 4:00 pm.

Sleeping Dune Trails:

Duneside Accessible Trail. A flat trail through a field and woods. A little less than two miles round trip, it is accessible to all visitors; including those using wheelchairs or with visual impairments. The trail is marked with signs denoting species of trees and other spots of scenic interest. Rated an easy trail.

Good Harbor Bay Trail is a flat trail mostly through a wooded section of the park. Approximately three-miles, this loop can be wet in sections. Rated an easy trail.

Old Indian Trail includes two scenic loops (each loop about 2½ miles) winding through evergreen and hardwood forests with majestic views of Lake Michigan. The start of the trail is off M-22 just north of Sutter Road. Rated an easy trail.

Alligator Hill Trail consists of three loops and is about nine miles through hilly old hardwood forests. The view of Lake Michigan and the Manitou Islands from one of its hills is perhaps the best in the area. Rated a moderate trail.

Bay View Trail. Several short loops through hardwood forests, farm fields and pine trees to a view of Lake Michigan. Rated a moderate trail.

Cottonwood Trail, a short mile and a half loop through moderately hilly dunes. A self-guided tour allows you to examine the grasses, shrubs and wild flowers that make up the dunes ecosystem. Rated a moderate trail.

Empire Bluff Trail is a two-mile round-trip route through hardwood forests with views of nearby Empire, Lake Michigan and the Sleeping Bear Dunes. The trail takes you across old farm fields and orchards and climbs to a perch of more than 400 feet on a dune that is used as the launch for hang-gliding. Rated a moderate trail.

Pyramid Point Trail. Short, but relatively steep trail that leads to an expansive view of Lake Michigan, Manitou Passage and the countryside. Rated a moderate trail because it is so steep.

Windy Moraine Trail. A short, hilly loop, only about a mile and a half, but relatively steep. You pass beautiful old trees and at the trail's highpoint you will see Glen Lake, Lake Michigan and the Sleeping Bear Dunes. At the start of the trail you can pick up a self-guided tour brochure that will identify the natural plant life in the area. Rated a moderate trail.

Dunes Trail, a 3½ mile round trip hike to Lake Michigan that goes up and over a 140 foot wall of loose sand making this a strenuous hike that can take several hours in spite of its short distance. Rated a challenging trail.

Sleeping Bear Point Trail is a three-mile trail that loops through rolling sand dunes. The path is adorned with dune grasses, shrubs and wildflowers. The trail includes Devil's Soup Bowl and a ghost forest. Because of the loose sand this is a difficult and challenging trail. (See p. 350 Part II for related story.)

Charters, Kayaking, Tubing and Canoeing
Finicky Fishing Charters, 11709 Lake Street, (231) 645-0020. Captain Steve Nowicki takes you fishing for salmon, trout or steelhead.

Riverside Canoe Trips, 5042 Scenic Highway, Honor, MI (midway between Frankfort and Empire), (231) 325-5622, www.canoemichigan.com. Family kayaking, tubing and canoeing on the Platte River. Open 7 days, May 1st to mid-October.

Sleeping Bear Surf and Kayak, 10085 West Front Street, (231) 326-9283. Surfboards, Kayaks and lessons. Also sells beachwear. Open Summer Mon to Sat 10:00 am to 8:00 pm, Sun noon to 6:00 pm.

Festivals

Empire Anchor Days, July. Commemorates the sailing ship *Empire*. Two day festival marked by games, a dance on the beach, pancake breakfast and a chicken BBQ.

Empire Asparagus Festival, May. The spring asparagus harvest is celebrated with a parade, car show, cooking contest, games, and the "Ode to Asparagus Contest" which challenges contestants to create the most touching (or perhaps delicious) ode to the skinny green veggie.

Sleeping Bear Dunegrass and Blues Festival,, August. In addition to bluegrass you will be treated to folk and rock and roll music. Also features: arts and crafts, food and shuttle to the beach.

Golf

Dunes Golf Club, 6464 West Empire Highway, (231) 326-5390. 18-hole course featuring 5730 yards of relaxing golf in the Sleeping Bear Dunes Area. Amenities include a pro-shop, snack bar, club rental, pull and power carts, practice green and sand trap and a driving range.

Contacts

Empire Chamber of Commerce, P.O. Box 65, Empire MI 49630, www.empirechamber.com.

For Empire Days information call (231) 326-5287.

For Sleeping Bear Dunes information call (231) 326-5134.

Glen Arbor
-including Historic Glen Haven

Population: Glen Arbor 788 as of 2000.

Directions: On M-22, 31miles north of Frankfort. **Traverse City**: M-72 West 19 miles turn north on M-22, 3 miles. It is 27 miles from Traverse City.

Background and History

Like nearly all Michigan coastal communities, Glen Arbor and Glen Haven followed the pattern: fur, lumber, farming and resort/tourism. However, the current day status of these two villages, located just a few miles from one another, diverges significantly. Glen Arbor is a quaint and busy little village known for its annual art fair and galleries, friendly people and lack of chain restaurants and motels. Glen Haven, located entirely within Sleeping Bear Dunes National Lakeshore exists only as a historical village with an operational blacksmith shop, an inn and a general store where you can purchase souvenirs and get a history of the Glen Haven of earlier days.

John LaRue, a fur trader from South Manitou Island, moved to the Glen Haven/Glen Arbor area in 1848 to set up a trading post at Sleeping Bear Bay. From his post he traded with Native Americans camping in the area. Gradually settlers followed and in 1854, Mrs. John E. Fisher named the area Glen Arbor because she felt it was a pleasant "glen" surrounded by beautiful Michigan forests.

Also in 1854 John Dorsey set up a cooper shop where he made fish barrels to ship to fishermen along the coast. About the same time, John Fisher purchased 1,000 acres of land on the north side of Glen Lake and with his brother-in-law, C.C. McCarty, built the Sleeping Bear Inn which was originally a residence for lumbermen.

George Ray built a dock in 1856 to permit the small villages to hook up to the shipping highway. Ray later became the tiny settlement's first postmaster.

W.D. Burdick established a sawmill and a grist mill southeast of Glen Arbor in 1864. He gave the location his name and it became known as Burdickville In 1878, David Henry Day, a land developer and agent for the Northern Transportation Company moved into Glen Arbor, which by then had about 200 residents, three docks, two hotels, four stores, a blacksmith shop, and a cooper. Wood products from the surrounding forests became the area's primary source of revenue. Both Glen Arbor and Glen Haven provided fuel for the schooners and steamers that traveled Lake Michigan carrying cargos of lumber.

In 1983 Glen Haven was added to the National Register of Historic Places. During its heyday in the logging era (late 1800s and early 1900s), Glen Haven was a bustling community, but the tiny village had

196

a hardscrabble existence – starting when it was burned in the fire of 1871. It fought to remain alive, but most of the residents moved when logging suffered its final death blow in the early 1900s. The village limped along trying to survive on agriculture and tourism, but began slipping into a state of disrepair with no one to watch out for its health.

The Department of the Interior bought the land on which Glen Haven sits for the Sleeping Bear Dunes National Lakeshore and required the few remaining residents to sell after twenty-five years or, if they died before twenty-five years, their estate would have to sell the property to the park. By that time the village had lost many of its historic points of interest including the dock, sawmill and railroad. Still, the Park Service acquired a remarkably intact 1920s-era village which brings the "ghost harbor" back to life.

The National Park Service is committed to restoring and maintaining Glen Haven. The buildings allow you to take a fascinating stroll back in history. The maritime museum is worth a stop. In 1901 the Coast Guard established a lifesaving station at Sleeping Bear Point. In 1931 it was moved east to its present location near Glen Haven. It closed in 1944, and now is part of the Maritime Museum.

Glen Arbor survived the setbacks that turned Glen Haven into a ghost town. Today the year-round local residents welcome the summer tourists and the boost they bring the local economy; they also relish the advent of fall and an opportunity to reclaim their quiet village and the relative solitude of winter's cross-country skiing and snowmobiling.

Food/Restaurants

Art's Tavern, 6487 Western Avenue, www.artsglenarbor.com, (231) 334-3754. Established in 1934, this bar has a surprisingly varied menu. Consider the Whitefish Dip to start. Soups, salads, sandwiches, burgers, Mexican, pizza and home-made dessert of the day. Cash or personal checks only. Open 7 days, breakfast, lunch, and dinner.

Barb's Country Oven, 5921 South Lake Street, (231) 334-3686. Place to get your morning donut.

Boone's Docks, 5858 South Manitou Boulevard, (231) 334-6444. Hard to resist appetizers with such interesting names as: Battered Bear Toes, Toasted Black Bean Twigs or Toasted Axe Handles. Sandwiches and burgers, but also full dinner entrees (fish, pork, chicken and steaks) and burritos. Open 7 days, 11:00 am to 10:30 pm.

Cherry Republic, 6026 South Lake Street, (231) 334-3150. Fresh cherry pastries every morning. Lunch and dinner menus carry entrees with cherries playing a major or at least supporting role. You can try cherry chili or a cherry chicken salad. You can top off a meal with cherry pie with any one of 14 flavors of cherry ice-cream. Summer hours: Sun to Thurs 9:00 am to 9:00 pm, Fri and Sat 9:00 am to 10:00 pm and Sun Brunch 10:00 am to 1:00 pm. Open year-round, reduced hours off-season.

Good Harbor Grill, 6584 Western Avenue, (231) 334-3555. The owners came up with the concept for this casual restaurant when they were sailing the Caribbean. They asked themselves what kind of restaurant they hoped to find in the next harbor and what would they do if they opened an establishment in Northern Michigan. The menu features fresh local produce with an international flavor in soups, salads, nightly seafood specialty and vegetarian entrees. You can order Seafood Mediterranean, Basil Tofu and Indian Curry or maybe just Whitefish or a steak. Open May to October, 7 days, Breakfast: Mon to Sat 8:00 am to 11:30 am, Sun 8:00 am to noon. Lunch: 11:30 am to 5:30 pm, Sun noon to 5:30 pm. Dinner 5:30 pm to 9:30 pm.

Leelanau Coffee Roasting Company, M-22, Downtown Glen Arbor, toll-free (800) 424-JAVA. Nearly 100 varieties of coffee as well as gift items. Open summer 7 days, 7:30 am to 9:00 pm. Spring and fall, April to June and September to January, 7:30 am to 5:00 pm. Winter, January to April, 8:00 am to 3:00 pm.

Western Avenue Bar and Grill, 6410 Western Avenue, (231) 334-3362. Bar and grill that offers outside seating. On the pricey side, but nice menu with such options as Cioppino Fish Stew and Pecan Encrusted Walleye with Sweet Jalapeno Glaze. Also steaks and chicken. Children's menu. Open daily, 11:00 am to 9:30 pm (approximately).

Lodging (Also see Campgrounds below)

Glen Arbor B&B and Cottage, 6548 Western Avenue, (231) 334-6789 or toll-free (877) 253-4200. The B&B is a 19th Century Inn with six rooms and a cozy cottage with a fireplace. Walking distance to boutique shopping, dining, beach and hiking. Minutes to Sleeping Bear Dunes. Award Winning Breakfast.

Glen Arbor Lakeshore Inn, 5793 South Ray Street (M-22), (231) 334-3773. Two-story colonial-style motel. The twelve rooms have two double beds and private bath. All are non-smoking and have either a DVD or VCR. One room is handicap accessible.

The Homestead, Wood Ridge Road, (231) 334-5000. A full range of lodging options including two small hotels, a lodge, an inn, and several privately owned homes and condominiums. Registration for all types of lodging is at the reception center.

Leelanau Vacation Rentals, 6546 State, (231) 334-4634. Offers a variety of types of rentals in Leelanau County.

The Sylvan Inn, 6680 Western Avenue, (231) 334-4333. 14 guest rooms, spa, sauna, expanded continental breakfast, close to beaches, shops, and restaurants. Seven rooms in the historic section of the inn each have a washbasin and share three modern baths. The Great House has six additional rooms and the Treetop Room; these rooms are larger and contemporary, but traditionally decorated, each with separate bath.

White Gull Inn B&B, 5926 Manitou Trail (M-22), (231) 334-4486. Ten rooms in a century-old farm house in the village. Continental-plus breakfast. Enclosed front porch, rear deck, and close to restaurants, beach, hiking trails and shops.

Museums and Galleries

Forest Gallery, 6023 South Lake Street, (231) 334-3179. Wildflower sculptures inspired by nature. Open June to September and a few special days like the day of their Thanksgiving Sale when the store opens 5:00 am, and you get 50% off if you are wearing pajamas!

Glen Lake Artist Gallery, 5968 South Lake Street, (231) 334-4320. 30 artists display their work here. Open Mon to Sat 10:30 am to 6:00 pm (Friday open 'til 9:00 pm) and Sun 11:00 am to 9:00 pm.

Historic Glen Haven (Sleeping Bear Dunes National Lakeshore):

The **General Store** looks much like it did in the 1920s and the Leelanau Ranger Station is upstairs. Open from Memorial Day to Labor Day noon to 4:00 pm. In June only open Fri to Sun. Closed off-season.

The **Blacksmith Shop** is fully restored and provides demonstrations of transforming bars of iron into beautiful, useful items. The blacksmith will also give you a history of the area when it depended upon logging and farming. Open from Memorial Day to Labor Day noon to 4:00 pm. June only open Fri to Sun.

The **Cannery Boathouse** was first built as a warehouse and converted to a cherry cannery in the early 1920s. In recent years it has housed a museum of historic boats that were used around Glen Haven and the Manitou Islands. It offers the largest collection of Great Lakes small craft for viewing anywhere. Open end of May until Labor Day weekend 11:00 am to 4:00 pm.

The exterior of the **Sleeping Bear Inn** has been restored and there are plans to restore the interior. For now, you can only view it from the outside. The best estimate of the Inn's original construction date is between 1864-67 when Charles McCarty built it as a frontier hotel.

Paradiso Studio Gallery, 5964 South Ray Street, (231) 334-3128, www.kristinhurlin.com. Wood furniture, detailed art drawings and watercolors. Everything made on location. Open Mon to Sat 11:00 am to 4:00 pm from May through August. By appointment off-season.

The Ruth Conklin Gallery, 6632 M-109, (231) 334-3880, www.ruthconklingallery.com. Nationally recognized as the source for *Sticks* furniture and also *Design Elements* by artist Sarah Grant-Hutchinson. Gallery owner, Ruth Conklin creates acrylics to capture the beauty and history of the Leelanau peninsula and she carves wood *Story Stool*s. Open 7 days, May 1st to October 31st.

Sleeping Bear Point Coast Guard Station Maritime Museum, (Just West of Glen Haven in Sleeping Bear Dunes National Lakeshore). This is the original Sleeping Bear Point U.S. Life-Saving Station which was moved to its present location because of the encroaching sand dunes. During the summer each day at 3:00 pm there is a reenactment of the breeches buoy rescue drill using a Lyle Gun *(*See p. 357 for description of this rescue.*)* Open May through Labor Day, 7 days, 10:30 am to 5:00 pm. Labor Day to September 30th daily, noon to 5:00 pm. October 1st to 15th, weekends only from noon to 5:00 pm.

Synchronicity Gallery of Michigan Art, M-109 (231) 334-4732, www.synchronicitygallery.com. Features work of 100 Michigan artists with collections of contemporary paintings, original prints, pottery, sculpture and jewelry. Open 7 days, 10:00 am to 5:00 pm May through October.

Theatre

The Beach Bards, on the Lake Michigan Shore near Glen Arbor. These are Michigan's home-grown poets who light a campfire on the shore and invite everyone to gather round. The hearty blow of the conch shell wails into the warm summer night. When the last sound fades the show is ready to start. The various bards proclaim stories of love-lost, or mother bear and her cubs,, or a soulful ballad, or maybe a demon/ghost or two. Verse after verse fills the air until the last words fade; leaving only Lake Michigan waves to break the night's silence.

Shopping

The Cherry Republic, 6026 Lake Street, toll-free (800) 206-6949, www.cherryrepublic.com, info@cherryrepublic.com. A store devoted to cherry delicacies including: jams, candy, soda (pop in Michigan), dried cherries, gift baskets and more. (Also see Food/Restaurants above). Open 7 days, 9:00 am to 10:00 pm. Reduced off-season hours.

Becky Thatcher Designs, 5795 Lake Street, (231) 334-3826, www.beckythatcherdesigns.com. Nationally renowned goldsmith, Becky Thatcher, creates unusual jewelry pieces with clean lines and perfect combinations of natural stones and precious metals. Open summer 7 days, Mon to Sat 10:00 am to 8:00 pm and Sun noon to 6:00 pm. Also stores in Harbor Springs, Leland and Traverse City.

Dune Wear, M-22 at the Village Sampler Plaza, (231) 334-3411. Comfortable, colorful, casual clothes. Open June to August, Mon to Sat 9:00 am to 9:00 pm and Sun 11:00 am to 7:00 pm. September to May 10:00 am to 5:00 pm and Sun 11:00 am to 4:00 pm.

Leelanau Coffee Roasting Company, toll-free (800) 424-JAVA, www.coffeeguys.com, info@coffeeguys.com. See above under Food/ Restaurants.

Petoskey Pete's, 5972 Lake Street (231) 334-3505. Sandals, hats, t-shirts, sweats and fleece. Open summer, 7 days, Mon to Fri 10:00 am to 9:00 pm, Sat 10:00 am to 10:00 pm and Sun 11:00 am to 6:00 pm.

Tiny Treasures and Tiny Treasures Toys, 5919 M-22 (Village Sampler Plaza), (231) 334-2100 or (231) 334-3874, www.tinyt.com. Frames, candles, books, journals, photos, jewelry, paper goods, lighthouse art, gifts for men, wall art and knickknacks. Also in Tiny Treasures: a variety of toys including: Legos, puzzles, Milton Bradley games, Klutz, educational toys, Hello Kitty and die-cast cars. Open 7 days, year round.

Wildflowers, 6127 Manitou Trail (M-22), (231) 334-3232. Merchandise from the whimsical to the elegant. Crabtree and Evelyn potions, specialty soaps, jewelry, home accents, purses, mirrors, lamps, prints, tableware, linens and more. Also a store in Traverse City. Open summer 9:00 am to 7:00 pm. September to May, 10:00 am to 5:00 pm.

Parks, Beaches and Campgrounds

Glen Arbor Municipal Beach. Amenities: beach with picnic facilities, restrooms and a playground.

Glen Haven Beach. In Sleeping Bear Dunes National Lakeshore. This may seem like your own private Lake Michigan beach when there are not many others around - a situation that is not unusual here.

Old Settlers' Park. East shore of Glen Lake off Highway 675. Amenities: playground, restrooms and picnic facilities.

Marinas and Boat Rental

Glen Craft Marina and Resort, 6391 Lake Street, (231) 334-4556. Lake front lodging on Big Glen Lake and boat rentals.

Charter Fishing

Wattabite Charter Fishing, (231) 228-7417 or Cell: (231) 409-0963. Sunrise, daytime or sunset fishing charters on Lake Michigan with Captain Bill Winowiecki who departs from Glen Arbor.

Other things to See or Do

Farmer's Market, behind the township hall, Tues 9:00 am to 1:00 pm, late June through August.

Festivals
Spring in Bloom Wine Tour, May.
Annual Dune Climb Concert, June.

Contacts
Glen Lake Chamber of Commerce, 6304 West Western Avenue, Glen Arbor, (231) 334-3238.

Photo Courtesy of Joe Jurkiewicz

Leland
-including Fishtown

Population: Unincorporated Township with population slightly in excess of 2,000.

Directions: Eighteen miles northeast of Glen Arbor on M-22. Twenty-seven miles northwest of Traverse City: **From Traverse City**: Take M-72 West 1.3 miles then, slight right on M-22, left on M-204, right on North Manitou Trail (M-22 again). 282 miles northwest of Detroit, 205 miles northwest of Lansing and 343 miles northeast of Chicago.

Background and History

Leland was born of the lumbering era, but fishing was also an integral part of its early economy. Its name originated from the nautical term "lee ward" or "lee land" which refers to the side sheltered from the wind. Leland offers protection from the north winds of stormy Lake Michigan. Leelanau, the peninsula on which Leland sits, is believed to mean "delight of life' in the Native American Language of the Ottawa.

Not far from the Carp River (now the Leland River) that flowed into Lake Michigan, bark-covered shelters, gardens, and fishing sites marked the settlement of Mishi-me-go-bing or the "place where canoes run up into the river to land because they have no harbor." Today Leland is the site of the oldest and largest Ottawa village on the Leelanau Peninsula. It is also the site of a man-made harbor.

In 1853, Antoine Manseau brought his family from North Manitou Island to the Leland area. Manseau, his son Antoine Jr., and John Miller built a dam near the outlet of the Carp River. Next to the dam they erected a water-powered sawmill to use in cutting timber to build a small city. After building the city, they used the mill for commercial lumbering. Docks were constructed as wooding stations. Steamers and schooners tied up at these docks, bringing more and more settlers. In 1882, Leland became the county seat and by 1887, it boasted 200 residents.

As the area grew more popular, hotels and other businesses were established and resort clientele began making the trek to the charming village and countryside. Some tourists returned summer after summer; others made Leland their permanent home. By 1900, the county population was over 10,500, or nearly five times the current population.

Fishtown, an integral part of Leland; is a 140-year-old commercial fishing complex on the river's edge. Its weathered, cedar-shingled, shanties, fishing tugs and docks create a living legacy to the area's maritime culture and provide a glimpse of early fishing life. The shanties remain intact and look much as they did when first built.

In 1906 Nels Carlson moved from his home on North Manitou Island to Leland to escape the excruciatingly harsh effects of winter on the small island. Nels, a farmer by trade, transplanted his family into the thriving fishing community that was Leland at the turn of the century. Nels and his four sons, Will, Gordie, Ed and Erwin took to fishing like ducks to water. Son Will opened Carlson's Fisheries. Today, the Carlsons continue to remove racks of fish from their smokers and offer them for sale in Fishtown where the family began its historic fishing tradition so long ago. A taste of that fishing tradition can be sampled at several local restaurants, including the Riverside Inn and the Leland Lodge which continue to get delicious whitefish from fifth generation fishermen at Carlson's commercial fishery in Fishtown.

Historic Fishtown   *Photo Courtesy of Rick Lahmann*

Before refrigeration, fishermen chopped and hauled mammoth chunks of ice from the solidly frozen lake and drug them to shore where they were covered with sawdust in a large ice house. During the summer, the ice was chipped to cool the daily catch of whitefish and lake trout.

By the 1940s many commercial fishermen gave up fishing because they could not support families with the empty nets they brought up from the icy Lake Michigan waters each day. The Lamprey Eel extracted a huge price from these fishermen. (See p. 348, Part II of this guide.) The Carlsons managed to survive during a decade when most of the others abandoned their shanties.

In addition to purchasing a package of fish for supper, you can enjoy the galleries and unique little shops that occupy some of the remaining shanties. Historic preservation efforts are in place to ensure Fishtown will always be alive with history.

Leland attracts many writers and artists who draw inspiration from the spectacular beauty of the area. If you are a simple tourist looking for a place to spread your beach towel and soothe your jangled nerves, you can try an area that locals call Van's Beach (follow the road behind Van's Garage towards Lake Michigan).This often secluded piece of Lake Michigan shoreline may prove to be your own personal paradise.

Food/Restaurants

Bluebird of Leland, 102 East River Street, (231) 256-9081. Drawing locals and tourists alike for over 70 years. Opened by Martin Telgard, a boat builder and his wife, Leone, in 1927 as a small sandwich and soda shop. It has remained in the family ever since. Enjoy a cocktail at the 100 seat bar or dinner in the more scenic dining room overlooking the Leland River. Specializing in seafood (especially the whitefish), homemade soups and desserts. Extensive wine list. In the winter, they feature ethnic specialties on Wednesday and Thursday. Sunday Brunch 10:00 am to 2:00 pm. Open 7 days a week for lunch and dinner.

The Cove, 111 River Street, (231) 256-9834. Waterfront dining on a deck overlooking beautiful Lake Michigan from historic Fishtown. Try a cup of their delicious seafood chowder and if you feel like imbibing, they are known for their "Chubby Mary." Seasonal hours. Open in the summer, 7 days, 11:00 am to 10:00 pm.

Cyber Express, 110 North Lake Street, (231) 256-0184. 20 varieties of whole bean coffee, by the pot or by the pound. Check your e-mails or print your digital vacation pictures while enjoying their fresh donuts or rolls.

Dam Candy Store, 205 River Street, Fishtown, (231) 256-7766. Enjoy ice cream, caramel corn, or maybe a handful of Swedish Fish candies. Open summer 7 days, 10:00 am to 10:00 pm.

The Early Bird Restaurant, Main Street, (231) 256-9656. Leland's only breakfast spot. For a great breakfast or lunch, this is the place to go. Daily specials and homemade soups. Friendly service. No credit cards. Open 7 days, 7:00 am to 2:00 pm.

The Leland Lodge, 565 East Pearl Street, (231) 256-9848. Large deck overlooking the golf course. Serves breakfast, lunch and dinner. Live music and a Perch Fry on Fridays. Open 7days, 7:00 am to 10:00 pm.

The Riverside Inn, 302 River Street, (231) 256-9971. Intimate ambiance and beautiful views of the Leland River. Fresh local ingredients used in creative entrees. A bit pricey but many who eat there regularly, consider it the best place to eat in Leland. Open 7 days summer, 5:00 pm to 10:00 pm. Reservations strongly recommended.

Sisson's Main Street Specialties, 203 North Main Street, (231) 256-9201 or toll-free (877) 284-3466. Specialty cookies, pastries, desserts, breads, coffee, dressings, homemade pastas and pasta sauces, dips, whitefish pate and gift baskets. Also sandwiches, homemade soups and salads at lunch. Special dinners to order and take home so you do not have to cook. Open Mon to Sat 7:00 am to 5:00 pm.

Stonehouse Bread, 407 South Main Street, (231) 256-2577. A sourdough bakery with Artisan breads, great sandwiches, homemade soups and pastries. Open summer 7 days, 7:00 am to 6:00 pm. Winter hours: Mon to Thurs 7:00 am to 3:00 pm. Fri to Sun remain the same.

The Village Cheese Shanty, Dockside in Fishtown, (231) 256-9141. They describe themselves as "*A never trendy, tourist friendly, palate pleasing, neighborhood store offering fresh, made-to-order sandwiches, over sixty imported cheeses, local cherry and related products, nourishing Leelanau County with better-than -ever food for over twenty-five years!*" That pretty much sums it up, except to say it is a great place to grab a lunch if you are going to the Manitou Islands where food will not be available. Open every day May through October, 9:00 am to 6:00 pm.

Lodging (Also see Campgrounds below)

The Aspen House B&B, 1353 North Manitou Trail, (231) 256-9724 or toll-free (800) 762-7736, www.aspenhouseleland.com. Charming 1880s farmhouse offers four rooms each with down comforter. Full breakfast. Between Lake Leelanau and Lake Michigan.

Falling Waters Lodge, 200 West Cedar Street, (231) 256-9832. Located in Fishtown, the rooms of this scenic lodge present views of Lake Michigan, Lake Leelanau, the waterfalls and the Leland River. Extras: kitchens, loft suites and a penthouse with a spiral staircase. Right in the middle of everything.

Jolli-Lodge, 29 North Manitou Trail West, (888) 256-9291. This lodge sits on the shore of Lake Michigan's Good Harbor, nestled amidst the trees, three miles north of Leland. A variety of options are available: lodge with six rooms and sixteen cottages/apartments.

Leland Lodge, 565 East Pearl Street, (231) 256-9848. 18 rooms each with private bath and 5 cottages. Extras: cable TV, continental breakfast, close to beaches and golf course access available.

Riverside Inn, 302 East River Street, (231) 256-9971, www.riverside-inn.com. Five rooms, some with river views, each with bathroom, although one accesses its bathroom through common hallway. One suite.

Snowbird Inn B&B, 473 North Manitou Trail, (231) 256-9773, www.snowbirdinn.com. Tucked into 18 acres of rolling hills, meadowland and cherry orchards, this turn-of-the-century farmhouse even has a secluded pond. Close to Lake Michigan. Closed for remodeling at the end of 2006, but should be open with five rooms available by the time the 2007 season starts.

The Whaleback Inn, 1757 North Manitou Trail, (231) 256-9090. The Inn certainly did not get its name because you can expect to look out your window and see whales surfacing in Lake Leelanau - begging the question of how exactly it did get its name. The Innkeepers describe their philosophy of inn-keeping as "Northern Exposure meets Southern Hospitality." In addition to four rooms they have a deluxe whirlpool room and fireplace cottages. Breakfast is served in the summer only, but they are open year round.

Museums and Galleries

Aurora Borealis Jewelry Store, 106 North Lake Street, (231) 256-0170. Leland Fish Tug Jewelry designed to commemorate Leelanau fishing legend Ross Lang. Hand-made jewelry crafted of sterling silver and beach glass, Petoskey stones and Leland Blues. Open 6 days in the summer. Hours may vary slightly.

Florentine Ceramics, 110 Lake Street, (231) 256-9780. Italian and majolica ceramics, made the same way they were 500 years ago. Beautiful hand-painted plates, pitchers, bottles and other decorative pieces. Open summer 7 days, 10:00 am to 6:00 pm (or later). Closed October to mid-May.

Leelanau Historical Museum, 203 Cedar Street, (231) 256-7475. The museum exhibits reflect the cultural history of the Leelanau Peninsula and the nearby islands from the time man first stepped foot in this area. One display is a collection of Anishnabek traditional arts. Open June 10th through September 2nd, Mon to Sat 10:00 am to 4:00 pm, Sun 1:00 pm to 4:00 pm. Open September 2nd through June 10th Fri and Sat 10:00 am to 4:00 pm.

The Main Street Gallery, 307 South Main Street, (231) 256-7787, www.mainstreetgalleryleland.com. The gallery displays all original art including metal sculpture by Bill Allen; oil, acrylic painting, pastels, watercolors, woodcarvings and glass. Open summer, 7 days, 10:00 am to 6:00 pm. Reduced winter hours. Open during the holiday season. Call for other hours.

Mary Frey Gallery, 106 North Lake Street, (231) 256-2015. Gift shop and gallery with ink and watercolor paintings of local artist, Mary Frey. Also clay pots and flower arrangements. Open summer, 7 days, 10:00 am to 5:00 pm. After Labor Day call for hours.

The Mimi Nieman Fine Art Gallery, 110 North Lake Street (Harbor Square) (231) 256-9910 or (231) 932-8455. Original oil and watercolor paintings by American Impressionist Mimi Nieman. Her work draws its inspiration from the northern Michigan countryside and she has paintings of Fishtown and local farmhouses. Open summer 7 days, Mon to Sat 10:00 am to 5:00 pm and Sun 11:00 am to 5:00 pm.

Nell Revel Smith Studios, 107 North Main Street, (231) 256-7689. Originals, glicees and prints. Open summer, 7 days, 10:00 am to 5:00 pm (with slight variation). Call for reduced winter hours.

Reflections Art Gallery, 199 West Street, Fishtown, (231) 256-7820. An intriguing gallery with a nautical flair. The space is filled to brimming with local artwork, boat replicas, CD music, lovely jewelry, sculpture, framed photographs and accent pieces. Treasures peek out from every nook and cranny. Open summer 7 days, 10:00 am to 10:00 pm. Spring and fall open to 6:00 pm. Closed in the heart of the winter.

Shopping

Americana Collection, 104 West River Street, (231) 256-9350, www.americana-collection.com. Something for everyone from your toddler to your great-grandmother. Handcrafted items for your home, cottage, boat or garden. Ceramics, jewelry, purses, prints, decorative tiles, coasters, cards, Christmas and clocks. Open summer: Mon to Sat 9:00 am to 10:00 pm, Sun may open slightly later and close earlier.

Becky Thatcher Designs, South Main Street, (231) 256-2229. Also located in Glen Arbor and Traverse City. Necklaces, bracelets, earrings and other jewelry using beach stones. Open summer, 7 days, 10:00 am to 5:00 pm. Weekends only in the fall. Call for other hours.

Benjamin Maier Ceramics, 104 Main Street, (517) 775-1418. Pottery and ceramics Open Memorial Day to Labor Day, 7 days 11:00 am to 5:00 pm.

The Blackbird, Pearl and Main Street, www.blackbirdshops.com (231) 256-0650. Country, folk art, primitive home décor, rugs, lamps, furniture, baskets, pewter, candles, greeting cards, note cards, nautical, prints, ships, walking sticks, canes, ducks, birdhouses, mirrors, shelves, tables, wreaths and garlands. Open 7 days, Mon to Sat 10:00 am to 6:00 pm and Sun 11:00 am to 5:00 pm.

The Crib, 203 West River Street, Fishtown, (231) 256-7962. Clothing and an eclectic collection of jewelry and "gifty" things. Open summer, 7 days, 10:00 am to 9:00 pm.

Diversions, on the Docks at Fishtown, www.hatsearch.com. Thousands of hats and caps for everyone. Open Memorial Day through October, 7 days, 10:00 am to 9:00 pm.

Harbor House Trading Company, 101 North Main Street, (231) 218-9427, www.lelandharborhouse.com. Sportswear including Fresh Produce, North Face, Maui Jim, Lily Pulitzer, Panama Jack and Raisins among others. Open summer, 7 days, 9:00 am to 10:00 pm. Reduced hours in the winter.

Haystacks of Leland, 103 North Main Street, (231) 256-9675, www.haystacks.net. Clothing designed and sewn in Leland. Open 7 days, 10:00 am to 10:00 pm in the summer and reduced to three or four days in the winter.

Leelanau Books, 109 North Main Street, (231) 256-7111, www.leelanaubooks.com. A spacious, welcoming book store, all light and open, not musty feeling like so many bookstores. They will try to locate hard to find books for you. Open summer, 7 days, Mon to Sat 10:00 am to 9:00 pm and Sun 10:00 am to 5:00 pm.

The Leland Toy Company, 201 North Main Street, (231) 256-7575. Papo figures, games, puzzles and other things to delight and amuse your children. Open 7 days through October, 10:00 am to 9:00 pm, (Sat closes at 6:00 pm). Winter 7 days, 10:00 am to 6:00 pm.

Manitou Outfitters, 104 North Main Street, (231) 256-7231. Also 203 B West River Street, Fishtown (231) 256-9254. Shoes, outerwear, leather. Open summer Mon to Sat 10:00 am to 9:00 pm (roughly).

Molly's, 105 Main Street, (231) 256-7540, www.mollysleland.com. A unique women's boutique with hand knit sweaters and artist made jewelry and sportswear. Open 7 days, Mon to Sat 10:00 am to 10:00 pm and Sun noon to 6:00 pm.

Nature's Gems, 106 Main Street (Above Haystacks), (231) 256-7570. Beading shop with Petoskey Stones and a variety of interesting fossils. Open summer 7 days, usually 10:00 am to 10:00 pm. Fall 10:00 am to 5:00 pm. In the winter, call first.

River and Main, 102 North Main Street, (231) 256-8858 or (231) 947-4580. Candles, candy, wine, coffee, nautical accents, bears and gift items. Open summer 7 days, 9:00 am to 10:00 pm. Reduced winter hours (may close at 8:00 pm).

Rustic Roots, 106 North Main Street (231) 256-0054. "*Funk-tional finds and eclectic art for the slightly insane at heart.*" That is the way they describe their establishment which features women's clothing and accent pieces. Open summer 10:00 am to 8:00 pm (sometimes closes at 6:00 pm). In the fall open long weekends. Off-season hours may vary, call first.

Tampico, 112 North Main Street, (231) 256-7747. Northern Michigan's largest selection of silver jewelry. Gifts and handmade treasures of the southwest, old Mexico and from around the world. Oaxaca and Navajo folk art, Zapotec, hooked rugs, rustic furniture, pillows, garden accents, and copper and pewter items. Open summer 7 days, Mon to Sat 10:00 am to 9:30 pm and Sun 10:00 am to 8:00 pm.

Tin Soldier of Leland, 113 North Main Street, (231) 256-9886, www.thetinsoldier.com. Gift shop with flair: household accents, ties, gift trays, books, lotions and cards. Open Mon to Thurs 9:00 am to 9:00 pm, Fri and Sat 9:00 am to 10:00 pm and Sun 9:00 am to 8:00 pm. Hours reduced in winter.

Tug Stuff, 201 West River Street, Fishtown, (231) 256-7140, www.tugstuff.com. Leland is one of three fishing ports to still use the old-fashioned fishing tug. The owner is proud of his city's fishing heritage and named his shop "Tug Stuff." You can find ladies', men's', kids', and infants' "stuff" including caps, bags, scarves, belts, bags and *gifty* items. Open summer 7 days, 9:00 am to 10:00 pm. Closed winter.

Downtown Leland   *Photo Courtesy of Rick Lahmann and Leland*
                          Michigan Chamber of Commerce

Parks, Beaches and Campgrounds

Neddows Beach, Lake Leelanau at the east end of Pearl Street, near Downtown Leland. Nice beach with a dock.

North Manitou Island Camping, (231) 326-5134. Low impact, open camping. 15,000 acres of wilderness with the emphasis on self-reliance. (See below for information about Manitou Island Transit to get to the island.)

South Manitou Island Camping, (231) 326-5134 for reservations. Camping is permitted at three locations on the island: the Bay, the Weather Station and the Popple Campgrounds. Low impact camping is the rule to prevent damage to the fragile ecosystem. Remember keep all food stored in hard containers to avoid thievery from the Northern

Miniature Tiger (chipmunk). There is no transportation from the lakeshore to the campgrounds and all gear must be trekked in and out. (See below, Manitou Island Transit for information on how to get to the island.)

Van's Beach, Lake Michigan just south of the Leland River (Behind Van's Garage). Often secluded, lovely beach.

Marinas and Boat Rentals

Leland Township Harbor, (231) 256-9132. Full service marina on Lake Michigan, Harbormaster on duty from 5/1 to 10/15. 48 transient slips.

(**Canoes and Kayaks** can be rented in the nearby village of Lake Leelanau.)

Cruises, Charters, and Ferries

Charter Boats, there are more than a dozen charter boats in Leland waiting to take you on a fishing or sightseeing adventure. Carlson Fishery in Fishtown (231) 256-9801 can help you arrange one.

Fishtown Charter Services, (231) 256-9639. Offers full and half day fishing charters on Lake Michigan.

Manitou Island Transit, P.O Box 1157, Leland, (231) 256-9061, manitou@freeway.net. A variety of ways to experience the beauty of the islands.

Other Things to See and Do

Gill's Pier Winery, 5620 North Manitou Trail, a few miles north of Leland, (231) 256-7003. (See listing under Northport, p. 218.)

Good Harbor Vineyards and Winery, 34 South Manitou Trail, Lake Leelanau, a few miles south of Leland, www.goodharbor.com, (231) 256-7165. Tasting room offers free self-guided tours and tasting. Open May to November, Mon to Sat 11:00 am to 5:00 pm and Sun noon to 5:00 pm. November to May open Sat 11:00 am to 5:00 pm.

Manitou Passage Underwater Preserve/Scuba Diving, can be arranged through Scuba North (231) 947-2520. You can explore historic docks and the shipwrecks of two centuries. The most popular dive site is the wreck of the *Francisco Morazan*, a freighter than ran aground in December 1960. It lies in only 15 feet of water. Scuba North is the contact, Carlson's Fishery is the local connection (231) 256-9801.

South Manitou Island. In addition to the tours offered by the Manitou Island Transit, you can strike out on your own to see areas that cannot be reached by vehicle. A self-guided tour of the perched dunes and the Valley of the Giant takes you along miles of sandy shoreline and provides unparalleled views for the hardy hiker.

St. Wenceslaus Church and Cemetery, located a few miles north of Leland where the community of Gill's Pier once stood, at County roads 626 and 637 in Leelanau Township. In the 1860s and 1870s Bohemian settlers came to the area and in 1890 they built the St. Wenceslaus Catholic Church and also established the cemetery. The membership increased and in 1914 an additional brick church was constructed to provide for the needs of the larger congregation. The two churches, old and new, stood side-by-side for many years. Now only the 1914 church survives and it is about all that remains of Gill's Pier. A walk through the cemetery with its tranquil views of the surrounding farmlands can be a refreshingly quiet moment in otherwise hectic travels. The original settlers to the area worked at the Leland Lake Superior Iron Foundry and the Gill sawmill. When one of their own died, to mark the grave, they hand crafted an ornate metal grave marker, reminiscent of their Bohemian heritage. The church is a current historic site.

Festivals

Leland Wine and Food Festival, June. Call (231) 256-9971 for further information. The event is held from noon to 6:00 pm. Admission includes an etched festival wine glass and two wine tickets. Smorgasbord of epicurean delights, served under a big tent overlooking Lake Michigan. The event features wines from 14 local wineries and food from 10 local restaurants. This is the "really big one" as festivals go in Leland.

July 4th Festival includes fireworks over Lake Michigan and a parade through downtown Leland.

Leland Heritage Celebration, September.

Contacts

Leelanau Community Cultural Center, (231) 256-2131.

Leelanau Historical Society, Leland, (231) 256-7475.

Leland Michigan Chamber of Commerce, PO Box 741, Leland, MI 49654, (231) 256-0079 or toll-free (877) LELAND-1, info@LelandMI.com. You can also get information from the following websites: www.LelandReport.com, www.LelandMi.com and www.Fishtown.info.

Northport
-Including Omena

Population: 648 as of 2000.

Directions: Twenty-three miles north of Traverse City, (M-72 West 1.3 miles to M-22 North) on the West arm of Grand Traverse Bay.

Background and History

Before there was a Northport, there was Waukazooville where a Native American mission was established in 1849 by the Reverend George Smith. Originally located in Southwestern Michigan, the mission was moved to the Leelanau Peninsula so the parishioners could escape a smallpox epidemic. The mission served the Ottawa and Chippewa and was named in honor of Chief Peter Waukazoo.

The move did not end the struggles endured by these hearty first settlers. Trying to produce enough food was a life and death battle that required enormous labor. The planting and growing season was relatively short; often crop failure left the tribes and early settlers threatened by starvation. If there was a silver lining, food preservation was aided by large chunks of ice that could be chopped from the lake.

In 1852 or 1854, depending upon the historical account you read, Deacon Joseph Dame and his son Eusebius, platted the land just north of Waukazooville. They named their plat Northport because it was the northernmost port on the Leelanau Peninsula.

The availability of land brought more settlers to the area and soon the mission village became a bustling center of activity and Northport annexed Waukazooville.

When the United States recognized the Grand Traverse Ottawa and Chippewa reservation on the Leelanau Peninsula in 1855, Northport was excluded from the boundaries.

William Voice built the first sawmill in the area in 1856. As with most small Michigan harbor towns, Northport lumbering supported the population. Northport's location as the first harbor in the Grand Traverse Bay gave it strategic maritime importance.

Northport served as the first county seat of Leelanau County from 1863 to 1883. It was incorporated as a village in 1903. Today the hills around Northport are dotted with cherry and apple orchards. Hotels and motels fill with seasonal visitors transforming the quiet village into a tourist spot during the summer.

Tiny Omena lies in sheltered Omena Bay about six miles south of Northport. Credit goes to Chief Shab-we-sung for establishing the small village and to his tribe for the name, Omena. According to legend, in 1852, Reverend Peter Daugherty started a small mission/Presbyterian Church in the area and many of the Ojibwe or

Chippewa became friends with the minister. They shared their news and problems with him. When told of some recent happening he always asked, "Is that so?" and O-me-nah allegedly translates to "Oh, is that so" in the Ojibwe native tongue. The Presbyterian Church is a historical building in Omena. (See below under Other Things to See or Do).

Another possible explanation for the name is that the word *omena* means apple in Finnish and apples are plentiful in the area. There is no evidence, however, that Finns were early settlers in Omena, A post office with that name, whatever its origin, opened in February 1858.

Northport and Omena welcome you to spend some of your precious vacation time with them: exploring galleries, sipping the local wines, sampling the local whitefish, soaking up the sun and maybe even catching Northport's off-beat Dog Parade.

Food/Restaurants

Barb's Bakery, 112 North Mill Street, (231) 386-5851. You need to buy a cinnamon twist and find a place to properly savor it. There are two large round tables and you can join whoever is already there. Great way to learn what is going on. Check out the historic building too. If you prefer, you can eat your pastry and enjoy a cup of coffee as you walk the small village. You may find others doing the same thing. Open Mon to Sat 6:00 am to 5:00 pm and Sun 6:00 am to 1:00 pm.

The Eat Spot, 215 Mill Street, (231) 386-7536. Makes their own bread, so a terrific place to get a sandwich or pizza. Open summer, 7 days, Sun to Thurs 11:00 am to 9:00 pm, Fri and Sat 11:00 am to 10:00 pm.

Fischer's Happy Hour Tavern, 7100 North Manitou Trail (231) 386-9923. Described as a *"Cheers Up North"* kind of place with homemade soups, (chili in chilly weather) and strawberry pie (when in season). The Happy Hour Ground Beef Burger Deluxe is always a good choice if you just want a sandwich, but they get fresh Whitefish from Carlson's Fishery in Leland and it just may be the best whitefish you have ever eaten. Open Mon to Sun 11:00 am to 10:00 pm.

The Galley, 110 Nagonaba Street, (231) 386-7929. Pizza and Ice Cream. Seasonal.

Stubb's Sweetwater Grill, 115 Waukazoo Street, (231) 386-7611. It has a Culinary Institute of America trained chef and has been written up by the Galloping Gourmet. The Grill evolved from a tavern to casual, fine dining. Start with the Thai Dragon Rolls and give serious consideration to the Parmesan Crusted Whitefish. A bit on the pricey side but excellent food. Extensive wine list. Open 7 days, 11:30 am to 10:00 pm (kitchen) and 2:00 am (bar).

Lodging (Also see Campgrounds below)

Old Mill Pond Inn, 202 West 3rd Street, (231) 386-7341. A Victorian Gothic built in approximately 1895 as a summer cottage, filled with unusual antiques and art. The Inn is located on three acres with flowers and formal gardens. A screened-in porch allows you to overlook a pond. Located in a residential neighborhood you can easily walk through the village from here. Two rooms have separate baths and two rooms share a bathroom.

Omena Sunset Lodge B&B, 12819 East Tatch Road, Omena (231) 386-9080, www.omenasunsetlodge.com Gourmet breakfast featuring locally grown fresh produce and a chance to view the Grand Traverse Bay. Built in 1898, the Country Victorian Lodge has four guest rooms, each with a private bath. The Shedd Cottage has five rooms available with a variety of lodging options. The Dixie LeMieux Cottage has three large suites, a fireplace, wet bar and breakfast brought to your door.

A Place in Thyme B&B, 13140 Isthmus Road, Omena, www.leelanau.com/lodging/placeinthyme. (231) 386-7006 or toll-free (866) 386-7006. Three rooms all on the second floor, private baths and air-conditioning. Open year round. Deck, gardens and a two minute walk to the harbor. Gourmet breakfast included.

Sunrise Landing Motel and Resort, 6530 Northwest Bayshore Drive, (231) 386-5010. Extras: sandy beach, daily/weekly rates, kitchenettes and housekeeping. Basic motel, open year round, near shops, restaurants, wineries and casino.

Museums and Galleries

Bay Street Gallery, 109 Rose Street, (231) 386-7428. Purses, jewelry, scarves, sculptures and more. Open Thurs to Sat 11:00 am to 5:00 pm (sometimes longer hours). Also by appointment.

By the Bight Gallery and Studio, 12271 East Woolsey Lake Road, (231) 386-7019. Owners promote the art of local artists as well as their own works. Jewelry, sculpture, prints, paintings, clay and rakku. Open Wed to Sat 11:00 am to 5:00 pm and Sun noon to 4:00 pm.

Grand Traverse Lighthouse and Museum, 15500 North Lighthouse Point Road, (231) 386-7195. You can tour the keeper's home, climb to the tower and visit the gift shop. (For more information see p. 363 in Part II of this guide.) Open June through Labor Day 7 days, 10:00 am to 7:00 pm. May, September (after Labor Day) and October noon to 4:00 pm.

Tamarack Craftsman Art Gallery, 5039 North West Bay Shore Drive, Omena, (231) 386-5529. A special shop where you will find an amazing assortment of merchandise including art of contemporary American artists working in glass, wood, porcelain, oil paintings and folk art. Open year round. Summer: 7 days, Mon to Sat 10:00 am to 5:00 pm and Sun noon to 5:00. Closed in the winter Mon to Wed.

Rantz Fine Art Gallery, 205 East Third Street, (231) 386-7734 or (231) 286-7628, www.rantzgallery.com. Displays the Leelanau landscapes of painter Gene Rantz and the lovely jewelry and fabric designs of Judy Rantz. Open Tues to Sat 11:00 am to 5:00 pm. Closed Sun and Mon, except by appointment.

Theatre

The Northport Community Arts Center and Theatre Company, (231) 386-5001, www.northportcac.org or www.leelanau.com Check the website for tickets and information about what is playing. Local citizens raised a million dollars and built the auditorium and gave it to the school. The school gets to use it whenever they need it, but there are also many theatre company performances each year. Usually there is a banner by the blinking light in town describing what is playing.

Antiques

By Chance or Design Antiques, 118 East Nagonaba Street, (231) 386-7444. Antique store featuring furniture, pattern glass, ironstone, brass, kitchenware, linens, baskets, sewing, jewelry and more. No set hours. During the summer open most of the time or by appointment.

Other Shopping

Dog Ears Books, 102 West Nagonaba Street, (231) 386-7209. New, used and antiquarian books. Open 7 days, summer Mon to Sat 10:00 am to 5:00 pm and Sun 11:00 am to 5:00 pm. Call for hours after Labor Day.

Dolls and More, 104 West Nagonaba Street, (231) 386-7303, www.northportdolls.com. They make, dress, repair and sell dolls. They also make real-fur teddy bears and sell yarn, knitting supplies, quilting and rug making materials and other craft supplies. Generally open Mon to Sat 10:30 am to 5:30 pm.

Nature Gems Gift Shop, Northport Marina, (231) 386-7826. Specializing in Petoskey Stones and natural gifts. Open summer, 7 days, 9:00 am to 9:00 pm.

Pennington Collection, 102 Mill Street (231) 386-9890 or toll free (888) 386-9890. Colorful and whimsical gifts. Open 7 days in the summer, Mon to Sat 10:00 am to 6:00 pm and Sun 11:00 am to 4:00 pm. Reduced winter hours.

Parks, Beaches and Campgrounds

Haserot Beach Park, Enjoy the beach in a sheltered cove. Amenities: swimming, playground, picnic facilities and restrooms.

216

Leelanau Conservancy's Kehl Lake Preserve, Kehl Road, (231) 256-9665. This 180 acre preserve is open to the public and features easy hiking on its trails (two loops that total about two miles), perfect for birding in the spring or cross-country skiing in the fall. The area combines shoreline, mixed forests and wetland habitats. Smallmouth bass and northern pike thrive in the lake. Along the property's 1,800 feet of undeveloped lakeshore you may be lucky enough to see herons, kingfishers and loons at the viewing platform. Native Americans gathered medicinal herbs from the wetlands. An ancient campsite sits in the middle of the trail. For a guided hike call (231) 256-9665.

Leelanau State Park, 15390 North Lighthouse Point Road, (231) 386-5422. Sitting at the top of the Leelanau Peninsula this 1,350-acre park includes coastal dunes and beaches where Petoskey stones are prevalent. The park is filled with wildlife including: deer, raccoons, porcupines and opossums. There is an eight and a half mile hiking and cross country ski trail meandering through the park to the beach. The Grand Traverse Lighthouse, built in 1852 and now a museum, is in this park. Camping is available and you can set up a tent at beachside.

Peterson Park, off Peterson Park Road outside of Northport. The Lake Michigan Coastline in West Michigan is generally known for its sugar sand beaches, but this is a rocky beach. You can find Petoskey stones as you walk the shore and the sunset is beautiful.

Marina

G. Marsten Dame Marina, (231) 386-5411. Harbor master on duty 5/15 to 10/31. 57 transient slips.

Other Things to See and Do

Gill's Pier Vineyard and Winery, 5620 North Manitou Trail, (231) 256-7003. Produces Merlot, Sauvignon Blanc, Riesling, Chardonnay, and Apple and Cherry wines. Open Summer 7 days, Mon to Sat 10:00 am to 6:00 pm and Sun noon to 5:00 pm. Reduced winter hours. (For additional wineries in the area see Sutton's Bay, Other Things to See or Do, p. 226.)

Leelanau Wine Sellers, 5019 North West Bayshore Drive (M-22), Omena (231) 386-5201. Although many of their wines are available at retailers throughout the state some are only available at their tasting room in Omena. Also many gift items. Hours: summer 7 days, Mon to Sat 10:00 am to 6:00 pm and Sun noon to 5:00 pm. Open all year but reduced off-season hours.

Omena Presbyterian Church, (On the National Historic Register as Grove Hill New Mission Church), 5066 North West Bay Shore Drive. Omena. A white clapboard church with an attached shed resting on a fieldstone foundation and constructed of pine lumber. Originally the church had two front doors but no front windows. The bell is original. The manse (a Presbyterian minister's home) is a Sears-Roebuck home. The church is open to the public.

U.S. Post Office, 117 East Nagonaba. Not a traditional tourist site, but something to look at as you are walking about.

Festivals

Music in the Park

Northport Wine and Food Festival, August. Haserot Park is the site of this epicurean festival with music and great food from local restaurants and wine from local vintners. The ***Dog Parade*** is a featured event of the festival.

Contacts

Leelanau Peninsula Chamber of Commerce, 5046 S. West Bayshore Drive, Suite G, Suttons Bay, MI 49682 (231) 271-9895, www.leelanauchamber.com, info@leelanauchamber.com.

Suttons Bay

Population: 589 in 2000.

Directions: Seventeen miles north of Traverse City. M-72 (1.3 miles) West to M-22 North (15.5 miles). Suttons Bay is 273 miles north of Detroit, 195 miles north of Lansing and 333 miles northeast of Chicago.

Background and History

In 1854, Harry C. Sutton founded a small village at the site of his wooding station in the Leelanau Peninsula near Traverse City. The efforts of Harry and his crew of woodsmen supplied fuel to wood-burning steamboats. Harry named his little settlement Suttonsburg, but in spite of honoring himself in that manner, the village was renamed Pleasant City shortly thereafter. In the end Sutton prevailed and the village was renamed Suttons Bay in 1861.

Before the first road connecting Traverse City to Suttons Bay was built in 1862, mail was delivered by boat every two weeks.

The second enterprise to locate in Suttonsburg, after Harry's wooding station, was a sawmill built in 1870. It was operated by Sutton's son-in-law, George Carr.

By 1876, a railroad ran through the center of town behind Lars Bahle's Drygoods and Clothing store. The railway provided a means to transport lumber from inland to the deep water harbor.

By 1880 there were 250 residents in the small village and they had the services of four stores, three docks, two hotels, a brick schoolhouse, the sawmill and a brand new Catholic church.

In 1920 voters of Leelanau County approved moving the county seat to Suttons Bay from Leland, but the move never materialized.

The mill run by George Carr changed hands and was operated by the Greilick brothers until 1902 when E.R. Dailey purchased the business and operated it as a stave and heading mill. A stave is part of a wooden keg or barrel; generally the thin, narrow-shaped pieces of wood that form the sides of a cask or keg, and the ends of a barrel were called the heads. The factory burned in 1907.

In 1914 Olaf Olson and Charles Chadsey disassembled a large building in nearby Thompsonville and moved it by rail to Suttons Bay where they erected and operated a planing mill until 1944. A planing tool is used to shape wood by flattening, reducing the thickness or smoothing the surface of a rough piece of lumber. In 1944 Gerald Selby purchased the business and named it Northern Lumber Company which continues to operate today as a lumber company and hardware.

Time brings changes to everything it touches, but in the small village of Sutton's Bay, time's touch has been gentle. Sutton's Bay is still a safe harbor serving boats and ships that dock there. It also serves its tourists and visitors to some old-fashioned charm in a slow-paced, charming little place away from it all.

Food/Restaurants

45th Parallel Café, 102 South Broadway, (231) 271-2233. (Also has a candy store). Wonderful breakfast and lunch served in a blues style café. Menu includes: homemade breads, a variety of baked goods, wraps, sandwiches, soups, salads and hummus. Consider one of their great omelets or the Smoked Bacon and Potato Special for breakfast. For lunch maybe the Perfect Grilled Cheese. This restaurant is a local favorite. Open 7 days, 7:30 am to 3:00 pm.

Boone's Prime Time Pub, 102 St. Joseph Avenue, (231) 271-4205. The menu includes steak and fish dinners as well as several lighter items. This is a busy pub with a family-friendly atmosphere. Kitchen open 7 days, Mon to Thurs 11:00 am to 10:00 pm, Fri and Sat 11:00 am to 10:30 pm and Sun noon to 10:00 pm.

Café Bliss, 420 St. Joseph Avenue, (231) 271-5000, www.cafebliss.com. Written up in "*Bon Appetit*," Café Bliss serves a variety of seafood, ethnic and vegetarian dishes. This café was an unexpected pleasure. Everyone will find something to suit their taste. Garden dining is available when weather permits and reservations are recommended. Open Tues to Sun 5:00 pm to 10:00 pm. Closed Mon.

Double Eagle Restaurant, M-22 at the Leelanau Sands Casino, (800) 922-2WIN. Buffets Friday and Saturday.

Ice Cream Factory, 403 South St. Joseph Avenue, (231) 271-6788. Soft serve and hand dipped Moomers Ice Cream. Also serves hot dogs and brats. Seasonal. Closes mid-September. Open Mon to Fri 11:00 am to 9:30 pm, Sat 11:00 am to 10:00 pm and Sun noon to 9:00 pm.

O'Keefe's Firehouse Pub, 303 St. Joseph Avenue, (231) 271-2999. Busy and inviting pub. Outside dining available. Sandwiches and wraps all day and dinners after 5:00 pm. Open Mon to Sat 11:30 am to 2:00 am.

Samuels, (formerly Hatties), 111 St. Joseph Avenue, (231) 271-6222, www.hatties.com. Experience upscale, fine-dining in downtown Suttons Bay. Everything is prepared from scratch with seasonal ingredients like morel mushrooms, fresh whitefish, and organic farm produce. The Ginger Snap Encrusted Walleye or the Two Way Duck would be excellent choices. The business card for Samuel's describes owner Elbertus (Sam) Hybels as "dishwasher, chef and owner." That pretty much says he is working hard to make the experience perfect. His efforts show. Open 7 days July and August from 5:00 pm. The remainder of the year closed on Sunday.

The Roman Wheel, 116 St. Joseph Avenue, (231) 271-4176. Pizza, subs, and fresh broasted chicken. A place to consider when you just want to grab a pizza or sandwich and head to the beach. Dine in or take-out. Open 7 days, 11:00 am to 11:00 pm.

Silvertree Deli and Gourmet Market, 119 St. Joseph Avenue, (231) 271-2271, www.thesilvertreedeli.com. Wine store with the largest selection of Michigan wines in the area and wines from 22 other countries. Great deli sandwiches and specialty coffees, but save room for one of their awesome desserts. One stop here and you can fill your picnic basket and head for the beach. They will even prepare your dinner to go. If you prefer, they have inside dining. Open 7 days, Mon to Thurs 7:00 am to 8:00 pm, Fri and Sat 7:00 am to 9:00 pm, Sun 9:00 am to 6:00 pm. (Only open Sun from Easter through December 31st.)

Village Inn Tavern, 201 St Joseph Avenue, (231) 271-3300. Features American and authentic Mexican food and full dinners after 5:00 pm. If you feel like throwing dieting caution to the wind, consider Granny's Pot Roast Open Faced Sandwich made with slow roasted beef. Daily drink specials. Open 7 days for breakfast, lunch and dinner.

Lodging (Also see Campgrounds below)

Black Star Farms, 10844 East Revold Road, (231) 271-6534, www.blackstarfarms.com, innkeeper@blackstarfarms.com. A beautiful inn with eight contemporary rooms. Tucked away below the vineyards. Extras: fireplaces, spa, TV, sauna, full breakfast, house wine during hospitality hours, nearby hiking trails and riding stables. Wine tasting.

Century Farm Country Cottages, 2421 North Jacobson Road, (231) 271-2421, www.centuryfarmcottages.com. A rustic feel, but with most of the modern conveniences you have come to rely on. Perfect for those who want privacy (29 acres of hills and forests) and a more old-fashioned, roughing-it feel to their vacation. Internet has pictures of the inside of the two cottages; each of which accommodates four to five and the owners permit up to two well-behaved dogs as well.

Guest House B&B, 504 North St. Joseph Avenue, (231) 271-3776, www.leelanau.com/guesthouse. Three guest rooms, each with private bath. Self-serve continental breakfast. Also a two-bedroom, two-bath Bayview cottage available.

Korner Kottage B&B, 503 North St. Joseph Avenue, (231) 271-2711, www.kornerkottage.com. Restored Craftsman-style home with three guest rooms, each with private bath. Extras: in-room refrigerator, full breakfast and open year round.

Leelanau Sands Casino, The Lodge, 2579 North West Bayshore Drive, www.casino2win.com, (231) 271-6330 or toll-free (800) 930-3008. 51 rooms at the Lodge next to the casino. Extras: satellite TV, free shuttle service, and central location. Also available: the Chalet, 1/8 of a mile away, and the Cedar View directly across from the casino. The Chalet and Cedar View are two separate houses and each sleeps up to eight people. Each has a private bath, full kitchen and living room.

Red Lion Motor Lodge, 4290 Southwest Bayshore Drive, (231) 271-6694, www.redlionmotorlodge.com, redlion@traverse.com. More of a standardized, basic motel experience, but at lower prices than many facilities in the area. Rooms, efficiencies, and townhouses. Extras: daily or weekly rates, pets welcome and views of the West Bay.

The Vineyard Inn, 1338 North Pebble Beach, (231) 941-7060, www.vininn.com. The site of many weddings, this Inn offers twelve guest suites and many amenities including specially crafted baskets waiting in the room if requested.

Museums and Galleries

Michigan Artists Gallery, 309 North St. Joseph Avenue, (231) 271-4922. Known for its canvases of local scenery by area artists, but also carries a mix of fine art from award winning artists in a wide selection of media including: folk art, shadow boxes, tile work, photography, jewelry, woodcuts, paintings and more. Great wooden fish. Open year round. Summer open 7 days, Mon to Sat 10:00 am to 5:30 pm and Sun 11:00 am to 4:00 pm. Closed Sun and Mon in winter.

The Painted Bird, 216 South St. Joseph Avenue, (231) 271-3050. With an emphasis on contemporary, this gallery displays crafts of over 100 area and American artists: jewelry, candle holders, decorative and functional art for the home, mirrors, tiles, glass sculpture, clothing, leather, furniture and rugs. Open 7 days, Mon to Sat 10:00 am to 6:00 pm and Sun 11:00 am to 5:00 pm.

Treeline Gallery, 103 Jefferson Street, (231) 271-5363, www.leelanau.com/gallery/treeline. Contemporary original fine art and paintings with area scenes of Leelanau County. Also ceramics, greeting cards, Greek jewelry and art. Open 7 days, Mon to Sat 10:00 am to 5:00 pm and Sun 10:00 am to 4:00 pm.

Theatre

The Bay Theatre, 216 St Joseph Avenue, (231) 271-3772. The last thing you would expect to find in the tiny harbor village of Suttons Bay would be a foreign film theatre. But, housed in a renovated Victorian movie house (where you will enjoy the atmosphere and architecture almost as much as the film), the Bay has been attracting discriminating film buffs since it opened in 1978. Besides offering foreign classics, you may happen upon a fascinating documentary or a live stage presentation. The owner hand picks the films presented and runs films that have captured his attention and imagination. The sophisticated sound system enhances your viewing and listening pleasure.

Antiques

Applegate Collection, 305 St. Joseph Avenue, (231) 271-5252. Exceptional, nationally recognized wicker as well as a variety of gifts, home furnishings, and accents. Carries both old and new. Open Mon to Sat 10:30 am to 5:00 pm and by appointment.

Up North Antiques, 311 St. Joseph Avenue, (231) 271-5400. Antiques and collectibles including: primitives, arts, crafts, furniture, etchings and sterling silver. Open 7 days, Mon to Sat 10:00 am to 5:30 pm and Sun 10:00 am to 4:00 pm and closed February and March.

Other Shopping

Anchor Cottage, 7179 North Swede Road, (231) 271-6614. A selection of home accessories including: mirrors, some sleepwear, lamps, quilts, rugs and folk art. Open 7 days, Mon to Sat 10:00 am to 6:00 pm and Sun 11:00 am to 4:00 pm. Winter hours reduced by one hour and closed Sun.

Bahle's Department Store, 210 St. Joseph Avenue, (231) 271-3841. Selling authentic Northern Michigan sportswear to loyal customers since 1876 when it opened. This is one of the areas very oldest stores; established and operated by the same family for over 100 years and officially recognized as a Michigan Centennial Store and registered historical site. Open Mon to Sat 9:30 am to 6:00 pm and Sun during summer, color season and Christmas from noon until 4:00.

Bayside Gallery, 204 North St. Joseph Avenue, (231) 271-4975. More store than gallery, you will find garden art and jewelry, but you will also find Swiss Army knives, dry and real flower art, pottery, wall art, mirrors, unusual home furnishings and perfect gift items. Open 7 days, Mon to Sat 9:30 am to 8:00 pm and Sun 10:00 am to 6:00 pm in the summer. Reduced off-season hours: 9:30 am to 6:00 pm during the week and 10:00 am to 4:00 pm after the color tour and closed Sun.

Bay Wear, 224 St. Joseph Avenue, (231) 271-4930. Sports and casual clothing for men, women and children. Open 7 days, Mon to Sat 9:00 am to 9:00 pm and Sun 10:00 am to 8:00 pm.

The Blackbird, 405 St. Joseph Street, (231) 271-4350. Several rooms of interesting merchandise. Country and folk art, home décor, greeting cards, candles, rugs, walking sticks and lodge décor. Open 7 days, Mon to Sat 10:00 am to 5:30 pm and Sun 11:00 am to 5:00 pm. Closed February.

Case-Daniels Jewelry, 305 St. Joseph Avenue, (231) 271-3876. Located behind the main street (St. Joseph) shops. Will Case has been crafting beautiful silver and gold jewelry with simple, sculpture-like lines for more than a quarter of a century. In addition to interesting jewelry you will find weathervanes and other pieces of artwork. Open Mon to Sat 10:00 am to 5:30 pm. Closed Sun.

Enerdyne, 223 St. Joseph Avenue, (231) 271-6033. A store filled with fun toys with a serious side, encouraging a love of science and education. High-quality telescopes, binoculars, garden-décor, games, books, gems, puzzles, bird-watching items, Petoskey stones and weather monitors among the selection. Open 7 days, Mon to Sat 10:00 am to 5:30 pm and Sun 11:00 am to 4:00 pm. Closed Jan to March.

Front Porch, 207 St. Joseph Avenue, (231) 271-6895. In addition to gourmet coffees, a wide selection of specialty foods, greeting cards, glassware, table linens and kitchen gadgets. Open summer 7 days, Mon to Wed 9:30 am to 5:30 pm, Thurs to Sat 9:30 am to 8:00 pm and Sun 11:00 am to 5:00 pm. Until Christmas open Mon to Sat 9:30 am until 5:30 pm and Sun 11:00 am to 5:00 pm. Closes Sun after the New Year.

The Happy Woman, 309 St. Joseph Avenue, (231) 271-0094, www.thehappywoman.com. "Stuff for Chicks of all ages." Gifts to amuse encourage and indulge all women. Open 7 days March to December, 11:00 am to 5:00 pm. Weekends only some winter months.

Hats and Haberdashery, 301 St. Joseph Avenue, (231) 271-5226, www.hatsandhaberdashery.com. Browse funky vintage clothing and accessories for both the body and the home. Treat yourself to luxury bath and beauty items. Open 7 days, Mon to Fri 10:00 am to 6:00 pm, Sat 10:00 am to 8:00 pm and Sun 11:00 am to 4:00 pm.

Lavish, 419 St. Joseph Avenue, (231) 271-1600. The place to stop when you absolutely must find a gift for a special woman. They carry jewelry, lingerie and robes, candles and spa products. Open summer 6 days, Mon to Fri 10:00 am to 6:00 pm and Sat 10:00 to 4:00 pm. Closed Sun. Call for winter hours.

Leelanau Cheese Company (at Black Star Farms). Homemade European-style, cellar-aged cheese. Visitors and customers can watch the cheese-making process and sample the results. (See above under lodging for further information.)

Lima Bean, 222 St. Joseph Avenue, (231) 271-5446. The quirky name reflects the quirky (although some traditional) merchandise which includes women's clothing, and whimsical gifts and treasures. Open summer 7 days, Mon to Sat 10:00 am to 6:00 pm and Sun noon to 5:00 pm. Some extended hours on Fri and Sat during the peak season.

Michigan Peddler, 219 St. Joseph Avenue, toll-free (800) 729-3180, www.michiganpeddler.com. All Michigan products including wine, books, dried cherries, jams, coffee and more. Open 7 days, Mon to Sat 10:00 am to 6:00 pm and Sun 11:00 am to 5:00 pm. Closed one month during winter.

Misfit Toys, 310 North St. Joseph Avenue, (231) 271-0600, www.misfit-toyz.com. Interesting name since the toys, games, and puzzles perfectly fit the imagination of youngsters and the young at heart. You will find a few unusual toys but there is also a large selection of traditional playthings along with penny candy like we remember from eons ago. Open 7 days, Mon to Sat 10:00 am to 7:00 pm and Sun noon to 5:00 pm.

Murdick's Fudge Shoppe, 209 St. Joseph Avenue, (231) 271-4445, www.murdicksfudgeshoppe.com. It is a Northern Michigan tradition, so give in and become a Fudgie (as tourists are often called), by trying their famous fudge or, if fudge is not your first choice, consider milk chocolates, brittles, caramel corn, and cherry products. You can watch fudge being made. Always a sweet experience. Open 7 days, Mon to Sat 10:00 am to 8:00 pm and Sun 10:00 am to 6:00 pm. Closes for a month in the winter.

Muriel's, 217 St. Joseph Avenue, (231) 271-4854. Distinctive clothing for the fashion conscious woman. Open 7 days, Mon to Sat 10:00 am to 5:30 pm and Sun noon to 4:00 pm.

New Kids in Town, 220 St. Joseph Avenue, (231) 271-6606. Infant's and children's clothing. Open 7 days, Mon to Sat 10:00 am to 6:00 pm and Sun 11:00 am to 5:00 pm. Closes Sun in winter.

Red Ladder, 326 St. Joseph Avenue, (231) 271-3231. A few furniture and lighting antiques, but mainly home accessories, accents and new gift items. Open 7 days, Mon to Sat 9:00 am to 5:30 pm and Sun noon to 4:00 pm.

Parks, Beaches and Campgrounds

Bahle Park, North end of West Street, (231) 271-3051. Thirty acres of walking trails, skiing, sledding and a warming house.

Suttons Bay Marina Park, (231) 271-6703. Sandy beach, nice playground, volley ball nets, picnic areas, tables, grills, boat launch and 30 transient slips.

Marinas, Water Sports, Boat and Jet Ski Rental

Suttons Bay Marina, (231) 271-6703) Harbormaster on duty 5/15 to 10/15. See Suttons Bay Marina Park above.

Other Things to See and Do

Leelanau Sands Casino, 2521 North West Bayshore Drive (two miles south of Omena), (231) 271-4104 or toll-free (800) 922-2946. Gaming, rooms (see lodging above) and restaurant (see food above).

Leelanau Farmers Market, North Park, M-22 and M-204 (Corner of Lincoln and Broadway), (231) 256-9888. If you are in town on a Saturday morning between May and October, it is worth a stop at this fresh produce market. You will also find gourmet items and crafts. Open Saturday 9:00 am to 1:00 pm, mid-May through mid-October.

Visit a Winery:

Black Star Farms, 10844 Revold Road, (231) 271-4970. (See above under B&B). Spend a bit of your vacation time sampling the wine and spirits at this lovely winery. Open 7 days, Mon to Sat 11:00 am to 6:00 pm and Sun noon to 5:00 pm. Closes one hour earlier during the week in the winter.

Chateau de Leelanau Vineyard and Winery, 13505 South High Point Drive, (231) 271-8888, www.chateaudeleelanau.com. Estate bottled wines grown on 30-acres of vineyards. Year round tasting. Wines include: pinot noir, merlot, cabernet franc, chardonnay, riesling, pinot gris, and newer varieties of bianca and regent. Large gift store with wine-related items. Summer open 7 days, Mon to Sat 10:00 am to 6:00 and Sun noon to 5:00 pm. Reduced off-season hours.

Ciccone Vineyard and Winery, 10343 East Hilltop Road, (231) 271-5553, www.cicconevineyards.com. Their harvest and winemaking rely on age-old-techniques to produce award winning wines: Lee La Tage, Dolcetto, pinot noir and cabernet franc reds and riesling, pinot grigio, chardonnay, pinot blanc and gewurztraminer whites. Summer open 7 days, noon to 6:00 pm. Reduced off-season hours.

L. Mawby Vineyards, 4519 South Elm Valley, (231) 271-3522, www.lmawbry.com. Methode Champenoise and sparkling wines. Tasting and sales. Open June to August 7 days, noon to 6:00 pm. May, September and October open Thurs to Sun noon to 6:00 pm. November to April, Sat noon to 5:00 pm.

Shady Lane Cellars, 9580 Shady Lane, (231) 947-8865. A prime vineyard producing award-winning table and sparkly wines including: chardonnay, riesling, vignoles, and pinot noir. Shady Lane cellars are located on a historic 150-acre farm between Traverse City and Suttons Bay. The buildings are stone and the Chicken Coop, which houses the tasting room, was built in 1914. Well kept grounds and the unique architecture enhance the wine tasting experience. Open May 1st through October 31st, Mon to Sat 11:00 am to 6:00 pm and Sun noon to 6:00 pm. Fall and winter hours Fri to Sun noon to 5:00 pm.

Willow Vineyard, 10702 East Hilltop Road, (231) 271-4813. They invite you to come and enjoy their spectacular views and sample their delicious chardonnay, pinot noir, and pinot gris. Open 7 days, May through October noon to 6:00 pm. November and December, Sat and Sun noon to 6:00 pm. January to April, Sat only, noon to 6:00 pm.

Festivals

Suttons Bay Art Festival, first weekend in August, Sutton Bay Marina. (231) 271-3050 for information. One of the most competitive shows in Michigan with more than 90 Juried Artists. Also a food tent.

Sutton Bay Jazzfest, July.

Sutton Bay Sidewalk Sale, 2nd Thursday and Friday of August. Downtown merchants sell all kinds of bargains.

Peshawbestowa Pow-Wow, 3rd weekend in August. The Grand Traverse Band of Ottawa and Chippewa Native Americans hold their Pow-Wow with Native American singers, dancers, artists and artisans.

Golf

The Leelanau Club at Bahle Farms, 3 miles south of Suttons Bay and 1 mile west of M-22. Take M-22 North from Traverse City to Fort Road, left onto Fort Road., then right onto County Road 633 (Center Highway) to Otto Road, then left, (231) 271-2020. The 11th hole is the signature hole of this course with its massively downhill par-3, a 90-foot drop from tee to green. If your game does not do you justice, the magnificent view will assuage your ego. This is a par 71 course with a course rating of 72.8 and a slope rating of 136.

Contact

Leelanau Peninsula Chamber of Commerce, 5046 S. West Bayshore Drive, Suite G, Suttons Bay, MI 49682 (231) 271-9895, www.leelanauchamber.com, info@leelanauchamber.com.

Photo Courtesy of Joe Jurkiewicz

Traverse City
-including Mission Peninsula and Old Mission

Population: 14,500, and several times that in the summer.

Directions: **From Detroit**: (257 miles) I-75 North, to M-72 East (exit 254) to US-131 North (Also called M-66 and M-72) and continue to follow signs for M-72 into Traverse City. **From Lansing**: (180 miles) US-127 North to US-10/M-115 West towards Ludington/Cadillac, right onto M-115, then right onto M-37 into Traverse City. **From Chicago**: (318 miles) I-94 East toward Detroit, merge onto I-196 North (exit 34) toward Holland/Grand Rapids, merge onto US-131 North (exit 77A) toward Cadillac, to M-115 exit (exit 176) toward Clare/Frankfort, to M-37 into Traverse City.

Background and History

Traverse City is a spectacular and vibrant city with a personality shaped by its location and intriguing past. Like all of Michigan, this area was originally inhabited by Native Americans, specifically the Ojibwa (Chippewa). The recorded history of the area began in 1838 when Protestant missionary, Reverend Peter Dougherty, was sent to the region to establish Old Mission, where he taught and provided religious training to the Native American population. By 1841, Dougherty was joined by John Johnson and together they created a small village consisting of five buildings at Mission Harbor.

Until 1845 Native Americans remained in the Grand Traverse Area, holding a considerable portion of the land. However, in that year, a government treaty expired and the Native Americans were forced to surrender the land if there was a demand for it by "whites." Property on the west shore of the Bay, in what is now Leelanau County, was settled by homesteaders in 1846. In 1852 Reverend Dougherty moved his settlement from Old Mission to New Mission (now Omena). In 1847, the village of Traverse City began to grow at the west end of the Bay. Traverse City was incorporated as a city in 1895.

On the heels of the missionaries came the settlers, some intending to live in the area and others merely following the money to be made in timber. Logging defined the area in the 1800s. Traverse City had forests to provide wood to the prairie states where the need for building materials was great. White Pine first caught the attention of lumberman because it was light, cheap and easily worked and crafted. Finding the timber to harvest was only half of the equation; it was also necessary to have access to shipping so lumber could be transported to its intended market. Grand Traverse Bay provided an excellent spot for schooners and other freighters to anchor. At this location they could take on the pine boards and planks and sail them to Chicago, Racine and other ports for shipment south and west.

The area's first sawmill was built at the head of the West Bay by Horace Boardman in 1847. His name reflected perfectly his occupation and today a river, a park and a street are named in his honor.

By 1893, fourteen sawmills operated in the county and shingle mills had gained importance. This was the high point of lumbering in the area. Timber continued to be cut in enormous quantities for two decades, but the number of mills and men involved in the lumbering operations slowly dwindled as forests became scarce.

By 1915 Traverse City boasted 14 churches and 21 saloons among its downtown buildings. The city was in for significant change. Lumber could no longer maintain the economy and another means to support the populace was needed. Attention turned to agriculture. The land that had been cleared of trees offered new soil that was particularly good for potato growth. In the early years of the 20th century, the Grand Traverse potato farmers found their niche.

Traverse City soon began producing diversified crops; hay and grain flourished. However, fruit became a particular boon to the area. Back when Reverend Dougherty first came to Old Mission, he found fruit bearing apple trees. Pioneer farmers planted their orchards experimenting with a number of fruits. Apples and cherries did particularly well and remain the important orchards of the region. Vineyards also do well on the Mission and Leelanau Peninsulas.

The cycle of the cherry crop made orchards a tremendous gamble; growers faced winterkill and early spring frosts. If their trees survived both, they still faced the bugs and other pests. By 1923, the cherry industry became so important it attracted more than local attention. It was in that year that the combined churches of the Grand Traverse Region were asked to pray for the success of the harvest. From that request came the "Blessing of the Blossoms" ceremony held in the orchards on a Sunday in May when the cherry blossoms are at their peak. From that early religious ceremony grew the National Cherry Festival which is held each year in July.

By 1926, only three years after the original Blessing of the Blossoms, the simple prayers had grown to a full-fledged festival with a parade and a queen. Three thousand people attended the celebration. Today the celebration lasts a week and is attended by more than a half million people who enjoy a wide range of events.

Traverse City is now a resort town. In the frenzied summer months its numbers swell as harried big-city dwellers crowd in to take advantage of the natural beauty and water activities the lake and bay offer.

In all your travels along the Sunset Coast you will not find better dining with more variety than in the epicurean center of Traverse City.

Food/Restaurants

Amical, 229 East Front Street, (231) 941-8888. Everyone loves this wonderful restaurant. It is difficult to choose between the many delicious sounding entrees: from Ravioli with Pumpkin Cream to Filet with Local Roasted Beets and Red Wine. Outdoor seating is an option when the weather permits. Open 7 days, lunch: Mon to Sat at 11:00 am, dinner: every night 5:00 pm to 10:00 pm. Sun Brunch 9:00 am to 3:00 pm.

Apache Trout Grill, 13671 South West Bay Shore Drive, (231) 947-7079, www.apachetroutgrill.com. The restaurant is named after the first fish to be put on the United States endangered species list. Extensive menu. "Up North" favorites like pan fried whitefish and Apache steak. Open year round for lunch and dinner.

Auntie Pasta's Italian Café, 2030 South Airport Road, Logan Landing Shopping Complex, (231) 941-8147. Casual atmosphere, traditional Italian dishes. Open 7 days, Mon to Sat 11:00 am to 10:00 pm and Sun noon to 10:00 pm.

Boat House, 14039 Peninsula Drive (231) 223-4030. Consider the Herb Marinated Boneless Pork Loin, grilled and accompanied by Couscous-Wild Rice Pilaf, Tart Apples, Smoked Bacon, Sautéed Chicory and Butternut Squash Coulis. A long name for a delicious meal. Open 7 days, May to October, Mon to Sat 5:00 pm to 10:00 pm, Sun Brunch 10:00 am to 2:00 pm. Open November to April, Wed to Sat 5:00 pm to 9:00 pm and Sun Brunch 10:00 am to 2:00 pm.

Bowers Harbor Inn, 13512 Peninsula Drive, Old Mission Peninsula, (231) 223-4222. Also the Bowery Bar and Grill. Fine dining to delight your palate. You will be tempted by delicious sounding entrees like the Morel Crusted Diver Scallops or the Ginger Crusted Rack of Lamb. (See p. 417, Part II for a related ghost story). Open 7 days, Sun to Thurs 4:00 pm to 10:00 pm and Fri and Sat 4:00 pm to 11:00 pm. In the off-season open Sun to Thurs 5:00 pm to 9:00 pm and Fri and Sat 5:00 pm to 10:00 pm.

Camp Critter Bar and Grille, 3575 North US-31, Inside the Great Wolf Lodge, (231) 941-3600. Serves breakfast, lunch and dinner.

Ciao Bella, 236 Front Street, (231) 929-1710. Italian influenced restaurant that prepares everything fresh from scratch daily. Wonderful house specialties. Open 7 days, Mon to Sat. Lunch: 11:00 am to 3:00 pm. Dinner: 5:00 pm to 9:00 pm. Sun special breakfast and dinner fusion with a different menu each time. Bar remains open Mon to Thurs until 11:00 pm and Fri and Sat until midnight.

Cold Stone Creamery, 240 East Front Street, (231) 944-1036. Ice cream and ice cream cakes. Open 7 days, Mon to Thurs 11:00 am to 10:00 pm, Fri and Sat 11:00 am to 11:00 pm and Sun 11:00 am to 10:00 pm.

C.W.'s Blue Water Bistro, 615 East Front Street, located in the Holiday Inn West Bay, (231) 947-3700. Casual but upscale dining for breakfast, lunch and dinner. Daily specials. Bar serves over 30 local wines. Sunday Brunch served until 1:00 pm.

The Dish, 108 South Union Street, (231) 932-2233. Salads, soups (four homemade selections daily), wraps, sandwiches, quesadillas, smoothie bar, vegetarian selections and specialty and organic coffee. Open Mon to Sat 10:00 am to 8:00 pm.

Espresso Bay, 202 East Front Street, (231) 941-9100. Any way you want your coffee, they have it. You have to wonder who dreams up things like Pumpkin Pie Latte? Also serves smoothies and gelato. Outside seating available. Open 7 days, 6:30 am to 11:00 pm in the summer. Winter hours: 7 days, 6:30 am to 10:00 pm.

Freshwater Lodge, 13890 South West Bay Shore Drive, (231) 932-4694, www.michiganmenu.com. Featuring rotisserie chicken, fresh fish (try the Huckleberry Glazed Salmon), wood-fired steaks, and sandwiches. The Freshwater Lodge prides itself on offering diners a unique experience reflective of the area. Early bird specials. Open Sun to Thurs 11:00 am to 10:00 pm and Fri and Sat 11:00 am to 11:00 pm.

Grand Traverse Pie Company, 525 West Front Street, (231) 922-PIES. 25 varieties of freshly made pies. You can enjoy a slice with their gourmet coffees or take a whole pie home for the family to enjoy with dinner. Lunch menu daily, featuring soups, salads, sandwiches, pot pies and quiche. Open Mon to Fri 7:00 am to 8:00 pm, Sat 8:00 am to 6:00 pm and Sun 11:00 am to 5:00 pm. Hours may be slightly reduced in the winter.

Greenhouse Café, 115 Front Street, (231) 929-7687. Open year round. Omelets, burgers, salads. Open Mon to Fri 7:00 am to 10:30 am for breakfast and 11:00 am to 3:00 pm for lunch. Also open Sat 8:00 am to 10:30 am for breakfast and 11:00 am to 3:00 pm for lunch.

Ham Bonz', 1108 East 8th Street, (231) 929-2356. Traverse City residents consider this the next best thing to eating in Mom's kitchen. Breakfast and lunch. Home style with southern style "pit" cooking (great ham and corned beef sandwiches) and homemade soups. Breakfast served any time. Open Mon to Sat 7:00 am to 3:00 pm, Sun 8:00 am to 1:00 pm.

Hanna Bistro-Bar, 118 Cass Street, (231) 946-8207. A century-old firehouse provides the ambiance for this casual bistro with fresh, simply prepared foods. Known for the fresh fish, they also have interesting appetizers, salads and desserts, as well as an interesting wine list. They make an Espresso Ice Cream that you have to try. Open for dinner, 4:00 pm to 11:00 pm.

Jonathon B Pub, 3200 South Airport Road West, Grand Traverse Mall, (231) 935-4441. Modeled after an old English Pub, they serve hearty sandwiches, delicious homemade soups, tender steaks, pasta, and barbeque ribs. Nice imported beer list. They also offer movie ticket/dinner specials. Open for lunch and dinner 7 days.

La Senorita Mexican Restaurant, 1245 South Garfield Lane and 2455 North US-31 (two locations), (231) 947-8820 and (231) 946-4545. Fajitas, burritos, quesadillas, chimichangas, and enchiladas, as well as American dishes including steaks, chicken, fish and burgers. Whatever your choice, it can be enjoyed with an icy Margarita. Open lunch and dinner 7 days.

Lobdell's, 715 East Front Street, (231) 995-3120. An interesting place if you want to experience something a bit different. Located at Northwestern Michigan College's Great Lakes Culinary Institute, you can sample the fare of future chefs. Open for lunch Tues to Thurs, 11:30 am to 1:30 pm. Reservations necessary and only open during school year. Sorry, closed in the summer.

Mackinaw Brewing Company, 161 East Front Street, (231) 933-1100. Ten house-crafted ales on tap to accompany any menu item you choose: Southwest smokehouse BBQ, fresh seafood specials and a full menu. During the summer season you can grab an outside table overlooking the Boardman River. Open Mon to Sat 11:00 am to midnight and Sun noon to 10:00 pm.

Mary's Kitchen Port, 539 West Front Street, (231) 941-0525. Gourmet treats to go. Great sandwiches, soups, salads and sweets. Open Tues to Fri 10:00 am to 5:00 pm and Sat 10:00 am to 4:00 pm.

Minervas, 300 East State Street, (231) 946-5093. Located in the historic Park Place Hotel; offers a full menu including: fish, seafood specials, pasta, steaks, salads, specialty pizzas and desserts. Happy hour specials. Open 7 days: Breakfast Mon to Fri 6:30 am to 10:30 am and Sat 7:30 am to 11:00 am. Sun buffet 7:30 am to 10:00 am. Lunch Mon to Sat 11:00 am to 4:00 pm. Sun lunch buffet 10:00 am to 2:00 pm or order from menu until 4:00 pm. Dinner 7 days, 4:00 pm to 10:00 pm.

Misheekeh Restaurant at Turtle Creek, 4 miles east of Traverse City on M-72, (231) 267-9574. Featuring BBQ ribs, prime rib, New York strip, center cut boneless pork chops and other creative entrees. Open daily at 4:00 pm.

Moomers Ice Cream, 7263 North Long Lake Road, (231) 941-4122. To anyone from Traverse City, this is the place to get ice-cream. It is a bit out of the way, but you are going to the farm and the ice-cream is truly home-made. You can even see the cows that contributed the cream! There are more flavors than you could possibly dream up. Open 7 days, Memorial Day to Labor Day, noon to 10:00 pm. Open

Labor Day to December 24th, 7 days, noon to 9:00 pm. Open April to Memorial Day Fri to Sun noon to 9:00 pm. Closed January thru March.

Mustards, 202 East State Street, (231) 929-0700. Place to get a great breakfast. Try the Mexican Jumble or Green Eggs and Ham. Open year round, Mon to Fri 7:00 am to 4:00 pm and Sat 7:00 am to 3:00 pm.

North Peak Brewing Company, 400 West Front Street, (231) 941-7325. Steaks, pastas, salads, sandwiches or wood-fired pizzas. Grab a mug of one of their handcrafted beers brewed on site. Mission Point Porter, full bodied with rich chocolate overtones - my kind of beer. Paired with BBQ Cherry Salmon, char-grilled with Cherry Porter BBQ sauce and served with barley pilaf and fresh seasonal vegetables, it will leave you one happy camper. The building was a candy factory in its former life. Open 7 days, Mon to Thurs 11:00 am to 10:00 pm, Fri and Sat 11:00 am to 11:00 pm and Sun noon to 11:00 pm.

Old Mission Tavern, 17015 Center Road, Old Mission Peninsula, (231) 223-7280. Fresh fish, prime rib, chicken artichoke, rack of lamb, pastas, steaks and an extensive wine list. Next door to Bella Galleria. Together they make this place worth a stop to and a bit of your time. Open 7 days for lunch and dinner.

Omelette Shoppe and Bakery, 123 Cass Street, (231) 946-0590. Established more than 30 years ago this restaurant and bakery has been voted "Best Breakfast" by area residents for 21 consecutive years. Extensive breakfast and lunch menu. The sticky buns are worth the calories and there is an assortment of pastries if you want something sweet with your coffee. Lunch menu includes burgers and a special egg salad. Fantastic breads and rolls made fresh in their bakery.

Patio, 615 Front Street (in the Holiday Inn), (231) 947-3700. Seasonal beachside patio offering live entertainment Thurs to Sun from 5:30 pm to 9:30 pm. Also serves grilled foods and has a bar. Open Mon to Thurs 2:00 pm to 10:00 pm and Fri to Sun noon to 10:00 pm.

Panda North, 2038 South Airport Road, (231) 929-9722. On the river at Logan's Landing. Asian food including: Vietnamese, Chinese, Japanese and Thai. Open 7 days, Mon to Thurs 11:00 am to 9:30 pm, Fri and Sat 11:00 am to 10:30 pm and Sun noon to 9:30 pm.

Poppycock's, 128 East Front Street, (231) 941-7632. Funky atmosphere. Poppycock's serves a variety of menu items including: fresh fish, pasta, prime rib, wonderful salads and sandwiches. Also has a full bar, extensive martini list and excellent wines by the glass. Entertainment Fri and Sat 9:30 pm. Open Sun to Thurs 11:00 am to 9:00 pm, Fri and Sat 11:00 am to midnight and closed Sun. Late night dining when there is entertainment.

Rancho Grande West, 3860 Long Lake Road, (231) 933-5420. Home made soup, great entrees and a bar. Open weekdays 11:00 am to 9:30 pm, Fri 11:00 am to 10:00 pm and Sat and Sun noon to 9:30 pm.

Randy's Diner, 1103 South Garfield Avenue, (231) 946-0789, randysdiner@yahoo.com. You can go from one extreme "all you can eat specials" to the other "low cal entrees" and many things in between. 100% smoke free dining. Open Mon to Sat 6:00 am to 8:30 pm.

Red Mesa Grill, 1544 US-31 North, (231) 938-2773. The Roasted Chicken Black Bean Burrito is a taste treat for lunch, and the Argentina Pork Churrasco an entrée to consider for dinner. Outdoor seating available, weather permitting. The Tequila Bar serves a perfect Margarita while you wait. Great place to eat if you feel like Mexican food; they also serve Cuban and International dishes. Open 7 days, Sun to Thurs 11:00 am to 10:00 pm and Fri and Sat 11:00 am to 11:00 pm.

Roma's Italian Restaurant, 830 East Front Street, (231) 946-6710. Many family recipes among the entrees offered by this casual restaurant geared to family dining. Open 7 days year round, Mon to Sat 11:00 am to midnight and Sun noon to 9:00 pm.

Schelde's Grill and Spirits, 714 Munson Avenue (231) 946-0981, www.michiganmenu.com. It may be a steak house at heart but how can anyone resist trying the Cherry Apple Whitefish and combining three taste treats unique and well-known in the area. Open 7 days, 11:00 am to 10:00 pm.

Sleder's Tavern, 717 Randolf Street, (231) 947-9213. A landmark in Traverse City for more than a century, serving lunches and dinners with choices of Mexican dishes, steaks, fish or a sandwich. It is traditional to "Smooch the Moose" while there. Open 7 days, 9:30 am to 9:00 pm or 10:00 pm (kitchen) in the summer. Off-season: Mon to Sat 10:00 am to 6:00 pm and Sun 10:00 am to 5:00 pm.

South City Limits, 1407 South Division Street, (231) 933-5420. Well established and popular with local patrons who keep coming back for the American food served in hearty portions. Open 7 days, Mon to Thurs 11:00 am to 11:00 pm, Fri and Sat 11:00 am to midnight and Sun noon to 10:00 pm.

Streeters Bar and Grille, 1669 Garfield, (231) 932-1300, www.streetersonline.com. Half-pound burgers, sandwiches, Mexican, pizza, appetizers, salads, and desserts. Lots to do including 9 billiard tables. Dancing and live concerts. Hangout for the college crowd. Open Tues to Sat 4:00 pm to 2:00 am and Sun 4:00 pm to midnight.

Sue's J&S Hamburger, 1083 South Airport Road, (231) 941-8844. A place to get old-fashioned shakes and malts. All-you-can-eat fish fries Thurs to Sat. Breakfast specials. Open 7 days, Mon to Sat 6:00 am to 9:00 pm and Sun 8:00 am to 4:00 pm.

Trattoria Stella, 1200 West 11th Street, (231) 929-8989, www.stellatc.com. Located in the infamous Building Fifty (now called the Village) of the old Traverse City Psychiatric Facility. The menu at Stella's changes daily and incorporates fresh local produce and seafood flown in each day from both coasts. Extensive wine list. This superb Italian restaurant was often noted as a "favorite" when local merchants were asked where they like to eat. Open 7 days, Mon to Thurs 11:00 am to 10:00 pm, Fri and Sat 11:00 am to 2:00 am and Sun noon to 9:00 pm.

U & I Lounge, 214 East Front Street, (231) 946-8932. Catch your favorite sporting event on eight large screen TVs while enjoying Greek food and a drink. Open 7 days, Mon to Sat 11:00 am to 2:00 am and Sun noon to 2:00 am.

The Underground Cheesecake Company, 406 South Union Street, (231) 929-4418. The *Food Network* called this the "food find" of gourmet desserts. The obvious is that they specialize in cheesecakes including their unique Cheesecake on a Stick: five flavors of cheesecake hand-dipped in chocolate. The less obvious is that they also offer two homemade soups, salads, muffins, brownies, cookies and espresso drinks. Open Mon to Fri 9:00 am to 5:30 pm, Sat 9:00 am to 3:00 pm and closed Sun.

Window's, 7677 South West Bay Shore Drive, (231) 941-0100. Wonderful French restaurant noted by many locals to be their very favorite restaurant for special occasions. Romantic ambiance and superb food. Fresh seafood is their specialty and you cannot go wrong if you try the Whitefish Pecandine or the walleye, but every entrée on the menu will make your taste buds smile. Open during the summer 7 days for dinner at 5:00 pm. In October they begin closing on Sunday.

Wingers Sports Bar, 615 East Front Street in the Holiday Inn, (231) 947-3700. High definition TVs for watching your favorite college or pro team. Wingers is located with views of the beach so prepare to be a bit distracted by the bay activity. Sandwiches and light fare. Open 7 days, 11:00 am to midnight.

Lodging (Also see Campgrounds below)

Several motels/resorts close after Labor Day so if you are traveling in the off-season, call first.

AmericInn of Traverse City, 1614 US-31 North, (231) 938-0262 or toll-free (800) 441-1903. 48 rooms. Extras: indoor pool, sauna, whirlpool, laundry, continental breakfast, some in-room fireplaces and whirlpools.

Antiquities Wellington Inn, 230 Wellington Street, (231) 922-9900 or toll-free (877) 968-9900, www.wellingtoninn.com, e-mail:

stay@wellingtoninn.com. Authentically restored neoclassical mansion offering nine guest rooms plus two 2-bedroom carriage house suites. All rooms with private baths. Amenities: walking distance to beaches, afternoon tea, carriage rides available, breakfast served in elegant dining room. Pricy but elegant rooms.

Baymont Inns and Suites, 2326 South US-31 North, (231) 933-4454 or toll-free (800) 301-0200, www.baymontinns.com. 119-rooms, located next to the Grand Traverse Mall. Extras: internet, indoor pool, fitness room, whirlpool, microwaves and refrigerators and breakfast. Two-room and Jacuzzi suites available.

Bayshore Resort, 833 East Front Street, (231) 935-4400 or toll-free (800) 634-4401, www.bayshore-resort.com, bayshore@bayshore-resort.com. 120 rooms in a lovely Victorian-style hotel located on the beach of the West Grand Traverse Bay. Extras: rooms with private balconies or patios and views of the bay, some in-room spas and fireplaces, indoor pool, spa, fitness room, game room, laundry, continental breakfast and free high-speed internet. Room prices go up to $300+, but they do have rooms at significantly lower rates as well.

The Beach Condominiums Hotel and Resort, 1995 US-31 North, www.beachcondohotel.com, (231) 938-2228 or toll-free (800) 778-2228. 30 privately owned condominiums on East Grand Traverse Bay. 267 feet of sandy beach, outdoor heated pool and spa and WIFI. Daily, midweek, weekend and 5-day specials.

The Beach Haus Resort, 1489 US-31 North, (231) 947-3560, beachhausresort@aol.com. 30 rooms, some with private patios overlooking 200 feet of sandy beach. Extras: refrigerators, computer compatible phones, spa units with king beds, VCR, HBO, wet bar, continental breakfast, microwaves and BBQ area.

Best Western Four Seasons, 305 Munson Avenue (US-31 North), www.traversecitylodging.com, (231) 946-8424 or toll-free (800) 823-7844. 74 recently renovated rooms. Extras: some deluxe two-story, loft spa rooms, continental breakfast and free local calls.

Chateau Chantal B&B, 15900 Rue de Vin, Old Mission Peninsula, www.chateauchantal.com, wine@chateauchantal.com, (231) 223-4110 or toll-free (800) 969-4009. Eleven units in a very scenic setting in the middle of a winery, vineyards and winding roads.

Cherry Tree Inn on the Beach, 2345 US-31 North, www.cherrytreeinn.com, cti@cherrytreeinn.com, (231) 938-8888 or toll-free (800) 439-3093. Beautiful, upscale inn with 75 rooms and suites. 400 feet of private beach on the East Grand Traverse Bay. A smoke free facility. Extras: refrigerators, microwaves, in-room coffee maker, safes, HBO and Disney, free WIFI internet access, bathrooms with 9-inch TV and telephone, indoor pool and spa, exercise facility, game room, laundry, whirlpool rooms with fireplaces available and many rooms with balcony. Jet ski rentals on site (231) 633-2583.

Courtyard by Marriott, 3615 South Airport Road West, (231) 929-1800 or toll-free (800) 321-2211, www.courtyard.com. 83 rooms designed with the business traveler in mind. Minutes from downtown. Extras: internet, whirlpool rooms with fireplaces available, indoor pool, whirlpool, fitness center, laundry, restaurant and lounge on premises.

Cross Creek Hotel, 877 Munson Avenue, (231) 946-7044 or toll-free (800) 678-1308. Located on 700 feet of beautiful, sandy Grand Traverse Bay. Extras: living area with sleeper sofa, one person Jacuzzi tub, microwave and small refrigerator. Only open Memorial Day through Labor Day weekend.

Days Inn and Suites, 420 Munson Avenue, www.tcdaysinn.com, hotelinfo@tcdaysinn.com, (231) 941-0208 or toll-free (800) 982-3297. 180 rooms. Extras: some two-room family suites, some two person Jacuzzis, some fireplaces, business rooms with microwave, refrigerator and data port, HBO, large indoor, heated pool and spa, exercise room, in-room wireless internet and continental breakfast.

Econo Lodge, 1065 M-37 South, (231) 943-3040 or toll-free (800) 553-2666. 47 rooms, seven miles from downtown Traverse City. Extras: continental breakfast, data ports, whirlpool tub rooms, indoor pool and spa, ample parking for vehicles hauling boats, snowmobile trailers and larger vehicles.

Fairfield Inn by Marriott, 3701 North Country Drive, (231) 922-7900, www.fairfieldinn.com. 85 rooms, 12 spa rooms. Extras: indoor pool, spa, exercise room, continental breakfast and free internet.

Gold Coast Inn, 4612 US-31 North, (231) 938-2538 or toll-free (800) 939-2538, www.goldcoastinntc.com. 29 rooms with views of the spectacular East Bay sunsets. Relax in your in-room spa and watch activity on the bay unfold before you.

Grand Beach Resort Hotel, 1683 US-31 North, (231) 938-4455 or toll-free (800) 968-1992, www.tcbeaches.com, gbeach@infinite.com. Beautiful resort with 97 rooms and 6 beachfront condos on over 300 feet of sugar-sand beach on the East Grand Traverse Bay. Extras: indoor pool, spa, continental breakfast, exercise room, laundry, video arcade, family suites, high-speed internet, HBO, VCRs and some rooms with in-room spa.

Grand Traverse Motel, 1010 East Front Street, (231) 947-9410. Basic motel with 18 rooms near downtown, shopping, dining and beaches. Extras: refrigerators, microwaves, VCRs, outdoor heated pool and sun deck.

The Great Wolf Lodge, 3573 North US-31 South, (231) 941-3600 or toll-free (866) GR8-WOLF, traverseinfo@greatwolflodge.com, www.greatwolflodge.com. 281 suites featuring north woods décor. This is a log-cabin style family retreat featuring a 52,000 square foot indoor entertainment area, large water park, outdoor pool, restaurants and 100 foot game arcade. Other extras: microwaves and mini refrigerators. Live buffalo on the grounds. You can enjoy casual dining at the **Loose Moose Cottage** inside the Lodge.

Hampton Inn, 1000 US-31 North, (231) 946-8900 or toll-free (800) HAMPTON, www.hampton-inn.com/hi/traversecity. Three miles from downtown Traverse City and across the street from the State Park Public Beach. Extras: complimentary hot breakfast bar, indoor pool, hot tub, fitness center, high speed internet, HBO and airport shuttle.

Heritage Inn, 417 Munson Avenue, www.heritageinn-tc.com, heritageinn@infinatecom, (231) 947-9520 or toll-free (800) 968-0105. 39 rooms, half with heart-shaped, two-person spas. Extras: VCR, HBO, Cinemax, continental breakfast, game and exercise rooms.

Holiday Inn West Bay, 615 East Front Street, (231) 947-3700 or toll-free (800) 888-8020, www.tcwestbay.com, sales@tcwestbay.com. A full service hotel on the waterfront in downtown Traverse City with 179 rooms. Extras: indoor/outdoor pools, sauna, whirlpool, fitness center, game room, nightclub with live entertainment, boat rentals, Nauti-Cat cruises, sandy beach and seasonal dock.

Island View Cottages, 853 East Front Street, (231) 947-2863, www.islandv.com. A variety of options including: 9 cottages, 3-bedroom beach house, 3-bedroom carriage house and a 4-bedroom colonial house. Great sandy beach.

Lakeshore Resort, 1897 US-31 North, (231) 938-1094 or toll-free (800) 968-1094. Standard type facility with 13 beachfront cottages and condos on the Grand Traverse Bay. Enjoy sandy beach and your choice of one or two-bedroom units. Extras: digital cable, VCR, fire pit, gas grill and picnic tables.

Mitchell Creek Inn, 894 Munson Avenue, (231) 947-9330 or toll-free (800) 947-9330, www.mitchellcreek.com. 13 rooms and two 2-bedroom cottages. Extras: views of Grand Traverse Bay and State Park, beach access, cable, kitchenette and trout stream. Knotty-pine décor.

Motel 6, 1582 US-31 North, (231) 938-3002, or toll-free (800) 4MOTELS, www.motel6.com. 43 rooms. Extras: indoor pool, whirlpool, cable TV, HBO, ESPN, cable hook-up, free local calls, coffee, laundry, game room and microwave and refrigerator available.

Neahtawanta Inn, North of Traverse City on Old Mission Peninsula. Opened in 1906 as the Sunrise Inn and guests arrived by boat. Began operating as Neahtawanta Inn B&B in 1985. More than 300 feet of beach on Bowers Harbor. Surrounded by woods and water, the inn is a place to enjoy serenity. Large living room/dining room has a sunken fieldstone fire pit and a library where you can grab a book and take a literary escape from the real world. Breakfasts are vegetarian and healthy. There is a wood-burning sauna behind the inn available to guests. Some rooms share a bath. Resident cat and dog allowed in common areas. Yoga studio available during your visit.

North Shore Inn, 2305 US-31 North, (231) 938-2365 or toll-free (800) 968-2365. 26 one and two-room condominiums in a pleasant New England-style beachfront hotel. Extras: 200 feet of sandy beach, outdoor pool, kitchens, HBO, VCR, laundry, WIFI and special packages available.

The Old Mission Inn, 18599 Mission Road, Old Mission Peninsula, (231) 223-7770, www.oldmissioninn.com. Built in 1869 the Old Mission Inn pays homage to the history of Old Mission, displaying a "Hall of History." Rooms are decorated in a Victorian motif.

Park Place Hotel, 300 East State Street, (231) 946-5000, or toll-free (800) 748-0133, www.park-place-hotel.com. 140 rooms and suites recently renovated and overlooking Grand Traverse Bay in the heart of downtown. Extras: indoor pool, whirlpool, sauna, fitness room, panoramic views from Beacon Lounge located at the "Top of the Park."

Park Shore Resort, 1401 US-31 North, (231) 947-3800, or toll-free (877) 349-8898, www.parkshoreresort.com. Great resort with 80 rooms on the East Grand Traverse Bay. Extras: refrigerators in each room, HBO, safes, deluxe whirlpool/fireplace efficiency suites, business class rooms, high speed internet, indoor pool, continental breakfast, video arcade, laundry, fitness room, whirlpool, walkout patios on first floor, private balconies with great views of the bay on the upper floors, and a beautiful beach with BBQ grills, volleyball area, bonfire pit and on-site jet ski, parasailing and boat rentals.

Petals and Pines B&B, 19963 Center Road, Old Mission Peninsula, (231) 223-4024. Beautiful B&B 18 miles north of Traverse City. Features giant century-old pine trees, Victorian garden, lovely views of West Grand Traverse Bay, large porch that begs a quiet hour or two of reading, and relaxing walks in the woodland across the road, biking and cross country skiing and snowshoeing in winter. Only a mile from Lighthouse Park. Open year round.

Pine Crest Motel, 360 Munson Avenue, (231) 947-8900 or toll-free (800) 223-4433. Basic 35 room, family-owned motel. King, queen or 2 queen beds. Direct dial phones with data ports. Extras: free local calls, VCR, HBO, refrigerators, outdoor pool, indoor exercise pool and spa, continental breakfast and two-person whirlpools in some rooms.

Pinestead Reef Resort, 1265 US-31 North, www.pinestead.com, pinestead@pinestead.com, (231) 947-4010 or toll-free (800) 968-1302. 46 beautiful waterfront suites situated on 700 feet of sandy beach and each with a fantastic view of the East Grand Traverse Bay. Extras: full kitchen with dishwasher, HBO, Movie Channel, VCR, DVD, indoor heated pool, whirlpool, sauna, exercise room, game room, internet access, laundry, movie rentals, weekly planned activities, BBQ deck with gas grills and located across from the Traverse City State Park. These condos are actually time shares, but the owners often put their units up for nightly or weekly rental. Open year round.

Pointes North Inn, 2211 US-31 North, www.pointesnorth.com, getaway@pointesnorth.com, (231) 938-9191 or toll-free (800) 968-3422. 51 suites/rooms on 300 feet of sandy East Grand Traverse Bay Beach. Each room has a balcony to insure that you will enjoy the view. Extras: refrigerators, VCR, heated outdoor bayside pool.

Quality Inn, 1492 US-31 North, (231) 929-4423. 96 rooms and suites, some with Jacuzzis. Extras: continental breakfast, free local phone calls, data port phones, safes, indoor pool and whirlpool.

Ranch Rudolf, 6841 Brownbridge Road, (231) 947-9529, www.ranchrudolf.com. 16 rooms and 25 campsites at this year-round ranch. Offers horseback riding, canoeing, tubing, horse drawn hay rides, snowmobiling, cross-country skiing and sleigh rides by season.

Sands Motel, 1465 US-31 North, (231) 946-6930, (800) 946-6930, www.thesandsmotel.com, thesands@voyager.net. Standard type motel with 21 rooms on the East Bay. Extras: microwave, refrigerators, VCR, private beach, deluxe breakfast bar and sports rentals.

Sierra Motel, 230 Munson Avenue, (231) 946-7720. Basic motel with 20 rooms close to downtown and the beaches. Extras: cable TV and free local calls. One of the lower priced motels in the area.

Sugar Beach Resort Hotel, 1773 US-31 North, (231) 938-0100 or toll-free (800) 509-1995, sbeach@sugarbeach.com, www.tcbeaches.com. Great resort with 97 rooms on East Grand Traverse Bay including: family suites, beachfront rooms with private balconies, deluxe rooms with in-room spas and deluxe 3-bedroom apartment. Extras: indoor pool and spa, continental breakfast, exercise room, laundry, game room, VCR and high speed internet.

Super 8 Motel, 1870 US-31 North, (231) 938-1887 or toll-free (800) 800-8000. 66 rooms three miles from downtown Traverse City. Extras: in-room spas and fireplace rooms available, HBO, ESPN, free local calls, free coffee, breakfast bar and laundry.

Tamarack Lodge, 2035 US-31 North, (231) 938-9744 or toll-free (877) 938-9744, www.tamaracklodgetc.com. A variety of lovely accommodations including: 29 rooms and 1, 2, and 3-bedroom luxury condominiums situated on 800 feet of beautiful East Grand Traverse Bay's sugar-sand beaches. Views of the bay from every room or condo. Condos: fully equipped gourmet kitchens, private balconies, fireplaces, cable, flat screen TV, DVD, VCR, WIFI, washer/dryer, jetted tubs, concierge, children's activities, airport shuttle and smoke-free.

Terrace Beach Motel, 841 East Front Street, (231) 946-9220. Standard motel with 33 rooms on 160 feet of Grand Traverse West Bay. Extras: HBO, free coffee and some water-view rooms.

Travelodge/Fox Haus, 704 Munson Avenue, (231) 922-9590, (231) 922-9111 or toll-free (866) 286-1621. 80 remodeled rooms. Extras: heated outdoor pool, whirlpool, game room, tennis courts, continental breakfast and some two-room suites with full kitchens.

Traverse Bay Lodge, 460 Munson Avenue, (231) 947-5436. 60 rooms, some with whirlpools. Extras: whirlpool and exercise room.

Traverse Bay Inn, 2300 US-31 North, (231) 938-2646 or toll-free (800) 968-2646, www.traversebayinn.com. 24 rooms, one and two-bedroom suites, and studios. Some rooms with Jacuzzis and fireplaces. Daily or weekly accommodations available year round. Extras: outdoor heated pool, hot tub, picnic area with gas grills, VCRs, game room, laundry, gift shop, beach access across street, and complimentary bicycles and snowshoes available for use on adjoining recreational trail.

Traverse Victorian Inn, 461 Munson Avenue, (231) 947-5525 or toll-free (Michigan only) (800) 506-5525, www.traversevictorian.com. 68 rooms each with a gas log fireplace. Extras: refrigerators, free local calls, HBO, indoor atrium style pool, hot tub and close to the beach.

The Warwickshire Inn, 5037 Barney Road, (231) 946-7176. Unique antique filled 1900s country farmhouse located two miles west of Traverse City next to Devonshire Antiques. Full breakfast.

Museums and Galleries

Art and Soul Gallery, 140 East Front Street, (231) 947-4888, www.artandsoultc.com. Contemporary gifts and fine art including: pottery, glass, metal, jewelry and wood. Open 7 days, 10:00 am to 6:00 pm in the summer. Reduced hours off-season.

Bella Galleria and Sculpture Studio, 17015 Center Road, (same building as the Old Mission Tavern on Old Mission Peninsula), (231) 223-4142. Showcases the works of over 75 artists, some well-known in the area and beyond. Bronzes, oils, watercolors, batiks, fiber art, blown glass, fused glass, direct metal, acrylics and prints. Open year round, 7 days, 11:30 am to 4:00 pm or 5:00 pm. Wait staff of the Old Mission Tavern can help customers anytime the Tavern is open.

By the Bay Nautical Fine Art Gallery, 172 East Main, (231) 933-4460 or toll-free (877) 933-4460. Original fine art, limited edition prints, model boats, relief maps, books, clocks, lighthouses and other unique items with a nautical theme. Open 7 days, Mon to Sat 10:00 am to 5:30 pm and Sun 11:00 am to 4:00 pm.

Dennos Museum Center, 1701 East Front Street (on the campus of Northwestern Michigan College), (231) 995-1055. The museum has a permanent collection that is one of the largest and most historically complete displays of sculptures, prints and drawings of the Inuit artists from the Canadian Arctic. They also have changing exhibits of historical and contemporary art and a hands-on Discovery Gallery that children will love. From September to May the museum presents more than 25 concerts in the 367 seat Milliken Auditorium. The Gift Shop carries the works of many local artists. Open summer 7 days, Mon to Sat 10:00 am to 5:00 pm and Sun 1:00 pm to 5:00 pm.

The Dougherty House, Eighteen miles north of Traverse City on Old Mission Peninsula. Built in 1842 by Reverend Peter Dougherty, it is the first frame building in the region. It is a replica of a log house used as a church and school for the Chippewa Native Americans.

Gallery 50, 830 Cottageview Drive, (231) 932-0775. Gallery 50 is located in the original Building 50 of the former Traverse City Regional Psychiatric Facility. (See p. 420, Part II for a related ghost story.) They carry *Art with Purpose*. Displayed are the works of many artists: jewelry, fine art, fiber, metal, ceramics, photography, glass and wood. Open Mon to Sat noon to 5:00 pm.

Grand Traverse Heritage Center, 322 Sixth Street, (231) 995-0313. Small museum showcasing the history of the area with emphasis on the Native Americans, railroads, the lumber era, local pioneers and the shipping industry. The Historical Society's research archives are open to the public. Open Tues to Fri noon to 4:00 pm and Sat 10:00 am to 4:00 pm. Not open on Saturdays January to May.

Great Lakes Children's Museum, 13240 South West Bay Shore Drive, (M-22 in Greilickville just north of Traverse City limits) (231) 932-4526, www.GreatLakesKids.org. Includes a great website with separate entrances for grown-ups and kids. The kids have a link to the yuckiest stuff on the internet (information about things most polite company prefers to ignore: pimples, belches, etc.). The museum has a variety of games, activities and interesting exhibits for your children. They will love the weather cart, the water table area and the art room. Open 7 days, Mon to Sat 10:00 am to 5:00 pm and Sun 1:00 pm to 5:00 pm. Closed Mon during the remainder of the year except school holidays when they open so children can enjoy this wonderful museum.

Watermelon Sugar Gallery and Gifts, 153 East Front Street, (231) 929-7426. Showcases the work of more than 200 local Michigan artists in crafted stoneware, pottery, jewelry, watercolors, photography, blown glass, gift cards, sculpture and hand painted windows. Open 7 days, Mon to Wed and Sat 10:00 am to 6:00 pm, Thurs and Fri 10:00 am to 8:00 pm and Sun 11:00 am 4:00 pm. Reduced hours off-season.

Wooden Gallery, 116 East Front Street, (231) 941-0823, www.thewoodengallery.com. Features the Wooden Gallery process of acrylic emulsion to bring out the very best in a print, lithograph, giclee, photograph or poster. Open year round 10:00 am to 6:00 pm.

Theatre

The City Opera House, 112½ East Front Street, (231) 941-8082, info@cityoperahouse.org. Constructed in 1891 the Opera House seats 720 people for a variety of performances and events. Call for details.

The Milliken Auditorium, 1701 East Front Street (Dennos Museum Center) (231) 995-1553. Provides a 365-seat theatre and brings in touring productions.

The Open Space Theatre, Corner of Union Street and Grandview Parkway, (231) 392-1134. A beautiful gathering place with its views of the spectacular West Grand Traverse Bay. Site of the Traverse City Film Festival.

The Old Town Playhouse, 148 East 8th Street, (231) 947-2443. Home to the Traverse City Civic Players that came into existence in 1960 to bring amateur theatre to Traverse City. The productions range from Broadway musicals to avant-garde, one-act plays. The season runs from fall to summer. The mainstage theatre can seat 358 and there is also an 80-seat studio theatre. Call for current information.

Traverse City Children's Theatre, 148 East 8th Street, (231) 947-2210, www.tcctheatre.org. Last year they produced *A Thousand Cranes*, *The Wind in the Willows* and others. Call for details.

Antiques

Americana Collection of Traverse City, 224 East Front Street, (231) 933-0297. Antiques, art, and accessories for home and cottage. Open 7 days, year round. Mon to Sat 10:00 am to 6:00 pm (8:00 pm on Fri) and Sun noon to 5:00 pm.

Antique Company East Bay, 4386 US-31 North, (231) 938-3000. Their slogan is *"If we don't have it, we will help you find it."* Open May to December, 7 days, 10:00 am to 6:00 pm. January to April open Fri to Sun 10:00 am to 6:00 pm.

Bay West Antiques, 221 West Grandview Parkway, (231) 947-3211. Antiques and collectibles, floor to ceiling. Open 7 days, year round, 10:00 am to 6:00 pm.

Cherry Acres Antiques, 12396 Peninsula Drive, (231) 223-4813. Antique furniture, tins, postcards, toys, graniteware, collectibles and advertising items. Open Mon to Sat 10:00 am to 5:00 pm (or by appointment or chance). Closed Sun.

Ella's Vintage Clothing and Collectibles, 157 East Front Street, (231) 947-9401. The name is an apt description. Open Mon to Fri 10:00 am to 8:00 pm, Sat 10:00 am to 6:00 pm and Sun 11:00 am to 4:00 pm.

Rolling Hills Antiques, 5065 Barney Road, two miles from downtown, (231) 947-1063. Two floors of antiques housed in a renovated 1870s barn. Specializes in Early American antique furniture, accessories and architectural pieces. Also carries lamps, light fixtures, glassware, pottery, area rugs, prints, framed paintings, fold art, tools, kitchen utensils, toys and more. Open year round, 6 days, 11:00 am to 6:00 pm. Closed Tues.

Walt's Barn Antiques, 2513 Nelson Road, Old Mission Peninsula, (231) 223-4123. An interesting and eclectic assortment of merchandise from vintage gas pumps and globes to furniture and a whole lot in between including: vintage clothing, jewelry, buttons, postcards, rare and common antiques. Three crowded floors with items from the 1850s to 1900s. Open 7 days, Mon to Sat 10:00 am to 5:30 pm and Sun noon to 5:30 pm. Reduced winter hours, call ahead.

Wilson's Antiques, 123 South Union Street, (231) 946-4177, www.wilsonantiquemall.com. Four floors of beautifully displayed antiques. Voted Traverse City's Best Antique Shop" four years in a row, 2000 through 2003, by the *Preview* (Traverse City Paper). Open 7 days, Mon to Sat 10:00 am to 6:00 pm and Sun 11:00 am to 5:00 pm.

Other Shopping

Backcountry Outfitters, 227 East Front Street, (231) 946-1339. Clothing and camping gear including: tents, footwear, backpacks, sandals, kayaks and outerwear. Open 7 days, Mon to Fri 9:30 am to 6:00 pm, Sat 10:00 am to 6:00 pm and Sun 11:00 am to 4:00 pm.

The Banana Tree, 120 East Front Street, (231) 941-0466. Clothes to hang out in. Open summer 7 days, Mon to Thurs 9:30 am to 9:00 pm (sometimes 10:00 pm), Fri and Sat 9:30 am to 10:00 pm and Sun 11:00 am to 7:00 pm. Reduced off-season hours.

Becky Thatcher, 541 West Front Street, (231) 947-5088. A downtown boutique featuring jewelry created with natural treasures of the region including beach glass, stones, and even pinecones and birch bark. Open Mon to Sat 10:00 am to 5:00 pm and closed Sun. Closed Mon in the off-season, but extended Christmas hours.

Boyne Country Sports, 101 East Front Street, (231) 941-1999. Coats, jackets and casual wear for the entire family. Ski wear, skis and snowboards. Open 7 days, Mon to Thurs 10:00 am to 5:00 pm, Fri and Sat 10:00 am to 8:00 pm and Sun 11:00 am to 4:00 pm. (Extended hours before Christmas).

244

By Candlelight, 336 West Front Street, (231) 947-1000. Amish Furnishings. Much of their business is custom ordered. So, if you need something special built just for you, this might be a place to consider. The items are all hand-crafted out of solid American hardwood. Open Mon to Sat 10:00 am to 5:30 pm.

Cali's, 242 East Front Street, (231) 947-0633. Two floors: a boutique downstairs and furniture and accessories upstairs. Open 7 days, Mon to Thurs 9:30 am to 6:00 pm, Fri 9:30 am to 8:00 pm, Sat 9:30 am to 6:00 pm and Sun noon to 4:00 pm.

The Candle Factory, 301 West Grandview Parkway on the West Bay Waterfront, (231) 946-2280, www.candles.net. A one-hundred-year-old building houses the Candle Factory and **Home Elements.** The Candle Factory carries seasonal candles, candles made in the sand of the Grand Traverse Beach and other beautiful candles for every occasion. Home Elements has linens, placemats, bright dishes, napkins, kitchenware and gadgets of every description. Open 7 days, Mon to Sat 9:30 am to 9:00 pm and Sun 10:00 am to 5:00 pm. Off-season hours Mon to Wed 9:30 am to 6:00 pm, Thurs to Sat 9:30 am to 9:00 pm and Sun 10:00 am to 5:00 pm. Reduced after Christmas.

Captain's Quarters, 151 East Front Street, (231) 946-7066. Fine men's clothing from casual to formal. Open 7 days, Mon to Fri 9:30 am to 8:00 pm, Sat 9:30 am to 6:00 pm and Sun noon to 4:00 pm.

The Celtic Rose Irish Shop, 140 East Front Street, (231) 922-2550. Carries Belleek Fine China, Guinness Merchandise, sterling jewelry, door knockers and more than 200 Irish items. Open Mon to Sat 10:30 am to 6:00 pm in the summer. Call for off-season hours.

Cherry Hill Boutique, 155 East Front Street (231) 929-3940, www.cherryhillclothing.com. Sophisticated and stylish clothing of Fresh Produce and Brighton. Open 7 days, Mon to Fri 10:00 am to 5:30 pm, Sat 10:00 am to 8:00 pm and Sun 10:00 am to 4:00 pm. Reduced hours in the off-season and closed in the dead of winter.

The Cherry Stop, 211 East Front Street, (231) 929-3990, www.cherrystop.com. Every cherry product you can imagine including: dried cherries, chocolate covered cherries, fruit blends, snack mixes, jams, condiments, canned cherries, cherry coffee, cherry truffles, gift boxes, pies, wines and baked goods. Open 7 days, 10:00 am to about 8:00 pm in the summer. Variable hours other seasons.

Children's World, 140 East Front Street, (231) 946-3450. A place to suspend reality and give free rein to the child in you. This shop is filled to the brim with teddy bears, puppets, miniature dollhouses, trains, wagons, games, rocking horses, dolls and simple things like marbles. Open July to August Mon to Sat 10:00 am to 8:00 pm and Sun

11:00 am to 4:00 pm. Off-season hours: Mon to Sat 10:00 am to 6:00 pm and closed some Sun. Extended holiday hours and by appointment.

The Cottage Garden, 205 East Front Street, (231) 929-9005. Lots of beautiful decorating accents for the home and garden. Open 7 days, Mon to Sat 10:00 am to 6:00 pm and Sun noon to 4:00 pm.

Cucina, 107 East Front Street, (231) 932-8787. A cook's paradise and the place to buy beautiful dishes, glassware or even take a cooking class. Similar to Williams-Sonoma, but smaller. Open 7 days, Mon to Sat 10:00 am to 6:00 pm and Sun noon to 4:00 pm.

Dandelion, 130 East Front Street, www.dandelionkids.com, (231) 933-4340. Clothing and gifts for kids. Open 7 days, Mon to Thurs 9:30 am to 8:00 pm, Fri 9:30 am to 9:00 pm, Sat 9:30 am to 7:00 pm and Sun 11:00 am to 5:00 pm. Winter hours: closes a bit earlier each day.

Del Sol, 154 East Front Street (231) 941-5030. Clothing (shorts, shirts and hats) and accessories (sunglasses, nail polish, watches, jewelry and hair accessories) that change color when exposed to the sun. Meant to be fun and make you smile. Open 7 days, Sun to Thurs 11:00 am to 7:00 pm and Fri and Sat 10:00 am to 9:00 pm. Slightly reduced hours in the off-season.

Diversions, 104 East Front Street, (231) 946-6500. More than 1,000 styles of hats. Something for everyone. Open 7 days, Mon to Sat 10:00 am to 6:00 pm and Sun 11:00 am to 4:00 pm.

Ella's, 157 East Front Street, (231) 947-9401. Cool vintage and retro apparel for men and women. Open 7 days, Mon to Thurs 10:00 am to 6:00 pm, Fri 10:00 am to 8:00 pm, Sat 10:00 am to 6:00 pm and Sun 11:00 am to 4:00 pm.

Euphoria, 139 East Front Street, (231) 922-9901. Embellishments for everyday, including handcrafted jewelry and accessories. Open 7 days, Mon to Sat 10:00 am to 6:00 pm and Sun (seasonally) noon to 4:00 pm.

Folgarelli's, 424 West Front Street, www.folgarellis.com, (231) 941-7651. Wine shop with excellent selection. Open Mon to Fri 9:30 am to 6:30 pm, Sat 9:30 am to 5:30 pm and closed Sun.

Grand Bay Kites, 121 East Front Street, (231) 929-0607, www.grandbaykite.com. Kites, plain and fancy. Open 7 days, Mon to Sat 10:00 am to 6:00 pm or later, and Sun noon to 4:00 pm in the summer. Reduced winter hours posted on web page.

Green Island, 116 South Union Street, (231) 933-8465. A store with a conscience: earth friendly merchandise that looks great while respecting the environment. You will find colorful tablecloths made in the villages of India, naturally-dyed carpets hand-knotted by Tibetans who live in exile in Nepal, soy candles that contain no lead in their wicks and recycled glassware. The children's clothing includes a line made from pesticide free cotton. Open 7 days, Mon to Sat 10:00 am to 6:00 pm and Sun noon to 3:00 pm. Off-season closes at 5:00 pm on Sat and closes some Sun depending on business.

Harbor Wear, 125 East Front Street (231) 935-4688. Casual cotton resort clothing. Open 7 days, Mon to Sat 9:30 am to 9:00 pm and Sun 10:00 am to 6:00 pm.

Home Essentials, 225 East Front Street, (231) 929-0799. Lots of wine-related merchandise and other gifts. Collegiate Tiffany lamps, wine racks, wine bars and wall art. Open 7 days, Mon to Sat 10:00 am to 6:00 pm and Sun 10:00 am to 5:00 pm.

Horizon Books, 243 East Front Street, (231) 946-7290. Coffee Bar, café and live music. Bookstore open 7 days, 8:00 am to 11:00 pm, Coffee Shop open 7 days, 7:00 am to 11:00 pm.

Items, 156 East Front Street, (231) 922-6787. Women's Clothing boutique with lots of accessories. Open 7 days, generally until 10:00 pm in the summer. Hours vary so a call would be wise.

Kay's, 219 East Front Street, (231) 941-3429. High-end women's clothing: lingerie, suits and accessories. Open 7 days, Mon to Thurs 10:00 am to 6:00 pm, Fri 10:00 am to 8:00 pm, Sat 10:00 am to 6:00 pm and Sun noon to 4:00 pm.

Kilwin's of Traverse City, 129 East Front Street, (231) 946-2403 or toll-free (800) 544-0596. Ice-cream, candy and other confections. Open in the summer 7 days, Mon to Sat 10:00 am to 6:00 pm and Sun noon to 4:00 pm.

The Leaping Lizard, 207 East Front Street, (231) 935-4470. Great linen dishtowels, jewelry, chimes, garden art, wall art and cards. Open 7 days, Mon to Sat 10:00 am to 5:30 pm, Sun noon to 4:00 pm.

ML & Company, 204 East Front Street, (231) 933-8454, www.mlandcompany.com. Women's boutique. Open Mon to Fri 10:00 am to 6:00 pm and Sat 10:00 am to 5:30 pm.

Momentum, 215 East Front Street. This is a customer driven store that does no advertising. They have become known strictly by word of mouth as customers pass along information about the great prices. They offer 40-70% off retail prices of resort wear and brand name clothing. They now have 7 locations in Northern Michigan and also have their own line of clothing which sells at terrific prices. It is their prices that keep their customers loyal. Tour buses actually stop to let shoppers check out the merchandise and purchase some bargains. Open 7 days in the summer, 9:00 am to 10:00 pm. Reduced fall hours, 7 days, Sun to Thurs 11:00 am to 6:00 pm and Fri and Sat 11:00 am to 7:00 pm. Hours further reduced after Christmas, Traverse City and Petoskey stores open 7 days year round.

Muriel's, 238 East Front Street, (231) 933-9745. Distinctive clothing for the mature woman who is young at heart. Fashionable and comfortable clothes. Open Mon to Sat 10:00 am to 6:00 pm.

My Favorite Things, 143 East Front Street (231) 929-9665, Gifts, accents, knickknacks, embroidered linen towels and miscellaneous. Open 7 days, Mon to Thurs 10:00 am to 6:00 pm, Fri 10:00 am to 8:00 pm, Sat 10:00 am to 6:00 pm and Sun 11:00 am to 5:00 pm. Hours change at the holidays.

Painted Door Gallery, 539 East 8th Street, (231) 929-4988. Antiques, gifts, folk art and collectibles. Open 7 days, 10:00 am to 6:00 pm. Some extended hours and closed Sun January to March.

Panache, 118 South Union Street, (231) 929-4225. A woman's shoe store with footwear the owner describes as appropriate for the lovelies of "Sex and the City." The shoes are fairly inexpensive and run from a mere $10. to maybe $70 at the high end.

Peppercorn, 226 East Front Street, (231) 941-4146. Kitchen store with lots of fun items - even carries treats for your dog and cat. Open 7 days, Mon to Sat 10:00 am to 6:00 pm and Sun 11:00 am to 4:00 pm.

Pop-Kies, 147 East Front Street, (231) 933-3000 or toll-free (877) 476-7543. 30+ flavors of great popcorn. Open 7 days, Sun to Thurs 11:00 am to 5:30 pm and Fri and Sat 11:00 am to 9:00 pm. Reduced hours in the winter: Mon to Sat 11:00 am to 5:30 pm.

Preferred Outlets at Traverse City, 3639 Market Place Circle, US-31, (231) 941-9211. If you are looking for discounted prices on familiar labels like Izod, Bass, Koret, Gap, Pendleton and more, you might want to give this place a try. Open 7 days Mon to Sat 10:00 am to 9:00 pm and Sun 11:00 am to 6:00 pm.

Pregger's, 417 South Union and 137 East Front Street, (231) 933-MAMA. Stores for Mom-to-be and baby. Maternity clothing, nursery furniture, baby clothes. Open 7 days, Mon to Sat 10:00 am to 6:00 pm and Sun 11:00 am to 4:00 pm.

Raven's Child, 220 East Front Street, (231) 941-8552. Contemporary clothes petite to plus size, casual to formal. Accessories and shoes. Open Mon and Tues 10:00 am to 6:00 pm, Wed to Fri 10:00 am to 8:00 pm, Sat 10:00 am to 6:00 pm and Sun noon to 4:00 pm.

Rue 101, 101 East Front Street, (231) 933-0101. Clothing store and boutique. Open 7 days, Mon to Sat 10:30 am to 5:30 pm and Sun noon to 3:00 pm. (Sun hours vary.)

So Many Books, So Little Time, 140 East Front Street, (231) 922-5916. Books, books and more books. Open Mon to Fri 10:00 am to 6:00 pm, Sat 10:30 am to 6:00 pm and closed Sun year round.

Spiral's, 121 East Front Street, (231) 929-7066. Resale shop that takes only name brand clothing in good condition. The accessories, purses, shoes and jewelry are new. Open Mon to Sat 10:00 am to 6:00 pm and Sun noon to 4:00 pm. Hours extended in the summer.

Stewart-Zack's, 118 East Front Street, (231) 947-2322. Home accessories and accents, area rugs and lovely things to make your home special. Open Mon to Sat 10:00 am to 5:30 pm.

Tiny Toes, 232 East Front Street, (231) 944-1051. Children's furniture, bedding and gifts. Open 7 days, Mon to Fri 10:00 am to 5:30 pm, Sat 10:00 am to 5:00 pm and Sun noon to 4:00 pm.

Toy Harbor, 221 East Front Street, (231) 946-1131. Creative, quality toys. Cutest puppets anywhere. Open 7 days, Mon to Sat 10:00 am to 5:30 pm and Sun noon to 4:00 pm.

Trains and Things, 210 East Front Street, (231) 947-1353. A place to let your imagination run wild. Trains, planes, ships, armor, cars, dollhouses and more. Open Mon to Sat 10:00 am to 5:30 and some Sundays.

Votruba, 112 East Front Street, (231) 947-5615. Leather goods including handbags, gifts and luggage. Open 7 days, Mon to Fri 10:00 am to 5:30 pm, Sat. 10:00 am to 5:00 pm and Sun noon to 4:00 pm.

What to Wear, 152 East Front Street, (231) 932-0510. Funky and stylish clothes. Open 7 days, Mon to Wed 10:00 am to 6:00 pm, Thurs to Sat 10:00 am to 8:00 pm and Sun noon to 5:00 pm.

Parks, Beaches, Trails, and Campgrounds

Archie Park, on East Shore Road of Old Mission Peninsula and a good place to start a bicycle tour. It provides the biker with a peaceful and scenic lookout.

Bowers Harbor Beach, tucked in Bowers Harbor on Old Mission Peninsula, 15 miles north of Traverse City. Amenities: swimming beach, picnic facilities, restrooms and a boat launch.

Brown Bridge Pond Natural Area and Nature Preserve, Garfield Avenue south to Hobbs Highway, left to Ranch Rudolf Road. Owned by the city, this is a local secret that most travelers miss. Easy hiking trails take you past a small lake created by a dam on the Boardman River. You will also pass two platforms that jut out over a steep slope affording spectacular views of the lake and the Boardman valley. You may see swans and even eagles during your hike.

Bryant Park, Peninsula Drive where Garfield and Front Streets intersect at the base of Old Mission Peninsula. Broad, sandy swimming beach. Amenities: play area, picnic area, charcoal grills and restrooms.

Clinch Park, Grandview Parkway, (231) 922-4903. 1,500 feet of sandy beach along West Grand Traverse Bay in downtown Traverse City. Its location guarantees a lot of activity. Amenities: swimming beach with lifeguards from mid-June through August, picnic tables and restrooms. Adjacent to the zoo and Clinch Park Marina.

East Bay Park, located at the foot of Front Street. A popular beach for families with children because of shallow water and gradual slopes. The park also has lifeguards, playgrounds and restrooms.

Elmwood Township Park, one mile north of the M-72 Junction in Traverse City. Beach, playground, restrooms and picnic facilities.

Grand Traverse Commons, 1200 West 11th Street. In 1885 this became the site of the State Psychiatric Hospital. In 1989, a century later, the hospital has been converted to a restaurant and gallery. The grounds (referred to as the Commons) remain open and are a favorite place for runners, walkers, cross-country skiers and bird-watchers.

Haserot Beach Park, 20 miles north of Traverse City on Old Mission Peninsula. Amenities: protected bay of Lake Michigan with sandy beaches, playground, picnic facilities, restrooms and boat launch.

Muncie Lakes Pathway, southeast of Traverse City, follow Supply Road to Remote Lake Road, turn right and continue to Ranch Rudolf Road intersection, turn left about a half-mile to the trail parking lot on the left. This trail has rolling hills covered with a variety of hardwoods and evergreens and is moderately difficult, but perfect for either hiking or biking if you are up to it.

Peninsula Township Park, Center Road all the way to the end of Old Mission Peninsula. Offers three miles of developed trails and another 500 acres of woodlands, old abandoned orchards and open highlands. You will be able to see both East and West Bay as you look out over the orchards. The sandy farm lanes offer a couple of invigorating climbs to get to higher land, but you will appreciate the effort when the magnificent view stretches out before you.

Power Island, accessible only by boat, located on West Grand Traverse Bay's Power Island off Bower's Harbor on Old Mission Peninsula. Amenities: picnic facilities, restrooms and hiking trails.

Pyatt Lake Nature Area, Neahtawanta Road, Old Mission Peninsula. Quiet and peaceful, this nature preserve provides hiking trails, boardwalks, wetlands, botanical diversity and observation points.

Sand Lake Quiet Area, M-72 to Broomhead Road then right (about 4 miles), parking is on the left. This 3,500-acre tract is perfect for a number of outdoor activities including: mountain biking, fishing, hiking, cross-country skiing, or just plain walking. It is called a quiet area because no motorized vehicles are allowed. It is considered a moderately difficult trail through scenic small lakes and woods brimming with wildlife.

TART (Traverse City Area Recreation Trail). Many access points throughout Traverse City. This ten mile, non-motorized trail is a popular cross city route for walkers, runners, in-line skaters and bicyclers. It stretches from M-72 on the West side of Traverse City to Bunker Hill Road in Acme winding through several popular parks along the way. You will pass restaurants, ice-cream parlors and a number of attractions along the way.

Traverse City KOA, 9700 M-37 (Buckley), (231) 269-3202. Campsites, cabins and lodge. Amenities: heated pool, game room, mini-golf, basketball, volleyball, playground and banana peel bikes.

Traverse City State Park, US-31 North (231) 922-5270 or reservations at toll-free (800) 44-PARKS. Amenities: quarter of a mile of sandy beach along the east arm of the Grand Traverse Bay, swimming, sunbathing, boating, fishing and camping, picnic tables, grills, beach house and children's playground are available. Open year round. 342 campsites.

Sleeping Bear Dunes National Lakeshore Park, There are numerous beaches along a 33 mile stretch of protected Lake Michigan shoreline. (See additional information about the Sleeping Bear Dunes under the Empire Listing, p. 192.). The Philip Hart Visitor Center is the place for information and is open 7 days a week from 8:00 am to 6:00 pm except for major holidays. The park operates on a year round basis.

Even the seagulls enjoy the Traverse City beaches   *Photo by Bob Royce*

Marinas, Water Sports, Boat and Jet Ski Rental

Blue Sky Rentals, Three locations: 2345 US-31 North (Peegoe's Restaurant, 525 High Lake Road (Beach Condominiums) or 1995 US-31 North (Cherry Tree Inn and Suites), (231) 633-2583 or (231) 633-2584. Rents personal water craft, jet boats, kayaks, water trampolines and more in the summer and in the winter you can rent snowmobiles.

Bowers Harbor Boat Launch, Neahtawanta Road, Old Mission Peninsula.

Duncan L Clinch Marina, Clinch Park, (231) 922-4906. 38 transient slips. Harbormaster on duty 5/15 to 10/20. Gas and pumpout available. Has a nice beach.

Great Lakes Scuba, 302 North US-31 South, (231) 943-3483, www.greatlakesscuba.com. All of the equipment you will need for scuba diving. Also provides dive trips, equipment repair, air fills, instruction, and sales. Rentals, charters and trips.

Sail and Power Boat Rental, at the Holiday Inn West Bay, (231) 922-9336. Rents power boats, jet skis, sailboats, pontoons, jet boats, paddle boats and outdoor motors.

Scuba North, 13380 South West Bayshore Drive (M-22), (231) 947-2520. Provides full scuba diving gear, snorkel equipment, underwater cameras, lights, instruction, dive charters and more.

Sunset Watersports, (231) 932-1800, sunsetwatersports.com. Ski boats, pontoon boats, tubes, water trampolines wake boards, knee boards, kayaks and jet ski rental. Free delivery.

Cruise, Charters, and Ferries

Bay Breeze Yacht Charters, 12935 West Bay Shore Drive, (231) 941-0535, www.bbyc.com. Yacht charters by the week, tugboat charters, day trips and sunset cruises. You can rent a sailboat (if you are qualified) or a crewed charter by the day or week. Primarily a sailboat charter organization with seventeen sailboats in their fleet. Offers sailing lessons and has a sailing school. Their learning vacation is very popular. You charter a sailboat for a week and spend four days with an instructor and three days on your own. Instruction is given on a 30-foot Catalina. The school runs every week mid-May to mid-September.

Big Kahuna Charters, Elmwood Township Marina, (231) 946-7457. Charter fishing and bay cruises on the West Grand Traverse Bay.

Blue Sky Guided Tours, (see above, Boat and Jet Ski rentals).

Dancing Bear Charters, 401 East Front Street on the Boardman River, (231) 883-7490. Charter fishing for salmon and trout on the Grand Traverse Bay.

Daydreamer Charter Service, operates out of several marinas. (231) 218-5176. Fish the Lake Michigan waters for trout and salmon with a fully-equipped charter fishing service that has over ten years of experience. Operates April to October.

Great Lakes Scuba, for dive trips, see above under Water Sports.

Scuba North, see above under Water Sports for dive charters.

Showtime Charters, West Side of Grand Traverse bay two miles from downtown, www.showtimecharters.com, toll-free (800) 817-5807. Catch and eat charter fishing with Captains Sam Worden and Cam Garst.

Traverse Tall Ship Company, 13390 Southwest Bay Shore Drive (M-22), (231) 941-2000 or toll-free (800) 678-0383. The 114-foot schooner *Manitou* offers three different two-hour excursions every day of the week. Passengers are provided with specially catered picnics during noon and evening sails. There are also special Wine Tasting Cruises featuring wines from the local area and entertainment cruises with local folk band, *Song of the Lakes*. You can spend the night on their "Floating B&B." In September they do four-day cruises that stop at several locations. Described as "like camping on the water, but the food is much better." Cabins are rustic, but you will eat like a king.

Other Things to See and Do
Grand Traverse Balloon Rides, 225 Cross Country Trail, (231) 947-7433, www.grandtraverseballoons.com. An exciting way to view the beautiful Grand Traverse Bay, surrounding lakes, and breathtaking countryside. The hot air balloons are multi-colored and seven stories tall. Enjoy your flight in any of the four seasons. Experienced FAA Certified Pilots glide your balloon effortlessly over the tree tops. The "in air" time is about an hour for either your sunrise or sunset flight and after landing you will be treated to a champagne celebration.

The Comedy Club, 738 South Garfield, (231) 941-0988. Live stand-up comedy. Open third weekend in September through May, Fri and Sat 8:00 pm and 10:30 pm.

Pirates Cove Adventure Park, 1710 US-31 North, (231) 938-9599, www.piratescove.net. Fun for the whole family with go-carts, water coaster, bumper boats and adventure golf where you can putt your way over footbridges and under cascading waterfalls.

Ranch Randolf, 6841 Brownbridge Road, (231) 947-9529. Sleigh rides, snowmobiling trails and other winter activities as well as summer fun. (See above under Lodging).

Traverse City Paintball, 1350 South Airport Road, (231) 933-0171. Paintball games. Call for hours.

Turtle Creek Casino, 7741 East Traverse Highway (4 miles east of Traverse City on M-72), (231) 267-9574. Features 1,200 slot machines from a penny to $100. Table games include blackjack, three card poker, four card poker, let it ride, roulette and craps. Open 7 days, 24 hours, year round.

Visit a Farm Market:
Cherry Connection/Edmondson Orchards, 12414 Center Road (cherries); 13451 Center Road (berries and currants), (231) 223-7130.

Downtown Farmers Market, Between Cass and Union Streets (across from Clinch Park) (231) 922-2050. Shop for fruits, vegetables, plants, flowers and baked goods. Open Saturday from mid-May through October. Wednesdays mid-June through September.

Elzer Farms, 12654 Center Road, (231) 223-9292. Homemade pies, jams, honey, syrup, cherry products, plants, perennials, hanging baskets, asparagus and cherries. You can also pick your own raspberries, apricots, peaches, apples, sweet corn and garden vegetables in season. Open May through September.

Groleau's Farm Market, 2100 Hammond Road East, (231) 929-9654. Fresh produce, jam, salsas, pies, maple syrup and fruit in season.

Visit an Old Mission Peninsula Winery:

Chateau Chantal Winery and Inn, 15900 Rue de Vin, Old Mission Peninsula, (231) 223-4110 or toll-free (800) 969-4009. (Also see Lodging above). Produces sparkling wines, pinot grigio, chardonnay, Trio, Naughty/Nice, riesling, gewürztraminer, Celebrate Bubbly and cherry wines. Has live jazz performances on Thursdays at sunset mid-June through August. Open 7 days, year round. Summer Mon to Sat 11:00 am to 8:00 pm and Sun noon to 5:00 pm. Closes slightly earlier in off-season.

Chateau Grand Traverse, 12239 Center Road, Old Mission Peninsula, (231) 223-7355. Produces riesling, chardonnay, gamay, merlot, pinot noir and cherry wines. Open 7 days, year round. Summer Mon to Sat 10:00 am to 7:00 pm, Sun noon to 6:00 pm. Closes slightly earlier in the winter. Also gives five tours a day in the summer.

Peninsula Cellars Tasting Room, 11480 Center Road, Old Mission Peninsula, (231) 933-9787. Produces pinot noir, chardonnay, gewürztraminer, riesling, pinot blanc, pinot grigio, and red and white fruit dessert wines.

(Also see wineries in Northport p. 218 and Suttons Bay p. 226.)

Winter Activities:

Cross Country Skiing. See parks above. Many of them are cross country ski sites in the winter.

Hickory Hills Downhill Skiing, (231) 922-4910 or ski info at (231) 922-4909. With its 240 vertical drop and eight runs (one beginner, 5 intermediate, and 2 advanced), this is a place to test the slopes. They also have cross country trails.

Timberlee Resort Tubing, 10484 South Timberlee Drive about 7 miles from Traverse City, (231) 941-4142. Short ten minute drive from downtown Traverse City amid rolling hills and forests, a place to take the family tubing.

Festivals

Blossom Days, May, (231) 969-4009. Beginning with the first prayer for a bountiful harvest (the Blessing of the Blossoms), this became one of the main festivals in the area. A time for food and fun amidst the blossoms from the vineyards and orchards.

The Annual National Cherry Festival, July, (231) 947-4230. For Traverse City this is the big one. An eight day festival with over 150 varied activities to keep everyone happy: air shows, parades, concerts, entertainment, fireworks, midway rides, games and lots of food.

Traverse Epicurean Classic, September, (231) 932-0475. This is a new festival to the peninsula and it invites top chefs, cookbook authors and wine experts to show their stuff in cooking classes, wine tasting, gourmet dinners and a host of other activities.

Golf

Bay Meadows Golf Course, 5220 Barney Avenue, (231) 946-7927. 9 hole course: carts, clubs, pro shop and driving range available.

The Crown Golf Course, 2430 East Crown Drive, (231) 946-2975 or toll-free (888) 921-2975. A 72 par course with a course rating of 72.2 and a slope rating of 136. Many players consider the eleventh hole the tough one.

Elmbrook Golf Course, 1750 Townline Road, (231) 946-9180. A 72 par, this is the oldest and busiest of Traverse City's golf courses. One of the few kid-friendly golf courses so take the family and everyone can have fun. Introduce the little ones to the joy of the game. You will be awed by the view from the sixth hole – you can see both the East and West shores of Grand Traverse Bay.

(*Also see Grand Traverse Resort under Acme listing p. 258*)

Also see Pirates Cove under Other Things to See and Do above for miniature golf.

Contacts

Traverse City Area Chamber of Commerce, 202 East Grandview Parkway, (231) 947-5075, www.tcchamber.org, info@tcchamber.org.

Traverse City Visitors Center, 101 West Grandview Parkway, (800) TRAVERSE. Open Memorial Day through Mid-October, Mon to Sat 9:00 am to 6:00 pm and Sun 11:00 am to 3:00 pm. Mid-October to Memorial Day open Mon to Fri 9:00 am to 5:00 pm, Sat 9:00 am to 3:00 pm and closed Sun.

Acme

Population: Township population 4332.

Directions: About 7 miles northeast of Traverse City on US-31. It is at the junction of US-31 and M-72 East.

Background and History

With no clear evidence of how Acme got its name, it seems reasonable to assume the word origin itself provides a clue: Acme, in Greek, means the peak, zenith, prime or best of something. That may be how the first settlers viewed this lovely area.

The village of Acme was established by L.S. Hoxsie in 1855 when he moved from downstate in Lenawee County. Acme was originally part of Whitewater Township and became a station stop for the Pere Marquette Railroad.

Three years after moving to Acme, Hoxsie built a sawmill that became part of the region's booming lumber craze. Acme soon had a hotel, a shingle mill and several stores to provide for the needs of its growing population.

John Pulcipher organized the area as a township and became its supervisor in 1891 - a position he held for nearly three decades. During his tenure he saw the depletion of the virgin timber in the area and banks foreclosing on many farms because the owners could not grow enough on the poor sandy soil to pay their taxes.

Hoxsie tried to make a go of a woolen mill in the area but in spite of his efforts, it failed. Eventually the few small stores closed and the hotel was razed. Acme's economy barely limped along. The government consolidated state lands and many farmers relocated; those that remained turned to fruit farming because cherry and apple trees actually flourished in the poor, sandy soil.

In the first part of the 20th century, railroads expanded and highways were built. The country's population was moving into cities and away from farms. This new trend fueled a desire for resorts where weary city-dwellers could get away and relax. Acme capitalized on the need this created. Relying on its spectacular location on the East Grand Traverse Bay and its proximity to Traverse City (which was rapidly becoming a premier tourist area), it became a major playground.

Today, Acme's claim to fame is its major resorts and golf courses. It is the gateway to fun. It is often considered part of the Greater Traverse City area and if you read the background of Traverse City and Elk Rapids contained in their respective chapters of this guide, you will also chronicle the similar history of Acme.

Food/Restaurants

Bayview Bar and Grill, 5074 US-31 North, (231) 938-2690. Appetizers, sandwiches, submarines, pitas, gyros, wraps, steaks, pizza and burgers. Friday night Prime Rib Special. Smoke free dining room. Open 7 days, Mon to Sat 7:00 am to 11:00 pm. Lounge open 11:00 am to 1:30 am and Sun noon to 9:00 pm.

Gio's Italian Kitchen, 6037 US-31 North, (231) 938-2222. Italian food: pasta, pizza, panini sandwiches, salads and a kids menu. Open 7 days, 11:00 am to 10:00 pm.

The Grille, located in the Clubhouse (Grand Traverse Resort). Overlooking the 18th green of the Jack Nicklaus Bear, spectacular views with a north woods atmosphere and a full bar and varied menu. Large outdoor seating area. Seasonal hours, but generally open during the summer months for lunch and dinner daily, 11:00 am to 10:00 pm.

Mountain Jack's Steakhouse, 5555 US-31 North, (231) 938-1300. Chain restaurant; house specialty is prime rib. Also good specialty steaks and seafood entrees. Sunday Brunch. Open 7 days, 4:00 pm to 10:00 pm.

Sweetwater Café, 100 Grand Traverse Boulevard, Grand Traverse Resort, toll-free (800) 236-1577. Casual dining in an open kitchen atmosphere. Breakfast entrees, sandwiches, salad bar, pastas and hearty entrees. Breakfast and lunch.

Travino Wine and Grille, 4341 M-72, located next to the Grand Traverse Resort, (231) 938-9496. Northern Italian Cuisine and a seasonal porch overlooking the golf course. You can also get steaks and sandwiches and enjoy an area wine. Open 7 days, Sun to Thurs 11:00 am to 10:00 pm, Fri and Sat 11:00 am to 11:00 pm. Bar open until midnight on Sat.

Trillium Restaurant, 100 Grand Traverse Boulevard (16th and 17th floors of the Grand Traverse Resort), toll-free (800) 236-1577 for reservations. Winner two years in a row of *Wine Spectator* Award for well-chosen selection of quality wines matched appropriately to wonderful entrees. Spectacular views of the golf courses enhance the ambiance and the chef has concocted an impressive selection of appetizers, salads, entrees and desserts. Live entertainment and some dinner theatre. Open 7 days, 6:00 pm to 10:00 pm (last reservation). Sun Brunch 10:00 am to 2:00 pm (they stop seating).

Lodging (Also see Campgrounds below)

Beach Club Motel, 5367 US-31 North, (231) 938-0000. Eleven guest rooms. 200 feet of East Grand Traverse Bay frontage with sandy beach. Boat launch next door. Extras: refrigerators and microwaves.

Grand Traverse Resort and Spa, 100 Grand Traverse Boulevard, (231) 534-6000 or toll-free (800) 236-1577. With 650 luxurious rooms, suites and condos this 4 star hotel is the largest lodging establishment in the area. It is also one of the nicest. It is not inexpensive, but a great place to treat yourself to a bit of pampering. The resort sits on 900 acres of gently rolling hills with views of Lake Michigan. With its fine dining (Trillium), casual restaurants, spa and championship golf course (and lessons), it **is** Acme.

Holiday Inn Express Hotel and Suites, 3536 Mount Hope Road, www.traversecitymi.hiexpress.com, (231) 938-0945 or toll-free (800) HOLIDAY. Nice rooms, moderately priced. Extras: kitchenette, indoor and outdoor pools, refrigerators, continental breakfast, high-speed internet, satellite TV, free local calls and laundry facilities available.

Knollwood Motel, 5777 US-31 North, (231) 938-2040, www.knollwoodmotel.com. Basic motel with 14 rooms, some kitchens, and cottages for two in a Victorian home. Extras: 175 feet of private beach and sundeck. Seasonal: Open May 1st through October 31st.

Sleep Inn and Suites, 5520 US-31 North, (231) 938-7000. Clean rooms, moderately priced. Built in 2000. Extras: overlooking Grand Traverse Bay, indoor pool, whirlpool, data ports, cable TV/HBO, in-house movie night, golf and casino packages and continental breakfast.

Museums and Galleries

Music House Museum, 7377 US-31 North, (231) 938-9300. Guests get a private tour during which instruments are explained and some are even played. The museum houses an extensive collection of fine, rare automatic musical instruments, antique radios, phonographs, nickelodeons, organs. music boxes and much more. Open 7 days, May 1st to Oct 31st, Mon to Sat 10:00 am to 4:00 pm, Sun noon to 4:00 pm.

Theatre/Entertainment

The Shores, at Grand Traverse Resort. A beach party every Friday and Saturday night during the summer. Guitarist takes requests from 9:00 pm to 1:00 am.

Showcase Dinner Theatre, M-72 East in Old Acme Cinema. (231) 938-2181. Dinner and Stage Shows. Box office opens Tues to Sat 10:00 am to 4:00 pm.

Trillium, (see above restaurants) has weekend entertainment and some dinner theatre.

Other Shopping

Gallery of Shops, 100 Grand Traverse Boulevard, (231) 534-1577 or toll-free (800) 236-1577. Grand Traverse Resort and Spa. Upscale, high-end merchandise in a variety of little shops at the resort.

Murdick's Fudge, 4500 US-31 (5 miles north of Traverse City), (231) 938-2330. Fudge and other confections. Open July and August, 7 days 9:00 am to 10:00 pm, May to October 7 days, but reduced hours.

Outdoor Adventures Down Outlet, 4144 M-72, (231) 938-9770 or toll-free (800) 722-3696, www.downoutlet.com. Bedding, pillows and featherbeds. Woolrich, Columbia and North Face outerwear. Open 7 days, Mon to Sat 9:30 am to 8:00 pm and Sun 10:00 am to 5:00 pm.

Camping

Traverse Bay RV Resort, 5555 M-72 East, (231) 938-5800, www.traversebayrv.com. Adult oriented RV resort and condominium development with individual lots for sale or rent on a daily, weekly or monthly basis. RVs restricted to motor homes and fifth wheels. RVs must be 10 years or newer and at least 24 feet. Amenities: paved streets, concrete pads, private restrooms and showers, laundry facilities, clubhouse, library, computer room, heated outdoor pool and spa, tennis courts, WIFI and next to the Grand Traverse Resort and Spa.

Marina

East Bay Harbor Marina, 5517 US-31 North, (231) 938-2131. Gas, pumpout and transient slips. Takes reservations.

Charter

Pisces Fishing Charter Service, marina in Acme, (231) 938-1562 or (231) 938-2165, piscesfishing@aol.com. Four-hour charters with Captains Gordon Boomer and Dale Elay on their 30-foot Sportcraft FlyBridge, docked at East Bay Marina.

Festival

Annual Subaru North American VASA, February. A premier cross-country ski race open to both classical and freestyle skiers. 12, 27 or 50 K distances on the well-known Vasa trail near Acme.

Golf

With three championship golf courses that have become Michigan's top golf destinations, The Grand Traverse Resort and Spa has put Acme on the map. Each course is 18 holes.

Spruce Run, The original Golf Course at Grand Traverse. 70 par, 18 hole course rated 70.9 and slope rating 130. It is the tamest of the resort's three courses. (See picture next page.)

The Wolverine, designed by Gary Player. Par 72 course with a 73.9 rating and a 144 slope rating.

The Bear, perhaps Michigan's best known course named for its famous architect, Jack Nicklaus, this is a challenging course. A par 72 course with a 76.8 rating and a 146 slope rating.

Photos Courtesy of the Grand Traverse Resort & Spa.

Contacts: See Traverse City Contacts. They have Acme information.

Elk Rapids

Population: 1700.

Directions: **From Detroit:** (253 miles) I-75 North, exit 254, left on M-72 towards Traverse City, right on US-31. **From Lansing**: (184 miles), US-127 North, merge onto US-10 West/MI-115 toward Cadillac, merge onto US-131 North toward Cadillac, left onto Fife Lake Road/CR-605, right onto US-31. **From Chicago:** (322 miles) I-94 toward Detroit, merge onto I-196 (exit 34) toward Holland/Grand Rapids, merge onto US-131 North (exit 77A toward Cadillac), left onto Fife Lake Road/CR605, right on US-31.

Background and History

Located in southwest Antrim County and bordered to the west by Grand Traverse Bay, to the east by Elk Lake, to the north by Bass Lake and with the Elk River running through it, picturesque Elk Rapids bursts with opportunities for day trippers, boaters, anglers and water worshipers. Whether you simply paddle or motor about absorbing the tranquil expanse of natural scenery or cast your line in the hope of catching dinner, you will never lack for something to do.

Elk Rapids was first home to the semi-nomadic Anishinaabek who likely migrated to the Great Lakes area from the East Coast. It is impossible to hike a Northern Michigan trail or paddle a Northern Michigan waterway and not follow a path taken by a Native American hundreds of years ago. Until the early 1800s the Original People enjoyed the vast, unbroken woodland around Elk Rapids without European influence. With the arrival of the French and English, the Anishinaabek became known as the Ojibwe, Ottawa, Chippewa and Pottawatomie. And change was inevitable.

The first Europeans to test the Elk River waters were the missionaries and the surveyors. The agenda of the former was saving souls, and that of the latter was laying claim to new lands for the United States government.

The first documented surveyor to the area was Abram Scranton Wadsworth, who according to local legend, discovered a pair of elk horns in the rapids near the mouth of the Elk River in 1847 and considered that an appropriate sign for naming the river. With Wadsworth were his family: wife, Martha, their three children and brother-in-law, Samuel Northam. Assisted by local Native Americans the Wadsworth family spent their first winter at Old Mission. Abram's thoughts, however, returned to the pleasant little river across the bay. He was a millwright by trade and the river seemed the perfect place to construct a mill.

Wadsworth returned to Elk Rapids and built a log cabin near the present site of the Town Hall. The family established a friendly relationship with their Native American neighbors who taught Wadsworth to strip the bark from trees; he then sold the bark for enough profit to build his lathe mill where operations began in 1850. Wadsworth platted the village in 1852 and sold lots for $25. Originally the village was called Stevens, but it was later renamed for its beautiful river. In 1853, a post office came to Elk Rapids and the first school opened. In 1863 the first issue of the *Elk Rapids Eagle* was printed. In 1864 the village boasted seven churches and seven saloons.

Geographically, Elk Rapid's growth was somewhat constrained. Wedged between the Grand Traverse Bay and Elk Lake there was little room for expansion. Farmers were limited to utilizing acreage to the north and south and although water travel was a blessing, land travel was impeded by the unbroken 75 mile chain of lakes to the north and east. The pathways that eventually became roads were twisted and contorted and even Traverse City seemed far away. Early residents of Elk Rapids must have felt isolated in their lovely countryside.

In 1872, the logging company of Dexter and Noble constructed a charcoal blast furnace forty-seven feet in diameter to produce pig iron; the vast hardwood forests surrounding Elk Rapids provided lumber that was converted to charcoal for firing the furnace. Iron ore was imported from the Upper Peninsula by freighter for use in the process. Dexter and Noble built a dock for ships bringing the ore. During its heyday, the furnace turned out 24 tons of pig-iron a day and employed 365 people. It closed in the early 1900s because the forests were depleted and cheaper smelting processes were developed.

Several plants and factories helped sustain Elk Rapids after the iron company closed. By the mid-1900s agriculture and orchards aided the economy and Elk Rapids relied for support on its cherry packing plants, but economic decline continued to grip the village until Grace Memorial Harbor and tourism brought needed revitalization.

Today Elk Rapids is a tiny gem, often overshadowed by the glitz of neighboring Traverse City and Charlevoix. Elk Rapids, however, beguiles with her own special charm and her slower, more peaceful pace. Fast food restaurants and chain motels have not made an appearance. Even in the heart of summer you can find a quiet patch of paradise along vast stretches of sandy Lake Michigan beach. Your eyes can feast on well-manicured flower gardens maintained by dedicated Garden Club volunteers. One place to view the results of their green thumbs is around the local library, a building worth a peek, and if you wander inside you can grab beach reading from their ongoing sale. The Elk Rapids District Library is housed in "The Island House" which Edwin Noble built for his family in 1865 on a small island overlooking the Elk Rapids marina. To the side of the Library in Library Park you can actually see one of the small rapids of Elk Rapids.

Local stores offer any tourist trinket you may need - from T-shirts to fudge. Elk Rapids' galleries, like the Twisted Fish, are special and feature some of the finest artwork you will find anywhere along Lake Michigan's coast. Before leaving, you must make time for dinner at Pearl's New Orleans' Kitchen. Call for reservations because it is one busy place. (See recipe at the end of this chapter for a special treat.)

Visit Elk Rapids during your summer vacation and you will leave with your spirit rejuvenated.

Food/Restaurants

Chang's Express, 114 River Street, (231) 264-9140. Chinese and Thai Cuisine. House specialties include: Two-flavored Chicken and Pad Thalay. Open 7 days, Mon to Wed 11:00 am to 8:00 pm, Thurs to Sat 11:00 am to 9:00 pm and Sun noon to 8:00 pm. Closes an hour earlier each day and Sun in the off-season.

Chef Charles, 147 River Street, (231) 264-8901. Pizza with pizzazz, by the piece or whole. The Chef Charles Special has six tasty toppings on a sesame crust topped with toasted pine nuts. If pizza is not what you crave, try a loaf sandwich. Open mid-June to Labor Day, Mon to Sat 11:00 am to 9:00 pm and Sun noon to 8:00 pm. In the fall and spring they close at 8:00 pm. Closed Sun in the winter.

Elk Harbor Restaurant, 714 South US-31, (231) 264-9201. Family style dining and serves breakfast all day. Open 7 days, 7:00 am to 9:00 pm. Closes at 8:00 pm each day in the winter.

Elk Rapids Sweet Shop, 108 River Street, (231) 264-9732. Great pastries if you can get there before they are gone! Open Tues to Fri 6:00 am to 4:00 pm, Sat 6:00 am to 1:00 pm and closed Sun and Mon.

Fish Bonz Café, 145 Ames Street (231) 264-8944. Not much from the outside, this prior bait shop fixes a mean breakfast. They also serve lunch and dinner. House specialty is the whitefish. Open 7 days, Mon to Sat 6:30 am to 8:00 pm (serving breakfast until 11:00 am during the week and until noon on Sat). Open Sun 8:00 am to 1:00 pm.

George's Frozen Custard, 103 River Street. Homemade and wonderful. People come from all over the area for this custard. Open 7 days, 8:00 am to 10:00 pm. Closes November 1st to mid-April.

Harbor Café, 129 River Street, (231) 264-8700. Small café with breakfast and lunch menu. Couple of outside tables for warm, sunny days. Open 7 days, Mon to Sat 7:00 am to 2:00 pm and Sun 8:00 am to 2:00 pm. Winter only open Fri to Sun.

Home Kitchen, 204 River Street (231) 264-5626. Fine foods to go. This is a new place with gourmet take out. It opened after the 2006 summer season and is getting rave reviews. Try Glenda's Crab Pie. The expected summer hours will be Mon to Sat 11:00 am to 8:30 pm or longer if demand is there. Winter Mon to Sat 11:00 am to 7:30 pm.

The Ice Cream Peddlers, 141 River Street, (231) 264-6866. Grab some frozen refreshment on a hot summer day. Open 7 days, noon to 10:00 pm. Closes for the season in October.

Java Jones, 131 River Street, (231) 264-1111. Coffeehouse and Internet Café. Specialty coffees, like Elk Rapids Cherry Mocha, espresso bar, smoothies, sodas, breakfast, soups, salads, quiche and sandwiches. Open 7 days, Mon to Fri 7:00 am to 5:00 pm, Sat 8:00 am to 5:00 pm and Sun 9:00 am to 2:00 pm.

The Moose, 127 River Street, www.ermoose.com, (231) 264-9266. Pizza, sandwiches, soup, salads and a lemonade slush that is perfectly refreshing on a hot afternoon. They also sell rustic furniture and are a state liquor store. Open 7 days, year round. Summer: Mon to Thurs 8:00 am to 10:00 pm, Fri and Sat 8:00 am to midnight and Sun 8:00 am to 9:00 pm. Winter: Mon to Thurs 9:00 am to 9:00 pm, Fri and Sat 9:00 am to 11:00 pm and Sun 9:00 am to 8:00 pm.

Pearl's New Orleans Kitchen Restaurant, 617 Ames Street, (231) 264-0530, www.pearlsneworleanskitchen.com. Cajun/Creole cooking served up in an atmosphere of Southern hospitality. It would be impossible to recommend just one item from the menu - everything is fabulous. Try to save room for one of their scrumptious desserts-even if you have to take it home in a box. Both the Sour Mash Blackberry Cobbler and the Cherry Pecan Bread Pudding were delicious. Serves lunch, dinner and Sunday Brunch. Open 7 days, Mon to Sat 11:00 am to 11:00 pm and Sun 10:00 am to 10:00 pm (brunch until 3:00 pm). See Pearl's recipe for Chocolate Pecan Pie on p. 269.

Portside Treats, 137 North River Shore, (231) 264-0343. Candy, caramel corn, soft serve, popcorn, sugar-free treats, fudge, nuts and other confections. Open 7 days, Mon to Sat 10:00 am to 8:00 pm (or later) and Sun 11:00 am to 4:00 pm. Reduced winter hours.

The Riverwalk Grill, 106 Ames Street, (231) 264-9121. Great Parmesan Whitefish. (They get their whitefish from Cross fisheries in Charlevoix daily). Located on Elk Lake this is one place to enjoy the million dollar sunsets. Boat docking and an outdoor deck. Music on Sunday nights. Open Sun to Thurs 11:30 am to 10:00 pm and Fri and Sat 11:30 am to 11:00 pm.

T. J. Charlie's, 135 River Street, (231) 264-8819. Hot grilled sandwiches, wraps and burgers, salads, soups and a piece of pie a la mode for dessert. Open 7 days, 7:00 am to 4:00 pm. Closed winter.

The Town Club, 133 River Street, (231) 264-9914. Bar with appetizers, munchies, sandwiches, burgers, Greek specialties, baskets and soups. Open 7 days, Mon to Sat 11:00 am to 2:00 am and Sun noon to 2:00 am. On slow days they may close earlier.

Vasquez Hacienda, 11324 US-31 North, (231) 264-5892. Mexican food and fish, shrimp, prime rib (Saturday), chicken dishes and a variety of salads. Open: Summer 11:00 am to 10:00 pm. Reduced winter hours.

Lodging (Also see Campgrounds below)

Cairn House B&B, 8160 Cairn Highway, (231) 264-8994 or toll-free at (866) 642-4262, hperez@cairnhouse.com. A stately colonial style home set in peaceful surroundings with elegant furnishings from around the world. 4 rooms available. View Elk Lake from front porch.

The Camelot Inn, 10962 US-31 North, toll-free (800) 761-4667, info@camelot-inn.com. Basic, one-story motel with single rooms, deluxe rooms with sitting areas and kitchenettes and master suites with fireplace and whirlpool. Twelve rooms, each with microwave and refrigerator. Other extras: free local calls and premium cable TV.

Elk Rapids Beach Resort, 8976 North Bayshore Road, toll-free (800) 748-0049. All units offer one-bedroom with a queen-bed and double sofa sleeper, living room with additional queen sofa sleeper, full size kitchen with microwave, refrigerator and kitchen utensils, one full bath with two-person Jacuzzi whirlpool tub, vanity, and shower stall. Great views along with sandy beach and outdoor heated pool. The units accommodate up to four adults and two children. Open year round.

Paradise Properties Vacation Rentals, toll-free (800) 977-3386, www.paradisevacationhomes.com. Brokers of delightful homes and condos located on Lake Michigan or nearby inland lakes, near-lake and golf course locations for weekly summer rentals, some monthly rentals, and some winter rentals. An inventory of about 120 properties.

Museums and Galleries

The Blue Heron Gallery, 131 Ames Street, (231) 264-9210, www.blueheronalleryer.com. Watercolors, pen and inks, oils, pastels, charcoal etchings, wood-cut prints, pottery, sculpture, jewelry, tiles textile art and photography by Michigan artists. Open 7 days, 11:00 am to 5:00 pm. January 1st to April only open weekends.

Elk Rapids Historical Museum, 401 River Street, (231) 264-8000, www.elkrapidshistory.org. In the 19th century, the port of Elk Rapids was Traverse City's major commercial rival. It was a prosperous town built around shipping, lumber and the local ironworks company. The lower level of the beautiful, restored Elk Rapids Township Hall has displays from that era. The hall faces the city's park and the beach on East Grand Traverse Bay. The building also houses the Elk Rapids

Historical Society. The Museum is open Tues, Thurs, Sat and Sun, 1:00 pm to 4:00 pm Memorial Day to Labor Day.

Guntzviller's Spirit of the Woods Museum, US-31, 2 miles south of Elk Rapids, (231) 264-5597. Native American artifacts, history, hunting and fishing gear and preserved animals including: bear, bison, deer, and mink. Open 7 days, Mon to Sat 9:00 am to 5:00 pm and Sun 11:00 am to 4:00 pm.

Mullaly's Studio and Gallery, 128 River Street, (231) 264-6660. Beautiful glasswork, metal sculptures and whimsical tables. Open 7 days, Mon to Sat 10:00 am to 5:00 pm and Sun 11:00 to 3:00 pm. Open year round but closed Tues and Wed from Labor Day to Memorial Day.

Twisted Fish Gallery, 10443 South Bayshore Drive, (231) 264-0123, www.twistedfishart@aol.com. One of the loveliest and most interesting galleries in west Michigan. Oils, watercolors, jewelry, pottery, wood crafts, stained, blown and etched glass, metal and paper works, indoor and outdoor sculpture, fabric art, flowers and the most outstanding kaleidoscope collection to be seen anywhere. In addition to revealing amazing color displays, these kaleidoscopes were themselves truly works of art. The gallery displays more two-dimensional paintings than any other gallery in the state. Next door they have special exhibits in the cottage gallery, and the outdoor garden is an absolute delight. The owner buys the best pieces of original art he can find, regardless of where it comes from. Open 7 days, year round, Mon to Sat 10:00 am to 5:00 pm and Sun noon to 5:00 pm.

Viola Gallery, 150 River Street, (231) 264-6250. Many regional and some national artists displaying works reflecting the Northern spirit in wall art, fine crafts and jewelry. Open 7 days, Mon to Sat 10:00 am to 6:00 pm and Sun noon to 3:00 pm. Reduced winter hours.

Theatre

Stone Circle, ten miles north of Elk Rapids turn right off US-31 onto Stone Circle Drive to the end, (231) 264-2443. Enjoy a night of oral poetry, music and storytelling in a unique setting around a campfire. Fri and Sat mid-June through Labor Day, starts at 9:00 pm.

Antiques

Elk Rapids Antiques, 603 Bridge Street, (231) 264-9192. More than 8,000 square feet of antiques, collectibles, vintage treasures and stained glass from 35 dealers. Open Mon to Sat 10:00 am to 6:00 pm and Sun 11:00 am to 5:00 pm. Winter 7 days, 11:00 am to 5:00 pm.

Harbor Antiques Mall, 151 River Street, (231) 264-6850, hrbrantiqus@aol.com. 6,000 Square feet of antiques and collectibles and vintage pieces from 50 dealers. Specializing in stained glass. Also, wicker, furniture, glassware, toys and wide range of other antiques.

Pleasant garden courtyard with Pinehill Nursery's annuals, perennials and garden accents. Open 7 days year round, Mon to Sat 10:00 am to 6:00 pm and Sun 10:00 am to 4:00 pm.

Lilacs Antiques, 965 Green Street (US-31 South), (231) 264-9491. In the purple building! Antiques, vintage collectibles, primitives plus a variety of other treasures. Open Mon to Sat 10:00 am to 6:00 pm and Sun 11:00 am to 5:00 pm. January to March, only open Fri to Sun.

Other Shopping

Cali's Cottons Boutique, 148 River Street, (231) 264-0817. Clothing, jewelry, and accessories for you and accents for your home. Open 7 days, Mon to Fri 10:00 am to 5:30 pm and Sun noon to 4:00 pm. Reduced winter hours.

Corner Druggist, 154 River Street, (231) 264-8033. Besides aspirin, sunscreen, Snicker's bars and a selection of gifts, you might want to take a look at the antique glass bottle collection and the old time pictures that grace the walls. Open 7 days, Mon to Fri 9:00 am to 6:00 pm, Sat 9:00 am to 5:00 pm and Sun 11:00 am to 3:00 pm.

Elk River Trading Company, 117 River Street, (231) 264-8060. Gift items, Christmas ornaments, toys, kids' books, linens, gourmet dips and fruit butter. Open 7 days, Mon to Sat 10:00 am to 8:00 pm (sometimes later) and Sun 11:00 am to 4:00 pm. Reduced winter hours.

Harbor Wear, 136 River Street, (231) 264-6404, www.harbor-wear.com. Casual cotton resort clothing. Open 7 days, Mon to Sat 10:00 am to 9:00 pm and Sun 11:00 am to 5:00 pm.

Mill Creek Gifts, 113 River Street, (231) 264-0807. Accents for the home and garden, one-of-a-kind mosaics, greeting cards, paper products and gift items. Open 7 days, Mon to Sat 10:00 am to 9:00 pm and Sun 11:00 am to 5:00 pm. Open five days in the winter, generally closed Sun and Mon and only open until 6:00 pm.

The Nature Connection, 137 River Street, (231) 264-6330. Practical, educational and fanciful merchandise for nature lovers. Open 7 days, Mon to Sat 10:00 am to 9:00 pm and Sun from 11:00 am to 3:00 pm. Winter hours Wed to Sat 11:00 am to 5:00 pm.

The Painted Door Gallery, 152 River Street, (231) 264-6875. Glassware, candles, and kitchenware. Open 7 days, Mon to Sat 10:00 am to 5:00 pm and Sun noon to 4:00 pm. Open winter Thurs to Sat 10:00 am to 5:00 pm.

The Princess and the Pea, 145 River Street, (231) 264-8031. Beautiful stuffed animals, handmade rugs, accent items, lotions. Open Mon to Thurs 10:30 am to 5:00 pm, Fri and Sat 10:00 am to 5:00 pm.

Scents and Nonsense/Gypsy Moon Soap Company, 124 River Street, www.gypsymoonsoap.com, (231) 264-9533 or toll-free (888)

644-9779. Soaps, handcrafted aromatherapy candles and merchandise to make you feel good about yourself. Check out the whimsical clocks. Open 7 days, 10:00 am to 6:30 pm (or slightly later). Open winter Tues to Sat 10:00 am to 5:00 pm.

Stuff and Such Curious Cargo, 142 River Street, (231) 264-9093. Boots, jewelry, bags, sweaters, clothing, hats and accessories, but emphasis is on shoes, shoes, shoes. Open 7 days, Mon to Sat 10:00 am to 6:00 pm and Sun 11:00 am to 5:00 pm. Hours reduced non-season.

A Summer Place, 125 River Street, (231) 264-6556. A collection of antiques, collectibles and gifts. Accents for a cottage lifestyle. Open 7 days, Mon to Sat 10:00 am to 5:00 pm and Sun noon to 4:00 pm. Call for off-season reduced hours.

Whirlygigs Toy Shop, 115 River Street, (231) 264-6885. Unique specialty toys in a great, tiny cobblestone building. Expect to find something different than typical mall kinds of playthings. Open Mon to Sat 10:00 am to 5:00 pm and some Sundays. Wed open until 9:00 pm. Hours have some variation (sometimes stays open until 6:00 pm).

The Whispering Willow, 141 River Street, (231) 264-4438. Gift shop with jewelry, pottery, candles, children's books, Christmas items, angels and gourmet food items. Open 7 days, Mon to Sat 10:00 am to 7:00 pm and Sun 11:00 am to 4:00 pm. Fall open Mon to Sat 10:00 am to 4:00 pm and closed Dec 24th to April 1st.

Parks, Beaches and Campgrounds

Elk Rapids Day Park, South Bay Shore Drive at the village limits, (231) 599-2778. Great park with awesome trails, Lake Michigan beach, picnic area and pavilion. During the week you may be the only one sunbathing on the beach. Open dawn to 8:00 pm, May to September.

Honcho Rest Campground, 8988 Cairn Highway, (231) 264-8548. Located on Bass Lake within walking distance of downtown Elk Rapids. RV Park and gated resort. Amenities: boat rentals, fishing, bathhouse and laundry, 50/30 amp sites with cable TV, concrete pads, BBQ and fire ring, store and playground.

Veterans' Memorial Park, River and Pine, on Lake Michigan. Tennis courts, picnic tables, grills, playground, slides, volleyball on the beach and great view of Mission Peninsula.

Marinas

Edward C. Grace Memorial Marina, downtown Elk Rapids, (231) 264-8174. 38 transient slips in one of the nicest marinas on Lake Michigan. Harbormaster on duty 5/15 to 10/15.

Elk River Marina, 118 Bridge Street, (231) 264-9500. Downtown Elk Rapids, serving Elk Lake.

(See also Honcho Rest Campground above for boat rentals.)

Other Things to See and Do

Farmers Market, at Chamber of Commerce, 305 US-31. Fridays at 8:00 am during the produce season it is the place to get flowers, plants, honey, vegetables, baked goods, fruits and much more.

Festivals

Harbor Days, August. Annual community dinner, open air movie in the park overlooking the Grand Traverse Bay, sandcastle building contest, carnival, music, art fair, food, Grand Parade and fireworks. It is Elk Rapids' big festival and people come from all over to attend.

Golf

A-Ga-Ming Golf Resort, 12890 McLachlan Road, (231) 264-5081 or toll-free (800) 678-0122, www.a-ga-ming.com. 36-holes of championship golf on 2 resort courses: The Torch and Sundance. Both are 72 par courses and the Torch has a course rating of 73.2 with a 133 slope rating. Sundance is new and not yet rated.

Elk Rapids Golf Course, 724 Ames Street, (231) 264-8891. Public golf course.

(Also see Grand Traverse Resort, Acme, p. 259)

Contact

Elk Rapids Chamber of Commerce, 305 US-31 Road, (231) 264-8202 or toll-free (800) 626-7328, www.elkrapidschamber.org, info@elkrapidschamber.org.

Pearl's Chocolate Pecan Pie
Recipe Courtesy of Chef J.W. Pascoe and Pearl's

4 eggs
¾ cup sugar
1 cup dark corn syrup
½ teaspoon salt
1 tablespoon vanilla

1¼ cups pecans
¼ cup melted butter
2½ tablespoons cocoa powder

2 single pie crusts

1) Pre-bake pie shells for 10 minutes before filling.
2) In a mixing bowl combine eggs and sugar. Add corn syrup, salt, vanilla and pecans.
3) In a separate bowl mix together melted butter and cocoa powder. Mix to dissolve, add to pecan mixture. Blend well and pour into the 2 pie shells.
4) Bake pies at 325 degrees for 45 minutes to an hour. Let cool.

Charlevoix

Population: Approximately 3,000, (ten times that in the summer).

Directions: **From Detroit:** (274 miles) I-75 North, exit 282, M-32 towards Gaylord, right on M-131 North (M-32) then left on C-48 and right on M-66 to Charlevoix. **From Lansing:** (215 miles) US-127 North to merge with I-75, exit 282, M-32 towards Gaylord, right on M-131 North (M-32) then left on C-48, and right on M-66 to Charlevoix. **From Chicago:** (358 miles) I-94 East toward Detroit, merge into I-196 (exit 34) toward Holland/Grand Rapids, merge onto US-131 North (exit 77A) toward Cadillac, then left on M-66.

Background and History

Charlevoix sits perched on an isthmus straddling Lake Michigan and Round Lake, and spreads east to Lake Charlevoix. The Pine River runs through the heart of the town.

Charlevoix County was part of the territory acquired in 1836 by the Treaty of Washington, an agreement between representatives of the Ottawa and Chippewa Nations and the United States Government. By this treaty, the Native Americans ceded nearly 14,000,000 acres in the northwest portion of the Lower Peninsula and the eastern portion of the Upper Peninsula to the United States. This land area, which represents slightly more than one-third of Michigan's current land mass, was known as Michilimackinac. After the land transfer, many of the Native Americans who signed the treaty were shunned and ostracized by other members of their tribes for their participation in ceding this land.

In 1840 the Michilimackinac territory was separated into several regions and the part that today includes Charlevoix was first called Keskkauko. When divided into counties, Charlevoix County was originally part of Emmet County. It was organized as a separate county in 1869 drawing part of its acreage from Emmet County and part from Antrim County. The name Charlevoix honors Pierre Francois Xavier de Charlevoix, an explorer and Jesuit missionary, who traveled the Great Lakes seeking the water passageway to the Pacific and China. Father Charlevoix lived from 1682-1761, dying at age 79 - an impressive life-span for an explorer of those days. It is not known if Father Charlevoix actually set foot in the area of Charlevoix, either the city or county.

Charlevoix County experienced slow growth until 1870, but in the years after the Civil War its economy was sparked by its natural bounty of White Pine. The Grand Rapids and Indiana Railroad brought a station to the area enabling the commercial lumbering of the old-growth forests.

In 1878, H.W. Page, a professor from the University of Chicago, formed the Belvedere Summer Home Association which was the first of many retreats to locate in Charlevoix. Even at that early date, the area was revered as a summer destination and the city became home to several extravagant summer hotels.

When the forests were exhausted the small town turned to farming, fishing, and tourism for sustenance. Many residents of the area believed that a sugar factory, a cement factory and a seed warehouse would spell ongoing prosperity. Ultimately resorts and tourism became a leading economic resource in the area.

Charlevoix was home to Michigan's first nuclear power plant, Big Rock Point, which operated from 1962 to 1997.

The city has had its share of notoriety because of its connection to the Loeb family of the infamous Leopold and Loeb case (See p. 434 Part II for a related story). Richard Loeb's father, Alfred Loeb built Castle Park, an experiment to create the perfect farm. Charlevoix is also the summer home of John Ramsey, father of Jon-Benet Ramsey.

Today Charlevoix is populated by a blend of longtime summer resorters and local residents who often work in the town's industrial park. Some year-rounders are descendents of early commercial fishermen from the area. In the summer the population swells to 30,000 as tourists flock to this beautiful area with its spectacular natural attractions. Locals call it "Charlevoix the Beautiful."

While in the area you will want to see the Charlevoix South Pier Light Station that marks the opening of the channel (See p. 365, Part II for more about the lighthouse) and the railroad depot that serves as a museum and home to the Charlevoix Historical Society. The State of Michigan purchased the track between Charlevoix and Petoskey from the Chessie Railroad System and in the 1990s the track was removed and the rail line paved as a bicycle trail between Charlevoix and Harbor Springs. Skaters, walkers and runners share the path with bicyclists. In the winter it is a popular cross country ski path.

It is only a short ferry ride to Beaver Island where you can explore the history of Michigan's only real king – King James Jesse Strang (See p. 443, Part II for a related story.)

A visit to Charlevoix presents opportunities for hunting, fishing, mushroom picking, apple festivals and downhill skiing in addition to beautiful harbors, beaches and quaint shops.

Food/Restaurants

Argonne Supper Club, 11929 Boyne City Road, (231) 547-9331. Family restaurant with both steak and seafood on the menu. Open for dinner only.

Chee-Peng Restaurant, 1411 Bridge Street, (231) 547-6060. Specializing in Chinese and Thai dishes; dine in or take out. Open 7 days, Mon to Thurs 11:00 am to 9:00 pm, Fri 11:00 am to 10:00 pm,

Sat noon to 10:00 pm and Sun noon to 9:00 pm. Off-season closes slightly earlier.

The Coffee Shop, 411 Bridge Street, (231) 547-9663. Coffee and pastries. Open 6 days, 7:00 am to 10:00 pm. Closed Sun. Hours reduced in the fall.

Duke Deli, 216 Bridge Street, (231) 547-7900. The house favorite is Chicken salad with dried cherries, cranberries, walnuts, finely chopped onions and their special sauce. Open Mon to Sat 10:00 am to 7:00 pm and Sun 11:00 am to 4:00 pm.

Giuseppe's Italian Grill, 757 Petoskey Avenue, (231) 547-2550. Italian and American dishes in a family type restaurant. You will love their famous breadsticks. Open 7 days, Sun to Thurs 11:00 am to 9:00 pm, Fri and Sat 11:00 am to 10:00 pm.

John Cross Fisheries, 209 Belvedere Avenue, (231) 547-2532. Not a restaurant, but if you are looking to purchase fish for your dinner, this market has them. They sell whitefish to the finest area restaurants.

Juilleret's Restaurant, 1418 Bridge Street, (231) 547-9212. This small town café and bakery is one of the little pleasures you will discover in Charlevoix. Customers rave about several dishes at the café including pancakes for breakfast and the whitefish served on their own homemade toast for lunch. Tip: always choose to have your sandwich grilled. You should leave with a loaf of any of their delectable breads for tomorrow's breakfast – that is if you can leave it alone until then. No credit cards. Open breakfast and lunch. (Hours not written in stone.)

The Landings Restaurant, M-66 near Ironton Ferry, (231) 547-9036. Lakeside dining on Lake Charlevoix offering burgers, salads and fresh fish dinners. Ample boat docking and a gas dock. The children's arcade will keep younger members of the family happy. Open 7 days from Memorial Day through Labor Day, 11:00 am to 10:00 pm.

Nanny's Pub, 230 Ferry Avenue, (231) 547-2960 or toll-free (800) 678-0912. Great view of Lake Charlevoix at this family restaurant. Varied menu, something for everyone. Sunday buffet and all-you-can-eat specials. Open 7 days in the summer: Sun to Thurs 11:00 am to 9:00 pm, Fri and Sat 11:00 am to 11:00 pm. Sun Buffet from 9:00 am to 2:00 pm.

Scovie's Gourmet and Catering, 111 Bridge Street, (231) 237-7827, www.scovies.com. Home-style cooking in a welcoming atmosphere. Made to order food from the freshest ingredients. The place to get a deli sandwich, full dinner or fabulous dessert. Specializes in Michigan wines and food products. Open Mon to Sat 11:00 am to 9:00 pm and closed Sun. Reduced off-season hours.

Stafford's Weathervane Restaurant, 106 Pine River Lane, (231) 547-4311. Tucked into the shoreline of the Pine River Channel in downtown Charlevoix, you can enjoy waterfront dining, savory regional cuisine and a relaxing atmosphere. Open 7 days, 11:00 am to 3:00 pm for lunch and 4:30 pm to 10:30 pm for dinner. Slightly reduced hours off-season.

Terry's Place, 101 Antrim Street (Behind the Villager Pub), (231) 547-2799. A small, intimate restaurant often mentioned as the favorite of locals. The signature dish is their widely appreciated and often ordered whitefish dinner. Located in the heart of town. Open 7 days, 5:00 pm to 10:00 pm. Winter closes an hour earlier during the week.

Truffles Bakery, 208 Bridge Street, (231) 547-5570. Boxed lunches, wonderful sandwiches, fabulous pastries, ice cream and, of course, homemade truffles from the finest imported Belgium chocolate. Chef James Simonsen has a Certificate of Patisserie Superieure.

Village Inn Pizza, 227 Bridge Street, (231) 547-4405. More than just pizza: Oven baked subs, stromboli, ribs, chicken, salads and a buffet. Open 7 days, Mon to Thurs 11:30 am to 11:00 pm, Fri and Sat 11:30 am to midnight and Sun 4:00 pm to 11:00 pm. Closes an hour earlier after Labor Day.

Villager Pub and Restaurant, 427 Bridge Street, (231) 547-4374. Whitefish reigns supreme, but you can also order Mexican dishes and sandwiches. Some entertainment. Open 7 days, 11:00 am to 11:00 pm, bar to 2:00 am. Reduced off-season hours.

Whitney's Oyster Bar of Charlevoix, 307 Bridge Street, (231) 547-0818. Besides fried oysters and oyster stew, you can get quesadillas, fresh fish, chicken, beef and vegetarian dishes. Open 7 days, Mon to Thurs 11:30 am to 10:00 pm, Fri and Sat 11:30 am to 11:00 pm and Sun noon to 10:00 pm.

Woolly Bugger, 204 Bridge Street, (231) 237-0740. Coffee shop and Internet Café. Open 7 days, 6:30 am to 9:00 pm (closes Sun at 5:00 pm). Reduced hours after Labor Day: Mon to Friday closes at 5:00 pm and Sun 7:00 am to 4:00 pm.

Lodging (Also see Campgrounds below)

AmericInn, 18000 US-31 North, (231) 237-0988. Extras: indoor recreation area, pool and spa, enhanced continental breakfast, free local calls and cable TV.

Aaron's Windy Hill Guest Lodge, 202 Michigan Avenue, (231) 547-6100, www.aaronswindyhill.com. Enjoy homemade breakfast on the stone wrap-around porch. Seven rooms with private baths, one suite can accommodate five guests. Close to Lake Michigan and shopping.

The Bridge Street Inn B&B, 113 Michigan Avenue, (231) 547-6606, www.bridgestreetinn-chx.com. Three-story, Colonial-Revival home with nine rooms, seven with private baths. Short walk to sandy beaches of Lake Michigan or downtown shopping.

Charlevoix Country Inn, 106 West Dixon Avenue, (231) 547-5134. Watch spectacular sunsets on Lake Michigan from the balcony or porch of this 1896 country inn next to the beach. Enjoy the breakfast and the evening beverage, wine, and cheese social hour. Ten rooms with private baths. The Inn can accommodate up to 24 if you have a family gathering planned. Open Memorial Day to mid-October.

Edgewater Inn, 100 Michigan Avenue, (231) 547-6044. Modern condominium hotel located at the bridge in downtown. Close to shopping, restaurants and attractions.

The Inn at Gray Gables, 306 Belvedere, (231) 547-2251. Seven rooms. King or queen feather beds. Each room with private bath. Plush bathrobes. Wonderful breakfast.

The Lodge of Charlevoix, 120 Michigan Avenue, (231) 547-6565. The Inn is constructed of native Michigan timber and stone. Extras: heated outdoor swimming pool, pets allowed, light, complimentary breakfast, VCR and movies.

Pointes North Inn, 101 Michigan Avenue, (231) 547-0055 or toll-free (866) 547-0055. Located at the bridge overlooking Round Lake and two blocks from Lake Michigan. One and two bedroom suites with lofts. Extras: Jacuzzis, VCR and indoor/outdoor heated pool.

Sleep Inn, 800 Petoskey Avenue, toll-free (888) 252-2505. Extras: free *USA Today*, continental breakfast, free local calls, indoor pool, whirlpool and spa.

The Weathervane Terrace Inn and Suites, US-31 at the Harbor Bridge, (231) 547-9955. 48 rooms and 4 suites. Extras: heated indoor pool, sauna, whirlpool and laundry.

Museums and Galleries

Bier Art Gallery and Pottery, 03500 US-31 South, 6 miles south of Charlevoix, www.biergallery.com, (231) 547-2288. Wonderful gallery and great place to stop on your trip between Elk Rapids and Charlevoix. More than 70 artists from all over the United States display their work here. You will find stoneware originals designed by Ray and Tami Bier. Also photography, glass, woodcuts, watercolors, batiks, dolls, sculptured wood, baskets and jewelry of other artists. Open 7 days 10:00 am to 6:00 pm April through late October. November and December closes at 5:00 pm daily. Call for off-season winter hours.

C2 Gallery, 327 Bridge Street, www.c2gallery.net, (231) 547-2228. Eclectic mix of intriguing art: local, regional and beyond. 130 artists, wide range of media and all prices. Beautiful glass art. Open 7 days, 10:00 am to approximately 9:30 pm or 10:00 pm in the summer.

Elements, 107 Bridge Street, www.elementsgalleryonline.com, (231) 547-5820. Unique home accessories, personal accessories, jewelry, wall art and handcrafted items by more than 200 artisans. Open 7 days, Mon to Sat 10:00 am to 9:00 pm and Sun 11:00 am to 7:00 pm. Open year round, but closes on Sun during March and April.

Harsha House Museum, 103 State Street, (231) 547-0373. Built in 1891 by Charlevoix businessman and community leader Horace Harsha, this lovely Victorian home was donated to the city by Mr. Harsha's granddaughter to be used as a museum. In addition to the museum, the building houses two apartments that provide the funds to maintain the grounds and building. Inside you will find three Victorian period rooms and over 9,000 historic photos and negatives along with local historical artifacts and collections. There is a 1917 working player piano. Open mid-June to Labor Day Mon to Sat 1:00 pm to 4:00 pm. Labor Day to end of December: Tues to Sat 1:00 pm to 4:00 pm and contact above telephone number for winter hours.

North Seas Gallery, 237 Bridge Street, (231) 547-0422. Lovely furniture, upscale accents and art. Open 7 days, 10:00 am to 6:00 pm in the summer and open weekends only in the winter.

Railway Depot Museum, East End of Dixon and Chicago Avenue on Lake Charlevoix across from Depot Beach Park Area. (North of the Coast Guard Station), (231) 547-0373. The Charlevoix Railroad Station was donated to the Historical Society by Robert Pew in June 1992 on the 100th anniversary of the first train arriving in Charlevoix. The Society has restored and preserved the Depot building which is only open for special exhibits. The Charlevoix Area Garden Club created and maintains the gardens and they are always open.

Zazen Gallery, 405 Bridge Street, (231) 237-0658. The owners are collectors and buy what appeals to them. Contemporary man-made and natural art including geodes, crystals, sculptures and wall art. Open 7 days, Sun to Fri 10:00 am to 6:00 pm and Sat 10:00 am to 8:00 pm.

Shopping

American Spoon Foods, 315 Bridge Street, (231) 547-5222, www.spoon.com. Gift baskets, preserves, condiments and other food items from the harvest of Michigan's northern fruit orchards. Summer open Mon to Sat 10:00 am to 5:00 pm and Sun 11:00 am to 3:00 pm.

Bridge Book Gallery, 407 Bridge Street, (231) 547-7323, www.charlevoixbooks.com. A bookstore where the staff actually discusses books. Open 7 days, 10:00 am to 10:00 pm in the summer. In the winter most days open until 6:00 pm.

Charlevoix Wear, 323 Bridge Street (231) 547-4359. Boutique carrying coordinated casuals. Open 7 days, Mon to Thurs 9:30 am to

5:30 pm, Fri and Sat 9:30 am to 9:00 pm and Sun 9:00 am to 10:00 pm. Winter hours reduced.

The Clothing Company, 339 Bridge Street, (231) 547-6361, www.myclothingco.com. Casual ladies' and men's clothing from such makers as Woolrich and Columbia. Also carries belts, purses, gloves, hats, scarves and other accessories. Open 7 days, 9:00 am to 10:00 pm; reduced in the winter to 9:30 am to 5:30 pm and Sun hours vary.

Color Wear, 222 Bridge Street, (231) 547-3136. Souvenirs, Up North and Life is Good clothing, Logo T's and sweats. Open 7 days, Mon to Thurs 9:30 am to 5:30 pm, Fri and Sat 9:30 am to 9:00 pm and Sun hours vary. Winter hours reduced.

Esperance Market and Café, 12853 US-31 North, (231) 237-9300. Specialty foods. They put together marvelous gift baskets. Place to get beer, wine and deli sandwiches if you are planning a picnic while in Charlevoix. Open Mon to Sat 10:00 am to 6:00 pm year round.

Glik's, 113 Bridge Street, (231) 237-9183. The main Glik's department store is in Manistee, but this one carries Quicksilver, Roxy and other young and casual fashions. Open 7 days, Mon to Thurs 10:00 am to 6:00 pm, Fri and Sat 10:00 am to 8:00 pm, Sun noon to 5:00 pm.

Halfway to the Top, 403 Bridge Street, (231) 547-9808. Contemporary blend of apparel, art and accessories. Clothing is youthful and moderately priced. Open 7 days, Mon to Sat 10:00 am to 8:00 pm and Sun 10:00 am to 6:00 pm. Hours reduced after Labor Day: 10:00 am to 5:30 pm and Sun 10:00 am to 4:00 pm.

J. Phillips, 317 Bridge Street, (231) 547-6072. Fashion forward women's apparel and accessories – from trendy through classic with an eye for the unusual. Open 7 days, 9:30 am to between 7:00 pm and 9:00 pm. Closes after Labor Day at 5:30 pm.

Kilwin's, 233 Bridge Street. Ice Cream, candy and other sweet confections. Open 7 days, Sun to Thurs 10:00 am to 10:00 pm and Fri and Sat 10:00 am to 11:00 pm. Reduced winter hours.

Maison and Jardin, 228 Bridge Street, (231) 547-0550. Bath accents, candles, architectural pieces, eclectic antiques, European influenced merchandise. Open Tues to Sat 10:30 am to 5:00 pm and Sun 11:00 am to 3:00 pm. Reduced winter hours.

Momentum, Bridge Street, (231) 599-3145. Casual clothing with great prices. (See listing under Traverse City, p. 247.) Open 7 days, 9:00 am to 10:00 pm. Reduced hours after summer.

Murdick's Famous Fudge Kitchen, 230 Bridge Street, (231) 547-4213. Also: peanut brittle, cashew brittle, taffy, caramels, pecan rolls and ice cream. Open summer, 7 days, 10:00 am to 6:00 pm.

The Rocking Horse Toy Company, 325 Bridge Street, (231) 547-5258, www.rockinghorsetoy.com. Interesting, challenging, and unique toys, games and puzzles. Carries Playmobil, Lego, Brio and more. Open 7 days, 9:00 am to 10:00 pm and Sun 10:00 am to 8:00 pm in the summer and at Christmas. Other off-season hours reduced to Mon to Sat 10:00 am to 5:30 pm and Sun 11:00 am to 4:00 pm.

Season's, 221 Bridge Street, (231) 237-9504. Sweatshirts to serving trays. Clothing and accessories. They try to combine trendy and classic. Michigan State and University of Michigan logo merchandise. Fun, humorous and unique products. Open 7 days, 10:00 am to 9:00 pm in the summer. After Labor Day closes Sun to Thurs at 6:00 pm.

Shop of the Gulls, 205 Bridge Street, (231) 547-9781. Kitchen shop, gifts, glassware, linens, Vera Bradley, rugs, potpourri, and candles in the store's two side-by-side shops with merchandise that spills over into the basement. Open 7 days, 9:00 am to 8:00 pm in the summer. Closes earlier in the winter.

Talula's, 115 Bridge Street, (231) 237-9711. Funky, chic boutique with women's clothing: jackets, jeans, skirts and shirts. Accessories: bags (many sequined), jewelry, belts and more. Open 7 days, Mon to Thurs 10:00 am to 6:00 pm and Fri to Sun 10:00 am to 9:00 pm. Reduced winter hours.

The Treasure Chest, 106 Park Avenue, (231) 547-5433. Gift shop specializing in nautical gifts and garden items. Open summer, 7 days, Mon to Sat 10:00 am to 9:00 pm and Sun 11:00 am to 8:00 pm.

Up North Kids and More, 220 Bridge Street, (231) 547-0444. A bookstore to encourage kids to read, play and explore. In addition to books you will find cute chairs, easels and other child-oriented merchandise. Open 7 days, 9:00 am to 9:00 pm. Fall hours slightly reduced until Christmas and then open only Saturday and Sunday.

Parks, Beaches and Campgrounds

Depot Park Beach, East End of Dixon and Chicago Avenue on Lake Charlevoix. Great park for children. Lifeguards during the summer and restrooms available.

Ferry Avenue Beach, Lake Charlevoix near downtown. Lifeguards on duty in the summer and restrooms available.

Fisherman's Island State Park, 16480 Bells Bay Road (just south of Charlevoix), (231) 547-6641. The park is not an island, but rather 2,678-acres with five miles of unspoiled Lake Michigan shoreline. Tiny Fisherman's Island is, however, encompassed by the park. Rustic campground with some sites nestled into the sand dunes. Amenities: picnic area, grills, firepits, hunting, cross-country skiing, swimming, fishing and hiking.

*And of course, you will always enjoy **Lake Michigan's beach,** close to downtown and with life guards on duty in the summer.*

Marina
   Charlevoix City Marina, 408 Bridge Street, (231) 547-3272. 60 transient slips. Harbormaster on duty 5/1 to 9/30, 8:00 am to 8:00 pm.

Cruises, Boat Rentals and Charter Fishing
   Beaver Island Boat Company, (231) 547-2311 or toll-free (888) 446-4095, www.bibco.com. (Also see Beaver Island below.)
   Island Hopper Charters Service, (231) 448-2309 or cell (231) 620-2058. A water taxi to take you wherever you want to go: Beaver Island or the outer islands. Your captain is Dan Higdon and his boat is a modern, fully-equipped, 334-foot Webbers Cover.
   Sunshine Charters, 402 Bridge Street, (231) 547-0266. A place to learn to sail, take a sailing charter or parasail.
   Ward Brothers Charters, 106 East Antrim, (231) 547-2371, www.wardbrothersboats.com. Fishing charters into Lake Michigan trolling for trout and salmon. Also rents ski boats, skis and tubes.

Other Things to See and Do
   Beaver Island. Enjoy a pleasant day on Beaver Island, the site of the former Kingdom of James Jesse Strang. Arrive aboard the **Emerald Isle** (231) 547-2311 or toll-free (888) 446-4095. You can arrange a day tour package at those numbers. If you prefer, you can take a 15 minute flight from the Charlevoix Airport on **Island Airways** (231) 547-2141 or toll-free (800) 524-6895, or take **Island Hopper Charter Service** water taxi to the outer Islands, (231) 448-2309 or cell (231) 620-2058. Beaver Island has a full service marina or you can pull into the Beaver Island Municipal Yacht Dock. You can rent a car on the island or take off on your own hiking excursion. There are bus trips available. (See p. 443, Part II for additional history of King James Jesse Strang.)
   Castle Farms-Historic Landmark, 5052 M-66 North, (231) 547-0884, www.castlefarms.com. The site for many local functions including wine tasting, theatre productions and even local weddings. This will prove an interesting and unique stop on your journey along the Sunset Coast. Tours of the castle provide visitors with the opportunity to see the exquisite courtyards and gardens, including a hedge maze and giant chessboard. (See picture next page.)

Photo Courtesy of Castle Farms

Ride the Little Traverse Wheelway. This 26-mile route takes you from Charlevoix to Harbor Springs. The trail is paved and you meander through beautiful parks and along spectacular shoreline on the way to your Bay Harbor, Petoskey or Harbor Springs destination. There is a ¾ mile boardwalk established to protect the wetland ecosystem of the area. There are many places to pick up the well-marked trail; one is the Charlevoix Township Hall at 12491 Waller Road. There is parking and trail access at that point. The trail is non-motorized and open to bikers, skaters, skiers, walkers or runners. So pick your favorite sport in any season and enjoy the views along the way.

Ski Boyne Mountain, Boyne Mountain Road, Boyne Falls, MI 49713, (231) 549-6000 or toll-free (800) GO-BOYNE. 61 runs await you and the Mountain has high-tech snowmaking and the slopes are well-groomed. They have the superpipe and 35 kilometers of cross-country trails. Lots of activities for children.

Surf and Turf Driving Tour, a 35 mile tour from Charlevoix that takes about 45 minutes. You will drive through rolling hills, typical Michigan farmland and the south arm of Lake Charlevoix. Depart Charlevoix along US-31 South to the Ellsworth turn in Atwood. Turn left on C-48, continue five miles and turn left on Church, then left again at the next stop, staying on C-48. In east Jordan, turn left on M-66 (you pass the Ironton Ferry, highlighted in *Ripley's Believe It or Not*). Stay on M-66 to US-31. A right on US-31 takes you back into Charlevoix.

Festivals
The Charlevoix Trout Tournament, June.

Castle Farms Fine Art Show, June.
Taste of Charlevoix, June.
Annual Craft Show, July.
Garden Clubs Garden Walk, July.
Street Legends Classic Car Show, July.
Annual Venetian Festival, July.
Ride the Charx, August.
Annual Waterfront Art Fair, August.
Annual Apple Festival, October.

Golf

Belvedere Golf Club, 5731 Marion Center Road, (231) 547-2611, www.belvederegolfclub.com. This golf course was built by 150 men with 5 teams of horses in the 1920s! Challenging 3 and 4 pars with 5 pars that reward aggressive play with birdie and eagle opportunities. Open to the public only during certain times.

Boyne Golf has eight courses in the northwestern Michigan area. Call toll-free (888) 66-Boyne for additional information.

Contacts

Beaver Island Chamber of Commerce, (231) 448-2505.
Charlevoix Area Convention and Visitors Bureau, 100 Michigan Avenue, www.charlevoixlodging.com, toll-free (800) 367-8557.

Bridge open for passing ship   *Photo by Bob Royce*

Bay Harbor

Population: No statistics separate from Petoskey but currently 580 families live in Bay Harbor.

Directions: **From Detroit:** I-75 North to the second Gaylord exit (exit 282). Turn left (west) at the exit ramp light onto M-32. Follow M-32 West for 13 miles, to dead end at US-131. Turn right (north) on Route 131. Follow US-131 for about 20 miles, to Petoskey. In Petoskey, just past the Big Boy (on the right), turn left at the light onto US-31 toward Charlevoix. Take US-31 four miles to Bay Harbor. **From Lansing:** (216 miles) US-127 North, merge with I-75 North and follow above directions. **From Chicago:** Take I-94 East to I-196 North to Grand Rapids to US-131 North. Take US-131 North to Petoskey. In Petoskey, just past the Big Boy (on the right), turn left at the light onto US-31 toward Charlevoix. Take US-31 four miles to Bay Harbor.

Background and History

The area that is now Bay Harbor was indistinguishable from Petoskey from the 16th to the 19th centuries. They were separated by only a couple of miles and shared a history common to nearly every shore community along Lake Michigan: Native Americans inhabited the land, fur became a lucrative business, lumber came on the scene to replace the fur industry when animals became too scarce for profitable hunting, and then the forests too were depleted. The citizenry of these little villages and towns awoke to the splendor of Lake Michigan every morning. There is a saying: *If you are lucky enough to live on Lake Michigan, you are lucky enough.* Unfortunately, that alone can not put food in your stomach or a roof over your head.

The death of lumbering meant drastic changes for shoreline communities. Harbor Springs became a resort community to wealthy families from all over the Midwest, including Chicago. It was the place to have your summer home. Petoskey grew into a bustling business community, but also had hotels and motels that accommodated a growing tourist trade. Bay Harbor's destiny took a different direction. About a century ago, limestone was discovered on the outskirts of Petoskey, in Bay Harbor, and it drew mining interests and became the site of a large cement manufacturing facility owned by Penn-Dixie.

For more than a century these mining operations defaced about five miles, and more than 1,000 acres of Lake Michigan shoreline along the Little Traverse Bay.

When mining operations were abandoned they left in their tracks scarred acreage, pockmarked by asbestos, coal and two and a half million cubic yards of kiln dust. It was not a benevolent way to treat the natural beauty of the Big Lake.

The scenic magnificence of the Traverse Bay, however, induced creative and enterprising folks to undertake a clean up effort to reclaim this eyesore and transform it into a first class resort area with wonderful tourist facilities.

By 1995 the toxic, hideous and deformed lakeshore became a luxury resort, the rival of any of her pretty, older neighbors. Today, instead of the reek of chemicals and carcinogens, Bay Harbor smells of elegance and money.

Food/Restaurants

Galley Gourmet Deli, 4181 Main Street, (231) 439-2665. Voted Best of Northern Michigan Reader's Choice for "Best Pizza." Also the place to get terrific portable meals for a local picnic or fishing trip. Open 7 days, 10:00 am to 10:00 pm. Hours reduced in fall.

Galley Gourmet Espresso Café, 4181 Main Street, (231) 439-2660. An interesting café with a nice selection of loose leaf teas, top quality espresso drinks, homemade ice cream and fabulous pastries. Computers and internet access or you can leisurely read the morning paper and get set for the day. Open 7 days, 7:00 am to 10:00 pm in the summer. During the off-season open 7 days: 8:00 am to 8:00 pm.

Knot Just a Bar, 820 Front Street, www.knotjustabar.com, (231) 439-2770. Located in the Harbor Master Building in the Bay Harbor Marina District, this bar offers a casual place to catch a quick bite, an icy brew, and maybe even see a bit of your favorite game on their big TV. The extensive menu takes a while to digest but the loaded potato boats are the perfect way to start. There are enough soups and salads to satisfy everyone's taste, a raw bar, wraps and sandwiches, burgers - or how about a Jack Daniels BBQ Pork Sandwich? If you want a full dinner, you will find a wide choice of entrees (Grilled Chicken Gorgonzola?). Save room for the Temptation Station (Big Al's Monster Fudge Sundae serves four!). Chosen Northern Michigan's Best Happy Hour. Open 7 days, Mon to Thurs noon "til we're done," Fri and Sat noon to 2:00 am and Sun noon to 8:00 pm.

Latitude Restaurant, 795 Front Street, (231) 439-2750, www.latituderestaurant.com. Enjoy the storybook yachts in Bay Harbor's Marina and watch the glorious sunset as you feast on top-notch seasonal cuisine that compliments the moods of Northern Michigan. The reputation of this restaurant is recognized throughout the area and it has received awards from several sources, including *The Observer and Eccentric* and *Wine Spectator*. Reservations suggested. Save room for one of the pastry chef's glorious desserts. Live entertainment in the lounge most weekends. Open May through September 7 days for lunch and dinner. Open October through May Tues to Sat 5:00 pm to closing.

The Original Pancake House, 4165 Main Street, (231) 439-9989, www.originalpancakehouse.com. One of their signature dishes is the Apple Pancake, a single large pancake smothered with sautéed apples and cinnamon sugar and baked to perfection to create a deliciously rich cinnamon sugar glaze. Open 7 days, 7:00 am to 3:00 pm. In the winter open 7 days but closes Mon to Fri at 2:00 pm.

Sagamore's Restaurant, 3600 Village Harbor Drive, (231) 439-4000. Fine French and international cuisine as well as picture-perfect views of the Grand Traverse Bay. Open 7 days, Breakfast: Mon to Sat 6:30 am to 10:30 am and Sun 6:30 am to noon. Dinner: Sun to Thurs 5:30 pm to 10:00 pm and Fri and Sat 5:30 pm to 11:00 pm.

South American Grill, 3600 Village Harbor Drive (231) 439-4000. A rich and relaxing bar/grill where you can order your favorite drink and enjoy appetizers or light fare (salads, sandwiches). Often has entertainment. Open 7 days, Sun to Thurs 11:00 am to 9:00 pm and Fri and Sat 11:00 am to 10:00 pm.

Lodging

Bay Harbor Resort and Marina, 4000 Main Street, toll-free (888) BAY-HARBOR. A wide range of suites with spectacular views of Lake Michigan. This upscale boutique hotel is pricy, but their fully furnished, luxury accommodations feature large, open floor plans ranging from 1,100 to 5,000 square feet.

Bay Harbor Vacation Rentals, 4000 Main Street, Suite 110, (231) 439-2400. Connected to the resort above and rents out premiere homes, town homes, and condos throughout Bay Harbor.

The Cliffs Condominiums at Bay Harbor, Cliffs Drive, (231) 342-3205 or toll-free (877) 492-1022, www.connectnorth.com. Two-to-four bedroom, two-to-four bath condominiums situated on a cliff overlooking Lake Michigan and the Little Traverse Bay. Extras: full kitchens, fireplaces, lakeside decks, garages and year round indoor pool. A wonderful place to stay. Call for rental information.

Cottages at Crooked Tree, Crooked Tree Drive, (231) 439-4000 or toll-free (800) 462-6963, www.boyne.com. Across the Street from Bay Harbor so not Bay Harbor proper, these cottages are perched atop a bluff overlooking Lake Michigan's spectacular sunsets and feature Northern Michigan architecture, cottage-style furnishings, equipped kitchens and fireplaces.

Inn at Bay Harbor, 3600 Village Harbor Drive, (231) 439-4000. A four-star hotel with great rooms, great views and a great staff. The Inn is reminiscent of Victorian inns of an earlier era and provides all of the comforts you could want or expect: pools, one and two bedroom suites with waterfront balconies, fireplaces, resort town with shopping, golf and entertainment.

Lakeside Cottages at Bay Harbor, 3600 Village Harbor Drive, (231) 439-4000 or toll-free (800) 462-6963. www.boyne.com. Two-and-three-bedroom cottages adjacent to The Inn at Bay Harbor. Extras: kitchens, fireplaces, access to the amenities of the Inn at Bay Harbor.

Museums and Galleries

Bay Harbor History Museum, 4245 Main Street (in the building with the Signature Store), (231) 439-2620. A maritime museum with the history of Bay Harbor's development. Open 7 days, Mon to Sat 10:00 am to 7:00 pm and Sun 10:00 am to 5:00 pm. Open in the winter, but hours reduced by season.

Gallery on Main, 4184 Main Street, www.galleryonmainbh.com, (231) 439-2745. The place to find a wide collection of regional fine art including: jewelry, abstract and traditional paintings, handcrafted furniture, ceramics, wood sculptures and bronze works. Open 7 days, Mon to Sat 10:00 am to 7:00 pm and Sun 10:00 am to 5:00 pm.

Antiques

Savoir Faire, 4245 Main Street, (231) 439-2614. Merchandise includes high-quality antiques, furniture, home accessories and gifts for anyone for any occasion. The store offers a blend of old and new. Open 7 days, Mon to Sat 10:00 am to 6:00 pm and Sun 10:00 am to 4:00 pm. Slightly reduced hours off-season.

Other Shopping

Bay Harbor Signature Store, 4245 Main Street, (231) 439-2620. Located in the Bay Harbor History Museum and featuring men's women's and children's apparel with the logo and spirit of Bay Harbor. Open 7 days, Mon to Sat 10:00 am to 7:00 pm and Sun 10:00 am to 5:00 pm. Open in the winter, but hours reduced by season.

J. Phillips, (231) 758-3450. Trendy, fashionable clothing in classic design. Casual to evening wear. Unique accessories from Rador to Sorrelli jewelry or Mary Francis to Timmy Woods handbags. Open 7 days, Mon to Sat 9:00 am to 8:00 pm and Sun 10:00 am to 6:00 pm. Reduced hours in the off-season.

Les Femmes, 4000 Main Street, (231) 439-2670. Boutique displaying classic clothing and luxurious gifts, Ashley Page swimwear and Oprah's favorite: Adam and Eve. Open Mon to Sat 10:00 am to 7:00 pm and Sun 10:00 am to 5:00 pm. Reduced off-season hours.

Monogram Goods, 4237 Main Street, (231) 439-9771, www.monogramgoods.com. Wide range of luxurious linens, clothing tableware, baby items and unique gifts. Monogram service offered.

Open: Mon to Sat 10:00 am to 7:00 pm, Sun 10:00 am to 5:00 pm. Hours reduced slightly in the winter and may close one day per week.

Northern Sole, 4176 Main Street (231) 439-2636. Men and women's shoes as well as handbags, belts and jewelry from such lines as Via Spiga, Maxx, Kenneth Cole, Lacoste, Puma and Carlos Santana. Open 7 days, Mon to Sat 10:00 am to 7:00 pm and Sun 10:00 am to 5:00 pm. Winter hours: closes Mon to Wed at 5:00 pm, Thurs to Sat at 6:00 pm and Sun at 4:00 pm.

Rocking Horse Toy Company, 4000 Main Street, (231) 439-2680. Brings out the kid in all of us. Kites, games, crafts and of course rocking horses, stuffed animals, vehicles, chairs, and even a plush rocking duck. Open 7 days, Mon to Sat 9:00 am to 10:00 pm and Sun 10:00 am to 8:00 pm. Open in the winter with slightly reduced hours.

Threads, 4234 Bay Street (231) 439-2626. Diverse blend of color, texture and style in women's clothing and accessories. Casual to elegant. Open 7 days, Mon to Sat 10:00 am to 7:00 pm and Sun 10:00 am to 5:00 pm. Reduced hours in the off-season.

Marinas, Water Sports and Boat Rental

Bay Harbor Lake Marina, 832 Front Street in the heart of the village, (231) 439-2544. You can dock for a week or a season. They offer 120 flotation docks. Amenities: ship store, restrooms, showers, ice, data port, paddle boat and kayak rentals, ASTM, seasonal access to Bay Harbor Swim and Fitness Club available and laundry.

Lake Michigan Yacht Sales, 801 Front Street, Suite B, (231) 439-2675, www.lakemichiganyachtsales.com. Though primarily a sales establishment, Lake Michigan Yacht Sales also rents Larson 18-and-21-foot boats and they are a place to rent a Kayak.

Bay Harbor Marina   *Photo Courtesy of Lloyd Pedersen*

Parks

Little Traverse Wheelway A 26-mile trail takes you from Charlevoix to Harbor Springs and can be accessed in Bay Harbor. See listing under Charlevoix p. 279, for additional detail.)

Charters

Great Lakes Charters, Bay Harbor Lake Marina, (231) 547-0700.

Other Things to See and Do

Bay Harbor Fun Factory, located at the Inn in Bay Harbor (231) 439-2728. Arcade games to keep your children happy even if the sun is hiding. Slot car races are scheduled every Saturday. They offer foosball, air hockey, retro-arcade games, pool tables, and flat screen TVs. Games include: Deer Hunting USA, Golden Tee 2K, 8 Lane Slot Car Racing, Hang On, Pump it Up, NBA Fast Break Pin Ball, Donkey Kong, Bubble Hockey, Pac-Man, Miss Pac-man, Dig Dug, California Speed Pole, Position II and more. Open noon to 8:00 pm. Off-season only open on weekends.

Festivals

Bay Harbor Concours d'Elegance, June 22 and 23, 2007. Vintage vehicles and classic boats make this an elegant and entertaining weekend.

Annual Bay Harbor Art Fair, August.

Taste of Bay Harbor, August.

Bay Harbor Fishing Tournament, September.

Bay Harbor Home Tour, October.

Bay Harbor Harvest Festival, October.

Golf

Bay Harbor Golf Club, US-31, (231) 439-4028 or toll free (800) 462-6963, www.boyne.com. Three 9-hole courses (Links, Preserve, and Quarry), any two of which can be combined to let you play 18-holes. *Golf Magazine* rated Bay Harbor Golf Club #8 of the Top 100 public U.S. courses its first season. You may be distracted by the panoramic views of dunes and bluffs of this Arthur Hills designed course.

Contacts

Experience Bay Harbor, 4000 Main Street, toll-free (888) Bay-Harbor, info@bayharbor.com for additional information and current schedule of festivals and outdoor concerts.

(Also see Petoskey contacts, next chapter p. 301.)

Petoskey
-including Bay View

Population: Just over 6,000.

Directions: **From Detroit**: (271 miles) I-75 North, exit 290 north toward Vanderbilt, left onto North Old 27/CR-C48, left onto East Thumb Lake Road/CR-C48, right onto US-131 into Petoskey. **From Lansing:** (212 miles) US-127 North, merge with I-75 North and follow above directions. **From Chicago:** (363 miles) I-94 East towards Detroit, merge into I-196 North via exit 34 toward Holland, merge onto US-131 North via exit 77A, to Petoskey.

Background and History

Antoine Carre, a descendant of French nobility, visited the Petoskey area in the late 1780s. Carre hooked up with John Jacob Astor's fur company and married a Native American princess from the Ottawa tribe. Carre so thoroughly assimilated into his wife's tribe that he became a chief and was given the name Neaatooshing.

In the spring of 1787, after spending the winter near what is now Chicago, Neaatooshing and his family began their long trek back to northwest Michigan. One night during this journey they camped on the banks of the Kalamazoo River. Before daybreak a son was born to the proud chief. As the sun rose in the morning sky, its rays fell on the newborn's face. Seeing the sunshine on his child's face, Chief Neaatooshing proclaimed, "His name shall be Petosegay and he shall become an important person." The Ottawa translation of the name is *"rising sun," "rays of dawn"* or *"sunbeams of promise."*

Chief Petoskey's son, Ignatius Petoskey, like his father and grandfather (Neaatooshing) before him, grew up to be a chief of his people. He was a leader in the Bear River Native American Village and made a selection of land in accordance with the provisions of the Treaty of 1855. He lived in a log home on this land and bought additional land from the government, ultimately owning much of the acreage on which the city of Petoskey, named in his father's honor, now stands. Ignatius served as a translator during church services, turning the words of the minister into the language of the Native Americans who attended the services along with their English speaking neighbors.

At 5:00 pm on November 25, 1873, the first steam locomotive penetrated the wilderness to the Little Traverse Bay. It signaled the start of an exciting era in Petoskey history. On board was George Gage, a reporter for the *Grand Rapids Times* who was awed by what he proclaimed: "the million dollar sunset." Lake Michigan's fabulous sunsets have been dubbed *Million Dollar Sunsets* ever since. The Grand

Rapids and Indiana Railroad played a huge role in transforming Petoskey into a busy city by the turn of the century.

Change came at a heavy price. In 1874 the railway had land to sell and vigorously promoted settlement in the area. The campaign championed the beauty of the wilderness: the clear, fresh, health-giving air, the pure, sparkling lakes and streams with abundant fish, and the unspoiled forests of pine and hard-woods. Would-be-settlers were swayed by the promises and for the next five years the numbers of people getting off the GRI at the last stop in Petoskey were impressive.

The claims that induced those early immigrants to relocate were all true, but the city was unequipped to meet their basic needs of food and shelter. Many of the new settlers were looking for a fresh start after losing everything in the "Panic of 1873." Others were Civil War veterans looking for a place to pick up the pieces of their lives. These uprooted transplants sometimes lived in holes dug in river banks until they could erect a suitable cabin. Even with long days spent toiling in the field; starvation seemed an ongoing and ominous threat.

By 1877, tales of the deprivation being suffered in Petoskey reached Grand Rapids and that city sent box cars full of supplies to sustain the populace of this northern outpost until it could get its fields tilled and producing.

At the same time the relief train was arriving from Grand Rapids, a miracle of sorts took place: great flocks of passenger pigeons flew across the northern Michigan skies seeking places to nest. They were trapped by the hundreds of thousands and became a desperately needed source of food. But, in addition to becoming dinner to starving settlers, they were hunted and exported to large city markets by the boat loads – until the passenger pigeon was extinct. (See p. 393, Part II of this guide for the story of Martha, the last passenger pigeon.)

In 1875, the Methodist Camp was established in Bay View. Summer homes sprang up and the wealthy residents of Bay View infused the Petoskey economy. Many other summer colonies followed.

Today Petoskey covers an area of approximately four square miles. While summer is its high season, winter sports are also popular. In fact, locals tell you that it is the year-rounder who is truly fortunate. He or she gets to enjoy each beautiful season in its turn.

Food/Restaurants

Andaste, 321 Bay Street, (231) 348-3321. Contemporary, art-filled restaurant near the Gaslight District of Petoskey. Views of the Little Traverse Bay. Menu offers Regional American, French, Asian, and Mediterranean entrees. Also has an excellent wine list. Open Tues to Sun 5:30 pm to 9:30 pm. Closed Mon. Call for winter hours.

Big Apple Bagels, 1125 North US-31, (231) 348-1110. Breakfast and lunch sandwiches. Bagels and muffins. Open year round, 7 days, Mon to Fri 6:00 am to 6:00 pm, Sat 7:00 am to 3:00 pm and Sun 8:00 am to 3:00 pm.

The Bistro, 423 Michigan Street, (231) 347-5583. Breakfast café with pancakes, omelets, cinnamon rolls and muffins to go with morning coffee. Open Mon to Fri 6:30 am to 2:00 pm and Sat 7:30 am to 2:00 pm. Closed Sun. Open year round.

Chandler's, 215½ Howard Street, (231) 347-2981. Daily specials, sandwiches, great drinks and desserts to tempt any palate. An upscale menu and a casual ambiance. Open Breakfast: Sat and Sun 9:00 am to 4:00 pm. Lunch: 7 days, 11:00 am to 4:00 pm. Dinner: Sun to Wed 5:00 pm to 9:00 pm and Thurs to Sat 5:00 pm to 11:00 pm.

City Park Grill, 432 Lake Street, (231) 347-0101. Established in 1910, this popular restaurant brags that Ernest Hemingway was a customer. Contemporary menu (maybe the Big Easy Linguine or fresh whitefish from John Cross Fishery in Charlevoix) with extensive wine list. Also a children's menu. Open for Lunch: Mon to Sat 11:30 am to 4:00 pm. Dinner: Mon to Thurs 4:00 pm to 9:00 pm, Fri and Sat 4:00 pm to 10:00 pm and Sun 11:30 am to 9:00 pm.

Flat Iron Deli, 313 Howard Street, (231) 347-5190. Build your own sandwich by choosing the breads, meats, condiments, toppings and cheese. Also: salads, homemade soups, cheesecakes and box lunches. Open Mon to Sat 9:00 am to 4:00 pm and closed Sun.

Gelato Café, 413 East Lake Street, (231) 347-7400. Great sandwiches, soups, salads and quiche along with coffees, teas and gelato. Open Mon to Thurs 8:00 am to 10:00 pm, Fri 8:00 am to 11:00 pm, Sat 9:00 am to 11:00 pm and Sun 9:00 am to 10:00 pm. Hours reduced slightly in fall: Mon to Thurs 8:00 am to 5:00 pm, Fri 8:00 am to 9:00 pm, Sat 9:00 am to 9:00 pm and Sun 9:00 am to 4:00 pm.

Hu Nan Chinese Restaurant, 629 Charlevoix Avenue, (231) 348-1848. You can indulge yourself on the large portions of Szechuan and Hu-Nan style cuisine in this friendly, family-owned Asian restaurant. Open 7 days, 11:00 am to 9:00 pm.

Johan's Pastry Shop, 565 West Mitchell Street, (231) 347-3815. Assorted baked goods including cakes, pastries, bread and bagels. Famous for the "J" Bun, a cinnamon bun that people take back as a gift to others from their visit to Petoskey. Open 7 days, Mon to Sat 5:30 am to 5:30 pm and Sun 6:00 am to 1:00 pm.

J.W. Filmore's Family Restaurant, 906 Spring Street, (231) 348-7500. Varied menu. Open 7 days, 6:00 am to 9:00 pm, closes slightly earlier in the fall.

Jesperson's Restaurant, 312 Howard Street, (231) 347-3601. Special is deep fried whitefish and coleslaw. Famous for their homemade pies, try the cherry-berry (cherries and red-raspberries). Open Mon to Sat 11:00 am to 4:00 pm. In the winter they close Mon.

La Senorita, 1285 North US-31, (231) 347-7750. Wide selection of Mexican favorites. Dining room is open Mon to Thurs 11:00 am to 11:00 pm, Fri and Sat 11:00 am to midnight and Sun noon to 10:00 pm. Reduced winter hours.

Mim's Mediterranean Grill, 1823 US-31, (231) 348-9994. Kabobs, gyros, combos, hummus, falafel, spanakopita and a variety of salads. The Mediterranean Plate allows you to sample the falafel, hummus, pita bread and tabbouleh. Open year round, Mon to Sat 11:00 am to 8:00 pm. Closed Sun.

Mitchell Street Pub and Cafe, 426 East Mitchell Street, (231) 347-1801. Nibbles, sandwiches, salads and burgers. Luncheon Specials Mon to Fri. Open 11:30 am to last call at 1:30 am, (kitchen closes 11:00 pm). Closed Sun. May reduce winter hours.

Northwood Restaurant, 4769 Ogden Road (5 miles north of the M-119 and US-31 intersection), (231) 347-3894. Steaks, ribs and chicken. Open 7 days 11:00 am to 10:00 pm (lunch served until 4:00 pm). Open year round, reduced winter hours.

Papa Lou's Pizza Pub and Grill, 317 East Lake Street, (231) 348-3668. Besides pizza, they serve appetizers, soups, salads and sandwiches. Open 7 days, Mon to Sat 11:00 am to 2:00 am and Sun noon to 2:00 am.

Rio Grand Steakhouse, 1315 North US-31, (231) 347-7747. *Big* steaks, chicken, fish, salads and sandwiches. Open year round, Mon to Thurs 11:00 am to 10:00 pm and Fri and Sat 11:00 am to 11:00 pm.

Roast and Toast Café & Coffee, 309 Lake Street, (231) 347-7767. Coffee freshly roasted on site. Menu includes award winning soups, sandwiches, homemade pot pies and bakery items. The veggie lasagna is a good choice for dinner. Open 7 days, 7:00 am to 9:00 pm. Winter closed Mon to Thurs at 7:00 pm, Fri and Sat at 8:00 pm. Off-season hours may vary so call to confirm.

Scalawags, M-119 and Petoskey Harbor, (231) 487-0055, www.scalawagswhitefish.com. House specialty: Whitefish and Chips. Variety of baskets and sandwiches. Open summer 7 days, 11:30 am to 9:30 pm. Winter closes at 9:00 pm Mon to Thurs and 8:00 pm on Sun.

Stafford's Bay View Inn, 2011 Woodland Avenue, Bay View, (231) 347-2771. Country-Style Victorian Inn provides elegant ambiance for this lovely restaurant. Views of the Little Traverse Bay. Best Sunday Brunch around. Open 7 days, 9:00 am to 1:00 pm and 5:00 pm to 9:00 pm. Sunday Brunch 8:30 am to 2:00 pm.

Stafford's Perry Hotel, Bay View at Lewis, (231) 347-4000. Elegant fine dining with fabulous views of the bay from the H. O. Rose Dining Room. The Rose Garden Veranda is perfect for summer outdoor dining. The Noggin Room is a full service pub. Open breakfast 7:00 am to 10:30 am, lunch 11:30 am to 2:30 pm, dinner Mon to Thurs 5:00 pm to 9:00 pm and Fri and Sat 5:00 to 10:00. Call for non-season hours.

Terrace Inn, 1549 Glendale Avenue, Bay View, (231) 347-2410. Enjoy dining in this historic setting. Chicken Hemingway is a tribute to Ernest, but you may prefer the Planked Whitefish or Artichoke Linguini. Open Tues to Thurs 5:30 pm to 8:30 pm, Fri and Sat 5:30 pm to 9:00 pm and Sun Brunch 11:00 am to 1:00 pm.

Villa Restorante Italiano, 887 Spring Street, (231) 347-1440. Upscale regional Italian cuisine featuring pastas, chicken, seafood, Naples-style pizza and veal. Consider their Tuscan specialty: Wild Boar. Extensive wine list and cocktails. Reservations recommended. Open Mon to Sat 4:30 pm to 10:30 pm.

Whitecaps Grill and Spirits, 215 East Lake Street, (231) 348-7092. Fine dining in a casual atmosphere. Menu includes wonderful appetizers, fresh seafood, choice cut meats, wood-fired pizzas, homemade pastas, great salads and homemade desserts. Raw bar during summer. Open 7 days, lunch and dinner and a seasonal Sunday Brunch.

Lodging (Also see Campgrounds below)

Apple Tree Inn, 915 Spring Street (US-131 South), (231) 348-2900 or toll-free (800) 348-2901, www.appletreeinn.com. 40 rooms, all with private balconies and view of the Little Traverse Bay. Extras: VCR, internet, refrigerator, suites and whirlpool rooms available, indoor pool, spa, continental breakfast, laundry, no pets, smoke free.

Bay Inn of Petoskey, 2445 Charlevoix Avenue (US-31), (231) 347-2593 or toll-free (888) 321-2500, www.bayinnpetoskey.com. Two story motel with 15 smoke free rooms. Reasonable rates.

Bay Winds Inn, 909 Spring Street (US-131 South), (231) 347-4193 or toll-free (800) 204-1748, www.baywindsinn.com. 50 rooms near Little Traverse Bay and Petoskey's Gaslight District. Extras: area's largest indoor pool, spa, exercise room, HBO, refrigerators, deluxe continental breakfast and internet. Whirlpool rooms available.

Best Western Inn, 1300 Spring Street (US-131 South), (231) 347-3925 or toll-free (888)-738-6753. 85 newly remodeled rooms. Extras: indoor pool, sauna, whirlpool, exercise room, game room, HBO, high-speed internet and continental breakfast.

Comfort Inn, 1314 US-31 North, (231) 347-3220 or toll-free (800) 228-5150, www.comfortinn.com/hotel/mi412. 65 guest rooms. Extras: lobby computers with free internet, HBO, exercise room, free Comfort

Sunshine breakfast, king rooms have refrigerator, microwave and two-person whirlpool bath. Two-room suite available.

Days Inn, 1420 Spring Street (US-131), toll-free (866) 439-9718, www.daysinnpetoskey.com. 134 rooms. Views of the Little Traverse Bay. Extras: HBO, DVD/CD, refrigerator, microwave, laptop in lobby, internet, data port phones, free local calls, laundry and exercise room.

Econo Lodge, 1858 US-131 South, (231) 348-3324 or toll-free (800) 748-0417, www.choicehotels.com/hotel/MI099. 59 rooms. Extras: indoor pool, whirlpool, refrigerators, continental breakfast and golf and ski packages.

Gingerbread House B&B, 1130 Bluff Street, Bay View, (231) 347-3538. National historic 1881 cottage with views of the bay. Four rooms. Full breakfast.

The Hampton Inn, 920 Spring Street (US-131 South), (231) 348-9555 or toll-free (800) 426-7866, www.hamptoninn.com. 77 rooms, many overlooking the bay. Extras: suites and rooms, internet, indoor pool, whirlpool, fitness center and complimentary deluxe breakfast bar.

Stafford's Bay View Inn, 2011 Woodland Avenue (US-31 North), Bay View, (231) 347-2771 or toll-free (800) 258-1886, www.staffords.com, bayviewinn@staffords.com. 31 individually appointed rooms decorated in Victorian motif. On the National Register of Historic Places. Extras: some suites with in-room whirlpools, individual climate control in each room and wireless internet.

Stafford's Perry Hotel, 100 Lewis Street, (231) 347-4000 or toll-free (800) 737-1899, www.staffords.com, perryhotel@staffords.com. On the National Register of Historic Places. 79 individually appointed rooms. Extras: pub with entertainment, fabulous views of the Little Traverse Bay, wireless internet and some rooms with private balconies.

Super 8 Motel, 2645 Charlevoix Avenue (US-31), (231) 439-8000 or toll-free (888) 439-8002, www.super8.com. 58 rooms and suites available; some with spectacular views of the bay. Extras: heated indoor pool, whirlpool, cable TV and continental breakfast.

Terrace Inn, 1549 Glendale, Bay View, (231) 347-2410, www.theterraceinn.com, info@theterraceinn.com. Built in 1911, this historic inn and restaurant offers 25 standard rooms, 11 deluxe rooms, and 4 Jacuzzi suites. Extras: wireless internet in all rooms, CATV in deluxe rooms and suites and some fireplaces. No smoking or pets.

Victories Hotel, 1444 US-131 South, (231) 347-6041 or toll-free (877) 4GAMING, www.victories-casino.com. 127 rooms and 10 suites. Extras: pool, whirlpool, exercise room and shuttle to Victories Casino.

Museums and Galleries

Art Tree Gallery, (See Crooked Tree Arts Center under Theatre below.)

Beyond Borders, 309 Howard Street, (231) 348-1176. International Trade Store that also features Michigan artists. Specializes in unique clothing, ceramics, collectibles and jewelry. Open 7 days, Mon to Thurs 10:00 am to 7:00 pm, Fri and Sat 10:00 am to 8:00 pm and Sun noon to 5:00 pm. Reduced off-season hours.

Cold Nose Productions, 437 East Mitchell Street, (231) 348-8271, www.coldnose-productions.com. A bright, fun gallery with lots of custom art and charming kid's furniture. Artist Kathy Mack designs and paints the furniture (even has a furniture company that makes her designs), and when she tires of painting furniture she crochets hats, she creates collages or turns to some other project that is sure to turn out beautiful. She also offers workshops in the summer from 1:00 pm to 3:00 pm, Mon to Fri. Gallery open Mon to Sat 9:00 am to 9:00 pm, Sun 11:00 am to 4:00 pm. Winter hours reduced: Mon to Sat 9:30 am to 6:00 pm and Sun 11:00 am to 4:00 pm.

Garwood Gallery, 438 East Mitchell Street, (231) 349-9610. The gallery showcases works and reproductions of well-known artists in acrylic, watercolor, oil, pastels, photography, ceramics, jewelry and blown glass. Open Tues to Sat 11:00 am to 5:00 pm, Fri open until 9:00 pm. Closed Sun and Mon.

Gaslight Gallery, 200 Howard Street, toll-free (866) 348-5079, www.gaslightgallery.net. Featuring works of over 200 local and national artists in a variety of mediums: painting, photography, sculpture, glass, jewelry and furniture. Open 7 days, Mon to Sat 10:00 am to 9:00 pm and Sun 11:00 am to 5:00 pm. Winter hours reduced.

Indian Hills Gallery, 1581 Harbor-Petoskey Road (M-119) (231) 347-3789. Beads, fine art, quill baskets, books, music and sterling silver jewelry. Open 7 days, Mon to Sat 10:00 am to 6:00 pm and Sun 11:00 am to 4:00 pm. Open year round, but reduced hours off-season.

Little Traverse Historical Society History Museum, 100 Depot Court (At Bayfront Park), (231) 347-2620. Museum is located in the historic Chicago and West Michigan Railroad Depot and features Native American Cultural Art, Emmet County genealogy, Ernest Hemingway exhibit, Petoskey Stone exhibit and the nautical history of the Little Traverse Bay. Open Mon to Sat 1:00 pm to 4:00 pm. Closed in winter (about November).

Northern Michigan Artist Market, 445 East Mitchell Street, (231) 487-0000, www.nmam.us. Broad spectrum of interesting art by more than 100 Northern Michigan artists: pottery, glass, oils, textiles, jewelry, prints and photographs - with something for every budget.

Open summer 7 days, Mon to Thurs 10:00 am to 5:00 pm, Fri 10:00 am to 8:00 pm, Sat 10:00 am to 5:00 pm and Sun 11:00 am to 4:00 pm. Sunday hours vary in the winter, call to confirm.

Ward and Eis Gallery, 315 East Lake Street, (231) 347-2750. Leather goods, jewelry and turquoise. Open 6 days, Mon to Sat.

Theatre

Bay View Association Concert Series, (231) 347-6225 for schedule and prices, or check the website at www.bayviewassoc.com. Several series of concerts offered in this little historic community just east of Petoskey. You can enjoy the Wednesday evening light classical music concerts, the student concerts on Friday afternoons or the Sunday evening vesper concerts. Concerts run mid-July to mid-August.

Crooked Tree Arts Center, 461 East Mitchell Street, (231) 347-4337, www.crookedtree.org. This renovated church with extraordinary original architecture is a treat by itself. However, it also offers fine art exhibits and performances by the Little Traverse Civic Theatre.

Antiques

Longton Hall Antiques, Mostly Scottish and English antiques, a few American and Western. Circa 1840s. Open 7 days, Mon to Sat 10:00 am to 5:00 pm and Sun noon to 3:00 pm. Reduced fall hours, closed in winter.

Other Shopping

American Spoon, 413 East Lake Street, (231) 347-7004. An assortment of jams, jellies and other food items. The American Spoon Gelato Café is next door, see above. Open 7 days, Mon to Sat 10:00 am to 5:30 pm and Sun 10:00 am to 4:30 pm. Closes at 4:30 pm in the fall.

Art and Soul Studio, 433 East Mitchell Street, (231) 348-7577. A studio where you can peruse or buy everything you can possibly need for art projects including stamps, stencils, sponges, paints, brushes and a wealth of ideas.

Back to Nature, 207 Howard Street, (231) 439-9135. Garden art, gifts, nightlights, stepping stones, polished and unpolished Petoskey stones, chimes, mini waterfalls and birdhouses. Open 7 days, Mon to Wed and Sat 10:00 am to 7:00 pm, Thurs and Fri 10:00 am to 9:00 pm and Sun 11:00 am to 4:00 pm. Closed some Sundays in the winter.

Bear Cub Outfitters, 321 East Lake Street, (231) 439-9500, www.bearcuboutfitters.com. Hiking and camping equipment for the entire family including the pooch. Duffels, clothes, sandals, running strollers, helmets; everything from the most basic to the rather esoteric. Open 7 days, Mon to Sat 10:00 am to 9:00 pm and Sun 11:00 am to 6:00 pm. Reduced off-season hours.

Bondurant, 206 Howard Street, www.shopbondurant.com, (231) 439-9181. Home accents, accessories, magnets, jewelry, wall art, bags, rugs, chandeliers and some furniture. Open 7 days, Mon to Sat 9:00 am to 9:00 pm and Sun 11:00 am to 4:00 pm. Reduced winter hours.

Chico's, 205 Howard Street, (231) 347-2999, www.chicos.com. Women's apparel and accessories. Sizes figured a little different than the traditional, but the clothing is worth a look. Open 7 days, Mon to Wed and Sat 10:00 am to 6:00 pm, Thurs and Fri 10:00 am to 7:00 pm and Sun 11:00 am to 4:00 pm. Open year round.

Clothes Post, 326 East Mitchell Street, (231) 347-4526. Men's clothing: hats to socks and everything in between. Open year round Mon to Fri 8:30 am to 5:30 pm, Sat 9:30 am to 5:30 pm. Closed Sun.

Christmas in the Country, 314 Lake Street, (231) 348-1225. Every imaginable Christmas ornament and decoration. On an 81 degree summer day the store was crowded! Open 7 days, Mon to Sat 9:30 am to 8:30 pm and Sun noon to 5:30 pm. Open weekends in the winter.

Country Clutter, 306 East Lake Street, (231) 347-6210. Everything that makes a house a home. Not just country, but French and other styles. Mary Hadley Pottery. Open 7 days, Mon to Sat 10:00 am to 8:00 pm and Sun noon to 5:00 pm. Reduced winter hours.

Cutler's, 216 Howard Street, www.cutlersonline.com, (231) 347-0341. Two great stores; one with every sort of cookware imaginable (pots, pans, espresso machines, glassware, dishes, baking pans, salad bowls, linens, etc.) and another that carries women's clothing. Some of the manufacturers you will spot in the home store: Kitchenaid, Cuisinart, Krups, Capresso, Waring, Henckels, Wusthof, Viking, Swiss Diamond, Calphalon, Staub, Le Creuset, Emile Henry and Waterford. In the women's clothing store you will find: Vera Bradley, Lilly Pullitzer, Geiger, David Brooks, Sigred Olsen and others. Cutler's home store is open 7 days: Mon to Sat 9:30 am to 6:00 pm and Sun noon to 4:00 pm. Cutler's women's clothing store is open Mon to Sat 9:30 am to 5:30 pm. A Petoskey gem!

Expressions, 332 East Lake Street (231) 347-6551. Clothing for junior-size women and girls, with men's clothing carried as well. A store aimed at youth. Shoes, jewelry, accessories and casual to dressy clothing. Open 7 days, Mon to Thurs 10:00 am to 7:00 pm, Fri and Sat 10:00 am to 8:00 pm and Sun 10:00 am to 5:30 pm. Reduced hours off-season.

Gattle's, 210 Howard Street, (231) 347-3982. Linens, sleepwear and Mackenzie-Child's dishes and pottery. Open Mon to Sat 9:00 am to 5:30 pm. Closed Sun. Slightly reduced winter hours.

Golden Shoes, 120 East Lake Street, (231) 347-0950 or toll-free (888) 465-3367. The place to find SAS or Birkenstock. Open 7 days,

Mon to Sat 9:30 am to 5:30 pm and Sun noon to 4:00 pm. Hours somewhat reduced in the winter.

Grandpa Shorter's, 301 East Lake Street, (231) 347-2603. In business for 60 years, Grandpa Shorter's is a Petoskey tradition. Interesting gifts, moccasins, Petoskey stone jewelry and Native American quill boxes are a few of the items you will find at the store voted *Northern Michigan's Favorite Gift Shop*. Open 7 days, Mon to Sat 10:00 am to 9:00 pm and Sun 11:30 am to 5:00 pm. Reduced hours in the winter, but open year round.

Harbor Wear, 319 East Lake Street, (231) 347-2664. Logo shirts, T's, sweaters and other casual clothing. Open 7 days, Mon to Fri 10:00 am to 9:00 pm, Sat 9:30 am to 9:00 pm and Sun 10:00 am to 7:00 pm. Reduced fall and winter hours.

Items, 316 East Lake Street, www.boutiqueemmuel.com, (231) 348-5890. Jeans, jackets, shoes, purses, blouses and accessories. Open 7 days, Mon to Wed 10:00 am to 6:00 pm, Thurs to Sat 10:00 am to 7:00 pm and Sun 11:00 am to 5:00 pm. Reduced winter hours.

J. B. Goods, 214 Petoskey Street, (231) 348-4663 or toll-free (800) 578-0544, www.jbgoods.com. Carries Life is Good product line of casual, relaxed and upbeat clothing for the whole family, even the dog. Open 7 days, Mon to Thurs 10:00 am to 6:00 pm, Fri and Sat 10:00 am to 8:00 pm and Sun 11:00 am to 5:00 pm. Reduced winter hours.

J. Phillips, 336 East Lake Street, (231) 347-6131. Actually five stores: Expressions (see above), Total Woman which carries plus sizes (on Mitchell Street), Country Casuals (see above) and a reduced-price store on East Lake in addition to this clothing store. Lots of options for your clothing needs. Open 7 days, Mon to Sat 10:00 am to 5:30 pm and Sun noon to 4:00 pm.

J. W. Shorter and Sons Mercantile, 311 East Lake Street, (231) 347-6540. This store is owned by Grandpa Shorter. The merchandise is a bit more upscale than Grandpa Shorter's and you will find china, bedding, handmade wreathes, accents and jewelry. Linen towels are embroidered with sayings that will make you laugh out loud. Open 7 days, Mon to Sat 10:00 am to 9:00 pm and Sun 11:30 am to 5:00 pm. Reduced hours in the winter, but open year round.

The Kid's Connection, 308 Howard Street, (231) 487-1881. A dangerous store for grandmas. Every kind of cute kid's clothing. Open 7 days, Mon to Sat 10:00 am to 6:00 pm and Sun 10:00 am to 2:00 pm.

Kilwin's Chocolates, 316 Howard Street, (231) 347-2635. Candy and ice cream. Open summer 7 days, Mon to Thurs 9:30 am to 6:00 pm, Fri and Sat 9:30 am to 8:00 pm and Sun 11:00 am to 5:00 pm.

McLean & Eakin Booksellers, 307 East Lake Street, (231) 347-1180, www.mcleanandeakin.com. I liked their bookmark which carried a warning, *"Never lend books, no one ever returns them. The only books I have in my library are those that other folks have lent me."* The store is open 7 days, Mon to Sat 9:00 am to 9:00 pm and Sun 9:30 am to 4:30 pm. Open all year but closes an hour earlier during the week in the off-season.

Mole Hole of Petoskey, 209 Howard Street, (231) 347-9959. Unique gifts including games, glassware, cards, jewelry and lots of college insignia merchandise for the University of Michigan and Michigan State. Open Mon to Sat 10:00 am to 7:00 pm and Sun 11:00 am to 5:00 pm in the summer. Winter hours shortened by one hour.

Momentum, 314 Howard Street, (231) 439-0530. Great prices on fashion apparel for the entire family. (See Traverse City p. 247) Open summer 7 days, 9:00 am to 10:00 pm. Reduced non-season hours.

Murdick's Fudge, 311 Howard Street, (231) 347-7551. Fudge, ice cream, caramel corn and snacks. Open 7 days 9:30 am to 10:30 pm. Closes earlier after Labor Day.

Pappagallo, 401 East Lake Street, (231) 347-5830. Only four Pappagallo stores remain in the country and they are each individually owned. High quality women's clothing. Open 7 days, Mon to Sat 10:00 am to 6:00 pm and Sun 11:00 am to 4:00 pm. Closes one hour earlier in the off-season and during the "deep" of winter closes Sun.

Parkside North Gifts, 407 East Lake Street, (231) 347-6292. Cards, lotions, mugs, goblets and other gifts.

Preferences, 208 Howard Street, (231) 487-9056. Silk florals, home accessories, pillows, lamps and lots of home detail items. Open 7 days, Mon to Sat 10:00 am to 5:30 pm and Sun noon to 4:00 pm.

The Rocking Horse Toys, 326 East Lake Street, (231) 347-0306. Fun and creative toys to make the little ones smile. Open 7 days a week during July and August, Mon to Sat 9:00 am to 9:00 pm and Sun 10:00 am to 8:00 pm. Reduced hours other times of the year.

Symon's General Store and Wine Cellar, 401 East Lake Street, (231) 347-2438. The General Store is on Lake Street and the Wine Cellar is around the corner on Howard, underneath the store. The store is a perfect place to buy cheese, packaged goods, candy and gourmet items. The Wine Cellar was named one of the top 20 wine stores in the country by *Food and Wine Magazine*. Open Mon to Sat 8:00 am to 7:30 pm and Sun 10:00 am to 6:30 pm. Non-season hours slightly reduced.

Toad Hall Fine Gifts, 215 Howard Street, (231) 347-5322, www.toadhallpetoskey.com. Large gift shop: crystal, wall art, glass, chess sets, pottery, kitchenware, gourmet foods, paper goods and every kind of knickknack. Do not miss the upstairs. Open 7 days, Mon to Sat 10:00 am to 9:00 pm and Sun 11:00 am to 4:00 pm, year round.

Trapper's Cabin, Behind Grandpa Shorter's on Petoskey Street, (see Grandpa Shorter's above). One of Grandpa Shorter's stores, this is the place to find unique and unusual items for the cottage, cabin or even your home. The furnishings are rustic as are the accessories.

Vintage to Vogue, 300 East Lake Street, (231) 347-7635. Vintage inspired, upscale women's clothing. Open 7 days, Mon to Wed 10:00 am to 7:00 pm, Thurs and Fri 10:00 am to 8:00 pm, Sat 10:00 am to 7:00 pm and Sun noon to 5:00 pm. Reduced winter hours.

Downtown Petoskey   *Photo by Bob Royce*

Parks, Beaches and Campgrounds

(At the corner of Petoskey and Bay Streets there is a tunnel under US-31 from the shopping district to the downtown parks and marina so you can avoid crossing the busy highway.)

Little Traverse Wheelway. This paved 26-mile trail takes you from Charlevoix to Harbor Springs. (See Charlevoix p. 279 for details.)

Magnus City Park Beach on the Little Traverse Bay in downtown Petoskey. Amenities: playground, restrooms, great views. Perfect place to find Petoskey stones; this is a rocky beach and not the place for swimming or sunbathing. Has camping sites that accommodate various size RVs, motor homes and campers.

Pennsylvania Park, 220 Park Avenue, (231) 348-9700. The park gazebo is the site of much summer entertainment.

Petoskey State Park, 2475 M-119, mid-way between Petoskey and Harbor Springs, (231) 347-2311 or toll-free (800) 447-2757 for camping information. The park has 305 acres along the Grand Traverse Bay. The day-use park offers picnic facilities and a playground, a mile long sun bathing beach, trails, access to the Little Traverse Wheelway, fishing and water sports. Lots of Petoskey stones. The park has two separate campgrounds: Tannery Creek offers 98 campsites and the Dunes has 70 campsites. All sites have electric hookups and the camps have modern bathroom and shower facilities. Camping facilities are open April 1st to December 1st. Modern toilets not available the first and last month. There are two mini-cabins with electricity (but pretty rustic) available for rent. There are no boat launches within the park.

Marinas, Water Sports, Bike, Boat and Jet Ski Rental

Bear Cove Marina, 3039 St. Louis Club, (231) 347-1994, www.bearcovemarina.com. A full service marina that also rents power boats with tow-rope and water skis and pontoons.

Bear River Canoe Livery, 2517 McDougall Road, (231) 347-9038. The place to rent canoes and kayaks. Call ahead to reserve your watercraft. You can spend a relaxing and revitalizing day soaking up the peaceful surroundings as you drift along the water.

Dee Z's Recreational Rentals, 1829 US-31 North, (231) 487-9579. Rents Yamaha personal watercraft.

High Gear Sports, 1187 US-31 North, (231) 347-6118, www.highgearsports.com. Rents all kinds of bikes including tandems.

Petoskey Marina, (231) 347-2500. 50 transient slips. Harbor master on duty 5/7 to 9/1. Amenities: grills, picnic tables, playground, dog run, launch, pump-out, showers, restrooms, gas and electricity.

Windjammer Marina, at the beginning of the Inland Waterway, 6 miles north of Petoskey on US-31, www.windjammermarina.com, (231) 347-6103. Rents pontoons, ski boats, houseboats with wet slides, waverunners and fishing boats.

Tours

Bay Breeze Tours, (231) 526-8888, www.baybreezetours.com. Hear fascinating stories about Victorian Bay View and Petoskey and enjoy a chance to learn about Ernest Hemingway's love affair with the area. Walking tours available Wednesdays during July and August. Walking and trolley tours are available year round by appointment.

Historic Trolley Tours, originate at Stafford's Perry Hotel in downtown Petoskey, (231) 347-4000. The tours last about 90 minutes and are offered twice weekly in the summer. Call for additional info.

Other Things to See and Do

Kilwin's Quality Confections, 355 North Division Road, (231) 347-3800. How sweet the tour of a candy factory. Kilwin's invites you to see how their delectable chocolates are made, including how the center *gets in there* (hint: think chocolate waterfall). The best part of the tour is sampling the wares. Tour times are: Mon to Thurs 10:30 am, 11:00 am, 2:00 pm and 2:30 pm. Other times call in advance.

Saint Francis Solanus Mission Church, 523 Howard Street, was built in 1859 and is often referred to as the "*Little Church by the Lake.*" The church was constructed under the directive of Bishop Baraga, the "Snow Shoe Priest" and was the religious home to Native Americans and early settlers in the area. It was named in honor of St. Francis Solanus, a Franciscan missionary working among the native people of South America. The years have taken their toll on the little mission church and it has been restored twice, but it still stands at its original location and is the oldest building in the Northern Lower Peninsula.

See-North Exploration Center, 220 Park Avenue, (231) 348-9700, www.seenorth.org. A wonderful place where you do not have to nag the children to keep their hands off – in fact just the opposite. There are 21 interactive learning stations which teach children (and their parents) about plants, animals and habitats of northern Michigan. During the summer there are also "Nature at Noon" programs held in Pennsylvania Park in downtown Petoskey. Center is open Mon to Fri 10:00 am to 4:30 pm and Sat 10:00 am to 3:00 pm.

Tri-County Driving Tour, 62 miles and approximately 1¼ hours driving time. Depart Petoskey east on Mitchell Street (C-58) to Wolverine. Take a right at the stop light onto Straits Highway and continue for seven miles to Thumb Lake Road (C-48), then right to US-131. Turn left on US-131 to Boyne Falls. Turn west on M-75 to Boyne City. Stay on M-75 North through Walloon Lake Village to US-131. Turn left and return to Petoskey. A pretty ride with one of the areas most spectacular views as your crest the hill re-entering Petoskey.

Victories Casino, 19967 US-131 South, (231) 439-6100 or toll-free (877) 4-GAMING, www.victories-casino.com. May Lady Luck smile on you as you challenge one of the 1,100 slot machines or place your bet on the table games. Frequent entertainment, promotions and other events.

Festivals

Petoskey Spring Arts and Crafts Show, May.
Gallery Walk, June.
Taste of the North, June.
Annual Bay View Play, July, Bay View.

Annual Bay View Musical, July. Bay View.
Art in the Park, July.
Sidewalk Sales, July.
Annual Bay View Opera, August. Bay View.
Annual Handbell Choir Concert, August. Bay View.
Petoskey Antiques Festival, August.
Petoskey Festival on the Bay, August.
Annual Juried Art Show, August.
Emmet County Fair, August.
Mopars by the Bay Car Show, September.
Michigan Hemingway Society Fall Weekend, September.
Petoskey Fall Kid's Fest, October.

Golf

Crooked Tree Golf Club, 600 Crooked Tree Drive, (231) 349-4030 or toll-free (800) Go-Boyne, www.boyne.com. An 18 hole course set in the middle of century-old pines and hardwoods of a northern farmstead. The last nine holes reward the golfer with breathtaking views of the bay.

Great American Adventures/Pro Am Miniature Golf, 2088 US-31 North, (231) 347-9566.

The Jungle Indoor Family Fun Center, corner of US-31 and US-131 (next to Big Boy), (231) 348-8787, www.junglefuncenter.com. Mini-golf and games for the entire family.

Pirate's Cove Adventure Golf, 1230 US-31 North, (231) 347-1123, www.piratescove.net. Miniature golf and family fun.

River Road Sports Complex, River Road, (US-131 south of Petoskey to Sheridan, east ¼ mile to a right on Clarion Street, park is a mile down on left). Course starts just to left of entrance. Disc Golf with 24 holes that follow a cross-country ski trail through relatively flat but challenging terrain in scenic river valley - creeks and a river come into play. Call for additional information (231) 348-0847.

Contacts

Petoskey Regional Chamber of Commerce, 401 East Mitchell Street, (231) 347-4150, www.petoskey.com.

Visitors Bureau for current schedule of festivals and outdoor concerts call (231) 348-2755 or toll-free (800) 845-2828 or check the web at www.boynecountry.com.

Harbor Springs
-Including Cross Village

Population: Harbor Springs slightly over 1,500. Cross Village, an unincorporated township, approximately 300.

Directions: **From Detroit**: 283 miles, I-75 North to left on MI-68, left on US-31, then right onto Conway Road. **From Lansing**: 224 miles, US-127 North, merge into I-75 North, and follow above directions. **From Chicago**: 373 miles, I-94 East towards Detroit to I-196 towards Holland (Exit 34), merge into US-131 North (becomes US-131), left on M-119 into Harbor Springs.

Background and History

Prior to the arrival of Europeans in the area, an Ottawa (or Odawa) village stood on an eminence between Cross Village and Harbor Springs; the coastline between them was called Wau-gaw-naw-ke-ze, which in the Ottawa language meant large crooked tree.

The French explorers translated Wau-gaw-naw-ke-ze to L'Arbre Croche and it became the site of the L'Arbre Croche mission.

The French also noted two deep indentations on Michigan's west coast; the smaller one, located where Harbor Springs now stands, they called La Petite Traverse, or the Little Crossing.

In 1823, the Ottawa Indians petitioned President James Monroe and the U. S. Congress for a religious teacher to serve their needs. Their request was honored and in 1827 Father Peter De Jean visited the mission at L'Arbre Croche and baptized twenty-one people. In 1829 or 1830, Father De Jean returned to the area and moved the L'Arbre Croche mission to Ville Neuve (New Village). The mission at the new location became known as New L'Arbre Croche, to distinguish it from the earlier or "Old" L'Arbre Croche on the coast. The New L'Arbre Croche mission in Ville Neuve was the beginning of Harbor Springs.

In 1853 Richard Cooper opened a general store and started commercial development of the little village. On March 27, 1862 postal service came to "Little Traverse" or "Bayfield," yet another name by which the settlement was known. In 1881, after many attempts to name it, the little village was incorporated and finally became Harbor Springs, a name that flowed from its natural harbor and the many springs in the area. In 1932 it became a city. The harbor was a tremendous asset to the area's development. It was deep and sheltered, offering great ships protection from angry storms.

To serve the lumber industry a branch of the Grand Rapids and Indiana Railroad located in Harbor Springs in 1837. The train depot was a stunning architectural structure that was intended to gain attention and entice passengers - and it did both. Its tall, ornate spire, bay window, and oversize roof brackets were part of the overall package designed by architect Stanley Osgood who also designed the Muskegon Union Station and the Mason County Courthouse.

The third weekend of July, model train and history buffs flock to Harbor Springs for Shay Days. This three-day event celebrates the life and inventions of 19th century Harbor Springs resident Ephraim Shay. During the annual event Shay's historic hexagon house at 396 Main Street, one block east of downtown Harbor Springs is alive with activity. The man honored by the celebration developed the Shay locomotive with its unique design specifically suited to the needs of the lumbering industry. Shay worked for many additional years while living in Harbor Springs to perfect his design. Besides being an inventor, Shay's resume included: physician, teacher, logger, civil engineer, merchant and businessman. He was also a veteran of the Civil War, serving under William Tecumseh Sherman.

Shay was born on July 17, 1839 in Huron County, Ohio and after living in many places throughout Michigan including: Ionia, Manistee, Haring, Portland, Lyons, Muir and Sunfield, he moved in 1888 to Harbor Springs. In addition to continuing work on his locomotive engine, Shay designed and operated a private water works for the city. He died in Harbor Springs in 1916 and is buried in a local cemetery.

By the turn of the century, resorts replaced lumbering. The Northland Limited, a special train serving northern Michigan resorts, brought passengers in sleeper and pullman cars from Cincinnati, Louisville, St. Louis, and Fort Wayne. Additional cars from Chicago were added at Kalamazoo for the trip north.

In Petoskey passengers transferred to "suburban" trains serving the resort towns between Petoskey and Harbor Springs. In 1915, the suburban trains ran each way eight times a day and over a half million tickets were sold. The trains' popularity ended in the 1930s when automobiles provided an alternate means of transportation to the area.

The Depot was eventually sold to private owners and became a dress shop, a dance hall and even an ice cream parlor. It has been restored and is currently Ward Gallery. A trip to the gallery is a trip back in history as you admire the amazing old depot.

Cross Village. Twenty miles from Harbor Springs, if you follow the magnificent Tunnel of Trees route along M-119, is Cross Village. The name Cross Village is the subject of local legend: Just before his death in 1675, French Jesuit Priest, Father Jacques Marquette, raised a large white cross on a bluff overlooking Lake Michigan at the site of modern-day Cross Village. Today a replica of that cross stands at the site and is visible off the shore and far into the lake.

In 1787, twenty tribes of Native Americans populated the region around Cross Village and held councils there. The Native Americans called the area "Land of the Cross" and it is one of the oldest settlements in the state with a rich history inextricably entwined with that of the Ottawa to whom it was home before Europeans arrived.

The French translated *Land of the Cross* from the Ottawa language to *La Croix*; the name by which the village was known from 1847 to 1875 when the English translated the name to Cross Village. Amos T. Burnett became the first postmaster on October 31, 1870.

This tiny hamlet would not normally merit much mention in a travel guide. The more touristy towns of Harbor Springs to the south and Mackinaw City to the north command the tourists' attention and Cross Village is not in the same league. But, the fascinating history of the area is tracked by a small, out of the way museum with displays of early artifacts. If you have an interest in the Native American history of the region, a stop at the L'Arbre Croche Museum might be worthwhile. If you drive the scenic Tunnel of Trees from Harbor Springs you will be ready for lunch at the Legs Restaurant when you arrive.

Food/Restaurants

Anchor Restaurant, 127 State Street, (231) 526-0744. Casual cuisine with flair. Stuffed French toast is a good choice for breakfast. The wraps make a perfect lunch and, of course, whitefish is a popular dinner entree. Open daily 8:00 am to 10:00 pm. Reduced hours after Labor Day and closes from mid-October to May.

Bar Harbor, 100 State Street, (231) 526-2671. A favorite stop for locals as well as resorters and a great place to enjoy a cold beer and burger after the morning on a boat or hitting 18 holes. Or, maybe if you have a salad (like the Caesar with blackened shrimp) you might have room for the hot fudge volcano cake with kiwi coulis sauce. Open 7 days, Mon to Sat 11:00 am to midnight and Sun noon to 8:00 pm.

Chang Cuisine, 1030 State Street, (231) 526-7107. Chef has several specialties including the Two Flavored Chicken with Sesame and Sweet and Sour. Open 7 days, 11:00 am to 9:00 pm. In the fall closes on Sun and closes at 8:00 pm during the week.

Chestnut Valley Golf Club Restaurant, 1875 Clubhouse Drive, (231) 526-9100, www.barharborharborsprings.com. This golf course restaurant has a full menu and you might wisely be tempted to start off with an appetizer like Shrimp Lenny (crab and shrimp wrapped in bacon and covered with hollandaise sauce - does it get much more decadent than that?). If you are not ready for a full dinner you can opt for the prime rib sandwich, quesadillas or something light. Open summer 11:00 am to 11:00 pm. Winter open Wed and Thurs 4:00 pm to 11:00 pm and Fri to Sun 11:00 am to 11:00 pm.

Cornichons, 248 State Street. (231) 242-0020. A European Market and Deli. Good place to stop and get a sandwich to take with you as you venture out for the day. Open 7 days, Mon to Sat 9:00 am to 6:00 pm and Sun noon to 4:00 pm. Reduced hours after Labor Day.

Crow's Nest, 4601 State Street, (231) 526-6011, www.crowsnest-harborsprings.com. Try a traditional favorite like whitefish which is fresh daily, or something completely new like the buffalo tenderloin. Open: Tues to Sun 5:00 pm to 10:00 pm. Closes an hour earlier in the fall and only open Fri and Sat from November through April.

The Fish, 2983 South State Road, www.thefishrestaurant.com, (231) 526-3969. Full bar, extensive wine list, sushi, daily specials and a full menu. If you are eating in a place that puts "fish" in its name it seems only appropriate to choose a seafood entrée so consider the Pan Roasted Walleye with tomatoes, feta cheese, and Kalamata olives served over garlic sautéed spinach. Reservations accepted, but walk-ins welcome. Open 7 days at 4:00 pm from Memorial Day to Labor Day. Open Wed to Sun at 4:00 pm from Labor Day to Memorial Day.

Gurney's Harbor Bottle Shop, 215 East Main Street, (231) 526-5472. State liquor store, but a great selection of wines and deli sandwiches made to order. Another place to put together your picnic lunch. Open 7 days, Mon to Sat 9:00 am to 7:00 pm and Sun 11:00 am to 3:00 pm. Winter Mon to Sat 9:00 am to 6:00 pm and closed Sun.

Island Bean Coffee Company, 110 West Main Street, (231) 526-9998. Located in a reclaimed and renovated 1930s brick gas station; it serves great coffee. Open 7 days, 6:30 am to 9:00 pm (sometimes a bit later). Winter hours: 7:00 am to 7:00 pm, 7 days.

Johan's Pastry Shop, 138 West 3rd Street, (231) 526-0907, johans@utmi.net. Main location is in Petoskey where Johan's opened in the 1940s (and for early risers that location opens at 5:30 am). This second location is in the Clocktower Plaza between Petoskey and Harbor Springs where they have a grill and also sell bagels. Open 7 days, 7:30 am to 1:00 pm.

Juilleret's Restaurant, 130 State Street, (231) 526-2821. Café style restaurant. Their Pea and Peanut salad is a favorite. Open mid-May to end of September, 7 days, 11:00 am to 9:00 pm.

Legs Inn, 6425 Lakeshore Drive, Cross Village, (231) 526-2881, www.legsinn.com. Polish cuisine and plenty of traditional American dishes. This famous historic site's exterior will cause a double take. It has been called a monument to nature. The architecture is not something you would expect to find in Northern Michigan. It glares at you with medieval looking stone, timber and driftwood. The odd-looking restaurant grows on you and takes time and perhaps several visits before you can properly appreciate it. The name comes from the furnace legs that decorate the roofline. The restaurant was created by Stanley Smolak, a Polish immigrant who fell in love with the area and the people living there: the Ottawa and Chippewa Native Americans. You can dine outside in the gardens when weather permits and there is often entertainment. This restaurant gets the nod of approval from food critics and guests. The Polish Combination Plate with Kielbasa and Golabki was wonderful. Open 7 days, noon to 10:00 pm. Closes from the 3rd week of October to the 3rd week in May.

Little Traverse Bay Golf Club and Restaurant, 995 Hideaway Valley Road, www.ltbaygolf.com, info@ltbaygolf.com, (231) 526-9662. Consider the freshly caught and planked Little Traverse Bay Whitefish with duchess potatoes. Open lunch and dinner, hours vary seasonally.

Lorenzo's, 7075 South Lakeshore Drive, (231) 526-1000. A newer restaurant to the Harbor Springs scene. Fine Italian cuisine served in a relaxed setting with magnificent Lake Michigan views. Full menu and wonderful Sunday Brunch. Open 7 days for dinner. Next year may open for lunch, call for hours. Closed Monday in the winter.

Mary Ellen's Place, 145 East Main Street, (231) 526-5591. This is the place where locals grab the morning paper and a cup of coffee. Many also treat themselves to Mary Ellen's wonderful breakfast of stuffed hash browns. Other times of the day you might want to try the homemade soup or any of the treats from the old-fashioned soda fountain. Open 7 days, Mon to Fri 7:00 am to 5:00 pm, Sat 7:00 am to 3:00 pm and Sun 7:00 am to noon. Open year round.

New York Restaurant, 101 State Street, (231) 526-1904. www.thenewyork.com, info@thenewyork.com. Enjoy fine dining with a view of the Little Traverse Bay. House specialties include Rack of Lamb, Crab Stuffed Chicken Breast, and Colorado Lamb Shank. Daily fish specials and award winning wine list. Open 7 days at 5:00 pm. Closes first week of November and the month of April.

Stafford's Pier, 102 Bay Street, (231) 526-6201, www.staffords.com, pier@staffords.com. Built on the original pilings over the harbor. The Pier's Pointer Room offers a delicious choice of fine cuisine and overlooks the historic Harbor Springs yacht basin. If you want a more casual setting you can enjoy your meal in the Chart Room, Wheel House or Dudley's Deck (weather permitting). Open 7 days, 11:00 am to 4:00 pm for lunch. Dinner on the deck 4:00 pm to 10:00 pm. Dinner in Chart Room, Wheel House Lounge and Pointer Room: 4:30 pm to 10:30 pm. Bar service to 1:00 am.

Tapperooney's, 3018 Harbor-Petoskey Road, (231) 439-0400. Upscale casual comfort food in distinctive Up North setting. Full menu including chicken, pasta, ribs, perch and walleye. Open: Sun to Thurs

4:00 pm to 10:00 pm and Fri and Sat 4:00 pm to 11:00 pm. Closes one hour earlier in the winter and one week in April.

Teddy Griffin's Road House, 50 Highland Pike Road, (231) 526-7805, www.teddygriffins.com. Check out your favorite sports event – golf, basketball, NASCAR racing, football or hockey while enjoying a sandwich or pizza and brew. The pub is decorated in Red Wings hockey memorabilia. In the main dining room try their signature Black Angus beef. Open 7 days, 4:00 pm to 10:00 pm. Reduced winter hours.

Tom's Mom's Cookies, 267 South Spring Street, (231) 526-6606, www.tomsmomscookies.com, smac@freeway.net. They have been making cookies using the same recipe since 1985. They hand-cut chocolate chunks from ten pound bars and use only the finest ingredients for their 14 varieties. They have been featured on the Food Network's "*Food Finds*" program and *Family Circle* rated them one of the three best cookies they tasted. Great place to top off a lunch or grab a bag of cookies to take with you on your travels. Open 7 days, Mon to Sat 10:00 am to 6:00 pm and Sun 10:00 am to 3:00 pm.

Turkey's Café and Pizzeria, 250 East Main Street, (231) 526-6041. The setting is a historic 110-year-old building; the fare includes: breakfast (omelets, bagels, French toast, etc.) or later meals of burgers, pizza, calzones and their featured turkey clubs. Open 9:00 am to 11:30 am for breakfast, 11:30 am to 3:00 pm for lunch and 4:45 pm to 9:30 pm for dinner. Reduced hours in winter and closes two weeks in April.

Woolly Bugger Coffee House and Internet Café, 181 East Main Street (231) 242-0592, www.wbcoffee.com. Freshly roasted gourmet coffees and specialty drinks. Broadband hot spot. Light menu with pizza, wraps and quiches. Open 7 days, Mon to Fri 6:30 am to 10:00 pm, Sat 7:00 am to 10:00 pm, Sun 8:00 am to 10:00 pm. Labor Day to mid-June closes Mon to Sat at 5:00 pm and Sun at 4:00 pm.

Yummies Ice Cream, 220 East Main Street. Over 60 flavors of ice cream and gelato. Open 7 days, noon to 10:00 pm in the summer and closes mid-October.

Lodging (Also see Campgrounds below)

Best Western of Harbor Springs, 8514 M-119, (231) 347-9050 or toll-free (800) 528-1234. 50 rooms. Extras: four two-room suites with fireplaces and kitchens, six with king-bed and in-room whirlpools. Also: indoor pool, hot tub, high-speed internet, fitness facility and laundry.

Birchwood Inn, 7077 Lake Shore Drive, (231) 526-2151 or toll-free (800) 530-9955, www.birchwoodinn.com. 48 rooms. Northern Michigan ambiance. Huge stone fireplace in gathering room, outdoor pool, game room, wireless internet, playground and ten acres, extended stay units. Upper lodge with two bedrooms, full kitchen, fireplace and deck. Many packages available.

Boyne Highlands Resort, 600 Highlands Drive, (231) 526-3000 or toll-free (800) 462-6963, www.boyne.com. 415 accommodations including hotel rooms, condominiums and cottages. Extras: 81 holes of golf with professional instructors, tennis courts, hiking trails, pond fishing, skiing, fitness center, outdoor heated pool, whirlpool and Young American Dinner Theatre (July and August).

Colonial Inn, 210 Artesian Avenue, (231) 526-2111, www.harborsprings.com. 40 rooms. Extras: outdoor and indoor pools, romance packages, king beds, fireplaces, porches, sun deck on Little Traverse Bay. Open late May to late October.

Graham Management, 163 East Main Street, (231) 526-9671. www.grahamrentalproperties.com. Rents cottages, houses and condos, weekly or longer. Some weekend rentals in the off-season.

Harborside Inn, 266 Main Street, (231) 526-6238 or toll-free (800) 526-6238, www.harborside-inn.net. 24 units in this boutique-style hotel in downtown Harbor Springs. Extras: each unit has a refrigerator, microwave and private terrace. Continental breakfast. Smoke free.

Hamlet Village Resort Homes and Condominiums, 5484 Pleasantview Road, (231) 526-2754 or toll-free (800) 678-2341, www.hamletvillage.com. One-to-four bedroom units with whirlpools, fireplaces, deluxe kitchens, gas grills, tennis courts, pool with whirlpools and sauna. Adjacent to Nub's Nob nature cross-country ski trail and chairlifts. Golf and ski packages available. These are homes and condominiums available for very short term rentals.

Highland Hideaway B&B Resort, 6767 Pleasanton Road, (231) 526-8100. Four rooms each with separate bath in this contemporary, secluded B&B. Situated on a hilltop, surrounded by spruce, hemlock, oak, and white birch trees. Fireplace rooms available during winter months. Also offers Sauterne House Vacation Rental which will accommodate families and small groups, and Sunset House B&B which is wheelchair accessible.

Museums and Galleries

Blackbird Museum, 368 Main Street, (231) 526-0612. Named for Chief Andrew Blackbird, the first postmaster of Harbor Springs, the museum displays Native American artifacts and crafts. It is on the Michigan State Historical Register and was the house in which Blackbird lived from 1858 until his death in 1908. Open Mon to Fri 10:00 am to 4:00 pm and Sat noon until 4:00 pm during the summer.

The Pierre Bittar Gallery, 188 East Main Street, (231) 526-6750, www.pierrebittar.com. Lithographs and original impressionistic artwork by Pierre Bittar. He paints landscapes and portraits. Open 7 days, Mon to Thurs 10:00 am to 5:00 pm, Fri and Sat 10:00 am to 5:00 pm and Sun 11:00 am to 2:00 pm. Winter call for hours.

By the Bay, 172 East Main Street, www.bythebay.com, (231) 526-3964. Largest nautical art gallery in the Midwest. Original and limited edition prints of sailing, yacht racing, lighthouses and harbors. Also: scrimshaw, telescopes and maritime history items, nautical antiques, models and books. Open Mon to Sat 10:00 am to 5:30 pm (Thurs until 9:00 pm), Sun 11:00 am to 3:00 pm. After Labor Day closes half hour earlier during week. Closes Sun and Mon after October.

Coyote Woman Gallery, 160 Main Street, (231) 526-5889. Artwork, jewelry, sculpture from more than fifty artists. Open 7 days, Mon to Sat 10:00 am to 6:00 pm and Sun 11:00 to 4:00. Winter Mon to Sat 10:00 am to 5:00 pm and closed Sun.

Elements, 107 Bridge Street, www.elementsgalleryonline.com, (231) 547-5820. Modern fine arts gallery metal work, wall art, jewelry, clothes and glass. Open 7 days, Mon to Sat, 10:00 am to 5:00 pm (at least). Sun noon to 4:00 pm. Closes some Sundays in the off-season.

Green Apple Blue Stem, 200 North State Street, (231) 526-0010. Fine art of Paula McNamara including fun and whimsical painted clothing. Also: furniture, floor cloths, acrylics, oils and pastels. Open Mon to Sat 10:00 am to 5:00 pm and Sun 11:00 am to 4:00 pm. Open year round, but reduced hours after Labor Day, call for specific times.

Hramiec Hoffman Fine Art Studio and Gallery, 6911 M-119, (231) 526-1011. One of the newer galleries in Harbor Springs displaying the oil scenes of Mary Hramiec-Hoffman.

Knox Gallery, 175 East Main Street, www.knoxgalleries.com, (231) 526-5377. Bronze works of G. Balciar, S. Scott, T. Corbin, Jensen, George Lundeen and Glenna Goodacre. Also displays paintings. This is a lovely gallery with a tranquil garden behind. Open daily, 10:00 am to 6:00 pm.

L'Arbre Croche Museum, M-119, Lower level of Father Al Parish Hall, Cross Village, (231) 526-2030. Reverend Father Al Langheim established this museum of Native American and Cross Village history after many years of collecting and identifying artifacts that tell a fascinating story. Open Sat from 1:00 pm to 3:00 pm or by appointment. (Closes October to May.)

Northern Possessions, 129 East Bay Street, (231) 526-7330. Great gallery with wearable art, jewelry, contemporary crafts and wonderful furniture. Open 7 days, 10:00 am to 6:00 pm with reduced winter hours.

Patricia Woods and Company, 120 East Main Street, (231) 526-9691. Handmade pottery and one-of-a-kind ceramics. Open 7 days Mon to Sat 9:00 am to 6:00 pm and Sun noon to 4:00 pm. Winter hours Mon to Sat 10:00 am to 5:00 pm.

Quarters Inc. Talents, 114 East Main Street, (231) 526-1122 or toll-free (888) ARTERS8. Fine art, fun art, wearable art, frivolous art, and functional art in a wide scope of media, in all price ranges. Quarters is a consignment shop (juried artists rent space) and cooperative (consigners can work there).

R. Frogs, East Main Street, www.RFrogsGallery.com, (231) 526-8884. Tim Cotterill is the Frogman. All kinds of artsy frogs. Also blown glass and jewelry. Open 7 days, Mon to Sat 10:00 am to 6:00 pm and Sun noon to 4:00 pm. Substantially reduced hours in the winter.

Three Pines Studio and Gallery, 5959 West Levering, Cross Village, (231) 526-9447. A working studio with approximately 60 artists with ties to the local area. Displays pottery, jewelry, furniture, paintings (oils, acrylics, watercolors), glass, quill boxes, and fiber art. An interesting array of lovely items. Open daily 11:00 am to 7:00 pm, closed Wed. Winter open Fri to Mon 11:00 am to 5:00 pm.

Ward Gallery, 111 West Bay Street, www.myfineartgallery.com, (231) 526-4366. Fine art and lovely antiques. Features the work of important contemporary artists: sculpture, post-impressionist still lifes and landscapes. The gallery is housed in the old Depot and the building is a treat. Open 7 days, Mon to Sat 9:30 am to 6:00 pm and Sun 11:00 am to 5:00 pm. Reduced hours beginning in September.

Whistling Moose Gallery, 273 East Main Street, (231) 526-5756, www.whistlingmoosegallery.com. Nature inspired art and crafts, including jewelry, pottery, fine woodworking, wall art, metal sculpture, and glass work. Open 7 days, Mon to Sat 10:00 am to 6:00 pm and Sun 11:00 am to 4:00 pm. Closed Sun in winter.

Witty Gallery, 236 East Main Street, (231) 526-1112. www.wittyart.com. Oils by Trisha Witty. Open 7 days, Mon to Sat 10:00 am to 5:00 pm and Sun 10:00 am to 3:00 pm in the summer. Open an occasional weekend after September.

Theatre

Young Americans, Boyne Highlands, (231) 526-3001 for information, www.boyne.com. Talented young actors and actresses (15-21 years old) present unique music and dance while serving as your waitstaff.

Antiques

Bishop's Antiques at Harbor, 378 East Third Street, (231) 526-8075. Lamps, chandeliers, furniture, boats, jewelry, linens, silver, beaded bags, wall art and architectural items. Open 7 days, Memorial Day to end of September 9:00 am to 7:00 pm.

By the Bay, 172 East Main Street, www.bythebay.com, (231) 526-3964. (See above under Galleries).

Huzza, 136 East Main Street, (231) 526-2128, www.huzza.net. Antiques, jewelry, home furnishings, primitives, contemporary art, clothing and more. Open 7 days, Mon to Sat 10:00 am to 6:00 pm and Sun noon to 6:00 pm. Winter closes Mon to Sat 5:00 pm. Closed Sun.

L'Esprit Antiques, 195 West Main Street and second location at 220 State Street, (231) 526-9888. Specializes in Country French antiques personally gathered throughout the French countryside, mainly from the Provence and Burgundy regions. Also has an on-line photo catalog. Antiques include: table linens, lighting, bath accessories, home accessories, French soaps, baskets and ironwork. Main Street Store open 10:00 am to 5:00 pm Mon to Sat, Sun noon to 3:00 pm. Closed on Sun after color season. 220 State Street shop open year around 7 days, Mon to Sat 10:00 am to 5:00 pm and Sun noon to 3:00 pm.

Pooter Olooms Antiques, 339 State Street, (231) 526-6101. Offers a wide selection of European antique furniture with the emphasis on French (from Louis XIV to Art Deco) and Danish. The focus is on the beauty of the item not a particular period or type of furniture, but primarily late 19th and early 20th century. You will find dining tables, settees, armoires, desks and beds. Accessories include everything from the exquisite to the downright funky as you discover mirrors, clocks, lamps, rugs, paintings and more. Open 7 days, Mon to Sat 10:00 am to 5:00 pm and Sun 11:00 am to 4:00 pm in the summer.

Other Shopping

American Spoon Food, 245 East Main Street, (231) 526-8628. (See Listing under Charlevoix p. 275.) Open Mon to Sat 10:00 am to 5:30 pm and Sun 11:00 am to 4:00 pm. Open only four days a week during winter.

Becky Thatcher Designs, 117 West Main, (231) 256-9336, www.beckythatcherdesigns.com. Becky draws her inspiration from the earth, water, sky and wildlife around her, capturing the essence of northern Michigan in her jewelry. Open May through December.

Between the Covers, 152 East Main Street, (231) 526-6658. Great little bookstore to pick up a "beach read." Open 7 days, Mon to Sat 10:00 am to 9:30 pm and Sun 11:00 am to 4:00 pm. After Labor Day Mon to Sat 10:00 am to 6:00 pm and Sun 11:00 am to 4:00 pm.

C.J.'s Originals, 189 East Main Street, (231) 526-7925. Gift store. Open daily in the summer. (See Little Cigar Factory below.)

Claymore Shop, 137 East Main Street, (231) 242-0134, www.claymoreshop.com. According to *Esquire Magazine*, one of the top 100 men's stores in the United States. Carries Ralph Lauren, Bill's

Khakis, Samuelsohn, Robert Talbott, Hickey Freeman and Lacoste. Free alterations. Open 7 days, 10:00 am to 6:00 pm from Memorial Day to end of September. Closed in the winter.

Contents, 141 North State Street, (231) 526-1800. Housewares, dishes, platters, kitchen accessories, gadgets and furniture with attitude. Open 7 days, 10:00 am to 6:00 pm. Winter closes an hour earlier during the week and noon to 4:00 pm on Sun.

Douglas Alan Bacon, 249 East Main Street, (231) 526-5245. Original pieces of custom designed jewelry. Open 7 days, Mon to Sat 11:00 am to 5:00 pm and Sun 11:00 am to 3:00 pm. Hours substantially reduced in the winter.

Frivolous Sal's, 201 East Bay Street, (231) 526-6006. Carries Jardin jewelry inspired by the most fabulous European designs and trends. Faux precious jewelry that is fun to wear without worry that you have significantly diminished your fortune if you lose it. Open daily, 9:00 am to 6:00 pm. Reduced hours after Labor Day 10:00 am to 5:00 pm. Closes December 1st to April.

Harbor Accents, 277 East Main Street, (231) 526-6860. Distinctive gifts, cards and accents. Open 7 days, Mon to Sat 9:00 am to 8:00 pm and Sun 10:00 am to 5:00 pm. Slightly reduced hours, but still open 7 days in winter.

Harbor Wear, 161 State Street, (231) 526-6922. Carries Fresh Produce, T-shirts, sweatshirts and casual clothing for men, women and children. Open Mon to Sat 9:30 am to 9:00 pm, Sun 10:00 am to 7:00 pm during the summer.

Hilda, 107 West Main Street, (231) 526-6914. Bright stylish fashions with a casual elegance for women. Also carries children's apparel and has a men's shop. Open 7 days, Mon to Sat 9:30 am to 5:30 pm and Sun noon to 4:00 pm. Open Fri, Sat and Mon in the winter.

Kilwin's of Harbor Springs, 139 East Main Street, (231) 526-9871, www.kilwins.com. Nationwide confectionary shop with ice cream and candy. Some outside seating. Open 7 days in the summer.

Little Cigar Factory, 189 East Main Street, (231) 242-0972. Back corner of the shop (CJ Originals is in the front). Place to find a wide variety of hand crafted cigars and a chance to design your own label. Open 10:00 am to 5:30 pm, 7 days, Memorial Day to Labor Day.

Momentum, 114 Main Street, (231) 526-5075. Great prices on clothing for the entire family. (See listing under Traverse City, p. 247.) Open 7 days, 9:00 am to 10:00 pm. Reduced off-peak season hours.

Monogram Goods, 223 East Third Street, (231) 526-7700, www.monogramgoods.com. A chance to personalize your gifts and a wide selection of interesting items in stock including: apparel, accessories, bed linens, towels, home accessories and children's items.

Open 7 days, Mon to Sat 10:00 am to 6:00 pm and Sun 11:00 am to 4:00 pm. Reduced winter hours.

The Outfitter, 153 East Main Street, www.outfitterharborsprings.com, (231) 526-2621. All brands and styles: sportswear, active wear, swimwear, winter wear, accessories and children's clothing. Rents kayaks, snowshoes and snowboards. Open daily, 9:30 am to 5:30 pm.

Ransom and Izzy, 106 East Main Street, (231) 526-8550. Women's upscale, high-end fashions. Open Mon to Sat 10:00 am to 5:00 pm and Sun 11:00 am to 4:00 pm. Winter closes on Sun.

Rocking Horse Toy Company, 326 East Lake Street, (231) 526-7236, www.rockinghorsetoy.com. Games, puzzles and toys for all seasons and all ages. Playmobil, Lego, Lamaze and Brio. Open 9:00 am to 9:00 pm (sometimes 10:00 pm) in the summer. Winter hours Mon to Sat 10:00 to 5:30 pm and Sun 11:00 am to 4:00 pm.

Tails on the Town, 101 East Main Street. Dog and Cat Boutique. Fashion accessories for the pampered pet. Open Mon to Sat 10:00 am to 6:00 pm (Closed Tues), and Sun 11:30 am to 4:00 pm.

W Wear, 185 East Main Street, (231) 526-9780. Women's apparel, men's apparel and accessories. Trendy, funky, contemporary with a passion for fashion. Open 7 days, Mon to Thurs 10:00 am to 6:00 pm, Fri and Sat 10:00 am to 8:00 pm and Sun 11:30 am to 4:30 pm. Reduced winter hours.

Parks, Beaches and Campgrounds

City Beach near Zorn Park, along the harbor front. This is the larger of two beaches with lifeguards in Harbor Springs. Also: a bath house, restrooms, swimming rafts and a sandy beach. You are guaranteed to love the view.

Deer Park, located on Zoll Street. A place to see deer that actually seem to look forward to human visits.

Little Traverse Conservancy Nature Preserve, 3264 Powell Road, (231) 347-0991, www.landtrust.org. This preserve is dedicated to protecting 25,000 acres of scenic land, but invites you to enjoy and appreciate it. You can wander through hardwood forests, walk sandy beaches, watch the activity of critters in and around the creeks and delight in the wildlife you are sure to encounter.

Thorne Swift Nature Preserve, 6696 Lowe Shore Drive, (231) 526-6401. With a naturalist on duty to answer your questions, this preserve provides a nature center, dune observation platform, beach on Lake Michigan and nature hikes. You can walk through stands of giant trees over a century old. According to the Odawa, this preserve is the home of the elusive water spirit. Legend says this water spirit creates storms on the lakes. You can hike around a Jesuit mission church built in 1889 and called Ah-pi-tah-wa-ing. The crosses surrounding the mission mark the graves of tribe members. The path to the right of the church leads to Lake Michigan where you can enjoy the small but pristine beach.

Zoll Street Beach, western edge of Wequetonsing. A small dog-friendly park perfect for swimming and kayaking. A long shallow area is great for younger children to splash around and enjoy getting wet on a hot day.

Marinas, Charters, and Boat Rental

Harbor Springs Municipal Marina, 250 East Bay Street, (231) 526-5355 (Harbormaster). 46 transient slips, restrooms, showers, water, pump-out, ice and launch.

The Outfitter, (See above under shopping. They rent kayaks.)

Trout and Salmon Charters-Ruddy Duck, (231) 347-3232.

Other Things to See and Do

Northern Lights Recreation, 8865 Harbor-Petoskey Road, (231) 526-3100, www.northernlightsrec.com. Bowling, billiards, arcade and bar and grill. Open 7 days, 10:00 am to 10:00 pm.

Pond Hill Farm, 5581 South Lake Shore, (231) 526-3276, www.pondhillfarm.com. An opportunity to visit a working farm and see how it really operates. Hay rides, scavenger hunts, a chance to meet the animals, and a farm market with extensive selection of locally grown produce and organic foods. Store sells fresh foods and canned goods. Gorgeous hanging baskets in the spring. Open year round, 7 days a week, 7:00 am to 6:00 pm.

Skiing. See Nubs Nob and Boyne Highlands above under lodging or below under Skiing.

Tunnel of Trees, If you only take one scenic drive during your travels of Western Michigan, consider making it this one. Snaking curves between Harbor Springs and Cross Village on M-119 are famous for their locking limbs that form a canopy over the road. Do not try to rush this 20-mile stretch or you may lose more than just the chance to inhale the gorgeous scenery - you may end up off the road. You can start your journey on Lower Shore Drive about 2½ miles north of Harbor Springs off M-119, directly across from Birchwood Farms. Consider stopping at Thorne Swift Nature Preserve (see above under parks). The drive is steeped in Native American History. Two miles south of Cross Village you will come to the Washout, a ravine that was allegedly created in a battle between sky beings and underwater spirits. As the underwater spirits tried to escape their watery dwelling place, the sky beings took the form of lightning and struck them down. As the lightning hit the ground it formed the huge ravine. On the south side of the ravine you can see the only remaining white pine trees from the historic Circle of Council Trees where in the late 1700s the British and Native Americans struck an alliance against the new United States.

Windsurf Harbor Springs, 5200 W. Lake Road, (231) 330-1001. Lessons, rentals and sales.

Festivals

Zoo-de-Mackinac Bike Bash, May.
Harbor Springs Cycling Classic, June.
Crooked Tree Arts Center Annual Home Tour, June.
Women's Club Art Fest at Nub's Nob, July.
Annual Shay Days, July.
Little Traverse Bay Regatta, July.
Annual Odawa Homecoming, August.
Harbor Springs Cycling Classic, September.

Golf

Chestnut Valley Golf, 1875 Clubhouse Drive, (231) 526-9100 or toll-free (877) 284-3688, www.chestnutvalley.com. 19-hole championship course. Full pro shop, driving range, practice green, and restaurant.

Donald Ross Memorial Golf Course, 600 Highlands Drive, (231) 526-3028 or toll-free (800) GO-BOYNE, www.boyne.com. Eighteen re-creations of the master's greatest holes: Pinehurst, Royal Dornoch, Inverness and others pay tribute to this course architect. Gets high marks from *Golf Digest*.

Harbor Point Golf Course, 8475 South Lake Shore Drive, (231) 526-2951, www.harborpointassociation.com. Originally opened as a private club, this course is now open to the public each day at 1:30 pm. It is worth golfing here just for the views of Little Traverse Bay.

The Heather, 600 Highlands Drive, (231) 526-3029 or toll-free (800) GO-BOYNE, www.boyne.com. Rolling terrain, water and hardwoods create the view.

The Hills, 600 Highlands Drive, (231) 526-3028 or toll-free (800) GO-BOYNE, www.boyne.com. The newest course at the Boyne Resort. Designed by Arthur Hill it tries your skill with enormous sand traps and intimidating water holes.

Little Traverse Bay Golf Club, 995 Hideaway Valley Road, (231) 526-6200 or toll-free (888) 995-6262, www.ltbaygolf.com. *Golf Digest* says it may be the most beautiful course on earth. Situated on a high bluff with magnificent vistas of Lake Michigan, Little Traverse Bay and three inland lakes.

The Moor, 600 Highlands Drive, (231) 526-3028 or toll-free (800) GO-BOYNE, www.boyne.com. Wetlands and undulating greens along with beautiful natural terrain.

Skiing

Northern Michigan is a natural wonderland in all seasons. The Harbor Springs area is home to some of the best skiing in the state.

Boyne Highlands, 600 Highlands Drive, (231) 526-3095 or toll-free (800) GO-BOYNE, www.boynehighlands.com. Expertly groomed hills. This is the place with the highest vertical, most skiable acreage and longest runs. The Highlands offers jumps, rails and a halfpipe. There is also tubing, cross-country skiing or snowshoeing.

Nubs Nob, 500 Nubs Nob Road, (231) 526-2131 or toll-free (800) SKI-NUBS, www.nubsnob.com. *Ski Magazine* readers rated this the Midwest's Best Ski area for three years in a row. Also great snowboarding. It provides 248-acres of skiing on 52 runs. The lift capacity is 15,000 skiers-per-hour.

Contacts

Harbor Springs Chamber of Commerce, 368 East Main Street, www.harborspringschamber.com, (231) 526-7999 or toll-free (866) 526-7999.

Boating, a favorite summer pastime   *Photo by Bob Royce*

Mackinaw City
-Including Mackinac Island

Population: Mackinaw City: 859. Mackinac Island has about 500 year-round residents.

Directions: **From Detroit**: north on I-75 to the very tip of the Lower Peninsula. **From Lansing:** US-127 North 139 miles merge into I-75 North 90 additional miles. **From Grand Rapids**: US-131 North towards Cadillac, M-55 East to US-127 North, merge into I-75 North. **From Chicago**: I-94 East towards Detroit, I-196 North towards Grand Rapids, US-131 North towards Cadillac, M-55 East to US-127 North, merge with I-75.

Background and History

Mackinac Island welcomed its first people as early as 2,000 years ago when Native Americans of the Woodland Period paddled canoes there to fish for trout, herring, whitefish, sturgeon and pike. Fish were so abundant that the early inhabitants referred to the Island as "*home of the fish.*" Artifacts confirm Native Americans in the Mackinaw City area at least 700 years before Europeans arrived. But, as with the Island, their actual presence in the area goes back much further.

The Original People, the Anishinaabe-Ojibwe, believed Mackinac Island was a sacred place and the home of the Great Spirit Gitchie Manitou. Its location in the center of the Great Lakes Waterway, between Lake Michigan and Lake Huron, close to both the Upper and Lower Peninsula, made the area a natural tribal gathering place. The first people believed that once the Europeans came to the area Gitchie Manitou abandoned the Island to dwell in the Northern Lights.

Several questions surround the name Mackinaw/Mackinac: Where did it come from? Does it end in a "c" or a "w?" And, how is it pronounced? The first question cannot be definitively answered although there are at least two viable theories. The latter two questions are relatively easy.

According to one prevailing legend, Native Americans, noting the island's elliptical shape with a hump on one side, called it "*place of the great turtle*" which in their language is said to be Michilimackinac. On the Island you will see many references to the turtle story; there is the Great Turtle Toy Shop, Great Turtle Cakes and turtle themed books peering out from shelves at local book stores.

According to a second account there is a different translation for the word Michilimackinac: **mish** means great, **inni** means connecting sound, **maki** means fault or crack and **nong** means land or place. The Ottawa and Ojibwa Native Americans described it as a place with a large or great fault. Over time the word Michilimackinac came to encompass the entire straits region, not just the Island.

French settlers who came to the area in the late 17th century had at least fifty-five spellings for the name, but Michilimackinac became the accepted one. Eventually the difficult to pronounce name was shortened to the far less tongue-twisting Mackinac. Later the British began spelling it as it was pronounced: Mackinaw. The "c" at the end is silent and the last syllable was always pronounced "aw" like in "aw, shucks" or awe.

When the city founders named the city they opted for the "aw" spelling to allow postal carriers to differentiate between the Island (which retained the "ac") and the occupants of the city. Both names, however, are still pronounced the same ("aw"). The bridge and the Straits also use the "ac" version.

In 1634 explorer Jean Nicolet was the first European to pass through the Straits of Mackinac and in 1665 French Jesuit Priest, Claude Allouez, was the first missionary to travel there. However, it was 1671, before the second Jesuit priest, Father Jacques Marquette, established a mission for the Huron Native Americans at St. Ignace. It is believed he was the first European to settle in the area and he is buried at his mission.

Around 1708, French soldiers constructed a strategic depot for the upper Great Lakes fur trade near present-day Mackinaw City. It became not only the headquarters for the fur trade, but also an important military post in the northwest.

Missionaries and fur traders occupy the same historical time period in both Mackinaw City and Mackinac Island history. As the missionaries attempted to convert Native Americans, fur traders sought their assistance in obtaining lucrative furs. Ships of European goods set out for Mackinaw City and Mackinac Island where they were traded for prized beaver pelts, and the less valuable muskrat, fox and otter pelts.

The fort at Mackinaw City passed from French to British control in 1761 after the last battle of the French and Indian Wars. In 1763 the British Garrison at Old Mackinac, as the fort near Mackinaw City was called, was attacked by the Ottawa and Chippewa during Pontiac's Rebellion. These tribes occupied the area and disliked British control. They staged a ball game outside the stockade to create a diversion and gain entrance to the post. They killed most of the British occupants.

During the American Revolution the beleaguered British were threatened by American General George Rogers Clark and the British retreated to Mackinac Island where they could more easily protect their position. In 1781 the Native American chiefs in the area sold Mackinac Island to the British in an attempt to protect their interests in the Great Lakes fur trade. In 1783 the Island and the Straits became United States property according to the terms of the Treaty of Paris. However, they remained in British hands until 1794 when the U. S. took possession.

In the War of 1812 the British recaptured Mackinac Island and forced an American surrender after a surprise landing on the north side of the Island allowed them to occupy the high ground of Fort Holmes. The Island continued to be a battleground during the War of 1812 and it was the site of many casualties. The 1814 Treaty of Ghent returned the Island to U.S. control.

After the war, Mackinac Island became a center of the fur trade operations for John Jacob Astor's American Fur Company which merged the Mackinaw Fur Company and the Southwestern Fur Company.

The area's fur industry gave way to fishing which ushered in a new economic era. By the 1830s fishing was the island's primary industry. Today the tourist trade generates significant revenue for the area.

Mackinac Island was designated the country's second National Park in 1875. Yellowstone had been designated a National Park three years earlier. When Fort Mackinac was decommissioned in 1895, the land was given to the state and it became Michigan's first state park, Mackinac Island State Park. Both the island and the city are great places to reach out and touch history.

You can sit in Alexander Henry Park and soak up a great view of the Mighty Mac which opened to traffic on November 1, 1957. The initial idea for Mackinac Bridge construction was discussed nearly seventy-five-years earlier in 1884. From then on, Michiganders never gave up the dream of a bridge to connect their two peninsulas. The bridge is five-miles-long and spans the shortest point between the Upper and Lower Peninsulas. Five men died during construction of the bridge, but contrary to myth, none are buried in the concrete supports.

Mackinaw City has wonderful shopping at the Mackinaw Crossing Mall, but fudge and T-shirts reign supreme along the shops on Central Avenue.

Mackinaw City is only partially on the Lake Michigan shoreline. Much of it peers out at Lake Huron - but its massive tourist appeal makes it the perfect spot to end a travel guide devoted to resort cities along the Lake Michigan coast. Mackinac Island is one of Michigan's premier tourist sites and just a short boat ride from Mackinaw City.

Food/Restaurants
Mackinaw City:

Admirals Table, 502 South Huron Avenue, (231) 436-5687. Casual dining, senior and children's menu, cocktail lounge. Located across from the docks. Menu includes Great Lakes fish, seafood, steaks and prime rib. Open 7 days, 7:00 am to 10:00 pm. Closes October through Mother's Day weekend.

Anna's Country Buffet, 416 South Huron Avenue, (231) 436-5195. Largest buffet in Mackinaw City. Offers down-home cooking using only fresh ingredients. Daily specials. Also has a gift shop and specialty food store. Open breakfast, lunch and dinner, 7 days, 7:00 am to 10:00 pm. Closes end of October until beginning of May.

Audie's Family Restaurant and the Chippewa Room, 314 North Nicolet Street, (231) 436-5744. Up-North atmosphere, but fine dining menu options. The Chippewa Room has received awards for their Great Lakes Whitefish and Perch. Rack of Lamb is a specialty and they cut steaks to order. Extensive wine list. Open 7 days at 5:00 pm, year round. The Family Room is open 7 days, 8:00 am to 10:00 pm, serving breakfast, lunch and dinner in a more casual setting.

Blue Water Grill and Bar, 918 South Huron Avenue, (231) 436-7818. Hand tossed pizza. Full bar. Open Mon to Sat 11:00 am to 11:00 pm, year round.

Cunningham's Family Restaurant, 312 East Central Avenue, (231) 436-8821. Nautical décor and home cooking. Features homemade pasties and pies. Open daily, 8:00 am to 10:00 pm. Reduced hours after Labor Day, 8:00 am to 9:00 pm. Closes 3rd week of October until May.

Darrow's Family Restaurant, 301 Louvigny, (231) 436-5514. Open since 1958 and serving food made from scratch using only the freshest ingredients. Homemade bread and soup. Open breakfast, lunch and dinner 7 days, 7:30 am to 9:00 pm. Closes in October.

Dixie Saloon, 401 East Central Avenue, (231) 436-5449. A favorite with locals and tourists since 1890. Specialty is their full slab of Dixie BBQ Ribs. Across from Shepler's Mackinac Island Ferry, so a good place to stop for dinner and a drink after spending the day on the island. Open 7 days, kitchen 11:00 am to 10:00 pm, bar until 2:00 am. Reduced winter hours.

Embers Restaurant, 810 South Huron Avenue, (231) 436-5773. Breakfast, lunch and dinner smorgasbords. Open 8:00 am to 9:00 pm (or later) and closed in the winter.

Historic Depot, Mackinaw Crossings, (231) 436-7060. Casual dining for lunch and dinner. Has a full bar, salads, sandwiches and fresh seafood. Indoor and outdoor seating. Open Mon to Thurs 11:00 am to 6:00 or 7:00 pm depending on business, Fri and Sat open until 8:00 pm. Closed Sun. Closed in the winter.

Lighthouse Restaurant, 618 South Huron, (231) 436-5191. Upscale menu but a casual, relaxed atmosphere. Fresh fish from local waters, nightly seafood special. Their lounge is a replica of President Teddy Roosevelt's favorite bar. Open daily 4:00 pm to 10:00 pm.

Mackinaw Bakery and Coffeehouse, 110 Langlade, (231) 436-5525. Full line of homemade baked confections including birthday cakes, breads, bagels, pies, muffins, doughnuts and pasties. Also offers ice cream cones, cappuccino and homemade sandwiches. Carries a selection of tea, teapots and tea accessories. Open 7 days, 6:00 am to 8:00 pm. Closes November to April.

Mackinaw Pasties and Cookie Company, 514 South Huron Avenue. They make fresh Cornish pasties from scratch daily in their own kitchen. *People's Choice* Winner in 2005 for best pasties. Open 7 days 9:00 am to 10:00 pm, closed in winter. Second location at 117 West Jamet where they are open 7 days, 9:00 am to 9:00 pm in the summer and 9:00 am to 6:00 pm in the winter.

Neath the Birches, 14277 Mackinaw Highway, (231) 436-5401. 35 years of serving fresh whitefish, steaks and chops. Stop in and see the wildlife: birds, raccoons and turkeys. Local favorite. Open 4:00 pm to 10:00 pm, 7 days. Closes mid-October to mid-April.

Nonna Lisa's Italian Ristorante, 312 South Huron Avenue, (231) 436-7901. Specializing in pasta and wood-fired pizza. You can start with any one of the many authentic Italian appetizers, then try a calzone or strombolis, panini sandwich, classic grille selection, pasta dish - and homemade dessert, if you can possibly save room for it. Open 7 days, 10:00 am until "late."

Palace Restaurant and Pizzeria, 316 East Central Avenue, (231) 436-5788. Full menu with daily specials. Tour groups welcome and children's menu available. Open 7 days, Sun to Thurs 11:00 am to 10:00 pm, Fri and Sat 11:00 am to midnight. May reduce winter hours.

Pancake Chef, 327 Central Avenue, (231) 436-5578. Salad bar and buffet. Breakfast anytime. Lunch and dinner menu. Open 7 days, 7:00 am to 9:00 pm (approximately) during the summer.

Mackinac Island:

A great side trip from Mackinaw City. Once you step off the boat on Mackinac Island you will find restaurant after restaurant, gift shop after gift shop, fourteen or fifteen fudge shops and more t-shirt shops than you can count. The original fudge establishments were Mays and Murdicks. Mackinac Island has a Victorian flavor and Victorians favored the flavor of fudge. How they loved their sweets. The first fudge maker is rumored to have wafted a huge fan over his cooling confection to carry the smell into the street and entice customers. Just walk down Main Street and you cannot miss the shops and restaurants. Hours for many establishments will vary with tourist traffic. Many close during the winter when the few full time residents take back their Island. There are dozens of additional fine restaurants and local hangouts, but for anyone needing assurance that restaurants will be there to feed their hunger a few are included:

The Carriage House Restaurant, Hotel Iroquois, (906) 847-3321. Elegant food enjoyed with beautiful views of Lake Michigan.

French Outpost, (906) 847-3772. Upscale, sophisticated, and varied cuisine in a casual setting. Entertainment throughout the day and evening.

Goodfellows Restaurant and Grill, Main Street, (906) 847-0270. A place where you will find locals hanging out at the bar and enjoying a brew. Pilot House Restaurant features American-style cuisine. Whitefish Dip is a choice way to start your meal.

Horn's Gaslight Bar and Restaurant, Main Street, (906) 847-6154, www.hornsbar.com. Established in 1933 the bar has an old-time flavor with modern entertainment and dancing. Southwestern favorites are a specialty, but you can get American food as well.

Mission Point Restaurant, toll-free (800) 833-5583. Four possibilities here: Euro Garden Café with European dishes, the Round Island Bar and Grill with casual dining, the Great Straits Seafood Company for seafood or steak, and finally, the Freighters Imports and Delicatessen for sandwiches and salads.

Pub and Oyster Bar, Main Street (906) 847-9901. American Grill serving three meals a day. Everything from their famous Pub Burger to the Thai YumYum Bowl.

Village Inn, (906) 847-3542, www.viofmackinac.com. Voted one of Northern Michigan's Best Restaurants by the *Detroit News*. Serving breakfast, lunch and dinner. House specialty is Planked Whitefish.

Yankee Rebel Tavern, Astor Street, (906) 847-6249. Updated American dishes in a casual, rustic atmosphere.

Lodging (Also see Campgrounds below)
Mackinaw City:

America's Best Value Inn, 112 Old US-31, (231) 436-5544 or toll-free (800) 647-8286. Amenities: indoor heated pool, spa, sauna, continental breakfast, internet, Jacuzzi rooms and one block to ferry.

Aqua-Grand Mackinaw Inn and Water Park, 907 South Huron Avenue, (231) 436-8831 or toll-free (800) 822-8314. Amenities: indoor water playground, sandy beach, microwaves and refrigerators.

Baymont Inn and Suites, 109 South Nicolet Street, (231) 436-7737 or toll free (866) 331-7737. Adjacent to Mackinaw Crossings and Mackinaw Theater. Amenities: continental breakfast, pool, spa, exercise room and two-room suites.

Best Western Dockside, 505 South Huron Avenue, (231) 436-5001 or toll-free (800) 998-0699, www.mackinawreservations.com. Lakefront rooms with private European-style balconies. Nightly laser show, concerts and live theater. Extras: breakfast bar, high speed internet access, indoor pool, whirlpool, access to new water park across the street, honeymoon suites with heart-shaped Jacuzzis and HBO.

Best Western Thunderbird Inn, 146 Old US-31, (231) 436-5433, toll-free (800) 633-1515, www.bestwesternthunderbirdinn.com. One block from ferry. Amenities: indoor heated pool, spa, sauna, deluxe continental breakfast, playground, refrigerators, microwaves and high speed internet.

Brigadoon B&B, 2007 Langlade Street, (231) 436-8882, www.mackinawbrigadoon.com. Beautiful guest suites all with private baths, marble floors, fireplaces, whirlpool tubs, balconies, TV, wet bars, king-size beds and full hot breakfast.

Clarion Hotel Beachfront, 905 South Huron Avenue, (231) 436-5539 or toll-free (800) 417-3795. Lakefront rooms with private balconies, private sandy beach, adjacent to Mackinac Island Ferry Docks. Great views of Mackinac Island and Bridge. Extras: family stays free with paying adult, in-room Jacuzzis, internet, indoor heated pool, whirlpool, microwaves, refrigerators, HBO, ESPN and CNN.

Comfort Inn, Lakeside, 611 South Huron Avenue, (231) 436-5057, www.comfortinnmackinaw.com. On the lake, next to the ferry. Views of the Straits of Mackinac. Amenities: private sandy beach, indoor pool, whirlpool and deluxe continental breakfast.

Comfort Suites, Lakeview, 720 South Huron Avenue, (231) 436-5929 or toll-free (800) 411-2871. New in 2005 and features an indoor water park. Extras: indoor and outdoor heated pools, two whirlpools, game room, exercise room, breakfast bar, 1400-feet of private sandy beach and honeymoon suites with Jacuzzis.

Courtyard of Mackinaw Inn and Suites, 202 East Central Avenue, (231) 436-5528 or toll-free (800) 978-5520. Downtown Mackinaw City. Amenities: indoor pool, spa, hot breakfast, internet, refrigerators and microwaves.

Deer Head Inn Bed and Breakfast, 109 Henry Street, (231) 436-3337, www.deerhead.com. Five rooms with fireplaces and private baths in a turn-of-the-century Arts & Crafts home. Full breakfast included.

Econo Lodge Bay View, 712 South Huron Avenue, (231) 436-5777 or toll-free (800) 410-6637. New in 2005. Extras: indoor and outdoor heated pools, two whirlpools, breakfast bar, exercise room, game room, private villas, block from town and indoor water park.

Hamilton Inn Select Beachfront, 701 South Huron Avenue, (231) 436-5493 or toll-free (800) 410-5302. Mackinaw City's largest lakefront hotel with indoor pool, oversized whirlpool and private sandy beach access. Extras: family stays free with one paying adult, honeymoon suites with in-room Jacuzzis, 25-foot breakfast bar, high speed internet, exercise room and tanning capsule.

Hampton Inn, 726 South Huron Avenue, (231) 436-7829 or toll-free (800) HAMPTON. Near shopping and water park. Amenities: hot breakfast, heated indoor pool, internet and 24-hour coffee bar.

Holiday Inn Express, "At the Bridge," 364 Louvigny, (231) 436-7100 or toll-free (866) EXIT-339. Amenities: hot breakfast, indoor heated pool, fitness facility, 2-room suites and some rooms with views.

Quality Inn and Suites Beachfront, 917 South Huron Avenue, (231) 436-5051 or toll-free (800) 410-6631. Newer motel with beach and a view. Beachfront rooms with balconies. Extras: access to indoor water park, indoor pool, spa, sauna, in-room whirlpools available, refrigerators, cable and hot breakfast in the Garden Room.

Ramada Limited Waterfront, 723 South Huron Avenue, (231) 436-5055 or toll-free (800) 852-4165, www.edgewater-mackinaw.com. Award winning property next to the ferry docks. Extras: refrigerators, 32-inch TV with HBO, private sandy beach access, indoor pool, indoor and outdoor whirlpools, honeymoon suites, Jacuzzi rooms and continental breakfast.

Super 8, Beachfront, 519 South Huron Avenue, (231) 436-7111 or toll-free (800) 515-7915. Downtown beachfront location, access to private sandy beach, unlimited access to indoor waterpark, indoor pool, whirlpool, sauna, honeymoon suites with in-room Jacuzzis and lakefront rooms with balconies.

Super 8 Motel, Bridgeview, 601 North Huron Avenue, (231) 436-5252 or toll-free (800) 654-0310. 65 rooms and log cabin-like exterior. Bridge and lake views. Amenities: continental breakfast, internet, indoor heated pool, spa, sauna, Jacuzzi suites available and HBO.

Travelodge Bay View, 900 South Huron Avenue, (231) 436-7900 or toll-free (888) 753-7900, www.mackinawcitytravelodge.com. Amenities: indoor heated pool with spa, outdoor pool with sundeck, microwaves, refrigerators and continental breakfast.

Mackinac Island:

Bay View on Mackinac Island, www.mackinacbayviewcom, (906) 847-3295. Built in 1891. Offering 16 rooms and 4 suites.

The Chippewa Hotel, on the waterfront, toll-free (800) 241-3341, www.chippewahotel.com. Walk off the ferry and into your hotel.

The Cottage Inn, www.cottageinnofmackinac.com, (906) 847-4000. One block from the ferry dock on Market Street. Extras: uniquely appointed rooms, private bathrooms and homemade deluxe breakfast. Smoke-free facility.

The Grand Hotel, www.grandhotel.com, toll-free (800) 33-GRAND. Named one of the top 100 hotels in the world; this hotel is the one that first comes to mind when you think Mackinac Island. You enter the inn through its nearly 900-foot porched entry with three-story columned supports. You are treated to afternoon tea and can play croquet on the expansive lawns. From its earliest days, it has been steeped in romance and tradition. A reminder of a more relaxed and genteel time. It was the location of the movie *"Somewhere in Time,"* starring Christopher Reeve and Jane Seymour. You might pick up the 1980 flick as a prelude to your trip to the island. Definitely the place to stay if money is not a concern.

The Beautiful Grand Hotel   *Photo by Bob Royce*

Haan's 1830 Inn, (906) 847-6244, www.mackinac.com/haans. Colonel Preston, one of the last officers at Fort Mackinac and the first mayor of the island at the turn of the century, called this home. Completely restored, it has six rooms and three suites available.

Harbour View Inn, (906) 847-0101, www.harbourviewinn.com. Originally built as the home of Madame La Framboise, one of Mackinac Island's wealthiest and most charismatic fur traders. 1829 structure provides a window to the past while offering the conveniences expected in today's fine hotels.

Hotel Iroquois, (906) 847-3321, www.iroquoishotel.com. Offers 46 rooms in the Victorian cottage design, including the flowers. Staying here is not inexpensive, but then nothing is on the island. This lovely hotel perches on a bluff overlooking the water. It was built as a private home just before the turn of the century. (Also see Carriage House Restaurant above.)

The Inn at Stonecliffe, www.innatstonecliffe.com, (906) 847-3355. You can enjoy a refreshing dip in the pool or just sit with a good book (while glancing up every little while to take in the beauty of the bridge and water). A European-style inn with many well-appointed rooms and suites to enhance your Island visit.

The Island House, www.theislandhouse.com, toll-free (800) 626-6304. The first summer hotel on the island. Built in 1852. As tourism grew, the hotel moved from the shore and expanded.

Lake View Hotel, toll-free (800) 207-7075, www.lake-view-hotel.us. An 1858 restored Victorian resort where you can enjoy a hearty dose of pampering.

Lilac Tree Hotel and Spa, Main Street on Downtown Mackinac Island, toll-free (866) 847-6575, www.lilactree.com. The goal is to make you feel special at this luxury hotel.

Main Street Inn and Suites, www.mainstreetinnandsuites.com, (906) 847-6530. The feeling of an intimate inn with the convenience of a modern hotel. One of the newer accommodations on the island.

Market Street Inn, toll-free (888) 899-3811. Extras: robes, allergy free feather bedding, cable and ceiling fans.

Metivier Inn, (866) 847-6234, www.metivierinn.com. Located conveniently on Market Street in downtown historic district. Offers 21 bedrooms all with private baths. Also an efficiency unit with Jacuzzi.

Mission Point Resort, www.missionpoint.com, toll-free (800) 833-7711. Exquisite views coupled with old-world hospitality.

Murray Hotel/The Inn on Mackinac, toll-free (800) 462-2546. www.4mackinac.com. When built in 1867 it was the Chateau Beaumont. The Inn retains its quaint, old-fashioned charm. Completely remodeled and redecorated, but maintaining its historic character, the Inn invites travelers to enjoy the beauty of its 43 rooms.

Museums and Galleries

Colonial Michilimackinac, along the waterfront in downtown Mackinaw City, (231) 436-4100, www.MackinacParks.com. Founded in 1715 this National Historic Landmark is a reconstructed fort and fur trading village. Staff dressed in period costumes wait to assist you and answer your questions. Enjoy the audio tour that brings to life the early inhabitants of Michilimackinac and watch a recreation of the British firing muskets and cannons. You may meet French voyageurs arriving at the fort's water gate. Open 7 days at 9:00 am, May to October.

Fort Mackinac, Mackinac Island, www.MackinacParks.com, (231) 436-4100. Park staff, dressed in period costume (1880s U.S. soldiers and Victorian ladies) show you around Michigan's only Revolutionary War-era fort. There are 14 original buildings at the site which sits on a bluff overlooking the small streets of downtown. Some things to see: Post Schoolhouse, North Blockhouse, Officers' Hill Quarters, West Blockhouse, Officers' Stone Quarters, Post Hospital, Soldiers Barracks,

North Sally Port, Post Headquarters and Quartermasters' Storehouse, East Blockhouse, Commissary, Gun Platforms, South Sally Port, Guardhouse and the Officers' Wooden Quarters. Open 7 days at 9:30 am, May to October.

Historic Mill Creek Sawmill and Nature Park, five minutes southeast of Mackinaw City on US-23, (231) 436-5563. This is a 1790s reconstructed sawmill, and given the importance of the lumber industry in Michigan's early development, it is worth stopping. You will see a woodworker demonstrate traditional craftsmanship. You can walk a 3½ mile wooded trail and there is a "Creatures of the Forest" program that will describe the critters you are likely to encounter along the way. Open May to September, 7 days at 9:00 am.

Theatre

Mackinaw Theater, 220 South Huron Avenue, located in Mackinaw Crossing shopping mall, (231) 436-2200 or toll-free (877) 43-STAGE, www.mackinawtheatre.com. An 821-seat, state-of-the-art facility. Past performances have included: *"Lost in the Fifties," "Men on Ice," "Forever Plaid," "Reflections," "The Rat Pack," "Heroes of Rock and Roll,"* and others. The season runs from May through October with two performances a day (closed Mondays). Matinee at 3:00 pm and evening performance at 7:30 pm.

Shopping

Mackinaw City:

Acatsgrin Tourist Trap, 301 East Central Avenue, (231) 436-6633. Unique gifts, collectibles, leather, shirts and old time photos. Scaredy Cat Horror House is on the second. Open 7 days, 10:00 am to 10:30 pm. Closes end of October to May 1st.

Allison and Ashley's Summer House, 314 East Central Avenue, (231) 436-5400. Casual home accessories, dolls, scarves, candles, quilts, jewelry, pins, wreaths, oil landscapes, purses and more. Open 7 days, 10:00 am to 10:00 pm, reduced fall hours and closes at the end of October and opens again May 1st.

Candy Corner/Windjammer Gifts, 331 East Central Avenue, (231) 436-5591, www.mackinawcitycandycorner.com. Mackinaw City Fudge, candies and a complete line of souvenirs, gifts and novelties. Open 8:00 am to 10:00 pm, 7 days. November to March only open weekends, 9:00 am to 5:00 pm.

Catch 22, 326 East Central Avenue, (231) 436-5329. Clothes for the entire family. Also carries colognes and accessories. Open 7 days, 9:00 am to 10:00 pm. Closes for the season 3rd week of October.

Devon's Delight, Mackinaw Trading Company, (231) 436-5356. Mackinaw Island Fudge, caramel corn, brittles, home-made jams, hand-made chocolates. Open 9:00 am to 11:00 pm, 7 days. Open weekends in the off-season, 9:00 am to 5:00 pm or thereabout.

Enchanted Knights, 248 South Huron Avenue in the Mackinaw Crossing, (231) 436-5650. A place where legends come alive. Mythical figurines, books, t-shirts, jewelry and renaissance clothing.

Fort Fudge Shop, 113 Straits Avenue, (231) 436-5650. Across from the fort. All kinds of candy with Mackinaw Fudge the mainstay. Full line of sugar-free candies. Also carries souvenirs, moccasins and gifts. Open 7 days, 7:00 am to 10:30 pm, fall 7:00 am to 10:00 pm and winter 9:00 am to 5:00 pm.

The Fort Gift Shop and Candy Kitchen, 400 North Louvingny, (231) 436-5453. In addition to a full selection of candy and gifts, you will find the Hockey Room and Mackinaw Mining Company, each worth a bit of your time. Open 7 days, 9:00 am to 10:00 pm, fall 9:00 am to 8:00 pm and winter 10:00 am to 6:00 pm.

Fran Murdick's Fudge, 222 Central Avenue, (231) 436-2665. The owners are third, fourth, and fifth generations of master candy makers in the Murdick family and they are carrying on the nearly 120-year-old tradition. In addition to their famous, creamy fudge you will find taffy, brittles and caramels. Open 9:00 am to 10:00 pm, 7 days, reduced hours in the fall and closed after October.

Island Bookstore, 215 East Central Avenue, (231) 436-2665. A full service bookstore with a wide selection of regional titles. Additionally, you will find gifts, toys, stationary, magazines, and newspapers. Open 9:00 am to 10:00 pm, 7 days, reduced in fall and spring. Closed October to May.

Joann's Fudge, 303 East Central Avenue, (231) 436-5611. Mackinac Island Fudge made daily using only natural ingredients. In addition to the 24 flavors of fudge you can get ice cream, English toffee, turtles, and hand dipped chocolates. Open 7 days, 9:00 am to 10:00 pm. Hours reduced in the fall. Closed in the winter.

Koko's Sportswear, 306 East Central, (231) 436-7999. (Also owns **Magic Fashion).** T-shirts, sportswear, coats. Both stores open 7 days, 9:00 am to 11:00 pm, May through October. Closed in the winter.

Mackinac Bay Trading Company, 312 South Huron Avenue, (231) 436-5005. Located across from Conkling Heritage Park, this location includes a number of shops under one roof, several of which are noted separately in this guide (Noona Lisa's, Devon's Delight), but also houses such stores as Nicolas Black River Vineyards and Wine Tasting Room and Woodland Creek Furniture.

Mackinaw Clothing, 319 East Central Avenue, (231) 436-5093. Clothing for the entire family. Features sportswear and outerwear (Woolrich and Columbia), and a large selection of unique sweaters, blankets and moccasins. Open 7 days, 9:00 am to 10:00 pm. Open year round, but reduced hours in the off-season.

Mackinaw Crossing, 248 South Huron Avenue, (231) 436-5030, www.mackinawcrossing.com. A quaint Victorian shopping village with 48 shops, 8 restaurants and entertainment. Entrance to the mall is downtown on the main strip. Brick pathways guide you from store to store. Stores include: Artists Corner Gallery, The Clothing Connection, Be You, Big Sail, Del Sol, Grandma and Me, Harbor Wear, Teysen's Moccasin Shop, Mackenzie's of Mackinaw, Mackinaw Shirt Co, Nadia's Fashion Shop, Sun Optics, Top Hats of Mackinaw, Tee Shirt Brothers, Canada Store, Christmas Store, Enchanted Knights, Michigan Peddler, Northwoods Harley Davidson, Paws Fur Fun, Pop Shop, Mackinaw City Soap Factory, Teysen's Gift Shop, True North Books, and the Mackinaw Theatre Gift Shop. Also the location of the Mackinaw Theater (see above under Theatres) and a Laser Show nightly as dusk. Open mid-June to early-August, 7 days, 10:00 am to 10:00 pm. May to mid-June and August through October open Sun to Thurs 10:00 am to 6:00 pm, Fri and Sat 10:00 am to 8:00 pm. Most shops close during the winter.

Mackinaw Crossing Shopping Center   *Photo by Bob Royce*

Mackinaw Kite Company, 307 East Central Avenue, (231) 436-8051. Single line and high-performance kites, windsocks, beach and flying toys all geared to nothing but fun. Open 7 days, 9:00 am to 10:00 pm. After Labor Day 9:00 am to 8:00 pm and closed October to April.

Marshall's Fudge and Candy Company, 308 East Central Avenue, toll-free (800) 343-8343, www.marshallsfudge.com. Dedicated to the proposition that not all fudge (even with dozens of stores selling it) is created equal. Open 7 days, 8:00 am to 11:00 pm. Non-season hours (beginning in October) 9:00 am to 6:00 pm.

Michigan Peddler, 219 St. Joseph Street, toll-free (800) 729-3180, www.michiganpeddler.com. All Michigan products including wine, books, dried cherries, jams and coffee. Open Mon to Sat 10:00 am to 6:00 pm and Sun 11:00 am to 5:00 pm. Closed one month in winter.

Momentum, 310 East Central Avenue, (231) 436-5839. Casual clothing at very reasonable prices. Lots of sweatshirts, t-shirts, jackets and fleece. (See listing under Traverse City, p. 247.) Open 7 days 9:00 am to 10:00 pm. Closed October to May.

Monadnock Gift Shop, 309 East Central Avenue, (231) 436-5131. Handmade Native American jewelry and authentic arts and crafts from more than 20 tribes. Merchandise includes Black Hills Gold, leaded crystal, stoneware, pewter, collectibles, Lake Superior beach granite and Petoskey stones. Open 7 days, 9:00 am to 10:00 pm. Closes the end of November and reopens in the middle of April.

Rainbow Sportswear, 317 East Central Avenue, (231) 436-5631. Perhaps the largest t-shirt store in the city with over 4000 images available. T-shirts made while you wait. Also carries swimwear, leather goods, knives, gift items, and the largest selection of belt buckles in the country (so they say, anyway). Open 7 days, 9:00 am to 10:00 pm. During the non-peak season from mid-October to May they open around 9:30 am and close at 7:00 pm, or later if there are customers.

Sign of the Loon, 311 East Central Avenue, (231) 436-5155, www.signoftheloon.com. Wildlife themed gifts to interest everyone. Lots of amber jewelry. Made by local Native American Tribes. Open 7 days, 9:00 am to 10:00 pm, Closes October 31st until May 1st.

Spag's Next Door, 113 North Huron Avenue, (231) 436-5309. Specialty foods, fine wine and imported beer. Create a gift basket from their merchandise. Also carries gifts, and cards. Open 8:00 am to 9:00 pm. In the fall they play it by ear. Closed in the winter.

Trail's End General Store, 305 East Central Avenue, (231) 436-8575. Assortment of merchandise from candy to film, dipping oil to batteries and a great deal in between. Open 7 days, 9:00 am to 10:00 pm. Closes in October for the season.

Twisted Crystal, 301 East Central Avenue, (231) 436-7020, www.twistedcrystal.com. Handcrafted jewelry boutique. Prices vary and start as low as $3.00. Open 7 days, 10:00 am to 10:00 pm. Closes in October and reopens in April or May.

Mackinac Island:
Great Turtle Toys, Main Street, (906) 847-6118. A frivolous, fun place for the entire family. The atmosphere encourages exploration and learning.

Island Bookstore, (906) 847-READ. Lots of books about the area and a place to grab a book if you plan to hang out and relax on the island.

Lilacs and Lace, located in the Carousel Shops on Market Street, (906) 847-0100. Victorian boutique with hand-made items, china, jewelry and fine art.

Love Shack, (906) 847-7777. Touristy clothing. Started in 1997 by two guys trying to sell the t-shirts off their back.

Mackinac Lapidary, located in the Carousel Shops on Market Street, (906) 847-1040. The owner, Frank Bloswick Jr, creates Mackinac-themed custom jewelry.

(*This is by no means a complete list; there are so many touristy kinds of shops that it becomes redundant to try to list them all. You will find them all around you on the two main streets of the island.*)

Parks, Beaches and Campgrounds

Alexander Henry Park, North Huron Avenue at the foot of the Mackinac Bridge. A pleasant little park where with great views of the Mackinac Bridge and Mackinac Island. Named after a fur trader and entrepreneur of the late 1700s.

KOA Campground, 566 Trailsend Road, (231) 436-5643 or toll-free (800) KOA-1738, www.koa.com. Fifty acre wooded setting, many pull-thru sites. Water, electric and sewer. Amenities: playground, nature trail, game room, and laundry.

Mackinac Island State Park, (The entire island is a park), (321) 436-4100., www.MackinacParks.com. This park is one of the few places in the country where cars are not allowed. You can take a horse-drawn carriage ride, stroll at your own pace, or bike the 8.1 miles around the island. You will access the island park by ferry (See Ferries below). You can explore 1,800 acres under canopies of cedars and birch. Limestone bluffs rise above sparkling blue water. The Visitors Center is probably the best place to begin your tour of the island. Some of the things you can see or visit while on the island (in addition to restaurants, lodging, and shops): Fort Mackinac (See above under Museums) Marquette Park, McGulpin House, Dr. Beaumont Museum/American Fur Company Store, Robert Stuart House, Michilimackinac County Courthouse, Biddle House, Missionary Bark Chapel, Trinity Episcopal Church, Mission Church, Arch Rock, Sugar Loaf Rock, Post Cemetery, British Landing, Lighthouse, (New and Old Round), the Butterfly House (*see below under Other Things to See and Do),* and Skull Cave. The nature trails on the island will take you past many of these sites. A stop at the Visitors' Center can provide you with good maps of walking tour options.

Mackinaw Mill Creek Camping, 2½ miles south of Mackinaw City on US-23, (231) 436-5584, www.campmackinaw.com. 600-sites, 200 with full hook-up. Amenities: playground, arcade, camping cabins, dump stations, flush toilets, showers and heated pool.

Tee Pee Campground, 11262 West US-23, (231) 436-5391, www.teepeecampground.com. Near downtown, beach with bridge view and nightly bonfire. 100 grassy and shady sites. Amenities: party store and hot showers.

Wawatam Park, North Huron Avenue next to Shepler's in Mackinaw City. A nice place to relax with a morning paper before deciding your day's agenda. The park is equipped with restrooms, picnic tables, grills and a playground. The park was named for Chief Wawatam, who on several occasions saved the life of Alexander Henry, a local fur trader and entrepreneur in the late 1700s.

Marinas

Mackinaw City Municipal Marina, (231) 436-5269. Harbor-master on duty 5/1 to 10/15. 78 transient slips available. Amenities: gas dock, pump out, restrooms, showers, laundry, picnic facilities, water, cable, boat ramp, casino shuttle and on-site mechanic.

Mackinac Island State Dock, (231) 847-3561. Operated by the Michigan Department of Natural Resources Recreation Division. 63 transient slips. Harbormaster on duty 5/31 to 10/20.

Cruise, Tours, Charters and Ferries

Arnold Line Mackinac Island Ferry Company, (ferries and catamarans), ferry dock, Mackinaw City, (906) 847-3351 or toll-free (800) 542-8528, www.arnoldline.com. Service to the island (ferry if you want to savor the ride, catamaran if you want a smooth, quick ride). Arnold's also offers sunset cruises. The fleet consists of three twin-hulled, triple-decked ferries with glass enclosed passenger lounges in case you prefer not to be on the open deck.

Dream Seeker Charters and Tours, (906) 647-7278 or toll-free (888) 634-3419, www.dreamseaker.com. Departs from Mackinac Island and will take you fishing for steelhead, northern pike, walleye, perch, salmon, lake trout or brown trout as they are in season. Also takes you on guided tours of Les Cheneaux Island and Martin's Reef Lighthouse. They provide historical narrative along the way.

Lighthouse Cruise, Sheplers Ferries, Mackinaw City Dock, 556 East Central Avenue, (231) 436-5023 or toll-free (800) 828-6157, www.sheplersferry.com. The same Shepler's Ferry Company that takes you to Mackinac Island can also take you on a lighthouse cruise showing you ten lighthouses in route. Or, you can consider the

Beaver's Connection, 2 day cruise. Call for details on the cruises available and to schedule reservations.

Mackinac Island Carriage Tours, Across from the Arnold Ferry Dock on the Island, (906) 847-3307. The alternative to the automobile or cabs on the island. The tour will provide interesting historical background and take you past the sites.

Shepler's Ferries to Mackinac Island, (See above Lighthouse Cruise).

Star Line, 711 South Huron Avenue toll-free (800) 638-9892. Mackinaw City/Mackinac Island Hydro-jet ferry service.

Vesper Cruises, Mackinaw City, (231) 597-0353. These services are aboard Arnold Ferries. A collection is taken to cover the cost of the boat. It is part of the Straits Area Resort Ministries. The services are Tuesdays and Sundays.

Other Things to See and Do

A-Maze-N Mirrors, Mackinaw Crossing, (231) 436-7550. Life sized maze of mirrors and glass.

Kewadin Casino, 3039 Mackinac Trail (St. Ignace). If you decide to cross the Mighty Mac, this is one of the entertainments you will find on the other side. Vegas-style gambling and over 2,300 slots, as well as blackjack, poker, craps, roulette, bingo and live keno.

Mackinac Bridge, Mackinaw City. The longest suspension bridge in America and third longest in the world with a total length of 8,614 feet suspended. A magnificent structure worth the time it takes to cross. The giant bridge turns fifty-years-old in 2007.

Mackinac Island Butterfly House, (906) 847-3972. Behind St. Anne's Church, not far from the ferry landing, fly 800 or more butterflies in a beautiful garden.

Old Mackinac Point Lighthouse, exit 339 from I-75 and follow signs, (231) 436-4100, www.MackinacParks.com. You can start your visit by meeting the lighthouse keeper and viewing a 1910 keeper's kitchen. The lighthouse features interactive exhibits that let you feel what it was like to pilot a ship. You can compare the architecture and style of area lighthouses and climb to the top of the tower for a panoramic view of the lake. (See p. 367, Part II for additional detail.)

Thunder Falls Family Water Park, Exit 338 off I-75, Mackinaw City, (231) 436-6000. The place to go for water fun, the park offers: a wave pool, tube slides, body slides, speed slides, a lazy river, arcade, and more. Situated on 20 beautifully landscaped acres.

Festivals

Colonial Michilimackinac Pageant, Mackinaw City, May.
Annual Lilac Festival, Mackinac Island, June.

"Big Mac" Spring Shoreline Bike Tour, Mackinaw City, June.

Corvette Crossroads Auto Show, Mackinaw City, August.

Annual Mackinac Bridge Walk, Mackinaw City, September.

Hopps of Fun-A Festival of Beer and Wine, Mackinaw City, September.

"Big Mac" Shoreline Bike Tour, Mackinaw City, September.

Golf

Animal Tracks Miniature Golf, 220 South Huron Avenue, (231) 436-5597. It is miniature golf with a learning twist, teaching about the animals of Northern Michigan.

Grand Hotel Golf Course, Mackinac Island, (906) 847-3331. 18-hole course, Tee times made 14 days in advance. Pro on staff.

The Greens, Mission Point Resort, Mackinaw Island, (906) 847-3312, www.missionpoint.com. 18-hole executive putting course. Open to the public 7 days a week.

Wawashkamo Golf Course, Mackinac Island, (906) 847-3871. The course is played on 9 greens from 18 tees and is open to the public. Built in 1898, the name Wawashkamo comes from a Chippewa phrase meaning "walk a crooked trail" and was coined by a local chief after observing a group of golfers on the links.

Contacts

Mackinaw Area Visitors Bureau, 10300 West US-23, Mackinaw City, (231) 436-5664, www.mackinawcity.com.

Mackinac State Historic Parks, www.MackinacParks.com, (906) 847-3328.

Mackinac Island Visitors Center. From the island ferry landing, turn right (east) onto Main Street and proceed to the end of town where you will find Marquette Park on the left and the Visitor's Center on the right. The Visitors Center has several interesting exhibits and is the place to pick up a map of the Island.

Horse and Carriage, Fort in Background   *Photo by Bob Royce*

PART TWO
-A Bit of History
-A Bit of Background
-A Bit of Fun

Introduction to Part Two

The next several chapters provide the traveler with some light vacation reading and a backdrop for Lake Michigan shoreline adventures.

The chapters *Lake Michigan: The Delightfullest Lake* and *Shipwrecks of Lake Michigan: Unlucky 13* provide a bit of history. The chapters *Sand Dunes of Lake Michigan: Glacier Created Wonders*, *Lighthouses of Lake Michigan: Soul of the Harbor* and *Flora and Fauna of Lake Michigan: Critters, Creatures and Other Living Things* offer a bit of background about what you may see during your travels. *Ghosts and Monsters of Lake Michigan: Haunting and Stalking the Sunset Coast* will add a bit of fun. What is better than a ghoulish story told around a campfire? *Legends of Lake Michigan: The Famous and Infamous with Ties to the Lake* contains all three: a bit of history, a bit of background and a bit of fun.

I am not a historian; I did no original research in preparing these chapters. I say that by way of disclaimer and simply to let you know that I believe the information contained in the following pages is true and accurate (well, maybe not the ghost stories). I have researched it to the best of my time constraints and abilities – and both were limited. The material was collected from many sources including: local libraries, conversations with residents of the featured shore towns and villages, newspapers, various booklets, encyclopedias, internet searches, discussions with many Chambers of Commerce and about anything else I could find. I do not include references because this is not meant to be a reference book. References would prove annoying and take up far too much space for a travel guide.

I hope you find this information interesting or entertaining and that it will enrich your travels along Michigan's Sunset Coast.

"The great fact in life,
  the always possible escape from dullness,
    was the lake.
The day began there; it was like an open door
  that nobody could shut.
    The land and all its dreariness
    could never close in on you.
You had only to look at the lake,
  and you knew you would soon be free. "

Attributed to Willa Cather by U.S. novelist Godfry St. Peter, in his book *The Professor's House* as the professor recalls his childhood on Lake Michigan.

Lake Michigan
"The delightfullest lake"

In the mid-1600s French adventurer and fur trader Pierre Esprit Radisson gazed at the vast sapphire waters of Lake Michigan and proclaimed it, "the delightfullest lake in the world." One of the five lakes collectively called the Great Lakes; Lake Michigan is part of the water highway known as the Great Lakes-St. Lawrence Seaway System, connecting North America to the Atlantic Ocean and the rest of the world.

In 1634 French cartographer, Nicholas Sanson, published a map of North American that included the Great Lakes. It is the first time Lake Michigan was identified, and it was unflatteringly labeled "Lac de Puans" which meant Lake of the Stinking Things. The name derived from the appellation "stinking people" given to the local Winnebago tribe. It was no reflection upon the Winnebago's personal hygiene; rather it was a reference to their migration from land near the ocean (stinking, or salt water). Fortunately, that original name did not stick. The legend of the tribe coming from a place of "stinking water" fueled the belief held by the French that if they pushed west far enough, they would reach the "stinking" ocean and the waterway to China.

Sitting on a sugar-sand beach in Grand Haven or Pentwater, mesmerized by the gentle waves as you watch the sun slip beyond the horizon, it is easy to lose yourself in the splendor of Lake Michigan. Statistics seem too cold, too trivial, and too impersonal to describe the grandeur of this great lake. However, the statistics are pretty impressive: By volume, Lake Michigan is the second largest Great Lake, next only to Superior. It is approximately 118 miles wide and 307 miles long with more than 1,600 miles of shoreline, or about the same distance as from Traverse City to Albuquerque, New Mexico.

The lake reaches 925 feet at its deepest point and its average depth is 297 feet.

Lake Michigan is the only one of our Great Lakes that lies completely enveloped by the United States. It has 22,300 square miles of surface water and its drainage basin covers portions of Illinois, Indiana, Michigan and Wisconsin and is twice as large as the area of its surface water. There is no separation of the waters between Lake Michigan and Lake Huron and the latter provides Lake Michigan's only natural outlet and connects it to the Atlantic Ocean and international trade by way of the St. Lawrence Seaway. The Illinois Waterway links Lake Michigan to the Mississippi River and the Gulf of Mexico.

Lake Michigan is the receptacle for the Muskegon, Grand, Kalamazoo, Fox and Menominee Rivers. The Chicago River at one time flowed into Lake Michigan, but its course was reversed in 1900.

Together the Great Lakes contain about 90% of the United States' fresh water supply and 18% of the world's fresh water supply. The lakes contain 5,500 cubic miles or six quadrillion gallons of water. Lake Michigan holds 1,180 cubic miles and approximately 1,287,272,400,000,000 gallons of water – give or take a few hundred thousand gallons. If the water from the Great Lakes could be spread evenly across the entire continental United States the depth would reach nine and a half feet. No matter how you look at it, that is a lot of water.

The history of Lake Michigan is also the history of the people and land at its shore. Rolling up to the water's edge are pastoral scenes painted by streams, barns, silos, dairy cattle, orchards, vineyards, farms, wheat fields, small vegetable gardens, harbors, ships and many small, quaint towns. They are all props in the drama of the great lake: Michigan.

In the very beginning. Even without humans to write the very earliest piece of its history, Lake Michigan left us its story etched in the rocks, sand, gorges, falls, dunes and beaches around its shores.

Three billion years ago, during the Precambrian Era, the world was a place of enormous volcanic activity. Earth shaking movement gave rise to the embryonic stage of Lake Michigan. Birth was a long, drawn-out process. Not until much more recently, a mere 600 million years ago, when the Paleozoic Era arrived, did water become an important part of the development process.

During the Paleozoic Era the Great Lakes region was repeatedly flooded by ancient marine seas. These seas contained the area's first life forms: corals, crinoids, mollusks and brachiopods. The early seas also left lime, clay, salt and sand which eventually became the limestone, shale, sandstone, halite and gypsum that we continue to mine today.

The Pleistocene Epoch, one time era back from the modern era, was known as the Great Ice Age. The Ice Age began about 1,000,000 years ago and lasted to a fairly recent 10,000 years ago. This was the time of gargantuan glaciers, up to 6,500 feet thick, steadily inched their way over the Great Lakes region.

As the glaciers receded, huge amounts of water melted in front of them, creating glacier lakes much larger than the Great Lakes we currently know. In a phenomenon called uplift, the land began to rise. This process continues today and means that Lake Michigan and the other four lakes will continue to see changes, but by a process so slow that to human experience it is imperceptible.

And then came man. About 10,000 to 14,000 years ago at the end of the Great Ice Age, there is evidence of prehistoric Paleo-Indian culture existing in North America. The prevailing theory suggests the first humans in North America traveled over a now extinct Siberian land bridge. Other theories continue to be explored, but the "land bridge" theory is based, at least in part, on the lack of significant evidence of earlier "pre-humans" on the continent.

The Paleo-Indian culture is marked by big-game hunting and the development of simple tools. Kill sites have been identified by artifacts including distinctive spearheads made of fluted, chipped stones. With these elemental spears, called Clovis stones, hunters stalked great mastodon, mammoth and bison.

Nearly 7000 years ago these early inhabitants discovered copper and began using it for hunting and ornamentation, as well as in religious practices. They also began to develop agriculture and further refined their method of killing game.

The earliest people to enter the Great Lakes Region of North America are believed to be the Anishinabe who are the forebears of the Ojibway and other Algonquin speaking tribes of the Great Lakes. They maintained a rich oral history that was passed from generation to generation over centuries, tracking important events and religious practices. Unfortunately, however, the written history of the Great Lakes' original people is sketchy. Although early French, Dutch and English explorers kept detailed journals beginning in the 1500s, they wrote from a European perspective, subject to cultural and language differences, and therefore much was lost in translation.

The oral histories suggest that originally the Anishinabe came from land near the Atlantic Ocean. According to one of the prevailing legends, a prophet to the Anishinabe warned his people "*if you do not move, you will be destroyed.*" The Anishinabe listened to their prophet and left their villages along the Atlantic seashore and embarked on an epic westward journey in search of a new home. The Anishinabe were guided by signs from the spirits that led them to a bountiful country where food was plentiful and they could avoid the prophesized disaster which some believe may have been a forewarning that the white man was coming.

The Anishinabe's courageous trek lasted for many generations and took them through the entire Great Lakes region down the St. Lawrence River and eventually overland through the heart of Michigan to the east side of Lake Michigan. They also went into the area around the whole of Lake Superior.

The Anishinabe broke into three groups. The Pottawatomie settled along the Lake Michigan shoreline where the abundant water provided them with food and waterways for travel. In southwestern Michigan they hunted the plentiful game and raised crops. The Pottawatomie pledged to safeguard the sacred fire for the Anishinabe.

A second group became known as the Ottawa. They remained in the area of the upper part of the lower peninsula of Michigan and on Manitoulin Island. They agreed to carry out major trading expeditions for their people.

The third group became known as the Ojibwa (or Chippewa). They settled in the Upper Peninsula of Michigan, Minnesota and Wisconsin. The role of the Ojibwa was to protect the spiritual beliefs of the Anishinabe and from their numbers came the Midewiwin, or religious leader, who would preserve the sacred lore of the people in words and songs and in the symbols they inscribed on their birch-bark scrolls.

Arrival of the Explorers and Missionaries. The story of the Anishinabe became inextricably entwined with the story of the Europeans who began arriving in Michigan in the 1500s. From the landing of Christopher Columbus in 1492, the New World and the possibility of a trade route to China by way of a Northwest Passage captured the minds of zealous explorers who believed they would be the lucky one to find it. They pleaded their cases to ruling monarchs, besieging them for authority to sail and for provisions to sustain them on their journey.

The first European to explore and map the St. Lawrence area was Sea Captain Jacques Cartier, born in St. Malo, France in 1491. In 1534 French King Frances I approved Cartier's travel to North America in search of gold or other riches and, more importantly, a passage to Cathay or China. Cartier never made it into the Great Lakes, but his was the first documented exploration of inland North America. He interacted with the Original People (Iroquois and Micmac Nations) in the area near present day Quebec. They regaled him with tales of wealthy kingdoms further up the river. Cartier boldly annexed the St. Lawrence River Valley to the Crown of France.

Samuel de Champlain was still a young man when his visionary king, Henry IV, granted him permission to sail to the area that had become known as New France. He was the first European to see the Great Lakes. He sailed into the top of Lake Huron, naming it the Great Sweetwater Sea in 1615. Of the five lakes, Huron was the first discovered, Michigan the last. Not an arrogant man, Champlain considered himself a geographer, although he was also a soldier, explorer, anthropologist, artist, author, naturalist and cartographer. He wrote profusely and drew maps to help future explorers. In one of his early maps, Champlain depicted all of the Great Lakes except Michigan. In some respects the map was quite accurate and his skill with navigational instruments and his dedication to accuracy (as far as he could determine it) made his maps the most respected Great Lakes maps of his time.

In 1634 Champlain sent his loyal follower, Jean Nicolet, to further explore the Great Lakes. Again, the motivation was to find the Northwest Passage, but instead Nicolet found the final of the five Great Lakes. Nicolet did not explore the entire lake and Nicholas Sanson's resulting map of 1634, based upon Jean Nicolet's explorations, presents a truncated and badly distorted Lake Michigan.

The late 1600s and early 1700s were the period of the Jesuits. As eager as explorers were to find new lands, missionaries, like Father Jacques Marquette, were equally enthusiastic about saving souls by converting the Anishinabe to Christianity. In 1670, as a result of their missionizing and exploring in the area, Father Marquette and Louis Joliet discovered the true, elongated shape of the lake. Further, they changed its name from the ignoble, "Lake of Stinking Things" to Lake Michigan. The name-game was still far from over. A map from 1675 labeled Lake Michigan, Lac St. Joseph, and another French explorer called it "Lac Daupin" in honor of the king's son. Jesuit Father Hennipin described it as Michigonong and local Native Americans called it Michigami. Ultimately, it was Lake Michigan that stuck.

Father Marquette founded the village of St. Ignace and it is there that his bones lie today. They were found on the shore of Lake Michigan near Ludington (or Frankfort or maybe even Cross Village) by Native Americans who cleaned them according to their custom, and then carried them back to the mission and planted them in a coffin of birch bark in a consecrated spot. Father Marquette allegedly died of exhaustion after a long and difficult exploration; but the best that can be said with some certainty is that he died of natural causes.

340

Although other Jesuits, as they explored the Great Lakes, brought the word of their God to the Native Americans, none is as well-remembered as Father Marquette. Cities, rivers, streets and churches are named in his honor and help his memory live on.

From 1669 to 1679 explorer Rene-Robert Cavelier Sieur de La Salle struggled with French bureaucrats and politicians to gain permission for his bold plan to expand the French Empire and increase trade in the New World. Finally, on August 7, 1679, La Salle after obtaining the necessary rights and financial backing to build his ship, the green timbered, 50-ton *Griffon*, set sail for the Great Lakes in search of the shortcut to China.

La Salle was the first explorer to sail all of the Great Lakes. It was his destiny to captain the *Griffon,* sailing her from Lake Erie at the head of the Niagara River, and continuing to travel with the winds westward from Buffalo, past Cleveland to Detroit, through the Detroit River and Lake St. Clair, up Huron to the Straits of Mackinac to Green Bay. There, on the shores of Lake Michigan, he left the *Griffon* in the charge of his pilot who would take her, loaded with furs, on a return trip that would hopefully earn La Salle enough money to clear his debts and finance future endeavors - as well as secure him a place in history.

La Salle, himself, continued exploring the east coast of Lake Michigan to Chicago and across the southern end of the lake by the sand dune country to what is now St. Joseph. Given the scarcity of food, inclement weather, uncharted course and other hardships endured by La Salle, it is a miracle he lived to tell his tale of the magnificent lake system he had navigated. His journey was assisted by friendly Native Americans who provided him with food and guidance.

In 1679, months after the *Griffon's* voyage began; La Salle was devastated to learn she had disappeared without a trace. It is generally believed the ship went down in a violent Lake Huron storm, but no sign of her crew or cargo was ever discovered. In spite of this tragic loss, La Salle's ventures were not wasted effort. They revealed a path for trading (although not to China), and made the Great Lakes seem accessible.

Jacques Cartier, Samuel de Champlain, Jean Nicolet, Father Jacques Marquette and Rene-Robert Cavelier Sieur de La Salle are but a few of the intrepid explorers and missionaries who are remembered for discovering and opening up the spectacular Great Lakes of Michigan. Their adventures fueled the ambitions of hordes of daring men who followed.

The Fur Traders. Today Lake Michigan is a resort paradise and a tourist destination featuring small quaint shops, gourmet restaurants, swimming, sailing, sand dunes, wineries and orchards. But for the first

200 years after Europeans arrived, Lake Michigan's shoreline was prized by the French for its importance in the fur trade. Although mink, muskrat, martin and even otter were hunted, beaver pelts were the coveted commodity of the day.

The wealth that accompanied the fur trade caused men to organize companies, recruit explorers, outfit ships and set sail for a land where they knew hardships awaited. They were warned of winters of ice and snow with freezing gales whipping with a ferocity unlike anything they experienced in France or England. The land was primitive. Food could elude them. Some Native American tribes, like the Iroquois, might fiercely try to thwart their efforts. Despite the many threats, early fur traders, knowing there were fortunes to be made, were not dissuaded from trying.

By the mid-1700s a trade route ran along the western coast of Lake Michigan between the forts at St. Joseph and Michilimackinac. The French, who caught the fur trade fever early, seemed less intent on colonizing and moving families into their new trade areas than their British counterparts who brought settlements to the new land. French, English and Native Americans spread themselves over a huge area of the Great Lakes with traps and trading posts. In the 1780s, it is believed that a million dollars of pelts were sold each year, and by 1800 six million pelts sold at fur markets in New York City, London and Paris for anywhere from a few cents to $500 for especially beautiful specimens.

The Hudson Bay Company, the Northwest Company and the Canadian Mackinaw Company were all formed to exploit the fur industry of the Great Lakes and Canada. Most prominent of the fur traders was John Jacob Astor. A butcher's son born in 1763 in Germany, he left at sixteen to seek a fortune. He made his way to the United States via London. For four months he was trapped in the Chesapeake Bay aboard a ship which had become solidly frozen in the January ice of 1784.

During his months aboard, Astor spent time listening to his fellow passengers and crew and learning the art of the fur trade. He discovered how furs could be picked up in odd lots at the wharves of New York. He stored away the knowledge of bartering with Native Americans for a few knives and beads and blankets to obtain the valuable pelts. He also learned how to judge the value of the furs, how to sort and pack them and how to sell them. Astor was a sharp student, keen on learning the tools of what would become his trade. Through his shrewd, if not always scrupulous business practices, he created for himself a fur monopoly and rode its economic wave until it broke beneath the crush of the lumbering tide. Astor bought out the Mackinaw Company and absorbed it into his new American Fur Company. By the late 1700s Astor's new company was operating twenty trading posts in Western Michigan, including his principal post, Gabagouache (Grand Haven).

Initially, many Native Americans saw the fur trade as an exciting way to obtain goods never before available to them. In time, however, the fur trade proved disastrous to the survival of the indigenous people. The fur trade depleted the local wildlife and caused violent conflict between tribes as they battled to curry favor with European fur traders. But perhaps the worst of the evils to befall the Anishinabe because of their contact with European fur traders was illness. Having no immunity to many of the diseases the Europeans carried, the Native Americans fell victim to new scourges including: scarlet fever, diphtheria, typhoid fever, whooping cough, measles and influenza. About half of the Huron population was wiped out by 1638 because disease accompanied the French into Native American villages. But small pox was the most pernicious disease. In 1639, the Ottawa were in the grip of a massive small pox epidemic.

Besides falling victim to disease, Native Americans became pawns in the fierce battle between the French and the British to control the lucrative fur trade. The War of Independence, in 1776, also had negative repercussions for the Anishinabe. Native Americans found themselves caught between two English-speaking groups, the British and those former British subjects who now identified themselves as Americans.

In the years following the war, Americans used questionable land deals and military force to claim much of Ohio. Alarmed by the advance of the Chemokmon, or Big Knives as some Native Americans called the American militiamen, the tribes around the lakes looked to the British for support. The British, who still held forts in the region, supplied the Native Americans with arms.

When the British and Americans found themselves again at war in 1812, the Native Americans sided with the British. They began battling Americans before the United States even declared war on Great Britain. Chief Tecumseh, who had lost most of his ancestral territory in Ohio to the Americans, convinced the tribes to the north and west that they would soon suffer the same fate if they did not band with him against the Big Knives. Tecumseh was joined in his fight by the Ojibwa, Ottawa, Pottawatomie, Winnebago, Menominee, Sauk and Fox.

The early battles favored the Native Americans and they overwhelmed the soldiers at the forts of Detroit, Mackinac (formerly Michilimackinac) and Chicago where some 600 Pottawatomie killed scores of American soldiers and a few civilians. These assaults provoked the Americans who launched devastating attacks against tribal villages in Michigan. By 1814, when the British were pushed back into Canada and defeated; the embattled tribes found themselves without allies.

Life for the Great Lakes tribes had always been a struggle, but now their very existence was endangered. After the War of 1812, the American hostility towards the tribes ensured that federal authorities would pressure them relentlessly to yield territory. The end of the war brought settlers across the Ohio border, many of whom were farmers attracted by the rich soil at the southern end of the Great Lakes. By 1830 the settlers outnumbered the native people by about twenty-five to one. Many tribes had already surrendered a great deal of their land.

In 1819, Michigan's territorial governor, Lewis Cass traveled to Saginaw to convince Ojibwa leaders to relinquish their remaining Michigan land. He brought along a company of U.S. Army troops and a shipment of "gifts" that included nearly 200 gallons of liquor. When the meeting was over the Ojibwa had signed away about six million acres of land in Michigan in exchange for tribal reserves of about 100,000 acres plus a small sum as an annual annuity.

In the 1822 Treaty of Chicago, Native Americans were divested of their remaining rights to the land in the area of Southwestern Michigan. In exchange they received $5,000 per year for 20 years. With that deal in place, the majority of Native Americans began their trek west of the Mississippi, but some who had adapted to European ways stayed behind and formed small communities of their own along the eastern shore of Lake Michigan where they had lived and hunted for so long.

Timber. In the 1800s when animals became scare and the fur trade was in its death throes, the entrepreneurial spirit was stirred by another natural resource. Michigan's 2400 miles of shoreline stood thick with virgin timber. Magnificent forests of walnut, oak, chestnut, spruce and the "King," white pine, stood ready for harvesting. More than 200,000 square miles of giant trees, whose rings recorded their centuries of patient growth, lured the lumbermen and lumber barons and signaled a new era of prosperity.

Men began swinging axes. With the Great Lakes providing a water highway for transportation, nearly every city along Michigan's coasts sprang up originally as a lumber mill and grist mill. America, still in her youth, was wasteful and believed the forests were limitless, so squandered this great natural resource. No one seemed worried about the time required to grow a forest. No one considered the cut and slash method of lumbering and the risks it posed for horrific fires. In many places the trees were cut only partway through, in a long row. This left them crippled but standing. Then a primary tree was cut so it would crash into the next, and the next, in domino fashion. Sometimes the timber was merely burned to make way for farming. Most of the time it was sold and when the land was cleared it became orchards, vineyards and fields.

Lumbermen scouted and purchased a "prime 40" which was 40 acres of land they could buy from the government at $1.50 per acre. They preferred land surrounded by other government land because it allowed them to clear their 40 acres of prime forest and continue clearing the perimeter of their property on government land. The government did not have rigid guidelines or much concern for the trees being felled.

The clearing by farmers, eager to make themselves a space for farming, played a minor roll in the massive devastation of Michigan's forests when compared to that of the great lumber barons who invaded port towns like Grand Haven and Muskegon. After the lumber barons completed their work, the cities they had created would have to look for a new way to survive. Manistee, for example, turned the cleared land into farms for fruit orchards, Traverse City turned to cherry canning and Muskegon turned to foundries.

Lumbering brought a cast of rough and tumble men to the western Michigan lakeshore region. "Silver Jack," as John Driscoll was known, was a huge man who traveled to the Saginaw mills when he was only eighteen. He lumbered in Muskegon and his reputation grew as he went from one lumber camp to the next. He was said to be an expert in the "Hell's Half Mile' school of fighting: gouging out eyes, head butting, kicking, fist-punching, wrestling and "putting the boots to a man," which meant driving the sharp calks or spikes of his boots into his opponent's face and giving him scars for life, or in some cases even killing him.

Still, most legends, including those that swirled about Silver Jack, insisted that the lumbermen, even those of fabled violence, had a good streak buried just beneath the surface. Jack's friends described him as lovable, generous and kindly and claimed he stood up against bullies on behalf of the weak. Someone with Jack's boot planted firmly in his face might have disagreed.

Jack was also said to be a staunch defender of his somewhat loosely interpreted Catholic faith. An old lumberjack ballad tells the story of a fight provoked by fellow lumberman, Bobby Waite's, assertion that the bible was fiction and hell nothing more than a lot of humbug. Apparently the slur on the religion of Jack's mother earned Bobby Waite a forty-minute fight with the not-so-gentle giant who pummeled him with iron fists, chewed off his ear and otherwise defended his religion as he believed any good Christian should.

While everyday-lumbermen were described as a bellicose, but benevolent bunch, those who became lumber barons were revered as the most prestigious citizens and founding fathers of coastal communities. They were cloaked in a mantle of 1800s genteel glamour. Charles H. Hackley was one such lumber baron and his benefactions continue to brighten the modern complexion of Muskegon today. He arrived in the spring of 1856 ready to seek his timber fortune. He was 19-years-old when his steamship pulled alongside the sawdust heaps of Muskegon harbor. He had seven dollars in his pocket and he began working in the mills the day he arrived. Three years later he and his father bought a share of a sawmill. Ultimately, like other lucky lumber barons, Hackley found his fortune. Homes of wealthy lumber barons still overlook Muskegon Lake and the sand dunes along Lake Michigan. Hackley's is one of the more elegant and is now a museum. (See p. 121 for a picture of the Hackley home.)

Lake Michigan Fishing. Fur trading, lumbering and farming all took a turn as the mainstay of Lake Michigan's shoreline economy. But, fishing predated these industries, co-existed while each reigned supreme, outlasted them and continues today as a source of income to the commercial fisheries and a source of joy to the sport fishers who will tell you there is nothing like a day spent angling.

We can not date the first Native American fishing attempt, but we can be relatively certain it did not take long for the Anishenabe to discover the Great Lakes' wealth of fish. Commercial fishing experienced a growth spurt in the early 1800s and by 1848 Lake Michigan fishing was an important source of food and income. The lake brimmed with trout, herring, whitefish, yellow perch, shiners, suckers and seven species of chub. These fish had evolved collectively to develop a finely balanced and mutually compatible system that began with the retreat of the glaciers. Key to the success of this eco-system was Niagara Falls, which served as a natural barrier to fish and other organisms coming from the Atlantic. The Falls prevented outside species from entering the Great Lakes and disrupting the Lakes' delicate balance.

In the mid-1800s Michigan's annual catch increased by nearly 20% per year until 1889 when the fishing industry produced a record 147 million pounds of fish. During the next 60 years the fishing methods improved, but the annual catch declined so that by the mid-1900s it was down 25% from its heyday.

Pollution of the lakes was a major factor in the decline of the fish population. Lumbering led to soil erosion and topsoil washed into the rivers and streams that eventually fed into the lakes. Pulp and paper mills caused chemical pollution and dumped sawdust into the lakes.

The sawdust rotted and used up oxygen. Mercury, used in the paper industry, was likely the most dangerous contaminant introduced to the lakes. Eventually mercury was banned in the production of paper, but it still found its way into the water because of contamination from power plants burning mercury-rich coal. Consumers began to worry about the mercury content of fish caught in the lakes. In 2002 every state bordering a Great Lake issued an advisory warning about the health dangers of consuming Great Lakes fish.

By 1850 there were more than a million Americans and Canadians living in the Great Lakes basin. Farming was a major industry and it exacerbated the serious erosion problem affecting the lakes. A century later, by the mid-1900s the problem was dramatically compounded by the addition of pesticides and fertilizer to crops. The fertilizers washed into the lakes and increased the growth of water plants, including algae. The decay of these plants, like the rotting of the sawdust dumped by mills, depleted the lakes of vital oxygen and in turn killed great numbers of fish.

The pollution of the Great Lakes increased dramatically with the rise of large cities like Chicago, Milwaukee and Detroit. Large industries coveted sites along the Great Lakes waterway exacerbating the pollution problem.

Like pollution, invasive species including the lamprey eel and zebra mussel took their toll on commercial fishing in the Great Lakes. The lamprey, first introduced to the lakes in 1936, attaches its sucking mouth with razor sharp teeth to a host and then feeds on its blood. Lake trout, once one of the most sought after species caught in the lakes, had no natural defense against the lamprey. By the mid-1950s, lamprey had nearly eliminated the native population of trout in Lake Michigan and significantly reduced other species as well. Even when the lamprey did not succeed in killing trout, the predator still wreaked havoc. Often sport fisherman reeled in a beautiful trout with lamprey hanging from its sides (see the picture next page) and were put off by the thought of eating the damaged trout as an evening meal.

Lamprey attached to a lake trout   Photo by United States Geological Survey

The zebra mussel was first discovered in Lake St. Clair in 1988. It was likely introduced to the lakes in the ballast water of ocean-going ships traveling the St. Lawrence Seaway, although it could have entered attached to chains and anchors of ocean vessels. The zebra mussel adversely affected the lakes ecosystem causing widespread economic loss running in the billions of dollars each year from damaged harbors, boats and power plants where the microscopic larvae make it directly into the facilities. The ruffe and spiny water flea may have also hopped a ride in the ballast of ocean vessels.

Each played a role in upsetting the delicate balance of the water's natural system. More than 140 non-indigenous species of plants and animals have been established in the Great Lakes since the 1800s. Even those that were intentionally introduced often came at the expense of something that was already there.

Native species have been replaced with introduced fish such as smelt, alewife, and Pacific salmon. The alewife entered the upper Great Lakes through the Welland Canal. It was first found in Lake Michigan in 1949. When the trout population in Lake Michigan was nearly destroyed by the lamprey, the alewife no longer had a natural predator and eventually became an estimated 85% of the fish population in Lake Michigan. Anglers no longer found fishing worthwhile since the herring, yellow perch and emerald shiner populations were all decimated. Predators to the alewife were desperately needed and resulted in stocking Lake Michigan with Coho salmon in 1966 and Chinook salmon in 1967. Sport fishing regained popularity as local anglers began catching salmon.

Pollution and non-native species dealt major blows to the Great Lakes' fish population, but recent reports from Lake Michigan suggest that commercial fisheries and sport anglers are again finding abundant populations of whitefish and trout. The status of the yellow perch is less certain. Hopefully the past has yielded valuable lessons about how to manage the fish population so that we can again boast successful commercial fisheries and world-class sport fishing.

Fruit, Farming and Flocks of Tourists. After the lumber industry was extinguished, like the fur industry before it, the Lake Michigan shoreline developed more stable and less environmentally destructive means of supporting itself. Today vineyards and orchards dot the countryside and resorts and tourism thrive. In fact, Lake Michigan is nicknamed the Gold Coast because of the expensive homes, cottages, upscale shops, gourmet restaurants and yachts that grace its shores. Resorts and tourism are major industries and every shore town caters to the whims and needs of visitors. But the *"million dollar sunsets"* cost nothing and are there for everyone to enjoy.

All in it together. The Michigan shores are a melting pot. Originally they were home to the Anishinabe: Ojibwa, Ottawa, Pottawatomie, Winnebago, Menominee, Sauk, Fox and other Native American tribes. In the 1800s Europeans from more than twenty nations came in large numbers. They endured life-threatening, and often life-ending, hardships. They left behind loved ones and crossed the Atlantic. Some, like the Irish, were wretchedly poor and came to escape extreme poverty or outright starvation. Others, like the Germans, Dutch, Finns and Swedes came to escape political turmoil. Still others, like the Danes, Poles, Italians and Norwegians came to create a new life.

The Germans came in highest numbers. They were actively recruited by the state of Michigan, which published and sent a guide to the Commissioner of Immigration, E. H. Thompson, in Germany during years of revolution. The book urged Germans, who needed little convincing, to buy Michigan land. They settled everywhere there was fertile soil and they began farming. Many Norwegians settled in the port towns of Lake Michigan and resumed the work they knew: shipbuilding. The Dutch settled in Holland and northward on Lake Michigan into the area that is now Leland. These immigrants came from many countries and retained many of their customs and traditions. But, in many other ways they assimilated. Because of them, Lake Michigan was transformed from the lonely wilderness of the fur trappers to the vast agricultural area and tourist center that it has become. Today, we enjoy the fruits of our forefathers' labors – from the orchards, to the wines, to the grains - and we enjoy their enduring celebrations – from the Tulip Festival in Holland to the Greek Festival in Muskegon to the Peshawbestowa Pow-Wow in Sutton's Bay.

"Those dunes are to the Midwest
what the Grand Canyon is to Arizona
and the Yosemite to California.
They constitute a signature of time and eternity.
Once lost, the loss would be irrevocable."
-Carl Sandburg

Sand Dunes of Lake Michigan
-Glacier Created Wonders

The Dunes along the eastern shore of Lake Michigan are the longest assemblage of freshwater dunes in the world. They create Michigan's magnificent sand playground. But they are also a complex and unique ecosystem worth exploring.

We all see the images: A toddler packs his or her red plastic pail with wet sand and tips it over to make a sand cake. A ten-year-old, advanced in sand construction, builds castles complete with water filled moats. A thirteen-year-old picks up a handful of dry sand and lets it slip mindlessly and slowly through her fingers, as she worries about how she looks in her first bikini. An eighteen-year-old couple sits on a beach towel; he reaches forward and with a stick draws R.L. loves J.K. in the damp sand. A young mother sorts the grains of sparkling color on the palm of her hand – an absentminded distraction in her otherwise furiously paced life. An elderly couple walks hand and hand at the water's edge, feeling the sand massage the bottoms of their wrinkled feet. Precious moments of life all washed away with the evening waves, but leaving behind memories and a certainty that the sand will be there for a repeat performance the next day, and all the days after, for each stage of our lives.

The most famous of Michigan's dunes is Sleeping Bear in the Sleeping Bear Dune National Lakeshore, sweeping more than sixty-four miles in a golden arc along the shimmering blue waters of Lake Michigan. The Legend of the Sleeping Bear Dune is known to most Michigan school children even today. It is an integral part of the dunes history:

According to Ojibwa legend, a long, long time ago in the land that is now Wisconsin, there lived a mother bear and her two precious cubs. A raging forest fire forced the mother and cubs into Lake Michigan. The cubs were brave and swam strongly towards the Michigan shore. The distance and the swirling water proved too much for them and they fell further and further behind their mother. Eventually they slipped beneath the waves and drowned. Mother Bear reached safety on the Michigan shore and climbed atop a bluff to peer back across the water in search of her cubs. They were nowhere to be seen. The Great Spirit saw her grieving and pitied her devastating loss. He raised North and South Manitou Islands to mark the spot where the cubs vanished and laid a slumber upon Mother Bear. (The "Mother Bear" was a tree-covered bump in the shape of a bear on the dune. It was eroded away by wind and water in the mid-1900s.)

Michigan boasts 275,000 acres of dune formations and half of them are parks or preserves managed by governmental entities or land conservancies. They are there for the public to enjoy.

The ancient bedrock that produced the dunes was buried beneath mile-thick glaciers for a million or so years. About 12,000 years ago the ice began melting and, over time, the glacial waters broke down the bedrock turning it into the sugar-like sand that covers the lake shore today. As they melted, the glaciers also acted as mammoth steam shovels dredging the huge holes in the earth that would eventually become the Great Lakes.

About 5,000 years ago, Lake Michigan's water level was twenty feet higher. Water levels rose and then slowly dissipated, causing erosion and flooding. This activity and the resultant currents carried the sand to the gouged out areas of our five Great Lakes. Dunes formed where the sand could collect and the lakes offered the perfect place for it to accumulate. Loose sand with no "receptacle" would widely scatter. Waves on the lakes moved the sand towards the shore. Breezes, even the gentle ones, whisked the sand into steep dunes. Wind activity causes "migrating" dunes. Movable dunes are not found much further than a mile from the lakeshore because the lake breezes die down by that point, allowing plant life to take hold and cover the dune, anchoring it in place.

From the naked sand at the shoreline to the forest inland, you can see the four zones of the dunes: *beach, foredune, trough* and *backdune.* The first dune zone is the **beach zone** where the sand is simply an infinitesimal number of tiny granules of crushed rock at the water's edge. The waves and the foot traffic of the beach worshipers prevent vegetation from growing. This zone is easily identified; it is the area scattered with beach towels on any hot summer day. Lake Michigan is famous world-wide for its vast beaches or dune beach zone.

The second dune zone, the **foredune**, is the next area you come to as you walk away from the lake. In these low-ridge areas, beach grass or marram grass sprouts bravely on the sand. This sharp grass, although unpleasant to walk through barefoot, is extremely important to the ecosystem because it provides some protection from the wind, allowing sand accumulation and additional vegetation. After the beach grass has gained a foothold, the juniper, dune willow, sand reed, milkweed,

Pitcher's Thistle and other plants take root. With the growth of vegetation the spiders and other burrowing animals, like toads and snakes, begin crawling forth. To survive on this extremely hot patch of land, these creatures burrow deep into the sand where the moisture keeps the inside of the dune cool.

The third dune zone, the **trough**, is the next area you encounter as you walk away from the lake. The troughs are depressions in the land. They become gullies and small ponds for the part of the year they are filled with water. The trough area is also called swale or wetland. Here you will find rushes, and in the more protected areas poplar, cottonwoods and even oak trees. Animal life becomes more abundant in this zone of the dune. It draws birds and, if the pond remains filled with enough water, muskrats find it a suitable habitat. Fox, weasels and other forest mammals slink into the trough to hunt.

The fourth and final dune zone, the **backdune**, has less accumulation of sand because of the decreasing winds. The backdunes prove a suitable place for trees to become a forest. On the edge of the backdunes, closer to the water where the soil is less rich, oaks and aspens grow. Further inland, with less exposure to the harsh winter winds and with the benefit of richer soil, magnificent deciduous forests develop. Here the sugar maple, hemlock, beech and the famous Michigan white pine create beautiful woodlands.

In addition to zones, dunes can also be described by type: linear, perched, parabolic, transverse and falling dunes. **Linear dunes** are the low area that parallels the waters edge. These are the beach dunes or the dune/swale areas. This type of dune is generally less than fifteen feet high. In Sleeping Bear Dunes National Lakeshore, however, these linear dunes reach more than 100 feet.

Perched dunes exist where the glacier has left behind moraines: areas that look as though the waves have cut steep, jagged edges into the land. Winds carry sand against these bluffs, and while the dunes themselves may be less than 100 feet in height, when they lie "perched" atop these glacier-created moraines or cliffs, they may tower more than 400 feet above the waters edge.

Parabolic dunes are u-shaped dune formations common along the eastern side of Lake Michigan. Periods of high water destroyed the plant cover of a linear dune and left the sand exposed to west winds. This "destabilized" dune ends up in a crescent shape called a "blowout." Strong winds blow the sand inland often eroding the next dune. Marram grass takes root along the edges and on the crest causing the sand to accumulate vertically. Mt. Baldy in P. J. Hoffmaster State Park, more than 200 feet high, is a parabolic dune.

A **transverse dune** is linear or scalloped in shape and formed in shallow bays along the edge of the ancient glaciers. They are found mostly in the Upper Peninsula.

Falling dunes are migrating dunes of sand that spill from perched dunes into neighboring lowlands. The Dune Climb at Sleeping Bear Dunes National Lakeshore is a falling dune. When these falling dunes drift completely beyond the plateau to the lowland they are called de-perched dunes. Sleeping Bear Point is a de-perched dune. Twice in the last century sandslides at Sleeping Bear Point have sent large land masses plunging into Lake Michigan. In June 1998 a large slide at Pyramid Point took thousands of tons from the point. In their movement, the dunes can cover and kill trees forming "ghost forests" such as the one on North Manitou Island.

Lake Michigan's great treasure, these famed dunes, are not impervious to wanton disregard and abuse. Just as Michigan's forests were felled and its animals hunted to near extinction, the cherished dunes can be damaged and destroyed. The dunes are beloved as a recreational area for hikers, climbers and walkers. Visitors must be environmentally conscious and leave vegetation intact, keep pets in check and pick up the trash they bring with them.

The bigger threat to the dunes has come, however, from sand mining. Up to one-third of the dunes are at risk from mining. During the rise of the Industrial Age in the early 1900s, various industries discovered Lake Michigan's dunes were a perfect source of high quality sand. Foundries used the sand in castings to make metal car parts. Railroads used the sand in laying tracks. The dunes provided accessible, cheap, and easily transported sand, and there were no legal barriers to its removal. And, at that time some people naively believed that ridding the landscape of the dunes would make the land more accessible and therefore more valuable for future development of homes and other projects.

Pigeon Hill in Muskegon vanished. Creeping Joe, near the Manistee River disappeared - gone forever because the railroads hauled away all of his sand. Maggie Thorpe, an immense dune system located north of the Manistee River from what is now Harbor Village, lay close enough to watch her brother dune, Creeping Joe, vanish. Maggie's own demise came soon after. Although these dunes may have looked barren and desolate to the casual observer, life thrived. For example, Maggie was home to many plants and animals including sandpipers, gulls, and the endangered Piping Plover that hopped about her surface. In earlier days she was covered with Passenger Pigeons that like Maggie, are now extinct. Maggie's foredune contained sea rockets and the endangered Pitcher's Thistle which in turn provided food and shade to snakes, turtles, ladybugs, butterflies and mice. The trough was home to toads, heron, raccoon and the dwarf lake iris, another endangered species. Finally, Maggie's backdune was a mixed forest perched on a rich layer of soil with sand underneath.

Sand mining destroys the ecosystem for any aquatic or terrestrial organism living in the mined area. Ultimately, the dune itself disappears. As a result of sand mining and other industrial use, many of Lake Michigan's dunes vanished.

By the 1960s, it became apparent that mining the dunes was negatively impacting the shoreline. As the dunes took on an important role in drawing tourists (two million visitors annually to the Sleeping Bear Dunes National Lakeshore and more than half a million to P. J. Hoffmaster State Park), it became imperative that efforts be made to save them. A 1991 study by the National Park Service calculated the economic benefit of the Sleeping Bear Dunes National Lakeshore over the years at a total of $38,910,000 in tourist revenue and the creation and support of a thousand jobs. Currently the dollar value has increased significantly and it is now estimated that each visitor to the park spends $64 a day, creating a regional cash flow of about $128 million annually.

Those numbers drew serious attention to dune preservation. In response, the State of Michigan passed the Sand Dune Protection and Management Act in 1976. However, even when efforts at reclamation are successful, they cannot bring back the dunes that have been lost. The forces of nature that created them can never again be duplicated. Their loss is irreparable.

Nowhere else on earth will you find the unique beauty or majesty you can experience in Michigan's dunes. The iridescent water shining its many hues of blue, murky gray and even black provide a dramatic backdrop for the dunes while the delicate and brightly colored flowers receding into forests are a visual feast. Hopefully this beauty will be preserved for future generations to enjoy.

To experience the Michigan Dunes, you can visit the following parks (beginning with the southern-most dunes and traveling north): Warren Dunes State Park (269) 426-4013, Weko Beach (269) 465-3406, Grand Mere State Park (269) 426-4013, Van Buren State Park (269) 637-2788, Mt. Baldy and Oval Beach (269) 857-2603, Saugatuck Dunes State Park (269) 637-2788, Laketown Beach Township Park (616) 335-3050, Holland State Park (616) 399-9390, Tunnel Park County Park (616) 738-4810, Kirk County Park (616) 738-4810, Rosy Mound Natural Area County Park (616) 738-4810, Kitchel-Lindquist Dunes (City of Ferrysburg Preserve) (616) 842-5803,

P. J. Hoffmaster State Park (231) 798-3711, Kruse City Park (231) 724-6704, Muskegon State Park (231) 744-3480, Duck Lake State Park (231) 744-3480, Meinert County Park (231) 894-4881, Silver Lake State Park (231) 873-3083, Charles Mears State Park (231) 869-2051, Ludington State Park (231) 843-2423, Nordhouse Dunes Manistee National Forest (231) 723-2211, Magoon Creek Natural Area (231) 723-2211, Sleeping Bear Dunes National Lakeshore (231) 326-5134, Old Indian Trail (231) 326-5134, Platte Plains (231) 326-5134, Empire Bluffs (231) 326-5134, North Bar Lake (231) 326-5134, Pierce Stocking Scenic Drive (231) 326-5134, The Dune Climb (231) 326-5134, Sleeping Bear Point (231) 326-5134, Pyramid Point (231) 326-5134, Good Harbor Bay (no phone information), South Manitou Island (231) 326-5134, Zetterberg Preserve Nature Conservancy (517) 316-0300, Leelanau State Park, (231) 386-5422, Wilcox-Palmer-Shah Grand Traverse Regional Land Conservancy Nature Preserve toll-free (888) 929-3866, North Point Preserve Township Park (231) 547-3253, Petoskey State Park, (231) 347-2311, Thorne Swift Conservancy (231) 526-6401 and Sturgeon Bay Dunes State Park (231) 436-5381.

Sand Dunes near South Haven: water, beach and foredune
Photo Courtesy of Joe Jurkiewicz

355

I had a classmate who fitted for college by the lamps of a lighthouse,
which was more light we think than the University afforded.

-Henry David Thoreau

Lighthouses of Lake Michigan
-The Soul of the Harbor

The first recorded lighthouse graced the harbor of the Egyptian city of Alexandria more than 2,200 years ago. It was the tallest lighthouse ever built, stretching 450 feet into the Mediterranean sky. It continued beaming its illumination for sailors until an earthquake tumbled it a thousand years later.

Michigan's first lighthouse was the Fort Gratiot Lighthouse near Port Huron, established in 1825. For more than a century, Great Lakes lighthouses kept lonely vigil from the edge of a sand dune, a perch high on a precipitous bluff, the end of a long pier, or an isolated shoal. These silent sentinels brought many ships to a safe harbor during a winter storm or misty fog.

From the earliest days of European exploration along Michigan's shores, shipping was integral to the economy. To aid shipping it was critical to have the ability to warn sailors of shoals and other dangers when visibility was impaired. In 1789, President George Washington created the United States Lighthouse Service. One of the duties of this new agency was to carry food, fuel, equipment and spare parts to the lighthouse keepers at remote stations.

Wicks fueled by whale oil and, later, kerosene were the original source of lighthouse illumination. But by 1900, electric-powered lamps began shining from the towers. Light beams were magnified by simple metal reflectors until the mid-1800s when the superior Fresnel lens became available. The Waugoshance Lighthouse, in Lake Michigan waters near the Straits of Mackinac, was the first on the Great Lakes to use the revolutionary Fresnel lens, made of glass prisms that directed beacons much farther and brighter than lamps alone.

Keepers lit lamps at sunset and extinguished them at sunrise. Maintenance was critical; lights could not be allowed to go out because of malfunction or oversight. There was no day of rest and illness did not excuse the performance of duty. Vacations for lighthouse keepers were non-existent, yet the lighthouses were home not only to the keeper, but often to the keeper's entire family.

Lighthouses were steeped in romance and intrigue and the keeper was frequently a hero; saving lives as routinely as the rest of us fix an evening meal. Arguably the keeper enjoyed a perfect life: sit around and drink coffee, read endless classics, gaze out at the beautiful lake, make sure the light was lit and be a hero. The reality was often quite different. Lighthouse keepers were a unique breed, able to withstand a primitive, and at times, dangerous lifestyle. They endured loneliness with no close neighbors and endless hours with little to do. After the invention of the television, many keepers left it blaring just for the sound of other human voices. This isolation imbued the lighthouse with a special mystique.

Even the best efforts of the lighthouse keepers and the growing number of lights along more than a thousand miles of shoreline could not prevent many ships from running aground or sinking. In the 1870s, the U.S. Life Saving Services began operations in Michigan. Each station was responsible for a section of coastline and the crews regularly walked the beach checking for signs of trouble or, in some cases, the wreckage of ships already lost. When a ship was sighted too close to land, flares were fired to warn the captain of the danger. If a ship foundered near shore a Lyle gun (like a small cannon) fired a thin rope across the water to the stranded ship. The mates on the ship used the rope to haul over a much thicker line. A sling called a "breeches buoy" could then be attached to the sturdier line. The buoy rode above the water and hauled the ship's crew to shore. Demonstrations of the breeches buoy are offered during the summer at Sleeping Bear Point Life Saving Museum. If disabled ships were not within reach of the Lyle gun, the crew of the Life Saving Station had to consider whether the conditions would permit rescue by a small motor boat.

Today the lighthouse keeper is obsolete; by the 1920s they began losing their jobs to advancing technology. One by one, Michigan lighthouses continued to be automated or abandoned until 1983 when the last Michigan keeper, at Point Betsie, left his light. Global positioning, sensors, solar powered beacons, helicopters, advanced radar, sonar, fixed wing aircraft and even satellites have taken us far beyond the solitary keeper who climbed the winding stairs to light a lamp. Although there are no longer manned lighthouses on Lake Michigan, most of the lighthouses continue to illuminate the shores. During a storm, when power can be cut and global positioning gone awry, they remain a final line of protection guiding ships to safety.

It is an interesting side note that many of Lake Michigan's lighthouses are painted red, a feature unique to this side of the state. While the reasoning behind painting these towers red is not entirely clear, speculation suggests that making red lighthouses unique to Lake Michigan made it easier for sailors to note their position. It seems, however, that any sailors worth his/her pay would know which Great Lake they were sailing. If the color simply made the lighthouses stand out more clearly as markers along the shore, one has to wonder why all lighthouses were not painted red.

We will never know how many lives were saved by the efforts of the remarkable men and women who served as lighthouse keepers over the years. For most of them their job was simply a way of life. Today dedicated volunteers work to preserve the lighthouses and keep alive the memory of their keepers.

Wherever you travel in Michigan you are never more than about ninety miles from a beach, and where you find a beach you will find lighthouses nearby. It is easy to visit a lighthouse when the sun is shining and the weather is warm. However, some of the most hauntingly beautiful pictures of lighthouses are taken during the worst winter storms, ice clinging to their brave exteriors making their critical jobs even more difficult.

St. Joseph North Pier Lights

There is a story suggesting that even before there was an official lighthouse, a Great Lakes captain from the St. Joseph area established his own system to steer him home safely. He lived close to the lakeshore and when he was arriving in port his family would hang lanterns in the second-story window of their home to guide him. In 1832, an official lighthouse was constructed on a bluff overlooking Lake Michigan. It was the first lighthouse on Lake Michigan's shores and it remained in operation until 1924 and was demolished in 1955. In 1846, a wooden pier was built extending into the lake at a point between St. Joseph and Benton Harbor, and at the end of this pier a new lighthouse was erected. It is a two-story steel structure with a red hip roof and white siding. An octagonal tower rises two additional stories above the base building. A black iron parapet tops the tower. A raised walkway extends about 1,000 feet from the shore to the second story of the lighthouse. This allowed the keeper to attend his duties even when waves blew over the pier. In 1907, the pier was extended and a steel outer light was added. This lighthouse still stands today and continues to send beacons into the dark. (See photo by Gary Martin on the next page.)

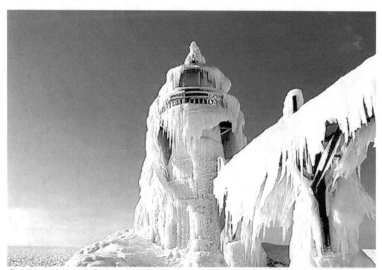

St. Joseph Lighthouse during a winter storm
Photo Courtesy of Gary Martin Photography

South Haven South Pier Light

Standing solemn at the end of a concrete pier that stretches several hundred feet into Lake Michigan is the South Haven South Pier Light. The tower was originally constructed in 1871 by the United States Lighthouse Board. It was a wood edifice, with a square tower and an open base. It had two stories, the upper for the lamp and the lower for storage. It stood 37 feet tall. The tower was reconstructed of steel in 1903 and is two feet shorter than the original version. It remains in use today. South Haven was prominent as a shipping port and the Army Corps of Engineers assumed responsibility for harbor improvements in 1867. As the construction of the second lighthouse came to an end, the Lighthouse Board requested an appropriation for the construction of a pierhead beacon and a keepers dwelling. A site was selected and plans were made to begin construction of the station in early 1870. However, Congress, short on money that year, recalled all unexpended funds from federal agencies and without the necessary financing, the work on the South Haven Lighthouse was put on hold until a new appropriation could be made. After this short delay, construction started in 1871. In 1932, Robert Young was the last keeper assigned to South Haven. That same year responsibility for the nation's lighthouses was turned over to Coast Guard personnel but Young remained until 1940, at which time he turned the keepers dwelling and the light over to the Coast Guard. The South Pier Light is a red steel structure topped by a black parapet. Like the St. Joseph Light the lighthouse in South Haven was accessible by a special catwalk that led from the shore to the second floor. The now automated light is still active. (See related ghost story, p. 412, Part II of this guide.)

South Haven Lighthouse   *Photo by Bob Royce*

Holland Harbor Lighthouse

Better known as Big Red, the Holland Harbor Lighthouse is a three-story building with a two-story square tower rising out of its gray shingled roof. Its name comes from the fact that the entire structure is painted bright red. It rose from its simple origins as a wooden tower to the present steel model of today. The lighthouse's lower story housed giant boilers to power the steam fog signal. From the third story of the building are twin gables with three windows in each gable. The lighthouse sits on the pier that runs along the south bank of the channel connecting Lake Michigan and Lake Macatawa. Melgert Van Regenmorter was appointed the first keeper on December 3, 1870 and the first beam went out sometime shortly thereafter. A keeper's dwelling was built in the 1870s, and in 1874 a 550-foot elevated walkway was constructed to lead from the beacon service room to the shore. The lights were electrified in 1932. In addition to its architectural interest, Big Red is popular because of its proximity to pleasant parks and sand dunes. One of the best views is from Holland State Park. Direct access to the lighthouse, however, is severely restricted because you have to pass private property to get to it.

Grand Haven Lights

Two small red columns rise from the azure water of Lake Michigan at Grand Haven State Park. The South Pier Light and the South Pier

360

Inner Light are a striking sight, standing several hundred feet apart on a long stone pier. The cylindrical inner light was built on shore in 1839. It is fifty-one feet tall, bright red, and steel, with a parapet and a lantern room. In 1905 it was rebuilt and moved to the pier. The second light, the squat South Pier Light, stands on a large, white concrete base, a square red building with a smallish tower on the top. It would have been large enough to accommodate a keeper's family, but was actually built to house the huge marine boilers that powered steam fog signals. The two lights are connected to each other and to the shore by an elevated walkway or catwalk and although now automated, they continue shining. (Also see back cover photo by Gary Martin.)

Grand Haven Pier Lights; the South Pier Light barely visible behind the
Inner Light   *Photo by Bob Royce*

Muskegon South Pier Light

Two breakwaters form an arc to protect the thin strip of water that connects Lake Michigan to Muskegon Lake. A short pier juts out to the south side of the mouth to the channel to form the base for the Muskegon South Pier Light. Muskegon's original lighthouse was built in 1852, and the current lighthouse was built in 1903. It is a cylindrical steel-sided tower painted red. Two smaller lights are located on the breakwaters farther out from shore. The site is still an active aid to navigation, but it is not open to the public.

White River Light Station

Built in 1875 by Captain William Robinson, this lighthouse currently houses a maritime museum. You can see many 19th and early 20th century photographs related to the lighthouse and area, and also view the collection of maritime artifacts. The lighthouse tower is octagonal shaped, 38 feet tall and made of limestone. Climbing the old spiral stairs, you will be rewarded by a spectacular view of Lake Michigan and White Lake. The lighthouse was first automated in 1945 and was deactivated in 1960. (See p. 135, Part I for a picture of the lighthouse and hours of the museum.)

Little Sable Point Light

Little Sable Point Light stands 107 feet tall in Silver Lake State Park surrounded by dunes. It is a simple lighthouse that reflects the tall cylindrical structure so common to Michigan lighthouses. It is one of the oldest brick lighthouses on Lake Michigan. Its red brick tower is topped by a black cast-iron parapet with arc-shaped supports. In 1874 it was considered one of the loneliest stations for a keeper because there was no village nearby. But, for anyone seeking solitude and space in the middle of unsurpassed beauty it was an ideal assignment. The keeper's house was demolished during the 1950s. Although no longer manned, the tower still sends its light out into the night. The lighthouse is open to the public on weekends during the summer.

Pentwater North and South Pier Lights

The Pentwater lights stand at the mouth of the Pentwater River, the southern boundary of Charles Mears State Park. The south light is situated on a breakwater and looks skeletal with its stark functional steel construction reminiscent of a water tower base, or a giant erector set creation. The steel is painted red and white and rises about 25 feet above the water. The north pier light is about the same height, but its tower looks more like a traditional cylindrical shaped lighthouse. In 1917 the north pier light was automated by an acetylene power system. It was equipped with a sun valve which automatically turned the light on when the temperature went down at dusk and turned it off with the increasing temperatures of daylight. Both lights continue to send out their illuminating signals today.

Ludington North Pierhead Light

First established in 1871, the Ludington Light is a three story square tower with a base wider than its top. It sits at the end of the pier on a black concrete base angled towards the shore. The base was constructed in the shape of the bow of a large ship to fight off waves and ice. The steel sides are painted white. In August 1994 the light was being repaired when it suddenly listed six inches to one side, but the shift caused no serious damage. It is still an active lighthouse.

Big Sable Point Lighthouse

The Big Sable Light would look very much like any grand two-story beach house if it did not have the soaring tower behind it. That huge 112 foot tower has a parapet with widow's walk sitting atop the column. The lighthouse is white with a wide black band in its middle section, giving it a candy cane appearance. In addition to the light, Ludington used a horn to guide sailors when the harbor was blanketed in thick fog. A bugle shaped, metal horn stood near the train track and when fog rolled in, the local citizens brought a steam locomotive up to the horn and gave a blast of the train's whistle. The whistle, magnified by the horn, could be heard for miles into the lake.

Manistee North Pierhead Light

At the mouth of the Manistee River, at the end of the north pier stands the white column steel tower of the North Pierhead Light. Established in 1873, it is 39 feet tall and has a catwalk stretching about 300 yards from shore to the side of the structure to make life easier for keepers during rough weather. Originally the walk was made of wood, but it took such a beating from Lake Michigan's waves that it was replaced by a modern structure with lots of steel and wire. The Manistee North Pierhead Light continues to light the dark.

Point Betsie Lighthouse

Built in 1858, Betsie was not fully automated until 1983. The name, Betsie, did not come from a desire to honor someone's wife or mother. Instead, it came from the French name Pointe Aux Becs Scies meaning "Saw Beak Point." The English speaking settlers in the area shortened and slurred the Becs Scies to Betsie. It was the last manned lighthouse on Lake Michigan and marked the end of an era. After automation, Betsie became a Coast Guard residence until 1996 when her boiler failed and the families living there were forced to abandon her. The two-story white keeper's house sits on a slight knoll offering an expansive view of the area. The red-shingled hip roof with dormers adds an element of drama to the 3000 square foot dwelling that could accommodate two families. Covered porches add a homey touch. Attached to Betsie's side is a three story tower, tall enough to allow someone looking out from the parapet to see over the house. At 37 feet, she is one of the shorter lighthouses on the lake. Steel breakwaters were constructed from the base of the tower toward the lake in an attempt to minimize the power of angry waves. Located a mile and a half from the campground in Ludington State Park, Betsie and keepers cottage are in need of some repair, but efforts are being made to restore them. They are surrounded by shifting dunes and the tranquility of the location makes it one of the more scenic and peaceful lights on the lake. The lighthouse remains active today.

Grand Traverse Lighthouse

Located on Cat's Head Point, and itself nicknamed Cat's Head, this lighthouse marks the entrance to Grand Traverse Bay. It sits in Leelanau State Park. Erected in 1853, this stately light is an imposing structure and boasts a two-story dwelling with additional basement and attic. At one side of the house is a square mounted tower with a parapet atop. The first keeper was Phil Beers, who was also a U. S. deputy marshal. It seems his law enforcement expertise was a necessary qualification for the job. During its construction in 1852, the lighthouse was burglarized by the religious followers of James Jesse Strang, the self-proclaimed king and religious zealot of nearby Beaver Island. Strang and his band of crooks apparently ignored "Thou Shalt Not Steal," and took everything that was not too heavy to carry, including some of the lighthouse equipment. Sheriff/keeper Beers was able to drive them off before they managed to steal the precious Fresnel lens. A new light was built in 1972 out a bit further on the tip of land that juts into Lake Michigan. While functional, it lacks character and is not nearly as impressive or as elegant as the original light. The grand white brick house with red shingles stands behind the new skeletal version. Fortunately, the original lighthouse has been preserved and is today an interesting museum with antiques, toys, early photos and other memorabilia. Visitors step back in time and imagine what it was like to be a keeper of the light. They can climb into the tower and retrace the steps of keeper Beers as he lit the light.

Old Mission Point Lighthouse

Construction began in 1870 on the Old Mission Point Lighthouse. A small tower stands on the crest of the roof on the front side of the building. Atop the tower sets a black cast iron parapet. It has the outward shape and appearance common to many of Michigan's old one-room schools and country churches. A lighthouse was a necessity at this location because shoals projected two miles from the northern tip of Old Mission Peninsula making it treacherous for sailors seeking their way south into Grand Traverse Bay. The first keeper was Jerome Pratt Sr. who officially sent out the first beam on September 10, 1870. The lighthouse is secluded: enveloped in dense forest. The light is located on the 45th parallel of latitude, equidistance between the equator and the North Pole. It is currently a residence for park employees and not accessible to the public. The beach in front of the lighthouse and the area on all four sides of the old station are public and afford views.

Old Mission Point Lighthouse   *Photo by Bob Royce*

Petoskey Pierhead

This modern structure remains active and replaced earlier lights dating from the late 1880s. It is a steel tower painted white sitting on a concrete square base at the end of Petoskey's west pier.

Charlevoix South Pier Light

A mere hundred feet from shore, on a concrete pier, stands the Charlevoix South Pierhead Light. It rests atop a short squat looking tower, the bottom third of which is open steel frame. A solar panel on the front of the tower provides the source for automated light. The first lighthouse was established in 1885 and was moved to the pier in 1914. The current square tower was built in 1948 and sits a little more than 100 feet from shore. Charlevoix's light is federally owned and is automated, but it is not open to the public.

Charlevoix Light   *Photo By Bob Royce*

Waugoshance Lighthouse

In the early 1800s sailors frequently ran aground in the shallow waters of Waugoshance Shoal. Safety required a lighthouse to mark the danger and guide ships into the Straits of Mackinac. The lighthouse had to be constructed on an underwater crib and that presented a daunting challenge. It had been tried on the East Coast, but it would be difficult in Northern Lake Michigan with its thick winter ice. In 1832 a lightship was stationed on the shoal to protect ships from the dangerous waters until the lighthouse could be constructed. In 1850 the decision was made to begin construction of a more permanent lighthouse. The lighthouse was dropped into place in 1851 and was rebuilt in 1867. By October 1891 the crib and pier supporting the Waugoshance light had again deteriorated and were in danger of toppling. A second lightship was called into service while repairs were made. The 76-foot Waugoshance lighthouse was the first on the Great Lakes to use the Fresnel lens that directed beacons much farther and brighter than lamps alone. Waugoshance was decommissioned in 1912 when the more powerful White Shoals light a few miles north made her beam redundant. During WWII the hapless, abandoned lighthouse became the bombing target of hotshot flyboys during military pilot training. One hit is believed to have started a massive fire that gutted the interior of the tower and the keeper's dwelling. The forces of nature continued battering the lighthouse, but the valiant light, a bit worse for the attacks, continues to stand. In spite of the severe damage, there is a

Waugoshance Lighthouse Preservation Society attempting to restore the lighthouse to her former grandeur.

Old Mackinac Point

Constructed in 1890 to house a fog signal, the light was added in 1892. The lighthouse is located in Fort Michilimackinac Park at the southeast foot of the Mackinac Bridge. It has a stone foundation and a round, cylindrical tower that stands forty feet high. A two-story brick dwelling is attached and served as the keeper's house. The light was deactivated in 1957 and currently serves as a maritime museum open to the public. It has been proposed as the site for a national lighthouse museum.

Lighthouse with the Mackinac Bridge in the background
Photo by Bob Royce

"Say that 'I loved old ships',
write nothing more upon my tombstone
and they who read it will know
that I loved the roar of the breakers
in bygone sailing days"
                                        -W. H. Van Dyke

Shipwrecks of Lake Michigan
-Unlucky 13

Ocean sailors speak of Great Lakes sailors with derision. The latter are not *real* sailors. They do not face the challenge of the mighty salt water oceans with their tides, unpredictability and sudden storms. And for the lakes sailor, the shore and escape are always nearby.

But the ocean sailors' ridicule evaporates the first time they sail the Great Lakes and face the tempestuous wrath these great inland seas can blow their way. Legion is the number of ocean sailors caught in a freshwater hurricane who have sworn "never again" to sailing the Sweetwater Seas. Lake Michigan has single-handedly claimed 800 ships, slightly more than 20% of the ships that have gone down on the Lakes.

The Great Lakes lie in the heart of the country at a point where cyclonic storms come from nowhere, bearing down with a ferocity that flips giant freighters like plastic toy boats in a bathtub. The cause for such cyclones is often the collision of two or more massive weather fronts. Frigid air masses come rushing down from polar-chilled northern Saskatchewan and Manitoba. These icy squalls collide with the warmer, moister air jetting east from the Rockies, or on occasion a front speeding up from the Gulf.

The "Big Blow" of 1913 was the result of weather fronts from all three (Canada, Rockies and the Gulf) smashing into each other directly over the lakes, causing the loss of ten giant freighters and their crews on that hellish night in November. Eight ships were lost in Lake Huron which bore the brunt of the weather disaster, and two more went down on Lake Michigan. There is a great deal of lake lore about the Storms of November. One of those demon storms destroyed the Edmund Fitzgerald on Lake Superior in 1975.

In November, when winter is threatening, but fall has not quite given up the fight, sailors play Russian roulette to complete a last trip of the season. Often they push the limits. Often they ignore the warnings. And while infrequent, it is still too often, that they do not come home alive.

368

The shipwrecks described in this chapter all belong to Lake Michigan. Some went down on the Michigan side of the lake at places like Grand Haven, St. Joseph and Pentwater, some went down near Chicago and others went down near Wisconsin harbors. All were claimed by the same lake and she knows no boundaries. All are her victims. Although many hundreds of ships sank beneath her raging waters, a complete listing is not possible here. These are the stories of 13:

The Phoenix   **November 21, 1847**

In medieval times the mythical phoenix was common in Egyptian, Asian and Greek culture. When the eagle-sized Phoenix grew old, it made a nest and set it on fire. The flames would consume the bird which would then be reborn from the ashes.

In a stroke of macabre irony, the steamer *Phoenix*, namesake of that mythical bird, was one of the first vessels to burn on the Great Lakes. She caught fire November 21, 1847, but nothing rose from her smoldering ashes. At the time of her demise, the *Phoenix* was still in her infancy, a mere two years old.

Almost all westbound travel in those days was by boat through the Great Lakes. The wave of immigration headed westward caused ships to stretch their capacity. On her final voyage of the season, the *Phoenix* was packed to bursting with 275 passengers, about seventy Americans and more than two hundred Dutch immigrants. Only a handful of the latter had cabins. The remaining passengers crowded in steerage or found space wherever they could on deck. Even the cargo hold was filled to bursting. The crew of 29 looked forward to this last trip of the season, but their anticipation was tempered by the knowledge that late November trips were fraught with danger.

The *Phoenix* left Buffalo on November 11th. On the 13th she was still in Lake Erie. A week later, on Saturday, November 20th, the *Phoenix* finally arrived in Manitowoc with her cargo of coffee, molasses, sugar and hardware destined for that port. Ugly weather forced her to remain in harbor for several hours after the cargo was removed. About 1:00 am on November 21st, Captain Sweet gave the order to continue the voyage that was intended to end at Chicago. Sheboygan, however, was the next stop and it was only twenty-five miles away. Captain Sweet expected to make it by daylight.

It was about 4:00 am when flames were noticed on the underside of the deck over the boiler. About the same time, flames sprouted out of the ventilators that moved hot air from the boiler room. Crew members, with the assistance of some passengers, immediately started fighting the blaze. Bucket brigades were set up, but the fire had a good start and raged out of control in spite of the efforts.

The ship was doomed. Some passengers continued trying to extinguish the flames; others threw themselves into the water. The only two lifeboats on board were launched. Captain Sweet manned one and his first mate the other. Their stated intent was to ferry people back and forth from the burning ship to shore. The lifeboats together could accommodate slightly less than 50 of the passengers at a time. The fire spread so quickly that there would never be a second trip. From the doomed vessel shrieks of terror sang to a backdrop of crackling fire and a softer chorus of unanswered prayers.

The passengers still aboard, deserted by their captain, had to literally choose between the devil and the deep blue sea – remain on board and burn or jump overboard to a certain death in the frigid waters. The Hazelton sisters, returning from school in the East to their home in Sheboygan, jumped. They clasped each other in a tight embrace and leapt to their deaths almost within sight of their home harbor. A young mother hugged her wailing infant close to her body and dropped from the burning deck into the restless waters that claimed them both. Family members kissed and hugged one last time before dropping to certain death in the churning waves.

Other ships hovered in the area and rushed to offer assistance to the blazing *Phoenix*. The *Delaware*, first to arrive, found only three survivors: three half-dead crewmen clung tenuously to the rudder chains of the charred hull. Everyone else was dead. Lake Michigan was littered with bodies. The final death toll was estimated at 258, most of whom were Dutch immigrants.

The high casualty rate was attributed to the lack of sufficient life boats, but the cause of the fire fell squarely on the shoulders of the Second Engineer who negligently allowed the boilers to overheat. *Why* he did not properly monitor the boilers is the subject of much speculation. Perhaps he fell asleep. Perhaps he imbibed in a few too many drinks when they were delayed in Manitowoc that afternoon. Perhaps his attention was merely directed elsewhere. Whatever caused him to shirk his duty, a diligent engineer would have tended the boilers and averted the disaster.

The Niagara   **September 24, 1856**

The *Niagara* was built in 1846 and during her decade of sailing she earned a legacy that would endure after her tragic demise. She had brought thousands of German and Scandinavian immigrants from Canada and New York to start new lives in Wisconsin and Michigan. She was one of the strongest and most powerful ships built in the mid-1800s. As her strength sapped the night of her death she witnessed heroism; she witnessed evil; and she witnessed rank, unmitigated terror.

The *Niagara* left Sheboygan, Wisconsin bound for Chicago with one-hundred cabin and nearly two-hundred steerage passengers aboard. Captain Fred S. Miller, expecting a calm and uneventful trip, had decided to grab a quick afternoon nap. In the late afternoon, just as the village of Port Washington came into sight, he was awakened by screams of "Fire!" A cloud of black smoke and blazing flames rolled up from the engine room. Captain Miller wasted no time getting the fire hose in position and the engineer began feeble attempts to douse the flames. The Captain rushed to the pilothouse and ordered the ship turned toward shore. Within a few minutes the engine had stopped and the burning ship was left floundering - safety just a short distance away.

It was not uncommon in the mid-1800s for a ship to lack any life preservers and insufficient lifeboats, so the frantic Captain, assisted by several passengers, began pulling down stateroom doors and pitching them, along with gangplanks, chairs, washstands and anything else that the looked likely to float, into the lake. They had only a few short minutes to accomplish these last-ditch efforts before the center portion of the boat was completely engulfed in fire. Most of the crew was trapped forward with no movement possible between the stern and the bow. Fear crazed passengers began attempts to launch lifeboats on their own. The largest of the life boats capsized upon hitting water.

Acts of courage and cowardice commingled that night. One lifeboat, safely lowered into the water with women and children aboard, was rushed by a group of men who jumped into it from the deck above. The flimsy little lifeboat flipped, sending all but four of its occupants to the depths of Lake Michigan.

An even more remarkable act of cowardice was attributed to former Wisconsin congressman, John B. Macy, who on his better days was described as a brave man with a cool head. Perhaps the scenes he witnessed that night addled his normally clear brain. Macy, a rather portly gentleman who could not swim, is said to have screamed, "Oh, God, someone save me. Ten thousand – a hundred thousand to the man who will save my life." Getting no takers he spotted a life boat filled with women and children being lowered into the water; one end was lower than the other. He jumped, and his prodigious weight caused the ropes to break, casting everyone inside the unbalanced lifecraft to a watery grave. The ex-congressman was never seen again. Mishaps with lifeboats may have been the single largest cause of death from the disaster.

Standing at the railing next to Macy when the congressman made his ignoble offer of reward, was a tiny lad maybe two years old. His parents were nowhere in sight. A deck-hand ignored Macy's pleas, but picked up the child and jumped into the water clutching the toddler tightly. The deck-hand managed to grab a piece of floating gangplank and courageously paddled them towards shore. By the next morning the two were found where they had drifted onto the beach at Port Washington. Both lived, but the deck-hand left town and his name was never known. He remains the anonymous hero of the tragedy.

The child was taken in by a couple in the area and identified as Frank Willette by the name on a small gold cross that hung from his neck. His new caretakers took out ads in papers throughout the country, but no one claimed the child. Several decades passed and the young man, who now went by the name of Frank Willis, made his own attempt to locate family by running ads similar to those initially run so many years earlier. Defying all odds, he was contacted by an aunt residing in Nebraska and a cousin in Manitowoc. They confirmed his real name was Frank Willette, as had been suggested by his cross. His parents, a brother and a sister had died in the shipwreck.

Aboard the *Niagara* the evening of September 24th, with safety only a mile or so away and beaches clearly in sight of those slipping under water for the last time, at least 150 either drowned or burned. If that is not a sad enough ending to this story, there was also speculation that the fire was intentionally set. On a previous trip, just after the ship had left port, a steward found a note on the table of his room: "Look out. Save yourself. The boat will be burned tonight. Everything is in readiness." Had a mad-person sent the note and then lacked the courage to carry out the threat until the next trip? Some questions will never be answered.

The Lady Elgin   September 7, 1860

All ships lost, sunk, or gone missing are cloaked in sadness, loss and despair. Some even engender rage or anger when it is revealed that human carelessness or plain stupidity like in the stories of the *Phoenix* and the *Niagara* above played a significant role. Other catastrophes could not have been avoided. Some of these disasters are steeped in irony like the *Chicora* below. A few capture our imaginations like the *Christmas Tree Ship* because of the cargo she carried and the human circumstances surrounding her last voyage. But there is no other ship that carries the overtones of intrigue, espionage or possible sabotage like the *Lady Elgin*.

The *Lady Elgin* was a monster-sized, side-wheeled steamer, 252-feet in length and boasting more than a thousand ton displacement. She was one of the largest vessels afloat on the Great Lakes in the mid-1800s. She was built to honor the wife of the Governor General of Canada, Lord Elgin.

The *Lady* had her detractors. They charged she was cursed from the day of her launching in 1851. Her boilers and engine had been salvaged from the *Cleopatra*, an ocean slave trader that was confiscated by the U.S. Navy. The *Cleopatra* was clouded in grim stories of human beings torn from their homelands to be sold as chattel in a strange land. Perhaps the evil that clung to and shrouded the *Cleopatra* marked the *Lady Elgin* because she dared to use those tainted parts.

When the *Lady* went down, stories hinted, or in some cases boldly asserted, she was rammed intentionally by the schooner, *Augusta*, which was sent to destroy her. The slavery issue seemed again entwined with the *Lady Elgin*. This time perhaps a reckoning was demanded. A number of southern states had already pulled out of the union and more would follow by the end of 1860. Michigan and Wisconsin were threatening secession, but on anti-slavery grounds. The country appeared to be coming apart at the seams and the political climate was going against President Buchanan.

Wisconsin Governor Alexander Randall felt Buchanan was useless since he refused to take a stand against slave owners. Within the borders of his own state, however, Randall had problems with a state militia called the Independent Union Guards that backed President Buchanan. In early March, 1860, Randall ordered all guns and munitions of the Union Guard surrendered to the state and per that order, they were seized.

The Union Guard, furious at losing their weapons scheduled a special excursion trip aboard the *Lady Elgin* to raise money to replace their arms. With many Union Guard members and a large number of their supporters aboard, the calamity led to suspicions of conspiracy. A persistent allegation making the rounds claimed the sinking of the *Lady Elgin* was no accident.

This much is fact: On September 7, 1860, the day the *Lady Elgin* went down, she was headed north from Chicago with about three hundred excursionists, fifty ordinary passengers and a crew of thirty-five officers - all bound for Milwaukee. Most of the excursionists were members of the Milwaukee Light Guardsmen, the German Black Jaegers or the German Green Jaegers, all of whom were returning from a week in the Windy City where they tried to raise money for guns and equipment. This group was preparing to join Southern forces in the Civil War.

The storm into which the *Lady Elgin* headed when departing Chicago turned into a full blown, northwesterly gale by 2:00 am. The *Lady Elgin* was captained by Jack Wilson; he was experienced and unconcerned about the storm. He headed directly into the wind and seemed to be handling the turbulence with relative ease.

At 2:30 am the two-masted, lumber schooner, *Augusta*, burst from the darkness and crashed into the *Lady's* port side. Darius Malott captained the *Augusta* and he was traveling downward on Lake Michigan with a heavy load of lumber he had picked up in Port Huron. His crew may have been busy getting the sails reefed and the ship under control and simply failed to spot the lights of the *Lady Elgin* in time to avoid disaster. Captain Malott ordered the wheelsman to put the wheel over hard to starboard to bring the big schooner around to the wind. The *Augusta* turned, but too slowly to prevent her from slamming hard into the port side of the *Lady Elgin* and driving a large hole in the *Lady*'s hull at the mid-ship gangway, just forward of the wheel.

The *Augusta* was also badly damaged in the crash. Captain Malott, who should have been celebrating his birthday that day, instead headed his limping vessel to Chicago where he reported the accident. He claimed he had backed off the scene of the collision and he could not return because his own foresails were wrecked and his bow was badly crushed and leaking. He denied knowing the collision had grievously injured, let alone sunk, the *Lady Elgin*.

In the meantime, Captain Wilson was trying to salvage his wounded ship. He tried to get her into shallow water. To gain time he ordered the cargo and passengers moved to the starboard side. He hoped that if he could get the ship to list in the other direction, he might be able to repair the hole to her port side. The crew stuffed mattresses into the hole in the hull. The damage, however, was so extensive that these pathetic gestures proved useless. Many passengers clung to wreckage from the deck and cabins which floated away from the hull as the ship sank under their feet.

As the *Lady Elgin* hobbled towards the beach, two of the ship's four lifeboats were launched. The first was immediately swamped and in spite of desperate attempts to keep her afloat she went under. On the second it was discovered too late there were no oars. The remaining two lifeboats were never used. Perhaps time just ran out. Only 20 minutes passed between the initial strike and the time the *Lady Elgin* vanished in the murky water. Even if the additional lifeboats had been thrown into the thrashing lake they could have offered only a long-shot at survival to no more than thirty or so passengers of the nearly four-hundred aboard the *Lady*.

Most of the passengers were still alive after the ship sunk. They clung hopefully to their pieces of flotsam. The Lake granted them only a brief reprieve. The gale flung high waves over their bodies bobbing in the icy water. Many of the short term survivors were exhausted after hours of fighting for their lives and simply gave up. They were among the many drowned. Many more were dashed to their deaths on rocks when they reached the shore. In the brutal game of life and death, the score stood at 98 survivors and more than 300 dead.

A three-month-old infant's body was one of the first to wash ashore after the disaster. Its size and weight undoubtedly made it easy to toss about the waves. The tiny girl's face was said to look content and showed none of the horror that was etched into the faces of many of the other bodies eventually recovered.

A woman living south of Milwaukee heard the news of the disaster. Believing it had claimed her son, a brother and a sister she set out walking, seventy five miles, following the railroad track all the way to the morgue set up in Chicago. The Chicago and Milwaukee Railroad had offered free passage to anyone traveling to Chicago to identify bodies, but this poor woman was unaware of the offer. With her she carried her nine-month-old son and five dollars to buy coffins for her family. She reached her destination, but her money was sufficient to purchase only one coffin and in it she buried her sister. Her brother and son were interred in a pauper's graveyard. Having done what she could, she headed home. She had not gone far when good Samaritans stopped her and assisted her and the baby aboard a train.

An unknown poet pleading for assistance for the families who lost loved ones in the *Lady Elgin* disaster, described in a long poetic saga how the mood changed from gaiety to terror that awful night. It reads in part:

"How changed every feature, how wild the confusion!
Despair in the darkness and death on the wave!
Some wail for the missing, some plunge, in their madness,
Swift into eternity and their own grave.
"My child!" shrieks a mother; "My daughter," "My father."
And a hundred shrill voices in agony call;
While black grow the waves, with the frantic and struggling,
And faster the boat sinks, beneath her dark pall.

In a postscript to the story of the *Lady Elgin*, the *Augusta* changed her name to the *Colonel Cook* to avoid the stigma of being the ship that sank the *Lady Elgin*. Still people remembered her for her part in the awful tragedy. Three years later, in 1863, Captain Malott was commanding another ship, the *Major*, when it sank in Lake Michigan. In a strange quirk of fate his bones are believed to have come to rest within ten miles of the *Lady Elgin*.

The Chicora   **January 21, 1895**
If other ship wrecks sustained more casualties, if other ships suffered more economic loss, if other ships more poignantly captured

the public's imagination, probably none was drenched in more irony than the wreck of the *Chicora*.

Mid-January may not seem like the optimal time to be crossing Lake Michigan, but the steamship *Chicora* was an especially stout ship designed for winter passenger and cargo runs. She was made to cut through an ice-packed lake and she rode violent waves that would have destroyed lesser ships. The wooden-hulled *Chicora* traveled at 17 miles per hour. She had been tied up for winter at St. Joseph when her owners were asked to deliver a shipment of late winter flour from Milwaukee to St. Joseph. On Sunday, January 20, 1895, Captain Edward C. Stine readied his boat and struck out for the Wisconsin harbor. Aboard was a crew of twenty-three including Captain Stine's 23-year-old son who was pressed into service by his father to replace the second mate who was too ill to make the trip. Only one passenger was aboard and he was said to be a friend of one of the ship's officers.

It was an unusually pleasant January day and the *Chicora* reached Milwaukee without problem. The next morning, January 21st, with cargo aboard, she readied for the return trip. The *Chicora* left port at 5:00 am, just minutes before a messenger arrived with a telegram from the ship's owner ordering the captain to hold off sailing. The barometer was falling fast in St. Joseph. One story reported that Captain Stine was ill and hurrying to get back to his doctor in St. Joseph.

Midway across Lake Michigan, the *Chicora* encountered winds that had shifted to the southwest bringing with them an awful January fury. Those anxiously awaiting the *Chicora's* return to St. Joseph tried to stave off panic when she did not arrive as scheduled. It made sense that the storm hampered her progress and she might be a bit late. As hours passed, and with fear gnawing at their guts, they finally reported her overdue. Telegrams were sent up and down the Lake Michigan coast alerting all harbors to keep watch for the lost ship.

From South Haven came a report that the night of the storm a ship had been spotted heading towards shore. Its stern was down and sinking. A second report described a distressed ship blowing its horn and seeking assistance. When the storm finally abated and it was safe to venture onto the water again, a group of men from Saugatuck began a search. What they found was disheartening and bode ill for the chances of the Chicora: less than a mile from shore, and embedded in ice, was a line of wreckage stretching from Saugatuck to South Haven.

A month later a tug reported sighting a hull floating on open water with men still clinging to it, apparently still alive! The *Chicora's* second mate, who had been lucky enough to be ill when the *Chicora* sailed, rented a tug and investigated the sighting. He reported finding only a dark iceberg covered with sea gulls.

No bodies ever washed ashore and other than the small pieces of wreckage including spars, the ship was never found. There was a report that the ship's dog was found wandering along the beach near St. Joseph a few days later. The crew of the *Chicora*, however, were not so fortunate. Their ship, with their bodies entombed, likely lies at the bottom of Lake Michigan between Saugatuck and St. Joseph.

The survivors were left to contemplate the ironies: The *Chicora* had already been tied up for winter when called into service. The Captain pressed his own son to replace the second mate who was too ill to make the trip. And, the saddest irony of all, the message telling the *Chicora* to stay put until after the storm, arrived just minutes too late to save her and her crew.

Nixon Waterman wrote a ballad, "Song and Sigh," popular in the lower lakes region of Michigan, commemorating the sinking of the *Chicora*:

"Here's a sigh for the Chicora, for the broken, sad Chicora;
Here's a tear for those who followed her beneath the tossing wave.
Oh, the mystery of the morrow! From its shadows let us borrow
A star of hope to shine above the gloom of every grave.

The Pere Marquette No. 18   September 9, 1910

On September 9, 1910 the railroad car-ferry *Pere Marquette No 18* took twenty-nine passengers and crew to the bottom of Lake Michigan. However, the remaining thirty-three of the sixty-two aboard managed to escape with their lives.

What caused the *Pier Marquette* to sink is still a mystery. She was not victim to a vicious storm, and although the waves were high it is not likely they caused her to go down. She was not overcrowded and to all appearances she was in excellent condition. We might know more if Captain Peter Kilty had survived. He and all of his officers went down with the ship.

It is known that the *Pere Marquette No 18* was riding low in the water and at some point she was steering with difficulty. Seven feet of water was discovered in the stern and water was pouring into the ship through portholes that may have been broken by the punishing waves. Twenty-nine rail cars were pushed overboard to lighten her load. The captain ordered his ship due west at full steam hoping to hit shoal water near Sheboygan in time to avert disaster. During this drama he also sent what may have been the first ship-to-shore radio distress signal in history. *"No. 18 is sinking in mid-lake, for God's sake, send help."* That terse plea, sent at 5:20 am, may have saved the thirty-three survivors who might otherwise have perished.

The *Pere Marquette No.17* responded to the distress signal and was maneuvering around the side of the stricken steamer to be in position to take additional people aboard when the *Pere Marquette No. 18* sank without warning. The bow bucked high in the air and the ship slid stern first into the great sea. As it sank there was an explosion that may have killed many of those still aboard. Fortunately, the *Pere Marquette 17* was able to assist some of those floundering in the water.

After that first wireless message was received, seven additional messages were dispatched describing for the first time, the horror of a ship going down as it was happening. The message above and the first two that follow came from the *Pere Marquette 18*, the remainder from the *Pere Marquette 17* as she responded to offer assistance:

"No. 18, sinking between Ludington and Milwaukee, for God's sake save us." *(Also at 5:20 am, same time as original message.)*

"Help, quick, Carferry 18 is sinking." *(Also at 5:20 am)*

"Steamer 18 went down." *(From Pere Marquette 17 at 7:30 am.)*

"Steamer 18 is gone. No 17 standing by. Will stay until all are saved." *(7:35 am)*

"Frank Young, James Fray and Cochrane were saved. All officers of No. 18 lost. Not one saved." *(9:00 am)*

"We have picked up thirty of crew of 18." *(11:00 am)*

"Thirty-three lives saved altogether. We picked up five bodies. Captain Kilty, Purser Sczypank, Mrs. Turner, Cummings and one unknown. Bodies on board No. 17 to be taken to Ludington at 4:00 pm." *(1:00 pm)*

In the aftermath of the tragedy, passengers who were saved, described the efforts of the *Pere Marquette 18*'s crew and accorded them the highest praise for their actions under harrowing conditions. According to survivor Seymore Cochrane of Chicago, he was reading a magazine in his berth when he heard shouts that the boat was sinking. He wrestled a door from its hinges and floated on it until he was picked up more than an hour later by *No. 17*. Later in an interview, Cochrane said, *"There is no other way of reasoning than to say the crew sacrificed their lives to save the passengers. The boat was well-equipped with life boats and the members of the crew might have saved themselves and let the passengers perish. But, thank goodness, they were not that kind of men."*

Rouse Simmons, "The Christmas Tree Ship"   November 23, 1912

The *Rouse Simmons* continues to stir imaginations nearly a century after her November 23, 1912 wreck and may be the best known of all Lake Michigan disasters. Her story is the stuff of legend and she is immortalized in songs, plays, a book and continuing attempts to trace her last route. She is one of the genuine ghost ships of the Great Lakes.

A ghost ship is more than a ship that goes down with a loss of lives, because such is not an uncommon occurrence. Most of these shipwrecks remain buried and quiet. A true ghost ship, however, is one that is sighted sailing after her demise. There have been *Rouse Simmons* sightings by sailors for decades. Her sails are tattered as she continues to limp along the Lake Michigan horizon.

The *Rouse Simmons* was a three-masted schooner bound for Chicago with a very special cargo that lent her the nickname "*The Christmas Tree Ship.*" She carried 5,500 fresh cut Christmas trees piled deep in her hold and lashed to the deck. She was a "floating forest." The trees would be sold from the dock in Chicago and would spread the Christmas spirit to holiday revelers who purchased them.

The ship was the namesake of Kenosha industrialist Rouse Simmons of Simmons mattress fame. She was built in 1868 and her 153-foot-length weighed 205 tons.

The doomed voyage started with an omen grave enough to cause one crewman to abandon ship. Rats were dropping into the water from the hawser pipe. While landlubbers may think it is a good thing to get rid of rats, when they abandon a ship, sailors take note. The filthy vermin inhabit ships galleys, and legend warns they always desert a sinking ship. If you see them leaving of their own volition, beware, the ship is going down. In this case it proved all too true. The *Rouse Simmons* was last spotted on Saturday afternoon five miles off Kewaunee, Wisconsin; with distress signals flying she was sailing south into a blinding snow storm.

For many years after she sank, the only evidence of the *Rouse Simmon's* fate was the pine trees that would occasionally become tangled in the nets of commercial fishermen. Then a cork-stopped bottle washed ashore. The message inside read: "*Friday. Everybody goodbye. I guess we are all through. Sea washed over our deckboard Thursday. During the night the small boat washed overboard. Leaking bad. Ingvald and Steve fell overboard Thursday. God help us.*" – Herman Schuenemann. The note appeared to be part of the Captain's log.

In 1924, twelve years after the *Simmons* went down, Captain Schuenemann's wallet popped up in a fishing net. The contents were intact and legible due to the oilskin that wrapped it and the rubber band that held it tight. It rekindled memories of the sweet-natured and beloved man who dealt in Yuletide cheer. But, the Captain, as decent a man as he was, may have had a fatal character flaw that contributed to his undoing. Whether it was greed, hardheadedness, or just a desire to spread some happiness, it was reported that the Captain overloaded the boat with trees, to the point where one crewman warned that if they encountered a storm, the boat would be too top heavy to pull through. The warning was ignored.

In 1927 a second bottle washed ashore. Inside was a note that read, *"These lines are written at 10:30 p.m. Schooner H.S. ready to go down about 20 miles southeast of Two Rivers Point between fifteen or twenty miles off shore. All hands lashed to one line. Goodbye."* Charles Nelson. (The H.S. refers to Herman Schuenemann.)

While the *Rouse Simmons* had no radio and the wreck left no survivors, it was as though the ghosts of this tragedy reached back from the watery grave and communicated their story to the living through two notes in bottles and an intact wallet.

The site of the wreck remained a mystery until 1971 when salvager Ken Bellrichard of Milwaukee discovered the *Rouse Simmons* grave in 180 feet of water off Rawley Point. Her bones remain nearly intact and she lies at rest, upright on the floor of her lake. Her cargo hold is still filled with the shrunken remains of Christmas trees.

Captain Schuenemann's wife and daughters continued selling Christmas trees from the deck of a schooner in the Chicago harbor for many years after his death. But, the time of Christmas Tree Ships was almost at an end. Wholesale tree farms and better transportation on railroads and highways led to the end of the holiday tradition where revelers headed to the harbor to choose their tree from the deck of a ship.

Captain Schuenemann's widow lived for more than twenty years after his death, but eventually was laid to rest in a Chicago cemetery. Their joint headstone bears a tiny engraved Christmas tree between their names.

The Plymouth   November 13, 1913

The questions will always be asked: Did the tug, James A. *Martin*, desert the *Plymouth* in her hour of need? Or, believing the *Plymouth* was stable, did the *Martin* merely seek shelter, intending to return for the *Plymouth* when weather permitted?

The *Plymouth* was a lumber barge with a seven man crew aboard when she met her fate. The tug, *Martin*, with the *Plymouth* in tow, had cleared the Menominee Light on Thursday afternoon bound for Search Bay in Lake Huron. Before they could get there, Lake Michigan waters raged, forcing the ships to anchor at St. Martins Island until Saturday morning.

In an effort to keep the barge from crashing on the rocks, the little tug towed the *Plymouth* to nearby Gull Island where it was anchored. What happened after that depends upon which story you accept. It is undisputed that the *Martin* left the *Plymouth* and headed for the shelter of Summer Island passage, where the *Martin* anchored to wait out the storm.

A few days later Captain Louis Stetunsky caused a sensation when he arrived in Menominee with his tug battered and bruised, looking much worse for the storm, but still miraculously afloat. Bystanders thought they were seeing ghosts. Everyone assumed the *Martin* and the *Plymouth* had gone down in the maniacal gale.

Captain Stetunsky described the horror that he and his crew of eight had suffered in the preceding days. The storm had started on Thursday and Stetunsky could make no headway hauling the barge against the worsening storm. He recounted his attempts to anchor both vessels in the lee of St. Martins Island. Unable to achieve the degree of security he wanted, he said he hauled the barge to a spot he felt offered better anchorage, just off Gull Island.

Here the two versions of this story diverge; Stetunsky insisted that only when the barge appeared to be riding safely, did he seek better refuge for his tug in the Summer Island passage. He was adamant that he was not leaving the *Plymouth* to whatever fate might befall her. His tug was not powerful enough to fight the storm and tow the barge at the same time. It was evident to him that both ships would founder if they tried to make it together. As it was, he had barely survived. (*Note, he never mentions why he did not take the crew of the Plymouth aboard his tug but perhaps he did not consider one ship any safer than the other.*)

On Tuesday, three days later, after the storm had burned out, Captain Stetunsky claimed he returned to the spot he had left the *Plymouth* anchored. The barge had vanished so he sailed on to Menominee.

After several more days, parts of the lost ship began washing ashore – a hatch cover here, a piece of the cabin there. Broken lifeboats from the *Plymouth* were found in Ludington.

The second version of the story suggests the Captain Stetunsky abandoned the *Plymouth* and left her crew to perish. The evidence supporting this second version arrived almost two weeks after the *Plymouth* vanished. A bottle was found five miles from Pentwater. Inside was a message: "*Dear wife and Children. We were left up here in Lake Michigan by McKinnon, Captain James H. Martin, tug, at anchor. He went away and never said goodbye or anything to us. Lost one man yesterday. We have been out in storm forty hours. Goodbye dear ones, I might see you in Heaven. Pray for me. Chris K.*" Chris Keenan's body was found several days later on a beach near Manistee.

While parts of the note seem to have the facts wrong (Captain McKinnon instead of Stetunsky?) the authenticity of the message has never been questioned and under any interpretation it seems clear the author of that note felt abandoned, whether, in fact, he was or was not.

The Eastland July 24, 1915

Perhaps the oddest tragedy to ever befall a ship on Lake Michigan did not happen during a raging storm or even in open water. The *Eastland* was tied to the dock at the Clark Street Bridge in the narrow channel of the Chicago River when tragedy befell her. She was a relatively young ship, with only ten years of service on the lakes. She weighed 1,900 tons. Captain Harry Pederson was at her helm.

The channel was as unlikely a spot for this senseless mishap as anyone could have envisioned. The *Eastland* was preparing to transport 2,500 Western Electric Company passengers to a pleasant holiday across the beautiful lake to the sand dunes. Some estimates conclude that perhaps there were actually 3,000 aboard and the ship designed to carry only 2,500. Regardless, the final investigation determined that overcrowding was not a significant issue in the disaster.

Passengers began boarding at 7:00 am to get an early start on the day's festivities. Ragtime music floated on the air as happy revelers stowed picnic baskets and engaged in lighthearted chatter with friends and colleagues. It was overcast with spitting drizzle, but the precipitation could not dampen the spirits of travelers on holiday. Only those on the main deck could hear the cries: *"Look out, the boat's turning over!"* For the moment it barely caused a pause in conversations, so certain were those aboard that the cry must be in jest.

But something was definitely amiss. The great ship began tilting towards the dock. Captain Pederson attempted to correct the situation and ordered the sea cocks opened to trip the ship. She came back upright, but then listed at a dangerous angle away from the dock. Passengers who had gone below found themselves smashing against the bulkheads. Bottles and other loose items began crashing about. Chairs on deck slid from starboard to port. The icebox in the refreshment stand tore loose and skidded across the deck.

Many passengers, fearing for their lives jumped overboard. By 7:30 am the demon-possessed ship turned over in the river with her starboard side facing upward above the water. Passengers caught in the confusion panicked. Many drowned with the dock just a few feet out of reach. Hundreds more were trapped in cabins below the decks. A few lucky ones crawled through portholes and a few more were still alive when rescuers with acetylene torches cut them a path to safety.

No satisfactory reason has even been offered to explain the erratic behavior of an otherwise predictable ship. One of the first theories was that the passengers all crowded to one side to watch a tug pass. That theory was discarded at the inquest. Improper ballast may be the answer, but no one will ever no for sure. The ship itself was in fine condition and continued to sail after the tragic incident. She was renamed the *U.S.S.Wilmette* and converted to a naval training ship. Most who saw her moored at her Randolph Street dock in Chicago had no idea that the *U.S.S.Wilmette* was the *Eastland* in her prior life. They simply stood and admired her clean lines and sharp appearance.

Captain Pederson and steamship company officials were charged with criminal negligence, but a U. S. Circuit Court of Appeals ultimately issued a decision that the boat was seaworthy and the operators had acted appropriately. That decision closed the legal aspect of the case. It did not close the public's indignation that the ship had caused the loss of half as many lives as had been doomed on the *Titanic* just three years earlier and no reason satisfactorily explained it. The *Titanic* could be rationalized: an iceberg, a cocky attitude that she was unsinkable, a speed to set records and lack of visibility. But, the *Eastland*? She had never made it out of the channel. It was unthinkable.

The ship, however, had been the target of ugly rumors about her safety for years. So persistent were the rumors, that the owners of the *Eastland* resorted to taking out a half page advertisement in the *Cleveland Plain Dealer* on August 9, 1910. The ad praised the ship for her strength, her safety record and the joy her excursions had brought to thousands of happy, satisfied passengers. It went on to offer a $5000 reward: *"we offer the above reward to any person that will bring forth a naval engineer, a marine architect, a ship builder, or anyone qualified to pass judgment on the merits of a ship, who will say that the steamer, Eastland, is not a seaworthy ship, or that she would not ride out any storm, or weather any condition that can arise on either lake or ocean."*

Whatever the cause, on one hot, steamy day in July, the *Eastland* became possessed and more than 800 people died, among them 22 entire families. Those gruesome statistics earned her the dubious distinction of "worst loss of lives in one accident on the Great Lakes." It was a record that would hopefully never be broken.

The Desmond December 8, 1917

The wooden-hulled propeller D*esmond* was in the business of extracting sand from the bottom of Lake Michigan and selling it for profit. December is late in the shipping season and the *Desmond* was on her last trip of the year when a monster winter storm sank her off the South Chicago Lighthouse. Captain Emil Thorsen departed St. Joseph in the afternoon headed northwest for Racine with his load of sand. Gale winds blew the *Desmond* off course hurling her into the path of a nasty squall out of the north blowing high waves and subzero temperatures.

Thorsen realized the danger and headed for the safety of the Chicago Harbor. Everyone aboard feared this would be their last trip – not for the year, but of their life. A survivor later said crew members tried to persuade the captain to run the ship on a beach, but he refused. He had been sailing for thirty years and never lost a ship. He declared that if the *Desmond* went down, he would go down with her.

The continued rocking of the waves shifted the cargo of sand causing the *Desmond* to list to starboard. The crew began shoveling furiously, trying to get the ship back on an even keel. They remained optimistic, inspired by the lights they could see in the Chicago Harbor. Surely with safety so close, they would be rescued?

At 2:00 am the ship developed a leak in the stern. The engines had to be shut down to operate the ship's steam pumps. The crew continued working all that long, terrifying night to keep their ship afloat. At the same time they frantically tried to get someone's attention to their plight. The water was gaining on them. One of the coal bunkers collapsed and pieces of coal began clogging the pumps and siphons.

The Captain decided his only chance to save his ship was to launch a lifeboat and row for help. He desperately needed a tug to haul them in. As the lifeboat headed away, the *Desmond* tipped on its side and its stack hit and capsized the lifeboat, throwing its occupants into the water. The eight men still aboard the *Desmond* scrambled up top as the ship tipped. The *Desmond* floated that way for several hours, buying them critical time. The men still aboard the ship threw ropes to the five they spotted floundering in the icy water. Captain Thorsen and Frank Kipper managed to grab the ropes and were pulled along side the ship, but Thorsen froze to death as he lay there. Kipper survived, along with the eight still on board. They were rescued by the tug, *William A. Field*. The *Desmond* finally sank at 7:00 am. Seven men died in the disaster.

The Andaste   September 9, 1929

On September 9, 1929 the *Andaste* disappeared beneath the waters of Lake Michigan. Twenty-five men went to their deaths with her. The *Andaste* was not the most elegant ship to sail the lakes. She was a semi-whaleback, slope-sided, 266-foot-long steam ship built in 1892. With a cargo capacity of 3,000 tons, she was built for function not beauty.

The *Andaste* was captained by Albert L. Anderson of Sturgeon Bay and on the day of her demise she was docked in Ferrysburg taking on a load of gravel. She cast off and passed the Grand Haven piers at 9:03 am headed for Chicago where she was scheduled to arrive the next morning. Her voyage was routine; it was a trip she had been making four times a week for years.

By 10:00 am winds kicked up and quickly morphed into a full blown gale. The *Andaste* did not arrive the next morning as scheduled, but her tardiness was not given much thought since the old ship had been late before. By Wednesday, a full day late, simple delay could no longer explain her tardiness. By Thursday it was assumed the *Andaste* was lost. She had no radio and there was no way to determine what had happened until the ship, herself, decided to speak.

Wreckage began to drift ashore at beaches from Grand Haven to Holland. At Castle Park, just south of Holland, the first body was recovered. Mr. H. H. Stibbs was scanning the water in front of his cottage and saw debris. His son, J. H. Stibbs, a competitive swimmer, swam out to recover what he could. He returned, towing a life ring with a dead sailor. Other bodies washed ashore at Jenison Park in Grand Haven. Of the bodies of the initial 14 victims to float to shore, 11 were wearing lifejackets. Continued search efforts during the next two weeks recovered the remaining bodies, as well as considerable flotsam: cabin doors, several hatch covers and part of a stairway. Much of the wreckage was tangled in fishing nets. The youngest victim was 14-year-old Earl Zietlow, a sailor on his first and last voyage.

The best evidence suggests the *Andaste* went down 25 or 30 miles out on the lake. A cottage owner, between Grand Haven and Holland, testified at an inquest that he was awakened by a violent storm at 1:00 am of the night the *Andaste* went missing. Looking out his window he could see the lights of a ship not too far from shore and the lights remained visible until about 4:00 am. And then, nothing.

The Milwaukee   October 22, 1929

The *Milwaukee*'s captain, Robert McKay, recklessly ignored the second chance luck graciously dealt him and the price tag for his ingratitude was death. Fifty-two additional crew members went down with him. The man responsible for the foolhardy decisions that night was alternately called a madman or dubbed "Heavy Weather McKay." On October 22, 1929, he guided his 383-foot, railroad car-ferry *Milwaukee* into the safety of the harbor for which she was named.

Rarely had a seasick crew been more relieved to step foot on solid ground than the queasy men who had just had their stomachs turned upside-down and knotted inside-out by a bullying storm. Bruising north winds had tried to take them under with every wave that washed over them on their way to port. But, the crew emerged victorious.

Once they tied up in the harbor, the seasick crew, like the troopers they were, began pulling boxcars ashore. When that was finished, twenty-five additional cars bound for the Grand Trunk Western's rail station at Grand Haven stood waiting to be loaded onto the ferry for the return trip. The crew again set directly to the task. Time was money and car ferries made the most of it. However, as the crew reloaded the *Milwaukee* they must have considered the worsening weather and hoped McKay would postpone the return trip long enough to let the storm burn itself out. They knew better than to bet their paychecks on it. The Grand Trunk Western Railroad did not like to see their ships idle, storm or no storm, and this storm would go down as one of the worst to ever hit Lake Michigan.

With the final eastbound railcar loaded and in position, Captain McKay, to no one's real surprise, announced his decision to depart immediately. Barely out of the harbor, the ferry was already rocking and rolling. The captain of the lightship three miles from Milwaukee watched the ship bouncing east until the rain and spray enveloped and erased her from sight.

A second Grand Trunk Ferry departed Milwaukee four hours after Captain McKay. It reached the dock in Grand Haven on the morning of October 23rd, having staggered into harbor after a fifteen-hour battle with the killer storm. It had taken nine hours longer than usual to cross. The crew of the second ferry was surprised to learn McKay's *Milwaukee* had not arrived before them. Everyone hoped she had been forced to abandon her normal course and that she had sought shelter or turned north seeking an easier route.

The morning of October 24th, Michigan and Wisconsin Coast Guard stations were finally alerted that the *Milwaukee* had not arrived and was long overdue. Debris was spotted floating in the water near Racine, Wisconsin, but it could not be definitively identified as wreckage from the missing *Milwaukee*.

On the morning of October 25th, two bodies were found floating off Kenosha, Wisconsin, both wearing lifejackets from the *Milwaukee*. Bodies began rolling in. On the 26th a lifeboat was found, but the four crewmen inside were dead of hypothermia. A second lifeboat was found later in the day, but its canvas cover was still lashed in place and no one was aboard. It was obvious the *Milwaukee* was lost.

Grand Haven was home to thirty of the ferry's crew and the little community was devastated. Earlier that fall, on September 11th, the *Andaste* had gone down in a storm while making its Grand Haven to Chicago run with a load of gravel. Thirteen of the twenty-five crewmembers who disappeared with the *Andaste* were also from Grand Haven. (See the story of the *Andaste* above.)

Several days after the first bodies were found, a surfman at the South Haven station discovered the *Milwaukee*'s message case floating along the shore. Inside was a note signed by the ship's purser: "*S.S. Milwaukee, October 22, '29, 8:30 pm. This ship is taking water fast. We have turned around and headed for Milwaukee. Pumps are working, but sea gate is bent in and can't keep the water out. Flicker is flooded. Seas are tremendous. Things look bad. Crew roll is about the same as on the last pay day.*"

The note explained much of the mystery concerning the sinking of the *Milwaukee*. If the sea gate was damaged there was nothing to stop water from flooding onto the main deck. The sea gate is a heavy steel gate that is dropped into place to close off the end of the main deck after the cargo of rail cars has been loaded. Without a functional sea gate, water would eventually fill the entire ship. Later investigation concluded that the sea gate may have broken when Captain McKay attempted to turn the ship around, perhaps causing one of the rail cars to come loose and crash into the gate. The "flicker" referenced the crews' quarters that were located below the main deck near the stern of the ship. The Purser referenced the crew roll so the ships owners would know who had been on board.

Later a second note, sealed in a bottle, washed ashore. "*This is the worst storm I have ever seen. Can't stay up much longer. Hole in the side of the boat.*" It was signed McKay. The note may have been a macabre joke. No one would ever know if there really was a hole in the side of the *Milwaukee,* but it seems that if there was, the purser's entry would have mentioned it. It was suspected that the note was a fake.

The Novadoc   **November 11, 1940**

The gales of November raged in full fury on November 11, 1940 in the Great Armistice Day Storm. It sank five vessels and claimed 66 victims.

There is a twenty-mile span of Lake Michigan between Little Point Sable at Silver Lake and Big Point Sable north of Ludington that has earned a reputation as the "Graveyard of Ships." It claimed its first ship, the *Neptune*, in 1848. The five that went down on Armistice Day 1940 brought the Graveyard's total to nearly seventy vessels.

The first two boats to go down in the 1940 storm were small commercial fishing tugs from South Haven. The *Indian* departed harbor about 7:30 am to pull in its daily catch. It never returned. The *Richard H*, an aging steam tug was last seen trying to make shore in the early afternoon.

It would take more than a few gusts of wind to destroy the remaining vessels: the *Novadoc, Anna Minch* and the *Davock*. The *Novadoc* was a 250-foot-canaller. A canaller is a ship small enough to fit through the Welland Canal. The doc at the end of her name stood for

Dominion of Canada. She had departed Montreal enroute to Chicago where she would pick up a load of sulphite coke intended for Quebec.

In Lake Michigan, Captain Steip had tried to set the *Novadoc* a course along the eastern shore to take advantage of the shelter it provided from wind. The obstinate wind shifted to the southwest and increased in speed. The ship ended up perilously close to the center of the lake and the waves became too high to allow the tossed vessel to make any harbor on the east side of the lake. The crew had no choice but to ride out the storm.

Near Pentwater at Little Sable Point, Lightkeeper, William Krewell, watched the masthead lights of the floundering ship as she rolled in the mountainous, foamy waves. The men aboard the ship later described seeing the lighthouse in the distance, but only when they were perilously perched at the crest of each new wave.

The *Novadoc* ran aground on a shoal at 7:00 pm, November 11th. The crash severed the ship in two, and buried each half in sand. All electric lines were cut. In this broken condition, the storm continued to pummel her. The crew spent the night huddled in the Captain's cabin. Just before daybreak the door to the cabin gave way and rushing water forced the men into the Captain's inner office. There they prayed that the wall separating the office from the rest of the quarters would hold. With daylight the weary crew found they had no lifeboats remaining to carry them to shore.

The stranded men sent up rockets to let potential rescuers on shore know they were alive. In return the crowd on shore built a fire so the crew would know they had not been forgotten. Help would get there as soon as it was safe to send a boat out. The storm abated somewhat as darkness fell the second night. The cold men aboard the *Novadoc* found a container and began cutting up pieces of kindling from chairs and other furniture to start a fire to warm their frozen limbs.

The next morning Captain Steip made his way to the far end of the boat and discovered two of the cooks had washed overboard. Later that morning the surviving crew was rescued by the *Three Brother,* a little fishing boat willing to brave the still churning sea to save the marooned men.

On shore, as the *Three Brothers* readied to launch, their crew was warned the proposed rescue attempt verged on insanity - it could not be done. Their boat was too small and the waves still too high. The *Three Brothers* pushed off in spite of the dire warnings. They reached the *Novadoc* where the grateful crew embraced them as heroes. Once safely ashore, Captain Steip is said to have reached in his pocket and produced a roll of bills, handing it to Clyde Cross, captain of the *Three Brothers*, in gratitude for his life. Cross, in an "aw shucks" way, is alleged to have responded, "Hell no, captain. Glad to be of service." Cross later said he saw that there was a job that needed doing and he did it. The press hailed him as an All-American hero.

The Coast Guard was not as generous in its praise; denouncing Cross as a glory seeker who had ignored the unwritten law of the sea by refusing to come to Coast Guard's aid when they had asked for his help in launching their lifeboat. Whatever anyone's position on the wisdom of the *Three Brothers* going to the aid of the *Novadoc* when it did, the cold, wet and frightened survivors were grateful.

In an unfortunate footnote, the little fishing tug, *Three Brothers,* became a victim of Lake Michigan a few years later. Fortunately no lives were lost and during her sailing days she could brag that she rode out the Great Storm of 1940 and saved seventeen men.

The *William B. Davock* and the *Anna C. Minch* were also lost in the Armistice Day Storm. There were no survivors on either and therefore the story of their last minutes or hours remains a mystery. They went down not too far from where the *Novadoc* was stranded. The *Minch*, a 380-foot-steel-propeller sits in 20 to 40 feet of water about 8 miles off Pentwater. Because she broke in two it is believed she collided with the *Davock*. The 310-foot-steel-hull-propeller, *Davock,* rests in about 150 feet of water, also 8 miles from Pentwater.

The Carl D. Bradley   November 18, 1958

The *Carl D. Bradley* holds the record for largest ship to sink in Lake Michigan. When she was launched in 1929 she was the most powerful ship on the Great Lakes. This giant tangled with a gale on November 18, 1958 and proved no match for the mighty lake. Thirty-three men went down with her that night; two survived to tell the story. Twenty-five of the crew hailed from the small town of Rogers City. Most were of Polish descent, many knew each other's families and many were related. The cook often served the sailors kielbasa purchased from a neighborhood market in the 'Polish town' section of Rogers City.

Ship Captain, Roland Bryan was a bit of an outsider. He still made his off-season home in Loudonville, New York, but he had been sailing with the Bradley Transportation Line for twenty-four years and even when his crewmen sprinkled their conversation with Polish, he usually understood.

The night it went down, the *Bradley* was returning empty after delivering its last shipment of limestone for the 1958 season to Gary, Indiana. It was a happy day. Captain Bryan had a sweetheart in Port Huron. For the eight-month shipping season he rarely saw her unless he picked up a load in Lake Huron and could blow his horn in salute as he passed by. In just a couple of more days he would see her again. He wished the weather forecast was less ominous, but he had endured many storms in his career. He knew if he delayed leaving Gary his entire crew would be unhappy. They, too, wanted to get back to families and loved ones.

The *Bradley* was in her thirty-first season and she was due for inspections; inspections that would reveal she needed a bit of work. But that was what winter was for.

Captain Bryan headed northwest, seeking protection from the winds along the west shore of Lake Michigan. The next day the weather worsened and winds reached sixty to sixty-five miles an hour. Waves rose at least twenty-five feet high. It might not have been the worst storm to ever hit Lake Michigan, but it was more than the *Bradley* could endure.

The ship's Mayday signal was picked up at the Charlevoix Coast Guard station at 5:30 am on November 18th. The message described the *Bradley*'s position twelve miles southwest of Gull Island. The radio operator listened to the crewmen shouting, "*Run, grab life jackets. Get the jackets.*" Then came another "*Mayday. The ship is breaking up.*"

It was the terrified voice of Elmer Fleming sending the Mayday calls. He and Frank Mays, the two survivors, were found the next morning in the life raft they shared. Two additional crewmates had clung to the raft until a huge wave flipped the frail vessel, drowning Dennis Meredith in the brackish water. Fleming, Mays and Gary Strzelecki managed to climb back aboard. Just after dawn, Strzelecki declared he had enough. The men were sending up flares, but had no reason to believe they had been spotted. Strzelecki jumped off the pontoon-like raft and began swimming towards shore.

Fleming, too, doubted his Mayday signals had been heard. He was a very happy man when he saw the Coast Guard rescue ship *Sundew* headed his way only an hour after his crewmate had given up and begun swimming to his death. Mays admitted to doing a lot of praying that night and said he had never being so cold in his life. His numb hands did not want to continue hanging on to the ropes attached to the raft, but his mind did not want to let go. Ice formed on the hair and clothing of the two surviving men who endured fourteen hours before their rescue.

When news reached Rogers city that two survivors had been found, the city rejoiced, hoping the remaining thirty-three missing were also alive. Instead, search vessels began retrieving bodies.

The survivors gave the following accounts: Mays was working below deck when the ship started breaking up. He was thrown into the water just as the *Bradley* capsized. He had the good fortune to surface a few feet from the raft and was able to get aboard. From there he watched the stern of the ship go straight down. An explosion followed as the ship slipped under and water hit the boilers.

Fleming had been in the pilot house with the ship's Captain when he was first alerted to trouble by a loud thud and an alarm. When he saw the stern sagging he knew it was bad. Instinctively he knew the ship was going down. He stepped out on deck as the *Bradley* rolled to its side, throwing both him and a raft into the water.

While many casualties on shipwrecks from the 1800s and early 1900s were attributed to lack of lifeboats, lack of life jackets and the lack of radio communication; all of which were no doubt important in saving lives, Lake Michigan made it very clear there were times when even those were not enough!

Photo Courtesy of Joe Jurkiewicz

"The ages of seven to eleven are a huge chunk of life, full of dulling and forgetting. It is fabled that we slowly lose the gift of speech with animals, that birds no longer visit our windowsills to converse. As our eyes grow accustomed to sight they armor themselves against wonder.   -Leonard Cohen

Flora and Fauna of Lake Michigan
-Critters, Creatures and Other Living Things

Some are beautiful. Some only a mother could love. Some are gone never to return and some are going. Some are making a valiant comeback. All share or shared our beautiful western Michigan.

A trip to Lake Michigan provides an opportunity to see fascinating plants, reptiles, butterflies, birds and mammals that share the shoreline and countryside. Listen closely to the sounds about you. Keep a watchful eye. Have your camera ready. There are no guarantees you will spot some of the rarer and more elusive of our living friends, but some interesting creature is certain to cross your path and delight your senses. A few of our more colorful characters are extinct – forever gone.

The Mastodon and Mammoth. Most of us use the terms mastodon and mammoth interchangeably, but they were two distinct, though related, members of the elephant family. Mastodons, although generally the smaller of the two, could stand ten feet at the shoulder. Mastodon fossils are most often discovered in regions that were forested during the Late Pliocene and Pleistocene epochs, four million to a mere 10,000 years ago. Mastodons roamed about eating the foliage of prehistoric trees. During certain periods when Michigan was covered by glacial ice, it still hosted extensive spruce forests similar to those found in Canada or Alaska today.

The extinction of the Mastodon has been attributed to the warming of their natural habitat, the disappearance of early forests and possibly over hunting by early Paleo-Indians. Early hunting has been documented by cut marks on fossilized bones.

The first report of mastodon bones in Michigan came in the early 1800s. Then, for more than a century after, bones and teeth of the extinct mastodon and mammoth were uncovered, often by farmers tilling their fields. There have been 250 discoveries in Michigan. The two most complete skeletal remains of mastodons are housed at the University of Michigan and Oakland Community College in Union Lake – one skeleton at each location.

In 2002, Michigan became one of only a handful of states to have two "official" fossils when Governor John Engler designated the American mastodon as our second official fossil. The Devonian Coral known as the Petoskey stone is Michigan's original state fossil.

Mammoths, larger than mastodons, could weigh between four and seven tons. They were comparable in size to the largest currently living elephant, the Savannah Elephant of Africa. A mammoth's teeth were adapted primarily for grazing on ground vegetation; their trunk had a hand-like tip that was effective for scooping snow off the ground and exposing plants buried beneath.

Both the mammoth and the mastodon had large, curved tusks which were really incisor teeth, and both had long shaggy hair that suited them to cold climates.

The Woolly Mammoth

The <u>Story of Martha</u>, the more recent extinction of the Passenger Pigeon. On September 1, 1914 at 1:00 pm at the Cincinnati Zoo, the last surviving passenger pigeon, Martha, died at the age of 29. Her legacy, if any good comes from her extinction, demonstrates the need for strong conservation laws to protect endangered species.

It is estimated that when Europeans began arriving on the North American continent there were three to five billion passenger pigeons. They made up 25% to 40% of the total bird population in the United States. Huge flocks, a mile in width and requiring several hours to pass overhead, were reported by early explorers. Stories were told of flocks darkening the sky from morning until night or even for several days during their migration. In three centuries humans eliminated this graceful bird from the face of the earth.

Passenger pigeons flew to warmer climates for winter roosting sites and sometimes they even changed their nesting location during the season; seeking more favorable spots to find food and raise a family. Their natural range was central Canada south to the uplands of Texas, as well as most of the southern United States. The main nesting area, however, was in the Great Lakes region. The habitat they required was mixed hardwood forests that provided them with spring nesting sites and a food source of pine nuts, acorns and seeds.

This wild pigeon had a small head and neck, a long, wedge-shaped tail and long pointed wings - all of which were ideally suited to speedy (up to sixty-miles-per-hour) and elegant flights. The female, at about 15½ inches, was slightly shorter than the male. The male sported a bluish gray coloring on its head and upper body. He wore iridescent pink patches at the sides of his throat with the patches blending to include bronze, green and purple at the back of the neck. The lower throat and breast were dusty, purplish-pink gradually fading to white on the lower abdomen. As with many species of birds, the female coloration was duller.

The clearing of Michigan's woodlands caused these birds to shift their nesting and roosting sites to areas where dense forests remained. Eventually they were forced to utilize grain fields for sustenance. When they began damaging the farmer's crops, the wholesale shooting began. Professional hunters indiscriminately netted and shot birds to sell in city markets. There were no laws to regulate the number killed and even when flocks noticeably dwindled the slaughter continued.

In Petoskey, in 1878, 50,000 birds a day were killed over a continuous five month period. When surviving birds attempted to nest, hunters slaughtered them before they could raise any young.

Legislative attempts to salvage the species caming too little and too late - proved futile. Survival of the species required massive numbers of birds that could survive natural predators with little harm to the overall flock. This worked until man became the ultimate predator.

The nearest surviving relative to the passenger pigeon, and the one closest in shape and coloring, is the mourning dove. Because of the similarities there were many false sightings of passenger pigeons long after their extinction. From 1909 to 1912, the American Ornithologists Society offered rewards to anyone who could find a nest or colony of passenger pigeons. The reward was never collected. Failed attempts were made to breed the few passenger pigeons that remained in captivity.

In a double tragedy, during the 1800s millions of passenger pigeons rested on the peak of Pigeon Hill, one of the largest sand dunes on Lake Michigan. Pigeon Hill was located on the Muskegon shoreline. It rose two hundred to three hundred feet high, dwarfing the surrounding landscape. Pigeon Hill is now gone; mined to death she passed into extinction like the millions of birds who perched on her sandy slope.

The Wolverine, still living but no longer in Michigan. Ernest Thompson Seton gave this most colorful description of the wolverine: *"Picture a weasel -- and most of us can do that, for we have met that little demon of destruction, that small atom of insensate courage, that symbol of slaughter, sleeplessness, and tireless, incredible activity -- picture that scrap of demoniac fury, multiply that mite some fifty times, and you have the likeness of a Wolverine."*

The powerfully built male wolverine is only about 18 inches high and 45 inches long. The female is equally powerful, but only about 14 inches high and 36 inches long. Yet when this "devil bear," bares its teeth a mountain lion will back away from its fresh kill. The wolverine is not above eating carrion and stealing the meat from the mouths of other predators. It also engages in its own kill of caribou, mountain goats and bear or other animals with which it shares its habitat.

The wolverine's bear-like appearance includes thick, dark, glossy, brown fur with skunk-like markings of yellowish bands from its shoulders down its back to the tip of the tail. If cornered the wolverine also sprays like a skunk. Its oversized claws offer defense against larger predators.

The wolverine walks on the soles of its feet as do bears and humans. Its jaw muscles are so strong it can eat meat that is solidly frozen. They prefer higher elevations and alpine habitats during the summer months and lower elevations, timbered-habitats during the winter. These preferences are likely related to the availability of food.

Historically, wolverine inhabited the northern part of Michigan's Lower Peninsula and all of the Upper Peninsula. Michigan was known as the "Wolverine State." However, our state animal disappeared from the area in the early 1900s (unless you count the breed living today in Ann Arbor and environs). The wolverine is well-suited for winter survival and continues to be found in the northern regions of North America and has a worldwide distribution that extends into sub-arctic areas of the northern hemisphere. Today there are still wolverines in Washington, Idaho, Montana and Wyoming and as this book went to press there were even alleged sightings of a lone female in Michigan.

Michigan's state animal, the Wolverine

Your treks to Lake Michigan will never result in sightings of Martha, a wolverine nor a mastodon, but there are plenty of interesting critters you can hope to see. Some are shy. Some are rare. Some are endangered. Some are so tiny you will have a hard time spotting them. The following animals, plants, bugs, snakes, reptiles and butterflies are out there and if you are lucky, your paths may cross.

Birds

The <u>Kirtland Warbler</u>. The endangered Kirtland Warbler nests in only a few counties in Michigan's northern Lower Peninsula. It also nests in Michigan's Upper Peninsula, Wisconsin and Ontario but no place else in the world. It is a ground nester that needs the mixed vegetation of grasses and shrubs below the living branches of five to eight-year-old jack pine forests. The soil in the habitat areas contains Grayling sand, an extremely well-drained sandy soil with low humus and nutrient content. Water drains through the sand so quickly that nests are seldom flooded.

In the late 1800s lumbermen and raging forest fires destroyed much of Michigan's forest land, but ironically these circumstances increased the range of jack pine. The fires removed older trees and rejuvenated the forest. The heat from the fire opened jack pine cones to release seeds and prepared the ground for germination. As a result, the Kirtland's warbler population reached its peak between 1885 and 1900 at the same time the passenger pigeon was disappearing. With better fire fighting efforts and limitations on lumbering, the warbler's habitat declined.

Michigan's Endangered Kirtland Warbler

In order to maintain a habitat for the Kirtland Warbler, the U.S. Department of Agriculture Forest Service and the Michigan Department of Natural Resources created four areas within the state and national forests to be managed specifically for Kirtland Warbler nesting habitat. Designated between 1957 and 1962, these areas contained 50% of the nesting population by 1973.

The male of the species is more colorful and easier to spot. He has a distinctive bright yellow-colored breast streaked in black and bluish-gray back feathers, a dark mask over his face with white eye rings and a bobbing tail. The length of the Warbler is less than six inches. Because of its restricted home range and unique habitat requirements, the Kirtland Warbler has always been a rare bird. It was first described in 1851 when a male was collected on the outskirts of Cleveland, Ohio. The new species was named in honor of Jared P. Kirtland, a naturalist who authored the first list of birds of Ohio.

The Warbler migrates from Michigan to winter grounds in the Bahamas a distance of 1,200 miles.

The Bald Eagle. Adopted as our national symbol in 1782, the Bald Eagle is unique to North America. It was in danger of extinction twenty-five years ago. The population of Bald Eagles throughout the United States had dwindled precipitously. By 1940 congress noted the precarious position of the national bird and passed the Bald Eagle Protection Act making it illegal to kill, sell, harass or otherwise harm a Bald Eagle.

Toxic pesticides and chemicals presented the greatest threat to the eagles' continued existence. DDT and other pesticides were sprayed on crops and washed into local waters. Eagles ate fish from the contaminated waters. The second-hand chemicals they ingested caused thinning eggshells that prevented the births of many chicks. But, the Bald Eagle's comeback is a success story. In 2004 there were between 300 and 425 breeding pairs in Michigan. That compares to fewer than the same number of pairs in the entire lower forty-eight states in the early 1960s. There are believed to be 4,500 breeding pairs in the United States today. In 1995 the Bald Eagle population had recovered to the point it was removed from the endangered list and upgraded to threatened. The increasing number of eagles in the state is a good sign for its complete recovery.

The turnaround is likely due to the substantial reduction of contaminants that previously affected the eagles' reproductive abilities. Captive-hatched Bald Eagles also played an important role in rejuvenating the wild population and helped establish a wider distribution of the bird. A third method of increasing the population was to introduce a "strong-shelled" egg obtained from captive birds into a wild nest of otherwise thin-shelled eggs. The wild eagle parents adopted the egg and raised the resulting chick.

It is hard to tell male and female eagles apart by their markings. Both have an easily identifiable white head with large, pale eyes and a strong yellow beak setting it apart from lesser birds. However, the white head and tail feathers only appear after the eagle is about four or five years old. An eagle may live to be thirty-years-old in the wild or even older in captivity. They have huge black talons capable of inflicting significant damage to their prey, but quite useful in catching fish, the staple of their diet. They also feed on injured geese, ducks and carrion along the roadside. Females are the larger of the pair and can weigh up to fourteen pounds and have a wing span of up to eight feet. Eagles mate for life and build large nests in tree tops near rivers, lakes, or wetland areas. They may reuse the nest for several years. Eggs are laid only once a year, two or three at a time. They hatch after a month and the young can fly within three months, and are on their own by the end of the season.

Bald Eagles can be found nearly anywhere in Michigan. They have been sighted in the Kalamazoo and Three Rivers area and along the St. Joseph River in St. Joseph County.

The Piping Plover. This small, sand-colored North American shorebird blends with the beaches which are its primary habitat. It generally weights only an ounce or two and is between six to six-and-a-half inches long. During the breeding season the legs are bright orange and the short bill is orange with a black tip. The plover has two single dark bands: one around its neck and one across its forehead between the eyes. In the winter the bill turns black, the legs are a paler orange and the black bands are lost. The female's neck band is thinner and less complete than the male's.

The Michigan population of Piping Plovers has decreased significantly in the last hundred years. They are still spotted along Lake Michigan's coastal shoreline. They were declared endangered in Michigan in 1985, but only classified as threatened along the Atlantic Coast. Because Piping Plovers nest on beaches where there is heavy human traffic, their eggs get stepped on and the presence of people may cause the birds to abandon their nests. Pets, especially dogs, are also a threat to these tiny birds. Much of their nesting territory has been lost to industrialization and they fall prey to raccoon, skunks and fox.

The Piping Plover on Nest

Reptiles and amphibians: Not ugh but ah!

<u>Mudpuppy.</u> The mudpuppy is a large permanently aquatic salamander ranging from eight to nineteen inches long with a flattened tail and reddish, fringelike gills behind the head. Body color is brown or gray-brown with darker scattered blotches. The mudpuppy is found throughout the state in inland lakes, Great Lakes' bays and marshes, rivers and reservoirs. It prefers shallow waters in the spring, but can be found in depths of up to one hundred feet at other times. Mudpuppies eat crayfish, insects and smaller amphibians. They are sensitive to chemical pollutants and are often destroyed by people who catch them

while fishing. The skin of the mudpuppy secretes a protective mucus covering that can make them very difficult to hold. Trying to grasp this creature is like gripping a wet bar of soap.

Copper-bellied Water Snake. This large brown or black snake has a reddish or coppery-orange belly for which it is named. The adult length is from three-to-five feet. The Copper-bellied Water Snake is found in or near river-bottom swamps, marshy ponds and wooded river banks. They feed on frogs, tadpoles and fish. They are found only in the southern third of the Lower Peninsula of Michigan. The Copper-bellied Water Snake is an endangered species.

Northern Water Snake. A two-to-four-foot snake, the dark bands or blotches on a lighter brown or gray background distinguish this snake. Old, adult snakes may appear solid black or brown. The belly is white with reddish half-moon shaped markings. The Northern Water Snake is non-venomous and found along shorelines of the Lower Peninsula. It is sometimes mistakenly called a water moccasin, but that species is not native to Michigan.

Northern Ring-necked Snake. This is a small black or gray snake only ten-to-twenty-four inches long sporting a yellow ring around its neck. The snake's belly is yellow, with a few black dots down the midline. It lives in moist woods and woodland edges, resting under logs or bark. It feeds on earthworms, salamanders and smaller snakes. They are found throughout Michigan, but they are rare. Some of the larger islands in Lake Michigan still have good populations.

Massasauga Rattlesnake. The Massasauga, Michigan's only venomous snake, is a heavy-bodied, gray or brown snake two to three feet long. It has dark blotches on the back and sides. It hibernates during the winter in swamps and marshes, but then moves to upland fields or woodlands in the summer, searching for mice and moles. Although venomous, these rattlesnakes are shy and avoid confrontation. Do not pester this critter, and if bitten you need prompt professional medical attention. This snake is found only in the Lower Peninsula and is listed as a "species of special concern."

Butterflies, a Special Kind of Fragile Beauty

Mitchell's Satyr. One of Michigan's rarest butterfly species, the Mitchell's Satyr inhabits fewer than twenty sites in Michigan. Satyr habitat is very specific to sedge grass, meadows and small wetlands called "fens." These wetlands typically have calcareous soils containing limestone, and are ringed with tamaracks, poison sumac and dogwood shrubs. Managing or containing land development is crucial to the survival of Mitchell's Satyr butterfly. Changes in watersheds surrounding fens can alter their fragile environments. The Satyr is an endangered species and harming one is a crime. Appearance: the Satyr is a small butterfly with a wing span of only one-and-a-half to one-and-three-quarters inches. The wings are dark brown with a powdery cast. The ventral (bottom) wing surfaces have a line of large, black, pale-yellow-ringed "eye spots" and are rimmed in orange bands. These butterflies are often seen flying low over vegetation in an erratic flight pattern. When disturbed they dart into grasses and shrubs. While on the ground with their wings tucked, predators have difficulty spotting them. Although rare, there are Mitchell's satyr butterflies in southwestern Michigan.

The **Karner Blue Butterfly**. One of Michigan's wildlife treasures, the endangered Karner Blue is found primarily in west Michigan in Mason, Oceana, Muskegon and Allegan Counties. Its habitat is open, sunny areas with sandy soil and scattered small trees called savannas or barrens. These areas support a variety of wildflowers including wild lupine which is the only food eaten by Karner Blue caterpillars. The Karner Blue is a small butterfly about one-inch in length. Males have a vibrant, silvery-blue color on the upper surface of their wings. The upper surfaces of the females' wings are blue close to the body, fading to grayish-brown towards the edges. The wing undersides of both sexes is light-gray to grayish-brown with rows of small, black spots. A single row of metallic blue-green, orange, and black spots rim the outer edges of the under-side of each wing, but are most distinct on the hind wings. There are several common butterflies that can be mistaken for Karner Blues, but most of them do not have orange markings on their under-wings.

Plants Worth Mentioning
The **Pitcher Plant, Dune Thistle** or **Pitcher Thistle**. This strange plant is usually found in acidic bogs or fens. It is carnivorous; feeding on insects that are trapped in its highly specialized bulbous pitcher-like leaves covered with downward-pointing hairs which keep insects from escaping. The doomed bugs drown, providing the pitcher plant with important nutrients.

The Carnivorous Pitcher Plant

This unique plant can only be found on the shoreline or sand dunes of the Great Lakes, and is primarily found along the Michigan side of Lake Michigan. Its roots can dig as deep as six feet into the sand dune. The Pitcher's Thistle has a special beauty with bluish-green leaves and white woolly hairs on its blossom. The flower blooms from June to September and is cream colored or carries a slightly pink hue. This thistle is no miniature plant, growing to three-and-a-half-feet; although flowering plants less than six inches have also been seen. The plant has a fragrant, but light smell.

The <u>Dwarf Lake Iris</u>. An exquisite miniature iris found only on the northern Great Lakes shoreline of Lakes Michigan and Huron where it may occur for miles, interrupted only by commercialization, buildings or rocky points and marshy bays unsuitable to its growth. It suffers loss of habitat due to increased human activity along the beaches. Human disturbances such as shoreline development and intensive recreation are major threats. It is currently listed as a "threatened" species by the federal government and the state of Michigan. The scientific name for this species is *iris lacustris*. "Lacustris" translates literally to "of lakes" and refers to the habitat of this special iris. It was first found on Mackinac Island in 1810 by Thomas Nuttall, a renowned naturalist. The Dwarf Lake Iris produces a single large, showy, blue flower, just below the height of the leaves. It is short in stature, perhaps six inches high. The leaves are light green and usually not more than one-half-inch wide.

A Triumphant Fish Tale

Lake Trout. Ask any Michigander what his or her favorite game fish is and often you will be told, "Lake Trout." Michigan is blessed with an abundance of cold, quality trout waters. The existence of popular game fish in Michigan waters was seriously threatened in the mid-1960s by the Lamprey eel. But with that problem coming under better control through the introduction of salmon into the lakes, the trout is making a welcomed comeback. The rainbow or steelhead trout lives, grows and reaches spawning size in the Great Lakes. The popular Great Lakes steelhead adult averages nine to ten pounds. Michigan's record is twenty-six-and-a-half pounds. The rainbow or steelhead trout can be distinguished from look-alike salmon species by the pinkish streak on its sides and the pepper-size spots radiating along the rays of the entire tail. Additional spots may or may not adorn the upper surface of the body.

The brown trout is a close relative to the Atlantic salmon and was brought to North American waters as an exotic (not native to the region). They can be distinguished from the Atlantic salmon by their upper lip which extends beyond the outer edges of the eye. The tongue is squarish with five or more strong teeth per side. The pectoral fins are light and the tail square. The name is somewhat misleading because for many Great Lakes brown trout, the predominant color is silver. On the average, lake-run adults weigh eight pounds. Michigan's champion catch weighed thirty-four pounds.

Michigan Mammals

Coyote. Most abundant in the northern Lower Peninsula and the Upper Peninsula where there is an adequate food, cover and water available, coyote can be found throughout the state. This member of the dog family is extremely adaptable and survives in virtually all habitat types common in Michigan. The size of a coyote's home range depends on the food and cover resources and the number of other coyotes in the area, but it generally averages between eight and twelve square miles. Mated pairs with pups occupy the home range during the spring and summer seasons in Michigan. An average litter is four to seven pups.

Coyote

From a distance a coyote can be difficult to distinguish from a German shepherd dog. Generally the upper body of the coyote is yellowish gray, although there is wide color variation, and the fur covering the throat and belly is white to cream color. The coyote's ears are pointed and stand erect unlike the ears of domestic dogs which often droop. When observed running, coyotes carry their bushy, black-tipped tail below the level of their back. A coyote's size and weight is often over-estimated because their thick fur makes them look larger. They are not usually taller than eighteen inches and their average length is slightly less than three feet. A coyote weighs between twenty-five and forty-five pounds. They are most often seen during their breeding period from mid-January into March.

Coyotes present no significant threat to humans. You are more likely to be bitten by a snake, rat or domestic dog.

Elk. Originally called "wapiti" meaning "white rump" in the Shawnee language, elk are members of the deer family, closely related to moose and white-tailed deer. An adult elk can weigh between 350 and 900 pounds. They stand four-and-a-half to five feet tall at the shoulder. They have distinct summer and winter coats. In the winter the head, neck and legs are dark brown while the sides and back are much lighter. The summer coat is a deep reddish-brown color. Both males and females have heavy dark manes extending to the brisket and a whitish rump patch. Each year male elk grow antlers used for dominance displays and defense. The antlers can weigh up to forty pounds when bulls reach maturity at five years. Elk are plant eating and consume a wide variety of vegetation.

Bull Elk

By 1875 elk had disappeared from the Lower Peninsula of Michigan. In 1918 seven elk were released in southern Cheboygan County as part of a restoration attempt. It proved successful. From that small beginning, the herd grew slowly, but by the early-1960s a large number of elk ranged over approximately six-hundred-square-miles. Crop damage problems and overuse of forest vegetation prompted the first public hunts for elk in Michigan in 1964 and 1965. Primarily due to poaching, elk numbers again began to decline. By 1975 the elk herd numbered only about two-hundred. The Department of Natural Resources increased protection through expanded enforcement efforts and by 1981 the herd see-sawed up again to an estimated 500. DNR developed a management plan with a goal of "a viable elk population in harmony with the environment, affording optimal recreational opportunities." The annual elk hunt is Michigan's most successful management tool. Hunters must apply and be selected through a random drawing in order to be eligible to hunt. These managed hunts keep the elk herd in the upper portion of the Lower Peninsula to about a thousand.

White Tailed Deer. Michigan's State Game Animal, the white tail deer is the shyest and most nervous of all North American deer. They range in size from two-and-a-half to three-and-a-half feet at shoulder, five-to-seven-feet in length and weigh between one-hundred-twenty-five to four-hundred pounds.

White Tailed Deer

They have characteristically brown fur with a white belly. The clearly identifiable tail, white on the underside, is raised when the deer is frightened and easily recognized as the animal bounds away. There is also a white patch on the throat and around the muzzle of the deer. Males have antlers that they shed between January and March and that grow back in April or May. Females are smaller and do not have antlers. White-Tailed Deer have scent glands on all four hooves, between the two parts of the foot. The scent is used for communication with other deer. Secretions become especially strong during mating season. The range of the deer is very small, only about one-third of a square mile. They do not migrate, remaining even in a cold winter climate like Michigan's. The White-Tailed Deer likes to live near farmland and in forests and they prefer to live near water. Their diet consists of vegetation, including buds, leaves, fruit and local gardens. Primarily a solitary animal, they herd in winter for warmth. Nimble and quick runners, they can reach speeds of forty-miles-per-hour. Less well known is the fact that they are excellent swimmers and plunge into waters to escape predators.

Porcupine, These rodents are covered with as many as 30,000 quills. The quills are hairs with a barbed tip on the end. The porcupine has quills over its entire body, except for the stomach. The quills are longer on the rump area and shorter around the face. They have hairless soles on their feet that help them climb trees where they spend much of their time. The porcupine is a good swimmer, buoyed by its hollow quills. It is a very vocal animal and has a wide-variety of calls including moans, grunts, coughs, wails, whines, shrieks and tooth clicking. They are solitary animals, although they may group in dens for the winter. They are not a hibernating animal, but will stay inside when the weather is particularly ferocious. A common myth warns you to stay away from the porcupine because it can throw those painful quills at you. That is not true. What actually happens is that a threatened porcupine will turn and lash out with its quill-covered tail. When that tail strikes, you can expect a painful reaction to those sharp quills. Porcupine are found in the western Lower Peninsula.

Northern Flying Squirrel. Although active all year and found in Western Michigan, these small furry mammals are nocturnal so you may never see one. They cannot really fly. They glide from tree to tree by stretching tight the membranes of furred skin between their front and hind legs. The tail has thick fur and is flat on the bottom and rounded on the top which provides additional lift for gliding by acting as a rudder and paddle, assisting in both up-and-down and side-to-side movements. This allows the squirrel to change direction while soaring through the air and set down on a perfect four-point landing. Thickened toe pads help cushion landing impact. The gliding ability makes the squirrel's search for food easier and also helps it escape natural enemies. Most often our contact with this squirrel is not in the wild, but rather when they scurry into our attics to store food or prepare a nest.

And even a bug

Whirligig Beetles. Beetles are the largest single order of insects in the world and they total a mind-boggling 360,000 or more species. They may constitute 25% of all animal species. Whirligigs look like plumped up watermelon seeds. They bob and skate and dart about on the water's surface with amazing speed. The beetles carry an air bubble on the posterior tip of their abdomen that serves as an oxygen tank allowing them to breathe underwater. Their elongated forelegs are tucked as they swim. Two other pairs of legs, shorter and flat, allow the Whirligig to control its movements in the water. It is easier to observe these insects on the surface of the water, where they may congregate in large number, than to look for them as they flit about the air on their membranous wings. Whirligigs reside in ponds or slow-moving streams where they search for smaller insects to eat. The beetle has four compound eyes, two flattened on the upper part of its head and two rather round ones on the underside.

And a word of thanks...

To the Michigan Department of Natural Resources for providing much of the information used in this section.

For time is inches
And the heart's changes,
Where ghost has haunted
Lost and wanted.
-Wystan Hugh Auden

Ghosts and Monsters of Lake Michigan
-Haunting and Stalking the Sunset Coast

Taylor Heath Salon, New Buffalo. It is after the sun goes down and everyone has left for the day that the ghost or ghosts of the Heath Salon are most at unrest. Whether it is the darkness, the moon's rays streaming through the upstairs windows or just being left alone, the disembodied souls, who struggle to escape this earth, wander about the salon trying to find their way. The staff and clients have had numerous run-ins with the spirits that haunt the salon. No one knows what causes the agitation of their resident ghosts; only that they make themselves known in disconcerting ways. One evening, stylist Jennifer Kasper (*names changed throughout*) remained late to finish up Margie Howard's shampoo and cut. They were the only two humans left in the salon as Jen guided her client to the shampoo bowl and began lathering Margie's hair. Kasper heard the unmistakable jangling of keys and the rattle of the door up front. She knew she had locked the door, so tried to ignore the suspicious sounds until Margie, who heard the ruckus over the sound of running water, insisted, "There's someone up there." Reluctantly, Jen went to investigate, but there was no one else in the building; the front door was locked just as she knew it would be.

Another evening, as darkness crept in, Bonnie Phillips remained in the building finishing paperwork long after her co-workers had left. She turned off the music that provided a pleasant backdrop to the day's busy activities. The quiet enveloped her and she was heavy in concentration when the sounds of footsteps and gnarled mumbling filtered down from the first room at the top of the stairs. Initially Bonnie wondered if someone had accidentally been locked in that tiny room. But, she knew that was not possible. She continued working, dismissing the noise to an overactive imagination. Then she heard an unmistakable cough. Bonnie was neither fainthearted nor easily rattled, but it was time to grab her purse and get out of there.

The ghost sometimes says "hi," to employees who look up to find no one there. These occurrences are so frequent that clients hearing unexplained noises remark, "Oh, the ghost is here."

Recently a former owner of the building stopped by and the staff questioned him about the odd occurrences. He shared with them peculiar experiences from when he lived in the building. He would hear noises like children crying upstairs; doors would open. He would check and find no one. Unfortunately, he could offer no explanation about who the ghosts were or why they continued to rustle about the haunted building.

Hannah's, New Buffalo. This popular restaurant serves food that brings 'em in by the busload, but behind its cheery façade lurk the ghosts of two former residents who lived there when Hannah's was a magnificent and expansive home in this lovely harbor town.

James Janata brought his Czechoslovakian bride to her dazzling new domicile shortly after they were married. Mrs. Janata proved a handful. A former beauty queen, whose stunning looks captivated and enthralled her bedeviled husband, she felt a sense of entitlement. Her inexhaustible demands left the beleaguered James weary and frustrated by his inability to satisfy her whims. Her spoiled antics were so relentless that the sweet-natured James, worn-down and heartsick, swore he would return in the afterlife to haunt her. It is suspected that he carried out his threat and that until the day she died James capitalized on every opportunity to make his widow as miserable as she had made him during his life. If Mr. Janata's ghost still spends time in his former residence, it may be that he enjoys the warm, friendly feelings that abide there now that Mrs. Janata is gone.

Hannah's was also home to a rugged sea captain who sailed from the port at New Buffalo. While at sea the captain lived a stark life barren of any luxury. He can hardly be blamed, then, if he wanted a grand and opulent home to make up for the deprivations he endured while sailing. He heard of a newfangled, ostentatious, luxury item known as a bath tub. The captain took a trip to Chicago to purchase this extravagance and once installed, it became the object of his great admiration. So much so, that even in the afterlife the captain came back to gaze upon its beauty. He appeared in the bathroom occasionally, wearing his skipper's uniform, and fondly, but vacantly, staring at his tub. He is a bit melancholy and causes no harm, although he may have brought a bit of consternation to ladies bathing as he looked on.

Timeless Treasures Antique Store, Sawyer. The proprietor of Timeless Treasures was surprised a few years ago when a group of high schoolers stopped by and asked about the ghost that lived in the building. The owner could not provide them with much information and the details are sketchy. The ghost's name is Joe and this is the bare-bones of his story:

Joe owned Blackstone Grocery which many years ago occupied the building where Timeless Treasures now stands. Joe and his wife had a tempestuous relationship. After one particularly unpleasant argument, the distressed wife escaped to Grand Rapids to visit their son. When Joe realized she had truly abandoned him, his emotions kicked into overdrive. He was angry, hurt, provoked and indignant. More than anything he wanted to retaliate; he wanted to upset his wife as much as her departure had upset him. Acting on his first hunch, he called one of his wife's friends. He was assured his wife was not staying with any of them. But, Joe did not believe the friends. The thought that his wife was playing games with him only further infuriated Joe, and he became more agitated. He went in the back room and retrieved his gun. It is unclear whether it was a hand gun or a shotgun, but either would have sufficed for what he contemplated.

After sitting for a while and reflecting on his situation, Joe decided he could not just kill himself; he needed to make his errant wife suffer. Joe decided to call their son to see if the son knew his mother's whereabouts. Joe was surprised when his son said, "She's here." Joe asked to speak to her. As she listened, Joe said, "Look, what you have made me do." And with that, he blew off his head. This suicide was believed to have occurred in the 1940s and Joe's ghost has found no peace since. Maybe it serves him right.

The Mansion Grille, St. Joseph. The Mansion Grill began its life as home to the Smith family from Chicago. The house was built in 1892 as their summer home and, from what we know, it was a place of joy and renewal for them until 1929. That gloomy year brought the stock market crashing; and Mr. Smith, dejected and beyond consolation, jumped from a building to his death. The widow Smith sold the property to Otis Colby in the early 1930s. The Colby family operated a used car lot to the north of the house; the family also operated a produce stand across the street on the lakeside for many years. The house became known as the Colby Mansion. The Colbys remained in the house for sixty years, celebrating many happy occasions there, including their 50th wedding anniversary. In 1990 the home was purchased as the site for an upscale restaurant. The new owners spent nearly three years renovating and preparing the mansion for its new incarnation. The goal was to restore the magnificent old home to its original character.

Apparently the resident ghost, likely that of Mr. Smith, appreciated the renovations which made him feel at home. So, he continues to inhabit the basement. He is a shy and considerate ghost and the current owners only became aware of his presence through a book about ghosts in the Midwest.

Ghost of the Lakeside Inn, Arthur Aylesworth and his brother first discovered the Lakeside Inn Resort when they were just boys on a family camping trip. In 1901 they persuaded their parents to buy it and the thirty acres of land surrounding it. The total cost of the purchase was $4,500. In 1917, Arthur's father died and two years later his mother deeded the property to him.

The hotel/inn is located on a sand dune and stands three stories high with an English basement at the rear. There are half a dozen ground floor entrances around the perimeter. As far as is known, no architect was involved in the Inn's design. It has two, large, stone fireplaces, back-to-back, one in the lobby and the other in the ballroom.

Arthur Aylesworth not only operated the hotel, but owned much other property in the Lakeside area. He was always buying, mortgaging and selling land. The Inn had beautiful gardens and a mini-zoo in back with a pet bear, raccoon, deer, goats and peacocks. During its heyday there was gambling just off the lobby; and much alcohol was consumed insides its walls during Prohibition. Supposedly bootleggers' boats from Canada would beach in front of the hotel and guests would wade out into the lake to help unload the cases of whisky. It is alleged that Al Capone visited the place to relax.

Arthur Aylesworth was a world adventurer who traveled extensively in South America and Alaska. He produced films about his big-game hunting expeditions. Aylesworth also toured with Buffalo Bill's Wild West Show, operated a gambling hall and bar in Las Vegas, and married and divorced Florence Young, the sister of movie star, Clare Kimball Young.

During the 1930s Aylesworth went bankrupt more than once, but somehow managed to maintain ownership of the Inn until the 1950s. By then he had married a second wife, an actress named Virginia Harned. Mrs. Harned-Aylesworth toured the country in the play, "The Woman He Married," produced by her husband. Years before her death she was shot by Arthur who insisted it was an accident. Sentiment in the local community ran contrary. No charges were filed and both Mrs. Aylesworth and the marriage survived. During massive rehabilitation of the Inn in 1995, a bloodstained towel was found hidden in a wall. It bore the initials AA.

During the later years of his life, Aylesworth, whose second wife had predeceased him (naturally we assume), still lived in the Inn. He became a lonely figure watching a tiny television set in the lobby until sleep finally numbed his mind. At about 10:00 pm each evening, the handyman who lived in an out-building behind the Inn would be awakened by the ghost of Virginia Harned-Aylesworth. She urged the handyman to go inside and awaken Mr. Aylesworth and tell him it was time to undress and go to bed. Through the subsequent decades many visitors have detected the presence of the ghost of Mrs. Aylesowrth - especially in or near room thirty.

There is less agreement over whether there is also a male ghost on the premises, presumably Mr. Aylesworth. A guest at a recent wedding in the ballroom swears she observed Mr. Aylesworth's silhouette with pet raccoon on his shoulder. All indications suggest these are harmless ghosts, pleased to continue residing in their Inn. It seems that even bankruptcy, death, and familial squabbles (if shooting a spouse can be called a squabble), cannot keep them away.

In an interesting aside to the ghost story, Aylesworth eventually lost the Inn to foreclosure by the Niles Bank. He died in the University Hospital at Ann Arbor, where no one knew his illustrious background. His cadaver was almost used for experimentation by medical students. A doctor from the hospital mentioned, during a phone conversation to the township lawyer of Lakeside, that one of their citizens had died at the hospital. When people from Lakeside realized what had happened several men went to Ann Arbor to claim the body which was then buried it in a plot Ayesworth had purchased at the Lakeside Cemetery.

The Lakeside Inn   *Photo Courtesy of Connie Williams*

South Haven Keeper's Ghost. Dr. Susan Scully, a university scholar and doctoral student, was researching old lighthouses and thrilled to be granted permission to study documents kept in the South

Haven keeper's house. *(Names are fictionalized since they varied in different accounts.)* Susan read all day and as night closed in she was still feverishly absorbing the documents spread out before her on the table. She laid her head down for a moment to rest her burning eyes, and must have dozed off.

When she awoke the keepers dwelling was pitch black. She fumbled to flip the light switch, but no illumination rewarded her effort. Her fingers explored the table for the telephone, but lifting the receiver she heard no dial tone. She rose to feel her way out of the house, but before she could take her first step a bone-chilling scream pierced the silence. It was the sound that accompanies horrible agony. Susan responded with her own scream demanding, "Who is there?" The only reply was a second wail that shook the walls of the small room. The lone voice was then joined by a chorus of muddled words coming from men, women and children. Susan could make out: "Help," "Take my child," "Please, Captain, save my children," and "Good-bye my love." The rest was unintelligible.

Dr. Scully was paralyzed by fear. The voices continued, stronger and stronger, pleading to be saved. Scully felt an icy mist on her skin. A gush of air blew against her. A bearded figure wearing a Civil War uniform and carrying a cane in one hand floated towards her and landed inches from her trembling body. The apparition was missing one leg from the knee down and the wooden peg that replaced it was noiseless as it tapped against the floor, moving the wraith closer to the ghoulish crowd that continued its frightful groaning.

Around the peg-legged Captain appeared more ghouls; misshapen and grossly deformed. Some wore black hooded cloaks. Their cries were muffled by the sound of crashing waves and splintering wood. Bodies floated and clung to pieces of debris. Susan saw the specter of a sinking ship with a gaping hole in its port side. Then she watched as the peg-legged man stepped into a small boat and rowed towards the terrified crowd hanging from the deck of a great steamer.

The hooded creatures lowered the coverings from their heads revealing leathery skin drawn tightly over skulls with gaping holes where eyes had once been. Lips contorted into evil grins and the crowd pitched towards the wooden-legged man in the boat. "Captain, how could you leave us to die?" the macabre group accusingly asked in unison.

"I did not leave you. I did what I could. There were too many. Stop torturing me. Be off with you. Can't you be grateful for those I was able to save," the Captain besieged them.

The creatures fell to the floor as the Captain began thrusting his cane about and striking them. As the image of the boat came closer to her face, Susan recognized it from a picture she had seen earlier that day during her research. It was Lars Johansson, a former keeper who had saved many shipwreck victims during his tenure at the lighthouse.

South Haven Lighthouse on a stormy day
Photo by permission of Gary Martin Photography

Postscript: To try to understand this strange and haunting story I attempted to verify any of the names I had heard applied to the Captain in this story. None was listed as a lighthouse keeper in South Haven. What I did find was astonishing: The lighthouse keeper with the longest tenure in South Haven was Captain James Donahue who tended the lighthouse for thirty-five years. Before he became a keeper, Donahue enlisted in the 8th Michigan Infantry and fought in the Civil War from 1861-1864, losing a leg in battle! In 1874 his appointment as lighthouse keeper at South Haven was compensation for his loss. While lighthouse keeper he was elected village president. During his service at the lighthouse, several ships went down in Lake Michigan near South Haven. The Chicora (see Shipwrecks, p. 375.) was one. However, the

414

Chicora had a crew and only one passenger so would not meet the ghostly description of voices of men, women and children ranting against the Captain.

Felt Mansion, Saugatuck. Dorr Felt began construction of his luxurious summer home in 1925, six years after he purchased the property. The house was his gift of love to his wife Agnes. The story ended tragically when Agnes died of a stroke in her room, shortly after the mansion's completion in 1928. Dorr Felt remarried, but his second wife hated being in the house where she felt Agnes' eyes watching her. The ghost of the first Mrs. Felt was not happy that Dorr had remarried.

The Felt family continued to own the mansion for an additional two decades before the daughters sold the estate to the St. Augustine Seminary and school. Buildings were added by the seminary in the 1960s, but declining enrollment forced closure in the 1970s.

The State of Michigan began using the seminary school as the minimum security Dunes Correctional Facility, and the Felt Mansion was converted to a State Police Post, along with offices and storage space for the prison. When the prison closed, the township purchased the land and buildings from the state with the agreement that the mansion and grounds would remain "for public use only." This limitation made selling the property to a private buyer or enterprise impossible. Although the mansion is a Michigan Historic Landmark, its future is not certain. There are attempts to raise funds for its restoration, and in the past these efforts have included "Ghost tours." Inside the house doors open and close in Agnes' room and voices can be heard whispering and groaning. Visitors take pictures that reveal wispy white streaks, orbs and mists. The ballroom is felt to be the most "haunted" area of the home. It is believed that Dorr's ghost has joined Agnes in wandering the mansion. Perhaps he always missed his first wife.

Near the mansion and behind the railroad tracks is the last remaining building from the Dunes Correctional Facility. It was used as the Trustee Building and housed eighty inmates. This building was reputedly an Asylum for the criminally insane, but that rumor is based on false information. Still, that is not to say that the silhouettes of figures walking the grounds, and the screams you hear, may not be ghosts who have some agonizing connection to the correctional facility or other ancient history of the grounds.

The Castle, Castle Park, near Holland. German born Michael Schwartz left his homeland because of Prussian militarism. Mr. Schwartz made an early fortune in real estate in Chicago which permitted him the luxury of retiring at a young age. He settled in Castle Park, a small community a few miles south of Holland where he hoped to build his dream manor, a replica of an estate he recalled in his native Germany. He wanted to insulate his wife and six daughters from the incivility of the big city and the crude ways of this brash young country.

Building the brick and stone castle was the easy part. More difficult was keeping his lovely daughters away from the attentions of local boys, especially two years later when the family moved from Castle Park to Holland. One of the Schwartz daughters met a local Dutch boy from their new neighborhood and made plans to marry him. Her father was outraged and forbade the union.

The lovers, not to be thwarted, made covert plans to sneak away in the middle of the night and elope. With the plans complete and the buggy ready, they made their escape, but not without waking Herr Schwartz who grabbed a gun and was in quick pursuit by horseback. His horse made better speed than the buggy, and Schwartz was able to reach the young couple before the vows were spoken. He locked his errant daughter in the Castle's tower where she pined away heartbroken until the time of her death. On moonlit nights she can be seen in the tower window, facing Holland and searching for the lover she lost.

Blue Man, Grand Haven. There are reported sightings of an apparition, described as a blue man, at the top of Ferry Hill in the Lake Forest Cemetery. This is the special, old section of the cemetery where the city's founding fathers, including William Ferry, are buried. Winding stairs provide access to the plots of some of the most prominent families of Grand Haven and Ferrysburg's past. The Blue Man is speculated to be William Montague Ferry who was born in 1796. William became a Presbyterian minister and moved with his wife to Mackinac Island where they were missionaries before moving to Grand Haven in 1834. William planned to pursue his future and fortune in the heavily wooded Grand Haven area. The cities of Ferrysburg and Montague were named for him. He died on December 30, 1867 leaving an estate worth more than $100,000, a huge sum of money in those days. The inscription on his tombstone reads: "First toil, then rest; First grace, then glory." But, is there a chance he is not resting well? Maybe on some clear night, with the moon illuminating the way, a hazy blue figure will appear and clarify the mystery that surrounds him.

Ramsdell Theater, Manistee. The Theatre opened on September 4, 1903 with a performance of "A Chinese Honeymoon" which had been a big hit on Broadway. Over the years the Ramsdell continued as a successful theatre, although during some periods it resorted to showing movies. Currently it provides a stage for the Manistee Civic Players. It is a Michigan Historic Building.

The Theatre was named for Thomas Jefferson Ramsdell who throughout his adult life worked for the continuing improvement of Manistee. In 1883, the city had a large building on the corner of First and Greenbush that met the theatre and cultural needs of the local population. When this building burned, Ramsdell generously offered to replace the loss.

His new theatre opened three years later at a cost of nearly four times the original projected price. Detractors called it "Ramsdell's Folly" partly in recognition of the outrageous cost and partly because of its artwork. Ramsdell's son, Frederick, was an accomplished artist and he is believed to have painted the semi-nude Aphrodite adorning the auditorium's dome in the image of his own wife. Even more scandalous at the time were the lobby's murals of two nude goddesses frolicking in pastoral fields. Allegedly these goddesses have the faces of local 1800s gossips and were Frederick's way of getting even with Ramsdell detractors.

The theatre is well known for its ghosts who seem to enjoy the performances as much as the living audience does. There is a White Lady, as people call a long-haired ghost that supposedly roams the theatre. It is believed she is Ramsdell's daughter. Ramsdell himself makes occasional appearances, wearing a dapper, Victorian tuxedo.

A worker in the basement of the theatre reported a long-haired young girl in a white dress standing in the doorway. He leaned closer to get a better look. She turned to him and said, "Follow me to your fortune," and disappeared before his eyes. The frightened worker gave a description that sounds very much like the White Lady described by others. It is hard to decipher her message. How was the startled worker supposed to follow her if she disappeared?

The theatre may, indeed, be haunted, but it is also a place worth the price of admission just to see the opulent interior.

Bowers Harbor Inn. Old Mission Peninsula is an incredibly beautiful strip of land just north of Traverse City. Chicago millionaire J. W. Stickney and his wife Genevive chose this spot to build their dream home. Stickney made his fortune in lumber and steel, although one account also described him as a Captain of a Great Lakes shipping liner. The mansion the Stickneys built was befitting a queen and Genevive Stickney was known to act the part. She attempted to capture the feeling of grace and leisure of the era as she chose the expensive furnishings for her fabulous new home. One piece that she treasured until her death was a gilded mirror that made her look thinner. She could stand in front of the magical looking glass and see herself as she wanted to be.

Genevive was an eccentric character - if not downright weird. In her kitchen she preserved fruits, and made jams, wines and brandies that she then buried about the estate to prevent them from being stolen. She was a vain and jealous woman, an unpleasant combination in a woman who was both frumpy and plump. Adding to or perhaps causing her other character flaws was a lack of self-confidence in matters of the heart. The years merely added more pounds and self-doubt. Poor Genevive Stickney also suffered from a host of medical ailments. Her physical health deteriorated to the point that her husband hired a nurse to care for her. He installed an elevator so his wife could reach the upper floors of her beloved home.

Instead of gratitude, Genevive grew paranoid; convinced her husband was having an affair with the nurse. She obsessed that Charles would leave everything they owned to this tart – his lover. Time bore out Genevive's fears. Charles predeceased Genevive by only a few months and he left his entire fortune, with the exception of their Mission Point residence, to his mistress. Genevive was devastated and sick at heart as she contemplated the evidence of her husband's cruel betrayal. She slipped into a severe depression; quite possibly accompanied by a healthy dose of madness.

Genevive shuffled her corpulent self to the elevator rafters, tied a noose about her neck, and hung herself in the shaft. Ever since her ghastly death she has been reported haunting the Inn, opening windows, blowing out candles, and preening in front of her special mirror in the second floor ladies' room where her image nearly frightened one poor customer to death. Other visitors have reported a blurry female figure appearing in their vacation photographs.

Employees of the Inn also report seeing Genevive on the second floor, standing in front of the mirror. They confirm stories about lights switched on and off without human assistance. The elevator takes restless trips up and down, at no one's particular beck and call. An Inn manager reported closing the Inn for the evening as was his regular routine: He turned all of the lights off and locked the freezer door and then the front door behind him as he walked out. He arrived the next morning to find the lights blazing and the freezer door not only unlocked, but standing open. Patrons have insisted they witness the fireplaces lighting themselves. Pictures fall from walls. During one of Genevive's temper tantrums, patrons who were gathered in the dining room witnessed, first hand, her fury. No one was standing near the salad bar, but suddenly, a bowl of food flew off the table and shattered as though it had been deliberately hurled to gain attention.

Another manager, and a non-believer in ghosts, reported checking the ladies' room as he prepared to close for the evening. He flipped off the light and the door banged shut in his face. That seemed strange since he had experienced difficulty opening the door due to the newly installed carpet which caused it to stick. The door also had a self-adjusting arm that prevented it from slamming. In spite of the manager's skepticism regarding the spirit of Genevive Stickney, he knew the door could not have slammed - not without help.

Genevive is one of the more active ghosts you will encounter and her antics have earned her a slot on "Unsolved Mysteries" and a piece in several books.

The DogMan of northwestern Michigan. Dog man is a monster firmly entrenched in the lore of northern lumber camps and backwoods from the mid-1800s to today. Dogman walks upright on hind legs and looks a bit like his monster relative, Wolfman.

1887 is the first reported sighting and lumberjacks in Wexford County spotted an animal they believed to be a dog, and for lack of anything better to do, they began chasing it. To escape its pursuers the tormented animal ran inside a hollow log. One of the lumberjacks grabbed a stick and poked inside the log. The creature let out an unearthly scream, crawled out of the log and stood upright. There face-to-face and eye-to-eye with the men stood a creature with a man's body and a dog's head. The terrified men broke camp and never returned to the area. From then on, the beast made an appearance about every ten years.

In 1897, near Buckley, a farmer was found slumped over his plow. It was an apparent heart attack and probably would not have been considered unusual except for the huge dog tracks that ringed the ground about the deceased's body.

Exactly a decade later there was a report of a demented widow who reported weird dreams with dogs circling her house at night. These dogs walked like men and yelled like banshees. Ten more years passed before the next incident: A sheriff is alleged to have walked upon a wagon with dog prints in the dust around it. No driver could be found, but nearby four horses lay dead with their eyes wide open. A veterinarian was called to the scene, but he could find no medical reason for their deaths.

In 1937 there was a report by a boat captain that several of his crew saw a pack of wild dogs roaming Bowers Harbor. That same year, or possibly the next, Robert Fortney picked up his shotgun and killed one of a pack of dogs that lunged at him as he stood on the banks of the Muskegon River. One dog did not run off in fright. Instead it reared up on its hind legs and glared at Fortney with slanted, yellow eyes. Fortney was unsure what to call the animal that locked eyes with him.

He had heard the stories about the dogman, but did not want to feed those crazy tales. Still, he admitted, that was what it looked like: a man with a dog's head.

In 1957 a preacher found claw marks high on an old church door. If it was a dog, it was a mighty tall one, at least seven feet, he reckoned, to leave marks where they scratched the door. In 1967 a van of hippies reported being awakened in the middle of the night by a dog-man scratching on the windows. People wondered what they had been smoking. Ten more years passed and the next incident involved screams reported in the night near the Village of Bellaire when someone saw the creature. Again a decade passed, and in 1987 there was the report of an attempted break-in at a local cabin. The cuts on the door were believed to have been made by very sharp teeth or claws.

Two local fishermen became believers one evening at dusk when they were casting near Manistee. The sun was setting in its usual spectacular fashion when they saw an animal swimming towards their boat. One man immediately thought it was his old coon hound, coming to join them, but when it got closer he realized the beast had a dog's head and a man's body and was doing a human-style English crawl instead of a dog paddle. The two men, frightened nearly out of their wits, picked up their oars and began clubbing dogman until the creature finally retreated. The fishermen, not wanting to appear sissies, declined to talk further about their experience.

Dogman may be nothing more than a bunch of wild stories, but he stirs the imagination and frightens local folks around the upper part of Lake Michigan. Just to be safe, there are nights when you should not go out alone. And note: all of the years with reported sightings end in seven.

Traverse City Regional Psychiatric Facility. Psychiatric Hospitals are ripe with horror stories that make our skin crawl. Just the thought of Jack Nicholson in *"One Flew over the Cuckoo's Nest,'* sends chills down our spines. *Old* psychiatric hospitals are even more frightening. They existed at a time in history when shock therapy, brain tissue manipulation, implants, drug experimentation and lobotomies were treatments de jour.

Also known as the Northern Michigan Asylum, Traverse City State Hospital opened in 1885 and sat on a lovely piece of property with rolling meadows and steep, wooded slopes. Wetlands surrounded a central building area. Mules hauled yellowish bricks to the site on special flat cars that ran on wooden two-by-four tracks. The bricks were used in the construction of Building Fifty. Michigan quarries provided the slate needed for its roof. Building Fifty was the main and eventually most haunted building of the complex. It boasted three floors in addition to its basement and attic. It was designed by Gordon Lloyd, the architect of many churches and cathedrals during this period. The off-white walls and large windows presented a pleasant façade to all manor of horror that resided within.

The building had two wings, separated by a central staff and office area. The south wing housed male patients and the north housed female patients. At the back of the building were two infirmary wings that were originally separate buildings but later attached to Building Fifty. A chapel was added behind the center section of the building and it stood as a place of prayer and hope until the 1960s when fire destroyed it. It was replaced by a new section referred to as Building Fifty-A. This strictly utilitarian structure was typical of mid-1900s construction and cheapened the beauty of the original Building Fifty.

From the time it opened its doors, the population of the "asylum" grew until it became necessary to add cottages, each housing 60 to 125 additional patients to accommodate the need.

Within a few years of construction, attention turned to beautifying the grounds. The first superintendent of the hospital, Dr. James Decker Munson, contributed trees from his worldwide travels. He determined where the trees should be placed on the grounds and the "farm" manager saw that they were properly planted. One of Munson's trees became known as the "Hippie Tree" and supposedly near its trunk is an open, portal gate to hell itself.

The hospital carried out large farming operations during its early history. The resultant crops provided much of the food the patients ate. Championship cows were raised from the quality herd of Holsteins kept on the farm. The farm operation was discontinued in 1957, in part due to the high cost of labor and in part due to a lack of suitable patients to carry out the work.

To outward appearances, especially during the daylight hours, the lovely buildings and grounds were not creepy - at least not if you could avoid thinking of the misery of the residents therein. There are estimates of 30,000 people dying during the facility's century long history. That is likely an exaggerated number and obviously, many of the residents/inmates were there for their natural (or perhaps unnaturally shortened?) lives and would be expected to die there. Rumors of torture surfaced but, yesterday's treatment is often considered torture by today's arguably enlightened standards. Many ghosts of the pathetic souls who resided at the "Asylum" roamed the grounds. The presence of evil was described as so great that it caused holy relics such as bibles, holy water flasks, or crosses to be destroyed or harmed as people tried to enter the premises with them. The only place that was considered safe was the Chapel, but even in that most holy of spots a spirit was said to be present – that of a priest who committed suicide there. One can only speculate what manner of evil caused a priest to indulge that most unpardonable of sins.

Lights went on and off even when there was no electricity connected in the buildings. Voices and screams were commonplace and suggested the presence of those from the nether regions. Abnormal sightings included: a small baby left in one of the rooms, elderly patients shuffling inside the vacant buildings on various floors even after the facility closed, a ghostly figure that chased anyone brave enough to enter, and disfigured creatures roaming the basements and tunnels.

In the late 1970s the hospital closed. It has been recreated to house several businesses including an upscale restaurant with the best Italian food in Traverse City and a gallery offering local art. Plans continue to unfold for Building Fifty's new life. A few ghosts feel it should have been razed and covered with twenty feet of hallowed ground.

Building Fifty Today

The Ghost of Waugoshance Light. By day, Waugoshance Lighthouse looks like a bombed-out, worn-down old lighthouse that lacks the strength to harm a soul. Used as target practice during WWII, and further bombarded by the forces of nature, she turns a woebegone countenance to the midday sun. At night, alone, sitting on her crib in dark, roiling Lake Michigan waters, far from shore, she is an eerie and ominous presence. She is home to the ghost of John Herman, keeper of the light from about 1885 to October 14, 1990 - when the waters around Waugoshance claimed his life.

Herman was known to imbibe in spirits (of the alcoholic kind), maybe a side effect of his confinement on a distant, isolated shoal. He was also a practical joker, a personality trait not always appreciated by his assistant, who one moonless and windy night ascended the tower to light the lanterns and heard the lock click behind him. He was the target of yet another of Herman's attempts to be funny. The irritated assistant began yelling and rattling the door, "John, John, stop this nonsense. Let me down."

After he believed the joke had run its course, but before he believed his pal would be angry enough to do him bodily harm, Keeper John Herman drunkenly staggered along the pier intending to unlock the door. Instead, he slipped, and unable to regain his footing, plunged, screaming and flailing, over the edge into the churning waves where he drowned.

After several hours of patiently waiting for John to release him, the assistant signaled a nearby lighthouse and the keeper from that neighboring tower quickly arrived to see what the problem was. The two men searched for Herman, but his body was never recovered. For the next twelve years lighthouse keepers contended with Herman's ghost as it continued to play pranks. During checkers games keepers tipped over in their chairs, even when they had not been leaning backwards. The fallen men insisted that the ghost had given them a shove. Doors were locked, but not by a living soul. The lighthouse's reputation and the stories of its many strange occurrences spread, and the haunting kept many keepers from accepting the assignment. In 1912 Waugoshance was decommissioned, ostensibly because it was no longer needed. But everyone knows, Keeper John Herman walks the crib and continues to inhabit the lighthouse more than a hundred years after it killed him.

"What rage for fame attends both great and small!
Better be damned than mentioned not at all." -John Wolcot

Legends of Lake Michigan
-The Famous and Infamous with Ties to the Lake

People. The most compelling component of any destination. In this chapter you will discover an interesting and eclectic group; each of whom has either made it big, lost it big, enjoyed five minutes or decades of fame, or in a few cases made us shudder at their incomprehensible evil. Meet writers, athletes, criminals, scientists, comedians, musicians, a king, an abolitionist, and a former Miss America. Some you probably knew had Lake Michigan connections. Others may surprise you. A few may cause you to ask, "Who?" But, all of these characters helped flavor the Lake Michigan stew.

Muhammad Ali. He claimed he was the greatest and eventually the world came to believe him. Muhammad Ali was born Cassius Clay in Louisville, Kentucky on January 17, 1942. Today he rests his weary and pummeled bones on a farm in Berrien Springs, a small community about eight miles from Lake Michigan. Ali has owned the place for 27 years. He likes it because there is no traffic and few people. Rumors have long persisted that Al Capone owned Ali's farm in the 1920s and buried some of his ill-gotten gains on the property. Ali's cornerman, Drew Brown, hoping to find treasure, searched Ali's homestead, but came up empty-handed. If the farmhouse was owned by Al Capone, someone else held title for him. A records search shows no Capone in chain of title. It is speculated that the wife of one of Capone's bodyguards held the farm in her name. (See story below about Al Capone.)

There is no adequate way to summarize in a paragraph or two the life of this three-time, world-heavyweight, boxing-champion of the world. He was a braggart although most of his claims bore at least a resemblance to the truth. He was charming and he wrote outrageous poems that garnered him attention in the press and brought a sense of liveliness to the sport.

By age 18, young Clay won Olympic gold and developed an acute social consciousness. His first wife quoted him as saying, "*I was young, black Cassius Marcellus Clay who had won a gold medal for his country. I went to downtown Louisville to a five and dime store that had a soda fountain. I sat down at the counter to order a burger and soda pop. The waitress looked at me. 'Sorry, we don't serve coloreds,' she said. I was furious. I went all the way to Italy to represent my country, won a gold medal, and now I come back to America and can't even get served at a five and dime store.*" The story ends with Cassius Clay, who had been sleeping with the medal and proudly wearing it everywhere, throwing the meaningless gold trinket off a bridge. Ali, himself, does not confirm the bridge part of the story; he simply recalls losing the medal. Either way, his political conscience was stirred by a waitress at a coffee counter in Louisville.

He converted to Islam and was given the name Muhammad Ali by Muslim patriarch Elijah Muhammad. It meant "beloved of Allah." Ali was a conscientious objector to the War in Viet Nam. He said he had no reason to kill men he did not even know. For his refusal to serve in the armed forces he was stripped of his title and boxing license, and would not be allowed to fight professionally for more than three years. Ali went into exile. He appealed his conviction and remained in the public eye.

His boxing matches are legendary, especially his bouts against Sonny Liston and Joe Frazier. His career resulted in a total of 61 fights, of which he won 56. Of those 56, 37 were knockouts. Movies and books have been written about him. History has painted this incredible athlete with a softer, kinder brush than the newspapers and tabloids of the day.

In Southwest Michigan, in tiny Berrien Springs, he lives a modest life for one who called himself "The King of the World." He has a pool and a pond and a security gate with an intercom. He seems content to play with his adopted son; perhaps making up for the time he could not spend with his older children. Since his retirement, Ali devotes himself to worldwide humanitarianism. He remains a devout Sunni Muslim and lends his name and presence to hunger and poverty relief, supports educational efforts, promotes adoption and encourages people to respect and try to better understand one another. Perhaps that is as much his legacy as his boxing.

Al Capone has a number of connections to Western Michigan and the sunset coast. He is alleged to have owned a home on Flynn Road in Sawyer and a cottage on the Leelanau Peninsula. Title to the latter was held in his attorney's name and is located just north of Traverse City on M-72. Without a doubt the most famous home he reportedly owned in Michigan is the farm house now owned by Muhammad Ali. Title to this 88-acre farm, on Kephart Lane in Berrien Springs, is believed to have been held in the name of Charlotte Campagna, the wife of one of Capone's bodyguards. Whether it was truly Capone's home is open to speculation, but the stories are persistent and Muhammad Ali has not denied them. Instead Ali has added a few of his own details.

Capone played at least an occasional game of poker with his buddies at the Lakeside Inn. (See the ghost story about the Inn, p. 411.) It may have even been one of his favorite drinking and gambling spots during prohibition. The Inn provided sleeping quarters and entertainment to movie stars and Chicago politicians. Capone loved glitz and considered himself part of that flashy "in-crowd." Chicagoans stepped out their back door and into Michigan's playground. In practically no time they could leave behind the angst of the big city and relax on pristine Lake Michigan beaches as beautiful as those found anywhere in the world. Capone's life is written in ink on the pages of Chicago history; it is written much less indelibly in the sands of Lake Michigan's Gold Coast where he came to play, relax and hide.

It is irrefutable that Capone was a murderer, racketeer, drug dealer, pimp, brothel owner, bootlegger, political boss, gambler and perhaps the most successful gang leader in history. And yet, we are captivated by this cocky killer. To a select few he was even a modern day Robin Hood. Unlike Robin Hood, though, he generally took from everyone and killed along the way.

In 1917, at the age of eighteen, Al Capone earned the nickname he would carry throughout his life. He was waiting tables at the Harvard Inn in Brooklyn and was enthralled by a beautiful Italian girl sitting at one of his tables. Al was not sure if it was her body or her face that tantalized him most; his eyes were riveted to her. With the brash ignorance that accompanied his youth, he approached the table, leaned towards the stunning woman and blurted in a voice loud enough for her brother, sitting next to her, to hear, "Honey, you have a nice ass, and I mean that as a compliment." By today's standard that is not the raunchiest thing one can imagine; in fact, as Al suggested some might have taken it as a compliment.

But Frank Gallucio, the outraged brother, leapt to his feet. Frank was drunk and much smaller than Capone. But, he had the courage of liquor on his side. He also had a four-inch knife which he immediately brandished at Al. Gallucio aimed the knife directly at Capone's neck and made his first stab. Capone was hardly fazed by the cut and moved closer to Gallucio who got in two more slashes along Al's cheek. Then with uncommon good sense Frank grabbed his sister by the hand and made a hasty exit before Al, who was trying to staunch the flow of blood, could come after him. As the scars healed they left white, jagged ridges along Al's left cheek. Capone remained sensitive to his disfigured face and would turn his head so cameras would capture him from his right, or non-scarred side.

Gallucio, fearing for his life, went to Lucky Luciano who mediated the beef between the two hoodlums. The justice meted out by Luciano required Capone to apologize to Gallucio, adding insult to the very real injuries that would brand him Scarface forever. It was a learning experience for the young Capone – there were times when he needed to control his temper.

In 1920, Chicago was the second largest city in the United States with a population of 2,701,705. That same year, on January 16, the 18th Amendment, known as the National Prohibition Act, made it illegal to manufacture, sell or transport intoxicating liquor. The rowdy, rapidly growing Chicago was ready for Al Capone. He arrived one year later, in 1921 He was not the only bootlegger in Chicago but he dominated the business. There was Capone and then there was everybody else. Capone did not like *everybody else.*

His murders, bootlegging, prostitution and other crimes went unpunished. It is commonly accepted that Capone, from his home in Miami, orchestrated the St. Valentine's Day massacre that propelled seven mobsters of the Bugsy Moran gang to their death on February 14, 1929. To accomplish the hit, Capone enlisted the services of Machine Gun McGurn who was more than happy to do a favor for Capone. McGurn studied the movements of Bugsy's gang. To assist in the hit he called on Capone's occasional golfing partner, "Killer" Burke from St. Louis to lead the group. Although Burke spent much time in Chicago and in Benton Harbor, the nearby Lake Michigan resort, few associated him with Capone. Burke agreed to a fee of $5,000 for the hit and enlisted the services of a gunman named James Ray. The hit took place at 2122 North Clark Street in Chicago. The assassins dressed as cops and the Moran gang, obviously believing the charade, lined up against a wall as ordered. It was a brutal machine gun execution, but the intended target, Moran, was not present.

In December 1929 Burke sideswiped a car on Main Street in St. Joseph, Michigan, and during an ensuing altercation he fired four shots at a young police officer, Charles Skelley, who was attempting to arrest him. Skelley died in the hospital and police launched a manhunt for his killer. At that point Burke vanished for over a year. During his absence, Major Calvin Goddard was carefully studying the bullet patterns from the St. Valentine's Day massacre. He also studied the bullets and shells recovered in the Skelley shooting and matched their markings to the bullets retrieved from the bodies of the massacre victims. When Burke was finally found, hiding out at his father in law's farm in Milan, Missouri, he was just happy it was the police and not other mobsters "taking him for a ride." He was extradited to Michigan, where he stood trial and was sentenced to life in prison for killing Officer Charles Skelley.

The income tax evasion trial that finally resulted in Capone's imprisonment was presided over by Judge James Herbert Wilkerson who was intent on bringing the notorious gangster down. Although Capone's men had bribed the entire jury pool, their efforts were thwarted when the jury pools were switched. Capone's confident smirk crumbled when Judge Wilkerson entered the Courtroom and announced, *"Judge Edwards also has a trial commencing today. Go to his courtroom and bring me the entire panel of jurors. Take my entire panel to Judge Edwards."* With that the men who were supposed to sit in judgment of Capone left the courtroom, where they were replaced by a new set of prospective jurors whose names had not appeared on any list and who had not been approached with bribes or threats from the Capone organization. During the trial Wilkerson hid his young son in Southwest Michigan to protect him from the Capone gang. Capone was convicted of federal tax evasion and served seven years in prison.

Al Capone died January 25, 1947 of syphilis-related complications. He was forty-eight and a free man at the time. However, his mind was bedeviled by then and he was never more than a shadow of his former ruthless self.

Ernest Hemingway was a complex man who battled his personal demons using cathartic fictionalization and an alter-ego: Nick Adams. His stories drew heavily on his private turmoil and experiences. Hemingway was handsome, strong and intelligent. He loved hunting and the great outdoors. He was a womanizer and an alcoholic. He was macho and, at the same time, weak, self-destructive and troubled.

Earnest was a mid-western boy, born in Chicago in 1899 and raised, at least partially, in the rugged north woods of Michigan. His family's rustic cottage, named Windemere after Lake Windermere in England, sat on Lake Grove Road at Walloon Lake. For whatever reason, the Hemingways spelled it Windemere without the first "r". To get to Windemere from Chicago the family boarded a steamer destined for Harbor Springs. At the train station on West Bay Street near the Municipal Marina they transferred their baggage onto a "dummy train" to Petoskey and Walloon Lake. Even in the early 1900s, before the advent of automobile travel, the Petoskey/Walloon Lake area was so popular with Chicagoans that dummy trains ran every few minutes. The name "dummy train" referenced the small size, frequent stops and short routes of these locomotives.

Hemingway's mother, Grace, often dressed him and his sister Marcelline as twins, sometimes as boys, sometimes as girls. A picture of the two taken at Walloon Lake in August 1900 bears the admiring description, "Two sturdy little chaps in overalls." At Walloon Lake in

1900, the summer of Ernest's first birthday, he and Marcelline played on the narrow beach in front of their parents newly completed cottage. As an adult Hemingway professed an intense dislike for Grace.

Hemingway spent all but one summer between 1900 and 1929 around Walloon Lake and Horton Bay, Michigan. It was in Northern Michigan that he developed his love for hunting and fishing; both skills taught to him by his father, Doctor Clarence "Ed" Hemingway. Ernest hiked and camped and explored his north woods; feeling safe and at peace there before he became a famed writer. These early years provided a backdrop for much of his subsequent writing. In later life he was consumed by living the legend he had become, enjoying the enormity of his fame. But, he never again found the security and serenity he knew in Michigan's North Country. During the 1930s and 1940s, after he stopped summering in Michigan, Ernest's fame landed him in the news almost daily. Peace became elusive.

Gregory Hemingway, called Gig by his famous father, was Ernest's youngest son. After Ernest committed suicide, Gig authored a biography, simply entitled, *"Papa."* In his book he describes his childhood ordeal in the hospital with polio-like symptoms. Gig writes: *"Papa wouldn't allow anyone else in the room except for himself and the doctors, and he took my temperature every four hours and brought my meals in himself. He'd lie beside me on the cot at night telling wonderful stories about his life up in Michigan as a boy, how he'd caught his first trout and how beautiful the virgin forests were before the loggers came. He told me about a furry monster who would grow taller and taller every night and then, just as it was about to eat him, would jump over the fence. He said fear was perfectly natural and nothing to be ashamed of. The trick to mastering it was controlling your imagination, but he said he knew how hard this was for a boy. Mainly he just told me stories – about how he had fished and hunted in the Michigan north woods and about how he wished he could have stayed my age and lived there forever - until I fell asleep."* Ultimately, Gig recovered from his illness and became a doctor like his grandfather.

Hemingway's works based in, or influenced by, his summers in Michigan include: *"Up in Michigan," "On Writing," "Summer People," "The Last Good Country," "The Torrents of Spring," "Sepi Jingan,"* and several of the Nick Adams stories, most notably:" *Indian Camp,*" *"The Doctor and the Doctor's Wife,"* "*Ten Indians,*" *"The End of Something,"* "*The Indians Moved Away,*" *"Wedding Day,"* and "*Fathers and Sons.*" Ernest spent time in Petoskey, Harbor Springs, Lake Charlevoix, Horton Bay and Traverse City. Many of his early stories were inspired by these locations and the life he enjoyed there.

One of the first streams Hemingway fished was School Creek, close to Walloon Lake. The Horton Bay Township School appears in "*Up in Michigan*." The Horton Bay General Store established in 1876 became one of young Ernest's favorite spots and it still displays photos of the author and some of his memorabilia. Next door was the Red Fox Inn, one of the earliest homes in the area, later converted to a restaurant and then a bookstore. After Hemingway's marriage to Elizabeth Hadley Richardson, a local Michigan farmer drove the newlyweds from the Red Fox Inn in Horton Bay where they were married to Walloon Lake where they started their honeymoon. The wedding was attended by Hemingway's friends Dutch Pailthorp and Luman Ramsdell from Petoskey.

Both the real Hemingway and his fictional self, Nick Adams, stayed in the Pinehurst and Shangri-La cottages on Lake Street. The cottages were part of the Dilworth Resort in Horton Bay.

In 1916 Ernest stayed at the well-known Perry Hotel in Petoskey's famous gaslight district after a northwest Lower Michigan camping trip with his friend Lewis Clarahan. Hemingway wrote about Greensky Hill Indian Methodist Church on Old US-31 North Highway. Ernest lived in charming and quaint Petoskey during the winter of 1919-1920. In the cold, bleak months of that winter, after Ernest returned from World War I, he rented an upstairs room at Potter's Rooming House at 602 East State Street. He was trying to write fiction, but having a hard time staying focused. Billiards with old friends at the City Park Grill at 432 East Lake Street proved a tempting distraction. Hemingway also frequented the Petoskey Public Library at 451 East Mitchell Street that winter trying to get back on his writing track. Still unable to work, it is believed he fled the genial company of his friends and holed up in a small room in Evelyn Hall, an unoccupied women's dormitory at the Bay View Conservatory. Jesperson's Restaurant at 312 Howard Street is said to be a place that Ernest and his friend, Dutch, frequented often.

Near the end of 1924, Hemingway sent a lengthy letter to Bill Smith, another northern Michigan friend. In the letter, Hemingway noted that since he and Bill had last been in touch he had been doing a lot of writing, and of all the work he had thus far produced, "*almost everything worth a damn*" had been about Michigan. He was nostalgic about the country that he and Bill had known in their boyhoods and insisted. "*The swell times we used to have with Auntie (Mrs. Dilworth) at the farm, the first swell trips out to the Black and the Sturgeon and the wonderful times we had with the men and the storms in the fall and potato digging and the whole damn thing.*"

In a letter to his father he said, "*I've written a number of stories about the Michigan country - the country is always true - what happens is always fiction."* Ed Hemingway did not approve of his son's dirty writings.

While it is apparent that some of Hemingway's happiest, and fondest memories revolve around his time spent in Michigan, it seems he never returned to the state in later years. His life took him to Spain, Paris, Africa, and Colorado, all to "find his voice" and yet he seems to have abandoned the place where it may have spoken to him the loudest.

During his writing career, which spanned approximately forty-three years, Hemingway wrote nine novels, four books of non-fiction, over a hundred short stories, nearly four-hundred articles, poetry and a play. He participated in five wars, and sustained serious injuries during World War I. He suffered four automobile accidents and two plane crashes. The plane crashes occurred on consecutive days in East Africa in 1954; they prompted untimely obituaries throughout the world. He was married four times and had three sons. In 1954 he won a Nobel Prize for literature and a Pulitzer Prize for *"The Old Man and the Sea."*

He suffered grave depression and spent two months in 1960 at the Mayo Clinic undergoing the cure of the day: electric shock treatments. He was tormented by his father's suicide. Two siblings also committed suicide; and the family curse continued after his death when his granddaughter, Margaux overdosed, killing herself. Hemingway felt the electro-shock had addled his brain to the point where he could no longer write and to him that was worse than death.

In June of 1961 Hemingway attempted suicide and was hospitalized for more electroshock therapy, but he convinced everyone he was well enough to be released. On July 2, 1961 at 7:00 am on an otherwise quite ordinary Sunday morning, still dressed in pajamas and a bathrobe, Hemingway went to the basement and got a shotgun and a box of ammunition. He brought them upstairs to the foyer and loaded two shells into the twelve-gauge. He put the barrel into his mouth and pulled the trigger.

Today Petoskey has a Hemingway Society of devoted fans. They meet each year to discuss his writing in the location where so many of his stories took root. They focus on his happier days.

James Earl Jones' first performance was at the Ramsdell Theatre in Manistee. During his high school years at Brethren Michigan High School he was an outstanding student excelling in forensics and track. While still in high school, Jones worked as a carpenter for local productions at the Ramsdell Theatre. There Jones developed a passion for acting and proved to be a natural. In addition to spending four summers with the acting group at Ramsdell, he was Assistant Stage Manager, Stage Manager, director of a Children's Theatre play and acted in twenty-eight productions. Jones graduated from high school in 1949 and attended the University of Michigan with plans to study medicine; he found that theatre's call more compelling. He graduated cum laude, 1953, with a B.A. degree in drama.

Jones was born in Arkabutla Township, Mississippi in 1931, but moved to Manistee County where he was raised by his maternal grandparents. Jones, among the best known African American film and stage actors, is also part Irish and part Chocktaw/Cherokee. He is famous for his deep, authoritative voice. His was the voice of Darth Vader in "*Star Wars,*" a role for which he was originally uncredited.

As a child, Jones developed a stutter so severe that he refused to speak out loud for fear of ridicule. He recalls riding the train from Mississippi to Manistee and the trauma of being ripped away from his mother and the only home he had ever known. This, coupled with beginning school and his stutter, made talking too difficult. He was rendered functionally and intentionally mute until high school. Then Donald Crouch, one of his teachers, recognized Jones' gift for writing poetry and helped him begin the battle towards speaking coherently without the stutter. He convinced Jones that the words he was writing, the words that sounded so beautiful in his mind, would sound even more beautiful if spoken aloud. Crouch believed public speaking would help Jones gain confidence and he urged him to recite a poem each day in class. It is more than a bit ironic that the voice Jones refused to use as a child has become one of the most famous and widely recognized voices in Hollywood.

His first film role came in 1964 as a B-52 bomb room operator in "*Dr. Strangelove, or How I Learned to Stop Worrying and Love the Bomb.*" He was nominated for a Best Actor Award for his portrayal of Jack Johnson in the film version of "*The Great White Hope.*" While often cast as an African American, as in the mini-series "*Roots*" where he played author Alex Haley, his voice transcends ethnicity and is sought merely for its deep, resonate clarity. He was the voice of Mufasa in the 1994 Disney animated feature "*The Lion King*" and the sequel, "*The Lion King II: Simba's Pride.*" Jones had roles in "*Under a Killing Moon,*" "*Field of Dreams,*" "*Cry, the Beloved Country,*" "*Clear and Present Danger,*" "*Conan the Barbarian,*" "*Patriot Games,*" "*Coming to America,*" and "*The Hunt for Red October.*"

Jones has also starred on Broadway in such performances as "*On Golden Pond*" (during which he was hospitalized for pneumonia) and "*The Great White Hope.*" And, he was the first established celebrity to appear on Sesame Street.

Even now, Jones has to think carefully about what he is about to say to avoid stuttering. The slow, deliberateness of his speech is partially due to looking for the right word; the one that will not trip-up his tongue.

Jones admits that his grandfather was not thrilled with the idea that he wanted to be an actor, but his Grandma Maggie quickly came around. In Jones' words, *"This is a woman whose bedtime stories were about lynching and hurricanes and floods and rapes and murders. Those were her bedtime stories! For me to go into drama, that kind of turned her on a little bit. I got a job over at the little opera house in Manistee, Michigan, the county seat. We had a summer theater there. She was always the first to be there, in the front row. Wanted to see me in these dramas. So she opened the door, as far as the family was concerned, about allowing this to happen."*

James Earl Jones describes himself as a plodder, someone who just keeps heading toward his goal, one little step at a time. The only advice he offers anyone is the same as that offered by Carl Sandburg *"Take no advice, including this."*

Joseph Frank Keaton Jr. Back at the turn of the century, about 1902, at a time in Muskegon history when lumber was giving way to industry and tourism, a community of entertainers sprung up in the shadow of a massive sand dune known as Pigeon Hill in the Bluffton section of the city. Bluffton was located between Lake Michigan and Muskegon Lake and it became home to Joseph Keaton, his wife Myra Cutler and their son, Joseph Frank Keaton, who was better known as Buster. These entertainers performed at a summer show house, built by the elder Keaton and his friends, at Lake Michigan Park. The Keaton family discovered the beauty of the area while performing there and fell in love with the community. From 1907 they returned each summer and referred to Muskegon as their adopted home; the city, in turn adopted them as its most famous citizens.

Buster was born October 4, 1895 and by age three he was part of his parents' act, *"The Three Keatons."* The act resulted in accusations of child abuse against Buster's parents because the plot involved young Buster goading his father, who then threw him against the scenery, into the orchestra pit and sometimes even into the audience. Buster always denied any abuse, saying he was trained to take trick falls safely. His parents also ran afoul the law with child labor violations.

Later Buster gained fame as a silent film comic actor and a filmmaker. His comedy included a deadpan expression that earned him a second nickname as "The Great Stone Face." His most popular films were: *"The General," "Sherlock Jr.," "The Navigator"* and *"Our Hospitality."*

After Vaudeville and silent films, Buster turned to talking movies. He could write, produce, act and direct films. MGM bought out Keaton's filmmaking unit in 1928, and Keaton found his subsequent work too regimented and restrictive. He had successful TV series: *"The Buster Keaton Show"* (1950) and *"Life with Buster Keaton"* (1951). Keaton cancelled his own show because he could not keep up with the demand of producing a new show each week.

At age fifty-five Keaton appeared on the Ed Wynn Variety Show and recreated one of his vaudeville stunts that required him to prop one foot on a table, swing his other foot next to it and hold that impossible position in midair for a moment before he crashed to the floor. When asked by TV host Garry Moore how he did those falls, he opened his jacket and revealed the bruises. Buster died February 1, 1966.

Richard A. Loeb. The Loeb family owned Castle Farms in Charlevoix. It was built as their prestigious summer home. Richard Loeb, partnered with Nathan F. Leopold, to become half of the most notorious killing duo of the 20th century. These two near-genius college kids were rich, privileged and bored when they murdered Bobby Franks for sport on May 24, 1924. Franks was small for his age and unable to put up much of a fight. Like his murderers, he also came from an extremely wealthy Chicago family. His naked body was stuffed into a culvert near Wolf Lake. His father, Jacob Franks, was ready to pay a ransom when the body was discovered.

Dickie (as Leopold called him) Loeb was the handsome, eighteen-year-old son of retired Sears-Roebuck Vice-President and attorney, Albert Loeb. Richard was the youngest graduate ever at the University of Michigan, but spent much of his time reading detective stories and planning crimes. It was a game to him. The ultimate challenge was to contrive the absolutely perfect crime - just for the sake of getting away with it. He needed an escape from the mundane aspects of his life and he sought a way to establish his superiority.

Nathan Leopold, Loeb's nineteen-year-old partner in the vicious crime, was interested in ornithology and had already achieved recognition as the nation's leading authority on the Kirtland Warbler, an endangered songbird native to the Lake Michigan shoreline. Leopold was the son of a millionaire box manufacturer. At the time of the Franks killing he was a law student at the University of Chicago and was planning to begin studies at Harvard Law School after a family trip to Europe in the summer.

In the 1920s Chicago was a violent city where the citizenry continually questioned whether it was safe to simply walk the streets. For Bobbie Franks it was not. But, fears usually raged over the likes of

Al Capone and John Dillinger, not well-dressed, wealthy college boys. Even with crime running rampant, the heinous act of Leopold and Loeb drew special attention. It was easy to identify the enemy if they were bootleggers, mobsters and pimps. Besides, such unsavory sorts generally left the average folks alone. Sometimes, they even offered a few crumbs to them. But how could you protect yourself against someone as innocuous in looks and background, someone so seemingly unlikely to commit a crime as these two well-heeled boys? Clarence Darrow represented the accused in the first criminal case dubbed "the Crime of the Century," a killing for fun that outraged the public conscience.

Leopold, after his conviction, acknowledged: *"For some reason, back in 1924, the newspapers found in our particular case apparently something that would sell, something that would interest the public, whether it was our youth, the position of our families, the fact that we were college students, a combination of these things, I really don't know."* In Chicago, the Loeb family lived down the street from the Franks and it is even believed that Richard Loeb may have been a distant cousin of Bobby Franks. Loeb would later bristle at the suggestion that it was he, who led Leopold in committing the crime; Loeb insisted Leopold was the leader because Nathan was able to achieve a more subtle dominance by his force of will and his superior intellect. Yet psychologists believed Loeb was more of a natural leader with a more dominant social presence.

The psychiatrists, hired to examine the boys for the defense, insisted the Loeb family was not responsible for its son's transgressions. They offered the following conclusions: *"The father, Albert H. Loeb, is fair and just. He is opposed to the boys' drinking and often spoke of it; he is not strict, although the boys may have thought he was. He never used corporal punishment. In early childhood he was not a play-fellow with the boys."* Of Loeb's mother the psychiatrists concluded, *"A woman in good health, with excellent poise, keen, alert, interested."*

The psychiatric reports provided information that Loeb had been a sickly child until four-and-a-half-years-old. The problem, it seemed, was his tonsils and once they were removed his health improved. As a small child, he fell from his bicycle going downhill. At age fifteen at his parent's summer estate in Charlevoix, Michigan, he had an automobile accident, suffering a concussion. Stories spread that Loeb had killed someone in that accident and that he purposely caused it by ramming a buggy that blocked his automobile, and that his family was able to avoid any publicity about it through bribery. Those rumors were never substantiated and the more "official" story is that Richard did have the accident and it involved a collision with a horse and buggy on a dark street corner. A woman might have been injured. but Loeb, slightly injured himself, helped take the woman to the hospital. He visited her in the hospital and persuaded his father to pay all of the hospital bills, and to pay off a mortgage on the woman's house and send her on a trip that winter to mend her shattered nerves.

In an interesting aside, Carl Sandburg testified at Leopold's parole hearing in 1958 and said, *"He was in darkness when he came here, but he has made a magnificent struggle toward the light."* Sandburg had not testified at two earlier parole hearings and he was a new voice to proceedings that included Leopold's friends and family. Sandburg became interested in the case partly through the intercession of Gene Lovitz, who had written a biography of the great poet after Lovitz, himself, was released from prison. Sandburg said, *"I never thought it would get to the time I would make a winter morning journey to Joliet to face the Board of Parole, to plead for a Chicago Jewish boy who at nineteen was out of his mind."* Of Sandburg's plea it was said he rambled some (he was by this time 80 years old), but in the overall content of his discourse there was still something unbelievably magnificent. Two weeks later Leopold was released after serving 33 years in prison.

Loeb did not fare as well in prison. He died with at least fifty-six razor cuts to his body, killed by fellow-inmate, James Day. There were no witnesses other than Day so the exact circumstances will never be known. Day alleged that Loeb attacked him and made homosexual advances. There were no cuts on Day's body which somewhat refutes his version of the story. Loeb was gushing blood and attempts to save him by suturing the gashes and stopping the spurting blood failed. He died on January 28, 1936. Richard Loeb had spent his last morning of his life in prison with his friend, Nathan Leopold.

In *"Life Plus 99 Years,"* Nathan Leopold wrote about his friend's death, *"We covered him at last with a sheet, but after a moment I folded the sheet back from his face and sat down on a stool by the table where he lay. I wanted a long last look at him. For, strange as it may sound, he had been my best pal. In one sense, he was also the greatest enemy I have ever had. For my friendship with him had cost me my life."* Richard Loeb was thirty-three-years-old.

Castle Farms was originally constructed in 1918 for Anna and Albert Loeb. It was a 1600 acre farm on which Mr. Loeb dreamed of raising prize-winning livestock and creating the "model farm." He hired Arthur Heun, the architect who designed the primary Loeb home in Chicago to work on the project. The out buildings were to be modeled after stone barns in Normandy. The house was constructed in the architectural style of a French Renaissance Châteaux. Thirty-five masons were employed for the project. They used local fieldstone as the main building material. The farm was a big enterprise and helped support the local Charlevoix economy by hiring 90 employees. Albert died in 1924, shortly after Richard was sentenced and his oldest son, Ernest, took over the farm and ran it for many additional years. By 1927, the farm no longer operated at a profit and all of the livestock was sold. For several decades it was rented and many of the buildings were used for storage.

In the mid-1960s the farm was sold to John Van Havre who charged visitors a fee to walk through the property which he had renamed Castle Van Haver. No doubt part of the "charm" was its gory history of association to the infamous murder.

Van Haver could not make his venture pay and eventually sold the property to the Reibels in 1969. Their plan for the property, by then called simply "Castle Farms," was a major arts and crafts center. Later they added a stage for rock concerts and many performances took place there including: Aerosmith, Alabama, Kenny G, Kiss, the Monkeys, Ozzy Ozbourne, Rod Steward, Stevie Nicks and Sting. The local community, mainly wealthy summer residents, was not happy with the noise, rowdiness, traffic congestion, and general chaos of concert days.

In 1995 there was a failed attempt to purchase the property for use as a 4-H camp. The deal lacked adequate funding and Castle Farms was finally purchased at auction in January 2001 by Linda Mueller who planned to restore the buildings and open the property for public use: weddings, corporate meetings, antique and art shows and public fundraisers. It appears Castle Farms has finally outlived its infamy.

Jesse Owens once owned a home in Union Pier and spent many summers there. His given name was James Cleveland Owens and he was the seventh of eleven children of sharecropper, Henry Owens, and his wife Emma. He was the grandson of a slave. He was first called Jesse by a teacher who did not understand when he said his name was J.C.

Owens' junior high track coach, Charles Riley, found young Jesse on a playground and put him on a track team. Riley became Owens inspiration and mentor. Owens practiced before school because he had a job in a shoe repair shop after. Owens attended Ohio State University and got his first taste of fame at a Big Ten Track Meet in Ann Arbor on May 25, 1935 when he tied the record for the 100-yard-dash and set world records in the long jump, 220-yard-dash and the 220-low-hurdles. His performance, achieved in less than an hour, is still considered one of the most amazing athletic achievements of all time.

At Ohio State he was a member of Alpha Phi Alpha, the first Greek fraternity established for African Americans.

In the 1936 Olympics, Owens represented the United States. Adolf Hitler saw the games as a way to showcase Nazi Germany to the rest of the world. He did not intend them to promote the achievements of African-Americans whom he considered inferior. He called the dark-skinned children of German women, Rhineland Bastards, and their mothers he labeled whores and prostitutes. In Mein Kampf he denigrated these children as a Black Disgrace. Hitler was dismayed and shocked when Owens won four gold medals: the 100-meter-dash, long jump, 200-meter-dash (he beat Matthew Robinson, Jackie's brother), and the 4 x 100 meter relay. Jesse's records stood until the 1984 Summer Olympics when Carl Lewis won medals in the same events.

A story in the papers at that time of his victory noted that Hitler shook hands only with the German athletes who won medals and left early to avoid shaking hands with Cornelius Johnson, another African-American. In spite of Hitler's politics, the crowds in Berlin applauded Owens enthusiastically. Owens came back to the United States and had to ride a freight elevator to a reception in his honor at the Waldorf Astoria. Of the slight by the German Chancellor, Owens commented, "I wasn't invited to the White House to shake hands with the president either." After his incredible athletic victories, Owens had difficulty earning a living. He was a sports promoter, forced to rely on theatrics to keep his job. He challenged and defeated a race horse, later explaining that there was a trick to beating a racehorse; he had to find a high-strung horse that would be startled by the pistol, giving Owens a good head start.

By the 1920s Union Pier had developed into a tourist resort. Its proximity to Chicago, where Owens was engaged in public relations, allowed him to enjoy his home and still be close to his job. Owens was Union Pier's most famous resident - the one who used to run like the wind on its beaches. Posthumously he received honors that had eluded him in life: The Presidential Medal of Freedom in 1976 (by Gerald Ford) and the Congressional Gold Medal in 1990 (by George H. W. Bush). A 1999 Irish postage stamp bore his image and a street in Berlin was renamed for him. Owens, a heavy cigarette smoker, died of lung cancer at 66.

Harriet Quimby was a superstitious woman. She had her favorite lucky jewelry and she refused to fly on Sundays. In 1911 she became the first licensed female pilot in the United States, and a year later the first woman to fly across the English Channel. She was beautiful with a strong sense of style that made her a marketable commodity to the press. She designed her own trademark purple, satin flight-suit. There is no record of Harriet ever marrying or having children. She kept her private life very much to herself.

She was born in 1875 in Coldwater, Michigan but spent her early childhood in a modest home in Arcadia Township on M-22 in Manistee County. It is marked today by a Michigan Historical Marker. Between 1887 and 1890 the family moved to California and Quimby later claimed Arroyo Grande, California, as her birthplace. But evidence of the family's ties to Michigan are uncontroverted in spite of Quimby's failure to recognize them. Her mother, Ursula Quimby produced and sold patent medicines such as "Quimby's Liver Invigorator," which she advertised in the Manistee Daily News. The ads presented testimonials from satisfied customers.

For a while after moving to California, Quimby was an aspiring actress, but in spite of her physical beauty and flair for the theatrical, she chose to become a journalist. She was an independent woman with strong views. She wrote articles about child neglect, preserving endangered species and corrupt politics.

Quimby became interested in flying in late October 1910 when she attended the Belmont Park International Aviation Tournament on Long Island. At that event she came into contact with aviator, John Moisant, She decided to take flight lessons from John's brother, Alfred, who operated a flight school on Long Island. Being the private person she was, Quimby had no intention of revealing to anyone her ambition of learning to fly. Somehow the press discovered it, and since a woman learning to fly was considered a big story, she decided to capitalize on it herself and authored a series of articles about her experiences.

Flying the English Channel, in spite of its unpredictable weather and dangers, became Quimby's goal. One of her male aviator friends, Gustav Hamel, actually offered to don her purple suit and make the flight for her so she would not have to face the risk. He planned it out, insisting that he would land in a remote spot of France and quickly trade places with her so she could take the credit. She refused his offer, regardless of how well-intentioned it may have been.

On April 16, 1912, Harriet left Dover, England, flew across the Channel and landed about 25 miles from her target of Calais, France. It was a foggy day and she maintained altitudes between 1,000 and 2,000 feet. The flight lasted a minute short of an hour. Her feat did not receive the press coverage it might have otherwise garnered because the Titanic had sunk just two days earlier.

On July 1, 1912, Quimby flew her new 70 horsepower, two-seat, Bleriot monoplane in the Third Annual Boston Aviation Meet in Massachusetts. Prior to the meet, William Willard, the event's organizer, and his son Charles, flipped a coin to see who got the honor of being Harriet's passenger. William won. In flight the monoplane unexpectedly lurched forward ejecting both Quimby and the unfortunate Willard, plunging them to their death before more than 5,000 horrified spectators. The plane survived nicely, gliding to the ground and banking in a muddy field. The exact cause of the plane's lurch will never be known, although several theories were proposed: one that Willard, a very large man, had leaned forward to ask his pilot a question and his great weight threw off the plane's sensitive balance. Whatever the cause, Harriet Quimby was dead at age 37, less than a year after she had learned to fly.

Her legacy inspired Amelia Earhart and was a role model to young women wanting to venture beyond stereotypical roles. In 1991 a picture of Quimby, sitting in her Bleriot, graced a 50 cent U.S. Airmail stamp.

Carl Sandberg was the "People's Poet." Sandburg made Chicago real to the rest of the world through his finely chiseled poetic descriptions. His city was alternatively the *Hog Butcher of the World* and the *Freight Handler of the Nation*. Chicago was *A City with Broad Shoulders*, a *City of Cunning* and at times a *Laughing City*. He loved her *when the fog came in from the harbor on little cat feet*. His was an exciting Chicago; a Chicago full of mobsters and bootleg liquor; a city that seduced with opportunities of overnight wealth and shunned with oppressive poverty. Carl Sandburg attempted to capture it all. Many of the writers and poets of his time turned to London and Paris for associations with other writers, to find inspiration and to find their voice. Sandburg turned to Chicago and his beloved Lake Michigan and her dunes.

Early literary success from *"Chicago Poems"* and his *"Rootabaga Stories,"* a book of fanciful children's tales, convinced Sandburg's publisher, Alfred Harcourt, to encourage Carl to write a juvenile biography of Abraham Lincoln. For most of his life, Sandburg had been fascinated by Lincoln and collected information about the Great Emancipator. He had a complete, complex filing system of materials and a ten volume set of Civil War photographs, plus several biographies to start his research. After three years of intense work, the intended juvenile biography ended up a two volume biography for the adult market.

Sandburg maintained a frantic schedule writing and lecturing, and as a result his health suffered. His wife, Lilian (known by her middle name, Paula, to her husband and friends) looked for a place where her beloved husband could relax, take life easy, and regain his strength. Carl was in his mid-forties, making money and a respected author. He was also exhausted. He had not taken a vacation since completing the Lincoln biography. Paula wanted a place with tranquility and solitude –

a place where Carl could restore his soul. She found a summer cottage on Lake Michigan at Tower Hill near Sawyer. Carl had a rather schizophrenic relationship with the place. He would admire the beauty and relax, but then his compulsive nature would take over and he would give in to one or another of his many obligations and leave.

In 1926 Paula purchased the cottage and also the lot adjoining it which she intended to turn into a studio for her busy husband. Carl was forty-eight years old and working on the "*Songbag*" manuscript. In 1927 he earned $7,000 in lecture fees. Sandburg was on the road lecturing much of the time to earn what today would be an annual salary of approximately $140,000. His lecture schedule kept him away from home much of the time, and still, every spare moment was dedicated to his writing.

Paula again lobbied her husband to relax. The entire family looked forward to their leisurely summers on the dunes, escaping the pace and harsh obligations of Chicago. While Carl was in New York for a month on business related to *Songbag*, his wife moved the family to their new lakefront property, Wren Cottage at Tower Hill near Sawyer. Regarding the move Carl told a friend, "*I nearly went bankrupt in health*" referencing his work on the Lincoln biography. Wren Cottage was his safe haven; the place he would rest and recuperate.

Sandburg and his family, which now included three daughters, all loved their Lake Michigan bungalow, but Carl complained about the way, "invaders from Lakeside" transgressed his privacy. Still, by 1927 the Sandburgs had made the decision to live on the Lake Michigan shore year round. Concluding that Wren Cottage was too small and the area too heavily populated with summer visitors, they bought a large lot in nearby Harbert in Chickaming Township.

Paula designed their dream home which was to have a special place where Carl could work uninterrupted by the stresses of daily life. There would be his workroom, a bedroom and a deck where he could write outside when the weather permitted. His suite would be on the third level of the white clapboard home - away from the mundane bustle of an active family. Paula's plans even included a fifteen-by-thirty-foot steel and concrete, shelf-lined vault in the basement. Carl's research files, manuscripts and books could be safely stored in a fireproof and dehumidified mini-fortress.

Sandburgl turned fifty on January 6, 1928. He described his work to a friend, "*I've been laying off and protecting myself from the disease called civilization – amid the sand hills of Michigan.*" He had reached a point in his life where financial security was no longer a concern. He took long walks on the dunes he had grown to love. A journalist described him as "*a white-haired man in a disreputable old hat, knocking golf balls across the sand.*" It was likely a depiction that Sandburg would have favored. In Harbert, those he chanced to meet on his solitary walks either did not recognize him or discretely respected his privacy.

By 1928 Sandburg was again in robust health and began working feverishly in his new home on the secluded Lake Michigan shore. He turned his attention back to one of his favorite and recurring subjects: Abraham Lincoln. This time it was *The War Years*. By 1929 he was so engrossed in his Lincoln project that he rarely left home, even to lecture. He still wrote a column for the Chicago Daily News. This was the most prolific and productive period in Sandburg's life. He played guitar and sang. And, of course he wrote.

Paula, acknowledging, although not resenting, the time Carl spent on *The War Years*, purchased the lot next door so she could pursue some of her own interests – prime among them was the acquisition of a goat herd. Carl called it Paula's summer of the three "Gs": garden, geese and goats. Paula's herd provided the milk that allowed her to make all of the family's cheese and butter. The garden contributed string beans, spinach, corn, cantaloupe, squash, pumpkin and broccoli. It was a peaceful time for the Sandburgs. Paula's farm was running smoothly and Carl was writing feverishly. He continued working on "*Lincoln: the War Years,*" but also began devoting time to an epic, 112 page poem, "*The People, Yes.*"

Occasionally Carl would relax and visit with neighbors. Sometimes notables like Frank Lloyd Wright dropped in on the Sandburgs. But, in the late 1930s, Carl again returned his undivided attention to "*Lincoln: the War Years.*" Carl loved working in his dune paradise. Of Lake Michigan, he said, "*The Lake performs. The lake runs a gamut of all moods.*" Sometimes he would go up into his Crow's nest to watch a sudden, angry storm overtake his lake.

For days Sandburg would lose himself in Lincoln's world. He would perch on a sturdy wooden fruit crate and bend over his reconditioned Remington typewriter and peck away. When the weather was warm he moved the crates to the third floor sundeck where he enjoyed the sunshine on his skin as he lost himself in reflection. As a break he would indulge himself in a long walk on the beach. He often swam at noon. He drank coffee and smoked a cigar.

By 1938 Sandburg had incorporated every last note and shred of information into a document that was more than a million words long. He was finally ready to begin editing. His goal was to have the book ready for print in September 1939. Upon publication, Harcourt had to rush a second printing to meet the Christmas demand. Sandburg was awarded his first Pulitzer Prize in 1940 for "*Lincoln: the War Years.*"

With its completion he admitted, *"I'm slowing down. There's a weariness in the bones...the heave and the haul, the slime and the scum of a long voyage, is still on me."* He was by that time nearly sixty-two years old.

In 1943 Carl turned sixty-five. He was the celebrated author of poetry, biography, children's stories, a folk music anthology and a news commentary. The house on Birchwood Beach in Harbert that the Sandburgs had named Chikaming Farm, seemed strangely quiet with all three of his daughters grown and gone. It was time for Carl to take on another challenge. He had not yet written a novel and that became his next project. It was tentatively entitled, *"American Cavalcade."*

In 1945 Carl began actual work on the novel and decided to move from his beloved home on the Lake Michigan shore. He enjoyed the beauty of each new season, but the severe winters were brutal as they blew down with a fierceness that he no longer wanted to brave. The bleak gray and cold which endured from the fall color change through the budding spring every year made the Sandburgs yearn for a warmer, more accommodating climate.

Paula began searching for a new place to call home. It had to have space for her prize-winning goat herd. There had to be plenty of flowers and she wanted fruit trees. And there had to be privacy and solitude for her husband. She found the perfect place in North Carolina. The beautiful mountains to the north of what would be their new home were a bonus. By January 1946, the Sandburgs left Michigan forever. It had been their home for nearly twenty years. Their family had grown up there. Carl had earned his Pulitzer there. But, it was time to move on. Carl was sixty-eight.

James Jesse Strang was the King of Beaver Island. By proclaiming himself King he defied his country that swore it would never have a monarch. Strang was born in 1813 in New York State, joined the Baptist Church at twelve and began the study of law at twenty-one. He was admitted to the Bar, married, worked as a lawyer, minister and postmaster.

In 1844, he met Joseph Smith, founder of the Mormon Church and converted to the Mormon faith. That appears to have been the major turning point in his otherwise seemingly normal life. Within a month he was made an elder of the church. When Smith was assassinated three months later, while serving a jail term for destroying the office of a newspaper that angered him, Strang claimed succession to Smith's position, insisting that Smith had told him the leadership was to be his.

Brigham Young contested Strang's claim and eventually won the battle for leadership. Young excommunicated Strang who, with his dissident followers, went to Voree, Wisconsin. Strang was strict about his Mormon religious observances and when a bunch of non-Mormon settlers moved into the area he moved his group to Beaver Island off the northwest coast of Michigan's Lower Peninsula. Sitting smack dab in the middle of Lake Michigan, Strang declared himself king of "The Kingdom of God on Earth." As king he collected tithes from all residents of the island, Mormon or not. Eventually non-Mormons were forced off the island. Strang built a temple, theater, sawmill, school, and other businesses on the little island. Church was compulsory. He levied taxes, published books and founded his own newspaper. He initially denounced polygamy but eventually, when he wanted another wife, embraced it and decreed every elder of the church must have two wives. For a while living up to the decree was difficult – even for the king. When Strang took his second wife, a former school teacher from Eaton Rapids, his first wife, not pleased with this situation, left him. Strang remedied the situation by taking wife number three. Eventually he had five wives and twelve children.

As bizarre as he sounds, Strang was no laughing matter. By 1851 he controlled all of the political offices of Mackinac Island. Beaver Island was attached to Mackinac Island for judicial and elective purposes. Governor Kinsley Bingham was careful to cultivate the 700 votes of Strang's followers.

Strang's detractors were successful in getting attention to his misdeeds and Stephen A. Douglas advised President Millard Fillmore that the U.S. Attorney General should issue orders for the U.S. District Attorney of Michigan to begin prosecuting Strang. His alleged list of offences was long: cutting timber on public lands, tax irregularities, counterfeiting, interfering with the U.S. mail and more. Strang and his followers were taken by a U.S. Marshall and deputies to Detroit for a three week trial. Everyone believed Strang would be convicted and there was an air of incredulity when the self-appointed monarch emerged from the trial victorious. He returned to Beaver Island stronger than ever.

On June 16, 1856 Strang was ambushed, shot and mortally wounded. He lingered until July 8, giving him time to return to Voree where he died in the arms of his first wife who apparently had forgiven him. A drunken mob of Mackinac Islanders and Irish fishermen burned and looted Beaver Island and drove out all of Strang's followers. There is a legend that Strang sunk a huge trove of gold in Fox Lake on the island before his flight. So far the gold, if it exists, has not been recovered.

Jonathon Walker was known as the man with the branded hand. Walker is Michigan's most famous abolitionist. As a young man, Walker was a fifth generation sea captain from Massachusetts. Early in his life he swore to work towards ending slavery, a practice he described as an abomination. His goal was not unpopular in Massachusetts, but decidedly less acceptable when he moved his family to Florida in the 1840s to gain work on the railroad. In Florida his neighbors quickly pegged him as a slave sympathizer.

In 1844 Walker attempted to assist seven runaway slaves escape to the British West Indies in an open boat. Along the way, Walker became violently ill and unable to captain the ship. The crew of slaves knew nothing about sailing and it is likely all aboard would have drowned if they had not been rescued by a sloop that took them to Key West.

The rescue was not all good news, however, because Walker was sent to Pensacola where he was put in prison and chained to the floor. He was tried, convicted, fined and put on a pillory. His ill-fated mission also earned him the brand "SS" on his hand. The Double S, ordered by the United States government, stood for *Slave Stealer.*

At least one blacksmith refused to make the branding iron, saying brands were for animals. But another less principled smithy made the tool and a United States Marshall inflicted the burning iron to Walker's hand. Those nearby could hear the sizzling flesh. After being branded Walker was returned to jail where he served eleven months before northern Abolitionists paid his fine and secured his freedom.

In 1850 after his release Walker moved to Michigan and lived near Muskegon until his death there in 1878. He was seventy-eight-years-old. On August 1, 1878 a monument was erected to his memory.

And a few other names you may recognize:

- **Liberty Hyde Bailey** was born in 1858 in a simple frame house in South Haven. Bailey was a world-famous botanist and horticulturist who attended Michigan State Agricultural College (now MSU) and developed a curriculum that is still used for horticultural training. His home in South Haven is a museum. (See page 50 for museum details.)
- **Quacy Barnes** was born in Benton Harbor September 26, 1976. She played college basketball at Indiana and professional basketball for the Sacramento Monarchs, Seattle Storm and Phoenix Mercury of the WNBA. After her playing career she became Eastern Illinois women's head basketball coach.
- **Bruce Catton** was a journalist and historian best known for his work about the American Civil War. He was born in Petoskey and died in Frankfort, Michigan. He won a Pulitzer Price in 1954 for *A Stillness at Appomattox,* the story of the last battle of the Civil War.
- **George Armstrong Custer** reportedly had a summer home or other residence in the Suttons Bay or Omena area. Biographies about

the man best known for his catastrophic defeat at Little Big Horn do not substantiate that story, but the chain of ownership of the building that houses the Omena Historical Society can be traced to Custer's father-in-law and Custer.

- **John Dillinger** once said, *"I guess my only bad habit is robbing banks. I smoke very little and don't drink much."* Dillinger used to flee Chicago when the heat was too great and escape to the cooler beach front areas of southwestern Michigan. He was a guest at the Prussa Resort and the local gas station frequently serviced his car. Dillinger was dead before his 32nd birthday.

- **Nancy Fleming** was born in Muskegon and raised in Montague. She was crowned Miss America in 1961. After her reign she worked in the entertainment industry, as a program host and interviewer for ABC-TV, Cable Health Network and PBS. In 1978 Fleming married radio and television personality, Jim Lange, who remains best known for the *Dating Game.* She and Lange live in San Francisco.

- **Gene Harris** was born in Benton Harbor and was known for his soulful, blues-drenched piano style. From the late 1950s through the late 1970s, Harris was part of the jazz trio, *The Three Sounds.* After a short retirement from touring, he returned to record many albums for Concord Records. An annual festival in Benton Harbor continues to honor Harris and his music.

- **Arte Johnson**, the comedian most famous for his characters on *Rowan and Martin's Laugh-In,* was born on January 20, 1929 in Benton Harbor. While working in New York City, he impulsively joined an audition line and, to his surprise, was cast in a revival of *Gentlemen Prefer Blondes.* His two most memorable characters from *Laugh-In* are the Nazi soldier and Tyrone F. Horneigh.

- **Julie Krone** became the first female jockey in the National Thoroughbred Racing Hall of Fame in 2000. She was born in Benton Harbor on July 24, 1963. In 1993 Krone became the only woman to win the Belmont Stakes, a Triple Crown race, after which ESPN gave her an Espy Award as the year's top female athlete.

- **Madame Madeline (Marcotte) La Framboise** was born in Northern Lower Michigan about 1779, a descendent of celebrated Ottawa Chieftain, Returning Cloud. La Framboise and her husband, Joseph, managed John Jacob Astor's fur interests on the west side of Michigan and after Joseph was murdered in 1809, Madeline continued to operate the business until she retired to Mackinac Island in 1821.

- **Daniel Lewis Majerle**, known as Thunder Dan to his fans, was born in 1965 in Traverse City. Majerle played fourteen years in the National Basketball Association, primarily for the Phoenix Suns, although also for the Miami Heat and briefly for the Cleveland Cavaliers. He was named to the All-Star team three times.

- **Father Jacques Marquette** was a French missionary and explorer, born in 1637. He died in 1675 either in Ludington or Frankfurt. His name is synonymous with the history of Western Michigan. His exploits are covered in the individual histories of many towns in this guide.
- **Anthony "Pig" Miller** was born in Benton Harbor on October 22, 1971. The 6'9", 225 pound guard played basketball for Michigan State University and was selected by the Golden State Warriors in the second round, 12th pick of the National Basketball Association Draft in 1994. He played professional basketball from 1995 to 2005 for the LA Lakers, Atlanta Hawks, Houston Rockets and Philadelphia 76ers.
- **William Grawn Milliken** was born on March 26, 1922 in Traverse City. He was the longest serving governor in Michigan history. In 1965 he became governor when George W. Romney left office to join President Richard Nixon's cabinet. Milliken served three additional, elected, full four-year-terms in 1970, 1974 and 1978. Although a republican, he endorsed John Kerry against George W. Bush in the presidential election of 2004.
- **Carter Oosterhouse**, was born September 19, 1976, in Traverse City, and returns often to enjoy sailing - one of his leisure time passions. He was a carpenter on the reality TV shows *"Trading Space's"* and *"Three Wishes"* and has appeared on the *Tony Danza* and *Oprah Winfrey shows*.
- **Sinbad** was born David Adkins on November 10, 1956 in Benton Harbor, the son of a preacher. Sinbad became a stand up comedian and an actor. He played Coach Walter Oakes on *A Different World* and had his own show, *The Sinbad Show* in the early 1990s. Sinbad is ranked 78th on Comedy Central's list of the "100 Greatest Standup Comedians of all Time."
- **Martha Teichner**, CBS News Correspondent and journalist, was born in Traverse City. She covered the Cuban boat lift and the Shah of Iran's exile to Panama. She had two London assignments and was based for a period in Johannesburg during the struggle against Apartheid. She reported on Bosnia and the fall of Communism in Central and Eastern Europe.
- **Craig Thompson**, a graphic cartoonist from Traverse City, is best known for his 2003 *"Blankets."* He has contributed many short works to *Nickelodeon Magazine* under the name "Craigory Thompson." In 1999 he did the graphic novella *"Good-Bye, Chunky Rice"* and in 2000 the mini-comic *"Bible Doodles."*

- **Barry Watson** was born in Traverse City in 1974. As an actor he is best known for his role as Matt Camden in television series "7th *Heaven.*" He also appeared as the title character in the series "*What About Brian.*"

- **Robert Whaley** was born April 16, 1982 in Benton Harbor. He was voted Mr. Basketball of Michigan even though Benton Harbor missed winning the championship the year he received the honor. He was selected by the Utah Jazz as the 51st pick in the 2005 National Basketball Association Draft.

- **Jerome Woods**, known as Rome, was born in Benton Harbor March 5, 1970 and started singing in the church choir. In high school he joined a rhythm and blues band: *Fire & Ice*. RCA signed him and his first album, *Rome*, was released in April 1997, and made it to number 30 earning Rome gold certification. Two years later he released *Thank You*. More recently he released *Soul Snatchers*.

- **Earl Young** was a real estate developer in Charlevoix and a dropout from the University of Michigan's architecture school. He built several stone houses in the city over a span of 57 years. His structures continue to amaze and delight visitors. A local writer once described his three clusters of homes (26 in all) as looking like something from J.R.R. Tolkien's "*Hobbitown.*"

Photo by Bob Royce

INDEX

463

465

About the Author

Julie Albrecht Royce was born and grew up in Michigan. She attended elementary and high school in Sandusky, Michigan and received a Bachelor of Arts from Michigan State University. She attended graduate and law school at the University of Cincinnati where she received an M.Ed. and a J.D. but after graduation she returned to her home state and practiced law for 25 years in Lansing. Ms. Royce was a First Assistant Attorney General to Frank Kelley for several years and to Jennifer Granholm when Ms. Granholm was Attorney General.

After retirement Ms. Royce and her husband, Bob, moved to Lexington, Michigan where they live today. In 2004, Governor Granholm visited Lexington and spoke of the need to promote the unparalleled magnificence of Michigan's lakeshores. Ms. Royce took her former boss's words to heart and authored her first travel guide, "Traveling Michigan's Thumb." She and her husband enjoyed the project so much that she decided to write this second guide.